UNDERSTANDING SOCIAL PROBLEMS

The Contributors

Stan L. Albrecht, Brigham Young University

John E. Berecochea, Criminological Research Associates, Berkeley, California

Daryl D. Enos, Southern Illinois University

Nona Glazer-Malbin, Portland State University

Stuart C. Hadden, Indiana University

Alfred Himelson, California State University at Northridge

Marilyn Lester, Indiana University

Frank Lindenfeld, Cheyney State College

David W. Musick, Washington State University

Jane E. Prather, California State University at Northridge

Ray C. Rist, Department of Health, Education and Welfare, National Institute of Education

William B. Sanders, University of Florida

Royce Singleton, Jr., University of California at Riverside

Colleen J. Soares

Charles E. Starnes, University of California at Riverside

Jonathan H. Turner, University of California at Riverside

UNDERSTANDING SOCIAL PROBLEMS

DON H. ZIMMERMAN
University of California, Santa Barbara

D. LAWRENCE WIEDER
University of Oklahoma, Norman

SIU ZIMMERMAN

PRAEGER PUBLISHERS · New York

Theodore Lownik Library
Illinois Benedictine College
Lisle, Illinois 60532

Published in the United States of America in 1976
by Praeger Publishers, Inc.
111 Fourth Avenue, New York, N.Y. 10003

Library of Congress Cataloging in Publication Data

Main entry under title:

Understanding social problems.

    Includes bibliographies and index.
    1.   United States—Social conditions—1960–
Addresses, essays, lectures. 2. Social problems—Ad-
dresses, essays, lectures. I. Zimmerman, Don H.
II. Wieder, D. Lawrence. III. Zimmerman, Siu.
HN65.U49   362′.042′0973   75–36212
ISBN 0–275–22790–1
ISBN 0–275–85570–8 pbk.

Printed in the United States of America

Preface

A textbook is a synthesis of knowledge in a given area, usually written for students at a specified level by one or more authors. In the social sciences, introductory textbooks are typically surveys of the broad range of areas in a discipline organized around the author's judgment concerning what is central and what is peripheral.

As a supplement to a textbook (and in some cases, an alternative to it) is the edited collection of readings, usually selected reprints of journal articles arranged and introduced by the editors. Unless the collection is lengthy or the individual pieces shortened, it is often difficult to attain the coverage of the textbook, and the fact that the articles included were originally intended for a professional audience may pose problems of comprehension, particularly for introductory students.

The present volume is intended for use as a text or a collection of supplementary readings for students in introductory social problems courses (and for some introductory sociology courses). It is a collection of fourteen original essays by young sociologists writing on their topics of professional concern. Beyond very broad guidelines, no editorial control was exercised over an author's approach, nor was any attempt made to define "appropriate" problems according to some theoretical prejudice. Thus, concern for the consistency of the treatment accorded topics in the book was secondary to encouraging the autonomy and creativity of its contributors. As a consequence, the book simulates the lively discussion of a seminar within the framework of an introductory text.

Each chapter was written for the student, however, rather than the authors' professional colleagues, with a consequent reduction in jargon and an increase in readability. The point of each contribution is to *engage* the student in the study of social problems rather than to summarize and report the present state of knowledge in the area. Facts (and even some figures) are presented, but the emphasis is on developing a framework in terms of which relevant information can be discriminated, collected, and interpreted. Few students have ever experienced the sense of being in a dialogue with a text, although the effective classroom teacher can stimulate a critical attitude toward it. The articles in this book demand such an active relationship.

In Part I, Hadden and Lester furnish an overview of various approaches to social problems, throwing into relief not only the differences but also the tension existing between alternative perspectives. Unlike most texts, the introductory portion of this volume furnishes the student with the means for raising critical questions concerning the essays that follow (aided by the discussion guide in the accompanying Teacher's Manual). Part VI concludes the book with a clear discussion of the major issues involved in evaluating the effectiveness of social programs aimed at societal troubles while at the same time establishing a perspective for going beyond narrowly technical questions. The volume opens and closes with an invitation to the student to assume a critical stance, a stance which should be addressed to this volume itself.

Parts II through V cover the areas of poverty, inequality, alienation, racism, sexism, and an array of problems emerging from major institutions in our society. Each article was edited to avoid major overlap or repetition, but a considerable degree of convergence is present which provides a measure of integration between each essay while preserving the viewpoint of the author. Essays were grouped in terms of major themes, but alternative organizations of the table of contents were possible. The present arrangement seemed to afford the most unity with the least strain, although no collection entirely avoids a touch of artificiality in lining up its contributions.

This volume does not provide a survey of all that is known in the area of social problems, nor does it attempt a comprehensive coverage of the wide range of relevant topics. Missing here are such introductory staples as drugs, sexual aberration, crime (as such), urban problems, mental illness, and so forth. It is often difficult to justify fully the selection of particular issues over others, but part of the rationale involved in this book was the exclusion of areas which heavily overlap with the sociology of deviant behavior. The two articles dealing with the criminal justice system in Part V emphasize the problems of social control agencies and hence are compatible with the structural and institutional emphasis found in the other articles.

In editing this volume, there was no attempt to engineer a uniform point of view or to insist on particular ideological credentials. As mentioned in the introduction to Part I, there is a tendency, on balance, for the essays to be critical or radical in their analysis, although by no means could the collection be characterized as a venture in the radical analysis of social problems. There remain sufficient differences of both degree and kind among the several essays to ensure controversy if the student is encouraged to read each essay in light of what related essays have suggested. (Here again the Teacher's Manual can be of help.)

In undertaking the adventure of editing a collection of original works such as this, an enormous number of debts are incurred, most of which can never be adequately acknowledged. We must mention, first of all, the authors represented in this volume. Their talent in the first place, and their patience in the second, were unfailing resources for us. In particular we must mention Ray C. Rist, who alerted Praeger Publishers to the project, and Marilyn Lester, who in many ways improved the quality of the editing in this volume. Thanks are due to Charles Mohler, William Sommerfield, and Susan Horowitz for their support and encouragement of the project. Maureen Harrington de Vivas furnished invaluable editorial and all-around assistance. James Bergin of Praeger has helped to slay the remaining dragons on the path to completion.

D.H.Z.
D.L.W.
S.Z.

CONTENTS

PART III   Racism and Sexism   127

PART IV   Institutional and Environmental Problems   211

Part I

What Is a Social Problem?

The study of social problems is not the exclusive preserve of the sociologist, although a concern with society's troubles was one of the influential factors in the development of sociology as a discipline. It is sometimes difficult, however, to distinguish between social problems research and the broad range of sociological inquiry. Special areas of sociological interest abound, for example, the family, social stratification, education, population and ecology, minorities, and so forth, and the study of social problems cuts across many of them as the readings in this volume testify. The concepts and theories of one tend to overlap the other, research procedures are virtually identical, and a common literature is cited.

If there must be a distinction between the two, we may speak of the relatively greater emphasis accorded to the search for solutions to societal troubles characteristic of work in social problems, and the tendency to draw the initial definition of the "problem" from the society itself rather than from the puzzles provided by the scholarly literature or issues raised by current theory. As Hadden and Lester point out in their introductory article, even this relatively simple distinction quickly presents difficulties; what counts as a solution is subject to dispute, and the very definition of what a social problem is may itself be an aspect of a social problem.

Hadden and Lester provide an overview of a set of options available to the student of social problems: contrasting approaches to the problem of definition, how to regard the emergence of a social problem in public consciousness, the selection of different levels of analysis, and deciding on alternative types of solution. In one sense, their purpose is to furnish the reader with a typology by which to classify and better understand different styles of research in social problems. However, the subtitle of their essay, "The Sociology of Social Problems," suggests a concern that ranges beyond simply categorizing existing work.

Sociology has a long tradition of self-reflection and self-criticism, perhaps nurtured by its struggle to legitimize itself as an academic discipline. It is still a matter of concern whether or not sociology is or ought to be a science, that is, whether or not strict objectivity is possible in the study of society, including the study of social problems. From the perspective of some critics, the attempt at being scientific and objective masks a conservative commitment to the status quo which mystifies and thus obscures existing inequalities in society and the concentration of power in the hands of a few. The counterattack to this criticism is the charge that radical critics substitute ideology for theory and rhetoric for method, and hence politicize what should remain a dispassionate search for truth.

This controversy is too complex to be examined in this brief introduction. It should be noted, however, that there is an important resource to be tapped in addressing the continuing debate, namely, the *sociological vision.* Sociology as a discipline examines the structure, process, and change of collective activity, including sociology itself which is practiced by a specialized group of persons with their own location in society. If sociologists study social problems and seek their solution, that very activity itself is subject to sociological scrutiny.

It is in this context that Hadden and Lester raise questions concerning many sociologists' proclivity to take as given the existence of certain social problems, as defined by some segment of society, instead of investigating the vested interests of the persons raising the alarm and the differential access to resources with which to promote or suppress the definition of some trouble as a social problem. They suggest that it is often the rich and powerful or the strategically located who have the wherewithal to manage, through the media or other means, collective definitions of reality favorable to their interests.

Granted some resolution to the problem of definition, Hadden and Lester consider the issue of level of analysis. They argue that work in social problems all too often isolates the problematic situation and treats it without regard to its connection to other social issues. (The article by Charles E. Starnes suggests the advantages that accrue to the affluent classes in society by separating the problem of poverty from the issues of inequality.) Those troubles which appear to be defects in the personality or motivation of individuals often have their roots in larger structural issues, a lesson that must often be repeated despite its trenchant exposition by C. Wright Mills.

At the point of formulating solutions to social problems, the political implication (if not the political character) of the researcher's model of society is made quite evident. The most obvious commitments to the status quo are found in the "hands off" or *laissez faire* approach and the *punitive* response, for example, increasing the severity of penalties and the scope of law enforcement to deal with crime. The more subtle issues emerge from the contrast between the *ameliorative* and *radical* approaches to solving social problems in which attempts to "tinker" with the present organization of society are juxtaposed to recommendations for thoroughgoing structural change.

The succeeding articles in this volume cannot be neatly classified in an either/or fashion using the Hadden and Lester scheme, nor do they offer their typology in the expectation that such neat categorizations follow. The distinctions suggested by Hadden and Lester represent their analysis of tendencies in the study of social problems and should be employed as a means of critically assessing a particular piece of work rather than labelling it as one type or another. On the whole, however, the authors·in this book lean toward a critical or radical perspective on social problems. While several readings suggest what must be classified as an ameliorative or reform approach, the net effect of the collection as a whole is in the direction of a call for a structural analysis of society's troubles and the need for fundamental social change. These articles do not, of course, offer the last word or anything near it, but they do afford a basis for understanding social problems—or, at least, *an* understanding of social problems. That there are alternative understandings is made plain in Hadden and Lester.

Looking at Society's Troubles

The Sociology of Social Problems

Stuart C. Hadden and Marilyn Lester

For most members of society, including many sociologists, social problems are self-evident, objective "things." Most of us believe that social problems exist, and if asked, we could undoubtedly furnish some examples of specific troubles in American society (for example, crime in the streets, poverty, the crisis of confidence in the government). This common-sense view of the nature of social problems masks much of the ambiguity and complexity involved.

Consider for a moment the following behaviors: killing, drug use, and discrimination. Most persons in our society feel that these activities are wrong and favor repressing them. Moreover, each of these behaviors may be viewed as problems for a society—as counter to the best interests of both the people affected by such activities and the persons initiating them. However, if we vary the social context of each of these behaviors, we find sizable segments of society who will argue that the behaviors are not only justified but also necessary. Certainly, the police officer is duty-bound to use force—even lethal force—if the situation warrants such drastic action. Regardless of our individual positions on the use of police

power, we can recognize the role of police officer as one which requires the willful taking of life in certain circumstances. Similarly, few of us would deny the right of a patient to take prescription drugs, even though in some cases it might mean addiction to the drug, as in the case of reliance on painkillers in terminal cancer. In this instance, we would not only recognize the validity of the activity but perhaps also describe it as reasonable and humane. Finally, even the act of discrimination might seem reasonable if we were talking about the systematic exclusion of dwarfs from professional basketball teams.

The above examples highlight in a simplified manner some of the issues involved in trying to describe any behavior or phenomenon as an instance of a social problem. The point is that we do allow behaviors to occur which in certain situations we would consider problems and, in fact, often reward people for engaging in them. As such, it does not seem likely that it is the behavior itself which constitutes a problem for people but rather the performance of that behavior by inappropriate people, in inappropriate situations, for inappropriate motives. What this means to the sociologist studying social problems is that attention must be directed to the ways in which some behaviors in some situations are set apart for special attention by a society.

A distinction must be made at this point between the "relativism" implied

Portions of this article are drawn from Stuart C. Hadden, *The Social Creation of a Social Problem*, unpublished doctoral dissertation, Washington State University, 1973. Lloyd Fitts, D. Lawrence Wieder, and Don Zimmerman provided invaluable suggestions for this work. Joan Hadden helped in the preparation of the final manuscript.

in the characterization above and the common-sense notion that "everything is relative." To recognize relativity does not deny the existence of uniformity or patterns of behavior. Sociologists studying social problems are interested in specifying the conditions under which particular societies or units in those societies come to define particular activities or conditions as problems. Attention is drawn to the fact that "problems" are the result of collective human activity, that they are in a very real sense "created" through such activity, and that this process of creation can be systematically studied and detailed. Such a concern specifically takes into consideration variation in what is viewed as a problem by different groups of people in different places at different points in time.

Throughout the remainder of this article we will consider the various ways in which sociologists have conceived of and analyzed social problems. Just as there is considerable variation in what is considered a problem by lay members of society, there is also diversity in sociological approaches. We will find different questions being asked about social problems from different sociological perspectives which will, of course, provide us with different analyses of their causes and consequences. In turn, these divergent perspectives can be used to suggest radically different solutions. Therefore, we should start this investigation by looking at the general approaches sociologists have employed to determine the place of social problems within a society.

SOCIAL PROBLEMS THEORY

Drugs, food prices, war, hippies, energy, poverty, hair styles, racism and sex roles

are all issues which have received considerable attention in the last ten years. Debate on these matters has concerned not only appropriate preventive, treatment, and punitive responses but also the extent to which each is a problem, to whom, and why. The diversity of opinion surrounding these issues is well illustrated by the types of statements we have all heard in relation to one or more of these problems:

"America is rapidly depleting its major source of energy."
"The energy crisis is a tactic of the oil companies to increase their profits."

"Marijuana is becoming a serious problem among the youth of the nation."
"The only problem with marijuana is the laws which prohibit its use."

"The Equal Rights Amendment will allow women to compete on an equal basis with men."
"The Equal Rights Amendment will mean the destruction of the institution of the family."

Such statements highlight two facets of sociological consideration of social problems. There is held to be a set of activities, such as marijuana use or energy consumption (objective factors), which are open to differing evaluations of good, bad, inescapable, and so on (subjective response). These two elements form the basis for a broad definition of a social problem as: "an alleged situation which is incompatible with the values of a significant number of people who agree that action is necessary to alter the situation" (Rubington and Weinberg, 1971:6).

The relative emphasis placed on the two elements of this definition (the objective situation and subjective evaluation) provides both diversity and controversy in the theoretical treatment of social problems. For present purposes we can divide the study of social problems into two theoretical approaches following the distinction which Zimmerman and Pollner (1970) have made between *resource* and *topic*. The first treats social problems as a resource, as given. That is, common-sense conceptions (which create our perceptions of social problems) are left unexamined as the researcher endeavors to explain the causes of drug abuse, juvenile delinquency, and the like, all of which are simply taken as problems "out there." The second approach takes the opposite tack and considers the social creation of social problems per se as the topic for research, examining both common-sense conceptions and their consequences.

Social Problems as Resource

Taking social problems as a given emphasizes the objective factors which are assumed to constitute a social problem. Research efforts within this framework are usually concerned with the rates of occurrence, social characteristics of the persons involved, and the relationship between these rates, characteristics, and other features of the society.

In the sociological literature there are two principal kinds of definitions of social problems that fall within this perspective: (1) A social problem is any objectively troublesome activity or set of activities engaged in by some significant number of people and (2) A social problem is a deviation from some group norm, value, or rule in society.

SOCIAL PROBLEMS AS OBJECTIVE CONDITIONS   One approach to defining a social problem is that it is any objectively trou-

blesome factor in the world. (Cf. Bogue, 1963a; Hollingshead and Redlich, 1953; Homans, 1950; and Moynihan, 1967.) By "troublesome factor" is meant that some phenomenon is inherently problematic for the society or subgroups within (for example, it thwarts goals, injures people or groups). By "objective" is meant that a phenomenon is perceived as problematic by anyone who cares to look. In short, this way of conceiving of social problems is based on the idea that the factor, its "harm," and its pervasiveness are simply there. Some critical issues are at stake in employing this approach.

First, there are objective factors which are intrinsically harmful but are not intuitively and/or popularly recognized as social problems. The existence of these factors undermines accurate prediction of what will be treated as a social problem by society. Many factors that are objectively troublesome go unrecognized and untreated while other phenomena which appear to have fewer deleterious consequences are defined as social problems.

Table 1. Total U.S. Costs in 1969 for Some Selected Items (Millions of Dollars)

Item	Amount
Fraud, embezzlement	1550
Robbery, burglary, larceny, auto theft	600
Floods, property loss	601

Source: U.S. Bureau of the Census, *Pocket Data Book* (Washington, D.C.: U.S. Government Printing Office, 1971), pp. 79, 127.

In Table 1 note the dollar amount lost due to fraud, robbery, and floods. Greater public concern is expressed over robbery, burglary, and similar crimes than over fraud and embezzlement, although the latter type of crime is more costly.[1] Floods are usually not considered to be social problems at all, although their effects can be devastating.

The discrepancy between actual cost and societal concern is significant because the advocates of the "objective factors" approach tend to take as phenomena for study those that are publicly recognized as social problems. However, they often do not take as problems conditions that are most harmful or pervasive, even though that is their criterion for defining a social problem. The equation of degree of public concern with the pervasiveness or seriousness of a problem is not borne out by empirical study.

The issue being raised is precisely that of definition. A variety of activities could have "real" deleterious consequences, but not constitute social problems about which something should be done. Unless a factor is recognized as problematic, proposed solutions will obviously not be forthcoming. That is not to say that these factors must forever remain non-problems, but it is precisely the act of defining and publicly promoting a factor as troublesome that turns it into a problem.

The matter of *context* is a second major issue with respect to this mode of conceiving of social problems. C. Wright Mills (1963:531) suggests that "context," while crucial, is often ignored. Sociologists, he says, tend to take the least comprehensive phenomenon as their topic, so that very often social problems are conceived of as *individual pa-*

[1] A good discussion of the discrepancy between the public's fear of certain crimes and the actual extent of those crimes, based on materials collected for the President's Commission on Law Enforcement and Administration of Justice, can be found in "Task Force Report: Crime and Its Impact—An Assessment" (1967; see especially pp. 85–95).

thologies rather than as *social* or *public* issues. In his view, for example, sociologists would be more inclined to study the characteristics of "criminals" in the streets than they would the nature of urban life; and the urban area would be taken as a problematic phenomenon much more often than the structure of the economy. What we end up with under this guise is an array of social problems isolated from each other and analyzed separately. The ties between social problems are seldom analyzed, for this requires the adoption of a larger context. It should be emphasized that this separation of social problems into small bits and pieces is not endemic to this mode of conceiving of social problems. However, it tends to be the preferred method of inquiry.

Social Problems as Deviation from Social Norms

The second principal conception which takes social problems as resource gives slightly more weight to social definition but, in the end, it too leaves the social creation and maintenance of social problems unexamined (see Haskell and Yablonsky, 1974; Merton and Nisbet, 1971; Sutherland, 1961; and Wolfgang, 1958). This conception sees social problems as violations of group norms, cherished values, or the administrative rules and laws of society. As Merton and Nisbet formulated this position, a social problem is a "breakdown or deviation in social behavior involving a considerable number of people, which are of serious concern to many members of society in which the aberrations occur" (1971:11). These deviations are seen as objective, that is, "out there in the world" and thus not a product of definition. This dovetails directly with the overall perspective of social problems as resource and with the first variant which sees social problems as objective factors in the society. In this case, deviations from "normal" ways of doing things are the objective factors requiring attention.

A more general model of the social world and of the social actor lies behind this conception of social problems. Society is seen as having a set of prescriptions—in the form of values, norms, and rules—for appropriate conduct.[2] When one person deviates from any of these, it is taken as individual pathology or individual deviation. However, when large numbers transgress the normative or rule-governed boundaries of society, there is a social problem. In fact, the entire area of social problems was described for many years as "social pathology," meaning precisely "social deviation" from normative rules of conduct.

CONSENSUS THEORY A basic concept within this model is *social order*, which consists of compliance with the socially shared system of norms (and rules, values, and so on). These norms and rules make it possible for us to act without infringing on the rights of others, because the normative system specifically takes others into account. Without this socially shared system, according to this framework, there might be what Hobbes (1928) referred to as a "war of all against all" where force and fraud would be used to further one's ends. Consensus about those norms is seen to be indispensable

for the maintenance of social order. From the perspective of "order theorists," any breakdown in the normative system or in the tendency of persons to comply with its rules leads to assorted troubles. Order theorists refer to such a breakdown as *anomie* (Durkheim, 1951), and its consequence is the emergence of social problems.

It is this conception of social problems that is largely responsible for the kinds of phenomena typically taken to be problematic; for example, homosexuality is a problem because it deviates from the prescribed heterosexual orientation. We could add other known problems to the list. The use of marijuana and other illicit drugs are a cause for concern not only for the reason that they are illegal, but because they are thought to interfere with normal, socially conforming behavior. The association of drugs with the youth counterculture perhaps pinpoints the source of alarm, for the "hippie" or "freak" flouts the major values or norms of middle- and upper-class America (cf. Wieder and Zimmerman, 1974). The unemployed do not live up to ethics, values, and prescriptions for economic success in society and thus unemployment is considered a problem.

From the standpoint of this model, order in society is assumed as the "usual" state of affairs and social problems, in their simplest terms, signal temporary breaches of social stability. This level of investigation still focuses on explaining an objective condition as it exists as a problem without asking what would seem to be crucial prior questions: For whom is an activity a problem? In what manner is it a problem? Why is it considered such? How did it come to be so considered?

---

2 Values are the general, rather abstract beliefs about what constitutes the "good life," "the worthwhile person," and so forth. Economic success or religious salvation are examples of values. Norms are more explicit prescriptions for action and rules specify the very explicit guidelines for action.

CONFLICT THEORY   There is a theoretical alternative to "consensus theory" within this same perspective. We are referring here to what is often called "conflict theory." One part of conflict theory maintains that consensus in itself is not mandatory for society. Instead, it is argued that certain kinds and amounts of friction or fragmentation are necessary and desirable for the continued survival or "beneficent transformation" of the society. Deviation from prescribed goals and means can have positive outcomes. For example, new institutions and new modes of doing things can result from deviation, for example, population increase might be controlled if large numbers of couples decide not to have children. And the presence of collectives and communes can teach some of us about alternative forms of survival in a complex society, including the fact that economic success may not be essential to a useful and satisfying existence. With conflict, issues that might otherwise not surface may do so—and new priorities and new values might be established as a consequence.

A key concept for "conflict theorists" (for example, Marx, 1959, 1970; Horton, 1966) is *alienation*. In contrast to order theory's anomie (which is a disjunction between goals and means, or absence of stabilizing norms altogether), alienation refers to a relationship between the individual and society. It is a separation of the person, beginning in the economic sphere, from his or her productive activities, due to the control exerted over the production process (and over the product) by essentially a nonproductive class of capitalists. This form of alienation, because it is seen to be central to social life, proliferates into alienation from self and

from others. It is not an inability to follow the norms of society that is problematic, but rather the nature of key institutions. Features of these institutions are taken as the objective factors which are themselves social problems or whose *consequences* can cause social problems.

Further, conflict theorists often characterize many of the norms of society as not furthering the needs of most human beings, for example, the norms which support institutional racism. It is argued that one needs to question critically the norms of society because they are initiated by and support the interests of the wealthy and not humankind in general. What is problematic under this variant is the institutional structure of society, not the conformity or deviation from the normative order, because the latter is seen to reflect or mirror the former.

In the order model, the emphasis is upon consensus rather than conflict. The conflict theorist argues that there is systematic deviation from the norms and rules because they are not legitimized by certain subgroups in the society. For example, many youths see the struggle for economic success as an inappropriate goal. We may count this lack of ambition as deviance only if we take the value of economic success as legitimate.

There is a need to study the process by which norms and rules become legitimized and those processes by which norms come to be rejected or changed. At issue here are not social problems per se, but social problems which result from someone or some group's ability to legislate social reality. Adopting this concern considerably broadens the scope of inquiry into social problems. It moves beyond studying those phenomena that are widely held to be deviant and focuses instead upon the way in which norms come to be dominant in the first place. It also involves the study of what Becker (1963) refers to as "moral entrepreneurs," those who set the boundaries for legitimate behavior. Such inquiry could include analyses of the positions of moral entrepreneurs in different sectors of society and how they come to have the ability to define what is conforming and what is deviant or problematic. This mode of study should look at the conflicting claims of persons who are differentially situated in the society. This study might have important consequences for what will be taken as problems requiring resolution.

TOWARD AN ALTERNATIVE STANCE   That the questions raised above are important is illustrated by the recent emergence of the role of women as a problem in this society (or put another way, the problem of a male-dominated society). One issue revolves around the "fact" that women have been systematically discriminated against in terms of wages, employment opportunities, professional training, and the like. In turn, this has been linked to the oppressive and limiting social role of women in America. If we were to investigate this problem from a resource perspective, the central concern would be to capture the "objective indicators" of the phenomena, such as salary differentials, rates of mental illness, and so on. While such efforts may, in fact, be worthwhile in one sense, they tell us very little about the problem of women's rights. Certainly the conditions being studied did not suddenly emerge in full bloom on the social scene. Rather, as women's organizations are pointing out, the "oppressive conditions" have existed throughout most of the history of this and other societies.

The question is, "Why is the situation only now a social problem?" As will be argued in some detail later, answers to this question will illuminate the structure of society and the place of social problems within it.

A further example will serve to sharpen this point. In the recent movie, "The Exorcist," the audience is confronted with a twelve-year-old girl who begins to exhibit changes in her behavior. The mother becomes concerned and searches for an explanation. Since she "knows" her daughter to be a happy, creative child, the first explanation available to her is that "something is bothering" her daughter, that is, she is in some sort of stressful situation. However, as the behavior persists, the mother rejects her first interpretation and other equally plausible explanations and takes her daughter to a doctor who evaluates the problem as medical in nature (brain disorder). When the behavior persists (and indeed escalates), the mother once again searches for an explanation, this time taking the child to group of psychologists. Their interpretation is one of mental disorder (sympathetic possession) requiring lengthy psychological treatment. However, the mother is uncomfortable with this explanation also and continues her search. Enter the exorcist who defines the problem as one of possession by the devil and acts accordingly with some measure of success. In essence, the mother and the audience viewing the movie are finally told what the behavior "meant" all along.

The intent of this "analysis" of a popular movie is not to point out the pitfalls encountered in explaining problematic behavior. Rather, it is to demonstrate how differing evaluations of essentially the same phenomenon are dependent on the definitions available to people as they interpret the world. "Devil possession" is not an available explanation for the people engaged in medical and psychological practices. Their worlds are interpreted through a quite different set of meanings than the Exorcist's; and, consequently, the way they view behavior (even the same behavior) will necessarily be different. It should also be noted that these conceptions may vary over time. Hence, the same behavior that was considered by most people in society to be "eccentric" thirty years ago may now be interpreted as symptomatic of "paranoia" merely because such mental illness categories have been more widely disseminated to the public at large. One consequence of this would be an increase in the amount of "paranoia" in the society (since more people could identify eccentricities as "really paranoia"), even if the actual incidence of that behavior did not increase.

Failure of the resource model to attend to these matters prevents serious consideration of how and why the behavior is a social problem for society in the first place. The restrictive focus of this model, as outlined above, is the basis for Blumer's (1971:300) argument that

the so-called objective existence or makeup of the social problem is very secondary indeed. . . . The objective analysis made . . . may have no influence on what is done with the problem and consequently have no realistic relation to the problem.

Social Problems as Topic

The basic assumption of the social problems as topic perspective, which may also be called the *interpretive perspective*, is that social order is continually being constructed in the course of ongoing interaction. This framework focuses on the practices of people in creating their sense that a phenomenon has certain features, including its possible status as a social problem. In a less global sense, the interpretive perspective is concerned with the social construction of meaning. In this vein, sociologists (Becker, 1966; Blumer, 1970; Hadden, 1973; Mauss, 1975; and Reasons, 1972) argue that a social problem is not just an objective condition or set of objective conditions because not all objective conditions that pose real threats get defined and treated as problematic within the society. For example, while poverty has been with us for decades, only in certain periods of time is it defined as a social problem. Similarly, while cities have been polluted for years, only recently has pollution been taken up as a social problem. It is in this sense that the social problems as topic framework takes very seriously the idea that social problems are socially constructed, for regardless of the pervasiveness of a certain condition (highly visible to nonexistent) or its harmful effects, it requires social definition and action to become a social problem.

The interpretive framework is perhaps best known within the field of deviance which, as we have seen, is closely related to social problems theory. The tenor of this viewpoint, known as "labeling perspective", is best expressed in Becker's (1963) now classic work, *The Outsiders*.

Social groups create deviance by making the rules whose infraction constitutes deviance, and by applying those rules to particular people and labeling them as outsiders. From this point of view deviance is not a quality of the act the person commits, but rather a consequence of the application by others of rules and sanctions to an "offender." The deviant is one to whom that label has successfully been applied; deviant behavior is behavior that people so label. (p. 9)

The research focus required by the labeling orientation also receives Becker's attention.

It is an interesting fact that most scientific research and speculation on deviance concerns itself with the people who break rules rather than with those who make and enforce them. If we are to achieve a full understanding of deviant behavior, we must get these two possible foci of inquiry into balance. We must see deviance, and the outsiders who personify the abstract conception, as a consequence of a *process of interaction* between people, some of whom in the service of their own interests make and enforce rules which catch others who, in the service of their own interests, have committed acts which are labeled deviant. (1963:163; italics added)

A key word in Becker's statement is "process," which reflects the negotiated character of social reality and social order. Such a theoretical basis helps to resolve a major deficiency noted in the resource model discussed earlier—the inability to account for changing definitions of phenomena as deviant or as social problems. The interpretive model fully recognizes the fact that what is one person's problem may be another's pleasure. The important questions to be pursued are, "How are such interests resolved as a matter of socially constructed order?" and "Who can, under what conditions, with what success, get a problem defined?" Thus, rather than directing attention to the objective indicators of a given phenomenon, this perspective looks at the *societal reaction* to the behavior and the consequences of this reaction.

THE NATURAL HISTORY APPROACH The most frequent consideration of social problems within this model which takes process as paramount is the natural history approach. Here, the "histories" of various problems, usually discussed as a set of stages, are traced and analyzed. Initial impetus was given by Fuller and Myers (1941) with their conception of a three-stage model through which social problems were said to progress. These steps were "awareness," "policy formation," and "reform." While the particular categories of the Fuller and Myers model have been called into question (cf. Lemert, 1951), the idea of a developmental or natural history model for conceiving social problems has remained credible.

The most recent conceptualizations for assessing the general development of social problems have been advanced by Blumer (1971), Reasons (1972), and Mauss (1975), among others. In general, these formulations are quite similar. Recalling our earlier broad definition of a social problem as "an alleged situation which is incompatible with the values of a significant number of people who agree that action is necessary to alter the situation" (Rubington and Weinberg, 1971:6), we can note that those proposing developmental models agree that social problems do not spring onto the social scene full blown. Instead, they are seen to pass through a process of social development which includes competing definitions about the "alleged situation," debate over appropriate action, and so on. Typically, this process consists of periods of growing social concern, followed by agitation for corrective efforts which result in some form of action being taken. The process can be summarized as: A phenomenon is perceived as occurring, is evaluated and reacted to, at which time action is taken which tends to formalize and then maintain the phenomenon as a problem.

While such explanations do offer a description of natural histories of social problems, they do little more. Except in the broadest sense, little is offered to enable us to understand the internal dynamics of the process apart from the general stages. There is scant research within this framework to explain why one phenomenon "makes it" as a social problem while others do not. The reason for this deficiency is quite clear. Whether we are talking about social problems or someone's individual biography, stages merely serve as "bench marks" to allow us to trace change over time. For example, if we wanted to know how a person came to be a master criminal, we might look at the following "history."

He was a child from a broken home who fell in with a street gang as an adolescent. He was arrested, went to prison, where he shared a cell with an old safe cracker who "adopted" him. Released from prison, he could not find a job, so he decided to apply the knowledge his cellmate had taught him.

A stage analysis of this "history" might be set up as: (1) stressful childhood, (2) unsavory peer group influence, (3) arrest, (4) prison experience, (5) social rejection, and (6) criminal lifestyle. This "analysis" describes the individual by condensing what happened to him into six significant periods of his life. It has a certain logic to it as each stage seems to follow from the previous one. However, while the analysis describes what happened, it does not tell us why or how such experiences lead to the next. It is perfectly reasonable to ask why, after going through stages 1–5 (childhood to social rejection), our master criminal did not become a humanitarian, an inventor, go back to school, or any other possible adaptation.

In essence, what we are missing in a stage analysis is an appreciation of the intrastage dynamics. What happens within each stage that brings about the next or fails to do so? While it is not being argued that this deficiency is inherent in a developmental model, it is noted that most stage-oriented explanations do not analyze such internal processes. An attempt will be made later to demonstrate some aspects of the intrastage mechanisms which might allow a more complete understanding of the processes by which social problems are created.

A second possible flaw with the process orientation to social problems is that it attempts to explain the emergence of social problems themselves, and not the behavior in question. This distinction is crucial. Since the focus of the interpretive model of social problems is on *reactions* to phenomena, concern is not with why particular phenomena exist (as in the resource model), but only with why they exist as problems. For example, it makes little sense to study homosexuals apart from the meanings people attach to homosexuality. Actually, what counts as homosexuality, or for that matter any behavior, can be seen to vary according to time, place, and the purposes for categorizing the behavior.[3] In its barest form, the framework suggests the "problem" with homosexuality, and more generally with all behaviors we usually consider social problems, exists by virtue of the interpretations people lend to these be-

[3] This is to suggest that the interpretive model can be extended to cover not only evaluations of a behavior but also what the "behavior really is" in the first place. What may be homosexuality in one place may be "just juvenile play" in another (cf. Dundes and Leach, 1972). This kind of elaboration of the interpretive model falls under the perspective, ethnomethodology (cf. Garfinkel, 1967; Mehan and Wood, 1975; Turner, 1974).

haviors. This is not to deny any of the miseries, weaknesses, or even glories that might be associated with these behaviors, but rather to assert that all such activities rely on people to give them meanings of good, bad, mediocre, or whatever. In this sense, the underlying assumption of the interpretive model is that persons actively piece together the particulars of conduct into sensible patterns. Consequently, the analyst must attempt to understand how some activities get set apart as warranting special attention while others do not.

If one's concern is with the emergence and maintenance of phenomena as social problems, then the assumptions and focus of this model are productive guidelines. For the sociologist studying social problems, this entails "suspending belief" in the everyday world as common-sensibly known in order to treat as "strange" how drugs, for instance (and only some drugs at that), are set apart as social problems. Since no phenomenon has social meaning apart from that conferred upon it by members of society, everything in the world is a potential candidate for inclusion as a social problem.

Besides the emphasis given social meanings and actions, the interpretive model draws attention to another facet of social problems which warrants discussion. If social problems are dependent on social meanings and these meanings are subject to change (as was the case with witches), it is possible to talk about the *careers of social problems.*

A CAREER MODEL OF SOCIAL PROBLEMS [4]
In analogous fashion to the way we usually think about careers of individuals, we

[4] This material is drawn from Stuart C. Hadden, *The Social Creation of a Social Problem,* unpublished doctoral dissertation, Washington State University, 1973.

can look at social problems as successful and unsuccessful, of long and short duration, and having high and low points. In this context, we can initially note that concern over particular problems is of short duration for most of the society. This is not to deny that problems persist for many years nor that some issues such as crime, drug use, homosexuality, and so on seem to be always present. What is being stipulated is that concern over these topics waxes and wanes over the years. Consequently, the amount of resources devoted to dealing with the problem changes.

Furthermore, we note that as a phenomenon reappears as a matter of some concern, it has usually undergone a qualitative change with either new meanings or attributes being associated with it and perhaps old meanings being discarded. For example, what counts as an American "drug problem" in 1975 is not the same phenomenon which caused concern in 1920. In fact, consideration of the drug problem in the United States reveals four historical eras culminating in present-day attitudes and policy (Hadden, 1975). The shape of the career of this and other long-standing social problems resembles a wave pattern. Essentially, each era exhibits a period of growing concern over drug-related issues which peaks and then declines, leaving a legacy of social policies which will be sustained until the next era. At the point of "reawakening," the policies may be reasserted, modified, or completely abandoned.

Finally, we should note that just as people can have careers at different levels within a society ranging from bank presidents to janitors, so too can social problems. Although we will be confining the present discussion to what are usually considered issues of national concern, it should be realized that social problems occur at several organizational levels within a society at different points in time. Thus, drugs, for example, can be an international problem, national, regional, state, or even community concern. There need be no time relationship to the existence of the problem within these differing organizational levels. In other words, for whom something is a problem and when this concern occurs are further conditions which will influence the empirical study of social problems.

Since we have already asserted that the career of a social problem is dependent on the meanings persons attach to certain phenomena and the actions people take on the basis of these meanings, it is instructive to view the overall process as one of "sounding an alarm." In effect, we are saying that it takes people to convince other people that something is enough of a problem that action is warranted. To conceive of this as a process of alarming keeps us sensitized to the fact that persons are engaged in constructing meanings about facets of the world in the same fashion that Chicken Little ran about warning that the sky was falling. An alarm is intended to spur people to action.

Descriptively, four stages can be defined which trace this alarming process: (1) no concern, (2) onset, (3) mobilization, and (4) muting. Although the actual boundaries of these four stages are quite imprecise, a short description of each can be offered.

No concern. At this point in the career of a social problem, the phenomenon is simply not of social importance to the society. It may be that the actual effects of the condition are not well known, as was the case of opiate use in nineteenth-century America. On the other hand, the condition may be well defined as a problem, such as in the present case with illegal drug use, but not seen as a problem for a local community or region. The actual incidence of the phenomenon is not a defining feature of this stage. A given condition may be quite pervasive and still not be seen as warranting social action. For example, the history of the United States shows years of substantial racial discrimination before it became an object of intensive social concern. In any event, this stage is best characterized by a relative quiet—the alarm is not being sounded to any great extent.

Onset. This is the most difficult stage to specify. When does a phenomenon become a problem? While the actual time dimension is imprecise, two conditions appear necessary. First, the phenomenon must be set apart from that considered "normal." At this point, various consequences are attributed as properties of the particular condition. These consequences must be put forth in opposition to widely held social values in order to be effective. For example, it would not be enough to say a particular drug substance is "bad" and therefore ought to be eliminated. Rather, one must attach consequences of the drug's use which most persons would see as undesirable, for example, as a result of using the drug persons go insane, become violent, lose motivation to work, become enslaved, and so on.

The second condition necessary for the onset of the problem is a "demonstration" that the phenomenon is pervasive enough to warrant concern. Again, there need be no correspondence to the actual prevalence of the phenomenon. The problem, as it comes to be defined and set apart (the first condition) will be pronounced prevalent enough to warrant concern although what "counts" as alarming prevalence will undergo change during the career of the social problem. Although commonly conceived of as such by social groups, the pronounced prevalence of the problem and the actual prevalence of the phenomenon need not be the same.

This point will be returned to later, but for now it is enough to note that pronounced prevalence refers to what makes up the problem (the "consequences" established in the first condition) *and* how serious or widespread the problem is assumed to be (for example, no problem, growing problem, serious problem, and so on). It is not a statement of the occurrence of the phenomenon itself, such as the actual number of drug users in the community. To use an extreme case, consider the example of witches in Salem, Massachusetts, where the problem was pronounced highly prevalent (that is, serious) but the phenomenon itself was not present (that is, we suspect there were no witches).

The reason for focusing on the pronounced as opposed to actual prevalence of a problem is twofold. First, it is usually difficult to say exactly how many drug users, witches, and so forth exist at any point in time (actual prevalence). Second, one person may think a single drug user constitutes a serious problem while another person might feel there is no problem until we have a million drug users. Thus, it is again the definition of the scope of the problem that is of concern to the process analyst.

Mobilization. This stage refers to the marshalling of resources in response to the growing alarm. In other words, if an alarm is being sounded, something should be done. This is primarily a control stage which starts out with a rhetoric of eliminating the "problem" and usually ends with statements about containing the phenomenon. Besides the usual considerations of educative, preventive, and treatment efforts which are often seen as social responses to a problem, the alarm itself becomes very crucial at this stage. If the problem cannot be contained, the alarm will be changed. On the other hand, if the alarm itself cannot be sustained, programs designed to meet the problem will diminish, regardless of actual prevalence. In fact, the mobilization stage, irrespective of its success, sows the seeds for the demise of the social problem.

Muting. The tail end of the alarming process is muting. This marks the return to a stage of little or no concern. The muting stage occurs under two broad conditions. First, the problem can be said to be contained, therefore, concern is no longer warranted. In this case, the sounding of the alarm may be muted by reversing one of the conditions necessary for onset (statements about prevalence). The second condition entails changing the definitional makeup of the alarm. This usually occurs in situations of high prevalence. As such, if the problem cannot be adequately contained, what "counts" as a problem is changed. Thus, in the face of massive pollution, minimal standards are set up in lieu of elimination. Similarly, with 24 million people having smoked marijuana (National Commission, 1972), it becomes "reasonable" to redefine occasional use of the substance as not worthy of vigorous law enforcement efforts and to say instead that the "real" concern is with the drug dealers.

Before moving on, some general comments are in order which may be obscured by focusing on "successful" alarms throughout the rest of this article. First, it should be noted that the alarm need not be successful. The conditions to be described will primarily focus on facilitants to success, but are equally applicable to less noteworthy ventures. As is empirically obvious, some phenomena that start out on a social problem career falter. A social problem model should be able to account for these instances.

Second, alarms, whether they be successful or not, are created. This position is a reassertion of the interpretive model discussed earlier. By "created" is simply meant that alarms are produced by people as they interpret the world. However, this interpretation is accomplished within a social system with discernible properties which allows one to specify the conditions which facilitate social alarms. Subsequent development will try to move this somewhat bald statement from the assumptive level to an empirical one as the properties of the social problems career are given more detail.

To this point, we have been discussing how sociologists conceive of their object of study when investigating social problems. We have seen that the two major approaches, social problems as resource and social problems as topic, provide radically different modes of inquiry and consequently supply different answers to the place of social problems within the society. It is now time to turn to the answers sociologists have developed through these respective forms of analysis.

SOCIOLOGICAL ANALYSIS OF SOCIAL PROBLEMS

Sociological interest does not end with the definitions of social problems. Many different explanations for the emergence of social problems are found in the literature, locating causal factors in the natural environment, personal characteristics of actors, the social organization or social structure of specific institutions, the rapid pace of social change in an industrial society, and the social and economic structure of society as a whole.

To make sense out of these many and diverse explanations, some means of classifying them is needed. For example, analyses of social problems can be fitted into consensus (order) or conflict models, as mentioned earlier. One could opt for functional theory which relates one selected part of the social environment to other parts or to the whole society, as opposed to a Marxist scheme which views ideas, values, and so on as mirroring an underlying economic structure. There are thus a variety of possible schemes for grouping analyses together in order to talk in an organized fashion about the genesis of social problems.

One possible scheme has already been suggested in the distinction between the study of social problems as a resource and as a topic. The latter may be characterized in general as a type of *interpretive* analysis; the former, on closer inspection, can be subdivided in terms of the relative emphasis placed upon *natural, social-structural,* and *social-psychological* factors in explaining the emergence of social problems. We now turn to a discussion of this scheme.

Social Problems as Topic: Interpretive Analysis

Corresponding to the problems-as-topic approach to defining social problems discussed previously, there is a range of concerns that the sociologist will have in analyzing problems seen in this vein. Unlike the other analytic modes to be discussed in this section, the interpretive approach has little interest in the causes or roots of the troublesome factor itself, but rather seeks to understand how social problems emerge, how they are maintained, and how they wane as such. In other terms, the analyst who begins by viewing social problems as topics will be concerned with the factors which facilitate or inhibit the creation of a full-fledged social problem. Several kinds of inquiries can result from this foundation.

Given that anything and everything is potentially problematic for someone, an analyst could undertake an investigation of how people go about the work of making, creating, and solving problems in their everyday lives, since that is a very accessible arena for research. We might ask the question, "How does it happen that something comes to be seen as problematic by somebody?" What we would expect to find in everyday life, as well as in reference to social problems, is that people seek to make their worlds as predictable as possible. To accomplish this, they construct typifications of typical courses of activity to be undertaken in typical kinds of situations. When such typifications are breached, there is trouble insofar as people's interpretive work is concerned.

For example, one might have constructed a typical course of activity for his/her spouse: "kisses me before leaving the house for work, calls me from the office during the day, comes home and fixes some drinks before dinner, talks before bed. . . ." Were that typified scheme to be broken—no kiss, no phone call, comes home late at night—one and/or the other person would probably begin to see "trouble" in the home. By looking at interaction, at the ways in which "trouble" is perceived in this kind of setting, sociologists may come to understand some of the processes by which social problems are created.

This kind of work provides a very broad scope of inquiry. We would further want to know *why* certain phenomena get set apart as having consequences of relevance, which are defined as undesirable. That is, it appears that a necessary component to defining a problem (social or everyday) is to see a phenomenon as having consequences about which something can be done. A situation which affects millions of Americans on practically a daily basis can sensitize us to the importance of that component.

Most of our urban centers suffer to some degree from a very visible, very frequent malady commonly referred to as smog. Given the visibility, the effects, and frequency of smog, it would seem on the face of it to be very strange that persons did not become enraged and demand steps be taken to eliminate it. Yet, what can be done? Our "experts" tell us most of the smog is caused by car exhausts. But living in the Los Angeles Basin, for instance, everyone "needs" a car to get to work, to the store, to school, and so on. How would they get to work, since their jobs are spread here and there? How would they shop with the retail complexes and different types of stores being diffused throughout the area? In other words, how do you eliminate the car from a section of the country which is spatially designed for car-oriented communities? Through mass transit? But mass transit systems take years and billions of dollars to produce. Through "clean exhaust" cars? They are unavailable for mass markets. On a pragmatic basis, smog is a phenomenon about which "nothing" can be done. As a consequence, most persons "live with it," get used to it, and at a certain level, pretend it does not exist.

Even if one were successful in *pronouncing* smog *a problem* about which something could be done, it is usually not enough simply to state that social action can remedy the situation. There should also be a corresponding emphasis on the consequences of not taking such action. This theme is best accomplished by *proclaiming* the *potential spread* of the undesirable phenomenon to previously unaffected segments of the society unless some social action is taken. In essence, we would want to promote a "contagion" notion with connotations of inevitable spread and irreversible harm should the public not act. Hence, regardless of the scope of the original problem, we would want to say it has the potential to affect everyone unless safeguards are established. In this manner the problem is made a general concern rather than a particularized condition having interest only to a special group. Again, the "drug problem" in the United States provides us with an illustration in which proclaiming spread was more successful and thus where a social problem was conceived.

If we look at the imagery associated with the drug problem throughout the last 25 years, perhaps the most stereotypic element is that of the "pusher." Depicted as a shady figure lurking around schoolyards and preying on unsuspecting youth, the pusher transformed "good kids" into mindless drug addicts. The message promoted was loud and clear. Regardless of how well parents had raised their children, how nice the community was, or any other indicator of well being, the population was still vulnerable to the unscrupulous tactics of the pusher. It was not just poor kids, minority kids,

dumb kids, or any other subpopulation within a particular community who were vulnerable—it was all kids, regardless of their upbringing. In this case, only constant vigilance and vigorous law enforcement efforts could act as a safeguard.

Of course, we all know the mythology of the pusher has broken down in the last ten years. How then has the population been kept informed of its vulnerability? Consider for a moment the following newspaper report of a speaker at a drug education panel. The speaker is a prison inmate who identifies himself as a narcotics addict.

Don't kid yourself by saying it [addiction] won't happen to me. It can! It's not the suspicious looking pusher that gets you started. It's a friend that tried it and thought it was great. He's not trying to get you addicted, he's trying to share the kicks with you. You start by telling yourself, 'Man, I know what's happening. I can handle it.' It feels great, wonderful, fabulous, until you get hooked. (*Pullman Herald*, March 7, 1968, p. 8; as cited in Hadden, 1973)

What is obvious from this fairly typical account is that the threat of contamination has been significantly expanded from the pusher (whom we could now all recognize and avoid) to include one's friends who have nothing more malicious in their hearts than wanting to share some "good times." Certainly, the community is more vulnerable than ever before.

The features of this problem which are of interest to the interpretive analyst are the *processes* of pronouncing a problem and proclaiming its spread, and detailing its undesirable consequences. However, to the extent that we are concerned with the success or failure of the practices of pronouncing a problem, proclaiming spread, and so on, we must also be concerned with who communicates what and how the communication occurs. It is clear, for example, that desiring to participate in the defining process does not allow us to predict who will finally have successfully defined a social problem. By "successfully" we mean to suggest that not all definitions "stick." Not all definitions get *legitimized* as *the* definition of what is problematic. We will want to know the kinds of individuals and groups who are successful in this regard.

What this suggests is that it is quite possible that people who are located in some positions in the society have greater ability or access to defining social problems than do other people. Insofar as these groups have competing definitions about what is problematic, even about what is problematic about the same condition, it is important to look at what the final definition is, who formulated it, and to ascertain the definitions that were not accepted. This is not to suggest that everyone will accept the final definition. It is rather that some definitions are made to stick, for example, through being adopted by policymakers. Indeed, another important variable to consider is who accepts the definition.

The media is yet another crucial ingredient for successful promotion of definitions of social problems. Molotch and Lester (1974) indicate many of the reasons why the media must be taken into account in studies of the creation of social problems. They note that people who control our major institutions have what they refer to as "habitual access" to the media and thus to creating audiences' experiences which can be extended to include their perception of social problems. Certain people are situated to be routinely covered by the media. They are

thus in an advantageous position to promote their definitions of social problems and suppress others (see also, Edelman, 1964; Schattschneider, 1961). But those lacking habitual access to the media, but who do have definitions to promote, often must rely upon disruption as a way of generating public experience. "Coverage is received from the mass media by virtue of its 'obvious' intervention into normal functioning and its problematic challenge to the social world as constituted" (Molotch and Lester, 1974).

Becker (1966:241) writes in a similar fashion about a "hierarchy of credibility." He says, "In any system of ranked groups, participants take it as given that members of the highest groups have the right to define the way things 'really are.'" The upper groups in society are seen to have an intrinsic right to provide the most credible account of what a problem "really is." Thus credibility and the right to be heard are distributed differentially.

As we have seen, this mode of analysis is directed toward discerning conditions which provide for the social creation of a social problem with little attention given to the "reasons" why a "troublesome factor" exists. The next three types of analysis, on the other hand, take as their topic the search for causes of the trouble as an objective state of affairs.

Social Problems as Resource: Natural Causation

A flood occurs; thousands of people are displaced from their homes. Tornadoes, large fires, electrical shortages can threaten thousands of individuals. A severe drought can shorten a food supply and hundreds of thousands of people can starve. Natural oil seeps can blacken beaches preventing, as a consequence, the use of a major recreation area.

These are examples of seemingly natural "social problems." Something in the physical environment, independent of people's actions, creates a social problem. Such disasters are typically seen to lie beyond human control—"they just happen"—but their occurrence can deleteriously affect many, many people. The creation of a social problem out of one of these phenomena is enhanced when there comes to be a public issue. So, for example, if there is a belief that conservation could prevent power shortages, such a shortage is evidence of a social problem—the lack of conservation measures being implemented.

Sociologists are not usually concerned with social problems when their immediate cause is seen to arise in the natural environment, for that is the domain of the natural scientist. However, the sociologist can analyze the consequences or social ramifications of such a natural occurrence. For example, a sociologist will ask what happens to people when a major fire, flood, or some other seemingly naturally caused condition occurs.

An entire research center has been established to study such events. The Disaster Research Center located at Ohio State University has several teams of sociologists who go to the scene of natural disasters and conduct research. For example, they may study the communication channels among citizens and official agencies which emerge to deal with the consequences of a disaster. The role of rumor and of official news media is of importance in this type of study. Or they may investigate the types of social arrangements which emerge to deal with the consequences of a natural occurrence (cf.

Quarantelli, 1960b). How do people organize to confront their predicament? Or, the question might be asked, "Under what conditions will people panic or act 'rationally' in a natural disaster?" (Quarantelli, 1957; 1960a)

In short, the social problem is minimized or exacerbated depending upon the kinds of intermediary steps taken. The sociologist is not usually concerned with the precipitating event itself, which lies in the domain of natural science, but with the next set of conditions that maximizes or minimizes the consequences of such an occurrence. Although the initial occurrence has an environmental genesis, many social problems can and do arise as a result, and these social problems are open to study like any other.

There is a second and perhaps more important factor to consider under this approach. Some phenomena which at first appear to be naturally caused are in fact socially derived. For instance, in California there is a "fault line" which runs through more than half the state. Why is there continual construction on the San Andreas fault in California? What political and social processes prevent the control of such building which could save lives in the event of a major earthquake. The same kinds of questions could be asked about floods, fires, droughts, and the like. The point is that one might find that what initially appears to be merely a naturally caused event is in fact due in large measure to social and political factors. For the most part this has not been systematically attended to by sociologists, but it is an important area of research and may come to the forefront over the next several years as people learn more about the political, social, and economic factors which affect what was previously taken to be beyond human control.

Social Problems as Resource: Social Psychological Explanations

In the late 1800s, a widely publicized study of prisoners by Cesare Lombroso tried to demonstrate that the physical constitution of criminals was different from that of noncriminals. Criminals were seen to be anthropological throwbacks to a more primitive stage of the biological evolution of the race (Cohen, 1966:49–50), distinguishable by such characteristics as a thin beard, projecting ears, large jaws, and a square and protruding chin. Under this type of analysis, something in the nature of the individual was seen to predispose a person to engage in activities that were considered problematic.

Later evidence shows that Lombroso's supposed characteristics of "criminals" are evenly distributed throughout the population. That is, there are no major differences between the physical character of incarcerated criminals and other people. Nevertheless, the search for similar qualities continued. In 1920, an explanation for criminality was low intelligence. At that time, Dr. Henry Goddard said, "It is no longer to be denied that the greatest single cause of delinquency and crime is low grade mentality, much of it within the limits of feeble-mindedness" (1920:23). That explanation, too, was later refuted. Intelligence scores, as unreliable as they might be, have been found to be distributed about equally in "deviant" and "normal" populations.

While these explanations may seem crass, there are more sophisticated versions drawn from psychology that have continued to constitute a major type of theoretical explanation for social prob-

lems. While psychology offers no single, universal explanation, the preferred mode assumes that individual malfunction underlies crime, drug use, drinking behavior, and the like.

There is a sociological counterpart to individual-level analyses which deals with social experiences in which the individual participates that make him or her part of a social problem. This form of analysis is generally called *social psychological*.

Gagnon and Simon (1967:247–285) illustrate this approach in a study of lesbians. They suggest that one must look at the interaction of gay people with their families and early sexual encounters to discern the roots of lesbianism. That is, there is something in the *social situations* of actors that leads to a certain pattern of behavior. For example, for females, emotional involvements precede discovery of their "specialness" while the reverse is generally true for male homosexuals. In fact, females' discovery of their homosexuality usually occurs very late in adolescence or even in adulthood. It is emotional, nonsexual involvements with women that later brings about recognition of their lesbianism. Simon and Gagnon discuss one instance of this pattern:

This romantic drift into sexual behavior was typified by one lesbian who described the beginning of her first homosexual affair in the following way: The fall after graduation from high school I started at (a residential school). I met a girl there who was extremely attractive. She had a good sense of humor and I was drawn to her because I liked to laugh. Many of the girls used to sit around in the evenings and talk. As our friendship grew, our circle narrowed and narrowed until it got to be three or four of us who would get together at night and talk. Then there was only three. Then two —us. And maybe after a couple of months of this our relationship developed into something more. Starting out by simply kissing. Later petting. That type of thing. It didn't actually involve overt sexuality (genital contact) until February. (p. 251–252)

Thus homosexuality, and specifically lesbianism, is to be viewed as the result of social relationships. One does not begin life as a lesbian; one evolves into a lesbian.

In pursuing this line of inquiry, sociologists begin their move away from totally individualistic interpretations of problems into the realm of analyzing social action within a societal context and the effect that social interaction may have on behavior. For instance, at one time or another, sociologists have looked to the *patterns of interaction* among members of a group, the *values* of some group or institution, the *relation* of some group to individuals on the one hand and to society on the other, and various combinations of the above.

One explanation for the emergence of the delinquent gang, for example, sees it as a result of the values of "lower-class culture." The lower class in Miller's analysis (1962) is viewed as searching out excitement and thrills, physical competition, danger, and, in general, immediate gratification. These values can support the existence of youth gangs in the absence of other outlets. Thus conformity to the norms of a subculture can result in criminal behavior—a social problem.

Edward Banfield (1968) goes further in suggesting that the members of the lower class are located at the bottom of the economic scale due to their inability to imagine a future and/or delay present gratification for future reward. That valuing of the present, he suggests, can only lead to poverty. People that lack economic resources but who can envision and plan for a future are merely "unfor-

tunate members" of the middle class. Thus, for Banfield, not only gangs, but urban blight, dilapidated housing, and other urban problems are caused by a subculture of values held by people living in close proximity to each other. There is a "culture of poverty" generated by a value scheme that is at variance with middle-class success values. Banfield has been and can be criticized on several grounds (cf. Miller and Reissman, 1965), but nonetheless his study is a prime example of how social scientists look to the culture and values of groups to analyze the roots of a social problem. Analogously one could define a sub-cultural emphasis on success in the middle and upper middle class as problematic in many ways. Middle-class values can lead to neurosis, excessive competition, high blood pressure, rebellion of the young, over-possessiveness, and a variety of other "problems." Thus, depending upon the position that one takes, the middle-class culture could be as, or even more, problematic than the lower-class culture. What is of importance in all of these examples is their general concern with values, culture, and so on, in contrast to an emphasis on social structure as in the next mode of analyzing the genesis of social problems.

Social Problems as Resource: Social Structural Analysis

A final approach looks to the overall social organization of the society as the generator of social problems. It searches the structure of groups, of institutions, the class structure, and the economic organization of society as a whole for the roots of social problems.

One kind of explanation for social problems might look to the structure of the city or some other area as precipitating social problems. The matters of housing and transportation provide examples. In the central city, land values are higher than elsewhere, but the increasingly older housing located there has degenerated, partly due to economic motives of landlords which lead them to resist improving housing for poor renters, and partly because business has a tendency to expand outward from the central city. Thus what are now residential areas might in the future be taken over by business enterprises and so there is no incentive to improve dwellings. Rents are nevertheless high due to the high value of the land itself. Because the housing in the central city is largely substandard, wealthier people move to the suburbs, leaving the residential area of the city mainly to the poor. Middle-class suburbanites commute to work in the cities and have resources available to them to get transportation thoroughfares (new highways) built.

Jobs for the poor, when they exist at all, are increasingly in the suburbs where many large industries have moved. The poor, however, are locked residentially in the central city with inadequate transportation to get to available jobs, and they lack the economic resources to move to the suburbs. Since many of the poor are non-white, discrimination adds to their being locked into poor urban neighborhoods. We thus have a situation where the structure of the city helps to account for and sustain major social problems (though obviously political and social factors are also at work).

In essence this approach to analyzing social problems looks to a higher level of generalization than the social psychological level. It is concerned with the social organization, or patterned activities of organizations and institutions, and the structure of urban areas as roots of social problems.

Another type of structural analysis focuses upon the imbalance between one part of society to the whole culture, which is viewed as a system of interrelated parts. When one part of the system becomes maladjusted or dysfunctional, the whole system can be affected, thus generating major social problems. One example should serve to illustrate this perspective. The family is seen to be an integral institution in the functioning of society. It socializes the young to the values of American society, helping to incorporate them into other societal institutions. One explanation for the "youth problem" today is the failure of the family to conduct appropriately this socializing activity. It is either seen as too permissive or as confused about exactly what values to instill in light of the changes that have occurred in other sectors (Flacks, 1971; Keniston, 1962).

This explanatory approach posits the need for consensus about the values that are to be shared and about the way in which the system should function. It is in this fourth type of analysis that we confront most sharply two major kinds of explanations for social problems—order and conflict theories. While we have just examined the "order theory" mode of explanation, we will now examine conflict models.

THE CONFLICT MODEL   The income distribution of the United States, despite optimistic assertions to the contrary, has not changed substantially throughout the twentieth century. Since about 1910, the income of the top tenth of the population has been larger than that of the bottom five-tenths (Kolko, 1962, 1970). In fact, the two lowest tenths have experienced a decline in the percentage of the national income which they receive.

In 1918 the combined income shares of the two lowest poorest income tenths were about one quarter that of the richest tenth; by 1959 their share had dropped to one-seventh. During this same period the percentage of the next lowest tenth also decreased, while the fourth and fifth from the lowest (the sixth and seventh ranking) neither gained nor lost ground appreciably. Together these five groups which constitute the poorer half of the United States population received 27% of the national personal income in 1910, but only 23% in 1959. (Kolko, 1970:64)

This pattern of inequality can be seen to cause many of our social problems. By definition it is reponsible for poverty, creating housing and health problems. The rich live longer and healthier lives than the poor and live pretty much as they choose, while the poor are relegated to urban and rural ghettos with little opportunity to move geographically, socially, or economically.

An unequal distribution of wealth breeds an unequal distribution of power in the society. More than one study has shown that those who have the largest incomes have a disproportionate say in political matters (cf. Domhoff, 1967, 1970). Thus, the wealthy have the power to structure the political life of those with fewer resources. More importantly, with wealth comes the power to have certain kinds of "troubles" defined as problematic to the neglect of other "troubles."

One might ask, for example, "Why isn't the unequal distribution of wealth a problem in its own right?" It certainly threatens millions of people. It is certainly an objective condition in the environment. It is certainly defined by some significant number of people as problematic. It fits all the criteria for a social problem. However, few who have the resources consider it or promote it as a serious social problem.

Conflict theory can provide an understanding of how some values, norms, and administrative rules become dominant. Marx saw that those who controlled the capitalist economy also formulated and sustained by force, where necessary, the major ideologies and values of society. Thus it is no accident that the poor are defined as maladjusted in terms of the success ethic—it serves the economic system to define those who lose as individual failures rather than as the creation of capitalism itself.

This perspective analyzes a whole different range of social problems as well as providing a reinterpretation of social problems that are conceptualized from other approaches. It places the genesis of social problems within the widest possible context. It further provides for links between social problems rather than considering them as isolated phenomena.

Selecting one of these four approaches is contingent on how one has chosen to formulate a social problem (as topic or resource) and the features of the problem that the inquirer is interested in. Further, the researcher can select one of these modes of analysis or seek to integrate them. For example, one could analyze linkages between the structure of an urban or rural area and the economic base of society. Or one could link the subcultural values of the poor to lack of resources in the society. Or one might ask what an interpretive analysis may add to any of the other approaches. A combination of one or more of these approaches may create a more sophisticated and comprehensive analysis than any single mode provides in itself.

SOLUTIONS

Attempts to solve social problems may be undertaken by a variety of people. The single outraged individual who writes a letter to the editor of a local newspaper may be seeking to call attention to some problem and offer a solution. If other people are also upset about the problem, they may collectively pursue a solution, such as the recent formation of a national citizens' group, with chapters across the country, to combat child abuse. It is likely that the formation of a group or organization will be more successful in promoting and implementing a solution than will the lone individual. Further, when people with official responsibility for alleviating or controlling some phenomenon become involved, there will usually be more success in implementing most kinds of solutions than when they are absent. Thus the citizens' group just named was aided considerably when officials from the Department of Health, Education and Welfare commended the group's attempts to solve a "pressing problem." Just as success at defining a problem varies with *who* engages in the defining process, so the promotion and implementation of solutions varies by the number of people, their degree of organization, and participation by legitimized officials.

A second consideration with respect to resolving social problems is the access of multiple groups to getting solutions accepted and acted upon. Insofar as the alarming process is successful and where several individuals and/or groups become involved, multiple solutions are likely to be proposed. Blumer (1970) points out that debate and deliberation about how to cope with a social problem is analo-gous to the multiple interpretations and negotiations that often occur over the initial definition of a problem and its causes. Depending on exactly who gets involved in this stage (a few people, an organized collectivity, officials, and so forth), there will be more or less debate about solutions and more or less equal access to promoting and implementing a solution.

With these concerns in mind, four broad types of solutions to social problems may be identified: (1) laissez-faire approach, (2) the punitive approach, (3) the ameliorative approach, and (4) the change-oriented approach. The order of their presentation roughly corresponds to the sequence in which they are applied. For instance, if the laissez-faire approach fails, punitive strategies may be sought and so on.

The laissez-faire solution to social problems is basically the position that nothing can be done or nothing should be done about the problem. The punitive solution, on the other hand, involves fairly direct intervention as it seeks to punish or otherwise sanction those people who engage in "troublesome" behavior. Advocates of this approach believe that by punishing offenders, the scope of the social problem will be contained—"punishment serves as an example to other potential offenders about the consequences of their actions."

The third strategy in attempting to cope with social problems, the ameliorative solution, is chosen quite frequently by both citizens at large and by those occupying official policy-making and implementing positions. It is a "reform" approach which seeks to "fix up" the symptoms of a problem. As such, no attempt is made to effect major changes in society as a whole, but as its name suggests, it selects certain elements for a kind of first-aid.

The change-oriented approach might be termed a radical alternative to the laissez faire, punitive, and ameliorative solutions. Under this approach, the solutions just discussed are attacked for their lack of attention to the "real roots" of social problems. Advocates argue that our major social problems—poverty, health, housing, pollution, power differentials—can never be solved under capitalism (cf. Christoffel et al., 1970; Mankoff, 1973). Instead, America must be transformed into a socialist society where wealth is more evenly divided, and where there are adequate facilities to care for the health and well-being of all people regardless of individual resources or social status.

Such a transformation would not look like other socialist revolutions because America is an advanced technological society and would not have to undergo all the problems of industrialization that Russia, China, and Cuba faced, although there might well be other difficult problems. Due to this difference, there are conflicting analyses of how this change would occur, and about what form the society would take both during and after the intense period of transformation. No one believes such a change will occur overnight, not in the United States where capitalist institutions are so firmly entrenched. But those who advocate socialism of whatever form see it as the principal road to overcoming major social problems.

CONCLUSION

This article ends with a short discussion of two elements which should be considered in any introduction to the sociology of social problems. One of these elements is *power*. The other is the *values* of those who define, analyze, and seek to resolve social problems, including people in their everyday lives, as well as official definers, policymakers, and sociologists.

The definition of social problems often rests on the ability to have one's definition of a social problem accepted. But those with wealth, position, and other resources have a far greater likelihood of getting their definitions accepted than those who lack these resources. For low-status people to advance their definitions requires far more strategic work, organization, and time than for those with power. Those with wealth have ready access to problem-defining mechanisms (for example, media, policymakers) which greatly facilitates their problem-creating work.

This differential power raises a serious problem for the researcher: Which social problems deserve to be studied? The most obvious social problems may be those defined by the powerful to the neglect of other issues in need of study. The selection of a problem must be made and justified on some basis, but if obviousness is not a good criterion, then some other must be chosen. As an alternative to studying the most publicized social problems, one could choose problems that are less publicized but which other less powerful groups conceive to be problematic. Or, one could study the intentional creation of nonproblems. In any event, the student of social problems should attend to the issue of which group or groups in society control the definition of societal troubles.

Power and values also enter into a second phase of studying social problems. Whether one chooses an interpretive, social psychological, or social structural level of analysis has important consequences for the way the issues will be formulated and perhaps even consequences for the way other people see and cope with social problems. For example, the rich do not profit from an analysis that calls major societal institutions into question. Alternatively, other groups' interests lie in social problems being seen as a manifestation of the entire economic and political structure which has located them in a powerless position. On what grounds, then, is one to select an analytical mode? Such a decision is largely rooted in the personal preferences or values of the researcher.

Then there are questions of data and data collection. Often, researchers rely on data collected by other agencies. But those agencies may have certain interests in collecting certain types of data and not others. Merely to analyze some readymade data might involve the researcher in the goals of some administrative agency, for the goals of organizations determine what facts are relevant to the organizations' tasks (cf. Cicourel, 1968; Garfinkel, 1967).

Finally, we see that solutions to social problems, as well as the previous two phases, are a political choice. Once a problem has been selected and its context defined, scientific canons can provide the inquirer with guides to the next steps in the research process. The scientific method can lead us to a critical stance on the role of social problems in the society; it can inform us about ways to engage in systematic data collection and analysis. But science does not and cannot dictate problems of study, of context, nor of appropriate level of analysis. These matters result from the values and political interests of the researcher, from his or her theoretical leanings. In an important sense, it is the researcher's obligation to make such choices clear from the beginning. In John Seeley's terms, are we going to "take" our topics from the powerful, or "make" them by attending to features of the world typically ignored by the mighty?

References

Banfield, Edward. *The Unheavenly City.* Boston: Little, Brown, 1968.

Becker, Howard. *The Outsiders.* New York: Free Press, 1963.

Becker, Howard. "Whose Side Are We On?" *Social Problems,* 1966, 14, 239–244.

Blumer, Herbert. "Social Problems as Collective Behavior." *Social Problems,* 1971, 18, 298–306.

Bogue, Donald. "Population Control in the United States." In Phillip Hauser (Ed.), *The Population Dilemma.* Englewood Cliffs, N.J.: Prentice-Hall, 1963. (a)

Bogue, Donald. "A Theory of Why Skid Row Exists." In Robert Dentler (Ed.), *Major American Social Problems.* New York: Rand McNally, 1963. (b)

Christoffel, Tom, and Finkelhor, David (Eds.). *Up Against the American Myth.* New York: Holt, Rinehart and Winston, 1970.

Cicourel, Aaron. *Method and Measurement in Sociology.* New York: Free Press, 1964.

Cicourel, Aaron. *Social Organization of Juvenile Justice.* New York: Wiley, 1968.

Cohen, Albert. *Deviance and Control.* Englewood Cliffs, N.J.: Prentice-Hall, 1966.

Dohrenwend, Bruce P., and Chin-Shong, Edwin. "Social Status and Attitudes toward Psychological Disorder: The Problem of Tolerance of Deviance." *American Sociological Review,* 1967, 32, 417–433.

Domhoff, G. William. *Who Rules America?* Englewood Cliffs, N.J.: Prentice-Hall, 1967.

Domhoff, G. William. *The Higher Circles.* New York: Random House, 1970.

Dundes, Alan, and Leach, Jerry. "The

Strategy of Turkish Boys' Verbal Dueling Rhymes." In John Gumperz and Dell Hymes (Eds.), *Directions in Sociolinguistics*. New York: Holt, Rinehart and Winston, 1972.

Durkheim, Emile. *Suicide*. New York: Free Press, 1951.

Edelman, Murray. *Symbolic Uses of Politics*. Urbana: University of Illinois Press, 1964.

Flacks, Richard. *Youth and Social Change*. Chicago: Markham, 1971.

Fuller, Richard, and Myers, Richard. "The Natural History of a Social Problem." *American Sociological Review*, 1941, 6, 320–329.

Gagnon, John, and Simon, William. "The Lesbians: A Preliminary Overview." In John Gagon and William Simon (Eds.), *Sexual Deviance*. New York: Harper & Row, 1969. Pp. 247–285.

Gans, Herbert. *The Urban Villagers*. New York: Free Press, 1962.

Garfinkel, Harold. *Studies in Ethnomethodology*. Englewood Cliffs, N.J.: Prentice-Hall, 1967.

Glick, Brian. "The Limits of Liberal Solutions: The Case of Income Guarantees." In Tom Christoffel and David Finkelhor (Eds.), *Up Against the American Myth*. New York: Holt, Rinehart and Winston, 1970. Pp. 380–386.

Goddard, Henry. *Human Efficiency and Levels of Intelligence*. Princeton: Princeton University Press, 1920.

Hadden, Stuart C. *Social Creation of a Social Problem*. Unpublished doctoral dissertation, Washington State University, 1973.

Hadden, Stuart C. "Drug Use." In Armand L. Mauss (Ed.), *Social Problems as Social Movements*. New York: Lippincott, 1975.

Haskell, Martin, and Yablonsky, Lewis. *Crime and Delinquency*. Chicago: Rand McNally, 1974.

Hobbes, Thomas. *The Leviathan*. London: S. M. Dent, 1928.

Hollingshead, August, and Redlich, Fred-erick. "Social Stratification and Psychiatric Disorder." *American Sociological Review*, 1953, 18, 163–169.

Homans, George. *The Human Group*. New York: Harcourt, 1950.

Horowitz, Irving Louis, and Liebovitz, Martin. "Deviance and Political Marginality: Toward a Redefinition of the Relation between Sociology and Politics." *Social Problems*, 1968, 15, 280–296.

Horton, John. "Order and Conflict Theories of Social Problems." *American Journal of Sociology*, 1966, 71, 701–713.

Keniston, Kenneth. *The Uncommitted*. New York: Harcourt, 1962.

Kolko, Gabriel. "Inequality under Capitalism." In Chris Christoffel and David Finkelhor (Eds.), *Up Against the American Myth*. New York: Holt, Rinehart and Winston, 1970. Pp. 63–73.

Kolko, Gabriel. *Wealth and Power in America*. New York: Praeger, 1962.

Lemert, Edwin M. "Is There a Natural History of Social Problems?" *American Sociological Review*, 1951, 16, 217–223.

Mankoff, Milton. *The Poverty of Progress*. New York: Holt, Rinehart and Winston, 1973.

Marx, Karl. *The German Ideology*. New York: International Publishers, 1970.

Marx, Karl. *The Manifesto of the Communist Party*. In Lewis Fever (Ed.), *Marx and Engels: Basic Writings on Politics and Philosophy*. New York: Anchor, 1959. Pp. 1–41.

Mauss, Armand L. *Social Problems as Social Movements*. New York: Lippincott, 1975.

McDonagh, Edward, and Simpson, Jan. *Social Problems: Challenges*. New York: Holt, Rinehart and Winston, 1971.

Mehan, Hugh, and Wood, Houston. *The Reality of Ethnomethodology*. New York: Wiley, 1975.

Merton, Robert. "Social Structure and Anomie." In Robert Merton (Ed.), *Social Theory and Social Structure*. Glencoe, Ill.: Free Press, 1949. Pp. 128–133.

Merton, Robert, and Nisbet, Robert.

Contemporary Social Problems. New York: Harcourt, 1971.

Miller, S. M., and Reissman, Frank. "Poverty and Self-Indulgence: A Critique of the Non-Deferred Gratification Pattern." In Lewis Ferman and Joyce Hanbluh (Eds.), *Poverty in America.* Ann Arbor: University of Michigan Press, 1965.

Miller, Walter. "Lower Class Culture as a Generating Milieu of Gang Delinquency." In Marvin Wolfgang and Leonard Savitz (Eds.), *The Sociology of Crime and Delinquency.* New York: Wiley, 1962. Pp. 267–277.

Mills, C. Wright. *The Sociological Imagination.* New York: Oxford, 1959.

Mills, C. Wright. "The Professional Ideology of Social Pathologists." In C. Wright Mills (Ed.), *Power, Politics and People.* New York: Ballantine, 1963.

Molotch, Harvey, and Lester, Marilyn. "News as Purposive Behavior: On the Strategic Use of Routine Events, Accidents and Scandals." *American Sociological Review,* 1974, 39, 101–112.

Molotch, Harvey, and Lester, Marilyn. "Accidental News: The Great Oil Spill as Local Occurence and National Event." *American Journal of Sociology,* 1975, 81, 235–260.

Moynihan, Daniel. "The Urban Condition." *The Annals,* 1967, 371, 160–177.

National Commission on Marijuana and Drug Abuse. *Drug Use in America: Problem in Perspective.* Washington, D.C.: U.S. Government Printing Office, 1972.

President's Commission on Law Enforcement and Administration of Justice. *Task Force Report: Crime and Its Impact—An Assessment.* Washington, D.C.: U.S. Government Printing Office, 1967.

Quarantelli, Enrico. "Behavior of Panic Participants." *Sociology and Social Research,* 1957, 41, 187–194.

Quarantelli, Enrico. "Images of Withdrawal Behavior in Disasters: Some Basic Misconceptions," *Social Problems,* 1960, 8, 68–79. (a)

Quarantelli, Enrico. "Note on the Protective Function of the Family in Disasters." *Marriage and Family Living,* 1960, 22, 263–264. (b)

Reasons, Charles E. "An Inquiry in the Sociology of Social Problems; The Drug Problem in Twentieth Century America." Unpublished doctoral dissertation, Washington State University, 1972.

Rubington, Earl, and Weinberg, Martin S. *The Study of Social Problems: Five Perspectives.* London: Oxford, 1971.

Schattschneider, E. E. *The Semi-Sovereign People.* New York: Holt, Rinehart and Winston, 1961.

Seeley, John. "The Making and Taking of Social Problems." *Social Problems,* 1966, 14, 382–389.

Shibutani, Tamotsu. *Improvised News.* Indianapolis: Bobbs-Merrill, 1966.

Starr, Shirley A. "The Place of Psychiatry in Popular Thinking." Paper read at the annual meeting of American Association for Public Opinion Research, Washington, D.C., 1957.

Sutherland, Edwin. *White Collar Crime.* New York: Holt, Rinehart and Winston, 1961.

Sutherland, Edwin, and Cressey, Donald. *Principles of Criminology.* New York: Lippincott, 1955.

Turner, Roy (Ed.). *Ethnomethodology.* Middlesex, Eng.: Penguin, 1974.

United States Bureau of the Census. *Pocket Data Book.* Washington, D.C.: U.S. Government Printing Office, 1971.

Wieder, D. Lawrence, and Zimmerman, Don H. "Generational Experience and the Development of Freak Culture." *Journal of Social Issues,* 1974, 30, 137–161.

Wolfgang, Marvin. *Patterns in Criminal Homicide.* Philadelphia: University of Pennsylvania, 1958.

Zimmerman, Don H., and Pollner, Melvin. "The Everyday World as a Phenomenon." In Jack Douglas (Ed.), *Understanding Everyday Life.* Chicago: Aldine, 1970. Pp. 80–103.

Suggested Reading

BECKER, HOWARD. *The Outsiders.* New York: Free Press, 1963.
One of the early expressions of the "labeling approach" to deviance and still considered a major statement. This is especially important for background material on the social problems as topic and the interpretive analysis sections.

BECKER, HOWARD. "Whose Side Are We On?" *Social Problems,* 1966, 14, 239–247.
A cogent article which looks at the manner in which sociologists select their subject matter and the ties between this selection and the resultant models developed by sociologists.

BLUMER, HERBERT. "Social Problems as Collective Behavior." *Social Problems,* 1970, 18, 298–306.
One of the most recent articles which exemplify both the natural history model and the analysis of "what is a social problem?"

GUSFIELD, JOSEPH. *Symbolic Crusade: Status Politics and the American Temperance Movement.* Urbana, Ill.: University of Illinois Press, 1966.
A good example of the complexities involved in any phenomena coming to be "officially" recognized as a social problem.

HORTON, JOHN. "Order and Conflict Theories of Social Problems." *American Journal of Sociology,* 1966, 71, 701–713.
Provides an alternative framework for conceptualizing social problems. A recent statement about the roles of the two theories, order and conflict, in the study of social problems.

MERTON, ROBERT. "Social Structure and Anomie." In Robert Merton (Ed.), *Social Theory and Social Structure.* Glencoe, Ill.: Free Press, 1949. Pp. 128–133.
This highly influential article has provided the intellectual foundation for much of the work characterized in this article as the resource approach to social problems.

MILLS, C. WRIGHT. "The Professional Ideology of Social Pathologists." In C. Wright Mills (Ed.), *Power, Politics and People.* New York: Ballantine Books, 1963.
This article provides a historical foundation for understanding why the area of social problems, as conventionally seen, takes on its particular form and substance.

RUBINGTON, EARL, AND WEINBERG, MARTIN S. *The Study of Social Problems: Five Perspectives.* London: Oxford University Press, 1971.
A concise review and chronology of the changing modes of analyzing social problems employed by sociologists and the linkages of these conceptions to the discipline as a whole.

SHIBUTANI, TAMOTSU. *Improvised News.* Indianapolis: Bobbs-Merrill, 1966.
This book sets forth a series of propositions with many illustrations about communication in problematic situations.

Part II

Poverty, Inequality, and Alienation

Poverty, inequality, and alienation are fundamental problems that come to the fore in a critical examination of the structure of modern society. Charles Starnes points out that poverty and wealth are complementary, both emerging from the root conditions of inequality. He suggests that a key to understanding the problem of poverty is to juxtapose it to the problem of wealth. In his article, Starnes makes the point that both contemporary and historical conceptions of poverty tend to define it as a natural consequence of indolence or ineptitude or as an aberration in an otherwise serviceable social plan.

Poverty is often viewed as the consequence of defects in moral character. The poor are condemned as lazy or unmotivated deadbeats seeking something for nothing. Alternatively, they may be seen as innately incompetent, with few if any skills to sell in the labor market. With the exception of the "deserving poor"—the old, dependent young, and the infirm—the destitute are blamed for their condition, since poverty is a punishment for sloth as much as wealth is a reward for industry. Inequality is thus perpetuated and infused with moral standing.

Even when "the system" is accorded a portion of the blame for poverty, the poor remain stigmatized as a group. Basic liberal thinking on poverty retains the notion of individual accomplishment as a cherished ideal; it concedes only that particular and circumscribed problems in the current social order unfairly block access to the skills and opportunities needed to share in the society's wealth. Thus, various social programs are launched that target the poor as a group to elevate through training or other ameliorative efforts. Hand in glove with such social action schemes are various sociological accounts such as the "culture of poverty" notion that, instead of blaming the individual poor person for his or her plight, blames the poor as a group since they perpetuate their poverty over the generations by instilling the wrong values and attitudes in their children.

Whether the blame is placed individually or collectively, the fundamental source of the problem is obscured and the privilege of the more affluent classes preserved. Starnes' review of the history of the concept of poverty and the societal response to it reveals a remarkable continuity with present-day ideas. The distinction between the deserving and the undeserving poor goes back to classical times but is modernized with bureaucratic flourish in the maze of restrictive regulations that comprise our current welfare system. Reform in the social treatment of the poor where it has occurred at different times and places has tended to alleviate the most pressing distress while preserving the basic class system which is the source of the problem. The perspective Starnes provides furnishes the basis for a critical appraisal of both theoretical and practical approaches to the problem of poverty, for to the extent that either fail to speak to the issue of inequality, they do not really address the problem at all.

The essay by Starnes is broad in scope and historical in emphasis. The next article, by Stan L. Albrecht, is concerned with a specific issue: the lack of access by the poor to the legal system. Using data from recent studies, Albrecht analyzes the unequal distribution of legal services to various segments of the population. As it turns out, those who are most frequently processed by the criminal justice system are the same categories of people who encounter a number of barriers to attaining legal help, most notably the poor. Just as the welfare system and other poverty programs function to preserve the status quo which gives rise to inequality, the legal system also reflects and supports the stratification system within society.

Access to legal assistance per se is but the tip of the iceberg in any analysis of the legal system. For example, prior questions can be asked: What is the relationship between distribution of knowledge (about legal rights, laws, and the legal system generally) and utilization of, or involvement in, legal processes? What *kinds* of knowledge are most important for dealing with any agency in the legal system? Albrecht examines these relationships in detail as he suggests that the kind and amount of information that one has significantly affects what will happen in encounters with legal agencies, whether those encounters entail the role of defendant or plaintiff.

In this concern for the social distribution of knowledge one must be sensitive to the fact that such knowledge is not simply "out there" for free acquisition by anyone. That is, access to knowledge itself is dependent on such features as social class, education, and position in the work force. Albrecht's work can be seen as an empirical focus for later sections of this book which analyze those conditions which inhibit or facilitate access to resources in the society.

Sociology is sometimes divided into two large camps: social organization and social psychology. That is, one can examine structural features of the society at large (social organization); or one may be concerned with individuals and their interactions with each other. Sometimes these are called "macro" and "micro" sociology, respectively.

In the next article, Frank Lindenfeld unites an organizational and social psychological approach. On the other hand, issues related to work and industry are viewed as problems of social organization—composition of the work force and its relationship to the economic structure of society. Simultaneously, such structural features are seen to have significant effects upon individuals and their relationships to each other. People will feel satisfied or discontented, integrated or alienated, depending on their location in the world of work and on the overall economic structure of society.

Lindenfeld does more than merely analyze the relationship between social organization and social psychology in the present. He goes further to ask questions about the future, for example, "What kind of society would promote feelings of self-worth?" "What kinds of conditions most favor the individual's integration into, rather than alienation from, society?"

C. Wright Mills described the "sociological imagination" as the ability to link private troubles to public issues, to see individual biographies in their social-historical context. This is another way of saying that a sound sociological approach will jointly consider structural and social psychological dynamics. Lindenfeld attempts to follow through with this idea.

Contemporary and Historical Aspects of Officially Defined Poverty in the United States

Charles E. Starnes

At first, it appears easy to define "poverty" and to identify the "poor." We all possess cultural knowledge which enables us to talk with apparent authority about the poor. Such knowledge originates in ordinary experience and, hence, is dependent on our social and political interests, accomplishments, and sentiments. We sometimes forget that, while our views appear "natural," a matter of "common sense," definitions of poverty and the poor vary between persons, times, and places. As such, cultural knowledge about the problem of poverty must itself be subjected to study. Without prejudging the merits of particular efforts, we should recognize that up to now, even most scientific accounts remain ethnocentric (that is, grounded in a single society, or in a particular social class), ahistorical, and do not examine basic assumptions about poverty. To date, there has been only limited effort by academics to uncover definitions, accounts, or explanations of poverty offered by those who have historically suffered it. The most widely published and dearly held accounts are furnished almost exclusively by persons who are not "poor," have never been "poor," and are unlikely to ever be "poor."

A partial remedy to these limitations of current discourse on poverty lies, in part, in linking the concept of poverty to the nature of wealth, since it can be argued that poverty and wealth are complementary manifestations of a single condition—inequality. Moreover, a crucial corrective is available in recovering the history of conceptions of poverty and the poor, for it is often easier to detect the class-based and self-serving nature of earlier treatments of the poor than to acknowledge what turns out to be a modernized form of the same ideas. It is to these tasks that we now turn.

THE INCIDENCE OF POVERTY: AN OVERVIEW

Absolute versus Relative Constructions of Poverty

There are multiple and sometimes conflicting definitions of poverty. Examining these will demonstrate that the incidence of poverty not only varies by economic conditions in a society, but also by the criteria used to define it.

During the Kennedy administration, the task of defining poverty in the United States was given to the Council of Economic Advisors (CEA). The CEA used data collected by the Social Security Administration (SSA) to determine the income needs of a nonfarm family of four. The SSA had constructed a "low-cost" budget judged to satisfy the eating practices of the lowest earning third of the population. This budget amounted to $3955. But this level of income exceeded the amounts that welfare agencies were willing to provide. So, the SSA prepared an "economy" budget to meet this objective. The economy budget was to allow only a *"deficiency diet designed for temporary or emergency use."* It amounted to $3165. Unwilling to be even this generous, the CEA pared this budget to an even $3000 for families and $1500 for unattached individuals. These became the CEA's recommended poverty lines; persons having incomes below these lines would be judged in poverty. At the time, 1962, this resulted in the estimate that 35 million people, over 20 percent of the population, were in poverty.

In 1964, the SSA revised the official poverty lines to take into account variations within the population. Separate poverty lines were set for combinations of (a) residence (farm or nonfarm), (b) age of the head of the family (aged or nonaged), (c) sex of the family head, and (d) the number of persons in the family. So, for example, the poverty line for a farm family was set at 70 percent of the poverty line for a nonfarm family, as it was assumed that the farm family could grow much of its food. In 1969, the poverty line for farm families was adjusted upward to 85 percent of the nonfarm poverty line in recognition that this assumption was of doubtful validity. Also in 1969, the method of making annual "cost of living" adjustments was altered so that the Consumer Price Index,[1] rather

[1] The Consumer Price Index is a composite of prices of selected consumer items maintained by The Bureau of Labor Statistics. The items vary from time to time according to changing conceptions of what components make up the average family's budget.

than merely food prices, would be used. Because food prices had been rising more slowly than other prices, this resulted in an increase in the estimated poor population. Thus, we see that using one kind of cost estimate as opposed to another can result in different amounts of poverty.

The original SSA budget lines were largely based on a 1955 study of the United States Department of Agriculture (USDA) on the food buying habits of the lowest-income population. It was found that these low-income families spent, on the average, about 36 percent of their earnings on food. From this the SSA assumed that a budget in which food costs amounted to one-third would be in keeping with the poor's "preferences" for food. In the USDA study an attempt was made to determine how a family could minimize dietary deficiencies in an economic emergency. The "deficiency diet" cited above was developed as a guide to what could be accomplished by a family well-instructed in home economics and family finance under such an emergency. The USDA's Consumer and Food Economics Division estimated that 75 percent of all families spending the amount allowed under this budget for food would suffer dietary deficiencies —hence, the term "deficiency diet."

The SSA's "economy" budget merely multiplies the cost of the deficiency diet by a factor of three to arrive at the total budget. For example, if a yearly deficiency diet for a family of four was determined to be $1000, the total budget would amount to $3000. In this regard, it is noteworthy that a more recent USDA study, from 1960–1961, was available and had shown that a factor of four would be more reasonable. The official count of the poor in 1968 was 25.4 million people in poverty, approximately

Table 1. Persons below the Official Poverty Lines, by Race, 1959–1974

| Year | Number (millions) | | | | Percent | | | |
	White	Non-white	Black *	U.S. Total	White	Non-white	Black *	U.S. Total
1974	16.3	7.9	7.5	24.3	NA	NA	NA	12.0
1973	15.1	7.8	7.4	23.0	8.4	29.6	31.4	11.1
1972	16.2	8.3	7.7	24.5	9.0	31.9	33.3	11.9
1971	17.8	7.8	7.4	25.6	9.9	30.9	32.5	12.5
1970	17.5	7.9	7.5	25.4	9.9	32.0	33.5	12.6
1969	16.7	7.5	7.1	24.1	9.5	31.0	32.2	12.1
1968	17.4	8.0	7.6	25.4	10.0	33.5	34.7	12.8
1967	19.0	8.8	8.5	27.8	11.0	37.2	39.3	14.2
1966	19.3	9.2	8.9	28.5	11.3	39.8	41.8	14.7
1965	22.5	10.7	NA	33.2	13.3	47.1	NA	17.3
1964	25.0	11.1	NA	36.1	14.9	49.6	NA	19.0
1963	25.2	11.2	NA	36.4	15.3	51.0	NA	19.5
1962	26.7	12.0	NA	38.6	16.4	55.8	NA	21.0
1961	27.9	11.7	NA	39.6	17.4	56.1	NA	21.9
1960	28.3	11.5	NA	39.9	17.8	55.9	NA	22.2
1959	28.5	11.0	NA	39.5	18.1	56.2	NA	22.4

Sources: U.S. Bureau of the Census, *Current Population Reports,* Series P–60, No. 91, "Characteristics of the Low-Income Population 1972," Table 1; Series P–23, No. 48, "The Social and Economic Status of the Black Population in the United States 1973," Table 16; 1974 data from: Riverside, Ca., *Press,* July 24, 1975.
* Blacks are also included in the figure for nonwhite; separate statistics for blacks were not maintained until 1965.

12.8 percent of the population. Had the SSA chosen a factor of four, the official count would have been about 37.5 million persons, or 19 percent of the population in poverty (Gordon, 1971:240).

Table 1 gives the number and percent of persons officially acknowledged as poor for the years from 1959 to 1974 in the United States. The table shows the trend for the country as a whole and for racial subcategories. An obvious feature of these data is the generally consistent decline in the incidence of official poverty. Although the efficacy of antipoverty programs can be questioned, the decline has slowed as the war on poverty grinds into nonexistence in the 1970s. There is even some sign of a reversal. In particular, during 1974 there has been an increase in the percent of poor persons in each racial group. The poor in 1974 totaled 24.3 million or 12 percent of the population. Of the poor, 16.3 million were white and 7.4 million were black. Although whites have consistently comprised the majority of the U.S. poor, the rate of poverty among nonwhites, most of whom are black, is much higher than among whites. Indeed, the extremely high rate of poverty among nonwhites is the most striking feature of these official counts of the poor.

The official poverty lines presume an absolute definition of poverty, that is, there exists a fixed standard of living which divides the poor from the nonpoor. While changes in the *cost* of acquiring this standard are recognized, changes in the standard itself are not. Thus, the poverty standard (that is, an absolute) may be logically and empirically unrelated to the typical standard of living (relative to time and place). This means that the number of poor can be reduced without any necessary reduction in inequality as a whole. If the portion of the population with the lowest level of living is provided an income at or above the poverty cutoffs, then poverty may be technically eliminated even though these people remain far below the rest of the population. In fact, when adjustments in the poverty lines do not keep up with increasing costs but incomes do, or come closer to doing so, then an absolute definition of poverty will produce a decline in the number of persons counted as poor. There is some evidence that just such a process accounts for some of the trend in Table 1.

Even the federal government implicitly recognizes that its poverty lines may be arbitrarily low. Thus, it has defined a category of the "near-poor" consisting of those persons in households with income above the poverty line but below 125 percent of it. These persons are only slightly above the official poverty line and clearly in precarious economic circumstances. One could argue that the government's "near-poor" cutoffs offer a better poverty line than its official ones.

Many critics of the official poverty lines have called for a *relative* definition of poverty. A relative definition positively correlates the poverty line with the typical standard of living or some other index reflecting the standard of living of more affluent members of society. The primary recommendation for a relative definition is that it formally recognizes that poverty and affluence are two sides of the same coin. The most widely discussed proposal

for a relative definition of poverty has been offered by Victor Fuchs (1967). Fuchs argues that a poverty line taken at 50 percent of the median family income would be desirable because it would recognize changing standards of living. More or less conservative lines could be drawn by lowering or raising the percentage. Responses to various Gallup polls over the years reveal that most Americans volunteer a line about 70 percent of the median family income when asked how much income they feel is necessary to provide a decent living standard in the United States (Rainwater, 1974). Hence, the Fuchs line is on the conservative side of public opinion, although public opinion might very well provide two lines if citizens answered the question separately in reference to themselves and to "the poor." Table 2 provides comparisons between the official poverty line, the near-poor alternative line, and the Fuchs line.

Since the near-poor line is a constant 125 percent of the poverty line, we expect and find a parallel trend of decline in comparing the incidence of "poverty" under these alternatives. In each of these cases, the percent in "poverty" in 1973 was about one-half of the percent in "poverty" in 1959. But, as the last two columns show, these alternative poverty lines clearly reflect the absolute-level approach to a definition of poverty.

In 1959 the official poverty line (actually constructed later than 1959) was located at 54.9 percent of the 1959 median family income. It was, therefore, higher than the Fuchs line and, hence, results in a higher count of the poor. The near-poor line for 1959 was located at 68.6 percent of the 1959 median family income. It would, incidentally, about match the income standard for a decent living implicit in the results of public

Table 2. Comparison of Official Poverty Lines, Near-Poor Lines, and Fuchs' Poverty Line (One-Half of Median Family Income)

| Year | *Percent in Poverty* | | | *Poverty Line as Percent of Family Median Income* | |
	Official Lines	Near-Poor Lines	Fuchs' Line	Official	Near-Poor
1974	12.0	NA	NA	39.2	49.0
1973	11.1	15.8	NA	37.7	47.1
1972	11.9	16.8	NA	38.5	48.1
1971	12.5	17.8	NA	40.2	50.3
1970	12.6	17.6	19.0	40.2	50.3
1969	12.1	17.4	18.5	39.7	49.6
1968	12.8	18.2	18.3	41.2	51.4
1967	14.2	20.0	18.5	43.0	53.4
1966	14.7	21.3	19.2	44.2	55.3
1965	17.3	24.1	20.0	46.3	57.9
1964	19.0	26.3	19.9	48.2	60.3
1963	19.5	27.1	19.9	50.1	62.6
1962	21.0	28.8	19.8	51.9	64.8
1961	21.9	30.0	20.3	53.2	66.6
1960	22.2	30.4	20.3	53.8	67.2
1959	22.4	31.1	20.0	54.9	68.6

Sources: For 1974, Riverside, Ca., *Press,* July 24, 1975; for official line and near-poor line, 1959–1973, U.S. Bureau of the Census, *Current Population Reports,* Series P–60, No. 98, Tables 1 and 2; for the Fuchs' line, Lowell E. Gallaway, *Poverty in America* (Athens, Ohio: Grid, 1973), p. 10.

opinion polls. Under the near-poor line for 1959 over 31 percent of the U.S. population would have been counted in poverty as compared with the official count of over 22 percent and the implicit count of 20 percent under the Fuchs proposal. Adjustments to the official and near-poor lines have not kept up with changes in the median family income. By 1974 the official poverty line was only 39.2 percent and the near-poor line 49.0 percent of the median family income. The Fuchs proposal, which automatically adjusts for changes in the median, would now count more persons in poverty than either the official lines or the near-poor lines. Indeed, the Fuchs line suggests very little reduction in poverty (inequality).[2]

For another alternative, the Bureau of Labor Statistics (BLS) had kept a series

[2] Even the Fuchs line, however, builds in a certain inflexibility. It would be technically possible for the lower half of a distribution to lie wholly above the Fuchs line (one-half of the median). Further, the inequality above the median is ignored by the Fuchs line. In many underdeveloped countries the standard of living at the median is scarcely better than that at one-half the median, because nearly everyone faces a harsh and dismal existence. Nevertheless, in such presumably affluent countries like the United States, some relative definition of poverty, be it the Fuchs line or some alternative, seems preferable to the absolute approach of the official definition.

of estimates of the cost of a "moderate but adequate" budget for urban families. It has also kept series for parallel "minimum" and "higher standard" budgets. The moderate budget would strike many as rather austere. It allows a father to buy a new suit every two to four years, a mother to buy a new coat every five years, the family a *used* car every four years, a new refrigerator and stove every seventeen years. It does not allow any savings for college education or emergencies of unemployment or illness. The minimum budget allows for nothing but food, clothing, and basic rent. In 1971, the BLS moderate budget cost $10,971 and the minimum budget cost $7214. By comparison, the *average factory wage* for 52 weeks of work in 1971 was $7488—barely above the BLS minimum and well below the BLS moderate but adequate budget. The official poverty line for the same urban family of four was $4137. The 1971 median family income for white families was $10,672 and for black families $6440. Thus, well over half of the population in 1971 fell below the BLS estimate of a moderate standard of living. And, over half of the black population fell below the BLS estimate of a *minimum* standard of living. For those federal officials who actually make policy, something lower than the BLS's minimum ($4137) was preferred because roughly 25.6 million persons fell below it.

Who Are the Poor?

Who are the poor counted by the government? Anecdotes, case studies, and TV documentaries—to say nothing of direct experience—provide lucid depictions of poverty. Michael Harrington's *The Other America* (1962) is a good place to begin

for those who want an overview. (For other characterizations of life in poverty, see Armstrong, 1971; Coles, 1971; Gitlin and Hollander, 1970; Liebow, 1967.) The government, as well, provides descriptions of the officially acknowledged poor. While its account is in the dry language of statistical tables and analyses, the diligent student would be well advised to study these figures. We have abstracted a sample of the available descriptions and include them in Table 3.

In Table 3 we may see how the poor have differed from those not officially in poverty with respect to certain family characteristics. Comparisons are given for each of three selected years, 1959, 1967, and 1973. For example, we see that the poor and nonpoor differ sharply in racial composition. We already know, from Table 1, that the risk of being poor is consistently higher for nonwhites, especially blacks, than for whites. In 1973 nearly one in every three blacks was below the official poverty line, while only about one in every twelve whites was likely to be poor. This results, in Table 3, in blacks making up nearly one-third of all persons in poverty in 1973, but only about eight of every one hundred persons out of poverty. Nevertheless, because of their greater numbers, whites still account for fully two-thirds of the poor people of the United States.

It is obvious from these statistics that racial discrimination is a reasonable hypothesis for explaining a large portion of America's poverty. This is further suggested by inspecting the ratio of black median family income to white median family income. In 1973 this ratio stood at .58. Nor can this low ratio be wholly attributed to Southern racial prejudice. In the South the 1973 ratio was .56, but

Table 3. Selected Characteristics of Families by Poverty Status
(Percentage with Characteristic) in 1973, 1967, and 1959

Selected Characteristic	Families in Poverty			Families Not in Poverty		
	1973	1967	1959	1973	1967	1959
Race of Head:						
White	66.7	71.6	74.3	90.9	92.2	94.2
Nonwhite	33.3	28.4	25.7	9.1	7.8	5.8
Black	31.6	27.4	NA	7.8	6.9	NA
Sex of Head:						
Male	54.6	68.7	77.0	90.9	91.9	93.0
Female	45.4	31.3	23.0	9.1	8.1	7.0
Age of Head:						
Under 25	14.0	9.4	7.5	7.1	6.0	4.6
25–64	68.8	63.8	70.1	78.9	81.4	83.6
Over 64	17.2	26.8	22.4	14.0	12.6	11.8
Family Size:						
2 persons	35.1	38.2	34.3	37.6	33.3	31.7
3–5	46.1	37.7	42.1	53.0	54.0	58.2
Over 5	18.8	24.1	23.6	9.4	12.7	10.1
Number of Earners:						
None	38.1	33.0	23.8	7.8	5.2	3.7
One	41.9	40.1	48.4	35.0	38.6	47.6
Two or more	20.0	26.9	27.7	57.1	56.3	48.7
Work Status:						
Worked	51.4	56.7	67.5	85.0	88.2	89.2
50–52 weeks	21.7	30.8	36.6	69.7	73.3	70.1
1–49 weeks	29.7	25.9	31.0	15.2	14.9	19.1
Did Not Work:	48.3	42.0	30.5	13.2	10.0	8.4
Poor Health	15.5	12.5	9.5	3.6	2.4	1.9
Housework	20.7	14.0	10.9	1.8	1.8	2.2
Other	12.0	15.5	10.0	7.9	5.8	4.3
In Military	0.3	1.3	1.9	1.8	1.8	2.4
Occupation of Head:						
Prof. & Tech.	4.4	3.9	2.0	14.7	14.6	12.1
Managers & Adm.	6.2	6.7	6.4	15.2	15.3	15.5
Sales & Clerical	11.2	8.4	5.1	14.0	13.4	14.3
Crafts & Kindred	12.3	11.0	9.9	22.0	21.3	22.0
Operatives	18.9	19.1	18.9	17.4	19.4	19.7
Service Workers	22.2	16.5	13.0	7.8	6.8	6.6
Nonfarm Laborers	9.2	10.2	12.5	4.9	4.6	5.1
Farmers & Farmlabor	15.6	24.1	32.2	4.0	4.5	4.7

Source: U.S. Bureau of the Census, *Current Population Reports,* Series P–60, No. 98, "Characteristics of the Low-Income Population 1973," Table 4.

the ratio in the rest of the nation was only .64 and in the Northeast it was only .59.

Further evidence for the role of racial discrimination in producing poverty among blacks is found when we consider

Table 4. Education of Persons 14 Years Old and Older: Percent below Poverty Line by Sex and Race, 1972

Sex and Years of School Completed	All Races	Whites	Blacks
Both Sexes			
Education:			
No years completed	35.5	31.8	51.9
1 to 5 years	30.7	25.5	46.5
6 to 8 years	17.6	14.9	36.2
9 to 11 years	12.9	9.5	32.8
High school (12 years)	6.4	5.3	18.2
Some college	4.9	4.4	11.1
Males			
Education:			
No years completed	33.1	27.9	48.6
1 to 5 years	24.8	20.4	39.0
6 to 8 years	13.5	11.3	28.5
9 to 11 years	9.7	7.0	25.1
High school (12 years)	4.6	3.8	13.3
Some college	4.2	3.8	9.4
Females			
Education:			
No years completed	38.1	35.5	58.0
1 to 5 years	36.5	30.8	53.5
6 to 8 years	21.6	18.4	43.3
9 to 11 years	15.6	11.6	39.0
High school (12 years)	7.7	6.5	21.8
Some college	5.6	5.1	12.4

Source: U.S. Bureau of the Census, *Current Population Reports,* Series P–60, No. 91, "Characteristics of the Low-Income Population 1972," Table 13.

the effects of education on the risks of poverty. The myth of equal opportunity in the United States is often based on the belief that education is equally available and that higher education provides a direct escape from the hazard of poverty. Table 4 confirms that one's chances of escaping poverty are increased as one's education is increased.

The table also demonstrates that education is a less effective escape route for women than men, much less effective for blacks than for whites, and least effective of all for black females. Sex discrimination in incomes can also be documented by looking at ratios of median income of females to median income of males. Indeed, the ratio for 1969 is barely above the ratio for 1939—.59 to .58, respectively. In fact, for whites the 1969 ratio (.58) is lower than the 1939 ratio (.61). Just the reverse held, however, among blacks. The female:male ratio for black median income was .51 in 1939 but .69 in 1969. What has occurred in this period is that black males have been unable to expand their employment into higher paying jobs during a time when jobs for black women have been opening up. But, these jobs for black women, although better paying than in prior generations, are still low-paying jobs (like those to which black males are largely restricted). Hence, black women have improved their median income relative to the black male median. But neither women nor blacks have been able to crack the higher barriers with much effectiveness.

Other aspects of Table 3 reveal that the poor differ from the nonpoor in the age of the head of household, family size, and relationship to the employment market. But most important of these for analytical purposes is the latter. For example, multiple earners are important for keeping families out of poverty. The popular conception of the family views it as a one-earner family. The father holds down a job while the mother stays at home to care for the house and children.

But the 1973 data show that for nonpoor families, the majority have two or more income earners. Indeed, sticking to the popular conception may be asking for trouble, especially at the lowest income levels.

On the other hand, employment itself does not guarantee one enough income to escape poverty. Over half of the 4.8 million heads of poor families in 1973 worked during the year. Of these, 1.1 million heads of families worked 50–52 weeks full-time; another .7 million single individuals were poor despite this same level of employment. Many other poor persons worked part-time or full-time for part of the year. Fully one in five families in poverty even had two or more income earners in 1973. The work experience of the poor in 1973 was similar to that in 1971 as depicted in Figure 1. Clearly, employment is a major factor in escape from poverty, but it is not a sure route.

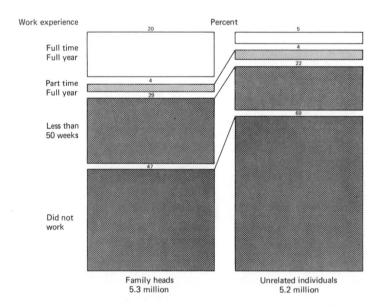

Figure 1. Work Experience of the Poor, 1971

Source: Sar A. Levitan, Programs in Aid of the Poor for the 1970s, rev. ed. (Baltimore: Johns Hopkins University Press, 1973), p. 120. © The Johns Hopkins University Press.

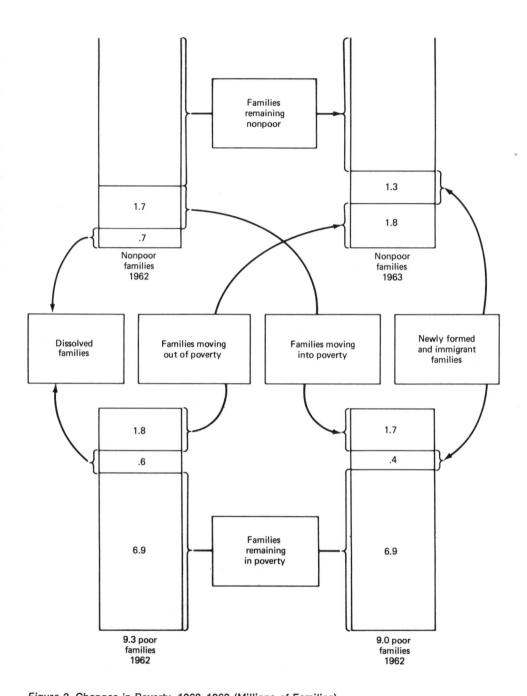

Figure 2. Changes in Poverty, 1962–1963 (Millions of Families)

Source: Robert J. Lampman, *Ends and Means of Reducing Income Poverty* (Madison: Institute for Research on Poverty, University of Wisconsin, 1971), p. 62.

When looking for routes out of poverty it is also useful to look at the record on aggregate flows in and out of poverty in recent years. Robert J. Lampman has provided the picture in Figure 2 for 1962–1963 from data given in the 1965 *Economic Report of the President*. What is striking about this figure is the evenness of inflow (persons newly poor) and outflow (persons escaping prior poverty). By way of comparison, Figure 3 shows the movement into and out of poverty for the years: 1968–1969 (Levitan, 1973:8). Again, we see counterbalancing flows. Apparently, the reduction of numbers of poor persons is an uneven process taking its toll on more people than the straightforward count would indicate. Further, it is evident that the concept of near-poor is more than mere academic double talk. An exit from poverty may be precarious, and those who fall into poverty may have been struggling just above for some time.

The difficulty of escaping poverty once in that circumstance is highlighted by the data behind Figure 2. Lampman (1971:63) reports that 69 percent of the families in poverty in 1962 remained in poverty in 1963. For poor nonwhite families in 1962, 76 percent remained in poverty in 1963. The fate of poor families headed by a woman was identical, in this respect, to that of poor nonwhites. And, fully 83 percent of the poor families in 1962 without employment for the head of the family were unable to rise above the poverty line in 1963. The data of Figure 3, for the years 1968–1969, suggest little change. Of those who were poor in 1968, over 64 percent remained poor in 1969.

Since the latter data derive from a period in the midst of the so-called war on poverty, they lend further evidence that little change has occurred in the basic structures generating poverty in the United States or in the welfare system designed to cope with it. We do not imply by this that social programs do nothing for the poor, only that poverty is very unlikely to be eradicated by current approaches. The fact that social insurance and public assistance programs do aid many people and, thereby, reduce the incidence of poverty is shown in Table 5.

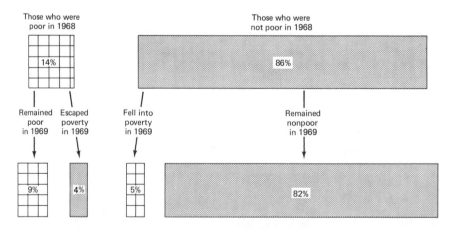

Figure 3. Movement Into and Out of Poverty

Source: Sar A. Levitan, *Programs in Aid of the Poor for the 1970s,* rev. ed. (Baltimore: Johns Hopkins University Press, 1973), p. 8. © The Johns Hopkins University Press.

Table 5. Poverty Status of Families Before and After Receiving
Social Insurance and/or Public Assistance Benefits, 1971

Family type	Total number (millions)	Families poor before benefits (%)	Families poor after social insurance benefits (%)	Families poor after social insurance and public as-sistance (%)	Percent of poor families receiving these benefits
All families	72.0	20.9	14.3	12.0	80
Family head aged 65 or over	13.0	53.8	25.8	22.9	97
With head disabled	3.6	57.2	46.0	36.3	89
Working age without children	24.1	9.8	8.0	7.5	43
Working age, male head, children	26.7	6.2	5.7	4.9	51
Working age, female head, children	4.7	43.1	38.5	26.3	83

Source: Barry M. Blechman, Edward M. Gramlich, and Robert W. Hartman, *Setting National Priorities: The 1975 Budget* (Washington, D.C.: The Brookings Institution, 1974), pp. 170, 174. © 1974 by the Brookings Institution, Washington, D.C.
Note: Families include unrelated individuals. Social insurance includes old-age, survivors, and disability insurance and unemployment compensation. Public assistance includes cash assistance from federal, state, and local sources, and the bonus value of food stamps.

From Table 5 we see that the effect of social insurance payments and public assistance reduced the incidence of poverty for families in 1971 from 20.9 percent to 12.0 percent even though only 80 percent of the poor received such benefits. The 20.9 percent of the population which would have been officially poor without these benefits totaled to roughly 15.1 million families. After receipt of benefits, roughly 8.6 million families remained in poverty. Thus, it could be said that social insurance and public assistance payments helped 6.4 million families escape poverty in 1971. These programs were more effective in reaching certain types of fam-ilies than others. For example, nearly all poor families whose official household head was over 64 years of age received some benefit from these programs. Social insurance and public assistance programs, however, were relatively ineffective in aid-ing poor families of working age without children, or those families headed by a male. Families in these categories are eligible for very little aid. The bulk of those benefits they do receive is in un-employment compensation.

An examination of the reigning official definitions of poverty and the character-istics of those defined as poor is but one facet of the study of poverty. Further questions remain, such as: "Why *this* set of definitions?" and "What interests are served by a particular conception of poverty?" To address the former question, a review of selected aspects of historical conceptions of poverty will be necessary. The latter question requires an examination of the relationship between poverty and inequality.

POVERTY AND INEQUALITY

There has long been a tendency to study the poor as if they constitute an independent rather than integral segment of society. Viewing the poor in such a fashion is consistent with theories of poverty that blame the victims. Such theories hold that the poor are poor because of fundamental flaws arising out of their own character. Whether these flaws are biological, psychological, or sociological is immaterial to the fact that such theories absolve, directly or indirectly, the nonpoor and society itself of any responsibility for the existence, persistence, or irradication of poverty.

There is an alternative view which suggests that the poor cannot be properly conceptualized apart from those structural features of society which distinguish them from the nonpoor. In this case, wealth as well as poverty must come under scrutiny. It is to this alternative that we turn for an explanation of poverty, followed by an analysis of "blaming the victims" theories.

Poverty and Wealth: Two Sides of the Same Coin

As a phenomenon, poverty depends upon the existence of an institutionalized system of *inequality* in which those who are most deprived are recognized and treated as a distinct social category. It follows that there are both material and ideological dimensions imbedded in the concept of poverty.

In its primary sense, poverty entails the condition of being unable to command those things thought to be minimal requirements for day-to-day physical well-being. Poverty is thus relative to some standard embedded in the social sentiments and relationships of members of some community or society. That standard itself is subject to variation over time as these sentiments and relationships change or the environment in which they operate undergoes transformations. Ancient and comparative evidence suggests that only in the most primitive economic conditions, where there is effectively no surplus of goods or services, does poverty fail to exist.

To understand poverty we must understand inequality. We must be able to account for the unequal distribution of desired goods and services in society. Correlatively, we must be able to account for the unequal distribution of degradation and coercion. Whereas "wealth" may be viewed as a quantity of goods and services which are positively valued and give enjoyment to those who possess or use them, "illth" may be viewed as a quantity of burdens and ill treatment which are negatively valued and give pain and degradation to those who carry or endure them (Walter, 1973). Both wealth and illth are dependent on the existence of social classes—hierarchical groupings; most people, however, do not make such a direct link between poverty and inequality.

Popular Conceptions

For obvious reasons, those who are free from the fear of permanent or acute poverty tend to take a conservative attitude toward the existence of social classes and the causes of poverty. They have long sought to restrict the definition of poverty to minimal standards of living and to locate the causes of poverty in the defects of individuals. As a result of this bias, there is a "dominant version" of poverty which can be abstracted from most theories.

First, the dominant version restricts attention to the bare economic necessities of life. It views material conditions of life as the criteria of concern and defines poverty as a condition which jeopardizes physical survival and social stability. The *social* problem of poverty, in this view, is to insure against organized revolt by assuring those at the bottom of the class structure the opportunity to obtain the necessities of survival.

Second, the dominant version views the misery of marginal survival as functional and proper, for in misery is felt to lie the motivational source of labor. Wealth is viewed as the product of work and talent; its absence, especially at the level of poverty, is seen as evidence of failure to work or absence of talent. The implicit voluntaristic bias in this "work ethic" rationalizes the moralistic evaluation of poor persons which is common in American society.

Third, the dominant version *translates the moral view of poverty as punishment and wealth as reward* into a causal view. American economic ideology is intimately grounded in the capitalist mode of production and distribution. Since Ricardo and Smith, classical economic theory implied that income depended fundamentally upon the amount of labor one expended. Capitalism, the economic system detailed by the classical economists, required the individuation of labor

in a mass labor market. For those not possessing ownership of productive resources beyond their own labor, economic survival became a matter of selling oneself. When one sells oneself as labor, he/she must treat himself/herself as an object. To recover a sense of subjective worth, one must identify with work. Work becomes a symbol of worth and working becomes the evidence that one is worth something. The wage rate, then, becomes the moral calculus by which people are judged. This "worth in work-and-wages" or "work ethic" simultaneously provides causal and moral explanations of poverty and wealth. Thus, the only way to ultimately explain poverty is to find its roots in individual defects of mind, body, or character.

This implicit conclusion leads the dominant version to its fourth principle: *that remedial actions must be addressed to the kinds of individual defects which can be found among the poor.* Such defects can be seen as biologically or physiologically determined or determined by the individual acting on his or her own initiative. Thus, the dominant version distinguishes two forms of appropriate remedy. Defects of the first kind are taken to justify charity and minimal maintenance of such individuals. Perhaps, also, some effort is approved for making these persons perform the menial labors which their defects still allow, thereby sharing in the costs and burdens of their own survival if not providing a source of labor for society's dirty work. Defects attributable to voluntary decisions, those not biologically or physiologically determined, are taken to justify remedies entailing punishment or retribution or, at minimum, moral reform. The "able-bodied" poor are found to be the cause of their own poverty and therefore are responsible for their own recovery.

These conceptions of poverty are not merely an isolated construct of twentieth-century American society. Rather they are rooted in centuries of European and American thought as well as political machinations.

HISTORICAL ROOTS OF AMERICAN VIEWS ON POVERTY: EUROPE

The Greco-Roman Tradition

The ancient Greeks and Romans anticipated certain modern notions about poverty. The concept of "philanthropy" comes originally from the Greek notion of the gods' love of man or, especially, the beneficence of the gods (Hands, 1968). Greek and Roman officials appropriated this concept themselves in trading gifts and public works for social honor and security. This practice reveals the implicit exchange behind such historic provision of social welfare, for exchange both symbolizes and specifies inequalities of status between donor and recipient.

Certain gifts came to be designated for the "poor" (*ploutos*), but this category was less restrictive than the term might imply today. The *ploutos* were simply persons with little or no property who worked long and hard to secure the frugal and dull life of the mass of citizens. Another class, however, was recognized to fall below the poor and was viewed contemptuously. This was the class of destitute unemployed forced to resort to beggary (*ptocheia*). In Plato's ideal state, beggary was to be outlawed; in practice,

beggars were often banished from Greek and Roman cities, a practice later institutionalized in Anglo-American poor law. In this distinction we see the formative stage of stigmatizing attitudes toward the poor and a nascent version of the division of poor people into the "moral, deserving poor" and the "immoral, undeserving poor."

During the Middle Ages, the Greco-Roman relief institutions were extended and improved by the Eastern Church in Byzantium. Special homes for the aged, orphans, travellers, the poor, and the ill existed in many cities. Although beggary was not fully approved, attitudes under the Church softened from those of the Greco-Roman eras. A "poverty line" was used in the sixth century to define the poor: those with income and property worth less than 50 nomismata. Occasionally, cities provided public works employment for the poor; beggars who refused such work were typically banished from the city. Houses for the poor ordinarily refused entry to those who were "able-bodied" (Constantelos, 1968).

Important developments reflected in these matters were (1) the specialization of relief by type of "problem," (2) the appearance of the concept of a "poverty line," and (3) the further refinement of moral evaluations along the line of assumed personal responsibility. Contemporary American poor relief is largely based upon categorical programs with categories presumably identifying types or causes of poverty, for example, Old Age Assistance and Aid to Families with Dependent Children. As we have seen, American poor relief and poverty policy also rely upon a "poverty line" definition of the poor. Finally, the concept of "able-bodied" as a basis for moral evaluation of the poor reached full flower in English poor law and continues with major impact in American attitudes and practice.

European Religious Tradition

Tierney (1959) has shown that canon (religious) law played an important role in providing both the administration of relief in the Middle Ages and the rationalization for relief programs in the transition to capitalism. While many scholars mark the onset of modern poor law with Edward III's "Ordinance of Laborers" in 1349 A.D., which sought to immobilize labor and reduce mendicancy —begging for alms—the Statute of Charlemagne, 800 A.D., had essentially the same objectives. It fined citizens giving alms to the able-bodied, threatened to forbid mendicancy, and tried to force serfs and rural laborers to remain in place, subservient to manorial lords.

The role of canon law in subsequent secular poor law may be seen in two examples. First, there is the canonical resolution of the conflict between the teaching of St. John Chrysostom (347–407), leader of the Greek Church at Antioch and Constantinople and that of St. Augustine. The former held that charity should give no thought to the motives or personal responsibility of those in poverty but rather to their need. St. Augustine, however, taught that aid should never be given where it might further sin or injustice. The conflict was over the issue of whether there were "deserving" and "undeserving" poor.

The resolution of the problem was to fall back upon a compromise offered by the leader of the Latin Church at Milan, St. Ambrose (340–397). He made no explicit distinction of "worthyness" but

provided that (unspecified) priorities should govern the giving of relief to the poor when funds were limited. This so-called compromise laid the legal basis for future distinctions between classes of poor people.

Second, the canonist debate on this matter filled in the gaps during the three-century struggle with the Mendicancy Movement. This movement arose in the first urban crises of the medieval era as a critique of the Church and its vast wealth and power. Roving preachers, often laymen, roamed towns and countryside condemning the wealth of the Church and adopting poverty as a testament to their Christianity. They spoke of themselves as "Christ's poor" and members of the "true" church. In response, Pope Innocent III (1161–1216) formed the Dominican Order (later, also, the Franciscan, Carmelite, and Augustinian orders) as an apostolic movement to coopt the heretics and win over their following. The orders were to adopt the life of poverty, including mendicancy, to enhance their appeal.

The "mendicant" orders were so successful that they began to arouse the fear of older orders of the Church as well as the secular elites. Eventually, these older elites obtained Papal regulation of the four mendicant orders. Yet, the controversy lasted for centuries. In 1349, the mendicants sought revision of a papal bull regulating their practices. Instead, they got a papal commission headed by a leading conservative, Richard Fitzralph. Fitzralph's report, *De pauperie Salvatoris*, condemned begging and promoted a lengthy series of morally graded distinctions between types of poverty which made presumptions as to the fault of the victim for his or her condition. Rapidly thereafter Fitzralph's distinctions entered the lexicon of secular poor law.

Political Codification of Poor Laws

The bubonic plague which swept across the Continent to England, 1347–1349, created a labor shortage for manufacturing and commercial businesses and forced many a former peasant onto the roads looking for work and higher wages, and also contributed to much vagrancy and medicancy.

In this context, economic and political elites were especially receptive to Fitzralph's moral rationalization of poor relief and its conservative implications. Edward III had already, in 1349, issued his Ordinance of Laborers and obtained a Statute of Laborers from Parliament to back it up in 1351. The Statute of Laborers fixed a maximum wage, required the unemployed to take whatever work was offered, forbade almsgiving to the able-bodied, and restricted the right of the worker to travel. By 1388, after a decade of peasant uprisings, additional restrictions were enacted. Servants were required to carry letters of permission for travel, stating the purposes and date of return. Healthy or "sturdy" beggars were only allowed to beg with permits. "Impotent" poor persons could receive aid only with longtime residency or in their birthplace. The Church's distinction between "sturdy" and "impotent" poor now entered the secular poor law. Other aspects of these developments have served as principles of poor relief into the present century: support ceilings; work requirements; residency requirements; and local responsibility.

Only minor changes were made in England's poor relief for over a century. By the early sixteenth century it was evident that the Church could no longer be depended upon by the emerging capitalists and nobility to provide the control of the poor which they needed. Even within the Church there were many who sought a secular solution to problems of social order and poverty. Thus began a century of secular codification of poor law, although much of these laws were drawn from canon law or Church practice.

Major reform of English poor law began with Henry VIII's order in 1531 that local officials investigate and register all applications by paupers, issue licenses to beg, and give public whippings to "sturdy" beggars. In 1536 an *Act for the Punishment of Sturdy Vagabonds and Beggars* completed the Henrician Poor Law. It provided for branding, enslavement, and execution for repeated offenses of vagrancy or begging by the able-bodied. In addition to punishment, "sturdy beggars" were to be forced to work and idle children aged 5–14 were to be taken from their parents and indentured. At the same time, however, the act required each parish to establish a fund in aid of "poor, impotent, sick and diseased people not able to work." Still, to limit relief expenses, paupers could not be registered for aid until they had resided in a community for three years.

Thereafter, several statutes supplemented these provisions. The 1562 Statute of Artificers attempted to fix wages and set forth indenturement for unemployed beggars aged 12 to 60. In 1563 local officials were given the power to make compulsory assessments on persons who refused voluntarily to contribute to the "poor boxes" set up in the parish church. By 1572 a general tax, called the "poor rate," was established for purposes of financing poor relief. But, to keep the poor rate low, all aided paupers had to be registered with the justice of peace so that indigent strangers could be "ordered out" of the parish. For much the same reason, "houses of correction" were established in 1576 and stocked with working materials for the poor. As their name suggests, these workhouses were viewed as moral training grounds for the victims of poverty.

A series of famines and peasant revolts near the end of the sixteenth century culminated in new statutes which systematized the poor law. The 1596–1601 Elizabethan Poor Law codified several principles which have guided and limited public policy on poverty up to the modern period. Among these are (1) that provision for the poor will be based upon moral evaluations as well as need, (2) that the administrative unit for poor relief is to be the smallest geographical subdivision of government, (3) that primary obligation of aid falls upon the relatives of the poor, and (4) that no locality has responsibility for aiding those poor persons who do not have long-term residency in it.

While the new codes finally established the principle of secular public responsibility for poor relief, they fixed this principle as consistently subordinate to the economic concern for a submissive, stable, and inexpensive labor force. For the next two hundred years the only changes in the Elizabethan Poor Law were those designed to strengthen the enforcement of these principles. Their net result was to institutionalize further the economic exploitation and moral stigma suffered by the poor.

By 1576 "houses of correction" were being used as devices for lowering relief costs and securing cheap labor. The Workhouse Act of 1696 made these houses of correction into general factories for pauper labor. In 1722 relief officials were empowered to contract out pauper labor to private workhouses and deny relief to any pauper who refused to submit to this degrading experience. Although problems with the workhouse caused many controversies, the logic of the workhouse test became engrained in English and American poor relief.

Adam Smith's *Wealth of Nations*, 1776, argued against all poor relief on the grounds that any payments to paupers reduced the welfare of the employed by interfering in the "natural laws" of the market for labor. Workhouses came under attack, therefore, from economic theorists. Others objected on moral or practical grounds. In 1788 Gilbert's Act abolished the contract system of private workhouses in favor of poorhouses for the impotent poor and "outdoor" relief for the able-bodied poor. Outdoor relief was to be given as wage supplements for paupers employed by private enterprises. However, little use was actually made of wage supplements, and even more stringent regulation of relief for the poor was in the offing.

The nineteenth century witnessed the systematization of the view which condemns the victims of poverty and exalts the work ethic. Jeremy Bentham (1797–8; 1811) had argued that humans have two masters, pain and pleasure, and the principle of utility by which these were balanced would determine behavior. Thus, he proposed a model penitentiary in which convicts "ought not be made more eligible than that of the poorest class of subjects living in a state of innocence and liberty." Chadwick, the chief author of an 1832 royal commission's report, applied a direct analogy to the reform of poor relief. He held that those receiving relief "shall not be made really or apparently so eligible as the situation of the independent laborer of the lowest class." "Eligibility" meant condition of life. Thus, relief would be refused the able-bodied except under such harsh and degrading conditions that none who could possibly escape the risk of starvation by other means would accept it and, even then, relief conditions must clearly place the recipient in circumstances below the most miserable independent laborer.

The principle of "less eligibility," as this mandate was called, required some method of "test" or enforcement. Unfortunately for the poor, a mechanism already existed: the "workhouse test." As early as 1722, overseers of the poor could refuse aid to any who refused to enter a house of correction. Although this power had been repealed in 1788, it was restored in 1820. The Chadwick Commission recommended, therefore, that harsh labor and miserly support in a workhouse be instituted as the primary mode of poor relief for the "sturdy" poor. Coupled with a centralization of poor relief policy at the national level and administration at the local level, the Poor Law of 1834 served as a model for poverty policy in both England and the United States until recent times.

Similar trends in conceptions and policies for regulating the poor are to be found in the United States, beginning with the thirteen colonies.

HISTORICAL ROOTS OF AMERICAN VIEWS ON POVERTY: AMERICAN DEVELOPMENTS

Early Colonial Experience

From the beginning of the American colonies the English poor law was transferred to the new territories. Obviously important in this regard was the English dominion, but conditions in the colonies probably played a direct part. While the new world may have been viewed as a land of milk and honey, as for example in Sir Thomas More's *Utopia*, the fact was that survival required a strong commitment and it was hardly a setting for the easy toleration of idleness. Furthermore, the heavy emphasis upon puritanical religion gave little comfort to the poor.

In Pennsylvania in 1718 paupers were forced to wear the letter "P" on their sleeve as identification of their pauper status. Almost everywhere paupers were disfranchised, required to swear the "pauper's oath," publicly flogged, and identified on "paupers lists" in newspapers or on bulletin boards. Although extensive use of almshouses did not develop until the 1800s, they appeared as early as 1657 in Rensselaerswyck, New York, and 1660 in Boston.

Particularly important in the American colonies was the disdain for "sturdy" poor persons. As early as 1619, the Virginia assembly demanded compulsory labor for those poor persons judged to be lazy. The Massachusetts Bay Company in 1633 enacted harsh punishments for idleness and "unprofitable" pastimes. By 1636 Boston had officially adopted the English Poor Law practice of forbidding visitors from remaining over two weeks without a certificate of permission. The practice of "warning out" suspected improvidents was adopted the same year, with forcible removal of those who did not immediately depart. By 1642, Plymouth Colony had legally defined a residency requirement for poor relief.

Eventually, however, disastrous events such as King Philip's War (1675–1677) created so many refugees that public officials had to begin providing some aid for the "sturdy" poor. Thus, Boston officials began to accumulate a general fund for the relief of "strangers." By 1701 local communities were generally being reimbursed from colonial treasuries for such programs. Even prior to this, some communities had used the compulsory labor laws to justify "farming out" sturdy paupers and older dependent children. The "farming out" system placed poor persons as indentured laborers or apprentices with the lowest bidders at public auction. Another system which was adopted rather early was that of "binding out" younger dependent children into guardian families in the western territories.

Poor Relief in the Nineteenth Century

Paralleling the English experience, the United States saw a series of investigations by commissions on poor relief during the first decades of the nineteenth century. The Yates Report of 1824 in New York served a similar function in the United States (except for nationalizing poverty policy) that the Chadwick Report did in England. The Yates Report recommended the virtual abolition of outdoor poor relief, denial of relief to healthy males aged 18 to 50, residency requirements for poor relief, punishment of citizens who helped paupers enter the state, a workhouse test for relief, enforced labor in the workhouse, and establishing the county as the administrative unit for poverty policy.

Following the Yates Report, most states set the workhouse as the primary approach to relief of poverty. However, rather than dividing the sturdy poor from the impotent poor, the workhouse became a common scrap heap for the ill, abandoned, aged, insane, criminal, desti-

tute, and other misfortunate souls of society. Within twenty years renewed investigations were detailing the appalling failure of the poorhouse system. However, the issue was still focused upon the "immoral," that is, able-bodied, poor.

This concern with morality meshed with a flowering of nativist and religious charities which Schlossman (1974) identifies as the origin of one of the most popular theories of poverty in America, the "culture of poverty" theory. This theory holds that poverty arises out of defective cultures or subcultures which fail to socialize people to the values, beliefs, and life styles necessary to successful participation in modern economic life. Implicit in the culture of poverty thesis is the notion of a cycle of poverty across family generations. Thus, the defective socialization of children produces defective parenting which, in turn, produces defective socialization, *ad infinitum*. The critical problem becomes that of breaking the cycle.

Schlossman attributes this thesis to the attempts of the old middle class during the decades from 1840–1960 to retain control of the cities and states in the face of a tremendous influx of Irish Catholic immigrants. He argues that the Irish refused to give up their ethnic identity or religious and community institutions. They were, therefore, "the first impoverished Americans wholly beyond the pale of missionary good works and evangelical inspirational teaching" (Schlossman, 1974:22).

Typical of the midnineteenth century response to poverty were the "friendly visitors" of such charity organizations as the New York Association for Improving the Condition of the Poor. These friendly visitors were sent into the homes of paupers with such instructions as:

The rule is, that the willingly dependent upon alms should not live so comfortably with them as the humblest independent labourer without them. . . . The evils of improvidence can never be diminished, except by removing the cause; and this can only be done by elevating the moral character of the poor, and by teaching them to depend upon themselves. (Komisar, 1974: 26)

By the 1880s these sentiments were being echoed in the powerful Charity Organization Societies which served as clearinghouses for all operating charities, made detailed investigations of poor persons, and pontificated widely on the moral and spiritual dimensions of poverty. With the motto "not alms but a friend," they gave the poor "friendly visits" complete with lectures on intemperance, indolence, and improvidence.

Around the turn of the twentieth century there were a few signs of changing views on poverty. The social gospel movement in religion, the institutional economists, the antitrust progressives, and the settlement houses all contributed to speculation that poverty was based in the structure of the economy. But this speculation never reached the point of consistent or fundamental application in practice.

The Great Depression and the "New Deal"

The first fundamental change in U.S. attitudes toward poverty came with the shattering effects of the Great Depression. For the first time, a depression had hit so swiftly and severely that no region or social class could escape unscathed. Even so, no major federal action was taken until nearly four years of suffering had passed. The political wing of the American ruling class vainly argued that the sit-uation was merely a normal and healthy adjustment of the economy. But continued suffering brought social unrest and some began to question whether capitalism could survive the crisis. Eventually, a reform movement emerged under Franklin Roosevelt to relieve the suffering and restore legitimacy to the capitalist system.

The story of FDR's "New Deal" rescue of American capitalism is best told elsewhere, but this rescue did entail innovations in the attack on poverty. Roosevelt himself was always more committed to "getting the economy going" than to solving the problems of poverty. Thus, his first actions as president were directed toward the banking system rather than the relief system. When he did turn to the reform of the relief system his concern was more with the unemployed than with the "impotent" poor. While this represented an historical shift in attacks upon poverty, in the end the attack was *not* directed at establishing a structural long-run approach toward eradicating poverty. The classic "work ethic" of historical Anglo-American poverty policy remained a strong element of FDR's programs. As the economic and political unrest of the Depression years began to fade, FDR was quite willing to back away from any major reforms affecting the distribution of wealth or income.

FDR's program for the relief of impoverished individuals and families focused on providing public employment and cash assistance to the unemployed. After trying to provide jobs through grants to states and localities via the Public Works Administration, FDR turned to the more effective Civil Works Administration (CWA) at the federal level. The CWA proved controversial, expensive, and short-lived. Although it lasted only four and a half months in operation, it employed as many as four million workers by January 1934.

Although public works employment was not new in the history of poor relief, it was new on this scale and level in the United States. For the unemployed not covered by public works employment, FDR established the Federal Emergency Relief Administration. The FERA provided matching and outright grants to state and local relief agencies giving cash assistance to the unemployed poor. Excepting the token agency of the reconstruction era, the Freedman's Bureau, FERA was the first national agency with direct responsibility for relief of poverty. As such, it finally laid to rest the old Elizabethan principle that poor relief was entirely a matter for local authorities.

Underlying FDR's social program was a strong belief in the work ethic. Thus, FERA was directed only to the relief of the able-bodied unemployed. Relief for the ill, aged, or otherwise incapacitated poor was left strictly as a local matter. Only later when FDR's political support was threatened by dissident movements did he turn toward general welfare programs. Even the cash assistance of FERA was designed to reinforce the work ethic, for it was thought that aid-in-kind would demoralize the unemployed.

Ironically, while FDR sought to save capitalism, capitalist elites began to organize against his programs. While the early years of depression had stunned them into acquiescence, it is evident that they never believed there was anything wrong with the economy except public confidence in it. Despite the work ethic they presupposed, public works employment and federalized relief were too much for the conservative capitalists.

Both entailed an implicit challenge to their control over labor policy. Further, the National Recovery Administration's efforts at rationalizing the economy through industry-wide plans or codes of practice was seen as an encroachment upon the domain of capital—even though, in fact, the NRA plan constituted an implicit pledge by the federal government to forego antitrust actions.

When the Supreme Court ruled NRA unconstitutional, the heartened right-wing capitalists formed the American Liberty League to openly fight the New Deal. Roosevelt's New Deal was also coming under attack from the left where impatience was building regarding the lack of fundamental long-run social programs. Communists, socialists, Musteites, Townsendites, Coughlinites, Upton Sinclair, Huey Long—the list of proletariat and populist reformers was rapidly growing.

With these challenges FDR moved toward the middle. He abandoned hopes for cooperation by the right-wing capitalists and turned toward centralization of government and a regulated economy. Most importantly for our account, he coopted the left-wing reformers by introducing an omnibus social security plan which has become the framework for welfare planning and practice up to the present.

The 1935 Social Security Act established three types of federal programs dealing with economic security. Social *insurance* programs were to provide security for the unemployed and aged. A relief fund was to be obtained from taxes (euphemistically called contributions) on employees and employers according to the employee's income with eligibility for benefits when retired or subsequently unemployed. The nominal tax on employers, of course, could be shifted to employees and consumers through wage rates and prices. Public categorical *assistance* programs were to provide security for the needy blind, dependent women with children, and those aged poor who were not covered by the insurance program. Finally, health and welfare *services* of limited scope and quantity were established. Social insurance and supplemental categorical assistance remain the foundation of contemporary welfare policy. Although they have contributed to easing the pain of poverty, they are basically remedial rather than preventive and, in any case, contain serious defects.

Social insurance programs have explicitly tied benefits to long-term labor force participation and level of earnings. Thus, those most in need receive the least. Further, the compulsory taxes which provide the benefit fund are regressive (that is, take a proportionately larger share of the income of the poor than of the more well to do). Finally, many workers were entirely excluded from coverage. Most of these, such as domestics and farm laborers, were in especially insecure occupations. The social insurance programs have become less a protection against poverty than a retirement fund for white collar and skilled blue collar workers with relatively secure employment histories.

The social insurance programs have come to be known as "social security." This reflects the fact that they were intended to be the central part of the Social Security Act. Assistance and services were intended to be supplemental, if not entirely phased out, as the insurance program became established. But, it also reflects traditional prejudices against aiding the poor. Benefits under social insurance are viewed as "earned" and due the recipient as a matter of "rights"; benefits

under the public assistance provisions are viewed as "unearned" and given only as a matter of "charity." Thus, the public assistance programs have retained much of the historic stigma of Anglo-American poor relief. Given that the social insurance programs are generally designed so as *not* to benefit the most needy, the result is that for many poverty remains the degrading experience it has always been.

The public assistance programs were to be "means tested." That is, nobody had a right to benefits. The privilege of benefit would only be granted on the burden of the recipient proving that he/she had no other means of subsistence. Further, administration of the assistance programs was given to the states and usually the states turned them over to local officials. Thus, states were able to set arbitrary payment and residency standards or even moral requirements of eligibility to suit the needs of local economic and political elites. Payment levels differed radically by state and no state paid assistance benefits sufficient to maintain an adequate living standard. The Elizabethan principle of "less eligibility" remained in effect in practice if not in law. As the legislation was only enabling, rather than mandatory, many states or localities refused to adopt the provisions for aid to dependent children or did so under most restrictive conditions.

Indeed, the Aid to (families with) Dependent Children (ADC or AFDC) program has remained a focus of controversy in the nation's poor relief system. It grew out of "mother's pensions" designed to promote family life by enabling mothers to remain at home to care for their children rather than going off to work. Thus, it had a definite moral premise from the beginning, a premise rooted in the ideology of the Puritan-Victorian family. It also contained an implicit contradiction of the classical work ethic. Those who were moved by the work ethic could note that "the place of the poor is on the job." Those moved by traditional family morality could respond "but the place of the mother is in the home."

The apparent moral stalemate has not yet been resolved, but from the beginning the weight of enforcement has favored the work ethic. First, the mother-in-the-home ethic was as much a euphemism for propriety as a plea for proper childcare. Thus, by 1942 over half of the states had enacted "suitable home" rules forbidding ADC payments where women did not have living arrangements to suit welfare officials. Second, "employable mother" rules in many states were used to deny benefits to women who might be needed as cheap field labor or domestics.

In almost all cases of special AFDC eligibility rules the applicant was either denied aid outright or forced to submit to degrading restrictions on her life and hopes. Whether a form of work rule or morality rule, it was often the case that rules were planned and implemented to maintain cheap labor for marginal jobs or to directly discriminate against minority women and children.

By 1943 Louisiana had adopted an "employable mother" rule which denied benefits to any mother with children over six years of age if there was a need for local cotton pickers. Georgia's employable mother rule denied assistance whenever any "suitable" employment was "available" so long as the mother's children were over three years of age. It further forbade local officials from supplementing her wage even if it fell below normal grant levels. Finally, it required all applications be denied and all cases be closed when demand for field labor was at a peak (Piven and Cloward, 1971:134–5). As recently as 1966 the U. S. Civil Rights Commission held hearings which revealed that such practices continue and are not restricted to the South (Komisar, 1974:83).

A national study of welfare terminations in 1961 showed that blacks were twice as likely as whites to be refused aid on the grounds of "unsuitable homes." (Komisar, 1974:76) In many cases suitable home rules appeared in hidden guise. In 1960 Louisiana enacted a law requiring mothers seeking ADC to *prove* they had ceased all "illicit relationships." The law was made retroactive and nearly 30,000 recipients were promptly kicked off the rolls. After a lengthy delay in hearing the protests that ensued, the Social Security Commissioner ruled that Louisiana's law was permissible. Later, HEW Secretary Flemming modified this ruling so that states could not deny aid to children in "unsuitable homes" so long as the children remained there. The usual state response was merely to declare homes unsuitable at the point of application. To prevent appeals of such declarations they could threaten to take away the applicant's children and file neglect proceedings against her. Eventually, such procedures were declared unconstitutional, though they were still being used in Maryland in 1967 (Komisar, 1974:77).

In recent years some of these arbitrary rules have been modified as welfare recipients and other political minorities have exerted organized pressure through the courts, in Congress, and on the streets. Yet, the basic framework of the welfare system remains intact. The 1935

Social Security Act's triparte division of "social security" into work-based insurance, need-based federal assistance, and local-option general assistance continues to define the scope and level of public aid for the poor and nearly poor in the United States. Amendments to this act have largely been *ad hoc*. They have expanded the population of persons eligible for aid and have marginally increased the levels of benefits. On the other hand, they have introduced great complexity and cost without greatly reducing poverty or altering the demoralized status of the poor.

FDR's Legacy: New Deal or "Old"?

Throughout the 1940s and 1950s most public and academic commentators felt that economic prosperity was pervasive in the United States and poverty was once again disappearing from the scene. Laissez-faire conservatives finally were out of the closets into which the Depression had driven them and with the Eisenhower years they were moving center stage. Even the liberal conservatives, those Keynesian capitalists with social consciences, were being persuaded that poverty was being reduced to a residual phenomenon.

Indeed, it was this sense that contemporary poverty was unlike traditional poverty that brought it once more to the fore of public discussion. The liberal economist J. K. Galbraith (1958) wrote in his *The Affluent Society* that poverty was no longer a "majority" problem. General poverty had been reduced through economic growth to the point that only "case" and "island" poverty persisted. Case poverty resulted from personal handicaps while island poverty resulted from "pockets" of underdeveloped regions in an otherwise expanding economy. But, said Galbraith, precisely because the remaining poverty was due to special rather than general circumstances it would be all the more painful for those who suffer it and the more difficult to solve. The "new" poverty would require new solutions.

Galbraith's speculations accorded well with other popular images held in the 1950s. Many believed that a "managerial revolution" had separated economic decisions from the owners of wealth and had thereby created a democratization of the economy (cf. Burnham, 1943). This was presumably followed by the rise of a "new class" of technical experts and bureaucrats bringing the middle class into political prominence. And there were reports that inequality of income and wealth had been on a long decline while popular ownership of corporate stock, "people's capitalism," was on the rise. Some even wrote of the "end of ideology" (Bell, 1960) which was at hand.

Unfortunately for traditional conservatives, these beliefs were half-truths at best and delusions at worst. While Galbraith's essay received sympathetic acclaim, others were soon to show that general poverty was far from disappearing. For example, Robert J. Lampman, one of the leading experts on income and wealth trends, found that the "low-income" population might comprise as much as 36 percent of the total U.S. population. His studies further showed that wealth was tremendously concentrated and showing signs of further concentration (Lampman, 1962). Similar findings were documented by the economic historian Gabriel Kolko (1962).

At the same time, Michael Harrington's book, *The Other America* (1962), gave a convincing and bitter portrait of America's "invisible" poor. Although not much noticed at first, Harrington's book gained national attention after Dwight MacDonald's sympathetic review in *The New Yorker* magazine in January, 1963. Various advisors to President Kennedy, perhaps Kennedy himself, read Harrington's book and were sorely distressed by the picture it painted. Walter Heller, chairman of the President's ·Council of Economic Advisors, brought the issue of poverty into the CEA's planning considerations. Supported by Lampman, then a staff member of CEA, Heller wrote a memorandum to President Kennedy that set into process exploration of the idea of making "widening participation in prosperity" a central focus of his coming legislative program. Legislative proposals from various departments were solicited and were being analyzed when word was received of Kennedy's assassination.

President Johnson immediately gave his support to the impending attack on poverty, saying "That's my kind of program" (Levitan, 1969:18). With this green light a "task force" of personnel from CEA, Bureau of the Budget, and various other departments began putting together a patchwork of programs, sometimes called the "War on Poverty."

In the end, the resulting legislation was quite traditional. The basic thrust was toward improving the capacities of the poor to take advantage of economic opportunities. This was, indeed, well expressed in the title of the legislation, The Economic Opportunity Act of 1964. Although the rhetoric might be new, the idea was old; it was less a "war" than a "skirmish," less concerned with poverty than incompetence. No fundamental doubt was cast on the structure of the economic or political system. The premise was that these systems were effective and just. By implication, the problem had to do with either personal defects, or, at most, a "subculture of poverty." In either case, the point was not to change the system but to change the poor.

Johnson's "Great Society" and the Culture of Poverty

The "culture of poverty" idea had been implicit in ethnic-class conflicts at least as early as the midnineteenth century. But, it had been popularized in academic circles by Oscar Lewis's (1959) anthropological studies of the Mexican peasantry during the 1950s. Lewis had persuaded many scholars that poor people were accommodated to their station through a rationally developed "culture of poverty." However, the intergenerational transmission of this accommodation results in a "vicious cycle of poverty" which might be extremely difficult to break and, in any case, would retard efforts toward economic development.

Various academic and political writers adapted Lewis's argument to serve their own purposes. The idea has been linked historically with racial and ethnic themes and, as Piven and Cloward (1971) have argued, the massive influx of blacks to the Northern slums during the 1950s was a major factor contributing to the rediscovery of poverty.

The central role of the culture of poverty thesis and its implicit cycle of poverty consequence is evidenced in a section of a CEA staff memorandum cited by Moynihan (1969:9; see also 1965) as "government staff work at its best." Because it so closely anticipated the structure of the subsequent "war on poverty" programs, it is useful to quote the passage at length. It reads in part:

The Poverty Cycle

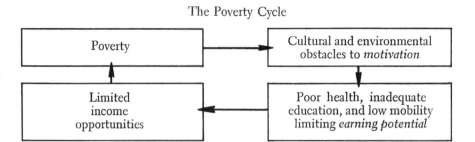

The sources of poverty are not listed in chronological sequence. The vicious cycle, in which poverty breeds poverty, occurs through time, and transmits its effects from one generation to another. There is no beginning to the cycle, no end. There is, therefore, no one "right" place to break into it: increasing opportunities may help little if health, educational attainments and motivation are unsuitable; making more education available may bear little fruit unless additional employment opportunities exist; altering adverse environmental factors may not be feasible or effective unless access to education and ultimately job opportunities is enhanced.

Programs to attack each of the three principal stages in the poverty cycle may be directed at one or more of three levels: (1) *prevent* the problem from developing, (2) *rehabilitate* the person who has been hurt, and (3) *ameliorate* the difficulties of persons for whom prevention or rehabilitation are not feasible. Each type of "treatment" is associated generally with a separate stage in the life cycle. Prevention of poverty calls for attention principally to youngsters (and to their parents, insofar as parents' attitudes and values affect the children). Rehabilitation of those missed by preventive efforts, or for whom these efforts were ineffective, seems best designed for adults in their productive work years. Amelioration of poverty seems called for in the case of the aged, the physically and mentally disabled, and those for whom prevention and rehabilitation are ineffective.[2]

[2] "The Poverty Cycle" from *On Understanding Poverty: Perspectives from the Social Sciences*, edited by Daniel P. Moynihan with the assistance of Corinne Saposs Schelling, © 1968, 1969 by the American Academy of Arts and Sciences, Basic Books, Inc., Publishers, New York.

Two aspects of this passage merit attention. First, the tone of the memo is pessimistic. The difficulty of breaking the cycle is stressed. It is feared that attacking poverty at one point will have little effect because of failures at another. Second, the "treatment" possibilities cited in the memo focus on individuals and not social structures. The discussion of the life cycle suggests that prevention efforts ought to be largely restricted to a focus on youth. By implication, once one is into middle age or older he/she is either beyond salvation (thus, the object is amelioration) or at least defective (thus, rehabilitation). However, this seems only to apply to the poor, for the rich and middle classes are not mentioned. Nor are social institutions.

Of course, if the plight of the poor is really seen as rooted in "their" culture, a culture of poverty, then why bother to break into the poverty cycle at all? "Doing nothing" about poverty is justified on several grounds. If that culture is viewed as a rational and positive way of coping with life, then one ought not to interfere. If, on the other hand, the culture is viewed as vicious but nonetheless intergenerational (that is, inevitable), nothing *can* be done short of removing young children from their parents (Banfield, 1970), which would be seen as immoral on other grounds. Thus, the culture of poverty cycle is a model which justifies traditional piecemeal approaches.

The Great Society's war on poverty was primarily a minor explosion of traditional programs for managing poverty. The initial (1965 fiscal year) authorization provided $947.5 million. The bulk of these funds went toward education, training, social services, and work experience for youth. Although some of these programs were novel in detail, nearly all of them were traditional in conception and effect.

Within the Economic Opportunity Act (EOA), however, there was one program which threatened for a time to produce a new approach to poverty prevention. Title II of the Economic Opportunity Act authorized "community action programs," a catch-phrase for almost any locally planned and executed program for reducing poverty which barred racial discrimination and provided "maximum feasible participation" by local residents and members of the groups served.

The community action program concept arose among a group of academics and social activists working in close contact with the Ford Foundation's "grey areas" project for rejuvenating urban slums and certain community organization projects sponsored by the President's Committee on Juvenile Delinquency and Youth Crime. The projects had experimented with grassroots organizing of slum residents through neighborhood action centers which did not fall under traditional lines of local political authority. The idea was to effect a wholesale mobilization of community resources, including participation of the poor, in a coordinated attack upon the many problems of people living in urban slums.

It was not long until Section 202(a)3 of Title II of the EOA was recognized as a critical challenge to traditional approaches to poverty policy. This section had slipped through the legislative process with only minimal attention even though it had inserted the requirement that local residents and persons served by the community action agencies must be provided "maximum feasible participation" in the development, conduct, and administration of community action programs (CAP). In effect, this meant local authorities must share with the poor powers which have traditionally been reserved to themselves and certain upper-class influentials. In the end, the problem of sharing power with the poor made the community action program the most controversial part of the so-called war on poverty.

Ironically, while participation by the poor became the focus of controversy, actual participation by the poor was largely a sham. In fact, most community action agencies (CAAs) were run by elected officials, welfare professionals, and leaders of various social causes. The EOA had set no criteria of eligibility for participation by the poor except local residence. Thus, local power groups could technically meet the legal requirement without any true representation by the poor. In addition, the percentage of CAP funds available for local-initiative programs, where the poor might influence program design, decreased as the years passed. This resulted from Office of Economic Opportunity directives making certain programs mandatory and transferring control to the national level—for example, Head Start, Upward Bound, and Legal Services.

No doubt the controversies over community action were related to the increasing importance of the movement for civil rights for blacks. The CAP requirement that the poor participate in the programs neither specified how this was to be done nor who could represent the poor. With black civil rights leaders and their organizations the primary indigenous vehicles available in the slums for defending the interests of the poor, it was inevitable that blacks should enter the fray. This obviously upset many racists, but the increasing militancy of black protest also led others to doubt whether black leaders could defend the interests of the white poor. Thus, even within the urban slums, representation of the poor was controversial. In this context, it is difficult to state the relative importance of class and race conflict in the controversy.

Piven and Cloward (1971) have argued that the social programs of the 1960s were intended to focus attention on race. They claim that the ghettoization in Northern slums of blacks had made their vote crucial for the national Democratic party. But, the gross neglect of slum problems by traditional urban institutions and political machines was, presumably, jeopardizing the Democratic tendency of the urban black voters. Thus, the war on poverty was designed to bypass these institutions and machines. A dual objective was to deliver services to the urban blacks and pressure local authorities and institutions into reforms which would sustain black loyalty to the Democratic party.

By this interpretation, direct participation by the poor was merely incidental to broader political objectives. Indeed, the concern with poverty itself was not fundamental. Though this judgment may be harsh, there is a plausible case for it. We have already noted the legal and operational equivocation on the meaning of maximum feasible participation. It should also be noted that the war on poverty rapidly faded into obscurity when it came into conflict with the war in Viet Nam. Finally, even granting a genuine war on poverty, the battle plan and weaponry were quite traditional. While CAP potentially could have evolved into a new approach, in fact, little innovation occurred.

The war on poverty left the country with essentially the same approach to the poor that it had inherited. The possibility of a structural explanation and attack was quickly dismissed. The poor were inspected for signs of individual defects which might explain their poverty.

Certain "no-fault" defects such as advanced age, physical handicap, mental deficiency, and so on have been viewed as unchangeable. Programs for the "no-fault" poor have increasingly sought to provide them with minimally adequate living conditions. Viewed positively, these programs have helped many unfortunate persons participate in life with security and dignity. Viewed cynically, they have eased the conscience of the affluent and purchased the quiescence of the disabled poor.

Many poor persons, however, do not suffer advanced age, physical handicap, or mental deficiency. To restrict explanation of their poverty to citing individual defects can degenerate into passing of moral judgments. This is largely what happens when many Americans speculate on the causes of poverty. When individualism becomes a cultural fetish, each person becomes morally responsible for his or her circumstances. The result is that we seem compelled to find fault with the able-bodied poor, to blame them for the poverty they suffer. The concept of the immoral or "sturdy" poor lives on in the United States even though the terminology may be forgotten.

For example, Feagin (1975:97) reports

that 88 percent of respondents in a recent nationwide survey felt that "lack of thrift" and "lack of effort" were important causes of poverty. Indeed, a majority felt these were *very* important causes. Eighty-five percent felt that "lack of ability and talent" were important causes, while 79 percent felt the same way about "loose morals and drunkenness." Although Feagin found some variation among types of respondents in this stress on individual defects as causes of poverty, he found only minor support for structural explanations. The poor appear somewhat more likely to offer structural explanations of poverty (Huber and Form, 1973), but even they tend to give surprising support to individualist accounts (Feagin, 1975:99; Williamson, 1974).

These sentiments echo the CEA memo quoted above. There, *motivation* and low *potential* were cited as key factors in the cycle of poverty causation. The subsequent poverty programs for the able-bodied poor directly correspond to these presumed deficiencies. CAP, VISTA, Legal Services, and other programs largely focused upon involving the poor, motivating them, and committing them to the existing political economy. Job Corps, Upward Bound, Head Start, Neighborhood Youth Corps, Work Experience, and the Concentrated Employment Program attempted to repair deficiencies of education, training, and work habits.

Thus, the war on poverty retained the three-pronged approach of the traditional welfare system. The "sturdy" poor were to be changed by improving their motivation and competence. The "impotent" poor were to be maintained by providing them with the essentials of quiet survival. Where necessary to change the sturdy poor, services might also be provided to them.

CONCLUSION

The welfare system which is taken by most Americans as our program for the poor continues to expand and contract with the flow of political moods and the needs of economic elites. Programs are tacked on to meet one problem while others are fed to the political wolves. Yet, many see a logic to the structure and trends of the welfare system. As we have noted, Piven and Cloward (1971) have vigorously argued that the function of relief-giving is to regulate the poor. The welfare system is seen as an institutional support for political and economic power. It has a dual structure or dialectic. Relief is initiated or expanded as necessary to mute civil discontent or disorder; it is terminated or contracted to reinforce or restore work norms.

A. Dale Tussing (1974) has seen this duality as internal to the logic and structure of the current welfare system in the United States. He believes the welfare system is not one but two systems. The one, built around the ideology of social insurance, is largely for the benefit of the nonpoor. It is camouflaged, well funded, and nonstigmatizing. The other, built around the ideology of public charity, is explicit, poorly funded, and stigmatizing. It is directed at the poor. This "dual welfare system" is not based upon meeting needs; it is designed to demoralize the illegitimate and reward the legitimate (that is, "proper behaving") people.

Piven and Cloward and Tussing are merely three of a growing number of scholars who are beginning to force a critical inspection of the complex structures for inequality in modern societies. Poverty must eventually be seen as an element of inequality with definite consequences for the whole of society and benefits for specific members of society. Just as sure as there is a welfare system for the lower classes (even if a dual system to distinguish the worthy and unworthy), there is an opposing wealthfare system for the affluent and superwealthy. In short, welfare and wealthfare are two sides of the same coin; and that coin is inequality.

References

Armstrong, Gregory. *Life at the Bottom.* New York: Bantam Books, 1971.

Banfield, Edward C. *The Unheavenly City.* Boston: Little, Brown, 1970.

Bell, Daniel. *End of Ideology.* New York: Free Press, 1960.

Bentham, Jeremy. "Pauper Management Improved: Particularly by Means of an Application of the Panoptikon Principles of Construction." *The Annals of Agriculture,* 1797–8.

Bentham, Jeremy. "On Houses of Safe-Custody and Industry." *Philanthropist,* 1881, 1, 228–236.

Blechman, Barry M., Gramlich, Edward M., and Hartman, Robert W. *Setting National Priorities: The 1975 Budget.* Washington, D.C.: Brookings Institution, 1974.

Burnham, James. *The Managerial Revolution.* London: Putnam, 1943.

Coles, Robert. *Children of Crisis,* 3 vols. Boston: Little, Brown, 1967–71.

Constantelos, Demetrios J. *Byzantine Philanthropy and Social Welfare.* New Brunswick, N.J.: Rutgers University Press, 1968.

Feagin, Joe R. *Subordinating the Poor.* Englewood Cliffs, N.J.: Prentice-Hall, 1975.

Fuchs, Victor. "Redefining Poverty and Redistributing Income." *The Public Interest,* 1967, 8, 88–95.

Galbraith, John K. *The Affluent Society.* Boston: Houghton-Mifflin, 1958.

Gallaway, Lowell E. *Poverty in America.* Columbus, Ohio: Grid, 1973.

Gans, Herbert J. "The Positive Functions of Poverty." *American Journal of Sociology,* 1972, 78, 275–89.

Gitlin, Todd, and Hollander, Nanci. *Uptown: Poor Whites in Chicago.* New York: Harper & Row, 1970.

Gordon, David M. "Trends in Poverty, Editor's Supplement." In David M. Gordon (Ed.), *Problems in Political Economy: An Urban Perspective.* Lexington, Mass.: Heath, 1971. Pp. 237–244.

Hands, Arthur R. *Charities and Social Aid in Greece and Rome.* Ithaca, N.Y.: Cornell University Press, 1968.

Harrington, Michael. *The Other America.* Baltimore: Penguin, 1962.

Huber, Joan, and Form, William H. *Income and Ideology: An Analysis of the American Political Formula.* New York: Free Press, 1973.

Kolko, Gabriel. *Wealth and Power in America: An Analysis of Social Class and Income Distribution.* New York: Praeger, 1962.

Komisar, Lucy. *Down and Out in the USA: A History of Social Welfare.* New York: New Viewpoints, 1974.

Lampman, Robert J. *The Share of Top Wealth-Holders in National Wealth 1922–1956.* New York: National Bureau of Economic Research, 1962.

Lampman, Robert J. *Ends and Means of Reducing Income Poverty.* Madison, Wisc.: Institute for Research on Poverty, 1971.

Lens, Sidney. *Poverty: America's Enduring Paradox.* New York: Crowell, 1971.

Levitan, Sar A. *The Great Society's Poor Law.* Baltimore: Johns Hopkins Press, 1969.

Levitan, Sar A. *Programs in Aid of the Poor for the 1970s.* Baltimore: Johns Hopkins Press, 1973.

Liebow, Elliot. *Tally's Corner.* Boston: Little, Brown, 1967.

Lewis, Oscar. *Five Families: Mexican Case Studies in the Culture of Poverty.* New York: Basic Books, 1959.

Matza, David. "The Disreputable Poor." In Reinhard Bendix and Seymour M. Lipset (Eds.), *Class, Status, and Power.* New York: Free Press, 1966. Pp. 289–302.

Moynihan, Daniel. *The Negro Family: The Case for National Action.* Office of Policy Planning and Research, U.S. Department of Labor. Washington, D.C.: Government Printing Office, 1965.

Moynihan, Daniel P. "The Professors and the Poor." In Daniel P. Moynihan (Ed.), *On Understanding Poverty.* New York: Basic Books, 1969. Pp. 3–35.

Piven, Frances Fox, and Cloward, Richard A. *Regulating the Poor: The Functions of Public Welfare.* New York: Vintage Books, 1971.

Polanyi, Karl. *The Great Transformation.* New York: Farrar & Rinehart, 1944.

Poynter, John R. *Society and Pauperism: English Ideas on Poor Relief, 1795–1834.* London: Routledge, 1969.

Rainwater, Lee. *What Money Buys: In-* equality and the Social Meaning of Income. New York: Basic Books, 1974.

Schlossman, Steven L. "The 'Culture of Poverty' in Ante-Bellum Social Thought." *Science & Society,* 1974, 38, 150–166.

Thurow, Lester C., and Lucas, Robert. "The American Distribution of Income: A Structural Problem." *Proceedings of the Joint Economic Committee of the Congress of the United States.* Washington, D.C.: Government Printing Office, 1972.

Tierney, Brian. *Medieval Poor Law.* Berkeley: University of California Press, 1959.

Trattner, Walter I. *From Poor Law to Welfare State: A History of Social Welfare in America.* New York: Free Press, 1974.

Tussing, A. Dale. "The Dual Welfare System." *Society,* 1974, 11, 50–7.

Walter, E. V. "Pauperism and Illth: An Archaeology of Social Policy." *Sociological Analysis,* 1973, 34, 239–54.

Williamson, John B. "Beliefs about the Welfare Poor." *Sociology and Social Research,* 1974, 58, 163–75.

Suggested Reading

FEAGIN, JOE R. *Subordinating the Poor: Welfare and American Beliefs.* Englewood Cliffs, N.J.: Prentice-Hall, 1975.

Focuses on the beliefs about poverty and welfare held by the American public and discusses the implications of these beliefs for public programs to aid the poor.

KOMISAR, LUCY. *Down and Out in the USA: A History of Social Welfare.* New York: New Viewpoints, 1974.

A good supplement to Lens' book, this work documents central points in the history of welfare law and practice and contains especially revealing accounts of the modern politics of public welfare.

LENS, SIDNEY. *Poverty: America's Enduring Paradox.* New York: Thomas Y. Crowell Company, 1971.

An excellent historical account of the United States from colonial to modern times with the problem of poverty as its point of departure. Shows that poverty is as American as apple pie and is rooted deeply in our social institutions and culture.

LEVITAN, SAR A. *Programs in Aid of the Poor in the 1970s,* rev. ed. Baltimore: The Johns Hopkins University Press, 1973.
A concise survey of current programs which have been officially viewed as aid to the poor and disadvantaged. Reveals the focus in American poverty policy on individuals rather than the institutional structure of inequality in social benefits and burdens.

PIVIN, FRANCES FOX, ANO CLOWARD, RICHARD A. *Regulating the Poor: The Functions of Public Welfare.* New York: Vintage Books, 1971.
The best analysis to date of the role of public welfare in manipulating the poor to the interests of the rich and powerful. A must reading for any serious student of poverty in American society.

ROBY, PAMELA (Ed.). *The Poverty Establishment.* Englewood Cliffs, N.J.: Prentice-Hall, 1974.
A reader which takes an essential step in the direction of combining an analysis of poverty with an equal analysis of wealth. Covers a wide range of provocative views relating these topics.

TUSSING, A. DALE. *Poverty in a Dual Economy.* New York: St. Martin's Press, 1975.
Public programs to deal with poverty are shown to be closely connected with a basic dualism in the American economy which separates people into the poor and the nonpoor with social stigma for the former and privilege for the latter.

The Distribution of Justice

Barriers to Equal Participation among the Poor
Stan L. Albrecht

The more fully developed a legal order, the greater the need for persons capable of formulating and challenging the reasons upon which the authority of claims, decisions or actions is based. The specialized responsibility for carrying out these critical functions may be located in a variety of social roles. In the Anglo-American system of law this responsibility has traditionally been assumed by the legal profession. (Carlin, Howard, and Messinger, 1967)

In recent years, more and more attention has been devoted to the topic of the changing locus of power in industrial and postindustrial societies. So long as concern with survival in one's natural environment has consumed so much of humankind's attention, the economy has provided the major resource base for exerting social power (Olsen, 1970:371). A number of influential social scientists and other commentators argue that knowledge will be the new resource base for power and influence (see, for example, Bell, 1970; Etzioni, 1968; Galbraith, 1967; Olsen, 1970). In Olsen's words (1970:371):

Some sections of this essay are adapted from two papers: Stan L. Albrecht and Miles Green, "Attitudes toward the Police and the Larger Attitude Complex: Implications for Police-Community Relationships," presented at the Fiftieth Annual Meeting of the American Association for the Advancement of Science, Laramie, Wyoming, April 1974, and Stan L. Albrecht and Miles Green, "Cognitive Barriers to Equal Justice before the Law," presented at the Annual Meeting of the Society for the Study of Social Problems, Montreal, Canada, August 1974.

A fully developed "post-industrial society" would undoubtedly contain a wide variety of important new power resources, including administrative and managerial abilities in operating complex organizations, scientific and technological expertise, teaching and mass communication skills, and perhaps even artistic and aesthetic talents. The common element in all of these kinds of resources is knowledge, since the fundamental functional requirement in such a society would be expert knowledge and accompanying skills.

However, even before reaching a "post-industrial" state, it is obvious that the gatekeepers of certain types of knowledge wield a good deal of power. Access or lack of access to these key types of information and to the roles that monopolize them is critical in determining the ability one has to influence decisions that affect, directly or indirectly, his or her life. This article will treat the general problem of inequitable access to the system of legal justice. A certain level of legal information, either on the part of the individuals concerned or on the part of "experts" who are readily available to represent their interests, will be seen as critical in determining one's ability to function successfully in the larger legal-political arenas of American society.

Legal services in a society such as ours have become very much a kind of "expert knowledge," requiring special training, skills, and credentials to make them work effectively. Cahn and Cahn (1968:218)

69

have noted rather cynically that "Legal services are basically a trade name product merchandised monopolistically by a small set of producers who jealously guard their profits against all potential competitors." Whether or not one is willing to go this far, it is clear that legal knowledge and expertise have become a valuable good as well as an important form of power in a highly technological society.

It is also clear that access to legal knowledge and expertise is not equally distributed in society. Evidence indicates that at each stage of the legal process, the poor, as well as many minority group members, have experiences that differ significantly from those of the more affluent. This holds despite the fact that, as noted by Sykes (1969:255): "It is a basic tenet of a democratic society that the protection of individual rights cannot turn on a matter of income or social class, since justice then becomes a luxury, available to a privileged few."

One of the important "rediscoveries" of the Great Society era of the 1960s, when so much concern was being expressed with equality of rights and opportunities, was that access to the law (and, consequently, to equal justice) was highly correlated with the socioeconomic characteristics of the individual involved. While the differential access to legal information and expertise is the primary focus of this article, important consequences of differential access for individuals as well as for the system more generally will be considered. We begin by identifying a series of barriers or hurdles that confront the poor person as he or she faces the legal system. Each of these must be seen as an obstruction standing in the way of the ability of the poor to obtain the same type of justice as that enjoyed by the more affluent.

BARRIERS TO EQUAL JUSTICE FOR THE POOR

The barriers impeding the ability of the poor or minority person to obtain equal justice in the American legal system are evident on several fronts. Three basic types will be discussed: (1) economic factors, (2) organizational and structural characteristics of the legal profession itself, and (3) social psychological factors.

Economic Barriers to Equal Justice before the Law

the law is not a neutral instrument, but rather . . . it is oriented in favor of those groups or classes in society having the power to bend the legal order to their advantage. The contention is that today as in the past the law primarily serves to protect and enhance the rights and interests of property holders and those in positions of wealth and authority. (Carlin, Howard, and Messinger, 1967)

A most thorough discussion of the severity of the problems faced by the indigent in confronting the legal system in this country has been developed by Patricia Wald (1967). She notes that from the very moment of contact with the police or some other representative of the system, the experiences of the poor are likely to differ significantly from those of the more affluent.

For example, if arrested the poor are much more likely to be detained because of the inability to raise bail. Prior to preliminary hearings, therefore, they are likely to have to spend their time in cramped and overcrowded cells. Instances in which persons have spent months languishing in jail waiting for a preliminary hearing are far too common. While the right to counsel and trial is reiterated at the time of preliminary hearings, the poor frequently waive these rights in order to avoid spending additional time in jail waiting for trial dates. As a consequence, a very high percentage of poor misdemeanants plead guilty. Even with counsel, Wald notes that the pressures for a guilty plea are great. Assigned counsel has little time to prepare his or her case; finding defense witnesses takes time and money which are frequently not available; expert testimony may not be available; and so on. In felony cases, where defendants are guaranteed a court-appointed attorney if they cannot afford their own, the system still works to the disadvantage of the indigent. For example, poor defendants who must rely on court-appointed lawyers serve on the average twice as long as those defendants with enough money to hire a private attorney.

Other problems are also evident. Promises to make restitution to the victim can be used to advantage by the affluent but such avenues are not available to the impoverished. A promise to seek private psychiatric treatment may gain release for the middle and upper class, while such an alternative is not open to the poor. When sentences are handed down, the more affluent may have the time and resources for an appeal, while the indigent may realize that the time spent in preparing an appeal for him or her must be spent in jail.

Wald (1967:151) concludes that

So long as the social conditions that produce poverty remain, no reforms in the criminal process will eliminate this imbalance. But we can ease the burdens of poverty by assuring the poor those basic procedural rights which our society ostensibly grants all citizens: the right to be represented by competent counsel early enough in the process to preserve other rights; the right to prepare an adequate defense; the right to be free until convicted; the right not to be jailed solely because of lack of money to remit a fine or make restitution; the right to parole; the right to a clean start after prison. In withholding these fundamentals from any citizen, society reveals a poverty of its own.

Several studies conducted during the sixties document the importance of economic barriers to equal access to the system of legal justice (see, for example, Carlin and Howard, 1965; Conrad, Morgan, and Pratt, 1964). Some of these studies found that the poor simply were not able to face the financial costs of seeking professional advice from an attorney. Carlin, Howard, and Messinger (1967) have found that the lower respondents' social class, the more likely they are to indicate that "price" or "expense" were their reasons for not consulting lawyers (cf. Hallauer, 1973).

As a consequence of these financial restraints, many Americans are convinced that the administration of justice depends in large part on who you are or how much money you have. For example, a task force report from the President's Commission on Law Enforcement and Administration of Justice (1967) found that half of the survey respondents studied in Washington, D.C., believed that people who have enough money for lawyers do not have to worry about the police. Similar numbers in other major cities feel that how the police treat you depends on who you are.

While it is readily apparent that the poor do not seek or receive the same kind of legal protection under the law as do the rich, it is just as apparent that they have just as much or even more need for such protection. Carlin, Howard, and Messinger (1967:2–4) have noted a number of areas in which the poor are likely to have grievances that have important legal implications:

(1) Illegal market practices—The poor, especially, have been susceptible to various practices that constitute consumer fraud. These include such things as misrepresentation of price and quality of goods, hidden credit costs, and collection practices that sometimes approximate extortion. Caplovitz (1963) reports that over 40 percent of his low-income respondents had experienced illegal consumer-related practices. While recent consumer laws have been designed to protect the public in the area of the cost of credit, there are still numerous related abuses.

(2) Contract laws—It is usually the slum landlord or the shady merchant who uses contract laws against his clients, rather than vice versa. However, there are probably just as many instances in which the poor would have just as much right to appeal to the legal processes for redress. For example, many landlords fail to fulfill obligations to keep up with services and repairs, and merchants often fail to honor warranties on poor quality goods. In other words, the landlord receives "favored party status" against the tenant, the lender against the borrower, and so on. Carlin, Howard, and Messinger (1967) also note that insurance settlements and cancellations involving the poor are often questionable or even illegal, but are seldom challenged through legal channels.

(3) Relationships with governmental agencies—Frequently, the poor are not provided the services to which they are entitled, such as garbage collection, police protection, street repair and upkeep, enforcement of housing codes, welfare payments, and so forth. Again, abuses in these areas constitute the basis for legal action but such avenues are seldom pursued.

The differential utilization of legal services in this country, then, cannot be seen as an accurate gauge of need. On the other hand, since legal participation is so closely related to economic and social characteristics, the legal system both reflects and supports the stratification system within the country.

Structural and Organizational Characteristics of the Legal Profession

While the economic barriers to obtaining equal representation for the poor are very great, the awareness has grown that there are other factors critical in determining the utilization of legal services. Furthermore, these noneconomic factors also help to account for nonuse of legal services by the nonpoor. Mayhew and Reiss (1969:311) argue that the resources theory simply cannot adequately account for the extent of use of legal services. According to these authors, "Access to resources, though it may account for the *adequacy* of legal services, is not a sufficient explanation of the patterns of contact between attorneys and the public, for attorney-client relations occur on the context of a complicated network of social organization." These authors are convinced that the social organization of legal institutions, as opposed to financial resources, best accounts for legal service utilization. They feel the legal profession is simply not organized to provide professional representation on a broad range of problems that commonly confront citizens such as welfare benefits, job and retirement rights, and civil rights. Such organizational deficiencies would account for lack of willingness to utilize legal services at all socioeconomic levels rather than just among the poor.

In a similar vein, Cahn and Cahn (1968:205) argue that new developments in such areas as the rights of juveniles, of tenants in public housing, of welfare recipients, as well as in other areas, has sorely challenged the capacity of the legal system to deal adequately with them. While a part of this challenge certainly lies in the provision of sufficient numbers of attorneys, much of it also lies in the problem of changing traditional ways of defining and responding to problems. These same authors argue that the legal system as it is presently structured will not suffice for the needs of modern urban society. More and more, lawyers as well as other legal professionals may increasingly find it necessary to become involved in assisting in the removal of "obstacles to the effective functioning of the democratic process," whether this be in the form of greater involvement in working for the rights of the poor in public housing, welfare, or whatever. Similar arguments are made by Henderson (1971) who feels that the legal profession must begin to look beyond its court-oriented functions in order to pursue the rights of the disadvantaged in other arenas.

According to Carlin, Howard, and Messinger (1967:55–59), the principal organizational and structural characteristics of the legal profession that work to limit its effectiveness in dealing with the problems of the poor include the following:

(1) The structure of rewards of the legal profession largely measures the success of practicing attorneys by the size of their income, which in turn, is likely to be closely correlated with the income of their clients. Prestige in the profession is associated with having high-status clients. Thus, having largely a lower-class clientele is viewed by much of the legal profession as a mark of failure. Such status considerations would likely curtail the better and more able attorneys from going into practice in neighborhood law offices or in other areas where their appeal would be primarily to the lower socioeconomic classes.[1]

(2) A second important organizational factor mitigating against use of the law by the poor is the requirement that legal action be initiated by the party concerned and not by the attorney. As will be noted later, the American legal system is largely passive in nature, meaning that legal mobilization must be initiated by other than the attorney. A consequence of this is that such a requirement decreases the likelihood of the poor initiating action.

(3) The third characteristic of the legal profession that limits its effectiveness in aiding the poor client is the tendency of lawyers to focus their attention on the particular case at hand. Carlin, Howard, and Messinger feel that the effective solution to many of the problems of the poor "may require the lawyer to

[1] There are, of course, exceptions to this. Henderson (1971) cites the example of a recent graduate of Stanford Law School, whose position as the president of the Stanford Law Review would probably guarantee employment with a top New York or Washington law firm, who chose, instead, to go to work for a Palo Alto "law commune" which pays salaries of roughly $300 per month for single persons. Numerous similar cases have occurred where the attorney is motivated less by the profit motive and more by a concern for being of some assistance to the disadvantaged.

direct his attention away from a particular claim or grievance to the broader interests and policies at stake, and away from the individual client to a class of clients, in order to challenge more directly and with greater impact certain structural sources of injustice" (1967:57). In other words, because of the tendency, reinforced in law school training, to focus on the individual client and his or her particular problem, many attorneys fail to see the possibility of challenging a regulation or a rule that has implications for many other persons. More recent emphasis on the use of the "test case" may indicate somewhat of a shift from such practices.

(4) Finally, conceptions of legal relevance on the part of attorneys may limit their ability to respond effectively to many of the needs of the poor. Carlin, Howard, and Messinger note that the lawyer is trained to view cases in the light of certain standards of relevance. Welfare and landlord problems do not, therefore, appear to many attorneys as matters requiring legal attention. "The attorney's legal training has prepared him to deal with creditor's rights, not debtor's rights; to represent clients before regulatory agencies, not before a local welfare agency or police department; to handle stock options and executive pension funds, not unemployment insurance benefits" (1967:58). The tendency, then, is frequently to define the problems of the poor as being social or psychological problems rather than legal problems. As a consequence, the legal profession is not particularly well-prepared to deal with them.

As was discussed earlier, the knowledge, ability, and confidence with which to confront the complex laws and bureaucracy of modern industrial society are a somewhat scarce resource. In fact, the resource rests largely in the hands of that small segment of society having legal training and competence. If those having such training are not sufficiently "geared-up" to deal with the specific problems of certain members of society, then it is obvious that those members are going to have special problems in gaining equal access to the law. This is the critical factor that becomes evident in assessing the organizational and structural characteristics of the legal profession. This is not to suggest that the factors discussed above are characteristic of the entire profession; nor is it to suggest that important changes are not occurring. Nevertheless, the unwillingness or inability in the past of the legal profession to concentrate sufficient effort on the legal problems of the poor has probably influenced the attitudes of distrust and powerlessness that many of them feel toward the system.

Social Psychological Barriers to Legal Service Utilization

A third set of factors that is important in determining level of legal service utilization is one that is basically social psychological in nature. Social psychological obstacles to legal service utilization are present at both the affective and the cognitive levels. At the affective level we are concerned primarily with the deeply ingrained negativism that many persons in this country feel toward the legal system. Our evidence here will be primarily from attitude studies. On a more strictly cognitive level, our concern will be with the problem of ignorance or lack of information as barriers to legal service utilization.

ATTITUDES AND THE DISTRIBUTION OF JUSTICE Many have argued that the so-called "crisis" in law and order in this country is largely an expression on the part of the poor and minorities that they have lost faith in their ability to get meaningful results by working within the system (see, for example, the report of the National Advisory Committee on Civil Disorders, 1968). The evidence is most pronounced relating to attitudes toward the police, although the few other studies that have been done in other areas suggest that many Americans, and more particularly the poor, view other representatives of the legal system with a good deal of suspicion and avoidance (see Hallauer, 1973).

A major source of information on public attitudes toward the police has been field studies and reports written primarily from observations in minority areas and in the ghettos of major cities. Such reports are important in pointing out the nature of the police image in these areas but do not generally allow quantification of the data. Survey data are scarce in the literature until the middle 1960s. Perhaps the single best source of such data can be found in the National Opinion Research Center (NORC) field studies conducted for the President's Commission on Law Enforcement and the Administration of Justice (Ennis, 1967b). In addition, Gallup polls provide national polling data collected in 1965 and 1967. Both of these sources are generally supportive of conclusions reached by field observation research. For example, Ennis (1967b:42) observes from his Presidential Commission data that "Negroes at all income levels show strong negative attitudes toward the police." Expressing a similar view, Lohman and Misner

(1967:ii) argue that "More than at any other time in our history, the police are estranged from other agencies and from groups within the community." [2]

Perhaps one indicator of the lack of public confidence in the police is found in the vast amount of unreported crime that occurs in this country. According to figures in a recently released study conducted by the Law Enforcement Assistance Agency (LEAA), almost half of the victims of such crimes as assault, robbery, burglary, and larceny above $50 did not report the incidents to the police. The nonreporting rate for larceny under $50 was 80 percent. Overall, only about 45 percent of the victims of crimes reported these crimes to the police. The most frequently stated reasons for not reporting criminal victimization was that the victim felt that probably nothing could be done. The third most important reason was the belief that the police would not want to be bothered. Overall, one would have to conclude that these findings indicate not so much apathy but lack of confidence in the willingness or

[2] It is important, however, that we keep the discussion of negative attitudes toward the police in a proper context. Both the NORC data and the Gallup poll data indicate that approximately 70 percent of the national samples studied view the police as generally effective, honest, and respectful. The question could be asked as to what percentage of the population must express positive attitudes before there is a "good" public image of the police. National polls have seldom shown 70 percent of the public agreeing that the president is doing an excellent job or showing satisfaction with the performance of Congress. In a poll conducted by the Gallup organization in June of 1967 it was revealed that only 45 percent thought that the Supreme Court was doing an excellent or good job, and only 47 percent felt that the court was impartial in its decisions. Recent polls show even more dissatisfaction with the president and Congress.

the ability of the legal system to get results.

It should again be emphasized that while most of the data available deal with attitudes toward the police, there is no reason to believe that confidence in the police differs significantly from confidence in other representatives of the legal justice and political systems. Perhaps there is more concern with police-community relationships because of the pivotal nature of the position occupied by the agencies of law and order. A mistake by a policeman can bring a city into a situation of riot and disorder. The police are also the representatives of the system with whom the average citizen is most likely to have contact. This is especially true in minority areas of the major cities and, as suggested above, it is in these same areas that negativism toward the police is most likely to be located.

While the application of findings from attitude studies dealing strictly with the police to other representatives of the legal system may be somewhat hazardous, there is some theoretical justification for doing so. Scholars now generally agree that the concept of attitude is most useful when it is studied in context and as a component of the broader personality of the individual. Any single attitude toward some attitude object does not exist in isolation but is a part of a broader set of attitudes which are sometimes assumed to constitute a value system. In other words, while attitude may be thought of as pertaining to single objects in the environment of the individual, they are likely to be organized into larger sets making up the value system of the individual.

In support of this, Albrecht and Green (1974a) have found that attitudes toward the police are strongly correlated with attitudes toward courts and judges, attitudes concerning the fairness of the legal system despite considerations of wealth and power and more general measures of political alienation and involvement. They found that a respondent who agreed with a statement such as "I have little respect for the police in this community," was likely to disagree with the statement "I have a great deal of faith in the American legal system," and to agree with the statement that "laws protect the rich more than the poor." These authors conclude that studies and polls showing negativism toward the police only touch the surface of a much deeper problem. The same people who express negativism toward their local police also have a tendency to feel most alienated from the broader legal and political process and to feel most clearly cynical about the effectiveness of the operation of that process, especially in terms of its relationship to them and to others like them.

If generally true, the implications of such findings are rather clear. Programs designed to change public attitudes toward the police (or toward attorneys, or judges, or laws) are not going to be generally successful unless they consider the broader, fundamental value system of which those attitudes are a part. Also, if negativism toward the police is closely intertwined with feelings of alienation and powerlessness toward the broader legal and political system, then the task is likely to be an even more difficult one. The solution will not lie in trying to convince the kids on the block that their local cop is basically a good guy. Rather, they must come to believe that they do, in fact, have some power over their own destiny, that they are not powerless and at the mercy of a system that appears to them to be frequently unjust and arbitrary in its operation. Only then will one truly observe less cynicism toward those who stand as representatives of that system.

As would be expected, the study by Albrecht and Green found that the most negative "attitude-set" toward the police, courts, and law was expressed among minority groups (in this instance, blacks and Chicanos in a middle-sized urban city) and among lower socioeconomic whites. Rural residents and persons residing in what were basically middle-class suburbs of the same city from which the minority sample was drawn exhibited much more favorable attitudes toward the police, toward courts and law, and toward other representatives of the legal justice system.

Negative attitudes which affect one's relationship to the system of legal justice and which act as barriers to legal service utilization cannot be viewed as wholly irrational responses. For many of the poor, and for what is probably a fairly high percentage of minority group members, they do have a rational base. The encounters the poor have with the law typically occur with such representatives of that law as police officers, probation officers, welfare workers, and others in similar positions. Too frequently, these contacts are with those representatives of the law who seek to control and/or punish. It is not surprising, therefore, that the conceptions of many of the poor and minorities toward the law are that it is something that works against them, rather than to protect them (Carlin, Howard, and Messinger, 1967:73).

As this implies, much of the problem is centered in the role that is played by the representative of the "system." This is especially true of the police. As noted by Wilson (1963:189–216), "the policeman is frequently in an adversary relation with his public. . . . The policeman in the routine case is often (though not always) dealing with his clientele as an antagonist: he issues summons, makes arrests, conducts inquiries, searches homes, stops cars, testifies in court and keeps a jail." Given the nature of the relationships that are likely to be established in such contacts, it is not surprising that police officers frequently perceive the public as hostile and feel that much of the citizenry holds them in contempt. Even in contacts occurring in a context that one would assume would contribute to somewhat more positive attitudes, it has been found that there is a certain amount of negative reinforcement. For example, in a study of contacts with attorneys, Hallauer (1973) found that negativism was little changed by experience. Three out of every four of his respondents (union members in Shreveport) who had used a lawyer still agreed with the statement: "Lawyers usually can't be trusted."

LEGAL KNOWLEDGE AND THE DISTRIBUTION OF JUSTICE

What does it profit a poor and ignorant man that he is equal to his strong antagonist before the law if there is no one to inform him what the law is? (William R. Vance, 1926)

While the data in this area are much more limited, it is becoming increasingly evident that level of legal information and knowledge is critical in affecting access to the legal process. While level of legal knowledge may be relatively low for the entire population, it is the poor, as well as members of minority groups, that are most frequently unaware that many of their problems are legal problems and that by appealing to the law they may have access to a means of obtaining redress.

This problem is obviously related closely to the attitude problem discussed above. In fact, if we were to define the concept "attitude" in the traditional sense, having affective, cognitive, and behavioral components, then the previous discussion has dealt largely with the affective level while the present one deals with the cognitive level. A majority of the theories of attitude organization (for example, Festinger's [1957] dissonance theory) also suggest that these components should be related in a positive manner. That is, affect should be positively related to cognition. Whatever their relationship in the present instance, the outcome is that injustice is often tolerated because people are reluctant to use the law, frequently resulting from a lack of trust and generally negative affect toward the system, or because they are ignorant as to what their rights are. As has been suggested by Williams and Hall (1972:100): "if law as a social tool is less effective than it might be, it is in part because many citizens are unaware of how legal processes may be used for their protection and for the solution of some of their problems."

Two major levels or types of ignorance that affect legal delivery will be discussed. Perhaps of most importance is the lack of information on basic rights. If blacks in Texas communities believe that there are laws prohibiting certain races from living where they may want to live (as was found by Williams and Hall, 1972), then such beliefs, despite their inaccuracy, will affect the likelihood of blacks seeking to obtain housing in certain areas of town. Again emphasizing the relationship between the cognitive and affective varia-

bles, the belief that such inequitable laws exist must also affect the attitudes that such persons hold toward the law and toward the political system in general. In other words, beliefs based on faulty information (or lack of knowledge) may very well lead to a high level of alienation from the system.

The second level or type of ignorance that seems critical is the lack of information as to the availability of legal aid and assistance for those problems that are defined as having legal consequences. Again, the evidence we will discuss below suggests rather clearly that even when problems are defined by the poor as being legal problems, they are frequently unaware of the availability of assistance in seeking redress for these problems. While ignorance of basic rights may lead to greater alienation from the system, it could be suggested that lack of knowledge of available legal avenues for redress of grievances may lead to a more widespread willingness to utilize and support extralegal means.[3]

Knowledge of basic rights. Henderson (1971:505–506) has noted, in discussing problems of equal justice in minority communities, that

the members of minority communities largely labor in ignorance and fear of the law and its processes. Though this condition also exists in the non-minority community under some circumstances, the problem is exacerbated in minority communities which have historically been subjected to discriminatory treatment under a

---

[3] It would be interesting, for example, to examine level of knowledge of legal redress channels of participants in violent and nonviolent protest. Of course, it is possible that participation in protest may also be engendered by frustration resulting from unsuccessful attempts to utilize established channels of redress.

system of laws which, unfortunately, are too often designed and administered for the advantage of those in power.

Data in support of this contention have recently been provided in the study done by Williams and Hall (1972) in Austin, Texas. Their results reveal that low-income minority groups did no better than chance in answering questions concerning important Texas laws. More advantaged persons missed over one-third of the questions, on the average. These findings held despite the fact that the knowledge questions used in the study dealt with items that were not complex but which were critical in terms of their implications for the average citizen.

Recent research undertaken by Albrecht and Green (1974, 1976) has sought to ascertain the frequency of ignorance of basic legal rights among different socioeconomic groups in a Rocky Mountain state. Data on legal knowledge were collected in a larger study dealing with public attitudes toward representatives of the legal system and the degree to which these attitudes were affected by various types of contact with the system. Four different populations were sampled in order to reflect socioeconomic, ethnic and rural-urban differences. Two of the samples were drawn from the second largest city in the state. One of these was selected from those census tracts having a heavy concentration of minority group members (primarily black and Mexican-American), while the second was taken from the middle-class suburbs of the same city. Of the other two samples, one was drawn from two contiguous rural counties and the second from a smaller urban community having a heavy concentration of mine laborers, many of whom were second- and third-generation southern Europeans. The ur-

ban middle class and the rural samples in the study most closely approximated each other in terms of education and family income. The small city sample ranked next on these variables with the urban minority sample ranking last.

Items were developed to ascertain knowledge of respondents toward a series of what were considered legal matters of varying degrees of importance. All of the items were assumed to be rather basic and not complex or difficult to understand. The respondents were read the items and then requested to answer with a true, false, or don't know. The "don't know" alternative was included to discourage guessing if the individual was not sure of the answer to any particular question. The knowledge items and responses to these items from the combined samples are included in Table 1.

Data presented in Table 1 should be interpreted with a certain degree of caution because of the inherent difficulties and hazards involved in attempting to develop a general measure of public legal knowledge. It is often argued, with some justification, that the law simply contains too many exceptions and too much flexibility to allow the development of statements that would elicit such information. The effort in the above case was to develop statements that were straightforward and unambiguous *in the general case*. This does not mean that there are not exceptions to what have been defined as the correct answers to some of the questions. For example, the statement that a loser in a case must pay the attorney fees of the winner is *true* in instances where such legal arrangements are specified by contract, when the judge in the case determines that fraud is involved, and in a few cases where the practice is provided by statute. Generally,

Table 1. Knowledge of Legal Rights

Questions	True		False		Don't Know		Correct Response	
	N	%	N	%	N	%	N	%
1. The loser in a civil case must pay the attorney fees of the winner.	208	52.7	98*	24.8	89	22.5	98	24.8
2. Attorneys for the plaintiff and the defendant do not appear in small claims court.	134*	34.1	119	30.3	140	35.6	134	34.1
3. Contract laws are generally not binding for minors. (A minor cannot be legally held responsible for a signed contract).	325*	81.9	54	13.6	18	4.5	325	81.9
4. Suppose you buy something on credit and the payments are $30.00 per month, but you are unable to pay that much and pay only $10.00 per month. The credit contract cannot be considered in default, nor can you be taken to court, nor have the item repossessed.	174	44.1	147*	37.2	74	18.7	147	37.2
5. If a court finds a person not guilty for a robbery and then the police find some new evidence, the person cannot be tried in court again for that robbery.	216*	54.5	128	32.3	52	13.1	216	54.5
6. In a trial, the presumption of innocence means that an accused person must prove the charges false.	201	50.8	158*	39.9	37	9.3	158	39.9
7. Police must advise a person of his constitutional rights whenever they perform an arrest no matter how serious the charge.	396*	92.9	15	3.8	13	3.3	369	92.9

8. Many credit contracts provide for a period of time in which the purchaser may change his mind and cancel the contract.	151*	38.0	172	43.3	74	18.6	151	38
9. Citizens of this country have the right to have an attorney present whenever the police question them.	340*	85.6	39	9.8	18	4.5	340	85.6
10. A *witness* in a trial must answer *all* questions even if they will establish his own involvement in a crime.	181	46.3	187*	47.8	23	5.9	187	47.8

-N size does not always total 398 because of an occasional failure to respond to all ten items.
* indicates correct answer

however, the practice of the losing party paying the attorney fees of the winner is not the rule in the U.S., although it is in many European countries.

With these cautions in mind, several comments can be made concerning the data. It will be noted that the percentage of the total sample giving the correct response to the items varied from 25 percent ("the loser in a civil case must pay the attorney fees of the winner") to 93 percent ("police must advise a person of his constitutional rights whenever they perform an arrest no matter how serious the charge"). Over half of all respondents gave incorrect or don't know responses to six of the ten items. This would seem to indicate a very serious lack of knowledge on what must be viewed as questions of basic legal rights. Most serious would seem to be the responses to two items: (1) item six, concerning the presumption of innocence, on which only 40 percent of the total sample gave the correct response, and (2) item ten on

self-incrimination, on which 48 percent gave correct responses. Almost as critical in terms of a combination of the content of the question and the percentage giving a correct response is item five concerning double jeopardy.

It seems especially interesting that the two items on which an overwhelming percentage of the respondents gave correct answers are items that are continually emphasized on the array of police, private eye, and courtroom drama TV programs. Fully 93 percent of the respondents knew that police must advise a person of his constitutional rights when performing an arrest, and 86 percent knew that a citizen has the right to presence of an attorney when being questioned by the police. Perhaps the cops and robbers menu to which the TV viewing audience is nightly subjected does have at least one latent positive consequence.

To facilitate comparisons between various segments of the population on legal knowledge, the ten items were combined into a single index. To develop the index, scores of two were assigned to correct responses, scores of one to "don't know" responses, and scores of zero to incorrect responses. The rationale for such point assignments was based on a logic similar to that employed by various testing agencies wherein penalties are assessed for guessing. In addition, it could be argued that incorrect responses are of far more serious consequence in terms of legal implications. A respondent who gives a "don't know" response indicates an awareness of his own ignorance, while a person giving an incorrect response apparently thinks he knows the correct answer but is wrong. The latter would perhaps be less likely to seek professional advice than would the person who is more aware of the limits of his own knowledge.

On this basis, knowledge scores were computed for each respondent. Total scores could vary between zero and twenty, with higher scores indicating higher legal knowledge. The actual range was from five to twenty with three of the 398 respondents obtaining perfect scores. Once total scores were obtained, respondents were divided into four categories.

As would be expected, knowledge of basic legal rights varied rather significantly between subcomponents of the original sample. Given the earlier socioeconomic descriptions of the four subsamples included in this study, it would be reasonable to predict that legal knowledge would be highest among the urban middle-class sample, followed, respectively, by the rural sample, the semirural sample and the urban poor sample. This is largely confirmed by the data presented in Table 2.

The highest level of legal knowledge as measured by the ten items included in the index is observed in both the urban nonpoor and the rural samples. The lowest level of knowledge is found among the urban poor and minority sample. The differences between these two groups are rather pronounced.

Other control variables that were most closely related to legal knowledge are those that would be highly correlated with social class. Specifically, in this study, these were the variables of education and income levels. As noted earlier, these variables also exhibited some rather important differences between the subsamples. The variable most strongly related to legal knowledge was education, followed by income.

The important difference on the education variable occurs between those completing a high school education and those going on for more advanced study, although high school graduates also did somewhat better than nongraduates. Overall, the higher a person's education, the more likely he or she was to be aware of basic legal rights. The same held true for income. In general, the higher a person's income, the higher his or her legal knowledge. The important dividing point in this instance was at the income level of $7,000. It was suggested earlier that persons of higher income are much more likely to have contact with various representatives of the legal system (other than the police). Part of the cause of this, obviously, is that greater income is associated with greater property holdings which are more likely to lead one into situations where legal advice is needed and sought.

Awareness of legal aid. A second type of knowledge that may have rather significant consequences in terms of utilization of the legal process is knowledge concerning the availability of agencies

Table 2. Legal Knowledge Compared by Area of Residence

	Area of Residence				
Knowledge Index	Urban Middle-Class	Rural	Semirural	Urban Poor & Minorities	TOTAL
1. (Low Knowledge)	28	24	34	36	122
2. ——————	21	26	24	36	107
3. ——————	20	24	18	28	90
4. (High Knowledge)	28	24	19	8	79
TOTAL	97	98	95	108	

$$x^2 = 19.90 \qquad p < .02 \qquad Gamma = -.163$$

which provide free legal assistance to those who cannot otherwise afford it. As will be discussed in more detail in the next section, various efforts have been expended to provide free legal assistance to the indigent. However, even when such aid is available, it will not be used by those who are eligible if they are unaware of its existence. The evidence at hand indicates that many of those most in need are so unaware.

Sykes (1969), in research conducted in Denver, found that despite the fact that a legal aid society had existed in Denver for almost 50 years, only one-third of his sample knew of its existence. Chadwick and his colleagues (1974) have demonstrated rather clearly that lack of information as to the availability of legal services is critical in decreasing the likelihood of American Indians living in urban settings seeking legal assistance. Native Americans migrating to the city frequently face serious difficulties in learning to conform with metropolitan legal norms. Chadwick and his colleagues found that one in every four of their sample Indians living in Seattle, Washington, had been arrested during the past year. Some of the persons studied who had finally come to an attorney seeking help had serious legal problems predating the consultation by as much as two years. Yet, this was the first legal counsel they had received. In fact, only ten percent of those reporting that they had been arrested had been represented by an attorney.

In addition to the arrest data, many of the respondents reported experiences with overt discrimination that may have called for legal advice. For example, one-third of the respondents reported they had been turned down when looking for housing because of their ethnicity. One-fifth had been denied welfare benefits in situations where there was a high probability of eligibility. In concluding their research, these authors (Chadwick et al., 1974:10) report: "The single most important deterrent to the use of legal service agencies by urban Indians seems to be lack of awareness, both of the existence of the agencies and of the types of services they provide."

In the research by Caplovitz (1963) conducted in New York settlement houses, it was found that almost one out of every three respondents did not know where to turn in situations where they had been cheated by a merchant or salesman. The percentage was highest among Puerto Ricans. In this case, only 24 percent indicated any awareness of sources of redress. The research by Albrecht and

Green (1974, 1976) discussed earlier also sought to ascertain the degree to which respondents were aware of the availability of various types of legal aid. Each person interviewed was asked if he or she was aware of any person, group, or organization which provided legal aid in that area, other than private attorneys. The rural-urban differences are even more pronounced than are the social class differences.

A total of 62 percent of the urban middle-class sample indicated that they were aware of individuals, groups, or organizations who provided legal aid. This was true of 43 percent of the urban poor and minority sample, but of only 8 and 5 percent of the semirural and rural samples, respectively.

Despite efforts to develop and publicize legal aid programs, it is apparent that a significant percentage of those who may be in need of legal assistance are not aware of the availability of programs that could help them, whatever their financial situation. The rural-urban differences noted in this study are perhaps not surprising since it has been noted that outside the major urban areas, there is a virtual absence of anything like the metropolitan legal aid societies to which individuals with problems, but not enough money to hire a private attorney, can turn.

The combination of lack of understanding of basic rights and lack of awareness of where to turn for assistance in protecting those rights when they are understood becomes critical in understanding some of the inequities of the system of legal justice. The quality which would best overcome the problems identified is closely related to what Carlin, Howard, and Messinger (1967:63) call "legal competence." In their words:

Broadly speaking [legal competence] would appear to consist of one part *awareness* and one part *assertiveness*. The legally competent person has a sense of himself as a possessor of rights, and he sees the legal system as a resource for validation of these rights. He knows when and how to seek validation. Beyond this, the legally competent person takes action: he not only "knows his rights" and how to validate them, but he turns to the legal system and uses it when his interests can be served by doing so. In the process, he tends to extend the rule of law.

In summarizing what we have defined as barriers to equal legal service participation, let us note again that each of the factors discussed must be considered as an important hurdle that must be cleared before there will be equitable legal activation and participation on the part of the poor and minority members of society. At the same time, these factors do

Table 3. Awareness of Legal Aid Programs by Sample Type

Aware of Legal Aid Programs	Area of Residence								TOTAL
	Urban Middle-Class		Rural		Semirural		Urban Poor & Minorities		
	N	%	N	%	N	%	N	%	
Yes	60	62	5	5	8	8	46	43	119
No	37	38	93	95	87	92	62	57	279
TOTAL	97		98		95		108		

not operate entirely independently of each other. Economic constraints are critical in and of themselves. They are also likely to affect the presence or absence of some of the other constraints. Since poverty is highly correlated with low educational attainment, economic means to utilize the law is also likely to be highly correlated with knowledge of basic rights as well as with knowledge of avenues for using the law. Starting from the other side of the equation, recognition of a problem as legal is a necessary but not necessarily sufficient condition for the activation of the legal process.

Other barriers, such as the availability of economic resources or the identification of legal professionals that are prepared to deal with the particular problems at hand may intercede between definition and participation. Such intercession may contribute to the search for alternative solutions to the perceived problem. This is rather critical because as Green (1974) has argued, nonparticipation in the legal process when the situation calls for legal action will result in increased levels of alienation and feelings of deprivation. Further, such experiences may reinforce or establish attitudes toward the legal system which act as barriers to further interest in or attempts at participation.

As can be seen, the problem is exacerbated by the fact that it frequently becomes a vicious cycle. The person with very limited economic means may have a problem that has important legal implications. If he or she does not define it as such, action will probably not be taken. On the other hand, even if the problem is defined as legal, no action will be taken if the person cannot afford an attorney and if he or she is ignorant of opportunities that may be available to obtain free legal aid. Inability to gain satisfactory closure may contribute to greater distrust and alienation from the system ("If I were rich, the problem would be taken care of"). While it is important to note that barriers other than economic constraints have been largely neglected or less systematically examined in the research literature, each of the factors will likely be found to some degree among those segments of the population exhibiting low legal participation.

RESPONSES AND PROGRAMS: THE LEGAL AID MOVEMENT

The starting point is to realize that the market is not for legal services; the market is for justice. (Cahn and Cahn, 1968)

Periodically, the recognition or discovery by reform groups and the public that the level of legal participation is inversely related to the distribution of wealth, leads to attempts at reform. The decade of the 1960s clearly exemplifies such a period of legal reform. Numerous legislative acts, court decisions, and social programs were initiated or expanded to correct what some felt were gross inequalities in the system of legal justice in this country.

The new programs of the sixties were made necessary by the failures of previous efforts to meet important legal needs of the poor and minorities. Henderson (1971:488) notes that "despite the traditional role of the lawyer in legal reform, lawyers [had] been strangely negligent in handling the affairs of those least able to pay the price for such representation." The legal profession had relied primarily upon Legal Aid societies and bureaus that had been established in most major cities to help meet some of the legal needs of the poor. However, Henderson feels that the Legal Aid bureaus frequently did little more than relieve the psychological guilt of many lawyers who may have recognized that they were not fully living up to their canon of ethics obliging them to accept clients on the merits of their case, whatever their ability to pay. Practically, the bureaus also gave them a place to refer clients "whom they could not simply kick out the door." Also, in discussing the Legal Aid and public defender programs, Carlin, Howard, and Messinger (1967:48) have noted:

With respect to the representation of criminal defendants, there is considerable evidence to suggest that neither the assigned counsel nor public defender system as now constituted is capable of providing adequate service to the indigent accused. A large proportion of poor defendants (particularly in misdemeanor cases) are not represented at all. Moreover, when counsel is provided he frequently has neither the resources, the skill nor the incentive to defend his client effectively; and he usually enters the case too late to make any real difference in the outcome. Indeed, the generally higher rate of guilty pleas and prison sentences among defendants represented by assigned counsel or the public defender suggest that these attorneys may actually undermine their client's position.

In short, it seems clear that the bureaus were woefully inadequate in meeting the needs of the people for whom they supposedly were established.

Partially in response to the failures and inadequacies of previous efforts, the Legal Services Program (LSP) was established by the Johnson administration as a part of a packet of amendments to the Economic Opportunity Act of 1964 (Henderson, 1971). Administered by the Office of Economic Opportunity, the Legal Services Program was set up to provide the poor with free legal assistance in those instances where they could not afford to pay for it themselves. Several related types of legal aid services, all evolving primarily out of OEO-administered grants made available by the Economic Opportunity Act, became available to communities and to various groups within communities. The purpose of the OEO grants was made quite explicit: to expand and improve legal representation for the poor (Silverstein, 1966). Neighborhood law offices, group legal aid programs, legal insurance and paraprofessional programs, many of which evolved from the OEO grants, were all designed to meet similar needs. The assumption behind all of these efforts seemed to be that if the poor were provided with assistance that would help them attain their legal rights, their situation could be significantly improved (Bamberger, 1966).

The initial impacts of the new programs seemed promising. Cahn and Cahn (1968) have noted that during the fiscal year 1967, neighborhood law firms processed over 300,000 cases. OEO reports indicate that in addition to the approximately 300,000 individuals served

834 community action groups, such as tenant associations, welfare mothers and farm worker communities received legal assistance. Members of these organizations, numbering an estimated 50 to 100 thousand poor people, received advice and representation to obtain their rights, to set up self-help institutions and to win their share of public services, such as health care, street lights, garbage collection, etc. (quoted in Cahn and Cahn, 1968:209)

Perhaps of even greater significance than the number of cases processed is the fact that in those cases that were carried through to trial, the results were favorable to the poor three-fourths of the time. In response to such a success ratio, Cahn and Cahn (1968:204) quote from the official publication of the Trial Lawyer's Association: "These are especially remarkable figures for the program's aid is withheld in any case that can be handled on a contingent basis or where there is an available source . . . for the person to engage a private attorney." While the most striking initial breakthroughs were in the area of welfare law, similar results were occurring in such areas as medicare, public housing, consumer frauds, bankruptcy, and public education.

However, the initial feelings of elation and success on the part of many soon gave way to the stark realization that the ideals they sought were still far from being realized. As noted by Henderson (1971:489):

The feelings of being in the vanguard of impending institutional change accounted for the sense of excitement and crusade expressed by so many of the early participants in the program. Soon they were inundated by divorces, wage attachments, automobile repossessions and the like. After five years of coping with staggering and demoralizing caseloads, LSP attorneys have come to suspect that a cruel joke has been played upon them—that someone in Washington, D.C. knew all along that a budget of $25 million, funding 551 offices and manned by 1,157 lawyers could not possibly begin to solve the legal problems of the nation's poor in the nation's core cities.

Lack of sufficient funding has always handicapped legal aid programs. Carlin, Howard, and Messinger (1967:49) have noted that in 1963, less than four million dollars was spent to finance the operations of Legal Aid organizations, or less than two-tenths of one percent of the total expenditures for legal services during that year. Even when clients were able to gain access to legal aid services, minimal time was too frequently spent on investigating facts, doing legal research, drafting legal documents and preparing for court work.

One consequence of the frustrations growing from impossible caseloads, inadequate manpower and budgets, and inundation with problems for which the program was not initially intended, was a growing belief on the part of many LSP officials and attorneys that if they were really going to have any impact, they must go beyond merely a service function to a greater concentration on the larger issue of legal reform. As Henderson (1971: 490) has put it: "to focus on the individual especially in view of the manpower and budgetary problems, is to largely ignore the greater problems now strangling our cities; that to file bankruptcy petitions for poor people does not solve the economic conditions that create the need for bankruptcy."

Other frustrations relating to the program were soon to be felt. Many in the legal profession itself felt that they should not be playing roles in providing free legal aid. Others, while recognizing the necessity of some type of legal assistance to the indigent, were strongly opposed to "judicial activism." The position of persons, both inside and outside the legal profession who opposed a more activist stance, seems best reflected in the work of Martin Mayer (1967). Mayer believes that the fight to improve the conditions of the poor as a group must be won in the legislatures and not in the courts.

In addition, powerful individuals and companies began to feel the consequences of providing federally funded legal services to the poor, especially in the form of class action suits. In talking about similar reactions to the earlier Legal Aid efforts, Carlin, Howard, and Messinger (1967:50–51) have noted that largely as a result of pressures from local businessmen, bankruptcy cases were eliminated from many Legal Aid offices. Such pressures also

resulted in a reluctance to press claims against local merchants, landlords and others whose interests would be threatened by more vigorous representation. The tendency, therefore, [was] for Legal Aid to become a captive of its principal financial supporters, who may well be considered its real clients. This leads to a cautious, passive and accomodative posture on the part of Legal Aid attorneys."

The consequence of this was that for the poor person, Legal Aid often became only "another line to wait in, another humiliating experience and a further reminder that the law is unresponsive to, if not opposed to, his interests." Powerful interests, in other words, began to realize that they were being affected by various legal action being initiated by attorneys for the poor who were hired and paid for by federal funds. This led to vigorous efforts to limit areas in which Legal Aid attorneys could function. Similar efforts have been directed by portions of the business community against the Legal Services Program.

In addition, the growing activism on the part of some LSP officials and attorneys did not endear them to a growing number of the members of Congress and particularly the Nixon administration that came to power following the Great Society of Lyndon Johnson. Continued efforts of the Nixon administration to disband the Office of Economic Opportunity were directed, in part, against such programs as legal services. All of these pressures have finally resulted in the termination of the OEO Legal Services Program and the replacement of it with a private legal services corporation. The Legal Services Corporation Act became law on July 25, 1974, creating a private, nonmembership, nonprofit corporation authorized to receive funds from both public and private sources and to operate a national legal services program through public financing, grants, and contracts. In a significant political move, the act prohibited the funding of outside back-up centers to perform research, technical assistance, and training for the program. Under the OEO program back-up centers, usually located at universities, had contributed to the growing activist image of LSP. The Corporation is still charged with providing legal assistance to those who would otherwise be unable to afford adequate legal council.

However, the notion of a private corporation was clearly designed to keep the provision of legal services out of the political arena and free from political influence. This is further evidenced by the restrictions placed upon the Corporation which include prohibition of LSC attorneys from involvement in matters involving class action suits (except in specifically identified situations), transportation of voters to polling places or related political activities, public demonstrations, civil disturbances, criminal proceedings, or cases involving desegregation, abortion, violation of selective service laws, and desertion. Supporters of continued governmental involvement in providing legal assistance to the poor have had to sacrifice these aspects of the controversial program in order to save what is left. It is obvious that such limitations will largely prohibit further efforts directed toward establishing important legal reform on the part of Legal Service attorneys.

One thing that is critical to note before leaving a discussion of governmental programs to provide legal aid to the poor and indigent is that these programs have been largely based upon the premise that economic factors are the most critical in determining differential participation in the legal process. Our earlier discussion, while recognizing the importance of economic means, also suggests that the barriers are more numerous. Implicit in much of the legal aid movement is the assumption that the poor and minorities correctly perceive many of their problems as legal and are willing to pursue these through traditional channels given the economic means (or the provision of free legal assistance through LSP, legal aid societies, or related programs). Only the lack of economic resources with which to consult and retain attorneys who, in turn, will initiate the legal process, acts as a barrier to legal participation.

As we have suggested above, and as has been argued elsewhere (Green, 1974), it may be quite likely that the economic barrier is the last in a series of obstacles. Prior to this would come a greater awareness of basic legal rights, an increased understanding of the process and channels through which one pursues these basic rights, and a breakdown of negative attitudes and beliefs that prohibit many from initiating action even when economic means are available. We would argue that if the goal of legal reform is to increase participation in the legal process, then removing the final barrier will increase participation only for those individuals who have surmounted those other barriers which precede it. Programs that will really have an impact on the system will have to concentrate on some of these other barriers as well.

It should be noted that some of these other barriers have not completely been ignored. There is, for example, growing concern with improving the level of legal knowledge among the lay public. Although efforts to educate the lay public on basic legal rights have not as yet received widespread attention from the legal profession itself, there is evidence that concern for such effort is growing. A recent paper by Whitler (1972–73) notes that the need to educate the lay public on various aspects of the law is now recognized by the "American Bar Association (ABA), the Association of American Law Schools (AALS), educators, reformers, the Congress and the lay public itself." The AALS is quoted in this report as stating that, "Basic legal concepts and institutions such as crime, contract, property, adversary presentation of claims and many others, which are fundamental to a social order, can and should be a part of the educational experience of all persons."

OEO-funded programs did place some emphasis on educating the poor about the law, in addition to providing funds for the establishment of legal aid services for those who could not otherwise afford them. Perhaps the most significant contribution of such information campaigns to this point has been the building of confidence in the law, leading to some erosion of the general tendency of many of the poor to try and avoid the law altogether (even in criminal law matters where the law could be employed as a safeguard to some very basic legal rights). However, the percentage of the poor influenced by the OEO programs is probably very low. In addition, it is no doubt true that the problems of educating middle-income groups as to their legal rights and needs do not differ significantly from those of educating the poor, and little effort has been directed toward middle-income groups. Finally, there continues to exist a critical problem in rural areas which generally lie outside the reach of legal services. New efforts will be needed to reach this important segment of the American populace.

A POSSIBLE SOLUTION: THE ESTABLISHMENT OF PARAPROFESSIONAL PROGRAMS

One solution to the problems identified above that is receiving more and more attention is the expanded use of paraprofessionals. Recent efforts in the medical field have clearly demonstrated the utility of paraprofessionals in meeting basic medical needs, particularly in areas where there is a shortage of physicians. In such areas, those physicians who are available have such heavy work loads that many problems either do not receive proper attention or draw the physician away from more serious concerns. Henderson has recently made a strong case for the increased use of paraprofessionals in the area of providing legal services to the poor. In his words (1971:494–495):

Increased use of paraprofessionals to perform legal work is a necessity, both to increasing the amount of legal work that can be turned out, given the chronic shortage of attorneys in this area, and also as an

approach toward decreasing the potency of the myth associated with attorneys and the law. Full use of volunteer help, including recruitment, both among lawyers and clients, serves to broaden the base of support for the office as well as providing real sources for use in serving client's needs.

Similar support has been expressed by Justice William O. Douglas for the utilization of paraprofessionals:

The supply of lawyer manpower is not nearly large enough. . . . It may well be that until the goal of free legal assistance to the indigent in all areas of the law is achieved, the poor are not harmed by well-meaning, charitable assistance of laymen. On the contrary, for the majority of indigents, who are not so fortunate to be served by neighborhood legal offices, lay assistance may be the only hope for achieving equal justice at this time. (quoted in Cahn and Cahn, 1968: 205–206)

One of the more impressive success stories in the utilization of paraprofessionals is found in the recent establishment of the Seattle Indian Paraprofessional Services program (IPS). Though very new (IPS first opened its doors to Indians living in Seattle in the summer of 1972), the program has already shown a good deal of promise. Funded by a grant from the National Institute of Mental Health, the program trained five Indian "ombudsmen" to act "as buffers between the Urban Indian and the alien city environment" in which he found himself (Halverson and Garrow, 1974). Recognizing the fears and frustrations so often experienced by the rural Indian migrant to urban America, the role of the five "ombudsmen" was to "seek out and assist Indians caught up in the criminal and civil legal process, entangled in and confused by bureaucratic red tape or simply in need of emergency food and shelter" (Halverson and Garrow, 1974:1).

Previous research had revealed to the originators of the program that many urban Indians were either not aware of, or were so distrustful of, available legal programs that few would use their services. Such groups as Seattle Legal Services, Seattle Public Defenders, and the Consumer Protection Branch of the State Attorney General's Office could have been of some assistance. However, distrust and ignorance led to the underutilization of such services by a minority that was badly in need of what they may have been able to provide. The organizers of the Seattle program also found that traditional utilization of private attorneys did not provide the answer to the social and legal needs they were identifying. Either lawyers were not interested in helping the Indians because of financial sacrifices involved or they were so unfamiliar with the culture of the natives that they had great difficulty in dealing with them.

The specific focus of the program, then, was to train lay Indians as paraprofessionals to intercede between reluctant clients and more traditional legal procedures. The training program was a rigorous one. Trainees spent three months taking law courses on such topics as consumer law, welfare rights, criminal law, housing rights, and so on. In addition, they enrolled in evening courses studying an experimental legal assistant curriculum approved by the American Bar Association. They also took classes from sociologists and others to help them develop counseling and related skills that would be useful in situations of marital and family conflict, alchohol problems, and emotional despondency.

In discussing IPS, Lowell Halverson (1974:9), an Indian attorney who played a critical role in establishing the program and training its participants, has concluded:

Success . . . cannot be measured merely by the number of Indian clients served or substantive law results obtained. In this author's opinion, the most profound impact of IPS was upon the attitude of urban natives toward the legal profession itself. For the first time, these forgotten peoples were able to witness skilled Indian advocates using tools of the established order to deal successfully with the mysteries of bureaucracy and courts, to ease the brutality of jailors and to expose the conniving of finance companies and used car dealers. The enduring lesson of IPS is that a dispossessed minority can, from among its own leadership, ease its people into their new urban life style while working within the established order.

The successes of the IPS program in Seattle merit continued evaluation and perhaps emulation in other areas, with other minorities, and with the poor more generally. As is true with medical and health care, it is frequently the rural resident in this country who has least access to the law. Paraprofessional legal programs established in rural counties and communities may meet a very basic need. Where problems are more serious, paraprofessionals could readily refer clients to their supervising attorneys who could then cover a much larger service area.

SOME IMPLICATIONS

The problem we have been dealing with in this article is basically a problem of mobilization of the law (Black, 1973). A citizenry able, willing, and ready to activate the legal process is necessary to retain effective power of the law. This is especially true when the legal system is basically passive in nature, as is the case of the legal system in the United States.

A passive legal system requires resources (in terms of such things as money, knowledge, and initiative) in order for an individual to make it work to his benefit (Whitler, 1972–73:271). If an individual lacks these resources, he is unable to utilize the law to further his own interests, and perhaps more importantly, to avoid the effects of the law when it is used against his interests.

Black (1973:139) notes that the legal system of the United States employs mechanisms to reinforce its passive nature (or in his terms, its reactive nature; both terms implying that mobilization will be "truly voluntary and entrepreneural"). According to Black, perhaps the best example of this is the general prohibition against solicitation by attorneys to obtain clients. "Were attorneys authorized to gather legal cases through solicitation, the input of legal business surely would change, since many otherwise passive victims of illegality undoubtedly would be persuaded to mobilize the law."

Largely because the law has been inaccessible to the poor, it has been used as an instrument of their oppression rather than as a means of combatting oppression (Alinsky, 1964). Too often it is the slumlords and the dishonest merchant or salesman in the ghetto who have used the law for eviction and repossession. However, the law can become a bulwark against oppressors only when the oppressed become knowledgeable of its workings and have access to its use.

The negative consequences must be felt by the system as well as by the victims. Lack of opportunities for obtaining redress when one has been wronged will contribute to feelings of alienation and estrangement from that source which fails to provide such access or opportunities. Political sociologists (see Lipset,

1963, for example) have argued that groups and individuals will accord a political or legal system legitimacy depending upon the degree to which they have access to the critical institutions of that system. Loyalty and support are frequently correlated with ease of access. When access is unjustly denied, crises of legitimacy must be seen as likely outcomes. This would imply that growing alienation from a political or legal system, along with the development of new ideologies opposed to that system (perhaps in the form of revolutionary social movements) are *natural* outcomes of the inequitable distribution of justice.

References

Albrecht, Stan L., and Green, Miles, "Cognitive Barriers to Equal Justice before the Law." Paper presented at the Annual Meeting of the Society for the Study of Social Problems, Montreal, Canada, 1974.

Albrecht, Stan L., and Green, Miles. "Attitudes toward the Police and the Larger Attitude Complex: Implications for Police-Community Relationships." Paper presented at the Fiftieth Annual Meeting of the American Association for the Advancement of Science, Laramie, Wyoming. Forthcoming, *Journal of Criminology*, February 1976.

Alinsky, Saul. *Reveille for Radicals*. Chicago: University of Chicago Press, 1964.

Bamberger, E. Clinton, Jr. "Legal Services to the Poor: Basic Principles." *Journal of the State Bar of California*, 1966, 41, 224–231.

Bell, Daniel. "Notes on the Post-Industrial Society." In M. E. Olsen (Ed.), *Power in Societies*. New York: Macmillan, 1970. Pp. 394–402.

Black, Donald J. "The Mobilization of the Law." *Journal of Legal Studies*, 1973, 2, 125–149.

Cahn, Edgar S., and Cahn, Jean Camper.

"Justice and the Poor." In W. Bloomberg and H. J. Schmandt (Eds.), *Power, Poverty and Urban Policy*. Beverly Hills, Ca.: Sage Publications, 1968. Pp. 203–222.

Caplovitz, David. *The Poor Pay More*. Glencoe, Ill.: Free Press, 1963.

Carlin, Jerome E., and Howard, Jan. "Legal Representation and Class Justice." *UCLA Law Review*, 1965, 12, 381–437.

Carlin, Jerome E., Howard, Jan, and Messinger, Sheldon L. *Civil Justice and the Poor*. New York: Russell Sage Foundation, 1967.

Chadwick, Bruce A., Stauss, Joseph, Bahr, Howard M., and Halverson, Lowell. "Confrontation with the Law: The Case of the Native American in Seattle." Unpublished manuscript, Brigham Young University, Provo, Utah, 1974.

Conrad, Alfred F., Morgan, James N., and Pratt, R. W., Jr., et al. *Automobile Accident Costs and Payments*. Ann Arbor: The University of Michigan Press, 1964.

Ennis, Philip H. "Criminal Victimiza- and the Police." *Trans-Action* 1967, 4, 36–44. (a)

Ennis, Philip H. "Criminal Victimization in the United States: A Report of a National Survey (National Opinion Research Center, University of Chicago)." A report prepared for the President's Commission on Law Enforcement and Administration of Justice. Field Survey II, Washington, D.C.: U.S. Government Printing Office, 1967. (b)

Etzioni, Amitai. *The Active Society*. New York: Free Press, 1968.

Festinger, Leon. *A Theory of Cognitive Dissonance*. Evanston, Ill.: Row, Peterson, 1957.

Galbraith, John Kenneth. *The New Industrial State*. Boston: Houghton Mifflin, 1967.

Gallup, George H. The Gallup Poll— Public Opinion 1935–1971, Vol. 3. New York: Random House, 1971.

Galvin, Raymond, and Radelet, Louis. "A National Survey of Police and Community Relations (East Lansing: Michigan State University)." A report prepared for the President's Commission on Law Enforcement and Administration of Justice. Field Survey V, Washington, D.C.: U.S. Government Printing Office, 1967.

Green, Miles. "Legal Participation: A Comparative Study." Unpublished dissertation, Utah State University, Logan, Utah, 1974.

Hallauer, Robert P. "The Shreveport Experiment in Prepaid Legal Services." *Journal of Legal Studies*, 1973, 2, 223–242.

Halverson, Lowell K., and Garrow, Tom. "Meeting the Social and Legal Needs of Urban Indians: An Experimental Program." Paper presented at the Annual Meeting of the American Sociological Association, Montreal, Canada, 1974.

Hazard, Geoffry C., Jr. "Legal Problems Peculiar to the Poor." *Journal of Social Issues*, 1970, 26, 47–58.

Henderson, Thelton E. "New Roles for the Legal Profession." In P. Orleans and W. R. Ellis (Eds.), *Race, Change and Urban Society*. Beverly Hills, Ca.: Sage Publications, 1971. Pp. 482–512.

Jacob, Herbert. "Black and White Perceptions of Justice in the City." *Law and Society Review*, 1971, 6, 69–89.

Lipset, Seymour Martin. *Political Man*. New York: Anchor, 1963.

Lohman, Joseph E., and Misner, Gordon. "The Police and Community: The Dynamics of their Relationship in a Changing Society (Berkley, University of California)." A report prepared for the President's Commission on Law Enforcement and the Administration of Justice. Field Surveys IV, Vol. II, Washington, D.C.: U.S. Government Printing Office, 1967.

Mayer, Martin. "The Idea of Justice and the Poor." *Public Interest*, 1967, 8, 75–115. (a)

Mayer, Martin. *The Lawyers*. New York: Harper & Row, 1967. (b)

Mayhew, Leon, and Reiss, Albert J., Jr. "The Social Organization of Legal Contacts." *American Sociological Review*, 1969, 34, 309–318.

National Advisory Commission on Civil Disorders. *Report of the Commission.* New York: Bantam, 1968.

Olsen, Marvin E. *Power in Societies.* New York: Macmillan, 1970.

President's Commission on Law Enforcement and the Administration of Justice. "Crime and Its Impact—An Assessment." Washington, D.C.: U.S. Government Printing Office, 1967. (b)

Santarelli, Donald E. "Police Failing to Gain Public Trust." Statement presented at a meeting of state crime administrators, Williamsburg, Virginia, January, 1974.

Silverstein, Lee. "Thoughts on the Legal Aid Movement." *Social Service Review,* 1966, 40, 135–151.

Sykes, Gresham M. "Legal Needs of the Poor in the City of Denver." *Law and Society Review,* 1969, 4, 255–277.

Task Force Report, President's Commission on Law Enforcement and the Administration of Justice. "The Courts." Washington, D.C.: U.S. Government Printing Office, 1967. (a)

Wald, Patricia M. "Poverty and Criminal Justice." In Task Force Report, President's Commission on Law Enforcement and the Administration of Justice. "The Courts." Washington, D.C.: U.S. Government Printing Office, 1967. Pp. 139–151.

Weiss, Jonathan. "The Law and the Poor." *Journal of Social Issues,* 1970, 26, 59–67.

Whitler, John. "Public Legal Education." *Journal of Family Law,* 1972–73, 12, 269–291.

Williams, Martha, and Hall, Jay. "Knowledge of the Law in Texas: Socioeconomic and Ethnic Differences." *Law and Society Review,* 1972, 7, 99–118.

Wilson, James Q. "The Police and their Problems: A Theory." *Public Policy,* 1963, 22, 189–216.

Wilson, James Q. "Police Morale, Reform and Citizen Respect: The Chicago Case." In David J. Bordua (Ed.), *The Police: Six Sociological Essays.* New York: Wiley, 1967. Pp. 137–162.

Suggested Reading

BLACK, DONALD J. "The Mobilization of the Law." *Journal of Legal Studies,* 1973, 2, 125–149.
A carefully reasoned treatise on the relationship between structural and social psychological variables and legal mobilization—for the more advanced student.

CAHN, EDGAR S., AND CAHN, JEAN CAMPER. "Justice and the Poor." In W. Bloomberg and H. J. Schmandt (Eds.), *Power and Urban Policy.* Beverly Hills, Ca.: Sage Publications, 1968. Pp. 203–222.
This entire volume contains an excellent set of articles on problems that poor and minority populations have in obtaining equal opportunities in American Society, and particularly in urban America. The piece by Cahn and Cahn is a well-reasoned treatise on the unequal distribution of justice evident in our society. Interested readers should look at other articles in the edition as well.

HENDERSON, THELTON E. "New Roles for the Legal Profession." In P. Orleans and W. R. Ellis (Eds.), *Race, Change and Urban Society.* Beverly Hills, Ca.: Sage Publications, 1971. Pp. 482–512.
Henderson highlights what the legal profession itself can do to increase equal access to the law for all socioeconomic groups.

WHITLER, JOHN. "Public Legal Education." *Journal of Family Law*, 1972–73, 12, 269–291.
Whitler proposes more extensive efforts to increase public knowledge of the law as a means of increasing access to equal protection before the law.

WILLIAMS, MARTHA, AND HALL, JAY. "Knowledge of the Law in Texas: Socio-economic and Ethnic Differences." *Law and Society Review*, 1972, 7, 99–118.
This study exposes the breadth of ignorance of very basic legal rights in a major city in Texas.

Work, Alienation, and the Industrial Order

Frank Lindenfeld

BACKGROUND

Since the Second World War, the American economy has been moving from an industrial into a "postindustrial" period (Bell, 1973; Bookchin, 1971; Reisman, 1958; Roszak, 1972; Touraine, 1971). This era is characterized by increasing use of computers and automation and decreasing need for human labor in industrial production; the employment of a greater proportion of the labor force in professional, technical, and service occupations; and an expansion of jobs provided by nonprofit agencies such as universities and hospitals, and by local, state, and federal governments.

The postindustrial economy provides greater material abundance than heretofore available, and so makes possible the establishment of a more equitable social order. If the abundance were shared, all persons in the society could be freed from the worries of subsistence. Freedom from economic insecurity would create the conditions under which men and women might find greater fulfillment in their work, instead of being forced to settle for meaningless or boring jobs that frustrate their creative energies. Instead of being controlled by management or machines, ordinary people would be in control of their own work.

To help the reader interpret this essay, I will make explicit some of my biases. (1) *Work*. All persons should have the opportunity to engage in work that is meaningful, creative, and fulfilling. Personal initiative, participation, and autonomy should be maximized. (2) *Distribution of rewards*. All persons deserve the guarantee of a minimum level of food, shelter, clothing, and medical care as a basic right. Great differences in wealth and income are undesirable. (3) *Ecological balance*. Continued consumption of nonrenewable natural resources is undesirable, as is continued growth of an economy based on such consumption.

A good case can be made for each of the above values, although I will not do so in any detail here. Logically, such a case would entail going back to still other values such as democracy, self-development, liberty, or happiness. I favor the maximization of what the psychologist Abraham Maslow terms the "higher" needs and values of all persons and believe that greater initiative, participation, and autonomy in work will enable more persons to attain fuller realization of their talents and capacities. I agree with Maslow that the human being appears to have a hierarchy of needs, such that his higher needs for creativity and fulfillment cannot be met unless creature needs are first taken care of (Maslow, 1968).

Great differences in wealth, income, and power are undesirable because they lead to the maximization of happiness for only a small number of persons. Such differences are based on the exploitation of the many by the few and subvert the possibility of a democratic society. Finally, growth of the gross national product based on increasing consumption of natural resources is dangerous for our well-being because of the possibility that our civilization will collapse when these resources are depleted (Daly, 1973). Moreover, it is immoral to expand our already high standard of living, while so many millions in other countries are starving.

Below, we shall examine some of the characteristics of the changing American labor force. The nature of available occupations and the characteristics of the persons who fill them are symptomatic of the problems that beset the current industrial order. Next, the enduring problems of work in industrial society will be discussed. These include unemployment, length of work week, income distribution, job satisfaction, and alienation. The chapter concludes with an examination of two types of "solutions" to the problems of work: (1) job enlargement and a guaranteed annual income—a reform approach, and (2) thoroughgoing structural change involving a shift in the locus of power—workers' control, socialism, and a dual economy consisting of subsistence and luxury sectors.

The Changing Labor Force

There were 94 million Americans in the labor force in 1975, out of a total population of 155 million persons 16 years or older. Some 7.5 million were unemployed and over 2 million in the armed forces, leaving about 84 million who held civilian jobs. About three-fifths of the work force were male, and two-fifths were female.

Men typically held different kinds of jobs than women (see Table 1). Two-fifths of the men were in white-collar jobs and almost half in blue-collar jobs. Three-fifths of the women were in white-collar occupations, while one-fifth was in blue-collar and one-fifth in service jobs. In all fields, from blue-collar work to the professions, the higher prestige and higher paid jobs are generally reserved for men.

Table 1 shows also that racism is still prevalent in the occupational structure. Only one-quarter of nonwhite men, compared with 44 percent of white men, held white-collar jobs in 1970. About 44 percent of nonwhite women, compared with 66 percent of the white women had white-collar jobs. Thirty-eight percent of non-white women versus 20 percent of white women worked in service jobs.[1] Although the occupational gap between blacks and whites, women and men, is still large, the difference has been narrowing in recent years. Hopefully, affirmative action programs to hire minorities and women in proportion to their numbers will further reduce such job discrimination.

The American labor force has changed considerably over the last century. One change is an increase in size, from 13 million to 84 million. In part this increase is attributable to population growth. In part it also reflects the increasing employment of women. By 1970, over 40 percent of women 16 years old or over were in the labor force, compared with about 20 percent at the turn of the century.

One of the main changes has been the "proletarianization" of the work force. More and more persons are employees,

[1] *Statistical Abstract of the United States,* 1974, p. 337; and U.S. Bureau of the Census, *Historical Statistics of the U.S., Colonial Times to 1957,* p. 70.

Table 1. United States Labor Force Composition, by Race and Sex, 1975

		Percent of group in occupational category among:					
	TOTAL		*MALE*			*FEMALE*	
Occupational				*Negro*			*Negro*
Category		*Total*	*White*	*& Other*	*Total*	*White*	*& Other*
White Collar	51	42	44	25	63	66	44
Professional &							
Technical	16	15	16	9	16	17	13
Managerial	11	14	15	5	5	5	3
Sales	6	6	7	2	7	7	3
Clerical	18	7	7	8	35	37	25
Blue Collar	32	45	43	54	14	13	17
Craftsmen	13	20	21	16	2	2	1
Operatives	15	18	17	24	11	11	14
Non-farm laborers	5	7	6	14	1	1	1
Service Workers	14	9	8	17	22	20	38
Farm	3	5	5	4	1	1	**
TOTAL *	100	100	100	100	100	100	100

Source: U.S. Bureau of Labor Statistics, *Employment and Earnings*, Vol. 21, No. 10, April 1975, p. 34. Data are for March 1975.
* Detail does not always add to total because of rounding.
** Less than 1%

working for others. The number of capitalists was and is small, never amounting to much more than 1 percent of the population.[2]

The self-employed middle class has been shrinking. In 1880, 37 percent of the labor force was self-employed. By 1970, this had dwindled to less than 10 percent (Reich, 1972). In part this is a reflection of the movement of independent farmers to factory and service occupations in the cities—only 2 percent of the labor force were small independent farmers in 1970. It also reflects the fact that increasing numbers of professionals, even in such traditionally independent

occupations as law and medicine, are now salaried employees.

It is still possible to start a small business today—small proprietors account for a third of the self-employed. However, it is difficult to survive as an independent within an economy dominated by the major corporations. (This is illustrated by the gradual replacement of independent "gas stations" by those franchised or operated by the major oil corporations.) The self-employed often work long hours and face considerable economic uncertainty. On the positive side, they do not have to worry about pleasing a boss.

Most of the work force are employees; they do not own or control the stores, factories, offices, hospitals, universities, and so forth, they work in. Some of them work in "fat" jobs, with high pay and job security, others in "lean" ones with sub-

[2] Capitalists are those whose incomes are obtained primarily from ownership or control of property, that is, from dividends, interests, rent, capital gains, and so on. Some capitalists are also managerial employees, and some put on greasy overalls. But they are not dependent on their jobs for their income.

sistence wages and little guarantee of steady employment. (Many, including unskilled blue-collar workers and clerical employees, are in between.)

Oligopolistic industry and federal, state, and local government bureaus provide most of the gravy employment. At its upper levels, this is the world of expense accounts, company cars, tax shelters, stock options, and so on. The fat work force includes scientists, engineers, and other professionals, as well as technical workers, teachers, and municipal employees. Common to these jobs are: short hours (except for some top executives); relatively high pay; job security; pensions; paid vacations; insurance plans; and other benefits.

But there is another force in the world of work, that of low-paid, seasonal, or "dirty" workers. These lean workers include domestics, car-wash attendants, dishwashers, migrant farm laborers, nurses' aides, and other menial occupations. The typical jobs are nonunionized, require few skills, provide little or no employment security, and few fringe benefits. Employment is usually intermittent, seasonal, or part-time. The pay is often at or below the legal minimum wage. Some of those in low-paid jobs are employed by small businesses that find it difficult to raise wages or increase benefits. Others, however, work for corporate giants or well-established "non-profit" institutions. The same corporations that pay their chief executives six figure salaries and large bonuses often give a pittance to the fieldworkers who pick the crops on which a portion of the company profits are based. We can include in the lean category the chronically unemployed, even though these are not usually a part of the officially defined labor force. A disproportionate number of the under-paid "dirty" workers are women and ethnic minorities.

Another trend has been the expansion of employment in the tertiary sector of the economy and the concomitant contraction of jobs in the primary sector. In 1850 more than two-thirds of the labor force was working in the primary sector, which involves extraction of raw materials from the earth (agriculture, forestry, fishing, mining). The remaining one-third of the labor force was equally divided between the secondary (manufacture and construction) and tertiary sectors (Clark, 1951). The latter includes all activities other than raw material extraction and manufacture (transportation, trade, finance, insurance, services, and government). By 1970 only about 5 percent of the labor force was still working in primary industries. The proportion of the work force in manufacturing and construction increased to a high point of about one-third during World War II and then began a gradual decline (see Table 2). The tertiary sector gradually increased until by 1970 it constituted almost two-thirds of the work force. This expansion in the tertiary sector, coupled with the greater use of automation and computers in production, is characteristic of what has been called the "postindustrial" society. Automation promises to free most persons from the drudgery and tedium of boring, repetitive work. Within the context of the existing capitalist economy, however, such increasing productive capacity also helps to create unemployment.

PROBLEMS

Unemployment

One problem of work is that many persons who want jobs cannot find them. In

Table 2. Historical Trends in the Composition of the American Labor Force

	1870	1900	1920	1940	1968	1980 (projection)
Size of total labor force (000's)	12,900	29,000	42,600	49,900	80,800	99,600
Percent distribution, by sector:						
Primary (agriculture, mining)	56	41	31	20	6	4
Secondary (manufacture, construction)	22	28	31	31	30	28
Tertiary (transportation, trade, finance, insurance, services and government	22	31	38	49	64	68
TOTAL	100	100	100	100	100	100

Sources: *Historical Statistics of the U.S., 1820–1940;* series D-57-71, p. 74; *The U.S. Economy in 1980,* Bureau of Labor Statistics Bulletin #1673.

a society where income is tied to jobs, extended unemployment means hardship and often poverty. The most severely hit by unemployment are those paid very low wages to begin with. The lower the wages, the less unemployment compensation received by those out of work. Many low-wage earners do not even qualify for unemployment benefits.

Official figures show some 54.3 million persons not in the labor force in 1970. This was just under 40 percent of the total population 16 years old or over. Most of them were "keeping house" or going to school. The number of unemployed was 4.1 million.[3] Such unemployment data are underestimates, because many of those counted as not in the labor force would be willing to work if there were jobs available. Official definitions of the unemployed include only those looking for work, but exclude those so discouraged that they have stopped

[3] *Statistical Abstract of the U.S.,* 1973, Table 347, p. 219.

looking for jobs. Nevertheless, government figures show general trends and are useful in pinpointing which groups have the highest relative joblessness. Among blacks, unemployment is about twice as high as among whites; it is higher among women than among men; it is highest in the age group under 20; and next highest among those aged 20–24. About one-quarter of all teenage blacks in the labor force in 1970 were officially unemployed! (See Table 3.)

The actual unemployment rate today may be almost as high as it was during the depression of the 1930s, when an estimated one-quarter of the labor force was out of work. The official rate of unemployment jumped sharply from 3.8 percent in 1967 to 9 percent by mid-1975, but such figures mask the full extent of joblessness. Counting not only the "unemployed," but also the underemployed and part-time workers seeking full employment, housewives and students who would work if they could find jobs, those between 55 and 64 not working, those in

Table 3. Unemployment Rates by Age, Sex, and Race
among Persons 16 Years of Age and Older (1970)

	Percent Unemployed among:			
	MEN		*WOMEN*	
Age	*White*	*Negro & Other Races*	*White*	*Negro & Other Races*
Total	3.8	6.8	4.9	8.5
16–19	12.5	19.6	11.8	30.7
20 and over	3.2	5.6	4.1	6.8

Source: U.S. Bureau of the Census, *Current Population Reports*, series P-23, No. 37, "Social and Economic Characteristics of the Population in Metropolitan and Non-Metropolitan Areas: 1970 and 1960," Table 13, pp. 55–57.

manpower training programs, and so forth, Gross and Moses (1972) estimate there were 25.6 million unemployed out of a real labor force of some 104 million persons in 1971.[4] If we add to this 2.8 million persons in the armed forces who would otherwise have been in the labor market, we arrive at a corrected unemployment rate of about 27 percent for 1971!

A major cause of unemployment is the continuing mechanization and automation of production. Under capitalism, labor is replaced by machines whenever it is cheaper to do so, and regardless of the social consequences such as increasing unemployment. Automation in the U.S. has sharply reduced the number of workers needed in primary industries such as agriculture and mining, and has made possible a continuing expansion of industrial output with a stable or declining number of production employees.

One of the chief difficulties of job displacement caused by automation is that many of those whose work is taken over by machines are relatively unskilled and uneducated. When they lose their jobs

they have difficulty finding other ones. Even when they obtain employment after "retraining," they may find their new jobs eliminated by automation within a few years. The growth of new service industries may take up some of the slack, but even here the trend is toward replacement of people by machines (Heilbroner, 1973).

The record of new jobs provided by private industry since World War II is not very good. The total number of persons in the labor force increased by about 22 million between 1950 and 1970. But private nondefense industry absorbed only 5–10 percent of this increase.[5] Unemployment increased by almost one million, while the size of the armed forces doubled. The fastest growing sectors during these 20 years were nonprofit institutions (for example, hospitals and universities) and government. In 1970 there were about 6 million federal employees, half of whom were in the armed forces; and about 10 million in state and

[4] Recomputation of 1930s statistics along similar lines for comparison would of course lead to higher estimates of unemployment for those years as well.

[5] During the middle six year period of time, between 1957 and 1963, Magdoff (1970) calculates total nonfarm employment increased by 4.3 million, while private demand (excluding jobs owing to government purchases from business) created only .3 million of these jobs, or 7 percent.

local governments (an increase of over 4 million in 20 years). Almost one-third of all the new jobs added in these two decades were provided directly by some form of government employment. Expansion of social services, especially education, provided one major source of employment. Expansion of the military establishment during the cold war, the Korean War, and the Vietnam War was the other main source.

Growth in the government sector slowed down by the mid-1970s, however. The winding down of the Vietnam War led to a slower increase in the military. This country seems to have reached a plateau in local, state, and federal government employment, beyond which it will be difficult to go without further tax increases. The current supply of trained teachers (one of the largest categories of government employees) greatly exceeds demand. According to the National Education Association, the number of jobs available for new teachers (through resignation, retirement, and so forth) in 1974 was about 111,000. But at the same time the total number of new teaching graduates was about 234,000. That means an oversupply of some 123,000 teachers. One out of every two teaching graduates in 1974 was unable to find a job in the field for which he or she was trained. (Los Angeles Times, 1974).

Can we provide enough jobs to go around? In the short run, probably not unless there is a major expansion in public planning and investment for presently unmet needs such as parks, low income housing, transportation, and so forth, and in human services such as medicine, child care, and social work, accompanied by major cuts in military spending. In the long run, not unless we replace the system of private profit with something that works better.

Continuing to pour billions of dollars into arms production and war-related industry will not create the jobs we need. Quite apart from undesirable social consequences, which include the militarization of the society and the greater likelihood of engaging in foreign wars such as the Vietnam War, there are detrimental economic effects of such investment for military purposes, as Melman (1971) documents in his work.[6]

(1) Producing more guns means we have less butter. Even the United States, the world's wealthiest economy, does not have infinite resources. More military production means less civilian production, as machinery, labor and talent, natural resources, and energy that could have been used for creating civilian goods and services are preempted by the military.[7]

(2) The Vietnam War and continuing massive military expenditures on the order of $80–100 billion a year have been a major factor contributing to inflation.

[6] Massive war production makes more probable the selection of military solutions to international problems and strengthens the influence of the military on the entire society. The vast operations managed by the U.S. Department of Defense make that agency the dominant industrial decision-maker in this country. Pentagon-controlled industrial output was about $44 billion in 1968, compared with net sales of $23 billion by General Motors and $14 billion by AT&T that year. (See Melman, 1970:7.)

[7] Melman (1970) estimates that the money spent each month of the Vietnam war could have financed the training of 100,000 scientists; or doubled funds expended for international economic development; or created four new Rockefeller Foundations; or paid for a full year's cost of all the state and local police forces in this country. In another comparison, he calculates that each polaris submarine costs the equivalent of 331 elementary schools, 6,811 hospital beds or 13,723 low-rent housing units. See also Melman (1965).

The purchasing power of the dollar has gone down because of military consumption of energy, resources, goods, and services.[8]

(3) The economy has been depleted by over-concentration of research and development, investment, and production into military channels. Some 64 percent of the metal-working machine tools in the U.S. in 1968 were 10 years old or older. American railroads and shipbuilding have been severely neglected. And only 37 percent of the engineers, scientists, and technicians engaged in research and development in this country in 1967 were working on civilian projects.

(4) A high level of military spending creates unemployment by providing fewer job opportunities than comparable spending on civilian uses. A conservative estimate is that between 1968 and 1972, when the military budget averaged $80 billion per year, the annual "loss" in jobs that would otherwise have been generated was 840,000. Each $1 billion spent on military instead of the civilian sector during those years resulted in between 10,000 and 21,000 fewer jobs (see Table 4) (Anderson, 1975; Russett, 1970).

[8] More civilian dollars chase fewer goods because so much production is consumed by the military. Hence, prices rise.

(5) Jobs created in either the civilian or military sector have a "multiplier" effect. (For example, schools provide jobs not only for teachers, but for others working to produce textbooks, films, audio-visual equipment, calculators, and so on, used by schools). The multiplier effect of military production in generating additional jobs, however, is far smaller than the effect of comparable civilian production.[9]

Even if the imbalance created by over-emphasis on the military were corrected, it is not certain that private industry could supply enough new jobs for those displaced by automation. Not all fields can or should be automated, however. There will probably be a continuing need for human service workers such as doctors, nurses, teachers, and psychologists in even the most technologically sophisticated economy. Further, there is plenty of work to be done in providing low income housing, mass transit, new energy systems, and so forth. Since there is not necessarily any profit to be made in such

[9] As Melman (1970:30) points out, "The product of the military-serving workers, technicians and managers is a product that does not enter the market place, is not bought back, and cannot be used for current level of living or for future production."

Table 4. Jobs Created per Billion Dollars of Expenditure

Jobs created by:	If spent to create jobs in:	
	Private Industry	Government
$1 billion spent in civilian sector	65,000	100,000
$1 billion spent in military sector	55,000	79,000
Net jobs foregone by military spending	10,000	21,000

Source: Marion Anderson, "The Empty Pork Barrel," WIN, 1975, 11, 4–8.

endeavors, most of them would have to be publicly sponsored or subsidized.

In summary, official figures for 1975 show almost 9 percent unemployment in this country. Such data are underestimates, actual unemployment may be three times as high. Hardest hit by unemployment in the United States are ethnic minorities, women, and the young. One cause of unemployment is the substitution of machines for human labor by capitalist business whenever it is more profitable to do so. During the 1950s and 1960s, jobs provided by government increased rapidly, but this expansion slowed down by the 1970s. New jobs have been created by government spending for military purposes, but the same money invested in civilian uses would have created many more job opportunities.

Income, Hours, and Productivity

LEISURE TIME The greater productivity resulting from the introduction of mechanization and automation in American industry means that less human labor is needed to turn out more goods and services. Productivity has risen at an annual rate of about 3 percent during this century. The gross national product (GNP) per capita increased from approximately $1700 in 1929 to nearly $2500 by 1950, and to $4000 by 1973 (in constant 1960 dollars). On the basis of present trends, it seems reasonable to estimate that by the year 2000 it could reach $7500.[10]

Such projections assume that our economy can (and should) continue to grow in the future at the same rate as it has in the past. They further assume little

change in our present habits of wasteful production and consumption. The growth in the GNP is based partly on the consumption of extravagant amounts of nonrenewable natural resources. Counted in the GNP are unnecessary and even harmful goods and services, including advertising, massive government military spending, and the production of millions of new model automobiles each year. It is questionable whether an ever-increasing American standard of living is desirable both in itself and in the face of a widening gap between the economically developed and the undeveloped countries of the world (Daly, 1973).

As we saw in the preceding section, higher productivity associated with the introduction of automation has exacerbated the unemployment problem in the context of a profit-oriented economy and the widespread acceptance of the 40-hour work week as a standard. Historically, part of the increased productivity of the labor force has been translated into higher wages; and part into more profits for employers. A third use of increased output has been to channel it into governmental social services and military uses through taxation. Finally, greater productivity has led to more time free from work. The average length of the work week in America declined steadily during the last century. Vacations are longer, there are more paid holidays, and job entry is postponed longer by going to school. Between 1890 and 1970, the average work week declined by about 14 hours in this country.[11]

[10] Kahn and Wiener (1973:142) estimate that by the year 2000, per capita GNP in the United States will rise to $10,160 (1965 dollars) at a 3 percent growth rate per year; or alternatively to $6750, at a growth rate of 1.8 percent per year.

[11] See Moore and Hodges (1971), Table 1, p. 5. As Wilensky (1963) points out, however, the decrease in the work week can also be seen as a return to the number of hours per year worked in medieval times, when the workday may have been long, but there were many holidays during the year.

Although average work hours have decreased over the last century, leisure time is unevenly distributed. Most American workers have considerable time "free" from work today (Moore and Hodges, 1971). Some, however, have a scarcity of time off and some work multiple jobs.

Certain professionals and many self-employed persons still work long hours. One-quarter of all managers, proprietors, and officials, and over half the farmers and farm workers put in an average of 60 or more hours of work per week in 1970. In Wilensky's study (1963), a third or more of the lawyers, professors, small business proprietors, and managers worked 55 or more hours per week. The same probably holds true for physicians, though not for dentists.

Others have more leisure time than they want. These are the involuntary retired, the chronic or intermittently unemployed, and those working part-time only because they cannot find any full-time jobs. The forced retirement of many persons able and willing to work even though they are past 60 or 65 is especially tragic, not only because they suffer from reduced income, but also because it deprives them of self-esteem.

Given the existing economic system, future gains in productivity will probably continue to be channeled into each of the aforementioned four avenues: higher wages, higher profits, more government services, and shorter working time. The 40-hour week may remain for some few years, with workers' share of productivity gains going into longer vacations, more holidays, and higher pay. Within a decade, however, there may be a "quantum leap" to a new standard of a four-day–32-hour, or five-day–30-hour work week. The higher the unemployment rate, the stronger may become the pressure to increase employment by cutting down on the average work week. A reduction of the average work week from 40 to 32 hours could be translated into 25 percent more jobs. As the work week decreases, the line between full and part-time jobs may gradually disappear, and the availability of shorter "standard" hours may enable even more women to enter the labor force.

INCOME DISTRIBUTION   There has been a long-run trend for income of American workers to rise, and for the relative number of impoverished to decline. Income, however, is still unequally distributed, and the extent of income inequality has not appreciably diminished during this century.

The median income of Americans increased steadily between the end of the Second World War and the early 1970s, even when inflation is taken into account (see Table 5). (The combination of inflation and high unemployment in the mid-1970's has reversed this progress.) This resulted primarily from the increasing productivity of the economy, but also through the gradual extension of government-provided welfare benefits. The average income of families in 1972 was over $11,000; for unrelated individuals it was over $3500. One-fifth of the families still had incomes below $5600 however, and one-fifth of the unrelated individuals had incomes between $0 and $1600!

While absolute income has risen in this country, the relative distribution of that income has remained fairly constant over the last 60 years. If we divide the population into fifths according to income, we find that the relative share of the bottom fifth is minute. If anything, the proportion of national income received by those at the bottom has de-

Table 5. Income for Total and Lowest Fifth, Families and Unrelated Individuals in the U.S., 1947–1972 (in Constant 1972 Dollars)

	1947	1960	1972
Average Income, Total Population			
Families	5,665	7,941	11,116
Unrelated individuals	1,866	2,442	3,521
Income of lowest fifth was below			
Families	2,966	3,932	5,612
Unrelated individuals	590	918	1,596

Source: Statistical Abstract of the U.S., 1974, Table 620, p. 384.

creased. (See Table 6.) The richest fifth of the population consistently received between 44–50 percent of all income between 1910 and 1968. The poorest fifth received 8 percent of all income in 1910, but only about 4 percent in 1968.[12] This inequality of income distribution has remained basically unaltered by income taxes. Income tax laws provide for progressively higher taxes on higher income, on paper. But because of the many tax loopholes and special provisions that apply to the wealthy, income taxes reduce

their relative share of income by at most one or two percent.[13]

The highest incomes in this country go to a handful of the top managers of corporate enterprises with six figure salaries, and to the capitalist class of which they are a part. This class, not usually included in standard comparisons of income from different occupations, derives most of its income from ownership of stocks and bonds, interest on bank deposits, rents from properties owned, or capital gains from selling them. The richest 1 percent of the population had on the average a net worth of $367,500 in 1969 (Smith

[12] When we look at the distribution of property and wealth, the differences between rich and poor are even more striking than when we examine income alone. In 1962, the top 2 percent of consumer units owned 43 percent of all the wealth in this country; the bottom 45 percent owned about 3 percent of the wealth. See Miller (1971).

[13] See data on before and after tax income, 1941–1957, in U.S. Bureau of the Census, *Historical Statistics of the U.S., Colonial Times to 1957*, pp. 163, 165. See also Miller (1971) and Kolko (1962).

Table 6. Distribution of Before Tax Income in the United States, by Fifths of the Population, 1910–1968

	Total	Richest Fifth	Middle Three Fifths	Poorest Fifth
1910	100%	46	46	8
1929	100%	51	43	5
1950	100%	44	52	4
1968	100%	44	52	4

Sources: Gabriel Kolko, *Wealth and Power in America* (New York: Praeger, 1962), p. 14; and Herman Miller, *Rich Man, Poor Man* (New York: Crowell, 1971), p. 50.

and Franklin, 1974:166). At 8 percent interest, this would have yielded an income of approximately $29,400 annually, to which would have to be added income from managerial or other income-producing occupations.

Next in income are the independent professionals, including doctors, lawyers, and dentists who work for themselves. According to the U.S. Census Bureau, the median income of male self-employed professionals in 1970 was about $20,200 (see Table 7). Just below them in income are professional, technical, managerial, and administrative workers in corporate or government bureaucracies. Around the middle of the income range are self-employed business persons, sales and clerical workers, craftsmen and foremen, and semiskilled operatives. The bottom of the income distribution includes service workers, laborers, farmers, and farm workers. Full-time, year-round farm laborers, nearly all men, earned a median income of only $3631 in 1970. Private household workers, almost all women, earned a mere $2203.

The income data presented make it

Table 7. Median Income of Civilian Labor Force, 1970, by Occupational Category and Sex

| Occupational category | Median income of full-time year-round workers (in dollars) | |
	Male	Female
Self-employed (nonfarm)		
Professional	20,209	B
Business	8,410	4,238
High salaried		
Professional & technical	12,144	8,019
Managers & officials	12,806	7,140
Other white collar		
Sales	10,243	4,268
Clerical	8,931	5,650
Blue collar		
Craftsmen & foremen	9,417	5,100
Operatives	7,786	4,589
Laborers	6,731	4,405
Service		
All except private household	7,234	4,035
Private household	B	2,203
Farm		
Farmers & managers	4,476	B
Farm laborers	3,631	B
TOTAL	9,184	5,440

B   Base number less than 75,000.
Source: U.S. Bureau of the Census, *Current Population Reports,* Series P-60, No. 80, "Income in 1970 of Families and Persons in the United States," p. 110.

clear that poverty still exists in our society. Poverty is a relative concept, but it is difficult to imagine how full-time domestics in this country earning $2200 could be considered anything but poor. The U.S. Census Bureau has worked out a formula for the "poverty threshold," based on current living standards, family size, residence, and sex. According to this definition, an urban family of four with an annual income of under $4000 in 1970 was considered poor.[14] About 35.7 million persons, or nearly a fifth of the population, were living near or below the officially defined poverty level in 1970. This includes many persons paid at or below the minimum wage, as well as the underemployed, the chronically unemployed, and those who depend on welfare, social security, or pension checks for their income.

Increasing productivity, in part the result of greater use of machines and automation, has enabled American workers to obtain both higher incomes and shorter working hours. Future gains in productivity may lead to longer paid vacations and an even shorter work week. And, as we have seen, income distribution remains unequal. For those who have jobs, well paid or not, further problems emerge as the next section demonstrates.

Satisfaction and Fulfillment vs. Alienation

JOB SATISFACTION How satisfied are Americans with their jobs? Which occupations are most satisfying, and why? By asking workers how they feel about their

[14] Definitions of where to draw the poverty line, below which a person is considered poor, can be made to vary depending on one's political sympathies. For the Census Bureau definition, see U.S. Bureau of the Census, *Current Population Reports*, Series P-60, No. 1, "Characteristics of the Low Income Population, 1970."

jobs, sociologists have gathered considerable information on these questions. Such data should be interpreted with caution because of the cultural norm which constrains us to say that we like our jobs (especially in the professions). To be dissatisfied with one's work is in a way to call into question some of the very meaning of one's life, and that is not something most of us want to do. In addition, questions on job satisfaction do not go far enough. If the pay is high, the job secure, and working conditions tolerable, many persons will report they are "satisfied" with jobs that are nevertheless alienating. What they *mean* when they say they are satisfied is that given the existing structure of opportunities, what they are doing compares favorably with other work that is available.

National samples of employed men in 1949 (Centers, 1949:172) and 1955 (Morse and Weiss, 1955) showed that most were satisfied with their jobs. Only 17–20 percent said they were dissatisfied. The data for women workers are inconsistent. On the one hand, many women's jobs require less skill and are more onerous and less interesting than those held by men. Women also usually receive less pay. On the other hand, women seem no more dissatisfied with the overall aspects of their jobs than men.

Among textile workers included in a 1947 national sample survey, for example, women disliked specific aspects of their jobs more than the men. On a general measure, however, women were more satisfied than men with their jobs. When asked whether they would choose different trades or occupations if they could go back to age 15, 62 percent of the men, compared with 43 percent of the women textile workers said they would choose a different occupation (Blauner, 1964).

One of the main variables associated with job satisfaction is occupational status. The higher the status of a job, the greater the proportion of workers who say they are satisfied with it. In one national survey of male workers the proportion who said they would continue in the same type of work even if they did not have to ranged from 68 percent of the professionals, to 40 percent of skilled manual workers, down to only 16 percent among the unskilled (Morse and Weiss, 1955). Similarly, data from a number of studies of job attitudes conducted since the Second World War shows that the proportion of those who said they would choose the same kind of work if they were to begin their careers again is directly related to job status. Between 70–93 percent of the professionals, 41–52 percent of the white-collar and skilled blue-collar workers, and 16–31 percent of the lower blue-collar workers would choose the same kind of work (Blauner, 1966:477; Wilensky, 1966:134).

Part of the reason for the correlation between job status and satisfaction is that many higher status jobs are in fact more interesting and challenging than lower status jobs. A second reason is the prestige attached to certain occupations. One of the things "wrong" with many blue-collar jobs is not so much the work itself as the fact that they are socially defined as lower than white-collar jobs, even at the same rate of pay. A third reason is that higher status jobs are associated with having more control over working conditions, pace of work, and other job-specific aspects of working.

Control over work is usually associated with higher job status. But even on the same status levels, the more control a worker has, the greater his job satisfaction (Blauner, 1966). A 1970 study by Sheppard and Herrick shows that job satisfaction among blue-collar workers is related to the degree of variety, autonomy, and responsibility they experience (Sheppard and Herrick, 1972). The survey consisted of a sample of 270 white, male employed union members in four Pennsylvania cities and 101 in Kalamazoo, Michigan. The authors devised a task index, based on workers' reports of the degree of variety, autonomy, and responsibility they felt they had on their jobs. They found that job satisfaction was directly related to task level. Those who said they were satisfied with their jobs most of the time decreased from 80 percent of those in the highest task level (most variety, and so on) to 27 percent of those in the lowest task level.

Thus, according to a number of studies, most Americans report they are satisfied with their jobs. Job satisfaction is positively linked with both high social status of an occupation as well as high task level (that is, a high degree of variety, control, and autonomy). The analysis of job satisfaction does not always go deep enough: Is it possible that workers may say they are satisfied with their jobs, and yet feel estranged from them? This possibility is explored below.

ALIENATION [15]   The conditions of work for many persons in contemporary industrial society are alienating. The drift is increasingly towards specialization, rationalization, and managerial control. In the offices and factories, major policies are determined by a few at the top; decisions made by those lower in the hierarchies concern only the means to achieve ends

[15] Portions of this and following sections are based on my article, "Work, Automation and Alienation." In Frank Lindenfeld (Ed.), *Radical Perspectives on Social Problems*, 2nd ed. New York: Macmillan, 1973.

predetermined by others, and often even the means are rigidly prescribed. Employees are confined to a strictly limited sphere of competence, where they merely carry out orders to make some part of a larger product they may never see in completed form. Men accept these alienating working conditions because of economic compulsion—they need jobs in order to live.

The modern division of labor is aptly described by sociologist Daniel Bell (1962):

The logic of hierarchy . . . is thus not merely the sociological fact of increased supervision which every complex enterprise demands, but a peculiarly technological imperative. In a simple division of labor, for example, the worker had a large measure of control over his own working conditions, that is, the set-up and make-ready, the cleaning and repairing of machines, obtaining his own materials, and so on. Under a complex division of labor these tasks pass out of his control, and he must rely on management to see that they are properly done. This dependence extends along the entire process of production. As a result, modern industry has had to devise an entirely new managerial superstructure which organizes and directs production. This superstructure draws all possible brain-work away from the shop; everything is centered in the planning and schedule and design departments. And in this new hierarchy there stands a figure known neither to the handicrafts nor to the industry in its infancy—the technical employee. With him, the separation of functions becomes complete. The worker at the bottom, attending only to a detail, is divorced from any decision or modification about the product he is working on. (pp. 234–235)

The logic of the division of labor is that of efficiency. The cooperation of many, each engaged in producing a small part, is thought to provide a greater output than the same number separately producing the whole item. The skilled worker who assembles a whole radio is replaced by semiskilled operatives who put together various subassemblies, and eventually these are replaced by automatic machines that make human labor superfluous. The skilled carpenter who makes and fits doors, windows, and floors is replaced by a crew with less complex skills, those who specialize in laying prefabricated sections of floor, for example. In medicine, the general practitioner gives way to specialists in particular diseases or parts of the body. In academia, the broad ranging intellect is replaced by more narrowly trained experts who explore subsections of arbitrarily defined areas of knowledge.

The technically most efficient methods are not always the most satisfying to those engaged in the work. Often one has to choose between technical efficiency (concentration on *production*) and employee happiness (concentration on the *producers*). It would be a lovely world if efficiency and happiness could always be reconciled, but this is not the case. When efficiency and happiness conflict, we have to choose one over the other. Until modern times, the choices have generally been in the direction of efficiency.[16]

What makes the age of automation unique is the possibility of consistently resolving conflicts between efficiency and happiness in favor of the latter. There is no need to dream of the efficiency of a

[16] Thus the Israeli *kibbutzim*, committed to a communist ideology of nonspecialization in work, have nevertheless found that economic pressures make the attainment of this ideal difficult in practice. Nonspecialization was found to be less efficient from the strict, short-run, technical point of view. When production values are given highest priority, as they are in contemporary Israel, being able to change jobs is likely to remain an unrealized ideal. See Vallier (1962).

full and rational "utilization" of human and technological resources when muscle power becomes superfluous and machines are readily available. We may consciously opt for *inefficiency*, for less "production" than is theoretically attainable, because we place other values first (Bell, 1962). Actually, decentralized organizations are often more efficient and less costly than centralized ones. But the important thing is that decentralization is a more desirable form of human organization because it promises to overcome the alienating conditions into which most employees are locked in industrial societies (Goodman, 1965).

What are these conditions? As Marx (1961) put it in 1844:

What constitutes the alienation of labor? First, that the work is *external* to the worker, that it is not part of his nature; and that, consequently, he does not fulfill himself in his work but denies himself, has a feeling of misery rather than well being, does not develop freely his mental and physical energies but is physically exhausted and mentally debased. The worker therefore feels himself at home only during his leisure time, whereas at work he feels homeless. His work is not voluntary but imposed, *forced labor*. It is not the satisfaction of a need, but only a *means* for satisfying other needs. Its alien character is clearly shown by the fact that as soon as there is no physical or other compulsion it is avoided like the plague. (pp. 98–99)

Contemporaries, including Seeman (1959) and Blauner (1964), have clarified the concept of alienation by distinguishing five separate dimensions, but the basic idea remains close to that of Marx (Blauner, 1964; Seeman, 1959). The most important aspects of alienation are powerlessness, meaninglessness, and self-estrangement.

Employees are powerless in that their voice does not count for much, they cannot say what should be produced, how, at what price, and for whom.

The growth of labor unions in the United States has provided many employees with the power to resist being pushed around and treated in a way that violates their dignity. Through collective bargaining, unions have resisted management pressures for speed-ups in production and arbitrary firing of employees. (In a number of nonunionized fields and in the smaller and marginal enterprises, however, many employees are still vulnerable to being pushed around.) But although unions can coerce employers into treating workers with more dignity, employees still accept the prerogative of management to decide what gets produced and what doesn't, what prices are set, and so on.

Meaninglessness refers to the fact that the employee in a bureaucratic organization is engaged in one small, standardized task, and rarely gets to see or understand the whole process or product. Only a few at the top know how all the highly subdivided jobs are interrelated. Self-estrangement occurs when work is undertaken for its extrinsic rather than its intrinsic value, when work is not done for its own sake, or for the sake of what the work itself accomplishes, but primarily for the money. Self-estrangement means that men do not express themselves fully or utilize their talents in their work.

The opposite of alienated labor is work pursued for its intrinsic worth and meaning. This, according to the radical sociologist C. Wright Mills (1951:220), is the Renaissance view of work as craftsmanship:

There is no ulterior motive in work other than the product being made and the processes of its creation. The details of daily work are meaningful because they are not detached in the worker's mind from the product of the work. The worker is free to control his own working action. The craftsman is thus able to learn from his work; and to use and develop his capacities and skills in its prosecution. There is no split of work and play, or work and culture. The craftsman's way of livelihood determines and infuses his entire mode of living.

It is helpful at this point to distinguish between objective social conditions and the subjective perceptions and feelings that arise in response to them. Alienation refers to the *objective* relationship of the employee to his work. To distinguish the subjective awareness of that relationship, Blauner (1966:473) suggests the use of the term *estrangement*. Estrangement is the subjective aspect of alienating working conditions. The condition of alienation may not necessarily be perceived or understood as such by the alienated. Thus, I doubt whether any great number of American employees *feel* alienated from their work. They accept doing something they may not entirely like in return for their paycheck. As Blauner (1966) points out, automation may help to diminish certain aspects of alienation from work. For example, those employed in continuous process industries may be much freer in their movement and may have more leeway in varying their schedules than those who tend machines or work on the assembly line. This freedom makes work in automated plants more satisfying. Blauner dismisses the question of workers' control by saying (albeit correctly) that most employees are generally not interested in taking on managerial responsibilities: they are being used, but as they are well paid it's a good bargain, and at least on the surface they don't seem to mind.

But the fact is that they are used.[17] With the exception of the self-employed, the ends of work are not determined by the worker but by others to whom he is subordinate. This is the typical condition of employees. Modern industrialism uses employees as means to the ends of those in control of industrial or governmental hierarchies.[18]

There are, of course, variations in working conditions, compensation, and employment security. These factors influence the subjective perception of workers, their satisfaction with their jobs, and the degree to which they *feel* estranged. Subjective awareness of alienation varies greatly. Some of those who are being used may be aware of the fact and resent it, in which case we can say that they feel estranged. But many who are used are not particularly aware of this, or if they are, they are not resentful because they receive high pay; are not closely supervised; can vary the pace of work; or because they are genuinely unaware of the possibility of alternatives.

Herein lies the paradox of the relative contentment of American employees. If

[17] I was tempted to use the term "exploited" instead of "used." But "exploited" is perhaps too strong. The larger American business firms do not generally have a policy of conscious exploitation of the domestic force. For on the contrary, many managers of modern industrial bureaucracies pride themselves on their sense of public responsibility and believe in looking after the welfare of employees as "good business." Nor do most American employees feel exploited. Exploitation is a more appropriate term for those with the lowest-paying jobs, such as auto-wash attendants or farm laborers in this country or for employees of American corporations in Latin America. In a similar context, Touraine (1971) speaks of "dependent participation."

[18] The hierarchical principle need not be intrinsically bad. Voluntary deference to a coworker on the basis of his greater knowledge and skill is quite different from deference based on the authoritative *position* of the coworker.

the work is dull, or even stupid and meaningless, at least the pay is high, the hours are short, and there are fringe benefits such as longer vacations, medical insurance, and pension systems. For meaning in their lives, people do not look so much to production as to consumption (of clothes, cars, television, homes) and they turn increasingly to do-it-yourself projects, gardening, travel, and so on.

American trade unions have not helped to develop the workers' consciousness of alienation. The role of the unions in the United States has been to raise wages and improve working conditions and fringe benefits through collective bargaining. The unions have never offered any serious challenge to management's prerogative of setting basic goals and policies. With the exception of groups such as the Industrial Workers of the World, unions have tended to accept the worker's powerlessness over broad policies in return for sharing with the managers a little bigger slice of the bread.

Unions have acquired a vested interest in the smooth running of business enterprises and often perform the very important function for management of "stabilizing" the labor situation. Moreover, the unions themselves have become large, bureaucratic structures over which the average worker has as little power as he has over management.

While most American workers say they are satisfied with their work, their working conditions remain alienating. The paradox of employees' apparent satisfaction may be explained by the fact that alienating work is not necessarily perceived as such by them. High pay, for example, may compensate for being used, so that they may not *feel* very estranged. American unions have by and large not raised the consciousness of workers beyond bread and butter issues. The unions themselves have become another bureaucratic instrument by which employees are kept in line.

TOWARD SOLUTIONS

Reforms

JOB ENLARGEMENT Perhaps the easiest of the work-related social problems to deal with is job satisfaction. A number of studies have shown that democratic forms of social organization are not only more satisfying to employees, but also that they can increase output and require fewer workers (Bennis and Slater, 1968; Jenkins, 1973; Maslow, 1965).

Progressive employers have successfully improved attitudes of employees toward their work through various paternalistically instituted job enlargement schemes. In enlarged jobs, workers participate in different phases of making a complex product, instead of engaging in only one repetitive task. Job enlargement typically provides more variety, more control over the pace of the work, and more flexible scheduling. In place of the extreme division of labor and hierarchical patterns characteristic of older style industry, some modern managers set goals for "teams" of workers to fulfill. Thus products may be partly assembled by work teams instead of on assembly lines, and worker suggestions incorporated into the work process, without diminishing quantity production and with a definite increase in both quality and worker satisfaction.

Jenkins cites a number of examples of successful experiments in industrial democracy. One of the most far-reaching job restructuring programs has been carried out in one of the divisions of Procter and Gamble. At a new, highly automated plant in Lima, Ohio, 125 employees worked in three shifts. In this factory, there are no barriers between jobs, in fact there are no job classifications. The workers are known as members of the plant "community." They have responsibility for hiring and firing, and in addition have a large degree of control over plant operations. There are no time clocks. Community members work out pay scales themselves, and all salaries are openly known (Jenkins, 1973).

In Sweden, both the Saab and Volvo companies have been moving away from assembly line production of cars. In place of the conveyor belt system, workers are divided into production groups, with each group responsible for assembling certain parts of the car. The teams of workers can vary the pace and divide the work among themselves as they choose (Jenkins, 1973).

To the extent that job enlargement programs involve a genuine shift in power from management to employees, they are a step in the right direction. But the new patterns do not necessarily alter the powerless and subordinate position of employees. This is illustrated by the results of a short-lived experiment in democracy at the innovative Polaroid Corporation. Because of a special rush job, 120 machine operators were put on a new schedule. In place of the usual eight hours at the machine, each one spent an hour in training and two in doing coordinating work. The program was *too* successful however, because it eliminated the need for managers. The managers did not want their workers *that* qualified, and so when the rush job was finished, they abolished the program (Jenkins, 1973).

Almost any change that gives employ-ees more control over the pattern and pace of their work promises to increase job satisfaction. Job enlargement, therefore, should be seen as a desirable, positive reform attainable within the existing capitalist system. Another type of reform that deals with the crisis most persons face when confronted by extended unemployment is the guaranteed income.

THE GUARANTEED INCOME The idea of the guaranteed income is simply to break the link between jobs and income by providing direct money payments to low-income persons (the poor and unemployed) *with no strings or conditions attached.* Originally proposed by economist Robert Theobold (1963) in the 1960s, the guaranteed income has been endorsed by policymakers and economic advisors in both major political parties. Samuelson, in the eighth edition of his widely read text, *Economics,* calls it "an idea whose time has come."

To make his proposal politically more acceptable, Theobold (1963) added the idea that payments to jobless persons should be proportionate to the level of income they were use to receiving. (This is similar to existing programs of unemployment compensation). Like the present welfare system, the guaranteed income would provide an economic floor. Unlike the present system it would not penalize the poor for earning money or make their subsidy depend on the judgment of a social worker about their morals or spending habits. The guaranteed income assumes that the main problem of the poor is lack of money and remedies it in an obvious fashion.

The guaranteed income deals indirectly with problems of job satisfaction by enabling those dissatisfied with their work to quit without having to worry that their families will starve. Put more directly, the guaranteed income is suggested as a solution to the interconnected problems of poverty, welfare, and unemployment.

The economic problem with which the guaranteed income deals is the imbalance between production and consumption in postindustrial capitalist society. The present economic system is based on the connection between jobs and income. As Theobold puts it,

Today's socioeconomic system . . . assumes that the overwhelming proportion of those seeking jobs can find them and that the incomes received will allow the job-holder to live in dignity. Such a distribution mechanism requires that enough effective demand exist to take up all the goods and services that can be produced by all the capital and labor that can be effectively used. (Theobold, 1973:136)

But in fact this system is breaking down. Not only are many uneducated and unskilled persons out of work, but increasing numbers of middle-class persons with both skills and education are being displaced by machines.

The negative income tax is a mechanism for implementing the guaranteed income that has been suggested by the conservative economist Milton Friedman and others. Above a certain income, taxes would continue to be progressively levied. Poor persons, below that income, would receive money from the government. Some negative income tax proposals incorporate a "work incentive" feature, while others do not. (Most present welfare systems do not have such a mechanism; low-income people who find jobs have their welfare benefits reduced by the amount of their income, leaving them with little economic incentive to work.)

The work incentive negative income tax would operate as follows. Assume that a couple with two children is socially guaranteed a minimum annual income of $4000. If the couple had *no* job earnings at all, they would receive a negative tax payment from the Internal Revenue Service of $4000. If they earned $2000 per year, they would receive a payment of $3000, so that the sum total of their "after tax" income would be increased by the fact that they had earned some money on their own; and so on with higher incomes up to a "break-even" point of $8000 (see Table 8).

Table 8. Negative Income Tax: Private Earnings, Tax, and After Tax Income, by Income Levels

Private Earnings	Tax		After Tax Income
$0	−$4000		$4000
$2000	−$3000	paid by govern-	$5000
$4000	−$2000	ment to family	$6000
$6000	−$1000		$7000
$8000	0		$8000
$10,000	+$1000	paid by family to government	$9000

Source: Adapted from Paul Samuelson, *Economics*, 8th ed. (New York: McGraw-Hill, 1970), p. 774.

The guaranteed income is a reform proposal that is both feasible and congruent with the existing political and economic framework. Under this system, taxes paid by the corporations and the rich would subsidize the poor. In its initial stages such a program might cost between $20–50 billion annually over and above present welfare expenditures. The exact cost would depend on the socially and politically acceptable definition of what constitutes the poverty line, below which no family or individual should have to live. Assume that on the average each of 25 million poor persons receives a net "subsidy" of $2000. The total gross cost of the income guaranteed would then be $50 billion annually. The *net* additional cost would probably be closer to $30 billion however, because the guaranteed income would replace a wide variety of existing costly social welfare measures. While such a sum is staggering, it represents only about one-third of the current military budget. It could be financed by using funds presently allocated for military purposes, without raising taxes a penny.

The guaranteed income would enable us to deal with the displacement of men and women by machines in a way designed to maximize human fulfillment. It is a program designed for an affluent society, which would enable all persons in the society to be guaranteed a minimum share of the social production. The guaranteed income avoids government make-work programs and replaces most of the present machinery of welfare assistance. It would probably reduce the degradation to which (poor) recipients of government subsidies are presently subjected.

A major side-effect of the guaranteed income would be to speed the elimination of low-paying and degrading jobs. It would help transform the relationship between employer and employee into one of voluntary cooperation instead of economic coercion. This will be especially true as the poverty "floor" is raised by an increasingly affluent society. In such a society, employees will feel free to leave unjust or exploitative employers, without the fear that they or their families will starve. The competition of the guaranteed income will force employers to be fair and will help to insure optimal working conditions. Such a subsidy would also be helpful in enabling more persons to be artists and craftsmen and to take advantage of opportunities for higher education. Yet by making minimum livelihood independent of jobs (and therefore independent of college "success") it will also force the colleges and universities to offer programs which are more relevant and intrinsically attractive to students.

This reform is radical in that it promises increasing freedom from toil, but it has conservative implications as well. It would stabilize the existing system by protecting it from the upheavals that accompany massive unemployment. The potentially discontented would be "bought off" by receiving the fringe benefits of being part of an affluent system. Contrary to Theobold's intentions, there might very well be strings of political conformity attached to the guaranteed income—dissidents might face the threat of having their income cut off by the government. Further, the proposal eliminates poverty but not extreme wealth. A few capitalists would continue to reap large profits from corporate operations in this country and abroad; because of their wealth, they would probably continue to have a disproportionately large influence on government domestic and foreign policies.

So far we have discussed two proposals for reforming the work-place: job enlargement and the guaranteed income. Job enlargement does away with the traditional division of labor in which each employee has one fixed, defined, separate function. The guaranteed income is a plan to break the link between jobs and income by providing an income subsidy to persons whose incomes are below a minimum level, without subjecting them to humiliating welfare interrogations or requiring them to accept any job at all.

Job enlargement provides workers with more variety and more control over the work-place. The guaranteed income would encourage employers to provide optimal working conditions; employees who do not like what the boss is doing would have less fear of leaving. Such reforms may diminish some of the alienating aspects of the work-place as well, although so long as control is vested in hierarchical managements, the work situation is still inherently alienating.

For more complete solutions, we may have to transcend the capitalist political economy. Two broader solutions that deal with this are presented in the following section. They are workers' control and the establishment of decentralized socialism within the framework of a "dual" economy.

Beyond Reform

WORKERS' CONTROL   Workers' control is based on the proposition that workers themselves should determine what products or services they will supply, how they will organize the work, and what they will do with the profits (Benello and Roussopoulos, 1972; Hunnius, 1973; Vanek, 1971). Under these conditions, alienated labor can be diminished. Under workers' control, all of those who work in an organization vote on production goals, wages, prices, and investments. All major decisions are shared: in small organizations, problems are resolved by the group meeting as a whole. In large organizations, the group may elect a rotating executive committee.

Workers' control must be distinguished from mere participation in management. The difference is a question of power. Comanagement means that workers are consulted, but the final decision still rests with the boss. *Control* means that the final decision rests with the workers. The *forms* of workers' participation in management appear similar to workers' control, but there is a vast gulf between these two systems. Thus in discussing the codetermination schemes (*Mitbestimmung*) instituted in the postwar capitalist system of West Germany, Clegg (1972:20) notes that:

Mitbestimmung, the ideology built round the works' councils, became a clear attempt to narrow the political and economic differences between capital and labour, management and workers, thus opening the way to harmonious social and economic reconstruction. *Mitbestimmung* developed as the particular German form of consensus created by capitalism to contain potential class conflict.

There have been attempts to implement workers' control during the Spanish revolution of 1936–37 and more recently in Yugoslavia and Algeria (Clegg, 1972; Guerin, 1970; Riddell, 1968). In all three countries, workers' management was hindered by government monopoly of banking and credit and by central government directives which set general policies within which local industries had to operate. Outstanding examples of workers' control in the United States are the 23 worker-owned plywood companies in the Pacific Northwest (Berman, 1967; Bernstein, 1972) and the 63-member farm-workers' Cooperativa Central near Salinas, California. The co-op was established through the initiative of a government-funded community action agency and did not grow out of any grassroots demand for democracy. The co-op policies are influenced by the Bank of America, which imposed a number of conditions on the organization for extending a large loan. In this, and in its paternalistic beginnings, it is a less-than-ideal illustration (Zwerdling, 1974).

One problem is that most proponents of workers' control assume that the average person is a morally responsible and autonomous agent. But it is not certain that the results of democratic participation would necessarily be superior to those of the present hierarchical system. For the average person has become conditioned to consider various alien needs as his own (Marcuse, 1964:6). Factory workers might upon due reflection decide that three-quarters of all their production should go into 500-horsepower automobiles, 49-inch color television sets, or even atomic missiles. Our assertion is simply the ethical superiority of democracy—making it *possible* for people to feel more responsible for their work, correct their own mistakes, and be the rulers of their own activity.

Workers' control is a remedy for alienated labor that goes beyond the palliatives of job enlargement by doing away with the usual hierarchical pattern of management over workers and replacing it with elected officials kept in check by democratic participation. The focus of this remedy, however, is mainly on the "microscopic" level of the individual work-place. The following section will consider the "macroscopic" level of the economy as a whole.

SOCIALISM Advanced technology has provided us with an enormous production capacity. In the context of capitalist industry, the use of this technology leads to alienated work, unemployment, and a continuing crisis of overproduction and underconsumption. Capitalist enterprises are run for the private profit of their owners and managers, which means that the decisions to displace workers by machines are made when the enterprise stands to make a larger profit thereby. Paradoxically, the wage gains of unionized workers have encouraged management to adopt automation at a faster rate: the higher the price of labor, the more attractive becomes its replacement by machines. But the more machines introduced to replace workers, the fewer jobs available in private industry, the higher the general level of unemployment. Unemployed workers do not have adequate purchasing power (in the absence of full employment benefits or a guaranteed annual income) and so inventories begin to pile up. This is a central contradiction inherent in a capitalist economy.

One answer is greater public planning and investment at the local, regional, and national levels; the replacement of private ownership/control of resources and industry with public ownership/control. This is usually referred to as socialism (Campen, 1974; Huberman and Sweezy, 1968). Such public planning and investment, and the conversion of military production to peaceful uses, could generate many new jobs. We need better urban transit systems, more low-income housing, better medical care for low- and middle-income families, more social services, and more public recreation facilities. We need to find alternatives to energy systems dependent on fossil or nuclear fuels. Such needs are not fully met at present because it is not profitable for private industry to do so.

Many persons erroneously equate socialism with centralized state control of all industry. Socialist economies can (and should) be decentralized to a large degree. The mere substitution of state socialism for capitalism will not eliminate alienation in work. Powerlessness, economic compulsion and subordination are just as likely to be the lot of the average employee under state socialism as under capitalism.[19] Indeed, these conditions may be even more pronounced in socialist economies. In a socialist society, the feeling of estrangement from one's work might be mitigated by the knowledge that one is working for the good of all, rather than somebody's private profit. However, it is doubtful whether knowing that industry is owned by the nation has given workers in the Soviet Union a sense of meaning and joy in their work. That feeling can come about only when work is freely chosen and when workers have a direct say in its organization.

There is little reason to expect that state socialist managers would be less likely than capitalist ones to treat em-

ployees as means to the ends of production. If anything, industrial discipline can be even tighter under *complete* socialism because employees have no place else to go. Under socialism, some of the excesses of capitalism would be avoided, but socialism has its own pitfalls, which can be avoided mainly by decentralization of industry and of economic control and by combining it with a democratic system of workers' self-management.

A DUAL ECONOMY   A variant of socialism is a dual economy with mass production of necessities on the one hand and a luxury market system on the other.[20] Such a dual economy would be based upon the principle that a certain proportion of social production must be set aside to provide for minimum subsistence needs of all. A subsistence guarantee, like the guaranteed annual income, would enable all persons to be free to do the kind of work they want to do, or not to do any at all if they so desire. Production of necessities would require the labor of so few that it could eventually be done by volunteers. This, however, presupposes a social consciousness different from the selfishness and individualism that we have been used to.

What makes the dual economy possible is that food, clothing, shelter, and basic tools can be produced cheaply, well, and in such quantity as to be given away freely. Mass-produced items do not have to be of inferior quality; if designed for human use instead of profit they can be functional and beautiful. In fact, automation can supply more variation in the end

[19] As Bertrand Russell (1963) put it, "When an industry is transferred to the state by nationalization it may happen that there is just as much inequality of power as there was in the days of private capitalism, the only change being that the holders of power are now officials, not owners." Bertrand Russell, *Authority and the Individual* (Boston: Beacon Press, 1963). For a solution to this problem, Russell comes close to advocating local "soviets" and workers control: "What is needed is local small-scale democracy in all internal affairs; foremen and managers should be elected by those over whom they are to have authority" (p. 50).

[20] See Goodman (1960). The dual economy idea is also found in the writing of earlier generations. See Russell (1966). This concept goes back as far as William Godwin's *Inquiry Concerning the Principles of Political Justice*, published in 1793.

products than older assembly-line techniques, and at no extra cost. The free distribution of necessities would allow more persons to be artists or craftsmen, because they would not have to depend upon selling their works. On the luxury side of the economy, those who did not want standardized goods could join with others to produce their own variants, or they could exchange their own products for those of others.[21]

A mere fraction of the present labor force would suffice to produce all the necessities within a dual economy. Only a few million persons in the United States are engaged in producing subsistence goods. Many of the rest are employed in packaging, selling, advertising, insuring, inspecting, and transporting the commodities produced by these few. Others work for the armed force, other government agencies or in war plants, or are unemployed.

A dual economy would not obviate the need to make certain political decisions. In fact it would clarify the political nature of economic decisions. When practically anything can be produced in large quantities and provided without charge it becomes a political question as to whether a particular item—automobiles for instance—should be made for general distribution.

In such an economy, some persons would have to volunteer for people-oriented services such as medicine, and others for building, maintaining, and operating such mass production machinery as

might be needed. If a community found itself short of volunteers for essential occupations, it might resort to a sales or production tax on the luxury economy to provide wages for workers in scarce supply in the subsistence sector. This would probably be a rare occurrence. People would work voluntarily because they wanted to help others, because the work was interesting to them, and because they felt they expressed and fulfilled themselves thereby.[22]

Given the opportunity to choose, many workers would leave large-scale organizations and form smaller voluntary associations, while some would work alone. If they were allowed by public policy, large bureaucracies such as General Motors could exist only if enough persons were persuaded to band together of their own free will. Certainly the lure of money or power would interest a number of persons sufficiently to devote their lives to such "old-fashioned" organizations. Nevertheless, their appeal would probably not be great if the basic necessities of life were freely available and nobody had to work for money. There would be many candidates for corpora-

---

[21] Another paradigm, described in Goodman (1960) consists of a decentralized system of independent communities, each relatively self-sufficient, where most persons are engaged in some form of craft or subsistence production. Isolated communities of this kind are beginning to form in the United States, but they are not likely to exist in large numbers in the forseeable future.

[22] To expect a continuing supply of volunteers for socially necessary work seems realistic on two grounds. (1) People work for more than just money, even in our present materialistic society. A consistent finding is that about four-fifths of employed men say they would continue to work even if they did not have to (although many would change the *type* of work they are doing if they could). See Morse and Weiss (1955) and also Tausky (1969). (2) Working for material rewards is *socially learned*. At present, materialist attitudes are inculcated by schools and mass media, and supported by corporate and government policies. In a changed political situation, social institutions would stress nonmaterial rewards. If there were enough social approval and prestige attached, many persons would volunteer for public service jobs, in much the same way that young persons volunteered for the Peace Corps in the 1960s.

tion president, but few would want to be junior executives or secretaries.

SUMMARY Both workers' control and socialism go beyond the reforms discussed earlier as remedies for problems of work. Workers' control would replace the power of managers with a more democratically organized system. Under some forms of workers' control, managerial jobs still exist, but occupants of these jobs are chosen by the workers, and major decisions are made in consultation with them. Workers' control places the direction, ownership, and profits of an enterprise in the hands of those who work in it.

The faults of capitalism stem primarily from production for *profit* instead of for social *use*. This leads to injustice in distribution and the perpetuation of class inequalities; to the neglect of community services; and to the decline of the "instinct of workmanship." The proposed remedy is a socialist economy with public ownership/control of resources, and public planning. One specific form of socialism described above is the dual economy. This would provide free basic necessities to all those who need or want them, from the subsistence side of the economy, while allowing the production of luxury goods on the other side. The labor for production of basic goods and provision of needed services would be supplied by volunteers imbued with the spirit of public service and motivated by much the same kind of enthusiasm that led so many to volunteer for the Peace Corps.

An economy where necessities are freely available, where work is voluntary, and where workers have control of the production process is more than a utopian dream. The technological capacity of America of the 1970s makes it a practical possibility that can be brought about when enough of us want it and join with others to bring it about.

References

American Friends Service Committee. *Democratizing the Workplace*. Cambridge, Mass.: American Friends Service Committee, 1973.

Anderson, Marion. "The Empty Pork Barrel." *WIN*, 1975, 11, 4–8.

Aronowitz, Stanley. *False Promises: The Shaping of American Working Class Consciousness*. New York: McGraw-Hill, 1973.

Bell, Daniel. *The End of Ideology*. New York: Collier, 1962.

Bell, Daniel. *The Coming of Post Industrial Society*. New York: Basic Books, 1973.

Bendix, Reinhard, and Lipset, Seymour (Eds.). *Class, Status and Power*, 2nd ed. New York: Free Press, 1966.

Benello, C. George, and Raussopoulos, Dimitrios (Eds.). *The Case for Participatory Democracy*. New York: Viking, 1972.

Bennis, Warren, and Slater, Philip. *The Temporary Society*. New York: Harper & Row, 1968.

Berman, Katrina V. *Worker Owned Plywood Companies: An Economic Analysis*. Pullman: Washington State University Press, 1967. Economic and Business Studies Bulletin #42.

Bernstein, Paul. "Democratization of Organization." Unpublished Ph.D. Dissertation, Stanford University, 1972.

Best, Fred (Ed.). *The Future of Work*. Englewood Cliffs, N.J.: Prentice-Hall, 1973.

Blauner, Robert. *Alienation and Freedom*. Chicago: University of Chicago Press, 1964.

Blauner, Robert. "Work Satisfaction and Industrial Trends in Modern Society." In Reinhard Bendix and Seymour Lipset (Eds.), *Class, Status and Power*. New York: Free Press, 1966.

Bookchin, Murray. *Post Scarcity Anarchism*. Berkeley: Ramparts, 1971.

Campen, Jim. "Socialist Alternatives for America: A Bibliography." Vol. 1 in *Resource Materials in Radical Political Economics*. Ann Arbor, Mich.: Union for Radical Political Economics, 1974.

Caplow, Theodore. *The Sociology of Work*. Minneapolis: University of Minnesota Press, 1954.

Centers, Richard. *The Psychology of Social Classes*. Princeton, N.J.: Princeton University Press, 1949.

Clark, Colin. *The Conditions of Economic Progress*, 2nd ed. London: Macmillan, 1951.

Clegg, Ian. *Workers' Self Management in Algeria*. New York: Monthly Review Press, 1972.

Cole, G. D. H. *Workers' Control and Self Government in Industry*. London: Gollanz, 1933.

Daly, Herman E. (Ed.). *Toward a Steady State Economy*. San Francisco: W. H. Freeman, 1973.

Edwards, Richard C., et al. (Eds.). *The Capitalist System*. Englewood Cliffs, N.J.: Prentice-Hall, 1972.

Friedman, Georges. *Industrial Society*. New York: Free Press, 1964.

Friedman, Milton. *Capitalism and Freedom*. Chicago: University of Chicago Press, 1962.

Fromm, E. *Marx's Concept of Man*. New York: Ungar, 1961.

Goodman, Paul. *People or Personnel*. New York: Random House, 1965.

Goodman, Paul and Percival. *Communitas*. New York: Vintage, 1960.

Gorz, Andre. *Strategy for Labor*. Boston: Beacon Press, 1967.

Gorz, Andre. *Socialism and Revolution*. New York: Anchor, 1973.

Gross, Bertram, and Moses, Stanley. "Measuring the Real Work Force: 25 Million Unemployed." *Social Policy*, 1972, 3, 5–10.

Gross, Ronald, and Osterman, David. *The New Professionals*. New York: Simon & Schuster, 1972.

Guerin, Daniel. *Anarchism*. New York: Monthly Review Press, 1970.

Heilbroner, Robert. "Work and Technological Priorities: A Historical Perspective." In Fred Best (Ed.), *The Future of Work*. Englewood Cliffs, N.J.: Prentice-Hall, 1973.

Hirschorn, Larry. *Toward a Political Economy of the Service Society*. Berkeley, Institute of Urban and Regional Development, University of California, Berkeley, 1974. Working paper No. 229.

Huberman, Leo and Sweezy, Paul. *Introduction to Socialism*. New York: Monthly Review Press, 1968.

Hughes, Everett C. *Men and Their Work*. Glencoe, Ill.: Free Press, 1959.

Hunnius, Gerry G., et. al. *Workers' Control: A Reader on Labor and Social Change*. New York: Random House, 1973.

Jenkins, David. *Job Power: Blue and White Collar Democracy*. New York: Doubleday, 1973.

Kahn, Herman, and Wiener, Anthony. "The Future Meanings of Work: Some 'Surprise-Free' Observations." In Fred Best (Ed.), *The Future of Work*. Englewood Cliffs, N.J.: Prentice-Hall, 1973.

Kolko, Gabriel. *Wealth and Power in America*. New York: Praeger, 1962.

Larrabee, Eric, and Meyersohn, Rolf (Eds.). *Mass Leisure*. Glencoe, Ill.: Free Press, 1958.

Lindenfield, Frank (Ed.). *Radical Perspectives on Social Problems*, 2nd ed. New York: Macmillan, 1973.

Los Angeles Times, August 15, 1974, p. 1.

Magdoff, Harry. "Problems of United States Capitalism." In Maurice Zeitlin (Ed.), *American Society, Inc.* Chicago: Markham, 1970. Pp. 306–7.

Marcuse, Herbert. *One Dimensional Man*. Boston: Beacon Press, 1964.

Marx, Karl. "Economic and Philosophical Manuscripts," T. B. Bottomore, trans. In Erich Fromm. *Marx's Concept of Man*. New York: Unger, 1961. Pp. 98–99.

Maslow, Abraham H. *Eupsychian Management*. Homewood, Ill.: Dorsey Press, 1965.

Maslow, Abraham H. *Towards a Psychology of Being*. Princeton, N.J.: Von Nostrand, 1968.

Melman, Seymour. *Our Depleted Society*. New York: Holt, Rinehart and Winston, 1965.

Melman, Seymour. *Pentagon Capitalism*. New York: McGraw-Hill, 1970.

Miller, Herman. *Rich Man, Poor Man*. New York: Crowell, 1971.

Mills, C. Wright. *White Collar*. New York: Oxford University Press, 1951.

Moore, Geoffrey, and Hodges, Janice. "Trends in Labor and Leisure." *Monthly Labor Review*, February, 1971.

Morse, Nancy C., and Weiss, Robert S. "The Function and Meaning of Work and the Job." *American Sociological Review*, 1955, 20, 191–8.

Perucci, Robert, and Gerstl, Joel. *Profession without Community: Engineers in American Society*. New York: Random House, 1969.

Reich, Michael. "The Evolution of the U.S. Labor Force." In Richard C. Edwards et al. (Eds.), *The Capitalist System*. Englewood Cliffs, N.J.: Prentice-Hall, 1972.

Reisman, David. "Leisure and Work in Post-Industrial Society." In Eric Larrabee and Rolf Meyersohn (Eds.). *Mass Leisure*. Glencoe, Ill.: Free Press, 1958.

Riddel, David. "Social Self Government: The Background of Theory and Practice in Yugoslav Socialism." *British Journal of Sociology*, 1968, 19, 47–75.

Roethlisberger, F. J., and Dickson, W. J. *Management and the Worker*. Cambridge: Harvard University Press, 1939.

Roszak, Theodore. *Where the Wasteland Ends: Politics and Transcendance in Post-Industrial Society*. New York: Doubleday, 1972.

Russell, Bertrand. *Authority and the Individual*. Boston: Beacon Press, 1963.

Russell, Bertrand. *Roads to Freedom*. London: Unwin, 1966.

Russett, Bruce. *What Price Vigilance*. New Haven: Yale University Press, 1970.

Samuelson, Paul. *Economics*, 8th ed. New York: McGraw-Hill, 1970.

Seeman, Melvin. "The Meaning of Alienation." *American Sociological Review*, 1959, 24, 783–91.

Sheppard, Harold L., and Herrick, Neal Q. *Where Have All the Robots Gone?: Worker Dissatisfaction in the 70's*. New York: Free Press, 1972.

Smigel, Erwin O. (Ed.). *Work and Leisure*. New Haven, Conn.: College and University Press, 1963.

Smith, J., and Franklin, S. "Concentration of Personal Wealth, 1922–65." *Proceedings of the American Economic Association*, 1974, 87, 166.

Sturmthal, Adolf. *Workers' Councils*. Cambridge, Mass.: Harvard University Press, 1964.

Tausky, Curt. "Meanings of Work among Blue Collar Men." *Pacific Sociological Review*, 1969, 12, 49–55.

Terkel, Studs. *Working*. New York: Pantheon, 1974.

Theobald, Robert. *Free Men and Free Markets*. New York: Clarkson N. Potter, 1963.

Theobold, Robert. "Guaranteed Income Tomorrow: Toward Post-Economic Motivation." In Fred Best (Ed.), *The Future of Work*. Englewood Cliffs, N.J.: Prentice-Hall, 1973.

Tilgher, Adriano. *Work: What It Has Meant to Men through the Ages*. New York: Harcourt, 1930.

Touraine, Alain. *The Post Industrial Society*. New York: Random House, 1971.

Vallier, Ivan. "Structural Differentiation, Production Imperatives and Communal Norms: The Kibbutz in Crisis." *Social Forces*, 1962, 40, 233–41.

Vanek, Jaroslav. *The Participatory Economy*. Ithaca, N.Y.: Cornell University Press, 1971.

Whyte, William F. *Money and Motivation*. New York: Harper & Row, 1955.

Wilensky, Harold L. "The Uneven Distribution of Leisure." In Erwin O. Smigel (Ed.), *Work and Leisure*. New Haven, Conn.: College and University Press, 1963.

Wilensky, Harold L. "Work as a Social Problem." In Howard S. Becker (ed.), *Social Problems*. New York: Wiley, 1966.

Zeitlin, Maurice (Ed.). *American Society, Inc.* Chicago: Markham, 1970.

Zwerdling, Daniel. "Managing Workers." *Working Papers for a New Society*, 1974, 2, 9–18.

Suggested Reading

ARONOWITZ, STANLEY. *False Promises*. New York: McGraw-Hill, 1973.
   Aronowitz says American workers are not very class conscious because they have been bought off with higher wages, because of ethnic divisions, and because of union preoccupation with bread and butter issues. The author stresses the need for workers' control and also for breaking the cultural monopoly of corporate capitalism reflected in such mass media as TV, movies, and educational institutions.

BEST, FRED (Ed.). *The Future of Work*. Englewood Cliffs, N.J.: Prentice-Hall, 1973.
   An anthology of short pieces on the meaning of work in an affluent society, including articles by C. Wright Mills, Abraham Maslow, Paul Samuelson, and Herman Kahn.

BLAUNER, ROBERT. *Alienation and Freedom*. Chicago: University of Chicago Press, 1964.
   Comparative analysis of American workers in four different plant settings. Blauner sees alienating tendencies as inherent in modern manufacturing organizations, but shows important variations by industry. Worker alienation is greater in more closely controlled settings (textile and auto factories) than in the craft-type print shop or automated chemical plant where workers have more control over their movements and the pace of their work.

BLUMBERG, PAUL. *Industrial Democracy*. New York: Schocken Books, 1973.
   Good survey of industrial relations literature. The author concludes: "There is hardly a study . . . which fails to demonstrate that satisfaction in work is enhanced or that other . . . beneficial consequences accrue from a genuine increase in workers' decision-making power." Blumberg sees workers' management as an integrative force that can help offset the fragmentation typical of modern industry.

BRECHER, JEREMY. *Strike!* San Francisco: Straight Arrow Books, 1972.
   An account of American labor history which demonstrates that workers have a long tradition of activism and militance. This militance, sometimes expressed in violent confrontations, is neglected or underplayed in "official" histories. When necessary, workers have defied both unions and managements in wildcat strikes, walkouts, etc.

JENKINS, DAVID. *Job Power*. Baltimore: Penguin Books, 1974.
Review of experiments in industrial democracy in the United States and other countries. Some of the most valuable examples are taken from the experience of American firms. Often, as Jenkins shows, workplace democracy leads to increased productivity.

HUNNIUS, GERRY, GARSON, G. DAVID, AND CASE, JOHN (Eds.). *Workers' Control*. New York: Vintage, 1973.
Best anthology available on workers' control. Includes sections on dissatisfaction of contemporary employees; a critique of collective bargaining (see especially Garson); models of industrial democracy abroad (including a good discussion of Yugoslavia by Hunnius); and a valuable theoretical section, with pieces by Gorz, Mandel, and the editors.

THEOBALD, ROBERT (Ed.). *The Guaranteed Income*. New York: Anchor, 1970.
An anthology on various aspects of the guaranteed income, with articles on the spread of automation, the concept of the guaranteed income, implications for the existing welfare system, and thoughtful comments by Erich Fromm and Conrad Arensberg.

Part III

Racism and Sexism

Generalizations by virtue of their breadth often suffer from many exceptions. Nevertheless, it is safe to say that three master statuses— each an accident of birth—exert a profound influence on an individual's life chances: race, social class, and sex. In the case of race, the dominant racial group is usually heterogeneous with respect to class, while the oppressed racial group tends toward homogeneity: it is at the bottom of the class structure. Sex, of course, cuts across both race and class, making it a particularly problematic status as Prather suggests in her essay. The American experience of the race issue is in many ways unique, and the robust character of institutional racism calls for an examination of the history of racism in this country. The decimation of Native Americans at the hands of white settlers is perhaps the logical starting point for such a review, but the experience of black people forcibly removed from their native lands by white slavers is more critical for an understanding of racism today.

In their article, Turner and Singleton examine the phenomenon of racism in its historical context, from precolonial English perceptions of race to present attitudes. They trace the development of the concept of race and the institutionalization of racism in terms of the interaction between cultural beliefs which legitimize racist institutions and the institutional patterns which give credence to those beliefs. If the heralded advances of the 1960s in the area of civil rights and equality between the races provide grounds for a certain white smugness, the account offered by Turner and Singleton is an effective antidote. They describe in detail the many contortions the idea of race has assumed in our culture and the ingenious transformation of one pattern of oppression into another during the course of the many conflicts that have focused on the issue of race. Like Starnes' discussion of poverty, in Part II, Turner and Singleton's treatment of racism reminds us that the problem has deep roots in history, and that what may look like a long awaited solution from a contemporary perspective may turn out to be yet another holding-action which offers surface gains but provides little in the way of basic social change.

At the root of oppression is advantage: the subordinated group is a source of wealth for the dominant group. As the article by Turner and Singleton documents in some detail, one mode of control is through the insidious concept of racial inferiority which furnishes the rationale for the systematic denial of full rights of humanity to whole groups of people. blacks, Native Americans, and Spanish-speaking peoples are held in bondage to the idea of race which serves the interests of those in power. These groups perform much of the "dirty work" that permits much of white America to keep its hands clean.

Rist and Soares analyze the situation of the Third World peoples in contemporary America employing a model of internal colonialism. At first glance, viewing blacks and other minorities in the United States as colonized peoples appears somewhat far-fetched. The image that often comes to mind when the notion of colonialism is discussed is that of a minority of foreign whites exercising military control over a country populated by multitudes of dark-skinned peoples. Rist and Soares argue, however, that as one moves away from the particular historical details of classical colonialism and focuses on the dynamics of colonialism itself, the comparison is apt. The political and economic domination of people's lives rationalized on the basis of racial and cultural superiority over the subjugated people is the heart of the process of colonialization. To the extent that the model of internal colonialism is appropriate, one is free to draw the same kind of conclusions that suggest themselves in the case of classical colonialism, namely, that the colonized peoples must be free to exercise control over their own fate and to enjoy the wealth they create rather than having it siphoned off by a dominant group. This view of the problem of poverty and racism suggests that the liberal reform approach which infuses money into one ameliorative program or another merely maintains the colonized people in a dependent and powerless position, a conclusion similar to that reached by Starnes in Part II.

Sexual status or gender is an ascribed role which influences almost every aspect of an individual's life. Societal expectations dictate the standard of appropriate behavior for male and female, and although there is considerable variation in these expectations by social class, ethnicity, culture, and historical period, it is often assumed that these prescribed behaviors are biologically ordained patterns. Thus, like class and race, gender role is transformed from a fact of social structure to a fixture of nature, thereby suggesting that it cannot be tampered with.

Prather suggests that the dominant role generally accorded males has its roots in environmental circumstances that have radically changed with the advent of modern technology. The advantage men have due to their generally greater strength plays a very minor role in the occupational sphere, and women's childbearing functions are now subject to volitional control by sophisticated methods of contraception. Nevertheless, in almost every area of social life, the evidence consistently documents the disadvantages of being born female. Longevity is one of the few advantages women enjoy in our society, although Prather points out that the differential in life expectancy between men and women found in the United States is less marked in more equalitarian societies. In this and a number of other aspects, the social definition of gender role is problematic for the male as well as the female.

Since gender role is socially defined, the strains and inequalities that result from those definitions and the institutionalized support for them must be viewed as a social problem. Sex role-stereotyping limits the range of productive and fulfilling behaviors for both genders. To the extent that the dissatisfaction and frustration felt by both men and women is recognized as stemming from such stereotyping, there is the impetus for change.

Contemporary definitions of appropriate sex role allocate to males the major rewards and power in society. Thus, it is not surprising that women have been the most vocal advocates of change. Prather analyzes the Women's Movement in relation to the history of feminism in this country and traces changes in social conditions as they have affected the recognition of sexism as a social problem. One of the more insidious obstacles to pressure for change emerges from the very institutionalized nature of sexism itself, which succeeds in indoctrinating women as well as men with a concept of "proper" gender behavior. One function of an article such as this is to provide not only an analysis of the problem, but also to alter the perception of it. The problems between men and women, as well as the characteristic complaints one hears from each sex, do not stem from the nature of male and female as much as from how society defines how those born with the insignia of one sex or the other must feel and behave. Here is a clear example of how individual fate depends upon a collective definition of reality.

Racism

White Oppression of Blacks in America

Royce Singleton, Jr. and Jonathan H. Turner

In recent years, America has been indicted as a "racist society." Inherent in this charge is the recognition that certain distinguishable categories of citizens have been systematically excluded from participation in the affluence of the wealthiest nation on earth. Those categories of citizens who are most often denied access to American affluence are racial and ethnic minorities, for while poverty is the fate of millions of whites, minorities are vastly overrepresented in the poverty ranks. Among minority categories, blacks, Chicanos, Puerto Ricans, Cubans, Filipinos, and Native Americans are the most overrepresented.

Knowing which minority groups exist in poverty helps clarify the scope and content of American racism: racism is "something" practiced against minority groups by the white majority, and it is related to the impoverishment of disproportionate numbers of some minorities. But what is racism? How does it operate? In what ways does the white majority oppress a "nonwhite" minority? In this paper, we hope to provide some tentative answers to these questions.

CONCEPTUALIZING RACISM

Prejudice and Discrimination

Two key concepts have been used by social scientists in the study of "racism": (1) prejudice and (2) discrimination. As we will argue, the lack of clarity about

racism is partly the result of adherence to these limited concepts, but for the moment, we should review what they offer the study of racism in America.

(1) Prejudice denotes the negative images or perceptions which individuals in a society have of certain social categories. These images are usually stereotypical, involving simplistic, crude, and rigidly held conceptions of the attributes of individuals cast into a prejudicial category. As such, prejudices are typically emotionally charged images expressing antipathy that persist in disregard of facts which contradict them. Social scientists have used the term prejudice widely in referring to negative and inflexible attitudes toward racial, religious, ethnic, and national groups. *Racial prejudice* connotes prejudice toward a group assumed to be biologically distinct and identifiable on the basis of physical attributes, while *ethnic prejudice* refers to negative attitudes toward groups identified primarily by cultural criteria, such as language, customs, and religion. Race is thus a biological category and ethnicity a cultural classification.

Yet, as neat and precise as this distinction may appear, it is difficult to maintain, for in the world of everyday human affairs, the two are commonly confused. For example, even though it is impossible to distinguish Jews biologically from non-Jews, many antisemites wrongly regard Jews as a race with peculiar physical and cultural traits. Hence, is antisemitism a racial or ethnic prejudice? Even where rough biological distinctions can be made, as is the case between many blacks and whites, are the prejudices based upon biological or cultural criteria, or some combination of both? These are not trivial distinctions, for it makes a great deal of difference if people are classified as biologically or culturally distinct. In general, prejudices are most negative when a social category is defined by people in racial terms, for then a biological and presumably unalterable basis for negative stereotyping of traits can be assumed. Studies of prejudice tell us that the study of "racism" is not a biological inquiry, but an examination of how and why a majority of people in a society will *define for themselves* certain minority groups as biologically distinct and then proceed to act toward them as if they were biologically inferior and undesirable.

(2) Discrimination is the most commonly used concept for denoting the differential treatment of persons "on grounds rationally irrelevant to the situation" (Antonovsky, 1960). When, for example, someone refuses to hire a fully qualified black candidate for a job because of the candidate's "race," that person has practiced discrimination, since merit, ability, experience, and other more appropriate standards for hiring have been ignored. Although discrimination has often been defined as the "behavioral manifestation of prejudice," the relationship between prejudice and discrimination is not always direct and rarely simple. For instance, employers may discriminate against a black applicant not so much because of intense racial prejudice on their part, but because of the anticipated reactions of others who, if they encountered a black, might take their business elsewhere. Or, prejudice

may never be overtly expressed if either situations allowing for discrimination do not present themselves or social constraints inhibit its direct expression. Knowing whether someone is tolerant or prejudiced, therefore, will not necessarily lead to accurate predictions about discrimination.

Even the assumption that prejudice is a cause of discrimination is oversimplified, for there is a good deal of evidence that the reverse relationship is just as likely to be the case: "that prejudice is in part the *result of discrimination*—a way of rationalizing and getting rid of guilt feelings that arise when one has treated an individual unfairly, according to one's own definition" (Simpson and Yinger, 1972:29). Studies of discrimination emphasize that "racism" involves actions against identifiable categories of people and that such action is not necessarily accompanied by prejudicial attitudes.

One of the problems with relying on the concepts of prejudice and discrimination is that they can inadvertently lead to a concern with *individual* attitudes and acts of discrimination against *individual* members of minority categories. Furthermore, when an entire society is examined, attitudes and actions can be viewed as forming complex patterns transcending individual thoughts and actions. For indeed, millions of minority citizens are not kept in bondage by the prejudices and acts of a few individuals; rather, it is the cultural and institutional patterns of *an entire society* which must be analyzed if the true magnitude and dimensions of prejudice and discrimination in America are to be understood.

In our analysis racism is viewed as a general concept pertaining to the complex institutional and cultural processes in a society which create and maintain the disadvantaged position of social categories which are defined by the majority as different not only in terms of culture but also in terms of biology. Such a perspective requires further elaboration.

Racism as a Cultural and Institutional Phenomenon

What is culture? What is a social institution? And how do these offer more insight into racism than the traditional concepts of "prejudice" and "discrimination"? Culture is a concept that focuses attention on patterns of ideas in society, such as values, beliefs, dogmas, and other symbolic systems which guide and direct human thought, perception, and action. Like all concepts, culture is an analytical artifact because it rips from a larger social context some things while ignoring others. At the same time, however, the concept is enormously useful because it gives analysts a way of visualizing "collective attitudes" of the individual actors in an entire society. When the individual is examined, only attitudes are evident; but when large numbers of individuals are studied as a group, then *patterns* of attitudes sometimes emerge. When such patterns do exist, it is useful to label them cultural beliefs and to study the consequences of the entire pattern on society.

Social institutions are the structural counterparts of culture in that they represent relatively stable and enduring *patterns* of social organization among human actors. To a great extent, institutions, such as the economy, government, education, and law, determine how, when and where humans will interact. Thus, to understand American society, it is necessary to comprehend the structure of those institutions guiding the actions of masses of Americans.

Culture and institutions reveal a complex, reciprocal relationship. On the one hand, the emergence and persistence of an institution creates certain ideas or systems of symbols which shape the thoughts, perceptions, and actions of those who must participate in the institution. On the other hand, because existing thoughts and perceptions shape social action, they can provide a source of resistance to institutional change and sometimes block the emergence of new institutions; or, if not actually blocking institutional change, they alter its course and shape the direction of its development.

The question of "which comes first, culture or institutions?" is not easily answered, nor is it always highly relevant. Changes in one can create pressures to change the other; and just which one changes first probably depends upon the institutional and cultural pattern in question and the unique historical circumstances of the change. What is critical in understanding a pervasive and enduring phenomenon such as racism is that cultural beliefs legitimize and justify institutional arrangements, while institutional patterns lend support and credence to existing cultural beliefs. At the individual level, prejudice justifies discrimination, while discrimination reinforces prejudices. Whether viewed at the individual level or at the societal level, the key point is that the reciprocity between cultural beliefs and structural arrangements provides both stability to existing arrangements and resistance to change in these arrangements.

To understand racism in America, it is necessary to analyze the reciprocal relationship between cultural beliefs and institutions. While the individual level of analysis can yield enormous insight into the precise interactions between cognitive and behavioral components of racism, it deflects analysis away from the consequences of prejudice and discrimination for the lives of large numbers of individuals in American society. Thus, initially, it is perhaps best to take a broad perspective on racism and visualize it as an institutional phenomenon which is legitimized by, while at the same time reinforcing, certain pervasive beliefs among white members of the society.

INSTITUTIONAL AND CULTURAL RACISM AGAINST BLACK AMERICANS

While racism has been perpetuated against a number of minority categories in America, nowhere are the cultural and institutional forces of racism more evident than in the treatment of black Americans. This takes on additional significance because of the large size of the black population, thus making racism one of the most conspicuous features of American society. White racism against black Americans is of critical significance in its own right, but the extreme cultural and institutional oppression of blacks can serve as a dramatic example of similar racist treatment of Chicanos, Native Americans, Cubans, Puerto Ricans, Filipinos, and other oppressed minority groups.

The Culture of White Racism: An Historical Overview

In June, 1942, a national survey asked, "In general, do you think Negroes are as intelligent as white people; that is, can they learn just as well if they are given the same education (and training)?" The responses reveal the scope of America's culture of racism at this time: 42 percent said "yes"; 48 percent said "no"; and 10 percent said they did not know (Simon, 1974:57). Over 200 years earlier, American colonists debated the issue of the capacity of black slaves to learn the principles of religion. The available evidence suggests that most believed blacks to be ignorant and unteachable (Jordan, 1968:187–190). This is not a case of history repeating itself, and the correspondence assumes heightened significance when we consider that the capacity for religious experience was extremely important in the eighteenth century, as innate intelligence is today. Indeed, the assumption of black "inferiority" has been a basic tenet of American culture for 350 years. Understanding its origin and tenacity means understanding the history of racial beliefs in America.

PRECOLONIAL ENGLISH BELIEFS   The culture of Elizabethan England formed the conceptions that shaped the early colonists' reactions to blacks. Winthrop Jordan (1968) identifies several aspects of this, beginning with English impressions of African "blackness." Early descriptions of Africans by travelers often began with their complexion, and the fact that the exaggerated term "black" was used suggests a powerful impact on English perceptions. The concept "blackness" at the time connoted baseness, evil, danger, and repulsion, whereas "whiteness" connoted such things as virtue, beneficence, peace, and beauty. Thus, Africans were identified in terms of a color that accentuated the Englishman's initial sense of his difference from Africans.

Religious speculations offered one way of "explaining" African blackness and inferiority. The adventurer George Best gave biblical authority to negative assumptions about Africans by reference to the story in Genesis, chapters 9 and 10, in which Noah curses Canaan, the son of Ham, making him a "servant of servants." Although the tale says nothing about skin color, Best concluded that a curse of blackness on Ham's son and all his descendants accounted for the color of Negroes. Such a belief was buttressed by African heathenism, since Christianity occupied a central place in European society. Christians held other religions to be defective, and to the English, who identified Protestant Christianity with English nationalism, heathenism was not easily separable from other African attributes. As Jordan (1968:23) notes: "Being a Christian was not merely a matter of subscribing to certain doctrines; it was a quality inherent in oneself and in one's society. It was interconnected with all the other attributes of normal and proper men. . . ."

English ethnocentrism expressed itself in other ways as well. Travelers took an active interest in the details of purported savagery, and by English standards of clothing, housing, language, government, and morality, African culture was inevitably found uncivilized. African behavior was described as "bestial." As Jordan points out, the terms "bestial" and "beastly" had strong sexual connotations in Elizabethan England and such terms were used widely in English accounts of West Africa. In addition, the Englishman's introduction "to the anthropoid apes and to Negroes at the same time and in the same place," and the long-standing myths associating apes with the devil, evil, and sexual sin—and with blackness—caused much speculation about the relationship between apes and Negroes. Sexual union was thought to occur sometimes between apes and Negroes.

In short, virtually every African trait invited the English to make invidious distinctions, and the negative image produced was given legitimacy through the ethnocentric prism of English society. The impact of this image was to be profound, for as long as Africans were considered less than human, the moral precepts of Protestant religion were not violated and inhuman practices could be defined as humane. Such was the case as the English settled in America and the first Americans began to oppress blacks.

RACIAL BELIEFS IN COLONIAL AMERICA
The first 20 Africans to arrive in America were traded for food supplies by a Dutch man-o'-war that put into Jamestown in 1619. Although they were bound over for some form of servitude, the precise status of blacks in America is not known until "Negroes" were declared slaves by Virginia and Maryland statutes. So, whether prejudice made slavery possible, or whether slavery was produced by economic forces and then caused racism, has been hotly debated by historians. (See, for example, Degler, 1959; Fredrickson, 1971b; Handlin and Handlin, 1950; Jordan, 1962). The most sensible position is that slavery and prejudice were mutually reinforcing. It is difficult to see how racial slavery could have evolved if English colonists had not made invidious distinctions between themselves and Africans before their initial contact. It is also clear that the development of slavery reinforced prejudice and elaborated it into an extensive belief system.

English conceptions of various forms of servitude are central here. The colonists were familiar in 1619 with other types of bondage. Many early settlers paid their passage with indentured servitude. Indentures were negotiable contracts that did not involve a complete loss of personal freedom, and were clearly differentiated from slavery. Slavery was a particularly degraded status, and "slave" was an epithet for the basest sort of person.

Long before 1619, the English had some knowledge, albeit imprecise, of the slave trade conducted by the Spanish and Portuguese. They knew that blacks, allegedly captured in tribal wars, were being transported to New World settlements for enslavement. More importantly, they tended to associate the slavery practiced in these settlements with the hereditary, lifetime service forced on Africans. The English clearly had in mind the sorts of distinctions that fostered racial slavery from the time of their first contact with Africans, and it is easy to see how this, added to the need for labor and the vulnerability of Africans dislodged from their homeland, made possible the evolution of black slavery in colonial America.

Soon after the statutory recognition of slavery, a series of laws, or slave codes, were passed stripping blacks of their rights until, by the early 1700s, they were no longer defined legally as persons but as chattel property. Once the cycle of interaction between slavery and supporting beliefs was set in motion, strong as the established forces were, it was to require constant revision and elaboration as slaveholders faced a host of problems and challenges.

The church continued to have a significant though paradoxical effect on racial attitudes during this period. African heathenism was contrasted with Christianity, although the church with its universalistic, proselytizing nature and its assumptions of spiritual equality, could have had a salutory influence. Among the

reasons it did not was the fact that many of the clergy endorsed slavery. More important were the infrequent conversions. In New England where the church was strong, there were few blacks, and the exclusionist strain in Puritanism tended to circumvent the process of conversion. In the South, where the church was less central to day-to-day affairs, the failure to convert was probably due in part to the practical problem of the instruction required for conversion. Some Southerners believed that conversion would make blacks worse slaves, and others contended that blacks did not have the capacity for religious experience, as we have noted.

This situation continued until about 1740 when a wave of religious revivals created a radical shift in church policy, and blacks entered the church in increasing numbers. The admission of spiritual equality eventually joined hands with secular beliefs about liberty to create a dilemma that was a source of heated controversy from the revolutionary era to the Civil War. However, physical distinctions had assumed central importance by the time religious equality arrived, enabling whites to justify continued enslavement of their "Christian brothers."

This is partly revealed by a shift in terminology. The distinction between "Negro" and "Christian" became a distinction between "Negro" and "English." Then, the latter term became interchangeable with "free" and "white" until, after 1700, the term "white" was adopted to unmistakably designate the racial distinction. For the most part, however, these distinctions preceeded nineteenth- and twentieth-century "scientific" racism, which began with speculations that grew out of the Linnean system of classification and the hierarchy imposed on the species, with several scholars theorizing about the varieties of men.

Interracial sex was the subject of eventually complex attitudes among the colonists. In the 1700s miscegenation was both common practice (especially in the South where there were fewer white women than white men) and a perceived threat to morality and to cultural integrity. Miscegenation was outlawed in Virginia and Maryland at about the same time slavery was instituted; and by 1776 all of the colonies had prohibited interracial sexual relations and marriages. This created a strong sense of guilt about the continued sexual exploitation of black women, expressed in beliefs about lascivious black women and well-endowed, sexually aggressive black men. Indeed, the fear that black men lust after white women persists to this day.

Attitudes about interracial sex revealingly express the colonists' sense of guilt about their enslavement of blacks. Such fears were further manifested in the elaborate slave codes erected to control the influx of black slaves in the first half of the eighteenth century. The colonists seemed to play the role of what Jordan (1968) calls "anxious oppressors," showing ambivalence about converting slaves to Christianity, and then emphasizing racial characteristics in order, it seems, to create a new justification for slavery.

CONFLICTING BELIEFS IN THE REVOLUTIONARY ERA Until the middle 1700s, most opposition to slavery and to racism came from the Quakers. Their strong sense of religious equalitarianism led them to object both to the treatment of slaves and to hereditary, lifetime servitude until, in the 1750s, two Quaker writers, Anthony Benezet and John Woolman, led an intensified attack which con-

demned slavery for its effects on the enslaved and for its corruption of white men.

These views became commonplace in the revolutionary era as abolitionists began to invoke the environmentalists' theory of human differences and the natural-rights philosophy which held that human nature is the same everywhere, but that character is subject to environmental forces. Thus, the purported ignorance and immorality of Negroes in America were due to their enslavement, and social conditions in Africa were similarly traceable to climate and natural environment. The most prevalent and influential abolitionist argument, however, was that of the inconsistency between slavery and the revolutionary principle that proclaimed the natural right of all men to freedom.

The basic natural right to private property, sacred goal of the Revolution, was the strongest antiemancipation argument. All but three of the Northern states that eventually abolished slavery adopted programs allowing for the gradual emancipation of *future* generations of Negroes, since the present generation was deemed unfit for freedom, and unable to support themselves. Finally, there were fears of inevitable miscegenation and outright revolt against whites (see Zilversmit, 1967).

Assuredly, a capital investment in slavery is here rationalized, but deep-rooted prejudice was an equally important impediment. Slavery was challenged often, black inferiority rarely. Indeed, the most popular abolitionist spokesman of the time, Thomas Jefferson, detested slavery because it violated natural law, but suggested biological inferiority and argued that natural differences produced inevitable and permanent white prejudice that would not allow blacks to be incorporated into white society on equal terms. The only practical program of freedom he could envision was the colonization of blacks in Africa or the West. The same proposal was justified later on the basis that inferiority was not inherent, but that white racial bias was (Fredrickson, 1971a). But in either case, the idea of colonization stemmed from an intolerance of blacks that precluded thought of assimilation.

Although limited, the antislavery campaign was not ineffectual. Much gross mistreatment of slaves was eliminated, importation was prohibited, and slavery was abolished in the North. Still, the congressional act that ended the slave trade in 1808 marks the effective closing of the first phase of antislavery attacks. By that time the sectional division was well defined. While gradual emancipation was underway in every state north of Maryland, the South was hardening its proslavery position and imposing greater restraints on free Negroes.

Whereas the North could not reconcile the practice of slavery with the revolutionary ideology, the South saw the "peculiar institution" as a practical economic necessity. In the North, the acceptance of black inferiority was to justify exclusion and racial discrimination following the demise of slavery.

IDEOLOGICAL RACISM IN THE ANTEBELLUM PERIOD   After a lull in the slavery debate, proslavery advocates were awakened in the 1820s by the resurgence of the colonization movement and the fight over the admission of Missouri to the Union. The earliest responses were traditional, with the Southerners apologetic about social and economic necessities and defending slavery in Congress on legalistic and constitutional grounds. For example, the argument of states' rights was used to oppose a federally subsidized colonization program. Toward the end of the 1820s, however, proslavery expression began to take on a more aggressive, self-righteous tone that forbode a particularly violent form of ideological racism.

The new defense of slavery came from the rebirth of the abolitionist movement in the North, where the phlegmatic opposition of the colonizationists gave way to the fervor of figures like William Lloyd Garrison. Morally outraged, they regarded slavery as an individual sin, demanded immediate freedom for slaves, and said that prejudice could be eradicated. This stimulated a defense during the next three decades that held that slavery was not a "necessary evil" but a "positive good."

The doctrine based itself on the permanent, biologically rooted inferiority of Negroes. This was not a novel assertion, but it had lacked respectability prior to the 1830s and had rarely been presented by articulate whites. Now, in the wake of the abolitionist attack, apologists brought "previously unarticulated assumptions" of white superiority "to the level of defensive ideological consciousness" (Fredrickson, 1971a:48).

The view that predominated defined the South as a *Herrenvolk* democracy in which democracy is reserved for the master race and tyranny for subordinated groups (Fredrickson, 1971a). A stereotype evolved to support the contentions of the slavery apologists which depicted slaves as happy, contented, and respectfully obedient to their enlightened, humane masters. Blacks were said to be better off in slavery than they had been in Africa, where, freed, they degenerated to their naturally savage natures. Such notions countered the abolitionist image of the wretched slave, assured Southerners that slavery was moral, and slavemasters fearful of rebellion that their slaves were controlled and contented (Fredrickson, 1971a; Takaki, 1970).

The case for white supremacy and slavery absorbed Southerners, and books, newspapers, periodicals, sermons, and lectures served to refine and invigorate traditional arguments (see Jenkins, 1935). The argument that the blacks had failed to develop a civilized way of life in Africa, the Biblical story of the curse of Canaan, the contention that abolition led to miscegenation, and biological arguments were all summoned to support slavery. However, the accepted opinion in scientific circles in the 1840s and 1850s, that blacks were a separate species, was probably peripheral to the defense of slavery since ethnological theories were beyond the ken of most laymen, conflicted with religious beliefs, and were generally not politicized by American scientists (Stanton, 1960).

Abolitionists, rather than basing their case on moral and intellectual equality, acknowledged vast racial differences and developed a distinctive conception of the Negro character. The "romantic racialists," as Fredrickson (1971a) describes them, simply interpreted differently the proslavery, paternalist image of "childlike simplicity," seeing the traits of meekness, affection, and loyalty as being the highest Christian virtues. The novel *Uncle Tom's Cabin* did much to popularize this benign image. The glorification of the Negro's superior aptitude for Christianity, as a function of permanent racial differences (implying the greater energy and intellectual superiority of whites) weakened moral objections to slavery and discrimination. Moreover, although abolitionists of this stripe were active and articulate, their demands for immediate emancipation and equal treatment of free blacks never won wide acceptance north or south of the Mason-Dixon line.

Abolitionists who demanded complete equality were actually a small "radical" minority in the anti-slavery coalition of the 1840s and 1850s. The majority were white nationalists who believed in manifest destiny and the desirability of a racially homogeneous society. This segment was motivated by practical aims rather than moral repulsion. They were both antislavery and anti-Negro. A few managed to uphold equal rights for blacks, but most did not. Concerned about racial purity and the competition of black labor in the western states and territories, white nationalists simultaneously demanded the prohibition of slavery and the exclusion of free Negroes from these areas (see Berwanger, 1967). They also endorsed the idea of repatriation. Abraham Lincoln himself reflected the public mind on questions of race. Indeed, if he had not, as Litwack (1961:276) notes, "his nomination and election would have been problematical." Lincoln vehemently opposed the expansion of slavery, but also vigorously denied opponents' claims that he favored full political and social equality; and he believed that colonization offered the only hope of solving the racial problem.

Northerners, rationalizing like Southerners, maintained that their own system of racial segregation and discrimination was the consequence of black inferiority. The comparatively less offensive nature of Northern racism never required the hard-core defenses constructed by Southern slaveholders. Still, scientific and Biblical explanations of the Negro's subordination were widely accepted in the North, with the threat of racial amalgamation supporting segregation, especially in schools. The press, black minstrels, and politicians pandering to insecure white psyches also popularized a stereotype of clownish, immature, lazy, immoral, and ignorant Negroes. As always, such racist beliefs interacted with repressive measures, each shaping and reinforcing the other.

By the dawn of the Civil War the inferiority of blacks was widely accepted, even among most abolitionists, in both the North and the South. Earlier ideas of black "bestiality" had been softened, but replaced by an equally damaging set of beliefs. Gentle, "Samboish" blacks had to be excluded from "adult" white society. In altered form, beliefs on black inferiority were to shape the institutionalization of discrimination in the latter half of the nineteenth century.

Although the Civil War brought about the demise of slavery and the extension of rights to blacks throughout the states, these were not the aims of the North at the outset of the war. Only a small minority of whites still clamored for emancipation, and among the latter, hardly anyone countenanced the idea of full equality. The Republican platform on which Lincoln ran pledged to protect the institution of slavery where it already existed. When war broke out, the immediate aim was preservation of the Union. As the conflict grew, slavery came to be understood as the root issue of the war, and it was believed that the North and South would be drawn into conflict again if slavery did not die with the Confederacy. The idea of a "new birth of liberty" evolved, providing Northerners with "an unclouded vision of the war that could engage their feelings and profoundest ideals" (Kincaid, 1970:53). Such beliefs paved the way for the Emancipation Proclamation and consequently the Thir-

teenth Amendment, which permanently abolished slavery throughout the Union.

RACIAL EXTREMISM IN THE POST-CIVIL WAR PERIOD   The nationalism thus stimulated did not eliminate the strong sense of racial differences. Unity and progress were associated with racial homogeneity, and the most liberal thought still tended to regard blacks as "temporary and inferior sojourners in a white America" (Fredrickson, 1971a:164). There were fantastic speculations about the future of blacks in America, many predicting their disappearance. The extinction of blacks as the result of "natural processes" was foretold, and Lincoln himself made several abortive attempts to establish black colonies. Northern fears of a massive northern migration of exslaves were allayed by the assertion that exslaves would prefer the more congenial climate of the South.

Emancipation and Reconstruction did nothing to change the caste status of Southern blacks; black laborers were as dependent as black slaves had been. Whites were the substantial majority in all but three states; they possessed nearly all of the money, land, education, social prestige, and political experience. Without full-scale revolution, it was inevitable that white Southerners would control the South. Northern protection was essential to preserve the newly acquired rights of blacks. During the period of Radical Reconstruction, Northern troops were stationed in the South, but in 1877, when its own ends were no longer served by protecting black suffrage, the North abandoned the South and left the freedmen to shift for themselves.

Northern abandonment of the South was rationalized by beliefs such as "equality before the law" and the dominant laissez-faire ideology. The staunchest promoters of black rights felt that blacks must make it on their own once they were extended basic rights, but this very idea suggests that blacks as a group were to find their social niche rather than being fully integrated (Fredrickson, 1971a: 179). The fact that blacks entered Reconstruction at a severe disadvantage did not seriously challenge the "equal opportunity" doctrine, because the failure of blacks was predicted by the prevailing belief in inferiority. By 1877 most Americans were willing to believe that blacks had been given their fair chance and had shown that they deserved their inferior status (see Fredrickson, 1971a:175–186).

In the South, Radical Reconstruction ultimately fostered the most extreme form of "Negrophobia" yet witnessed in America. Several factors contributed (Kincaid, 1970). First, blacks became the objects of the hatred and frustration defeated Southerners felt toward the North. Blacks were blamed for every imaginable ill, from the corruption of Reconstruction government (blacks being susceptible to demagoguery) to the failure of Southern agriculture (black labor being inefficient). The sudden collapse of the old social order with its traditional restraints on black people also rekindled racial fears and prejudices. Laws could not undo the 200-year-old image of black child-savages who, without the control of slavery, threatened life and civilization. Southerners, anxious at the thought of black men as free citizens, sought to reaffirm their supremacy through new forms of racial subordination. Finally, political competition between blacks and whites had two unfortunate effects: (1) it provided fuel to Southern fire-breathing politicians, and (2) it led supporters of the Confederacy who were denied the right to vote during Radical Reconstruction to resort to extralegal means to intimidate blacks, especially black voters and officeholders.

The South's new structure of white dominance consisted of the social and economic separation of the races. Segregation was rationalized by a new doctrine which differed from the proslavery argument mainly in a new undisguised hatred of the Negro. The benign "Uncle Tom" image formed no part of the segregationist dogma. According to this doctrine (see Johnson, 1949): racial segregation is natural and instinctive, for the good of and desired by both races; by virtue of superior intelligence and wealth, whites should hold the political power and blacks should not be granted suffrage; blacks are permanently inferior beings necessitating segregation to control their criminality and inordinate sexual passion and to guard against amalgamation or intermarriage which is sinful, unnatural and begets hybrid monstrosities.

In the 1890s the most extreme racism occurred. The decline of Southern agriculture and the political successes of Southern conservative extremists led to the complete disenfranchisement of blacks, legal codification of the system of racial segregation, and increasing lynching and other brutalities, to keep the Negro in his place (Gossett, 1963; Woodward, 1966). Racist beliefs also reached the nadir, perhaps in part to remove "the intolerable burden of guilt for perpetrating or tolerating the most horrendous cruelties and injustices" (Fredrickson, 1971a: 283). One popular view held that blacks had degenerated as freedmen, having retrogressed to their natural shiftless and licentious state. Lynching was an unfortunate practice necessitated by the beastly, brutal black nature. Such beliefs originated in the proslavery conception of the dual nature of blacks—childlike and docile when enslaved, but savage and criminal when free. Indeed, racist imagination at the turn of the century differed from that of the antebellum South only in its unrestrained expression.

"Social Darwinism" provided a powerful rationale for racist beliefs during the late nineteenth century.[1] The "failure" of blacks during Reconstruction, after Northern intervention on their behalf, "demonstrated" the futility of interfering with the natural forces of evolution. If blacks were a degenerating race with no future, the urgent need was to segregate them in order not to endanger or contaminate the white race (see Fredrickson, 1971a: Ch. 8; Gossett, 1963: Ch. 7).

Social Darwinism was attacked around the turn of the century by reformers and social scientists who argued for social progress based on regulation and cooperation. Because this group did not challenge some of the most basic racist assumptions, however, they had little effect on racial extremism in the South and little effect upon the development of "scientific" racism. Many "moderate" racists accepted the permanent inferiority of blacks, and most said that racial purity and the instinct of race prejudice demanded segregation. The essence of their

[1] Acceptance of the Darwinian theory of evolution at this time led to the notion of "evolving" groups and societies. The idea of varieties and species progressing to higher forms of life through a competitive process of natural selection was translated to a struggle between individual members of society and between different human groups. When applied to different races, the "survival of the fittest" could only mean the superior white race. And since the biological struggle for existence was nature's indispensable method for human progress, races should be left free to compete for the limited resources. On this basis, race theorists justified policies of neglect and repression.

argument for tolerant benevolence was that blacks, as a "child race," were naturally docile and kindly and could become useful, peaceful citizens, through white guidance and self-help. Since the Negro race was less advanced evolutionarily, the "wheels of progress" needed to be oiled by providing education, industrial training, and moral uplift. The model for racial moderates was Booker T. Washington, the founder of the Tuskegee Institute, who advocated self-help, industrial education, and black accommodation to racial segregation.

SCIENCE AND TWENTIETH-CENTURY RACIAL BELIEFS   At the start of the twentieth century, racist thought was respectable among all social classes and in all sections of the country. The South, defending its efforts to disenfranchise and segregate blacks, was inundating the nation with a mass of anti-Negro literature. The North, concerned with the nation's imperialistic ventures and channeling its reformist energies into other areas, mounted no serious challenge to Southern race polices. During the first quarter of the century, sociologists, psychologists, and biologists, among others, developed a comprehensive science of race which placed a stigma of inferiority on blacks more damaging and humiliating than slavery, and from which blacks still suffer (Newby, 1965:21).

The source of racism in biology was the science of heredity, whose task it was to explain the mechanisms underlying evolution. Experiments with plant genetics and hybridization were believed to demonstrate the overwhelming importance of heredity in determining human characteristics, supporting the notion of innate black inferiority. Eugenicists warned that racial intermixture led to biological abnormalities, and biologists who did not accept the idea of "abnormalities" reasoned that crosses between inferior and superior races produced mediocre offspring (Gossett, 1963).

In psychology there was a parallel development in the assessment of mental and emotional differences between the races, and the development of intelligence testing, which originated in France in 1905 and developed rapidly, placed a powerful tool in the hands of racists when blacks' scores turned out to be lower than whites' on the average. Racists would argue that black inferiority was an established scientific fact.

Sociologists also contributed to scientific racism. The famous University of Chicago sociologist William I. Thomas (1904:610) maintained that race prejudice was an instinct originating in the need for group solidarity and that it would "probably never disappear completely." Others argued that differences between the races fostered a "caste feeling" and "consciousness of kind" which was strongest in the "superior" white race. Finally, Robert Park (1918) celebrated the black artistic achievements during the "Harlem renaissance" of the 1920s as an expression of the black's superior emotionalism and sensuality.

Although many of these scientists maintained a purely academic interest in the subject of race, and argued against the use of their ideas to justify discriminatory policies toward blacks, their ideas became the foundation of sophisticated inequality.

Popular writers such as Lothrop Stoddard, who felt that as a "scientific humanist" he was morally obligated to warn the nation about the perils of race, made the "new 'truths' of science concerning race available to great numbers of people"

(Gossett, 1963:390), and against the backdrop of the events of this period, these "truths" gained heightened significance.

The mass migration of Southern blacks to the North during World War I had great impact. This movement caused deep resentment among the working-class members with whom blacks competed for jobs, resulting in the outbreak of several race riots in 1919. The great wave of foreign immigration in the late nineteenth and early twentieth century made restrictive immigration legislation the chief political objective of racists in the 1920s. In the end, such events were to make the problem of black-white relations national in scope and to cause reflective people in the sciences to question the scientific truths to which racists appealed.

The scientific backing which racists had long received was finally revoked in the 1920s and 1930s. There had always been a few whites who were able to see through racism, but not until the anthropologist Franz Boas led the attack in the 1920s did the opponents of racism gain a sizeable following. Boas forcefully exposed the mass of contradictory evidence, errors of judgment, and faulty generalizations associated with studies of race, while offering his own well-reasoned cultural explanation of why races all over the world reveal diversity.

By the late 1920s, the tide had turned against racism in all the sciences. Psychologists disclosed the biases inherent in mental tests, and careful analysis of the results of these tests clearly demonstrated the powerful effects of the environment, leading to the conclusion that there was no evidence of inherent racial differences in intelligence. Among biologists, arguments against the harmful effects of miscegenation gained force as did the idea that both heredity and environment collectively determine the traits of an organism. In a similar vein, sociologists shifted their emphasis from the biological, instinctive basis of human relationships to a social background, social process analysis, with the result that racial prejudice was no longer understood as an innate aversion but as a consequence of social conflict and tension (see Gossett, 1963: Ch. 16; Rose, 1968).

From these scientific developments there emerged a new enlightened perspective in white racial thinking which Fredrickson (1971a) has labeled "liberal environmentalism." The major tenet of this view is that all apparent social, cultural, and intellectual differences between the races are the product of environment.

By World War II such thinking completely dominated the fields of sociology and anthropology and was becoming increasingly influential among the liberal public. Adding force to this perspective was the growth of socialist thinking in the 1930s which recognized the harmful effects of economic and social deprivation, and the emergence of black political power as evidenced by the shift of black voters to the Democratic Party in the election of 1936 and the threatened March on Washington in 1942. During World War II, when the horrors of Nazi racism were revealed and the democratic-equalitarian ideology of the "American creed" was once again called forth, the liberal environmentalist doctrine finally triumphed as the respectable thought in intellectual and academic circles.

The importance of this triumph for race relations in America is inestimable. The new egalitarian doctrine provided the theoretical basis of the civil rights movement of the 1950s and 1960s and

was influential in the legislative and court decisions that this movement produced. Moreover, it offered the first serious challenge to the most fundamental racist belief in America—that blacks are inherently inferior to whites. Although millions of Americans still associate race with character, intelligence, and human worth, blatant racist beliefs are no longer respectable, and racists have found it increasingly difficult to invoke the authority of science to support their views.[2]

Still, there are other less hopeful portents. Efforts to remove inequality are still seen as a threat to white dominance and still meet strong opposition. In the 1950s, 60s, and 70s, Southern resistance to desegregation and Northern resistance to busing to achieve racially integrated schools have required federal intervention. Furthermore, many Americans who deny a belief in inherent racial inequality nonetheless endorse beliefs which have racist consequences. The majority of Americans now feel that blacks have been duly compensated for the injustices they suffered, that blacks are treated fairly, and that blacks themselves are to blame for the conditions in which they live (Simon,

[2] With respect to the concept of race, scientists now agree that: (1) All races belong to the same species—*Homo sapiens;* (2) Races are not discrete, stable units; that is, there are no "pure" races; (3) Races represent populations of people who share a common gene pool, or set of characteristics; (4) Thus, racial differences involve the relative frequency of genes, or traits, rather than absolute, mutually exclusive distinctions; and (5) Race as a scientific concept has proven useless for the analysis of most human differences. In the few instances where racial differences have been tied to different distributions of genes, such as in the analysis of blood types, the findings have underscored the adaptability and unity of mankind. For indeed, all races have demonstrated an equal potential for intelligence, an equal capacity to learn anything produced by any other race, and an equal capacity to adapt to the environment in which they live (see, for example, Osborne, 1971).

1974; Ch. 3). In addition, there is evidence of a "backlash" of prejudice among whites who are disturbed by the pace of change in race relations and who believe that current antidiscrimination policies have given blacks unfair advantages (Campbell, 1971). Such ideas reflect the latent interracial hostility that over 350 years of racism has imbued in American culture; and as long as this hostility persists among whites and manifests itself in sporadic flashes of racial violence, it will continue to threaten America's commitment to racial equality.

The Structure of White Racism: An Historical Overview

Cultural beliefs do not emerge and persist in a vacuum. White racism against blacks in America must be viewed as a changing sequence of oppressive institutional arrangements which have interacted with changing beliefs to perpetuate the disadvantaged status of blacks.

ECONOMIC RACISM   Prior to the Civil War, the economic organization of the South became heavily dependent upon a large slave population. While the historical record is vague on just when slavery was first institutionalized, it is clear that by 1670 most blacks in America found themselves, and their offspring, forced into life-long servitude. Slavery became rapidly institutionalized because of the agricultural economy emerging in the South. In contrast to the North which was beginning to industrialize and urbanize by the time of the American Revolution, the South was to remain heavily agricultural, relying on the export of cotton, tobacco, hemp, rice, wheat, and sugar. While different states tended to specialize in only some of these crops, they

all had one feature in common: the reliance upon an inexpensive and relatively large labor pool to cultivate large tracts of land. It is not clear whether or not slavery was the most efficient form of agricultural organization (see Fogel and Engerman, 1974; Genovese, 1965), but the shortage of labor and the abundance of land in the Southern colonies placed a high value on involuntary labor. As a result, slaves were used to initiate the plantation system, and once initiated, the system was used to "keep in line" a large and potentially revolutionary population.

The initial importation and enslavement of blacks in the seventeenth century was facilitated by the cultural beliefs which dominated precolonial America. Whether these beliefs made emerging slavery more palatable or were in fact the actual cause of slavery can never be known. But it is clear that the interaction between these beliefs and the economic imperatives of Southern agriculture of the eighteenth and early nineteenth centuries accelerated the pace of enslavement, while making Southern institutions highly resistant to change.

The distribution of slaves in the South reflected the economic priorities and power relations of the South (Stampp, 1956; Starobin, 1970:5). By 1860 there were about four million slaves in the South, but over 50 percent of them were owned by only 12 percent of the slaveowners who held the large tracts of fertile land which formed the base of the Southern economy. Slavery emerged and persisted largely because a small group of politically powerful landowners required cheap labor and made slavery acceptable in the agricultural sector of the economy, and then over time, in the industrial sector. Thus, by the dawn of the Civil War, every phase of the Southern economy had come to rely upon slave labor. It is such complete institutionalization of slavery into the Southern economy, plus fear of violence by oppressed blacks, which partially accounts for the resistance of this "peculiar institution" to change (Stampp, 1956).

The abolitionist attacks on the use of slaves in the Southern economy were countered by a further codification of antebellum beliefs emphasizing the "Sambo" stereotype. Even radical abolitionists acknowledged the intellectual inferiority of blacks. Differences in the Northern and Southern belief systems no doubt reflected the respective economic dependency of the Northern and Southern economies on slave labor. There were few blacks in the North, with the result that the economies of Northern states would remain unaffected by abolition or the colonization of the black population, whereas the loss of slave labor would cause widespread disruption of the Southern economy and lifestyle.

Only a war between the states was to penetrate the culturally legitimized economic system of the South. During the brief period of "Radical Reconstruction," large numbers of blacks gained access to many skilled trades and began to assume ownership of farms. But in 1877 Congress had a change of mind in matters of race. For thirty years thereafter the economic situation of blacks worsened as they were systematically excluded from skilled nonfarm occupations and thrust into tenant farming or low-wage labor for white landholders or into menial labor and domestic work in both rural and urban areas. Such a dramatic reversal of the economic policies of Radical Reconstruction was legitimized by a limited conception of "equality," by the then dominant laissez-faire ideology and by the

Social Darwinism of the late nineteenth century.

By the turn of the century, 90 percent of all blacks still resided in the South, with 75 percent living under oppressive conditions in rural areas. For a number of reasons, the plight of blacks, especially those in rural areas, worsened dramatically during the early years of this century (Hamilton, 1964): (1) The high birth rates of rural families began to exceed their ability to secure sufficient income in the depressed economy of the rural South. (2) The nature of agriculture changed dramatically with mechanization and the consequent displacement of black labor. (3) The cotton industry on which many blacks depended for survival became at first devastated by the boll weevil and then began to move to the Southwest. There were many "push" factors disposing blacks to migrate out of the South and into the urban areas of the North. By 1914, these "push factors" were combined with "pull factors" from Northern cities as the onset of World War I cut off European migrations while rapidly expanding the very industrial production which had for decades drawn European migrants to American cities. Suddenly, there were economic opportunities for blacks in Northern cities, with the result that between 1914 and 1920, nearly one million blacks migrated to urban areas in the industrial North. This migration was to be the first of a series of large-scale shifts in the black population, for by 1960 over three-fourths of the black population resided in cities, with only one-half still living in the South. Economic racism became an urban, as opposed to rural, and a national, in contrast to regional, phenomenon.

Many of the early migrants to Northern cities initially found jobs during the peak of wartime production, but they also encountered white discrimination and violence. Blacks were commonly forced into segregated tenements which early European migrants were abandoning because of their dilapidated and unsafe condition; and when blacks ventured into white neighborhoods and into certain occupations, acts of violence frequently occurred. There were, for example, 25 "race riots" in America between June and October of 1919. With the end of wartime production and the onset of the Depression, the economic situation of blacks worsened once again. Unemployment and hunger increased, and even welfare allocations were differentially bestowed on blacks and whites (Pinkney, 1969:33–34). The New Deal ushered in some changes, but the capacity of the then incipient civil rights groups to generate change was limited. Wage and job discrimination and exclusion from unions continued until well after World War II.

World War II, like World War I, caused a massive migration to urban areas in both the North and South. As blacks became concentrated in key wartime industries in urban areas, they began to exert some political pressure, forcing President Roosevelt to ban discrimination in wartime industries and pressuring the Congress of Industrial Organizations to allow some blacks into the union ranks.

The post-World War II period has seen many "apparent" improvements in economic racism, but much of this change is illusory. Blacks are still overrepresented in farm and service occupations; they are underrepresented in professional and managerial occupations; black unemployment is typically twice that of whites; black pay scales are still lower than whites; college educated blacks, on the average, still earn only a little more than high school educated whites; and black income as a percentage of white income actually declined between 1969 and 1973. The disadvantaged position of black workers in contemporary America cannot be explained as simply a lag phenomenon. Economic discrimination remains built into America's major economic institutions.

An examination of the three most general economic channels—(1) opportunities for running a business, (2) opportunities for securing jobs and promotions in the open job market, and (3) opportunities within union job markets to find work and be promoted—reveals that even in the face of clear civil rights laws, much discrimination can be found. This present discrimination will continue to maintain the disadvantaged position of blacks for some time in the future.

Business opportunities. For many white Americans, owning and running a business has been one path to affluence. For blacks, however, this path is hazardous; and even when blacks do own businesses, they tend to be labor-intensive proprietorships which are economically marginal. There are only 50,000 black businesses in America, a figure which would reach 500,000 if blacks owned businesses in proportion to their numbers. The absolute number of black businesses appears to be declining (Brimmer, 1966). Several obstacles hinder black businesses. It is more difficult for blacks than whites to secure credit, since the criteria used by lending agencies favor those with "white credentials" such as education, current collateral, high credit ratings, and white shopping center clientele. While all small businesses are high risk ventures, there is no evidence that black businesses in ghetto neighborhoods are any more risky than white ventures in white neighborhoods. For example, in 1964 the Small Business Administration began extending loans in terms of criteria other than credit history and collateral. Ninety-eight of 219 loans issued that year went to blacks, and, surprisingly, only 8 of all 219 loans became delinquent and none were liquidated (Foley, 1966; Knowles and Prewitt, 1969:17).

The barriers to black participation in the business sector have far-reaching consequences for the plight of blacks in other sectors of the economy. One of the most important consequences is for black Americans to become highly dependent upon employment in white-dominated organizations where, as the historical record shows, they are subject to intense discrimination. Such discrimination is reflected in the fact that since 1954 the black unemployment rate has consistently exceeded the 6 percent level which, in terms of conventional economic "wisdom," signals serious difficulties for the white work force. But equally important is the *under*employment of blacks who are able to find jobs, for as the Kerner Commission reported in 1966 figures, an additional $4.8 billion in income would be produced for blacks if their employment were upgraded to a level proportionate to whites with similar skills and credentials (Knowles and Prewitt, 1969:20).

The open job market. A number of structural forces have operated to economically oppress black Americans in the open job market. First, unskilled rural blacks migrated to the cities at just the time in America's economic development when large pools of unskilled industrial labor were decreasingly necessary. The black migrants' lack of skill was, of course, a result of *de jure* policies of

whites in the South, and the result was inevitably devastating. Secondly, just as blacks migrated to the deteriorating cores of America's cities the economic and demographic trend in America was in the direction of suburbanization. Thus, industry and commerce began to move out of the city, drawing with it the white population, at the very time that blacks were moving into the cities in search of new economic opportunities. Because of housing discrimination in the suburbs, blacks could not move with whites to the emerging suburban industries; and because mass transit systems began to deteriorate with America's growing dependency on the automobile, blacks could not easily commute to suburban jobs. Thirdly, black Americans became an industrial labor pool *after* trade and industrial unions had become organized and had begun to exclude both white and black members.

Dominant beliefs of the late nineteenth century focused attention on the character flaws of blacks who again "exposed" their inability to "take advantage of opportunities and compete successfully against whites." In turn, such beliefs could be used to systematically exclude blacks from full economic participation. In the private job market, this racism involved outright rejection of black applications for jobs in both blue- and white-collar occupations. The discriminatory practices of private business have been compounded by the policies of state and private employment agencies, as a number of studies have revealed (Turner, 1972:119).

Beyond such open racism is a subtle, and yet profoundly important, institutional racism in the job market: the biasing of criteria for what constitutes a good worker in favor of cultural traits of whites. For example, since written tests for jobs are constructed by whites, they discriminate against those of a different cultural background. Or, to take another example, white speech styles and personal demeanor which, in reality, are seldom related to actual job performance, are considered "appropriate" in certain jobs. Even the over-use of formal educational credentials discriminates against blacks and other groups who cannot afford higher education. Thus, there is an invidious racism built into the hiring practices of American economic organizations —a racism which perpetuates the disadvantaged position of black Americans.

The government sector of the economy has been almost as discriminatory as the private job sector. One form of discrimination has been the failure of government to enforce civil rights codes even for organizations doing contract business with the government. More directly, while blacks are slightly overrepresented in government jobs, blacks are highly underrepresented in the better paying managerial positions (Pinkney, 1969:80).

The union job market. Because unions are the only avenue for entry into most skilled blue-collar jobs and many unskilled occupations, racial discrimination in this sector of the economy has profound consequences. The fact that of the over 11 million black workers, less than 20 percent are members of trade unions documents the extent of union discrimination, especially when it is recognized that the vast majority of the black work force is blue-collar.

While the general policies of national labor organizations such as the AFL and CIO are antidiscriminatory, these policies are frequently ignored by union locals. Craft and trade unions, which have the strongest local structure, are the most discriminatory, with few blacks involved in trades as plumbers, carpenters, electricians, printers, metal workers, and machinists (Schaffler et al., 1970:44). The two most prevalent strategies for discrimination against blacks are: exclusion from apprenticeship programs and extracting from economic organizations the right of the union to employ, hire, fire, and promote.

Because industrial unions such as the United Automobile Workers organize all workers on an industry-wide basis and have a strong central administration and because much of the work performed involves no apprenticeship, many blacks have been able to join industrial unions and get jobs. However, the apprenticeship programs of these industrial unions which lead to higher paying, skilled jobs are often discriminatory. Thus, even in "liberal" industrial unions where blacks are union members, they are more likely than whites to be kept at the lower-paying positions.

In sum, these obstacles represent a massive form of institutional racism. Cut off from the normal channels of economic participation, blacks are often forced to take menial and seasonal work which offers only the minimal wage and few, if any, fringe benefits. Current beliefs in America support this situation, for "equal opportunity" beliefs, coupled with widespread "backlash" attitudes, allow employers, unions, and credit agencies to discriminate because blacks do not meet *the* criteria for economic participation. Equal opportunity has thus become a belief justifying "equal" and "even handed" treatment of blacks and whites in terms of criteria which favor whites. While dominant beliefs have become less severe and blatant, they still operate in a subtle and profound way to legitimize institutional arrangements which impede the full participation of blacks in the economy.

POLITICAL RACISM Despite the size of the black population, its capacity to generate political influence in America has been limited. The reasons for this are a reflection of historical political processes that have created a political system which is unresponsive to the plight of the poor in general and to the black in particular.

To understand just how this racism operates at both the local and national level of political organization requires, first of all, an understanding of a few historical facts:

(1) Prior to the Civil War, blacks held the right to vote or hold office in only five states (all Northern with very small black populations).
(2) In the last century, only during the brief period of Radical Reconstruction in the post-Civil War period did blacks vote and hold office in significant numbers.
(3) In the 1870s, however, Congressional commitment to Reconstruction waned, and when the presidential election of 1876 became deadlocked and was thrown into Congress, Republicans abandoned all Reconstruction in order to "buy" Southern votes. The result was for blacks to be systematically excluded from the polls, with virtually complete disenfranchisement in the South by 1895.
(4) Through a variety of tactics—from poll taxes to threats of violence—blacks in the South remained politically excluded until well into the 1960s (Daniel, 1972). Urban blacks in both the North and South had somewhat more voting power, but a number of tactics

have kept large numbers of urban blacks disenfranchised, while mitigating the power of those who have participated in local and national elections.

The legacy of the political past, coupled with the present unresponsiveness of the political system to all categories of poor, limits the exercise of black power.

At the national level black powerlessness is largely a result of the long history of political disenfranchisement. This continued with strategies such as the poll tax and the "literacy test" and "constitution test" which were differentially enforced for blacks and poor whites. When these measures were declared illegal, administrative obstruction—long lines, much paper work, elaborate documentation of residents, and so forth—effectively kept blacks from registering to vote. Underlying these techniques was the frequently implemented threat of white violence.

It was not until the mid-1960s that many of these exclusionary tactics were declared unconstitutional. The removal of these roadblocks and growing black political consciousness caused racist political strategy to be shifted from denying the vote to diluting the impact of black voting power frequently by means of gerrymandering Congressional districts in order to break up the ghetto and spread its votes into two or more districts where whites could be assured of outnumbering the divided black vote. In this way, very few black congressmen have been elected to the House of Representatives, and it is only in the last decade that representation has even begun to reflect the actual proportion of blacks. In senatorial and presidential races, white votes can always outnumber black votes, creating a situation where Congress has represented the will of whites and their interest groups— labor unions, trade associations, and large corporations.

In spite of signs of growing black power, the effects of nearly 200 years of exclusion from national politics cannot be easily undone. For example, how can new programs change the apartheid between urban and suburban areas? How can the effects of 40 years of union, employment, and business discrimination be undone as black representation becomes more proportionate? How is schooling to be made more equal in the face of rigid residential segregation and unequal tax assessments to finance schools? Only a massive financial and political commitment could eliminate the cumulative legacy of past disenfranchisement. Such a commitment, however, is unlikely because of the present structure of political decision-making in America.

Two general features typify this structure: (1) An inability to reorder national priorities, and (2) a difficulty in establishing and implementing effective national and change-oriented programs. In a *de facto* sense, the national political system is racist because it perpetuates the existing structural patterns which have for so long discriminated against black Americans.

Within the congressional branch of national government, at least four structural features preclude a reordering of priorities and the enactment of effective national legislation. First, despite "reforms" in the post-Watergate era, the election process in America will continue to be expensive, creating a situation in which elected officials are dependent upon the money of well-organized and financed interests, which are resistant to a reordering of na-

tional priorities. Secondly, Congress is also vulnerable to lobbying activities of any well-organized and financed group, regardless of whether or not it has helped finance a campaign. Labor unions, trade associations, large corporations, and departments of the executive branch (such as the Pentagon) are able to exert disproportionate influence.

A third structural feature of Congress is the seniority system which, despite some recent rule changes in the Senate, places the chair of key committees in the hands of those with the most seniority. The result is for many essential committees to be controlled by a chairperson who is from a stable constituency—typically rural with a South and Midwestern bias. A final obstacle inheres in the structure of representative government in a heterogeneous society: *any* new, expensive, change-oriented national program will threaten coalitions of interests which may have conflicts of interests among themselves, but which for any piece of comprehensive, national, and change-oriented legislation will perceive a threat to their position. For example, a national program to increase economic equality will threaten, for different reasons, the Defense Department (fear of losing money in support budget), labor unions (fear of losing jobs for current members), and business (fear of government interference in their affairs and profits). Similarly, a majority of white Americans of different backgrounds may exert influence to prevent drastic changes in priorities and to impede national programs.

The executive branch of government is subject to the same four pressures and has the power of enforcing court orders and of implementing congressional legislation, so that even if sound laws of national scope are ordered by the courts or enacted by Congress, enforcement and effective implementation may be blocked. Again and again, laws pertaining to school desegregation, housing, discrimination, fair employment, and job and union opportunities have only been partially acted upon by the Justice Department.

Thus, in looking at the structure of national decision-making, racism is clearly evident. This racism may not be related to prejudicial attitudes and bigotry, but its consequences for the lives of black Americans are no less profound.

At the local community level, similar patterns can be observed. While federal policies do indeed affect local political patterns, community political systems have exerted a parallel but autonomous form of racism. In the rural South, the same forces—disenfranchisement, poll taxes, eligibility tests, and violence—which kept blacks out of national politics operated even more effectively at the community level, since the local white power structure could exert immediate pressure on black residents.

When the numbers of blacks in cities began to increase to a point where old gerrymandering techniques would no longer work, a large "black ward" with one representative was sometimes established, with the result that black representatives could consistently be out-voted by the larger number of white representatives from smaller white wards. Thus, black representatives have been forced to make extensive compromises with the white majority in order to help their communities. Such compromising techniques often bring justified charges of "Uncle Tomism," but equally often, there has been no choice for black representatives.

Blacks have encountered even more problems in penetrating the nonelective civil service and patronage positions of local government where much of the actual decision-making occurs. One reason is the timing of black migration into the cities. Previous generations of Europeans had used the city political machines not only to secure benefits but also as a path of upward occupational mobility. But by the time blacks began to migrate to the cities, the patronage system had become closed, or, this system had been replaced by a civil service bureaucracy dominated by educated whites. In contrast to the political machines, this bureaucracy has been less corrupt, but it became more detached from the people it serves.

With growing numbers of blacks in large cities and with greater numbers of educated blacks who can meet civil service requirements, many of the historical obstacles to black participation in city governments have been surmounted. But again, timing appears to be operating against blacks, for just as blacks have achieved some degree of political power in the large core cities of metropolitan regions, there are pressures for regional and metropolitan governments. For increasingly, many of the patronage positions formerly run at the city level—planning, health, fire, sanitation, water, and so on—appear to be assumed by regional governmental bodies, with the result that they are more likely to be dominated by white suburbanites. The end result may be another form of *de facto* racism in which whites residing in the suburbs could conceivably control the fate of large black populations living in the core cities of metropolitan areas.

To the extent that blacks cannot have proportionate political power in the cities, a potential base of power in the national political arena is undermined. For the growing significance of the cities in federal fiscal policies—from revenue sharing to mass transit systems—could signal a period of black participation in elective and nonelective bodies in federal, state, and community governments. Yet, such participation is far from proportionate today; and it is not clear that it will become so in the near future with the likely trend toward metropolitan governance.

In the last few decades, the prominence of some black leaders gives the illusion that black political power is proportionate to its size or needs. But as is evident, opportunities are not equal, and even if they suddenly became equal, the current political system reveals little capacity to redress the institutionalization of racism in the economy and educational process.

LEGALIZED RACISM Dominant values and beliefs usually become codified into laws. And so it was with beliefs about, and acts of discrimination against, blacks in America, with the result that an intricate web of racism was drawn tighter as blacks languished in poverty. However, this gives only a partial indicator of legal racism. For underlying and often defying the law are informal discriminatory practices and many de facto forms of discrimination which are not formalized into law. For example, housing discrimination is currently forbidden by law, but the economically depressed situation of blacks, coupled with their isolation in ghettos, leads inevitably to widespread exclusion of blacks from white suburban housing, even if it could be assumed that no informal discrimination in the housing industry currently occurs (a most tenuous assumption). Thus, laws can allow people to affirm current "liberal" beliefs, while participating in a set of racist institutional arrangements.

What is remarkable, however, is that the legal system has openly legitimized discrimination. Much of this has come from blatantly racist legal codes, but a considerable amount stems from the failure of legislators and enforcers of the law to move against openly discriminatory practices. The legal system has legitimized discrimination by both open support of and inattention to racist arrangements in such key institutional sectors as housing, jobs, education, politics, transportation, and recreation.

It is difficult to determine whether the first blacks in America were slaves or indentured servants; the historical record is not clear on this point (Jordan, 1962). By the 1650s, however, some colonies evidenced laws distinguishing white and black servants, with blacks and their offspring consigned to servitude for life. By the early eighteenth century, the broad legal framework of slavery in the South had become clearly codified (Stampp, 1956; Starobin, 1970:7):

(1) Blacks were to be slaves for life.
(2) Slaves were *both* property and persons, with owners holding title to blacks as property, but at the same time, having some responsibilities to blacks as persons.
(3) Children would inherit their mother's status.
(4) Christian baptism did not automatically lead to freedom.
(5) Marriages between blacks and whites were prohibited.
(6) Blacks could not acquire or inherit property.
(7) Blacks could not engage in litigation or enter into civil contracts; they could not testify against whites in courts, nor could they sit on juries.

Such codes reaffirmed beliefs about the "bestiality" of slaves, and legitimized the economic imperatives of slavery by making it appear right and proper that all whites could buy slave labor. In the North, the laws were considerably more benign, but few questioned the biological inferiority of blacks or the necessity of economic, educational, and political discrimination (Litwack, 1961:30–38). With admission of border and Southern states to the union in the early 1800s, a considerable amount of debate in Congress ensued over the "legal rights" of blacks. The coexistence of free blacks in the North and enslaved blacks in Southern and border states presented a problem of how to define the constitutional rights of blacks in the growing Union. The problem was effectively avoided in 1821 when Missouri was admitted to the Union, for Congress enacted a vague platitude which allowed the states to legislate as they pleased, while giving the appearance that no citizens "shall be excluded from the enjoyment of any of the privileges and immunities to which such citizen is entitled under the Constitution of the United States." Thereafter, until the Civil War, Northern laws were increasingly relaxed, while Southern legislatures passed ever more restrictive laws.

Abolitionist pleas for at least "humane treatment" of the "inferior race" were beginning to have a small impact on public opinion, for those states having few black residents began to accord them broader citizenship rights. However, these formal laws contradicted informal Jim Crow practices of the North which, despite the lofty tenets of formal laws, prohibited access by most blacks to jobs, education, and housing.

It appears likely that the abolitionist ideology was used *ex post facto* to justify a massive Northern invasion of the South for economic and political reasons. Nevertheless, the War abolished forever the institution of slavery, and hence, the economic base of the South. In 1866, this was formally ratified in the Thirteenth Amendment.

In reaction, Southern states began to enact "black codes" restricting the rights of the now "free" slaves. The details of these codes varied but several restrictions were common to all Southern states: (1) blacks could not vote; (2) blacks could not serve on juries; (3) they could not testify against whites; (4) they could not carry arms; (5) depending upon the state, they could not enter certain occupations; and (6) black vagrants could be consigned to forced labor. Thus, after the Civil War, the South was unified in its attempts to impose new legal restrictions upon blacks.

In reaction to this and to Andrew Johnson's conciliatory approach, Radical Republicans in Congress began to assume control of Reconstruction. The Radicals in Congress assumed a two-front legal attack on racism in the South: (1) the division of the South into military districts and the enforcement of new constitutional conventions on each Southern state; and (2) the passage of the Fourteenth and Fifteenth Amendments which were ratified by Northern and reconstituted Southern states in 1868 and 1870, respectively. The Fourteenth Amendment was an extension of an earlier Civil Rights Act (vetoed by Johnson, and then overridden by Congress) which was designed to overrule the emerging "black codes." The Fifteenth Amendment extended suffrage to blacks. Reforms in the South were soon followed by the Civil Rights Act of 1875, which outlawed Northern "Jim Crow" practices.

In this way, Congress forced the South, and to a lesser extent, the North, to accept black participation in key institutional sectors. Had Radical Reconstruction been continued over several generations, institutional racism in America would have been markedly reduced. However, by 1880, the Radical Republicans had lost control of Congress and the presidency. In the 1890s, the Supreme Court legitimized the reemergence of Jim Crow practices. First, the Supreme Court declared unconstitutional the Civil Rights Act of 1875, thus condoning the denial of blacks' access to public conveyances and amusement facilities used by whites. Then, in 1896, the court ruled that segregated facilities for blacks and whites were not in violation of the Thirteenth and Fourteenth Amendments to the Constitution since, as the court declared: "If one race be inferior to the other socially, the Constitution cannot put them on the same plane" (Pinkney, 1969:28).

Codifying exclusionary and segregationist practices in the highest laws of the land gave added support to the culture and structure of racism in America. Exclusion and segregation in housing, recreation, and transportation was easily extended informally to jobs and politics.

It was with this *national* legal legacy that black Americans entered the twentieth century. During this period, blacks became increasingly urban. But in the North, a myriad of discriminatory laws were to prevent black integration into white institutions and black participation in American affluence. Such laws were not considered illegal or immoral by many, as they were legitimized by the highest court in the land and reflected the post-Civil War belief that blacks had been given a chance and had demonstrated their inferiority. Even when these decisions were subsequently reversed, informal practices of discrimination in

housing, jobs, education, and other spheres were to persist. It is against not only the formal legal barriers but also the informal climate of discrimination created by the long tenure of these legal barriers and dominant beliefs that black Americans have fought in the twentieth century. This fight has been primarily against discriminatory laws in housing, jobs, politics, and education—the key institutional sectors blocking equal participation for blacks.

Legal barriers in attaining equal housing have had profound consequences for black Americans, since place of residence determines, to a very great extent, their access to jobs and schools. Housing discrimination in America has involved a complex pattern of *de facto* and *de jure* processes which periodically have become codified into law.

In this cultural and legal milieu, the first black migrants to Northern cities were forced not only by their meager resources, but also by threats of white violence and landlord policies, into the decaying cores of the cities. While the wartime industries of World War I provided many jobs, and while the geographical concentration of cities allowed easy access from the ghetto to work, a *pattern* of residential isolation of blacks had been initiated. This pattern was often formalized in communities by restrictive covenants which forbade integrated neighborhoods. During the 1930s, when economic opportunities vanished in the North and elsewhere, black migration to the cities waned. Yet, it is during this period that the federal government enacted highly discriminatory legislation which was to forge the current profile of urban America.

The most significant piece of legislation was the federal act creating the Federal Housing Authority and the FHA mortgage loan guarantee program. White Americans were enabled to purchase single family dwellings in the growing suburbs of large cities. So, in the post-World War II period, FHA (and the related VA) mortgage guarantee program stimulated the rapid flight of white Americans from the cities to the suburbs. Black Americans, however, were prevented from joining whites by the explicitly discriminatory administrative rules of the law. From 1950 to 1962, when President Kennedy finally issued an executive order to the contrary, the practice of providing FHA and VA loan guarantees primarily to white neighborhoods continued. Even after 1962, FHA policy was "ineffectively integrationist."

Industry and commerce began to follow the population to the suburbs; and eventually, industry began to pull residents out of the cities as assembly line production with its need for large tracts of land came to dominate sectors of the economy. As industry and workers moved out of the city, commerce and service industries followed. Some blacks could commute out to these jobs; but as mass transit services in America began to deteriorate in the post-World War II period, commuting became even more difficult. At the same time, the tax base for financing city schools vanished, with the result that schools with heavy concentrations of black students languished for lack of financial resources. Furthermore, large suburban communities began to exert enormous political power in metropolitan and state-wide governmental bodies. Thus, urban-suburban segregation, as created by FHA law, has had profound consequences for blocking the

black American's access to jobs, quality schools, and political power, and has forced blacks to live in urban squalor.

To cope with this squalor, other federal laws have been enacted, but they have not eliminated slum conditions, and, more importantly, they have exacerbated patterns of segregation. One of the key legislative acts of the New Deal initiated Public Housing which, by 1937, had acquired the social purpose of eliminating substandard housing. Unfortunately, changes in the law in the late 1930s turned Public Housing project administration over to the cities, with the result that housing projects were built in existing slum areas, thereby perpetuating black confinement to the core city. Urban renewal was another major attempt to revitalize slum areas to restore the decaying downtown areas of cities and to attract middle-class suburbanites back to the city. But the result of the program was to destroy slum housing and force the poor into Public Housing projects where few wished to live. Model Cities programs have done little better, because they do not attack the basic problem —urban-suburban segregation.

A recent Supreme Court decision has made even more difficult the breakdown of urban-suburban apartheid. In 1973 the Supreme Court ruled that suburban communities do have zoning control over patterns of land use in their communities. The result of this ruling is to allow local suburban governments to alter the zoning of land tracts in a way designed to keep public housing or federally subsidized home ownership programs for blacks out of the suburbs—thus perpetuating urban-suburban apartheid. Such "zoning-out" techniques have been common practices for a number of years, as was the case in Milpitas, California, where the land for a union's black housing tract was suddenly rezoned "nonresidential," or as occurred in Deerfield, Illinois, where the land for an integrated housing project was condemned for park use. The recent Supreme Court ruling thus legitimizes these racist housing policies in much the same way as earlier Supreme Court rulings legitimized Jim Crow laws.

Important civil rights legislation of the 1960s has been ineffective in counteracting discrimination because: (1) It often goes unenforced since the civil rights division of the Justice Department is understaffed and underfinanced; and (2) It places the burden of litigation on the *individual* against whom discrimination has occurred—a personally and financially arduous process.

More fundamentally, it does not attack the problem—the need for *mass* migration of blacks to the suburbs (or vice versa). Of course, any such mass policy will encounter resistance of local communities which, under the 1973 Supreme Court ruling, can zone-out government-sponsored housing for blacks. One of the racist ironies of housing laws is that from the mid-1930s until the mid-1960s, whites were given mortgage subsidies (or welfare) by FHA and VA to move out into the suburbs en masse, whereas current laws prevent a similar mass exodus of blacks. Moreover, current Supreme Court rulings prevent massive federal programs of integration of blacks into suburban life, forcing integration of the suburbs to occur on a slow, individual by individual basis. Thus, current housing laws promote racism in housing. These laws further allow Americans to affirm "equal opportunity" beliefs which, in the context of housing, explain blacks' absence from the suburbs as a result of their failure to avail themselves of "equal" educational and economic opportunities that would allow them to buy a house there.

Legalization of discrimination in other institutional spheres has been prevalent, even without the exacerbating impact of residential segregation. In the economy, as already noted, discriminatory practices have blocked black occupational achievement. These practices were tacitly condoned by the absence of laws to the contrary, primarily because the Supreme Court decisions of the last century suspending the Thirteenth and Fourteenth Amendments' rights of blacks created a legal climate of racism. In the 1930s, some of the discriminatory practices were eliminated under political pressure, but it was not until after World War II that clear and enforceable antidiscriminatory laws were enacted. Even these laws were not federal; some states such as New York enacted a tough Fair Employment Practices Law in 1945, but others failed to enact any antidiscriminatory laws whatsoever. In fact, it was only a little over a decade ago—just one year short of 100 years since the Civil War—that a strong Civil Rights Act on job discrimination was passed by Congress. While some enforcement and voluntary compliance to this law is now in evidence, much informal and illegal discrimination occurs. Furthermore, current fair employment laws do not significantly address the question of how to correct and compensate for over a century of legalized job discrimination.

In education, a similar form of legal neglect allowed segregation of blacks and whites in unequal schools. Such segregation was compounded by the fact that there were few federal education laws, especially compulsory education codes; these matters were left to the states, with many states only recently enacting compulsory education laws. Thus, not only were blacks segregated by law, they were not even required by law to come to school, and, in fact, the laws often worked to discourage black school attendance.

Only with the 1954 Supreme Court decision outlawing *de jure* segregation of schools (the question of *de facto* segregation has yet to be completely resolved) did the federal government legally intervene in school system activities. As the post-1954 record reveals, even this Supreme Court decision has proven difficult to enforce. Just recently, in 1974, the Supreme Court ruled that only deliberate attempts to gerrymander school districts in metropolitan regions in order to achieve segregation came under the 1954 ruling. Since urban-suburban apartheid is so well institutionalized (by past *de jure* policies), this latest ruling is likely to forestall any future school integration within metropolitan regions. The irony is that *de jure* policies in one sector of the society (housing) have now become legally defined as a *de facto* situation in another sector (education)—a subtle form of legal racism which, coupled with legal inattention to the racism built into the internal structure of American schools themselves, will perpetuate the racist profile of American education.

In the political arena, similar legal inattention to informal and formal practices of black disenfranchisement and exclusion has existed. In fact, only in the late 1950s and 1960s was a significant legal assault made to give blacks fullfledged political rights. The Voting Rights Act of the 1960s was critical because it made illegal many of the tactics designed to keep blacks unregistered and hence disenfranchised. Somewhat earlier, the Supreme Court in its famous "one man, one vote" ruling struck a blow against blatant gerrymandering of Congressional districts along racial lines. But these laws and court decisions are now only a little over a decade old.

In sum, through existing statutes and statutory omissions, law legitimizes existing arrangements in a society. In the United States, a complex pattern of legitimization has occurred, but its overall profile is clear: Up until the last decades, laws tended to be explicitly racist in housing. In the political arena, state laws were indirectly racist by allowing differential enforcement of the supposedly universal voter eligibility requirements for blacks and whites, while the absence of federal laws sustained racist practices in the area of voter registration and political exclusion. In the job market, laws were racist by virtue of their absence in securing the Thirteenth and Fourteenth Amendment rights for black Americans. In education, legal uninvolvement allowed for local discriminatory laws and informal practices to prevail; and in all institutional spheres, current congressional acts and Supreme Court decisions consistently encounter resistance as they seek to change prevailing institutional arrangements. Thus, legal neglect and inattention to the rights of blacks, as well as direct legal discrimination, have helped create institutions and living patterns in America that will not easily be legislated away.

There are several reasons for this impotency of current laws: (a) Institutions do not change easily because they embody the beliefs and traditional actions of the majority. (b) The laws are not always enforced because of meager enforcement resources. (c) The laws themselves do not always address the problem of past inequities, thrusting the burden of change on individual blacks who have now suddenly been given "equal opportunity." And so, current laws allow white Americans to reaffirm egalitarian values, while at the same time to avoid significantly altering the structural arrangements which violate these values.

Institutional Racism: An Overview

From our brief analysis, it is clear that racism in America involves complex, reciprocal relationships between cultural beliefs and social structural arrangements. While many idiosyncratic prejudices and discriminatory acts among individuals can be observed, the plight of any minority is best explained by the ways attitudes become crystallized into society-wide beliefs and by the patterning of discrimination in key institutional sectors of the society.

In this cursory analysis of white racism against blacks, we have endeavored to portray the present historical record from this unified viewpoint: Racism is an institutional force built into the dominant beliefs and structures of American society. While the specific historical beliefs and structural arrangements oppressing other minorities will differ somewhat from those evident in the case of black Americans, the institutionalization of oppression will still remain the most conspicuous feature of their plight. By exploring the reciprocal relations between cultural beliefs and social structures for Chicanos, Puerto Ricans, Indians, Cubans, and Orientals, a picture of oppression will be evident at some, or as is the case with blacks, at *all*, periods of their history in America.

References

Antonovsky, Aaron. "The Social Meaning of Discrimination." *Phylon*, 1960, 21, 81–95.

Berwanger, Eugene H. *The Frontier against Slavery: Western Anti-Negro Prejudice and the Slavery Extension Controversy*. Urbana, Ill.: University of Illinois Press, 1967.

Brimmer, Andrew F. "The Negro in the National Economy." In John P. Davis (Ed.), *The American Negro Reference Book*. Englewood Cliffs, N.J.: Prentice-Hall, 1966. Pp. 251–336.

Campbell, Angus. *White Attitudes toward Black People*. Ann Arbor, Mich.: Institute for Social Research, 1971.

Daniel, Pete. *The Shadow of Slavery: Peonage in the South 1901–1969*. London: Oxford, 1972.

Degler, Carl N. "Slavery and the Genesis of American Race Prejudice." *Comparative Studies in Society and History*, 1959, 2, 49–66.

Fogel, Robert, and Engerman, Stanley. *Time on the Cross*. Boston: Little, Brown, 1974.

Foley, Eugene P. "The Negro Businessman: In Search of a Tradition." In Talcott Parsons and Kenneth B. Clark (Eds.), *The Negro American*. Boston: Beacon Press, 1966. Pp. 555–592.

Fredrickson, George M. *The Black Image in the White Mind: The Debate on Afro-American Character and Destiny, 1817–1914*. New York: Harper & Row, 1971(a).

Fredrickson, George M. "Toward a Social Interpretation of the Development of American Racism." In Nathan I. Higgins, Martin Kilson, and Daniel M. Fox (Eds.), *Key Issues in the Afro-American Experience*, Vol. 1. New York: Harcourt, 1971(b). Pp. 240–254.

Genovese, Eugene D. *The Political Economy of Slavery: Studies in the Economy* and *Society of the Slave South*. New York: Vintage, 1965.

Gossett, Thomas F. *Race: The History of an Idea in America*: Dallas: Southern Methodist University Press, 1963.

Hamilton, C. Horace. "The Negro Leaves the South." *Demography*, 1964, 1, 273–295.

Handlin, Oscar, and Handlin, Mary F. "Origins of the Southern Labor System." *William and Mary Quarterly*, 1950, 7, 199–222.

Jenkins, William Sumner. *Pro-Slavery Thought in the Old South*. Chapel Hill, N.C.: University of North Carolina Press, 1935.

Johnson, Guion Griffis. "The Ideology of White Supremacy, 1876–1910." In Fletcher Melvin Green (Ed.), *Essays in Southern History*. Chapel Hill, N.C.: University of North Carolina Press, 1949. Pp. 124–156.

Jordan, Winthrop D. "Modern Tensions and the Origins of American Slavery." *Journal of Southern History*, 1962, 28, 18–30.

Jordan, Winthrop D. *White over Black: American Attitudes toward the Negro, 1550–1812*. Chapel Hill, N.C.: The University of North Carolina Press, 1968.

Kincaid, Larry. "Two Steps Forward, One Step Back: Racial Attitudes During the Civil War and Reconstruction." Pp. 45–70. In Gary B. Nash and Richard Weiss (Eds.), *The Great Fear: Race in the Mind of America*. New York: Holt, Rinehart, and Winston, 1970. Pp. 45–70.

Knowles, Louis L., and Prewitt, Kenneth. *Institutional Racism in America*. Englewood Cliffs, N.J.: Prentice-Hall, 1969.

Litwack, Leon F. *North of Slavery: The Negro in the Free States, 1790–1860*. Chicago: University of Chicago Press, 1961.

Newby, Idus A. *Jim Crow's Defense: Anti-Negro Thought in America, 1900–1930*. Baton Rouge, La.: Louisiana State University Press, 1965.

Osborne, Richard H. (Ed.). *The Biological and Social Meaning of Race*. San Francisco: W. H. Freeman, 1971.

Park, Robert Ezra. "Education and Its Relation to the Conflict and Fusion of Culture: With Special Reference to the Problems of the Immigrant, the Negro, and the Missions." *Publications of the American Sociological Society*, 1918, 13, 38–63.

Pinkney, Alphonso. *Black Americans*, Englewood Cliffs. N.J.: Prentice-Hall, 1969.

Rose, Peter I. *The Subject Is Race*. New York: Oxford, 1968.

Schaffler, Albert, Schaffler, Ruth C., Ahrenholz, Gladys L., and Prigmore, Charles S. *Understanding Social Problems*. Columbus, Ohio: Charles E. Merrill, 1970.

Simon, Rita James. *Public Opinion in America: 1936–1970*. Chicago: Rand McNally, 1974.

Simpson, George Eaton, and Yinger, J. Milton. *Racial and Cultural Minorities: An Analysis of Prejudice and Discrimination*, 4th ed. New York: Harper & Row, 1972.

Stampp, Kenneth M. *The Peculiar Institution: Slavery in the Ante-Bellum South*, New York: Vintage Books, 1956.

Stanton, William. *The Leopard's Spots: Scientific Attitudes toward Race in America 1815–59*. Chicago: University of Chicago Press, 1960.

Starobin, Robert S. *Industrial Slavery in the Old South*. London: Oxford, 1970.

Takaki, Ronald. "The Black Child-Savage in Ante-Bellum America." In Gary B. Nash and Richard Weiss (Eds.), *The Great Fear: Race in the Mind of America*. New York: Holt, Rinehart and Winston, 1970. Pp. 27–44.

Thomas, William I. "The Psychology of Race-Prejudice." *American Journal of Sociology*, 1904, 9, 593–611.

Turner, Jonathan H. *Patterns of Social Organization*. New York: McGraw-Hill, 1972.

Woodward, C. Vann. *The Strange Career of Jim Crow*, sec. rev. ed. New York: Oxford, 1966.

Zilversmit, Arthur. *The First Emancipation: The Abolition of Slavery in the North*. Chicago: University of Chicago Press, 1967.

Suggested Reading

FREDRICKSON, GEORGE M. *The Black Image in the White Mind: The Debate on Afro-American Character and Destiny, 1817–1914.* New York: Harper & Row, 1971.
A study of the development of white racist ideology in America during the nineteenth and early twentieth centuries.

GOSSETT, THOMAS F. *Race: The History of an Idea in America.* Dallas: Southern Methodist University Press, 1963.
An historical survey of race theory and bigotry in the United States.

JONES, JAMES M. *Prejudice and Racism.* Reading, Mass.: Addison-Wesley, 1972.
An introduction to the sociological and psychological study of racism. Includes a critical review of recent literature and a discussion of the various perspectives on prejudice and racism.

JORDAN, WINTHROP D. *White over Black: American Attitudes toward the Negro, 1550–1812.* Chapel Hill: University of North Carolina Press, 1968.
An analysis of early American racial attitudes from the formation of beliefs about Africans in pre-Colonial, Elizabethan England to the solidification of the North-South split in the post-Revolutionary War era.

KNOWLES, LOUIS L., AND PREWITT, KENNETH (Eds.). *Institutional Racism in America.* Englewood Cliffs, N.J.: Prentice-Hall, 1969.
The product of a work-study group of Stanford University undergraduates, this volume catalogs examples of racism as found in major American institutions and suggests means for its elimination.

NASH, GARY B., AND WEISS, RICHARD (Eds.). *The Great Fear: Race in the Mind of America.* New York: Holt, Rinehart and Winston, 1970.
A collection of essays dealing with white racial attitudes from the colonial period to the twentieth century. Discusses attitudes toward Indians, European and Asian immigrants, and Mexican-Americans, as well as blacks.

PETTIGREW, THOMAS F. (Ed.). *Racial Discrimination in the United States.* New York: Harper & Row, 1975.
A recent symposium dealing with discrimination against blacks. Chapters document discrimination in housing, employment, education, income, administration of justice, and political power; analyze the human cost of racial discrimination; and offer some remedies to the situation.

The Oppressed in America

Poverty and Internal Colonialism

Ray C. Rist and Colleen J. Soares

The strong do as they may, the weak suffer as they must. Thucydides, Greek historian
"One-third of all dog food sold in some urban areas is eaten by humans." Headline to news article on testimony to U.S. Senate

It appears to be a particular characteristic of the American public consciousness that attention and concern for any social problem lasts only a very short time before something else, perhaps more exotic or more bizarre, comes to capture the attention and energy of the citizenry. One could offer a whole litany of the concerns of the past decade alone: civil rights, poverty, war, crime, prisons, drugs, political trials, political corruption, pollution, and energy. Each of them in and of itself is complex and demands serious analysis, discussion, and insightful responses. But it is as if we, as a nation, were on a wild roller coaster ride where at each high point we glimpse a problem only briefly before we are brought back down into the trough to come up again on another problem. Soon it takes something more and more crisis-ridden to gain our attention. Selma, Alabama; Attica prison; the jungles of Vietnam; Watergate; aged people freezing to death in homes without heat—all have blunted our sensibility. It is hard to keep a per-

The views of the senior author are solely his own and no official support or endorsement by the National Institute of Education or the Department of Health, Education and Welfare is intended or should be inferred.

spective and intelligent allocation of our time and concern. The task of recycling papers and bottles now seems as critical as were the efforts to end racism and poverty only a few short years ago.

It is the premise of this article that in spite of all the problems which surround us, the issues related to poverty and oppression are critical and must remain at the center of the national agenda. The inequalities inherent in poverty and oppression will not fade nor quietly pass away. Rather, they will grow and generate even more problematic conditions. As such inequalities increasingly pervade all aspects of American society, the gap between the rhetoric of what we say we are and the reality of what we actually are will widen to the point at which we are up against the wall and faced with one of two solutions: extreme repression or rebellion. Those are not pleasant choices.

POVERTY AS A SOCIAL PROBLEM

A social problem is some condition which affects a significant number of persons, is deemed undesirable, and thought to be amenable to change or resolution. Thus, to talk of poverty, urban decay, or pollution as social problems is to suggest that they all share in some degree these three attributes. But determining if some condition constitutes a social problem may not be as simple as it first appears. A process is involved whereby the particular condition is first recognized as a "problem" by a private or interest group whose audience is small and generally specialized. If that definition of the condition as a problem is accepted by others it then begins to move into the public domain where both the legitimacy and salience of the condition are evaluated. Here, pronouncements of the media and public officials play a key role in either propelling the condition into public awareness or sending it back into the oblivion of the small interested group.

Once the condition is in the process of being publicly discussed and analyzed, there emerges the conflicting interpretations and definitions of what constitutes the condition, what causes the condition, and what might resolve it. No longer is the condition the concern of just the initial group. Now elites, national professional organizations, the scientific community, public officials, and those directly involved begin to define and interpret the condition from their perspectives and in terms of their vantage points. How the contending groups resolve their various definitions and prescriptions is the result of a political process, of conflict and struggle among groups as to whose definitions become the "official" and legitimate pronouncements. Such a struggle over legitimacy is not unimportant, for it determines the responses to be made. How the problem is defined directly influences the kinds of solutions seen as appropriate.

But what about the presence of poverty? Does it constitute a social problem? Is it widely seen as an undesirable condition? Are there means to change or eradicate it? One might turn back to the Biblical injunction of "The poor you shall always have with you" as sufficient verification of the permanence and persistence of poverty, and the futility of efforts to have it otherwise. As Reissman (1973:9) has noted:

Social inequality is as old as human history, as universal as human societies. Everywhere and in every epoch there has existed some form of stratification with those at the top holding more privilege, power, and enjoying greater rewards than those at the bottom. Inequality, not equality, has been the predominant social rule by which most men at most times have lived. The rationales used by those in power to explain and justify inequality have varied throughout human history, even as the effects have turned out to be remarkably similar. . . . In one form or another, and at different times, God, the supernatural, nature, blood, tradition, and science have been used to explain why some system of stratification exists and why it is proper for some members of a society to have so much while others have less.

Although most Americans would more or less reject notions that the poor are poor because of genetics, or some Darwinist belief in a "survival of the fittest," or theological predestination, there is still a large segment of the population who would support the notion that poverty does come from being lazy and unwilling to find a job and hold it. In this view, poverty results from the absence of hard work, ambition, and the drive to get ahead. Consequently, to state that perhaps as many as 40 million Americans live in poverty is only to state that they have their just reward. We have no doubt but that this perspective is one held by many Americans, one in which the poor are blamed for being poor and inequality is viewed as a natural outcome of the differences among individuals. From this viewpoint, there is no social problem for there is nothing to be changed and nothing undesirable in the present arrangement.

The first of the three-part definition of a social problem, that it affects a significant number of persons, is critical, for the condition would not be considered a *social* problem if it affected only one or a very few individuals. Here a distinction by C. W. Mills (1959:8–9) is relevant. He discusses the differences between "troubles" and "issues."

Troubles occur within the character of the individual and within the range of his immediate relations with others; they have to do with his self and with those limited areas of social life of which he is directly and personally aware. . . . A trouble is a private matter.

Issues have to do with matters that transcend those local environments of the individual and the range of his inner life. They have to do with the organization of many such milieux into the institutions of an historical society as a whole, with the ways in which milieux overlap and interpenetrate to form the larger structure of social and historical life. An issue is a public matter.

Mills goes on to give examples of this distinction, using unemployment, war, marriage, the metropolis, and the economy as areas in which differentiations can be fruitfully made. Consider his comments on unemployment:

When in a city of 100,000, only one man is unemployed, that is his personal trouble, and for its relief we properly look to the character of the man, his skills, and his immediate opportunities. But when in a nation of 50 million employees, 15 million men are unemployed, that is an issue, and we may not hope to find its solution within the range of opportunities open to any one individual. The very structure of opportunities has collapsed. Both the correct state-

ment of the problem and the range of possible solutions require us to consider the economic and political institutions of the society, and not merely the personal situation and character of a scatter of individuals. (Mills, 1959:9)

Given that unemployment generates poverty, it is as if one could substitute the word "poverty" for "unemployment" in the above quote and remain accurate in the analysis. If one man is poor, that is a personal trouble, when 25 to 40 million persons are poor, it is a public issue. More importantly, solutions to the latter condition will not be found by simply expanding solutions for the former. There is both a quantitative and qualitative difference in the poverty of one or a few versus that of millions.

The second part of the definition of a social problem, that the condition be seen by many as undesirable, is self-evident. Desirable conditions are hardly considered problems. Furthermore, conditions which those outside the social context may think of as undesirable may not be so to those directly involved. If one's religious faith leads one to believe that inequalities are inherent in the world and that they are ordained from above, then so long as one held to the faith, the conditions would not be negatively evaluated. The classical caste system in India is a perfect example of a system in which inequality was not defined in negative terms. Everyone knew his or her caste position and there was no thought of changing or challenging it, for that was the way the universe was ordered.

The final part of the definition, that of the perceived problem seen as amenable to resolution, is at first glance perhaps less crucial, but in the end, most important. It is not enough to say that a condition which affects large numbers of people and is undesirable justifies calling it a social problem. Death and drought are but two examples of conditions which fit the first two criteria of the definition but not the third. If there is a belief in the inevitability of the event or condition, that it is outside the capacity of man to change or modify it, that it is a permanent aspect of the human existence, then such a condition is not a problem, but a given. One may fear death, but ultimately one cannot flee from it.

We have come to see that it is not the same with poverty. There has emerged, most strongly in the past four decades, the belief that poverty is a social condition which can be ameliorated through welfare programs, unemployment legislation, minimal redistribution of income, and the like. The allocation of funding for the war on poverty, for manpower training, and for education programs fitted for the "disadvantaged" all suggest a belief that poverty is not inevitable and inescapable.

It will be argued here that while poverty still persists, it is not the result of a placid acceptance of the status quo, but is due to the conscious effort by the powerful to perpetuate institutional arrangements which are to their own benefit and to the detriment of the poor. The programs which have been instituted are created not to alleviate poverty per se, but only its most extreme forms. In a very real sense, it is not poverty that is the most pressing problem, but the inordinate concentration of wealth and power in the hands of the few. The solution to the presence of poverty is not to do something to the poor, but to do something to the wealthy. So long as the top one percent of the population controls eight times the wealth of the bottom fifty percent, not much will be effectively done to eliminate poverty. When fifty percent of the population must share nine percent of the pie, no one gets much of a piece!

It is not surprising that the efforts to ameliorate poverty have failed and the inequality still persists. For not only has the analysis been faulty, but the American perspective is one which does not envision much of a payoff for the intervention in the social order to alleviate poverty. As Reissman has noted (1973: 12):

Why, indeed, have Americans even bothered to try? After all, they have for decades believed that social inequalities were corrected automatically by the formal functioning of their institutional system. Those inequalities that did exist were legitimate consequences of that system, and therefore, it was unnecessary to tamper or intervene with its functioning.

The belief in the constantly improving state of American society is not new. The notion of "things are getting better every day, and in every way" has had expression in America at least since the early nineteenth century in the writings of de Tocqueville. As he wrote in his major treatise, *Democracy in America* (1969:9):

No novelty in the United States struck me more vividly during my stay there than the equality of conditions. It was easy to see the immense influence of this basic fact on the whole course of society. It gives a particular turn to public opinion and a particular twist to the laws, new maxims to those who govern and particular habits to the governed.

Later on in the book he notes:

It is not that in the United States as elsewhere, there are no rich: indeed I know of no other country where love of money has such a grip on men's hearts or where stronger scorn is expressed for the theory of permanent equality of property. But wealth circulates there with incredible rapidity, and experience shows that two successive generations seldom enjoy its favors. (p. 54)

The highly optimistic tone of De Tocqueville's writing has found its latter-day adherents in a number of social scientists who have argued that social mobility in America is increasing, the distribution of income has become more even, and institutional discrimination is on the decline. As Lipset (1963:341) has written in a spirit of celebration of the American experience;

American values, more than those of other nations, have encouraged men to apply equalitarian and achievement orientations to the polity and its various institutions. . . . [T]he fact that this New Nation has succeeded in fostering economic growth and democracy under the aegis of equalitarian values holds out hope for the rest of the world. The consequence of this particularly unique American perspective is a faith in the premise of equality, i.e., "All men are created equal," and a faith in the current institutional arrangements to make that equality a reality. The bind comes when one recognizes that the present system cannot foster more equality, but in fact perpetuates inequality. Thus one is theoretically confronted with either rejecting the traditionally ideological belief in equality, or seeking to give expression to it by working towards institutional change. But there has been a loophole, and it is as if the entire national consciousness has slid through. The bypass in America has been to define "equality" as a political and not an economic condition. America can espouse a particular form of equality through the "one man, one vote" principal and the enfranchisement of all sectors of the society, save for the young. Equality becomes the rich and poor alike being able to go into the voting booth as "equals," though they

may go home to a mansion or a hovel. To be a "free person" is to be able to vote, it is not necessarily to have food, housing, clothing or medical care.

A consequence of equality having been defined in such a way within the United States is that the economic disparities have remained virtually unchanged for at least the last 45 years. Further, it has meant that the relation of wealth to political power has not been a point of much contention, for it has not been seen as related to a discussion of equality. The failure to elucidate this relation has resulted in the notion of democracy in America taking on a rather twisted meaning: Everyone is politically equal and free, although economic disparities allow some to buy and influence the course of political events more than can others. As Horowitz (1972:233) has noted:

The reciprocal interaction between economic change and social democracy is an important issue of our time. The power that an individual or group has to support the meaningfulness of his participation in the making of social decisions involves his ability to withhold something significantly necessary to the welfare of others in the group. *One source of such power is the control over economic resources necessary to the society as a whole or to individuals in the society. Democracy is related to the distribution of power in society. The more concentrated power is, the less democratic is the society. Contrariwise, the more widely and evenly power is distributed, the more democratic that society is likely to be.* (Italics added.)

That in America economic resources are so unevenly distributed that there are people eating dog food to survive while others partake in full of the American feast attests to the inequalities. Such disparities also attest to the reality of America being very undemocratic.

IDEOLOGICAL PERSPECTIVES ON POVERTY

As with so many other facets of our social existence, poverty is created in the eye of the beholder. This is not to say that there are not objective conditions involved or that such conditions are unimportant, but that how such conditions are evaluated is the result of the framework within which one looks at the world. Different people can look at the same individual, penniless and without visible means of support, and one could offer only contempt for failing to be employed, while another person would see the victim of a class system that perpetuates poverty and large numbers of low-skilled individuals who fill the seasonal and short-term jobs unwanted by others in the society. How one perceives poverty, its causes, and its remedies, is linked to how one has socially constructed reality. As Gouldner (1970:29) has noted, any formally explicated social theory carries within it a number of "domain assumptions" about the nature of man, reality, and social institutions. We believe that such a perspective can be fruitfully extrapolated to deal with the "metatheories" that each of us individually carries to help order our understanding of the social world. Such personalized metatheories would relate to whether we think humankind is ultimately good or evil, whether or not there exists free will, whether humans shape their institutions or are shaped by them, and the like. The presence of such metatheories results in a series of screens or filters through which we selectively view the world around us. Consequently, what we come to believe is "reality" is the result of a number of individualized perceptions and judgments.

When one moves from the individual to the collective level, and the debate becomes one of "what to do" about poverty, the multiplicity of perspectives immediately suggests that there is no uniformity of agreement as to what constitutes poverty, let alone how one should respond to it. The collective response which is finally forthcoming is the result of the definition of poverty having been established through the political process. As suggested in the previous section, contending groups contest for the right to impose their definition on the situation. These positions, admittedly reified, are the conservative, the liberal, and the radical. For each of these perspectives, there has emerged not only a definition of cause, but a prescription for response.

The Conservative Position

For the conservative, the presence of poverty is seen to be the result of a series of personal and individual character deficits which preclude the person from actively participating in the national market economy. In these terms, poverty is explained by the lack of personal motivation, ambition, desire to succeed, or goals for one's life. In addition, there is frequently the claim that contentment with government welfare programs inhibits any initiative on the part of the person to overcome his poverty.

When such a perspective has been theoretically conceptualized, it has emerged as some variation on the "culture of poverty" model. Here the poor, and sometimes the entire lower class, are characterized as possessing a distinctive set of values, beliefs, and practices which separates them out and away from the main cultural forces of the rest of the society. Although infrequently, it is sometimes argued that such a subculture is one with positive adaptive advantages for the poor (Rainwater, 1970:146):

This functional autonomy of the lower-class subculture is in the interest of both the larger society and of the lower class. The lower class requires breathing room free from the oppressive eye of conventional study, and, therefore, from the oppressive application of conventional norms. Conventional society is freed from the necessity to confront the fact that the norms are constantly flaunted and that the social control mechanisms that are supposed to insure observance cannot operate effectively.

However, the predominant view of the culture of the poor is one characterized by Lewis (1966):

. . . a strong feeling of fatalism, helplessness, dependency and inferiority. These traits, so often remarked in the current literature as characteristic of the American Negro, I found equally strong in slum dwellers of Mexico City and San Juan, who are not segregated or discriminated against as a distinct ethnic or racial group. Other traits include a high incidence of weak ego structure, orality and confusion of sexual identification, all reflecting material deprivation; a strong present time identification with relatively little disposition to defer gratification and plan for the future, and a high tolerance for psychological pathology of all kinds.

For the conservative, the means to eliminate this subcultural system with its endemic poverty is to eliminate those welfare programs which sustain people and prevent their being forced into the labor market. It is believed that by putting people into the labor force, the problems of poverty will be drastically, if not completely, eliminated. If people are not now motivated to work, it is reasoned that once they no longer have the support of welfare programs, they will of necessity have to begin working. What is overlooked in this view is that the large majority of poor people are not able to work. If one considers the numbers of children, aged, ill, blind, handicapped, and retarded who simply have no way of making it in the labor market, the notion of large numbers of able-bodied persons who are not working out of choice becomes inaccurate. Further, such a perspective implies that (1) the system is able to absorb all those who wish to work, and (2) that all will find employment sufficient to lift them out of poverty. It ignores the realities of millions of persons who are "underemployed" and still poor. If a man with a wife and three children worked 51 weeks a year, earning the minimum wage of $1.60 per hour, he and his family would still be in poverty. His income would be $3294 before taxes and social security, while the poverty line for an urban family of that size is approximately $4600. That family is still poor by more than $1300, and working full time! The conservative position places the blame for being poor on the poor themselves and absolves the economic and political system of any responsibility. There is no discrimination, no racism—just lazy people.

The Liberal Position

For the liberal, there is a modification of the above emphasis on personal pathology to include the notion that the bureaucracy and welfare programs are doing an ineffective job. Thus there emerges a blend of personal and systemic factors which are seen to generate the presence of poverty. Such was the prevailing notion during the 1960s as found in the federal attempts to wage a "war on poverty." The guiding assumptions of how poverty was to be eradicated were related to the rewarding of individual effort through providing opportunities for upward social mobility and economic gain. It was acknowledged that discrimination did exist and as such prevented some mobility. But it was also explicit that there were characteriological defects in the poor which needed to be overcome before they could make use of the new mobility opportunities being opened up for them.

Perhaps one of the best ways to visualize the liberal perspective is to consider part of a memorandum from the Council of Economic Advisors to President Kennedy in November of 1963 suggesting the following cycle as an explanation of the perpetuation of poverty and dependency:

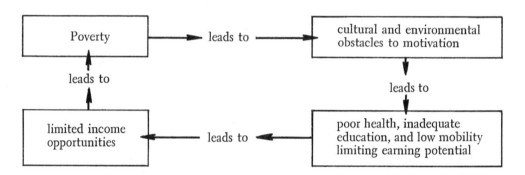

Implicit in this model is the liberal faith that with only slight modifications in the current arrangements of the system, the poor can find sufficient escape routes from poverty to join the nonpoor at the banquet table. Thus poverty ultimately exists in spite of the society, not because of it. The system is essentially sound and viable; what is needed is cosmetic surgery to smooth out the rough places and eliminate the last few vestiges of obstacles to mobility. Within this perspective the programatic approaches were that social welfare agencies would be "modernized"; educational programs initiated for the drop-outs and push outs; Headstart would provide the poor children with additional "enrichment" so they could compete more equally in the classroom; and job training programs would be begun to give the poor new skills. Also, racism and discrimination could be decried and the need to reduce prejudice espoused. Ultimately, as the dominants became more tolerant and the poor became more acceptable, poverty should disappear. But this has not been so.

The Radical Position

When the sources of poverty are defined as emerging not from personalistic or pathological sources, but from the structural arrangements of the society, one has reached the radical perspective. Within this framework, the presence of poverty results from class inequality; systematic discrimination and exclusion of the poor from other sectors in the society; from the self-interests of those who are in positions of dominance; and from the ability of the very wealthy to keep large sums of their wealth intact through the intergenerational transfer of funds. Furthermore, the radical perspective argues that the present political and economic arrangements in the society perpetuate such inequality and hinder attempts at a more equitable distribution of wealth. Thus poverty exists because America is as it is, and so long as the power and institutional networks remain as they are, there will be no change.

It is our view that a structural explanation of poverty is the most appropriate. We reject individualistic notions of cultural deprivation or even typical "social welfare" approaches to the explanation of poverty for failing to examine the relation of the poor to the remainder of the society and how it is that others benefit from the presence of large numbers of poor persons. As Reissman (1973:52) has noted:

The poor belong to the lowest social stratum of the American class structure. They lack any effective access to social, political, and economic institutions—a situation which makes the poor virtually powerless to challenge or to control their environment. This condition is further compounded by the inability of the poor to organize themselves into a coherent and conscious class that might pursue power. Far from being outside of the national mainstream, as the cultural proponents would have it, the poor as a class are very much a part of it.

An elaboration of the structural argument of origins and means of perpetuation of poverty follows. Particular emphasis will be placed on the nonwhite peoples of America. This group has often been referred to as the "third-world" or

"subordinate" minorities. This is to differentiate them from earlier immigrant groups who voluntarily sought America. It will ·be argued these third-world peoples exist within American society as a colonized sector—dependent, powerless, and exploited. Thus it is not to the migrant Chicano picking lettuce and berries, or the Native American on a desolate and barren reservation, or the black person contained in an urban ghetto to whom one turns to understand the origins of poverty, but to the power and wealth of the dominant sector of the society and how that position is preserved and protected at the expense of others. To know what has happened to the oppressed, one must know what has been done by the oppressor.

INTERNAL COLONIALISM IN AMERICA: THE OPPRESSION OF THIRD-WORLD PEOPLES

Using the internal colonialism model to better understand the oppression of third-world minorities in the United States is not new, and it is the contention here that it is the one model to date which best illustrates and puts into perspective the institutional oppression suffered by millions of third-world people in one of the richest nations in the world. The following discussion then is not to enhance the value of a colonial perspective as an end in itself, but only to use it as a tool to expose the extent of oppression and the necessity for structural change. One fear is that in reading about oppression, pondering statistics, and debating the relative values of various models, the real people are lost sight of, and their very real human suffering and despair becomes distant and unreal. We must not lose sight of the people and their day-to-day struggle to survive.

The central feature of the internal colonialism model for understanding the oppression of third-world minorities focuses on the political and economic control of their lives. What results is an extreme powerlessness to affect any change in their environments. Reactions to this powerlessness vary from group to group. Apathy, higher rates of suicide, or violence may be among the reactions, while economic and psychological dependence on the dominant group is frequently a corollary. Some theorists assert violence is one result of powerlessness. Richard Rubenstein (1970) contends that much of the violence of the 1960s can be understood in terms of the powerlessness of various groups. This violence may be recognized as the only option available to those attempting to gain some control over their lives.

As the use of the perspective of internal colonialism has grown, there has, likewise, been an increasing criticism of this approach by those who claim it to be obscurantist and misleading. Attention is called to the significant differences in historical and sociopolitical conditions between American society and the traditional imperial conquests of the nineteenth century. Although this criticism of the internal colonialism model does highlight some of the differences between these two contexts, it has also tended to obscure the common experiences and patterns of social organization which have been shared by American minorities and nonwhite peoples in other parts of the world. What appears divergent on first glance takes on a commonality and unity when examined more closely.

Blauner (1969) suggests there are five basic components to the colonization complex, regardless of whether it is internal or external in its manifestation. The processes are very similar; what differs are the specific institutional structures by which the patterns of relations are governed. First, Blauner posits the forced, involuntary entry into the relation on the part of the colonized. The transformation and attempts at destruction of the culture of the colonized peoples is the second characteristic. Third is the experience by the colonized of having their lives managed, manipulated, and administered by representatives of the dominant group. Racism, a principle of social domination designating superiors and inferiors, is the fourth characteristic. Finally, there is the separation in labor status of the colonized and colonizers. Jobs are designated for one group or the other. One does not by hard work move from a colonized to a colonizer position in the labor hierarchy, and wages and benefits are grossly disparate. What is striking about these five characteristics outlined by Blauner is the enormous sense of fatefulness which confronts a colonized group when they are brought into the society of the colonizers. Options are closed, power systems remain exclusive, and membership in the larger society is never offered. The colonized are viewed as alien, culturally deficient, and, frequently, biologically inferior.

The internal colonialism model is based upon certain key premises. First, the model casts aside the preoccupation with individual prejudice. It is still held by many people that by eliminating individual prejudice, the problems of racial oppression will be solved. Such is not the case, however, for as Albert Memmi (1965:38) maintains:

the style of a colonization does not depend upon one or a few generous or clear thinking individuals. Colonial relations do not stem from individual good will or actions; they exist before his arrival or his birth and whether he accepts or rejects them matters little. It is they, on the contrary, which like any institution determine *a priori* his place and that of the colonized and, in the final analysis, their true relationship.

While it is acknowledged that prejudice still exists, it is not the root of the problem, and by concentrating efforts on such offshoots of institutional oppression energies are wasted which are better utilized elsewhere. The consequences of concentrating on individual prejudice lie in the psychological resolution to the oppressive situation; for after all, proponents say, we cannot legislate attitudes out of existence, therefore there is nothing to do until attitudes change by themselves. The point to remember, however, is that behavior can be changed by legislation which in turn will eventually change attitudes. Robert Blauner (1972: 28) contends that such preoccupation ignores the fact that "ethnic and racial groups are first and foremost interest groups." As such they have "distinctive objective interests" which may be at variance with those of other groups.

Secondly, the colonial model rejects notions of cultural and racial assimilation and amalgamation as alternatives for they are idealistic and fail to confront the realities of colonial oppression. People raised in unique environments have unique value orientations to life. The supreme and arrogant misjudgment on the part of the government and other institutions is the tacit assumption that the Anglo value system is universal, and more than this, that it is the only natural way for anyone to live. An underlying problem then is an unwillingness on the part of the dominant group to understand and truly value other cultures. The crux is, of course, that this one culture, after obtaining by questionable means a disproportionate amount of power, assumes from this its inherent superiority over other cultures and refuses to see any value in other ways of life. The pressure for assimilation of minority group peoples according to the precepts of Anglo values and culture has dominated American majority-minority group relations since the beginning of research into the question.

The contention of the theory of assimilation $(A + B + C = A)$ is that over time minority groups will adopt or at least conform in large degree to the life style, mores, and values of the dominant group; in short, the culture of the dominant group. Amalgamation $(A + B + C = D)$ refers to the combination of different cultural groups, resulting in one group different from each of the originals. This is the classic "melting pot" theory of dominant-minority relations. There is no question that each of the above processes is occurring to some extent, however, many years after other ethnic groups have attained positions of control and influence over their lives, the overwhelming majority of third-world groups remain on the periphery when the "goodies" are distributed.

Amalgamation and assimilation do not confront the realities of dominant control of all institutions in America. There are too many institutionalized barriers against third-world participation for these to be viable solutions. Equality is not as simple as these theories imply. They are unrealistic, for they fail to acknowledge the privilege gained by the dominant group from the continual subjugation of third-world people.

It is important to note that all social and scientific theories and ideologies must be examined in the context of the milieu in which they emerge. Even the most detached scientist cannot escape being socialized into the specific cultural milieu in which he or she was raised. With this in mind what was the dominant ideology behind the emergence of assimilationist theory? The most simplistic and obvious assumption (and for this reason frequently taken for granted and not questioned) underlying the assimilationist view is that the culture of the dominant group is superior in most ways. Following from this is the belief that the culture of the minority group is inferior. The result is, of course, that there is no question as to which culture ought to predominate and which groups will be stigmatized and relegated to the lowest positions on the socioeconomic ladder.

Thomas F. Gossett (1971) documents that for the past several centuries there have been individuals in the scientific community who promote the view of one group being inherently superior to another. In addition, these views have frequently corresponded to and reinforced some popular beliefs and feelings of the period in which they arose. Some social scientists agree that Spencer's and Darwin's theories of evolution promoted the awakening ideology of superior and inferior groups, and historical evidence lends credence to such a position. William M. Newman (1973:61) contends that the most important ideological development lending strength to the assimi-

lationist viewpoint was the emergence of the concept of "race" itself. It was expected that over time all minority groups would adopt the culture of the dominant group in the United States, and little serious thought was given to the fact that some groups wished to retain their own culture, indeed, had to retain their culture to maintain any semblance of identity and self-esteem. This was especially true in the case of blacks in America, who, it was felt, had very little in the way of any culture at all, except that which some theorists suggested was "lower-class culture" or the "culture of poverty."

However, the underlying assumption of the assimilationist doctrine (regardless of from which school of thought it arises) is still the same and is no less serious for the plight of Spanish-speaking or surnamed, and Native American minorities. However, the assimilationist strategy of dominants with regard to these two groups has been somewhat different since their culture was at least acknowledged. It is the contention of Blauner (1972:7) that another misguided assumption underlying the assimilationist theory is that racial oppression is deviant behavior, considered in the context of present American society, and that it will eventually be eliminated with little or no change in that society. He feels this is an erroneous assumption and that, on the contrary, racial oppression is "a fundamental principle of American society" rather than an aberration, and subsequently, one which calls forth structural resolution.

In an impersonal, technological society, one's identity is precarious. It is thus an easy option, a form of escape, to identify with a powerful group and to project hostilities and frustrations onto other groups. Favorite targets throughout history have, of course, been powerless and this is perhaps the main reason for such projection. Only by the creation of a more just society in America will there emerge that consciousness and compassion necessary to truly eliminate prejudice and institutional oppression. No one is suggesting that decolonization is an easy process; on the contrary, it has usually been violent. But perhaps if America heeds warning, it may yet escape the culminations of a violent past. This will only be if those oppressed voices are allowed expression and only if America's diverse cultural minorities are at least allowed that right to reeducate all of those in America who would question the value of cultural diversity in the political and legal systems, in education, in the media and in all other facets of American life.

A third premise of the internal colonialism model is the notion of privilege. Memmi (1965:11) reasons that the colonizer must benefit from a system which he or she so readily and rigidly supports. All whites, however much they too may feel oppressed, benefit from the continual oppression of third-world people. Although small colonizers are frequently victims of the very "masters" they support, nevertheless, support is most often forthcoming:

If the small colonizer defends the colonial system so vigorously, it is because he benefits from it to some extent. His gullibility lies in the fact that to protect his very limited interests he protects other infinitely more important ones, of which he is, incidentally, the victim. But though dupe and victim, he also gets his share. (Memmi, 1965:11)

In America this "share" may be economically less relevant than the notion of status, that is, the idea that however

low one sinks, there is some group which is always lower still; yet there still remains economic privilege. An involved analysis of this privilege by Lester C. Thurow (1969:133) reveals a total white income gain of $15.5 billion. He calculates that these gains are realized via less unemployment; higher wages; larger investments in human capital, such as education; occupational discrimination resulting in more profitable occupations; and labor union monopoly discrimination. This averages out to a gain of $248 each year for each white member of the labor force and a loss of $2100 for each nonwhite member. As Thurow (1969: 134) asserts:

Since discrimination produces large economic gains, there are important vested interests in its continuation. Programs to eliminate discrimination must take these interests into account; economic self-interest cannot be counted on to aid in eliminating discrimination. The magnitude of the gains also indicates that elimination would have a powerful impact on the distribution of income for non-whites.

G. William Domhoff (1971) offers a striking view of how the upper class has managed to retain their privileged status in America, while seemingly acting many times for the common good. Domhoff maintains that the upper class represents only .5 percent of the population. However, through their cohesiveness and their economic power they are able to wield substantial influence on all sectors of the government. In fact, it is most likely due in large part to their small size that they have the necessary cohesiveness to affect policy.

We can be assured that the upper classes have very little notion of what it means to be a third-world group member and/or to live in poverty in America today. Thus we can also be assured that their ideas for amelioration would be substantially different from those of third-world groups. Even those in power who may be sympathetic with the needs of various people, after touring poverty-stricken areas, return to Washington "shocked" at the extent of deprivation and inequality still existing in the United States (cf. Javits 1969). Unfortunately, many of those in power have little real awareness of America's basic problems of oppression. Also, as Domhoff substantiates, the power elite are dominant in shaping social policy. That they would do so in their own best interests, while regrettable, is perhaps not surprising. What is surprising is that while continuing to uphold, indeed fight for, the ideology of democratic equality, the majority in the United States also continues to allow a minority of powerful monied interests to dominate the government, domestic policy, and foreign policy. The reality is thus making a sham of the ideology of equality. The internal colonialism model stresses the necessity for institutional change to decrease the gap between the reality and the ideology.

It is no accident that the elite structure has persisted: no privileged class bows out of power when there are still means to maintain that power. Illegal, as well as questionable but legal, means have always been used when power was threatened, and law and order in any society is the law and order which protects the established ruling class. When colonial privilege is threatened, those means necessary for regaining control are used.

Far from being surprised at the revolts of colonized peoples, we should be, on the contrary, surprised that they are not more frequent and more violent. Actually the colonizer guards against them in many ways: by continuous incapacitation of the leaders and periodic destruction of those who, despite everything, manage to come forward; by corruption or police oppression, aborting all popular movements and causing their . . . rapid destruction. (Memmi, 1965:127)

Although legally the government may be all of us, there are powerful groups which have an excessive amount of influence on policy. This influence is not usually achieved by outright violence, although violence is sometimes used: the influence is achieved through subtle and intricate methods and pressures. Federal money and contracts have sometimes been awarded where the payoff was deemed of highest political value. Senator Joseph Montoya (*Oregonian*, June 5, 1974) expressed concern that such action took advantage of Spanish-speaking minorities during the 1972 presidential election campaign. Various tax-free foundations (which include on their boards a majority of the upper class) grant money to commissions and academic people to study topics the power elite deems important. Most often these studies have little to do with questioning the distribution of wealth or the source of social positions (Domhoff, 1971:128). In this way the government is indirectly subsidizing the power elite while the lower classes take a back seat with ineffective and subsistence welfare programs. Through subtle manipulation of the media, the upper classes are able to control information while giving the appearance of promoting equal rights. Also, even through programs designed to help the lower-income masses (Wagner Act, 1934; Social Security Act, 1935; Welfare; Workmen's Compensation 1907–20; labor unions) the upper classes gave up proportionately little or no wealth. The distribution has remained the same for at least 40 years. The country as a whole has grown economically and, relative to earlier times, everyone is financially better off. The disparity remains, however, between the haves and the have-nots.

The upper class represents only that minority of whites benefiting directly from the continuation of an oppressive system. Not all whites benefit *directly* from colonial oppression. For example, only a minority of white business people owns buildings in ghetto areas. Nevertheless, all whites in America, whether they wish it or not, regardless of how much they rebel against an unjust system, are still received as more privileged persons by the institutions and the dominant culture, than are blacks, Chicanos, Puerto Ricans, and Native Americans. Therefore, there is still a very real threat to most whites that their status and wealth, gained at the expense of third-world peoples, would diminish if equality were a reality. In defense of their positions, whites practice ostracism accordingly. The reality then has become large ghettos and barrios as the predominant residences for blacks, Puerto Ricans, and Chicanos. It is important also to stress this containment policy is not simply one of social class, for in 1972, 47 percent of those blacks above the poverty level still lived in low-income areas (cf. U.S. Bureau of Census, 1973:4).

The early westward movement by Anglo-Americans was a process of imperialistic expansion from which Indians and Mexicans emerged with very little land holdings from their former large supply. D'Arcy McNickle (1973:4) briefly documents the war Native Americans waged for 300 years against Anglo-American encroachment. By 1850, this war had reduced the original population of various Indian peoples from 850,000 to 250,000. More than 100 years later, that original population has not yet been reached. A total today of 700,000 represents the official number of Native Americans for which the government has responsibility (McNickle, 1973:5). Stripped of their land base, Indians and Mexicans became economically and politically subordinant to a foreign culture which then attempted to "civilize" them, or to convert them to white culture. The black experience has been similar, the difference being that the colonized were transported to the new world for a long period of slavery. Rodolfo Acuña (1972:73) asserts "the land is at the crux of the Mexican's grievances against the United States government." By revealing a long-neglected history of Anglo domination and control, he demonstrates the existence of a colonial system. For instance, in those areas with a large Mexican-American population and only a few Anglo-Americans, it was the Anglos who had economic and political power. For example, by 1870, there was a population of 12,000 in El Paso County; eighty of these were non-Mexican; however, they held most of the wealth of the county and most of the elected offices. At this same time, the Spanish-speaking people were nearly all poor and had little or no power (Acuña, 1972:50). This trend was and is the rule rather than the exception throughout Mexican-American and Anglo-American interaction. He documents the "legal and illegal methods" by which the Anglo-Americans systematically took the land, methods by which "the Mexican in New Mexico lost 2,000,000 acres of private lands and 1,700,000 acres of communal lands" (1972:61–62). Similarly, Native

Americans were pushed further and further west and were successfully stripped of their land, resulting today in their possession of only 56 million acres from previous "holdings" of 146 million acres in 1897 (cf. Simpson and Yinger, 1972:713).

Several of the most important areas of inequality suffered by third-world minorities were initially caused and are now maintained by internal colonial oppression. These areas are employment, political activity, education, and health. Intersecting at every point in this discussion is the affirmation of a unique cultural base for each of the third-world groups, which must be allowed full expression for any real progress in any area to be made. We share with Blauner (1972:129) the more modern notion of culture as "one that locates ethnicity in certain distinctive values, orientations to life and experiences, and shared memories that coexist within the framework of general American life styles and allegiances." As long as the dominant group fails to acknowledge a necessary cultural diversity, fails to allow unique groups to apply their unique perspectives toward amelioration of oppression, there will be no progress, but only a continuation of costly and impotent social welfare programs. "For in American life, ethnic culture is identity, and there is no individual or group progress without a clear sense of who one is, where one came from, and where one is going" (Blauner, 1972:150).

By a systematic suppression of the cultural expression of blacks, Chicanos, Puerto Ricans, and Native Americans, which is still occurring today, whites were initially able to acquire political and economic power and are able to continue to maintain that power. Cultural exploitation works against third-world groups in numerous ways, but the result is the same: decreasing political power and continuing economic subordination. This is why the reawakening of various cultural expressions is such a crucial first step, for it alone can begin to break the brutal cycle in which third-world groups are enmeshed; it alone can provide the pride, the stimulus, and the strength needed to break the self-fulfilling prophetic cycle and to gain control over one's past, present, and future. Memmi (1965:128) asserts:

Assimilation being abandoned, the colonized's liberation must be carried out through a recovery of self and of autonomous dignity. Attempts at imitating the colonizer required self-denial; the colonizer's rejection is the indispensable prelude to self-discovery. That accusing and annihilating image must be shaken off; oppression must be attacked boldly since it is impossible to go around it. After having been rejected for so long by the colonizer, the day has come when it is the colonized who must refuse the colonizer.

Employment

Third-world groups have traditionally been confined to low-paying jobs frequently considered dirty and unfit for the majority of whites. Although a recent *Time* cover story (1974) applauded the fact that blacks hold 15 percent of all federal government jobs, it failed to acknowledge that only 3 percent of these are higher-grade jobs in the federal classification system. By 1970, nonwhites accounted for only 7 percent of craftspeople and foremen, and only 5 percent of industrial foremen. Less than 10 percent of government jobs which pay more than $8000 a year are held by nonwhites, while in the postal service, they held only 4 percent of the higher-grade positions (U.S. Bureau of Census, 1970:61, 67). Contrary to popular myths, there is evidence that more blacks living in poverty worked year-round, full-time than whites living in poverty (U.S. Bureau of Census, 1973:5).

An additional fact of being confined to the lower stratum of the working class is the insecurity suffered through the realization that unemployment and marginal employment are a frequent reality. Being concentrated in unskilled jobs, third-world people are expendable when there are slumps in the economy, or when technical advancement mechanizes their jobs. Thus the rate of unemployment has consistently run at least twice as high for nonwhites as for whites, and today black unemployment is 9.5 percent, and Indian unemployment is 40 percent, while the corresponding figure for whites is 4.7 percent. In the economy of 1974, with costs of basic foods, energies, and other necessities reaching alarming rates, the plight of minorities becomes not just increasingly bleak, but a day-to-day struggle for survival itself. The National Urban League, in a recently issued report entitled, "Inflation and the Black Consumer," indicated the overall inflation rate for blacks in 1973 was 2 percent higher than the rate for whites (*Oregonian*, August 4, 1974).

While it may be assumed that, until quite recently, most outgroups were pulling out of poverty and becoming more economically self-sufficient, such has not been the case. For example, blacks comprise an increasing proportion of the low-income population, while the national numbers of the poor are perhaps decreasing. While blacks were 26 percent of the low-income population in 1959, and 29 percent in 1971, by 1972 they constituted 33 percent of the 24.5 million poor in the nation, and one-third of all blacks were poor (U.S. Census, 1973:10). Considering they represent only 12 percent of the total population, this is a highly disproportionate figure. And while Spanish-surnamed people represent less than 4 percent of the population (approximately 7 million), they constitute 10 percent of those suffering poverty today, and again, more than 30 percent of all Spanish-speaking peoples are poor (U.S. Census, 1973:1). Statistics on Native Americans are more alarming still with an average median income of $1600 a year, far below the poverty line. The present poverty figure of $4500 for a nonfarm family of four is a cruel joke which hides the true poverty figures of those earning $5000 and $6000 a year, and just barely scraping by. One wonders what kind of "life" one is able to sustain for four people in an American city today on $4500.

Minority entrepreneurs have much more difficulty obtaining loans from banks and the Small Business Administration (SBA) than do their majority counterparts. For example, blacks constitute only 3 percent of the owners of all United States businesses (Reid, 1972: 203). Although the white-to-black population ratio in 1972 was 8.8 to 1, the white-to-black business ownership ratio was 46 to 1, while the white-to-black business dollar ratio runs as high as 336 to 1 (Camp, 1972:55). More than ten years after Federal economic programs were developed to help equalize this disparity, the gap has not diminished.

Philip Mason (1971:335) lends perspective to the problems:

If a man has neither work nor food, it is not enough to provide that he shall not be punished except after trial by his peers, and in accordance with law; it is not enough that he should have the vote if he can be refused a seat in a bus because someone does not like the colour of his skin. In each of these four dimensions—judicial and economic, political and social, which includes esteem—steps have to be taken in a just society to ensure that there is some balance between rights and duties, obligations and reward. It is in the fourth category of social esteem that we are most backward, and legislation to enforce minimum standards, which is clearly essential, is only just beginning.

It is obvious that minorities and other groups calling for recognition and reforms are not merely idly complaining with no just cause. While measurement may be difficult, "the differential distribution of positive feelings about oneself is perhaps the essence of inequality." (Miller and Roby, 1970:172). Therefore, statistics do not tell all, and in fact the most important aspects of inequality may be those which are hardest, if not impossible, to measure.

Blauner (1972) and Rist (1972) document the reality of colonial oppression behind ghetto revolts such as Watts and Detroit respectively. Blauner contends that enclosed minority communities which are owned and controlled by absentee, and usually white landlords (and these communities may be ghettos, barrios, and reservations alike) are not necessarily only complaining about the more easily recognized extreme forms of police brutality when they urge more community control, but in fact are protesting "the more subtle attack on personal dignity that manifests itself in unexplainable questionings and searches, in hostile and insolent attitudes toward groups of young Negroes on the street or in cars, and in the use of disrespectful and sometimes racist language . . ."

(Blauner, 1972:203). This discontent and frustration with police organizations have resulted in failure to recruit minorities into law enforcement programs. Thus for example, in Los Angeles in 1971, the proportion of black police officers was 5.2 percent, while blacks constituted 17.9 percent of that city's population (Blauner, 1972:206).

Politics

Above all, the colonization of third-world groups has meant the dominant groups must maintain control, for only then can exploitation take place. Third-world minorities have virtually no power in the political arena. Although blacks have made some inroads, the overwhelming majority remains outside the political process. Likewise, Mexican-Americans or Chicanos have little or no voice at the local, state, and national level. In California, with a large population of Chicanos, there were no Chicanos in state office in 1972, and there have been no Chicanos in the state senate since the 1880s (Acuña, 1972:247). It has been estimated that 1500 blacks held elective office in the United States in 1972. However, out of a total of 500,000 United States elected officials, this represents only three-tenths of one percent. In 1972, there was one black in the U.S. Senate and 12 in the House, and as Reid (1972:176) points out, "Twelve out of 435 congressional representatives may reinforce an image of powerlessness."

One of the many problems newly elected black mayors have is the economic crisis of the deteriorating inner city areas. Black mayors have "arrived" only to find their cities bankrupt. The Nixon administration's "new federalism" only added to the crisis. Thus, "Charles

Evers of Fayettville, Mississippi, had to wage a national campaign to try and make his city solvent and Hatcher of Gary, Stokes of Cleveland, and Gibson of Newark have all had to become fundraisers" (Reid, 1972:178).

Elected officials only represent one aspect of political oppression. Third-world groups are at the mercy of local economic and political policies which undermine their ability to control their own lives. In the Portland, Oregon, area, for example, 85 percent of the black community is zoned commercially.

The legal procedure itself is another aspect of institutional racism and colonial oppression. While jury selection, voter registration, and the like, would appear to be color blind, the realities point to systems which are so organized as to delimit the participation of people of color. While these systems operate under specific legal guidelines for all, the guidelines themselves must be questioned if they appear to limit such participation. These guidelines and processes are usually nonintentionally racist, and do not point to a racist outlook on the part of most of their initiators.

Nevertheless, this does not absolve the dominant communities from any responsibility in dealing with such systematic exclusion. It only points more glaringly to institutional reorganization for an institutional problem. For example, all nonwhite minorities are underrepresented on jury panels. Frequently the selection of jury members is via lists of registered voters, and just as frequently, third-world peoples are underrepresented on these lists. The underlying reasons revolve around the issues of poverty, geographical location and mobility, and a disenchantment with the political process. Blacks, Chicanos, Puerto Ricans, and

Native Americans have always been disproportionately represented among the poor more than other groups, and the poor have always been among those who do not exercise their vote, for reasons mainly stemming from poverty.

Native Americans, under the jurisdiction of the Bureau of Indian Affairs (BIA), continued to maintain their "special" relationship with the United States government. Controlled in all respects by the repressive tactics of the BIA, it remains their only link with the U.S. government, which has yet to honor treaties made and broken; "only the Bureau stands between the Indian and extinction as a . . . cultural entity . . . and total, unilateral renunciation of all federal treaty obligations" (Cahn et al, 1970:14).

The Bureau is the socializing agent in charge of transforming Indians into individuals acceptable to the white middle class, and it closely controls literally every aspect of the reservation Indian's life. The urban Indian is another special minority whose problems are somewhat different from those found on the reservation. Native Americans in the city have been an invisible minority until recently. Many face the city with ambiguous feelings about a tribal past from which they are physically removed. Also, many are psychically attached to their cultural heritage and thus remain culturally marginal—split between two very different worlds. Many urban Indians are no longer accountable to, nor financially protected by, the BIA; however, others work for periods in the city and return to their reservations with their earnings. The urban Indian is becoming an increasingly vocal minority and the American Indian Movement (AIM), founded in 1968, has become adamant concerning the rights of urban Indians for a share of BIA funding (Bahr, 1972:410).

Education

In addition to a lack of representation in the political realm, third-world peoples are poorly represented in education. Perhaps the majority way utilized by dominant groups to attain and retain control has been the suppression, as nearly as possible, of the cultural expression and traditions of third-world groups. This has been more prevalent in those institutions which hold "hostage" millions of children while attempting to convert them to white middle-class standards. As only one example of cultural oppression, it would be illustrative to examine the denial of any legitimacy to Black English. Third-world children from diverse backgrounds speaking Black English, Spanish, and various tribal languages, have been branded as failures in schools across the land simply because they cannot speak the foreign language of the dominant group. McNickle (1973:7) maintains that today, half of the original 300 Indian languages are in current use. And as Memmi relates (1965:107):

the colonized mother tongue, that which is sustained by his feelings, emotions and dreams, that in which his tenderness and wonder are expressed, thus that which holds the greatest emotional impact, is precisely the one which is the least valued. It has no stature in the country or in the concert of peoples. If he wants to obtain a job, make a place for himself, exist in the community and the world, he must first bow to the language of his masters.

Frequently, children who have unique cultural backgrounds or who have not learned "proper" or standard English, if they have learned English at all, are relegated to classes for the mentally retarded. The dehumanizing bureaucracy of the school system, in addition to ignorance on the part of many educators, make the system unable to deal with diversity of background and culture. Schools, with few exceptions, have historically been nothing more than great socializing "factories" where children of different class and radical positions were socialized to "know their place" and prepare for different slots in the class structure. However, schools are only extensions of the structures of the larger society and as Rist (1973:2) maintains, they have actually done their jobs quite well.

There is no crisis in American education if we accept American society as is. But one must recognize that inherent in its very existence are aspects of racism, class schisms, coercion, the continual erosion of freedom and destruction of the "humanness" of those insufficiently strong to resist.

Schools are unable to recognize and build upon cultural diversity, and this same problem is built into many other institutions in this society. By continually showing third-world children that their cultures and lifestyles are not valued, they successfully crush the spirit and retard the growth of many children who would otherwise succeed quite well.

The predominant reason behind a much lower educational attainment has been, and remains today, segregated facilities and a low expectation from third-world groups, coupled with a lack of respect for their unique backgrounds. In other words, schools teach the way teachers *suppose* children *ought* to learn rather than attempting to determine in what ways the children are *prepared* to learn. In addition, they are rarely held accountable for any resulting failures; that re-sponsibility is usually passed back to the child (the victim), or the parents, or the environment. These reasons, coupled with the vicious cycle of poverty in which many third-world families are enmeshed, ensures that low educational attainment will be a continuing reality for these children.

The BIA operates approximately 77 boarding schools which house nearly half of the reservation children, who often are forced to leave their families and travel across the country at a very young age. These boarding schools have a 60 per-cent drop-out rate compared to the na-tional average of 23 percent, and for those Indians under federal supervi-sion, the average educational level is five school years (Cahn, et al., 1970:28). It has been estimated that as few as ten Native Americans hold Ph.D. degrees in all fields (Blauner, 1972:174). In a com-parative study of white and Indian males in California, urban Indians had com-pleted a median of 9.7 school years, while for whites the figure was 12 years. In ad-dition, the unemployment rates for ur-ban Native Americans and whites were 15.1 percent and 5.5 percent respectively (Bahr et al., 1972:429).

Burma (1970:91) estimates that in 1970 perhaps 45 percent of the Spanish-speaking peoples living in five southwest-ern states have less than five years of schooling, and in these five states they make up 10 percent of the population. In California, half of the Spanish-speak-ing students drop out by the eighth grade (Ortega, 1972:159). Chicanos comprise more than 14 percent of the public school population in California and half the total population in New Mexico. Yet there are fewer than one-half of one per-cent, and eight percent respectively, en-rolled in the state universities (Ortega, 1972:167–8).

Blacks represent the largest minority in the nation with 12 percent, yet there are only .25 percent who have Ph.D.s, and their educational attainment continues to lag behind the national average (Gayles, 1974:7). Today, 20 years after Brown vs. Board of Education, there are still many effective barriers to equal edu-cational attainment. Thus, while there was a decrease in the gap for median edu-cational attainment for whites and blacks between 1960 and 1968, the gap between those whites and blacks graduating from college has increased (Miller and Roby, 1970:126). In addition, about 12 percent of those black family heads with some college education were poor in 1972, as compared to 2 percent for white family heads. Also, 76 percent of low-income blacks compared to 67 percent of low-income whites did not finish high school (U.S. Census, 1973:5). This is an impor-tant fact in our credential-oriented so-ciety, where it is becoming increasingly difficult to manipulate and fully utilize the advantages of a complex social and political system.

POSTSCRIPT: POLITICAL MARGINALITY AND DECOLONIZATION

The situation for third-world groups liv-ing under internal colonialism in the United States has been one characterized by enforced dependency and manifested by lack of command over resources. The dependency builds on itself in a circular fashion over time, for as whites hold out to third-world groups the enticements of the material benefits of the society, third-world groups find themselves economically falling further and further behind, thus diminishing the opportunities to partake of the feast. The only avenue that appears open for third-world peoples is that of vying for the opportunity of becoming one of the few talented "natives" allowed to trickle into the overwhelmingly white middle class. What this means is that the vast majority of members of these minority groups stand still or fall behind as the remainder of the society grows in wealth and affluence. So long as third-world groups are expected to adhere to the notion of mobility being an individualistic, one-at-a-time process, there will be no reduction in the inequality gap.

But minority communities are increasingly aware of the pitfalls inherent in an individualistic model of economic and political advancement. So long as minority group members are forced to become "acceptable" in order to trickle up according to the standards of the white dominant community, there is no real change. The colonial system will remain effective to the degree that the colonizers act in concert as a group, while splintering the colonized, thus forcing them to struggle as individuals. Decolonialization will come with group liberation, not individual mobility.

It is our assessment that the most effective ideological camouflage by which the dominants have been able to thwart the aspirations of the colonized for political and economic development has been through the use of the liberal "social welfare" model. This model posits that the most effective means of creating meaningful social change is to provide the conditions in which people are allowed to "help themselves." The notion of "self-help" is a pernicious and destructive means by which those in the dominant group reinforce the "boot strap" theory of economic and political development. One is expected to make something from nothing, and if one fails, it is the result of personal pathology!

In contradistinction to the perspective which emphasizes the poverty *per se* of the third-world minorities in America, we would suggest that an emphasis upon their *powerlessness* more accurately reflects their position in this society. To emphasize the powerlessness is in no way a denial or attempt to preclude a recognition that a response is also necessary to the poor housing, lack of medical care, sporadic police protection, and other denials inherent in being poor. Rather, a perspective focusing on the issue of power emphasizes that remedial welfare measures will not suffice. The time for band-aids is past. To move beyond treating the third-world peoples as if they themselves constitute a "social problem" requires that attention be given to the political realities which dictate the options for individual and group freedom. As C. W. Mills (1959:149) has noted:

Freedom is not merely the chance to do as one pleases; neither is it merely the opportunity to choose between set alternatives. Freedom is, first of all, the chance to formulate the available choices, to argue over them—and then, the opportunity to choose.

To stress that the third-world minorities have no power is to say they have no options.

It is a central trait of the colonial situation for the colonizers to restrict the options of the colonized. Thus any movement toward the decolonialization of the third-world communities would entail an increase in the options they possess and a corresponding decrease in the ability of dominant whites to dictate the options or "set alternatives." The implications for minority-dominant relations within the United States are profound. As Rubenstein (1970:149–150) suggests for the black community in particular, some of the consequences would be that:

the ghettos be treated, in certain respects, as cities in themselves: that business enterprises and real property within be turned over to black ownership (preferably by community organizations), that control over ghetto schools be vested in school boards representing ghetto parents, that police forces operating in black territory be made directly responsible to those inhabiting that territory, that the stranglehold of white dominated political machines over ghetto life be broken, and that local housing, health, education and welfare programs be administered, wherever possible, by blacks. Each of these proposals, it is recognized, will require serious shifts in the distribution of power in urban areas. Slumlords will be compelled to give up valuable property and businessmen profitable businesses. Urban political machines allied with racketeers will have to abandon a rich vein of political power and graft. An army of welfare workers will be forced to seek other employment and unionized schoolteachers will become responsible to local boards rather than to more acquiescent central authorities.

White resistance to decolonialization will persist, due not only to the very real loss of white authority and power, but also because of the inherent fear whites have of third-world peoples. We suspect that in the minds of many whites, there is a lurking distrust of the possibility of reprisals by third-world peoples should they have the opportunity. The threat of black violence and white fear runs through much of the literature in the late 1960s on the debate over decentralization and why it would not work (cf. Wilson,

1968). It is the chant, perhaps echoing the classical colonialist, that the colonized are not yet sufficiently "developed" to maintain an orderly society.

One consequence of white resistance to decolonialization is that by refusing to move towards the institutionalization (and legitimation) of such conflict, there is, in fact, an exacerbation of the very conflict that is feared. There would no longer be the need for a zero-sum game were whites willing to forego their reliance on cooptation through an apolitical social welfare model of change and instead allow third-world peoples to participate in all areas of decision-making, no longer on the basis of a pseudoconsensus model, but on the realities of legitimate political conflict.

Many whites have bought the social welfare model as the correct means for resolving inequalities between third-world peoples and themselves—failing to realize that this very model effectively "cools out" the political dimensions of decolonialization and thus engenders further dependency. But if the tumultuous events of the 1960s have been a lesson so far as subordinant-dominant relations are concerned, the lesson should be that any attempt to present an apolitical solution to colonialization has proved inadequate in the past and, one can surmise, will continue to do so in the future. As Horowitz and Liebowitz (1968:21) note:

The welfare solution has not erased the consequences of having a growing number of disaffected people in the midst of general affluence. Indeed, the very existence of affluence on so wide a scale creates demands that parallel those made by the "poor nations" on the "rich nations." Because of this, a political attempt to solve the problem is bound to emerge. If this attempt is not initiated from above within the legitimate political or electoral apparatus, it will be generated from below and probably take illegitimate para-military forms.

The emergence of an increased consciousness within the communities of third-world peoples suggests a political solution may be in the making, and a moment's reflection reveals it has not come from above through the "political or electoral apparatus." The gap between the rhetoric and reality of America is growing wider, week by week, and day by day. An answer to the realities of colonialization has to be found. The question remains when and how.

References

Acuña, Rodolfo. *Occupied America: The Chicano's Struggle toward Liberation.* San Francisco: Canfield Press, 1972.

Bahr, Howard M. "An End to Invisibility." In Howard M. Bahr, Bruce A. Chadwick, and Robert C. Day (Eds.), *Native Americans Today: Sociological Perspectives.* New York: Harper & Row, 1972.

Bahr, Howard M., Chadwick, Bruce A., and Day, Robert C. (Eds.). *Native Americans Today: Sociological Perspectives.* New York: Harper & Row, 1972.

Blauner, Robert. "Internal Colonialism and Ghetto Revolt." *Social Problems,* 1969, 16, 393–408.

Blauner, Robert. *Racial Oppression in America.* New York: Harper & Row, 1972.

Burma, John H. (Ed.). *Mexican-Americans in the United States.* Cambridge, Mass.: Schenkman, 1970.

Cahn, Edgar S., (Ed.). *Our Brother's Keeper: The Indian in White America.* New York: New Community Press, 1969.

Camp, Robert C. "Minority Business and the New Economy." *Black Enterprise,* 1972, 3, 55–58.

Dillard, J. L. *Black English: Its History and Usage in the United States.* New York: Vintage, 1973.

Domhoff, G. William. *The Higher Circles: The Governing Class in America.* New York: Vintage, 1971.

Galbraith, John Kenneth. *Economics and the Public Purpose.* Boston: Houghton Mifflin, 1973.

Gayles, J. N., Jr. "Health, Brutality and the Black Cycle." *The Black Scholar,* 1974, 5, 2–9.

Gossett, Thomas F. *Race: The History of an Idea in America.* New York: Schocken Books, 1971.

Gouldner, Alvin. *The Coming Crisis in Western Sociology.* New York: Basic Books, 1970.

Horowitz, Irving Louis. *Three Worlds of Development.* New York: Oxford, 1972.

Horowitz, Irving Louis, and Liebowitz, Martin. "Social Deviance and Political Marginality: Toward a Redefinition of the Relation between Sociology and Politics." *Social Problems,* 1968, 15, 280–296.

Javits, Jacob. "Hunger in America." *Playboy,* December 1969, 107–112.

Lewis, Oscar. "The Culture of Poverty." *Scientific American,* 1966, 215, 16–25.

Lipset, Seymour M. *The First New Nation: The United States in Historical and Comparative Perspective.* New York: Basic Books, 1963.

Mason, Philip. *Patterns of Dominance.* New York: Oxford, 1971.

McNickle, D'Arcy. *Native American Tribalism.* New York: Oxford, 1973.

Memmi, Albert. *The Colonizer and the Colonized.* New York: Orion Press, 1965.

Miller, S. M., and Roby, Pamela. *The Future of Inequality.* New York: Basic Books, 1970.

Mills, C. W. *The Sociological Imagination.* New York: Oxford, 1959.

Newman, William M. *American Pluralism: A Study of Minority Groups and Social Theory.* New York: Harper & Row, 1973.

Ortega, Philip D. "The Education of Mexican Americans." In Edward Ludwig and James Sontibanez (Eds.), *The Chicanos: Mexican American Voices.* Baltimore: Penguin, 1972.

Rainwater, Lee. "The Problem of Lower Class Culture." *Journal of Social Issues,* 1970, 26, 133–48.

Reid, Inez Smith. *"Together" Black Women.* New York: Emerson Hall Publishers, 1972.

Reissman, Leonard. *Inequality in American Society: Social Stratification.* Glenview, Ill,: Scott, Foresman, 1973.

Rist, Ray C. *The Quest for Autonomy: A Socio-Historical Study of Black Revolt in Detroit.* Los Angeles: Caas Publishers, 1972.

Rist, Ray C. *The Urban School: A Factory for Failure.* Cambridge, Mass.: MIT Press, 1973.

Rubenstein, Richard E. *Rebels in Eden: Mass Political Violence in the United States.* Boston: Little, Brown, 1970.

Simpson, George Eaton, and Yinger, J.

Milton. *Racial and Cultural Minorities: An Analysis of Prejudice and Discrimination.* New York: Harper & Row, 1972.

Thurow, Lester C. *Poverty and Discrimination.* Washington, D.C.: The Brookings Institute, 1969.

Time, July 1, 1974, 47.

Tocqueville, Alexis de. *Democracy in America,* trans. by Henry Reeve. New Rochelle, N.Y.: Arlington House, 1969.

U.S. Bureau of the Census. *Current Population Reports,* Series P-60, No. 91, "Characteristics of Low-Income Population: 1972." Washington, D.C.: U.S. Government Printing Office, 1973.

Wilson, J. (Ed.). *The Metropolitan Enigma.* Cambridge, Mass.: Harvard University Press, 1968.

Suggested Reading

ACUÑA, RUDOLFO. *Occupied America: The Chicano's Struggle toward Liberation.* San Francisco: Canfield Press, 1972.

The most comprehensive historical and contemporary account of the position of the Chicano in American society presented within the context of the internal colonialism framework.

BLAUNER, ROBERT. *Racial Oppression in America.* New York: Harper & Row, 1972.

An in-depth discussion of the notion of internal colonialism as it is applicable to the American context.

CAHN, EDGAR. (Ed.). *Our Brother's Keeper: The Indian in White America.* New York: New Community Press, 1969.

An extensive account of the current conditions of the Native American. A vivid example of white internal colonialism.

CESAIRE, AIME. *Discourse on Colonialism.* New York: Monthly Review Press, 1972.

A detailed and provoking discussion of the concept of colonialism by a major political figure for the West Indies.

CLARK, KENNETH. *Dark Ghetto: Dilemmas of Social Power.* New York: Harper & Row, 1965.

An account of the Harlem community in New York City and the manner in which this community is exploited by outside interests.

COX, OLIVER. *Caste, Class and Race.* New York: Doubleday, 1948.
A classic examination of the position of the black in American society. Argues from a Marxian position that black people form a separate caste which is created and sustained by whites.

PIVEN, FRANCIS, AND CLOWARD, RICHARD. *Regulating the Poor: The Functions of Public Welfare.* New York: Pantheon Books, 1971.
A damning critique of the way in which public welfare is used as a means of controlling and subduing the poor.

RUBENSTEIN, RICHARD. *Rebels in Eden: Mass Political Violence in the United States.* Boston: Little, Brown, 1970.
Extends the notion of exploitation and dependency to a number of groups in American society and then traces out their resistance through the political use of violence.

WILLHELM, SIDNEY. *Who Needs the Negro?* Cambridge, Mass.: Schenkman, 1970.
An examination of the political and economic marginality of the black in American society. Argues as economic and technological spheres continue to change, the colonized black falls further behind and becomes more irrelevant, thus becoming more vulnerable to white exploitation.

Sexism

Everyone's Social Problem

Jane E. Prather

Sexism refers to the practices or beliefs in a society which limit behavior, goals, or expectations because of the individual's sexual status.[1] In contemporary America, sexual status to a great extent defines which roles one should play, what emotions a person displays, what goals he/she should pursue, and what behavior should be emphasized or hidden. In some other societies caste or age or social status is even more important than sex for defining how people should act.

Sexism is a social problem because society establishes the appropriate ways of behaving for each sex. The individual growing up in a society learns these sex role expectations and learns she/he is rewarded when her/his behavior corresponds to the expectations. It is usually groups that deny privileges to a person because of sexual status. In addition, sexism is a social problem because it is found throughout all institutions of society, and it is only through changing them that sexism can be eliminated.

[1] Sex, in contrast to gender, refers to categorizing of an individual based upon biological factors such as anatomy, chromosomes, and hormones. Gender, on the other hand, refers to categorizing of an individual based upon social factors such as behavior, dress, mannerisms. Sex refers to an ascribed identity while gender refers to an acquired identity. The difficulty with using sex and gender interchangeably is that in American society there is an assumption that gender is determined by biological factors rather than social factors. In this chapter, the tie between sex and gender, or sex-role expectations, is assumed to be primarily cultural and social rather than biological. When biological differences between the sexes are socially significant, it will be pointed out.

The cost of limiting an individual's behavior solely on the basis of sexual category is high for both men and women. Men in the U.S. have a shorter life expectancy than women and also men in most other urban, industrialized societies (Sullerot, 1971:45–51). For example, a boy born in 1970 in the U.S. can expect to live an average of 66 years, while a girl born the same year is expected to live 74 years. In Sweden, men's life expectancy is 71.6 years, compared to an average of 75.7 years for Swedish women. Thus, in Sweden the differential life expectancy is approximately four years, while in the U.S. the difference averages eight years. Obviously biological consequences of being born male or female cannot account for the increased longevity of men in Sweden in contrast to that of men in the U.S. Instead, sociocultural factors—such as the fact that men and women occupy more of an equalitarian position in Sweden than they do in the U.S.—may account for these life expectancy differences. For example, psychologist Sidney Jourard argues that the roles of American men are lethal because men are not allowed self-disclosure—to freely express emotions, to display fear, to cry, or to admit failure (Jourard, 1971). One can only speculate on how much more creative men might be in the areas of music, poetry, art, and drama if they were freely encouraged to participate in these activities without threat to their masculinity.

For women, the cost of sexism is high

personally, economically, and politically. Women, regardless of their qualifications or job level, earn less than men. The U.S. Bureau of Labor (1969:133) Statistics estimates that women earn 60 percent of what men do and this difference has been increasing rather than decreasing during the past decade. According to the U.S. Bureau of Commerce (1970), the average salaries earned by full-time, year-round workers in 1970 were as follows:

White men	$9,375
Nonwhite men	6,598
White women	5,490
Nonwhite women	4,674

When advancement possibilities, fringe benefits, and retirement programs are compared, women fare far worse than do men.

Politically, as well as economically, women are at an extreme disadvantage. At local, state, and national levels, women are not visible in leadership positions. Despite some noteworthy attempts to promote change politically, few female candidates run for office. A recent issue of *Time* magazine, for example, featured 200 future leaders in the United States—for the 1980s. Only 18 women were represented.

Using a variety of mental health indices—admission to mental health clinics and hospitals, attempted suicides, visits to psychiatrists—women seem to suffer more mental health problems than men since World War II (cf. Barnard, 1972; Bart, 1970; Chesler, 1972; Gove and Tudor, 1973). These tensions appear even more pronounced among married women than single women, which has led Jessie Bernard (1972) to argue that marriage insulates men from various mental tensions while it accentuates tension for women. Women report more frequently than men that they experienced marital disillusionment because their imagined image of marriage was quite different from the actual experience. Sexist beliefs foster a greater commitment to marriage and family for women than for men and perpetuate a belief that familial experiences will be a very fulfilling dimension of women's lives but not men's.

A high psychological cost of sexism for women has been in the area of self-image. Women report having less self-esteem and self-confidence than do men (McKee and Sherriffs, 1957, 1959), and both men and women believe that men lead more fulfilling lives than women.

Thus, as will be shown throughout this article, the consequences of sexism have effects upon everyone—men and women. Although many of the groups have focused predominantly upon altering women's roles, more and more supporters in this social movement are pointing out the need for changes in men's roles as well.

CAUSAL FACTOR I: OUTMODED ROLE EXPECTATIONS

The Role of Biological Factors

In American society, children receive outmoded messages which define their adult roles as men and women. Different messages are sent to boys than to girls presumably because of sex differences; yet, within the past century, technology has diminished these differences. There are probably two important biological differences between human males and females: (1) men have, on the average, more musculature and physical strength than women, and (2) women bear and nurse children.

Regarding the first factor, the greater physical strength of men, modern society, with its automation and mechanization, has only a few jobs with physical strength as their principal prerequisite. Those differences, then, are not crucial for determining which sex can perform most tasks. For example, even in such traditionally strenuous occupations as mining and construction, women have demonstrated that they can perform the job when given the opportunity. Physical Performance Tests bar women from applying for many jobs where physical skill would rarely be required for meeting the daily work assignment. One California community recently hired women as fire fighters after several never-used physical strength requirements were eliminated. It should be pointed out that the belief that women are physically weak is recent. Throughout history, and in many societies in the world today, women have been and are expected to perform many physically demanding tasks such as transporting heavy burdens and carrying water (Murdock, 1935).

In highly prestigious and responsible positions such as that of corporate executive, physician, or university president, skills in communication, organization, decision-making, and human relations are requisite. Still, women competing against men for these jobs are often at a disadvantage, presumably because they do not meet the qualifications. Yet, there is no empirical evidence to show that women are less capable than men in performing these tasks.

The second important biological difference between men and women modified by technology is that women bear and nurse children. Technology now helps women to control their reproductive functions and to shorten or eliminate the time engaged in nursing infants. A woman engaging in regular sexual intercourse without use of any form of birth control is estimated to become pregnant every two years throughout her reproductive years (Bullough, 1974:326). Although not every pregnancy results in a live birth, the process of continual reproduction can be physically debilitating. Technology has increased women's life expectancy through safer childbirth procedures and through improved birth control measures which allow for the limiting and spacing of births. Now that a woman can control the number of pregnancies initiated, her life is less heavily tied to these biological functions. The development of artificial formula, vulcanized rubber for bottle nipples, and inexpensive ways of processing food for infants—all these have drastically shortened the time engaged in feeding an infant (cf. Bullough, 1974). Previously women nursed infants for one to two years. These technological discoveries have also had the significant effect of allowing persons other than the biological mother to be able to feed and rear a child.

Because advances in technology and medical sciences have diminished the effect of biological sex differences, sex role expectations based predominantly upon these differences are outmoded. Cultural beliefs, attitudes, stereotypes, and socialization messages about the appropriate roles for men and women often do not reflect these technological changes. In the remaining part of this section, the ways in which boys and girls grow up learning societal expectations about adult sex roles will be explored, followed by a discussion of the discrepancies which emerge between the role children expect to fill and the roles they actually experience as adult men and women.

The Socialization of Jill and Jack

Sexism begins at birth when usually the first question asked is, "What is the sex of the baby?" Sex determines a whole range of immediate and future events such as: the kind of name the child will receive, what toys relatives will give, the color of the nursery, and the style of clothing worn.

In some societies, the sex even determines whether or not the parents want the child to live. A recent newspaper article contained a picture of two children in India. They were twins, but of different sexes. The boy was healthy, robust, and well-fed, while the girl was suffering from severe malnutrition. The Indian parents had decided that it was more important for the boy to survive the famine than the girl. In India, as in some other areas of the world, the boy is regarded as an economic asset who may be able to improve the family's status or wealth, while the girl is viewed as a liability who can rarely make a significant economic contribution to the family. Although in American society, we may be shocked over such practices, we, too, share some of the same beliefs. Studies reveal that Americans prefer male babies and that prospective parents more often hope their first child will be a boy (Etzioni, 1968:1107–1112).

At birth, then, the "pink and blue" process begins. There are strong societal taboos against boys wearing clothing that might in any way, either through color, style, or decoration, be considered feminine. Girls have more latitude in crossing sex lines in their clothing. Dressing a young child in sex-specific styles is one of the very few ways of identifying the gender. There appears to be even more emphasis upon identifying the sex of the infant via clothing during recent decades than previously. Photographs of infants at the turn of the century show both boys and girls dressed in identical smocks and wearing long curly hair. During the past decade it has not been uncommon for parents to differentiate the sex of a newborn by placing a bow on the forehead of a female baby or by dressing an infant boy in plastic pants with fly fronts.

Although there are many items of clothing that are interchangeable between boys and girls, there can be slight differences in style, color, or decoration which, as some parents have complained, necessitate the purchasing of separate sets of clothing. There are also differences in durability. Girl-only clothes are more likely to be restrictive and binding and of a delicate fabric that is easily damaged or soiled. Thus, the stereotypes that girls are delicate, dainty, and neat and that boys are vigorous, rough, and dirty are often reinforced in early childhood through clothing.

Children's toys also reflect sex differences. Toys are designed for boys, for girls, or for either sex. A stroll through any toy store will reveal that packaging and advertising of toys reinforces notions of which sex should want each toy. Chemistry sets, astronaut outfits, and doctor kits—all are illustrated with boys; while girls are shown playing with make-up kits, doll houses, and jewelry boxes. One toy catalog illustrated a toy kitchen busily occupied by several girls with one boy sitting at a table, being served by a girl. By age three, boys and girls begin to select appropriate sex-linked toys, with girls being freer to select a "boy toy" than a boy is to choose a "girl toy" (Kagan, 1964a). Lower classes have been shown to be stricter than middle classes in reinforcing children's selection of the appropriate sex-linked toy or activity (Kagan, 1964b; Rabban, 1950). Lower-class fathers express vehemently their abhorrence of any form of "sissyish" behavior from their sons. Why are fathers more perturbed than mothers when children do not play with sex-stereotyped toys? One explanation is that the father's own masculinity is threatened or questioned if his son does not consistently adhere to masculine activities and toys.

Through toys, games, and play, children learn various skills, attributes, and values. If a child only plays with sex-specific toys, he or she is only gaining the skills of one adult role, a role which in many cases is highly stereotyped and outmoded. Both boys and girls can learn aspects of the parenting role by playing with dolls, yet often the only dolls considered to be appropriate for boys emphasize warlike or adventure activities, not the loving and caring for an infant. Although the tool chest or erector set could be beneficial for both girls and boys in learning to manipulate tools, there is a societal assumption that only boys will want these toys.

In children's mass media—comics, TV cartoons, movies—major characters are more likely to be male than female. In an unpublished study by this author, TV cartoons were found to have girls as major characters only one-fourth of the time, while boys, men, or male animals were the central figures the rest of the time. Boys and men did the exciting adventuresome activities while girls acted like scaredy cats!

Children's songs, nursery rhymes, and fairy tales abound with sexist messages. No child could mistake the theme of the rhyme that boys are made of "snakes, snails, and puppy dog tails" and girls are made of "sugar and spice and everything nice." Via fairy tales, a child learns that a woman should look weak and helpless in order to be protected by a gallant man, who validates his love for her through bold and adventuresome actions. The love of the charming prince and the beautiful princess is not based upon what they do together or even what they say, but rather on how attractive they both perceive each other to be. This message is particularly insidious for women because it implies that a woman should focus *only* upon being attractive in order to interest a man. In fairy tales, marriage is stereotyped as a blissful relationship created and perpetuated via romantic love, and enduring until death occurs.

There is speculation that parents treat sons differently from daughters. Empirical verification of these differences is difficult to obtain because the data is either gathered from parents' recall of how they treated their children, from children's recall of how they were treated by their parents, or from direct observations of how parents and children interact. (For an extensive review of this literature, see Maccoby and Jacklin, 1974). Differences between parental treatment of infant boys and girls as young as six weeks have been reported when parents were observed to cuddle girls and speak to them more frequently than boys (Goldberg and Lewis, 1969). Additional observational studies of parental interaction with infants, however, do not consistently reveal sex differences in warmth, affection, or touching (Maccoby and Jacklin, 1974:312–316). Numerous studies have sought to verify that boys are given more freedom to express aggression than are girls (Maccoby, 1966). The evidence is difficult to assess since there are differences concerning what constitutes aggression and how it is measured.

Consistent differences in childrearing do occur in two areas: chaperoning and physical punishment. Both boys and girls, when young, are limited in their independence and are frequently required to specify where they are and with whom (Maccoby, 1972). However, as children mature, parents are much more likely to be concerned about their daughter's than their son's location, and girls are more frequently subjected to chaperones than are boys (Newson and Newson, 1968). Girls report that parents gave them less privacy than their brothers in such areas as phone calls and letters received (Komarovsky, 1950). It has been documented that parents are more likely to subject their sons than their daughters to physical punishment (Maccoby and Jacklin, 1974:330–35). This differential treatment appears to be based on a feeling that boys need or are better able to tolerate physical punishment than are girls. This finding perhaps illustrates that parents feel masculinity requires the ability to take physical punishment.

Parents may also have different expectations concerning how boys and girls should act and hence reinforce behavior along the lines of these expectations. In American society there is an assumption that boys are much more physically active, inquisitive, and curious than girls, yet recent studies do not find clear cut sex differences in the amount of activity or exploratory behavior (Pedersen and Bell, 1970).

Boys and girls also learn about adult roles through observing their parents as models. One study of boys,[2] ages 8–11 from both middle and lower classes, found that boys felt parents expected them to be noisy, dirty, and messy. Boys were not to be like girls, cry babies or softies. The boys' images of adult women were not positive, as they perceived women as cleaning up messes, keeping things neat, and considering household chores a drudgery. According to the boys, women did these tasks because that's all they could do! On the other hand, men were seen by the boys as being very important to the household, being more fun than their mothers, and having more freedom than mothers to do what they wanted to do (Hartley, 1959).

Schools, too, promote sexism in a variety of ways. In textbooks, as in other children's books, the majority of characters are boys or men (Weitzman, 1972). More telling are the comments made about women. For instance, one primer had the comment, "Look at her, Mother, just look at her. She is just like a girl. She gives up!" (Hagan, 1970). Even animal stories differentiate the sexes: whether human or animal, males are presented as doing the exciting, adventuresome things while females are shown helping others and participating in more sedentary activities. Girls' ideas were either ignored or discounted in favor of those initiated by boys. Parental roles are also subject to sexism, with mothers doing housework and preparing meals, while fathers are "coming home" or playing with sons.

School systems are structured in a sexist manner in that the majority of ele-

[2] This particular study illustrates a common sexist bias found in sociological research, the bias of interviewing only boys. Throughout the social sciences one finds studies conducted with only male subjects and focusing only on male issues (Stoll, 1973:69).

mentary school teachers are women while the majority of principals, administrators, and college and university professors are men. The elementary school boy is often believed to suffer severely from this environment, particularly if there is emphasis upon obedience, neatness, and quietness (for discussion of femininity in schools see Howe, 1971; Sexton, 1969). Teachers report more prohibitions and disapproval statements in harsh or angry tones to boys than to girls (Meyer and Thompson, 1963; Sears and Feldman, 1974). At higher education levels the female students report put-down statements and professors' disapproval of their being students, such as, "You're so cute. I can't see you as a professor of anything," or, "A pretty girl like you will certainly get married; why don't you stop with an M.A." (Harris, 1974).

Boys frequently face a double bind in schools. Among peers, trying to excel in the classroom may be considered sissyish; yet to compete effectively for academic programs, academic achievement is necessary. In addition, the boy may be encouraged to excel in athletics at the expense of his academic pursuits. However, as one student complained to the writer, the stereotype of the brawny, but not brainy, athlete is very detrimental to the boy. Since he was not expected to be a good student, he strove for only minimal academic achievement.

Traditionally, school systems train boys and girls for different adult roles and different career orientations. Physical education, home management, drafting, have all been courses which have been established as sex-specific courses. Even when there have been attempts to open traditional sex-specific classes such as home economics or shop to the other sex, the classes are often not equivalent.

For example, classes in home economics could be integrated, instead of the creation of special male classes such as "bachelor living" or "chefs' classes" (Van Deventer and Bathurst, 1974). However, upon reaching high school, many students have already received such a large amount of sexist socialization that even if offered the opportunity to take sex-specific courses, they have lost the interest and skills to participate in these classes. Although recent federal government regulations forbid segregating on the basis of sex any class except sex education, it remains to be seen if there is enforcement of such regulations. Perhaps no other area of education shows sexism as much as physical education, where the amount of money, equipment, and instructors provided for athletic events for boys far surpasses that for girls. The federal government policies trying to decrease this difference have met with strong resistance and ridicule in many school systems. Counselors and advisors in schools, especially elementary and high schools, are shown to be sex stereotyped in their advice to males and females (Naffziger and Naffziger, 1974). In short, the philosophy of many school systems is probably similar to that expressed by a prominent director and founder of a national chain of private schools: "I run schools for boys, and girls may attend."

From the role models of parents, the influence of peers, the socialization messages, mass media and schools, boys and girls grow up with strong images about their appropriate roles as adults. Sex role messages imply that there are many things which girls physically and emotionally *cannot* do, and that boys can do anything, but there are many things they *should not* do. The consequence for girls is low self-esteem and inadequacy feelings, and for boys, a fear that they need constantly to monitor their behavior to verify that they are not doing any of the prohibited activities which might lead to a questioning of their masculinity.

By knowing the sex of a child at its birth, one can then make some predictions about whether or not the child learns to play football or to jump rope, takes elementary education or engineering courses in college, and if the child will be encouraged to get married soon after college or to enter business. The expectations for these events are different for Jill and for Jack.

Discrepancies in Women's Roles

Besides exaggerating and idealizing the adult sex roles, the socialization messages are for the most part incongruent with reality. In the remaining part of this section, the discrepancies between expected and actual sex roles of men and women will be explored.

MOTHERHOOD   Most American girls receive a complex of notions about women's lives, including the belief that motherhood provides the maximum self-fulfillment. When girls fantasize about motherhood, they are most likely to envision caring for a beautiful, clean baby. One critic argues that in our society we "reinforce babies as the sine qua non of existence" (Peck, 1971:65).

The life expectancy of women has increased at the same time that the number of years spent completely engaged in child-rearing has decreased. A baby girl born in 1970 in the United States is estimated to have a life expectancy of 74 years. More women now marry at age 18 than at any other age and have their last child by age 28. This means that for over 35 years of her lifetime, the woman is not primarily engaged in child-rearing. In addition, with improved contraceptives and with increasing desirability to control the number of children they have, women are opting for fewer children than did their grandmothers.

Women who exclusively identify with the motherhood role may encounter severe problems when their children finally leave home. Interviewing middle-aged women hospitalized for severe depression, Bart (1971) discovered that the onset of the depression was frequently caused by a change in a familial relationship. Most of the women identified only with their role as mother, and with their children grown and on their own, this role was without a purpose. When they were asked what accomplishments they were proud of during their lifetime, they listed accomplishments of others— their sons and daughters and their husbands. None listed any personal achievements. The living of a vicarious identity through family members is detrimental not only for the woman, but also for her children and husband. Levy found children suffered when they not only had to satisfy their own achievement needs but also to fulfill the accomplishment needs of their mothers (Levy, 1943).

Parenthood is reported to be a crisis for both men and women, with women reporting the most drastic change in their lives (Le Masters, 1970; Rossi, 1971). With the birth of a child, the woman usually relinquishes involvement in career or school, in contrast to her husband who usually does not experience the same drastic changes in his own lifestyle. The urban woman today may face a greater crisis during pregnancy than did her mother or grandmother, particularly if the latter lived in a rural area. A rural woman could continue her work on the farm regardless of her pregnancy (Turner, 1970:368). And a half-century ago, she was much more likely to be prepared for motherhood than today's middle-class woman, because she had experience in taking care of siblings and other younger children. These experiences are less common in today's small nuclear families.

Child-rearing may be more stressful for the urban wife than the rural counterpart of a generation ago. In contrast to the women in rural areas, the women in urban, particularly suburban, areas are usually solely responsible for the daily care of their children and are not likely to have extended families or close neighbors on whom they can rely for help. In urban settings children are not free to roam large distances from home; in some cases they even need adult supervision to go a block away from home or down the apartment elevator (cf. Barker and Wright, 1964).

A study of mothers in six different cultures (Minturn and Lambert, 1964) found that American mothers were the only mothers expected to supervise their children closely with little relief from any other adult. Perhaps because of the tension and frustration from this intense supervision, the American mothers reported that the best time of the day was when their children were in bed! According to Jessie Bernard (1974), only modern industrial societies can afford to allow an adult in a family to devote a life to caring for and rearing children and not be engaged in economic pursuits. Although one might argue that as societies became wealthy, mothers should engage in full-time child-rearing for the benefit of the children, a more plausible explanation is that the nonemployed wife is a status

symbol for the husband supporting her who now can say, "My wife doesn't have to work." The guilt arising from not enjoying full-time mothering or because of seeking employment is particular to the middle-class white woman. The wealthy have been able to hire childcare, and the poor have required the woman to be employed in order for the family to survive. The middle-class woman, then, is the one most likely to find a lack of community or familial support for her desire to be more than a full-time mother.

In summary, many of the responsibilities the contemporary mother faces in child-rearing—such as supervising younger children for hours, chauffering older children, and participating in organizations for planning children's activities—may be unrelated to the expectations, fantasies, and preparations for the motherhood role that the woman envisioned. Instead, the fulfillment expected in motherhood may be heavily diluted by the frustrations and tensions of child-rearing in a highly urbanized society.

THE MARRIAGE GAP   A second gap between the expected role of women and the reality is in marriage. In American society marriage is viewed as a lifetime commitment, an institution that women need much more than men, and an experience that creates an important, fulfilling role for women. For many American girls there is a Cinderella fantasy of finding an adoring, loving prince who will provide for and protect them. However, here again the marital roles have changed. Although 97 percent of all Americans marry sometime during their lifetime, American society is also one of the few modern societies where women and men marry at very early ages. Yet the most successful marriages are those that occur at ages later than the median age of marriage (Lasswell, 1974). With the increasing life span, there is the possibility of many couples being married for over 50 years. The notion that men and women would remain married for a lifetime is subjected to the pressures of high expectations for a meaningful, not just survivable marriage, highly differentiated roles of marital partners, and the lack of strong community supports for preserving marriages. Although divorce is still stigmatized, most Americans would probably agree that it is better to divorce than to be miserably married. Bertrand Russell (1929) argued that dissatisfaction with a marital partner is higher where there is a contrast between possible partners. That is, in a society where most of the women and men are very similar, there is less feeling that changing partners would be exciting or meaningful. However, in a very urban, mobile society where one can meet quite different people, there is present a feeling that another partner might be more interesting than the current mate. In fact, one sociologist claims American mate selection has "permanent availability," meaning that one can continually search for new partners regardless of any partner's current marital status (Farber, 1964).

Another difficulty which women may experience in their marital roles that differs from their expectations is that of not having or not exercising power in the family. As Jessie Bernard points out, "there is no research proof that equalitarianism has been increasing" (1972:127). Upper-middle-class couples are likely to believe they are equal partners in the family, yet in the actual operation of the family, the husband exercises much more power than the wife. The high status of the upper-middle-class husband in the work situation carries over to give him more status in the family than his wife (Wilensky, 1961). In blue-collar families the ideology that the husband is the head of the family often prevails, but in practice the wife has more power than her middle-class counterpart because the gap between the potential earning power of the blue-collar family wife and her husband is less (Martinson, 1970:119–120).

What appears to be a crucial determinant of family power is the economic earning capacity of each partner. Poloma and Garland (1971), however, found that among couples with dual professions, if the wife's earning capacity is greater than her husband's, she often compensates for this differential by strongly asserting that he is head of the household and by assuming more family and household responsibilities than her husband assumes. Not only is the power differential caused by the fact that few women (even with the same training) receive the same work opportunity as their husbands, but also that most women agree that they would select a partner to whom they can look up—who is taller, older, or more educated than they are (cf. Bernard, 1972; Rossi, 1965). Hence, few couples even select each other from an equalitarian perspective. Moreover, family studies have shown the wife tends to lose power and her husband to gain it as the couple progresses through the family life cycle (cf. Lewis, 1972; Safilios-Rothschild, 1972). American couples believe in and practice what might be called the male ego mystique. Folklore asserts that men's egos need to be protected and expanded, not just by the man himself, but also by the women who interact with him. Thus, the status of the man's ego becomes a woman's as well as a man's problem. Her ego, on the other hand, is likely to be treated, according to the folklore, as her problem.

The gap between the expected and actual role in marriage occurs when the woman finds that neither will she necessarily be provided for economically throughout her lifetime, nor will she find, in many cases, the high expectations of love, excitement, and fulfillment she may have hoped for in marriage. Since many women move from the protection of their father's house to that of their husband's, they are unprepared for the experience of living alone, dealing with financial matters, or economically providing for themselves—experiences they encounter with divorce, widowhood, or remaining single. In a traditional socialization, the woman is not prepared for any status other than marital status.

Discrepancies in Male Roles

While women envision their adult lives as being happily married and joyously involved with parenthood, men are taught to give work their first priority and their familial and marital roles a lower priority. Discrepancies in male roles thus occur in these two areas—work and family—where boys receive messages about these adult roles which are inapplicable to their adult experiences.

WORK   In early socialization, boys learn to have a ready answer to the question, "What do you want to be when you grow up?" In contrast to girls, who may answer the question by listing marriage and motherhood, the boy who responded he wanted to be a daddy would probably be ridiculed.

Boys learn that work involves time and commitment. In fact, men are rewarded for becoming so dedicated to their work

that they sacrifice all other interests (Slater, 1970:72). Work then is not perceived as a choice for men but rather an unquestioned duty. The message that for men work is essential, while it is optional for women, gives work a masculine connotation in American society. Work becomes that activity requiring one vigorously to attack, compete, strive, and achieve; the man who does not work is not only considered deviant, but his sexuality and masculinity may also be questioned.

The discrepancy between the expectations about work and the actual experiences of it partly occurs because the meaning of work is changing in American society. Boys may fantasize adventuresome, exciting, even dangerous activities on their future jobs, such as putting out fires, performing a critical operation, or saving the life of a circus tiger. The majority of jobs that a child perceives are not that common. Rarely do children see adults at work preparing memos, answering phone calls, or dictating letters. In fact, what the child conceptualizes as important work may sometimes be a low status occupation by societal standards.

Another discrepancy in the real versus expected work world is the definition of success. While the boy may consider success as accomplishing something or creating a better way of doing something, in adult life, success may indicate only the ability to surpass coworkers.

Traditionally, the man is expected to derive identity and pride from his work. Yet in contemporary American society, work is often alienating, meaningless, routine, or degrading. The man may find he feels powerless over his work, about the pace of work, or the quality of the product. Automation and specialization have created many tedious and repetitive jobs. As one assembly line worker stated to a sociology class, "I put the locks in car doors. The only variety in my job is when my partner and I switch sides—he does the right hand doors, while I do the left hand ones."

Even in the high status occupations, the man experiences alienation. His decisions may be inconsequential, or they may not be actualized. In addition, he may feel he does not receive credit for his efforts. All these problems are intensified because of the long chain of bureaucratic channels which plague contemporary organizations. With emphasis upon following procedures through multilevels of organizations, the worker loses his/her creativity and individuality. Competition for top positions in organizations may impose dehumanizing conditions such as long hours, frequent moves, excessive travel, or intense pressure. As technology advances in a highly specialized society, the man may find that within a short period of time his career, his skills, and training are outdated, and he is surpassed by someone much younger and with less experience.

American society via its socialization messages to boys perpetuates the protestant ethic that one should work hard to validate moral character and that one is successful who works hard. Yet despite how hard one works, many jobs for the worker are dead-end positions with few if any promotional possibilities.

FAMILY ROLES Traditionally men may have envisioned the father or husband role as very prestigious, in which they were revered by wife and children. In a modern industrialized society, education often creates deep generation gaps between adults and children. The young do not necessarily revere the old, and the father does not, on the basis of his status, necessarily obtain respect.

There is less importance placed upon being a father who relates well to his children. The notion of a family man once connoted a man engrossed in activities centered around the family; now the term family man is often reduced to mean only being a good provider for his family (cf. Brenton, 1966). Wives, too, perceive the man's responsibility as breadwinner surpassing in importance all other aspects of being a father or husband (Lopata, 1971:91).

In urban society, work and family may be in direct competition, for a man is pressured to commit his energy and attention to his career first. The smallness of today's nuclear family means that it can be transported to follow the husband's career. Family activities for a highly committed career man may interfere with his work or be seen as too inconsequential to merit his time. *Time-with-family* acquires the meaning of *time-away-from-work*. The man may possibly receive a bonus or at least recognition for additional time spent at work, but not for time at home.

Time-at-home does not necessarily mean the husband is participating in family or household activities. Instead, his time-at-home can acquire the dimension of being "R & R" time—rest and recuperation which is needed to prepare for the vigorous schedule of the next work-day or to recover from the alienation of work (cf. Goode, 1963). Since the husband's time is considered so important for economic status, the husband may devote less time to the family and delegate more family responsibilities and household tasks to his wife or others.

Among upper-middle-class families, Seeley et al. (1963) found the family hired someone to do household tasks that had previously been performed by the husband. Now his career was too demanding to allow time for him to do many household tasks or repairs. However, in order to pay for the work done, the husband now had to work ever harder than before. The man's significance to his family became greater when he was away at work than when he was at home.

In addition to the direct competition between home and work in the urban society, the skills that the man needs to emphasize at work may be antithetical to those he needs to demonstrate at home. The man may feel he is expected to be aggressive, domineering, assertive, rational, or unemotional at work; however, at home he is expected to display other characteristics such as being warm, understanding, compassionate, and tender. This emotional conflict has been described as leading to "the inexpressive male," particularly with women. According to this perspective, male models for relating to women fall into two categories —the playboy or the cowboy. The playboy is sophisticated in seducing women but does not risk becoming close with any one partner; the cowboy is strong, silent but awkward around women, as he cannot allow himself to express tender emotions since that is not considered masculine (Balwick and Peek, 1971).

In summary, both men and women today experience discrepancy between their expected adulthood and their actual roles. Lives of men and women today appear more complex and stressful than those of their parents. The roles of husband and wife, and mother and father, often require different behavior in today's family than in the families which men and women observed as children. The roles, although functional in a traditional society, are not viable in a modern urban society. Nevertheless, our socialization for familial roles is often still geared towards preparing children for the esteemed traditional roles.

CAUSAL FACTOR II: INSTITUTIONS PERPETUATING SEXISM

A second causal factor in the perpetuation of sexist practices is institutionalized sexism. In the United States the top positions of most major organizations are occupied by men, and if there are any women in the organization, they occupy only bottom-rung positions. To understand how institutional sexism operates, one needs to find why women don't make it to the top level.

As discussed in earlier sections, both boys and girls grow up in this society with the impression that men are employed and women are not. Children are raised with the images of men as leaders and women as helpers or followers. These images become norms, expectations supported by beliefs that women cannot handle and do not seek leadership positions.

Another aspect of this socialization is that boys are more likely than girls to develop leadership skills through participation in games and competitive sports. Girls usually lead other girls and younger children—not male peers. Thus, as girls reach adulthood they are well socialized into accepting, if not believing, that men should occupy leadership positions and that they cannot.

What happens to a woman who does strive for a leadership position in an organization? First, the top recruiting officer (most often a man) usually has an image of what category of person would best fill the leading positions. Secondly, studies in the area of social structure and personality have shown that bureaucracies and organizations tend to recruit people with particular personality traits. The image is most likely to be of men, not women. In systems where there are psychological tests and educational requirements—even when the woman meets these qualifications—she may not, in subtle, qualitative ways, pass the selection criteria. In short, she does not fit the recruiter's expectations of who will best fill the leadership position.[3]

If the recruiter believes that women do not have the attributes for the job, he/she feels justified in limiting the interviewing to men. For women seeking the position, this practice puts them in a double bind. If the woman desires to have the job, she must then try to emulate the masculine characteristics deemed necessary for the job. If, however, she does demonstrate these characteristics, she may then be told she is "unfeminine." Women may fear that being successful and getting ahead in a traditional man's field will be perceived as "unfeminine" (cf. Horner, 1972). Another technique that hinders a woman's advancement is the "buddy system" in which the recruiting is by word-of-mouth rather than explicit and widespread advertising. In contacting people the recruiter personally thinks might be interested in the position, he (since most recruiters for top positions are male) is likely to draw from his male friends—business buddies who belong to the same country club, tennis set, or college fraternity. This practice discriminates against women. Until women are in the recruiting positions, they are not likely to be recruited.

Other factors which limit the woman's advancement in the organization are a series of myths which prevail about working women.

Myth 1

Women do not need or want to work. This particular myth is based upon the premise that the woman has someone else to support her such as a husband, father, or son. Hence, she would only work for "extras." However, the Woman's Bureau of the U.S. Department of Labor found that most women are working because of economic need and that more American families would be at poverty levels if the women were not working (cf. Suelzle, 1971).

Despite the widely held belief that women do not work, 90 percent of American women work sometime during their lifetime, with 60 percent working more than 30 years. The majority of American women are participants in the labor force. However, their career preparation and commitment are often stifled because of beliefs that employment will not be a significant aspect of their life.

Myth 2

Women are not interested in advancement and promotions. Women have been shown to be just as interested in

[3] To counteract these practices, the federal government has initiated the affirmative action program in which any organization receiving contracts totaling $50,000 or more from the U.S. government must demonstrate that they are not discriminating against women and minorities.

advancements as men, particularly for top positions. The more education and training a woman has, the more likely she is to be committed to a career and the more likely she is to remain in that career (Wells, 1967).

Belief in this myth has serious consequences when employers only consider women to be available for low-status, low-paying jobs and not candidates for meaningful careers. Because of the male ego mystique, some husbands may de-emphasize the importance of the wife's economic contribution by arguing that his is the only important job in the family.

Black women more than white women are more committed to their careers and less likely to say that a career will interfere with marriage (Fichter, 1967). The contrast between black and white women is probably due to the different expectations they received concerning their adult lives—black women have been expected to work. Their families, schools, and community organizations have provided support and encouragement for them to work, while the white woman has received discouragement and even hostility when she sought employment. This is not to say that black women have not faced discrimination, for they have in fact faced two kinds of discrimination— racial and sexual. However, black women usually have not had to face the same psychological conflict as white women, who experience guilt within themselves and anger from their peers for seeking employment, particularly if they have young children. In contrast, the black woman who wanted to remain at home with her young children often experienced pressure to seek employment to help support her family.

Myth 3

Women have high absenteeism and high turnover. A Bureau of Labor study indicated absenteeism was approximately the same for men and women—women lost 5.3 days per year while men in the same time period lost 5.4 days (U.S. Bureau of Labor, 1969:80). Since people in low-status jobs have higher turnover than those occupying higher-status positions, status and skill level of the job are more important factors in determining turnover than sex of occupant (1969:76–80).

If the woman finally obtains a leadership position in a large organization, she still faces barriers. Although she serves as an example for other women—an extremely important function—her struggles may deter other women from striving for the top positions. She often encounters problems such as her superiors setting higher expectations for her performance than for men in comparable positions. She faces rumors about how she got ahead—that she didn't play fair, she had intimate relations with a man in a leadership position, or she threatened a suit with the Equal Employment Opportunities Office.

The top of an organization is considered such a male turf that the woman is treated as an outsider or stranger. She is frequently excluded from the male gatherings where decisions are really made— such as in locker rooms, executive restrooms, or golf courses. Not infrequently the complaint from a female at the top is that she is expected to carry out traditional feminine activities for her fellow co-workers such as making coffee, entertaining guests, or even typing (cf. Prather, 1971).

Because of her advancement, the

woman may be treated as deviant and even feel a need to validate her normalcy or femininity. Epstein, for example, discovered some female lawyers insisted on doing housework and marketing to prove themselves in traditional feminine activities (Epstein, 1970:30). Not only is the woman stigmatized, but her family also may encounter the stigma of having a working mother. Husband and children may receive pity because they have such an ambitious wife and mother. The working woman feels guilty that she is causing her children to suffer, despite the numerous studies that show that working does not have negative effects upon children (Nye and Hoffman, 1963).

Organizations, too, may discriminate between the working parents, with the woman being asked many more questions than the man about the number of children she has, pregnancy plans or preventions, and childcare arrangements. Organizations reinforce sexism by assuming only women are concerned with the care of their children. Similarly, when they give only maternity leaves and not paternity leaves also, they perpetuate the belief that only mothers are interested in caring for a newborn infant. A nonsexist society would exist when both mother and father are equally concerned about how their work affects their children. An indication of shared parenthood responsibilities is the demand for paternity leaves for new fathers as well as maternity leaves for mothers.

In summary, organizations predominantly hire one category of person—usually white male—for leadership; any other category of person has difficulty competing for the positions. Once the organization sets its rules, the fellow players and their successors perpetuate these rules. In this manner, sexism has persisted for generations, and only recently has the system been questioned.

THE WOMAN'S MOVEMENT AS A SOCIAL MOVEMENT AGAINST SEXISM

The movement against sexism has been principally led by feminists,[4] who emerged in the United States in the nineteenth century. One of the first cries for women's rights came in 1776 during the Continental Congress when Abigail Adams wrote her husband John that women would not be bound by any laws made by a group in which women were not represented. Rights for women was an issue at the founding of this country, even though European men described colonial women as having more independence than their European counterparts, because they observed that colonial women managed their own business and attended activities unchaperoned.

Through their participation in the abolition movement women became aware that they themselves lacked many of the rights they were demanding for slaves. When women were not allowed to be public speakers, or were denied the right to be official delegates at abolition conventions, the women grew cognizant of their own plight. In addition, the abolition movement provided an opportunity for women to gain leadership skills which they later applied to feminism.

In 1840 at an abolition meeting in England, two leaders of the American feminism movement, Elizabeth Cady Stanton and Lucretia Mott, first met. Excluded as official delegates because of

[4] For a review of the Feminist Movement see Eleanor Flexner, *Century of Struggle: The Woman's Rights Movement in the U.S.*, Cambridge, Mass.: Harvard University Press, 1959.

their sex, they vowed to work immediately for the rights of women. They organized the Seneca Falls Convention in 1848, the first conference ever held in the U.S. to discuss women's rights. The delegates passed all the women's rights resolutions except suffrage. Encouraged by enthusiasm about and attendance at the Seneca Falls Meeting, Elizabeth Stanton and Susan B. Anthony founded in New York the National Woman Suffrage Association, dedicated to achieving a wide range of rights for women through pressuring Congress.

In Boston, Lucy Stone and Julia Ward established the conservative American Woman Suffrage Association which focused only upon attaining the vote and developed the strategy of instituting change through each state rather than nationally. Although they had dissimilar tactics and philosophies, the groups finally merged in 1890 to form the National American Woman Suffrage Association to concentrate on what became the central issue—suffrage.

Women became united on the one issue of suffrage with the over-optimistic hope that with the vote they could begin to be influential in promoting other changes. In retrospect, this tactic was a mistake, because once they obtained the vote in 1919, women were unable to unite on other issues. Instead, the suffrage movement began to splinter and to focus on such related but not strictly feminist issues as labor reform, changes in working conditions for women and children, birth control, and prohibition.

By the decades of the 1920–30s and the 1930–40s, women were participating in many occupations and activities from which they had previously been excluded. During this era, women received proportionately more postgraduate degrees than at any time previously or since in the history of the United States (Blitz, 1974). Although women were making some strides toward equality, there were strong taboos, particularly among the middle class, against married women working. Women who pursued careers and professions did so by denouncing marriage. Although the Depression drastically decreased job possibilities for both men and women, for many years women would be denied jobs because of a belief stemming from the Depression that an employed woman was taking a job away from a man.

World War II brought sudden changes in employment opportunities for women. For the first time, women were vigorously recruited for employment in businesses and industries on a wide range of positions. So intense was the pressure to hire women to free men to serve in the armed forces that the U.S. Employment Service Offices even banned the hiring of men (Chafe, 1972:147). Female employees at this time shattered many of the stereotypes and myths concerning the kinds of jobs women could handle.

During the war, many factories streamlined and automated their plants which had the effect after the war of decreasing the number of available jobs. Following the war, there was heavy propaganda aimed at encouraging the women to quit work despite the finding that the majority of employed women did not want to relinquish their jobs (Gray, 1972). Women's roles were altered by two important governmental policies—the GI home loans which enabled the middle class to purchase homes in the suburbs, and the GI education bill which allowed men to return to college campuses.

The move to the suburbs encouraged the breaking of extended family and community ties. The wife, more than ever before, became a full-time homemaker. Full or part-time jobs were rare in the suburbs and the family lived too far for both the husband and wife to commute to the cities. Because the husband was gone for long periods of time from home, the woman became the head of the household in terms of responsibilities and decision-making. In addition, the woman was isolated—she was only in the company of other women within the same age range and backgrounds and their small children. Heavy emphasis was then placed upon being a good home-maker. Movies, mass media, magazines, all promoted the image of the wife who loved her responsibilities of cleaning the house, caring for her children, and greeting her husband (cf. Friedan, 1970:28–61). During the previous two decades, the career woman had been favorably featured in mass media, but now the career woman was portrayed as being miserable because she was not married and fulfilled through motherhood. Said Ashley Montagu in 1958: "No woman with a husband and small children can hold a full-time job and be a good homemaker at one and the same time."

The move to college campuses was significant for several reasons. For the first time older students were accepted in major universities. Married students and married-student housing became new institutions on college campuses. Although the move to campuses did allow some married women to become a part of the college scene, a more common situation emerged: the wife worked while the husband attended school. This trend took its toll on women. During the 1950s and 60s, fewer women received graduate degrees than during any other time period (Pietrofesa and Schlossberg, 1971).

The pressure upon the woman to concentrate on her responsibilities of housewife, mother and wife, plus the trend for families to move to suburbs, had a particularly compounding effect upon middle-class women. Despite mechanization of housework, women spent more hours in housecleaning than ever before because the standards of housekeeping increased (Goode, 1963:10–20; Vanek, 1974).[5] Because of the distance from schools and various centers of shopping and other activity, the wife began taking on a thankless and endless job of chauffering children. Many of the cleaning, shopping, and chauffering activities, however, did not provide her with tangible evidence of her labors. If she had any spare time at all the housewife was expected to participate in a variety of volunteer activities and/or community organizations. The effect of the suburban life-style upon the middle-class woman began to be described as the problem without a name, the feminine mystique (Friedan, 1970). The middle-class woman with a college degree described her life as frustrating and meaningless, while perceiving her husband advance his career and gain status among his peers, the community, and within the family. This woman, seeking a more fulfilling life, was ripe for a feminist movement.

The revival of feminism occurred among three groups—middle-class housewives, working-class women, and female

5 This trend continues. Women in the 1970s report spending more time in household activities than did women in the 1920s (Dubrin, 1972). Typical of how modern appliances have increased time spent in household activities is in the task of laundry. Because families today have many more clothes than families 50 years ago, women wash more clothes than previously and wash them more frequently.

students. The middle-class woman, as described above, suffered from the feminine mystique—the feeling of a loss of self-esteem and a lack of a fulfilling life despite her involvement in her wife and mother role. The working-class woman, too, was ready for a women's rights movement. She discovered she did not have the same advancement opportunities as her male coworkers, nor could she earn the same wages. Young college students participating in the civil rights movement also helped revive feminism. The female students found they could march alongside their fellow male students in protests but were not treated equally in decision-making sessions.

Feminism, like other social movements, began with a general feeling of unrest among women—an unrest that was difficult to define and that was diffuse in its symptoms. Two kinds of feminist organizations first emerged. The National Organization of Women represented initially middle-class women concerned about status of women legally, occupationally, and politically. Women's Liberation groups were formed by women who discussed their individual problems and participated in consciousness-raising sessions concerning the plight of all women and other oppressed minorities. As these two kinds of groups began to flower in the late 1960s, other organizations formed among professions or other special-interest groups.

Feminists have established their own newspapers in major cities. Pamphlets, drama, poetry, prose, and magazines—all have emerged to describe the plight of women. Not only have traditional women's magazines such as *Ladies Home Journal* or *McCalls* had many articles dedicated to the feminist movement, but even male-dominant magazines ranging from *Playboy* to *Fortune* have written about women's rights.

In the movement to eradicate sexism, men's liberation organizations are increasing, formed to work to change and to recognize the disadvantages of the traditional male role (Farrell, 1971). The members of these groups do not envision themselves as opposing the women's movement, but instead, joining with the women's movement to work for human liberation. Several legal cases for men's rights have been newsworthy, such as men seeking paternity leaves on the birth of their children or men applying to adopt children or to obtain custody of their children.

In conclusion, the effort to change traditional roles of men and women and to eliminate discrimination on the basis of sex is a viable movement with recognized leaders, established political supporters, and defined goals and tactics. Three goals are paramount for eradicating sexism. The first goal is the creation throughout society of nonsexist educational systems where educational policies, career and personal counseling, textbooks, classroom exercises, financial aids, and so forth, would be devoid of any sex stereotyping. Boys and girls would be allowed to explore the interests and classes which appeal to them as individuals, not just those which are open to them because of their sexual status.

A second goal for alleviating sexism would be the establishing of elaborate and creative child care centers for all children, regardless of social class. Ideally, these programs would include participation by parents of both sexes and would encourage nonsex stereotyping in curriculum and activities.

The third goal for the promotion of new roles for men and women is the institution of flexible work hours. Under this provision, individuals would have a variety of work schedules rather than the majority of the labor force adhering to an 8–5 workday. When flexible work plans have been created, employees report feeling more autonomy and independence on the job than when required to work at specific times. For families, enormous benefits emerge from flexible work hours since both parents and perhaps other concerned and interested adults can take an active part in child-rearing and child-loving. In addition economist Mary Rowe (1973) asserts that women and men could enrich their home and employment roles if both men and women worked a three-quarter work week, averaging 30 to 40 hours maximum. Under this scheme, both men and women would experience greater variety and self-esteem in their lives than under the present system of differentiating between men's and women's work.

When all three of these goals are accomplished, sexism should decline as a social problem since men and women would be free to choose the lifestyle they desire without feeling limited because of their sexual status. In a nonsexist society, both men and women would have the opportunity to enjoy a challenging career without stigma, to cry intensely without shame, to participate in any hobby or sport without ridicule, and to warmly embrace a person—of either sex—without guilt.

References

Balwick, J. O., and Peek, C. W. "The Inexpressive Male: A Tragedy of American Society." *The Family Coordinator*, 1971, 20, 363–68.

Barker, R., and Wright, H. *Midwest and Its Children*. New York: Harper & Row, 1964.

Bart, Pauline. "Mother Portnoy's Complaints." *TransAction*, 1970, 8, 69–74.

Bernard, Jessie. *The Future of Marriage*. New York: World, 1972.

Bernard, Jessie. *The Future of Motherhood*. New York: Dial, 1974.

Blitz, R. C. "Women in the Professions." *Monthly Labor Review*, 1974, 97, 34–39.

Brenton, Myron. *The American Male*. New York: Coward-McCann, 1966.

Bullough, Vern L. *The Subordinate Sex*. Baltimore: Penguin Books, 1974.

Chafe, W. H. *The American Woman*. New York: Oxford, 1972.

Chesler, P. *Women and Madness*. New York: Doubleday, 1972.

Dubrin, Andrew. *Women in Transition*. Springfield, Ill.: Charles C. Thomas, 1972.

Epstein, C. F. *Woman's Place*. Berkeley: University of California Press, 1970.

Etzioni, Amitai. "Sex Control, Science, and Society." *Science*, 1968, 161, 1107–1112.

Farber, B. *Family: Organization and Interaction*. San Francisco: Chandler, 1964.

Farrell, W. T. "Male Consciousness-Raising for a Sociological and Political Perspective." *Sociological Focus*, 1971–72, 5, 19–28.

Fichter, J. H. "Career Expectations of Negro Women Graduates." *Monthly Labor Review*, 1967, 90, 36–42.

Friedan, B. *The Feminine Mystique*. New York: Dell, 1970.

Goldberg, S., and Lewis, M. "Play Behavior in the Year-old Infant: Early Sex Differences." *Child Development*, 1969, 40, 21–32.

Goode, William. *World Revolution and Family Patterns*. New York: Free Press, 1963.

Gove, W., and Tudor, J. F. "Adult Sex Roles and Mental Illness." *American Journal of Sociology*, 1973, 78, 812–35.

Gray, B. M. "Sex Bias and Cyclical Un-employment." In N. Glazer-Malbin and H. Waehrer (Eds.), *Woman in a Man-Made World*. Chicago: Rand McNally, 1972. Pp. 235–37.

Hagan, E. "Sex Role Stereotyping in Elementary School Readers." Report of Central New Jersey Chapter of National Organization of Women, 1970.

Harris, A. "Second Sex in Academe." In J. Stacy, S. Bereaud, and J. Daniel (Eds.), *And Jill Came Tumbling Down*. New York: Dell, 1974. Pp. 293–316.

Hartley, R. "Sex Role Pressures and the Socialization of the Male Child." *Psychological Reports*, 1959, 5, 457–68.

Horner, M. "Toward an Understanding of Achievement-Related Conflicts in Women." *Journal of Social Issues*, 1972, 28, 157–75.

Howe, F. "Sexual Stereotypes Start Early." *Saturday Review*, 1971, 54 (October 16), 77–82, 92–94.

Jourard, Sidney. *The Transparent Self*. New York: Van Nostrand, 1971.

Kagan, J. "Acquisition and Significance of Sex Typing and Identity." In M. Hoffman (Ed.), *Review of Child Development Research*. New York: Russell Sage, 1964. Pp. 137–67. (a)

Kagan, J. "The Child's Sex Role Classification of School Objects." *Child Development*, 1964, 35, 1051–56. (b)

Komarovsky, M. "Functional Analysis of Sex Roles." *American Sociological Review*, 1950, 15, 508–16.

Lasswell, M. "Is There a Best Age to Marry?: An Interpretation." *The Family Coordinator*, 1974, 23, 237–42.

Le Masters, E. *Parents in Modern America*. Homewood: Dorsey Press, 1970.

Levy, D. *Maternal Overprotection*. New York: Columbia University Press, 1943.

Lewis, Robert. "Satisfaction with Conjugal Power over the Family Life Cycle." Unpublished manuscript presented at the National Council of Family Relations, Portland, Oregon, 1972.

Lopata, Helena. *Occupation Housewife*. New York: Oxford University Press, 1972.

Maccoby, E. E. *The Development of Sex Differences*. Stanford, Ca.: Stanford University Press, 1966.

Maccoby, E. E. "Differential Socialization of Boys and Girls." Paper presented at American Psychological Association, Hawaii, September, 1972.

Maccoby, E. E., and Jacklin, C. *The Psychology of Sex Differences*. Stanford, Ca.: Stanford University Press, 1974.

Martinson, F. *Family in Society*. New York: Dodd Mead, 1970.

McKee, J., and Sherriffs, A. C. "The Differential Evaluation of Males and Females." *Journal of Personality*, 1957, 25, 226–39.

McKee, J., and Sherriffs, A. C. "Men's and Women's Beliefs, Ideals and Self-concepts." *American Journal of Sociology*, 1959, 64, 356–63.

Meyer, W. J., and Thompson, G. C. "Teacher Interactions with Boys as Contrasted with Girls." In R. Kuhlens and G. Thompson (Eds.), *Psychological Studies of Human Development*. New York: Appleton, 1963. Pp. 510–18.

Minturn, L., and Lambert, W. *Mothers of Six Cultures*. New York: J. Wiley, 1964.

Montagu, Ashley. "The Triumph and Tragedy of the American Woman." *Saturday Review*, 1958, 41 (September 27), 13–18.

Murdock, G. P. "Comparative Data on Division of Labor by Sex." *Social Forces*, 1935, 15, 551–53.

Naffziger, C., and Naffziger, K. "Development of Sex Role Stereotypes." *Family Coordinator*, 1974, 23, 251–58.

Newson, J., and Newson, E. *Four Years Old in an Urban Community*. Harmondworth, England: Pelican, 1968.

Nye, I., and Hoffman, L. W. *The Employed Mother in America*. Chicago: Rand McNally, 1963.

Peck, E. *The Baby Trap*. New York: Bernard Geis Associates, 1971.

Pederson, F. A., and Bell, R. O. "Sex Differences in Pre-School Children without

Histories of Complications in Pregnancy and Delivery." *Developmental Psychology,* 1970, 3, 1–15.

Pietrofesa, J., and Schlossberg, N. "Counselor Bias and the Female Occupational Role." In N. Glazer-Malbin and H. Waehrer (Eds.), *Woman in a Man-Made World.* Chicago: Rand McNally, 1971. Pp. 219–227.

Pitcher, E. G. "Male and Female." In J. Stacey, S. Beraud, and J. Daniels (Eds.), *And Jill Came Tumbling Down.* New York: Dell, 1974. Pp. 79–90.

Poloma, M., and Garland, T. N. "The Married Professional Woman: A Study on the Tolerance of Domestication." *Journal of Marriage and the Family,* 1971, 33, 531–39.

Prather, J. "Why Can't Women Be More Like Men: A Summary of the Sociopsychological Factors Hindering Women's Advancement in the Professions." *American Behavioral Scientist,* 1971, 15, 172–83.

Rabban, M. "Sex Role Identification in Young Children in Two Diverse Social Groups." *Genetic Psychological Monographs,* 1950, 42, 81–158.

Ringo, M. "The Well-Placed Wife." Unpublished manuscript by Center for Urban Affairs, Northwestern University, 1970.

Rossi, A. S. "Barriers to the Career Choice of Engineering, Medicine or Science among American Women." In J. A. Mattfeld and C. G. VanAken (Eds.), *Women and the Scientific Professions.* Cambridge: Massachusetts Institute of Technology, 1965. Pp. 51–127.

Rossi, A. S. "Equality between the Sexes: An Immodest Proposal." In M. Garskof (Ed.), *Roles Women Play: Readings toward Women's Liberation.* Belmont, Ca.: Brooks/Cole, 1967. Pp. 145–64.

Rossi, A. S. "Transition to Parenthood." Pp. 331–341 In A. Skolnick and J. Skolnick (Eds.), *Family in Transition.* Boston: Little, Brown, 1970. Pp. 331–341.

Rowe, Mary. "Prospects and Patterns for Men and Women at Work." "The Right to Both Love and Work." Speech presented to the M.I.T. Alumni Association, Centennial Convocation, 1973.

Russell, Bertrand. *Marriage and Morals.* New York: Liveright, 1929.

Safilios-Rothschild, Constantina. "The Dimensions of Power Distribution in the Family." In J. Christ and H. Grunebaum (Eds.), *Marriage, Problems and Their Treatment.* Boston: Little, Brown, 1972.

Sears, P. S., and Feldman, D. "Teacher Interactions with Boys and with Girls." In J. Stacey, S. Bereaud, and J. Daniels (Eds.), *And Jill Came Tumbling Down.* New York: Dell, 1974. Pp. 147–59.

Seeley, J. R., Sim, R. A., and Loosley, E. W. *Crestwood Heights.* New York: John Wiley, 1963.

Seidenberg, R. *Corporate Wives—Corporate Casualities.* New York: Doubleday, 1975.

Sexton, P. *The Feminized Male.* New York: Random House, 1969.

Slater, P. *Pursuit of Loneliness.* Boston: Beacon Press, 1970.

Stoll, C. (Ed.). Sexism: Scientific Debates. Reading, Mass.: Addison-Wesley, 1973.

Stoll, C. *Female and Male.* Dubuque, Iowa: William C. Brown, 1974.

Suelzle, Marijean. "Women in Labor." *TransAction,* 1970, 8, 50–58.

Sullerot, E. *Women, Society and Change.* New York: McGraw-Hill, 1971.

Turner, Ralph. *Family Interaction.* New York: John Wiley, 1970.

U.S. Bureau of Labor. *Handbook on Women Workers.* Women's Bureau Bulletin, 294. Washington, D.C., 1969.

U.S. Department of Commerce. *Current Population Report,* Bulletin P-60, No. 80, 1970, 129.

Van Deventer, E., and Bathurst, C. "Home Economics A La Male." *Family Coordinator,* 1974, 23, 314.

Vanek, J. "Time Spent in Housework." *Scientific American,* 1974, 231, 116–20.

Walker, C. "Time-use Patterns for Household Use Related to Homemakers Employment." Reprint from U.S. Department of Agriculture, Hyattsville, Md. 20782, 1970.

Weitzman, L. J., Eifles, D., Hokada, E., and Ross, C. "Sex Role Socialization in Picture Books for Pre-school Children." *American Journal of Sociology*, 1972, 72, 1125–30.

Wells, Jean. "Women College Gradu-ates 7 Years Later." *Monthly Labor Review*, 1967, 90, 28–32.

Wilensky, H. "Orderly Careers and Social Participation: The Impact of Work History on Social Integration in the Middle Mass." *American Sociological Review*, 1961, 26, 521–39.

Suggested Reading

BERNARD, JESSIE. *The Future of Motherhood*. New York: Dial Press, 1974.
A provocative, critical look at the motherhood role in contemporary society; includes prophecies and plans for the future of motherhood.

CHAFE, W. H. *The American Woman*. New York: Oxford, 1972.
A detailed description of the historical position and current status of American women.

EPSTEIN, C. F. *Woman's Place*. Berkeley: University of California Press, 1970.
An overview of the problems, conflicts, and rewards experienced by women in the major professions, with an emphasis upon the legal professions.

FARRELL, W. T. *Liberated Man beyond Masculinity: Freeing Men and Their Relationship with Women*. New York: Random House, 1975.
A current analysis of the American male—his value orientations, his roles, his plight.

LOPATA, H. *Occupation Housewife*. New York: Oxford, 1972.
A definitive description of the housewife as an occupational role including a classification of housewives.

MACCOBY, E. E., AND JACKLIN, C. *The Psychology of Sex Differences*. Stanford, Ca.: Stanford University Press, 1974.
A scholarly review of contemporary research concerning psychological sex differences.

SEIDENBERG, R. *Corporate Wives—Corporate Casualties*. New York: Doubleday, 1975.
An indepth look at a select group—women whose lives are structured by the corporations which employ their husbands.

STOLL, C. *Female and Male*. Dubuque, Iowa: William C. Brown, 1974.
A sociological analysis of current gender/sex roles with recognition of the contribution of biology, psychology, and anthropology.

SULLEROT, E. *Women, Society and Change*. New York: McGraw-Hill, 1971.
An analysis of women's roles as defined by diverse societies and by changes occurring within societies.

Part IV

Institutional and Environmental Problems

While parental social class remains the best predictor of school achievement, and hence, personal and occupational success, it is still pertinent to inquire into the structure of public education in the United States. Public schools are expected to perform a multitude of functions and play a number of different and sometimes conflicting roles in the socialization of youth. The educational process is expected to be a transmitter for the values, attitudes, and manners of the dominant white middle-class culture. At the same time, Musick points out, those children who come to the schools lacking such a cultural background are differentially treated.

The schools are asked to instill curiosity and a love of learning in the student, but more often the effective pressure is toward maintaining discipline in the classroom and ensuring that its graduates are tractable, morally acceptable "products" with saleable skills. Modern concepts of pedagogy stress adaptation to the special learning needs of individual children and to the special problems of the so-called "culturally deprived," yet problems of funding, stemming from the property-tax base and variation in the wealth of school districts, lead to large class-sizes and cutbacks of special programs and bilingual education when funds are scarce. Teachers, moreover, are reluctant to take custody of the disadvantaged student, perceiving—perhaps quite correctly—that their role is to keep these youths off the streets and under control as long as possible. The tyranny of statewide standardized achievement tests applied in mass to students is felt when test scores slip in one area or another and more creative programs are scrapped in favor of a return to basics.

In his article, Musick analyzes the bureaucratic context of modern mass education and relates the persistent pattern of class and racial bias in education to the rigidity of a cumbersome bureaucratic structure. It is perhaps appropriate that the child's first experience in an institutional setting other than the family is in the school, for in due time, other bureaucratically organized settings will influence his or her life pattern. In the school, the child will learn that forces outside of his/her control will allocate praise or blame, generating enduring records of success or failure which may influence yet distant decisions concerning job, military service, and so on. Like other institutions, the rewards will be distributed unequally: The children of the poor, the black, the Chicano, and the Native American will be allocated little recognition as individuals with their own unique accomplishments, but will receive much attention as "problems" which interfere with the smooth running of the school bureaucracy. Social programs abound, but in each institutional sphere, including the school, the racial and class stratification of the society reproduces itself in specific and predictable handicaps for those who lack the power to control their own fate.

The introductory essay by Hadden and Lester identifed the ameliorative solution to social problems as a kind of first-aid in contrast to any fundamental revamping of the underlying conditions. Using bandages where major restructuring seems necessary aptly characterizes present attempts to solve the problems associated with medical care.

Enos lucidly demonstrates that a few more doctors (and some minority ones at that), a few more bandages, and a little more insurance cannot come to grips with the major problems associated with another important institution, the health care delivery system. These problems range from a lack of emphasis on preventive medical care, the different health care needs of various groups (for example, women, children, the aged), the hierarchical control of the health care profession, the impersonality of the doctor-patient relationship, to the crucial economic component which we confront once again in this article—the poor pay more and receive less.

The problems are not solved even when we adopt the often-questioned principle that all people, regardless of race or economic resources, are entitled to adequate and humane medical treatment. For example, it would be difficult to "socialize" medicine while leaving intact other capitalist, profit-oriented institutions. Besides, given its performance in other sectors of the economy, most people are skeptical of the possible benefits of governmental coordination of health care. Expanding prepaid health care will certainly benefit the middle classes, but its usefulness to the poor (who cannot afford medical insurance in the first place) is obviously dubious. Neither will a laissez-faire (do nothing) approach rectify health care troubles. In short, this essay confronts the difficulties, ·

contradictions and perplexities entailed in resolving social problems rooted in the major institutions of our society.

One of the concerns voiced by those alarmed by the feminist movement is over the effect of changing the role of women on family life. Glazer-Malbin's article documents the costly effects of *not* changing current conceptions of male and female roles to conform more closely with an equalitarian and open conception of the potential of individuals extending beyond the narrow confines of traditional gender expectations. She extends her analysis to the point of examining alternative solutions to the problem of sexism in the marriage relationship and ends with a discussion of a new structure for family life.

The burden of gender roles is perhaps most acutely felt when two potent myths shatter against the reality of family life. One myth is that the most satisfying relationship in modern society is between man and woman in a monogamous marriage. The other is that a woman is fulfilled in marriage and childbearing. The marital bond and the chore of childrearing have their rewards, but often the cost outruns the benefit.

The primary issue is not the existence of conventional marital and family role relationships, however, but their nonelective character. Many individuals find security in traditional gender roles and would choose them if a choice existed. However, women in particular may increasingly find that what conventional marriage and childrearing have to offer does not measure up to alternatives that are now perceived as possible. Being consigned to the often exhausting "nonwork" of housework and almost full responsibility for the daily supervision of children, coupled with dependency on the male for the family's economic survival, does not add up to an attractive pattern of life for many women. Glazer-Malbin is careful to point out that the work of the wife and mother is not in and of itself menial or degrading; childcare, for example, is an important function that must be performed. The heart of the matter is the way in which such pursuits are defined in capitalist society, namely, as low or lacking in exchange value. A male spending an equivalent amount of time in a "productive" pursuit is rewarded by prestige and money; his wife has only reflected glory and perhaps a modicum of esteem for keeping a clean house and raising mannerly children.

The burden of gender role is particularly heavy as women advance in age. A principal component of their identity, that of mother, is attenuated as children grow up and leave the home. Their husbands may have grown in their career and be reaching their peak, while they wonder what to do with the emptiness in their houses and lives. If they should be widowed or divorced, they find themselves at a competitive disadvantage, since men of their own age may seek and can attract younger women. While men bear some of the burden of gender, women bear most.

Glazer-Malbin opts for a socialist solution based on a communal organization of family life encompassing ties extending beyond the nuclear family. The individualistic ideology prevalent in modern society may make it difficult for many to entertain seriously a collectivist solution, but it is clear that Glazer-Malbin's proposal directly addresses the problems of contemporary marriage and family life.

The relatively recent explosion of technological control and rapid economic growth in Western industrial societies (particularly in the United States) may be hailed by some as an unparalleled triumph of a rational bureaucratic capitalism over the recalcitrance of nature and the indolent and superstitious side of the human character. For the privileged in these societies, material affluence has become a taken-for-granted fact of life. For those of lesser privilege, while perhaps better off than their counterparts in poorer societies, there is the indignity of being in the presence of a feast to which they are not invited. Yet precisely to the extent that the Western industrial order has been successful, it has brought countries rich and poor, and persons privileged and deprived, near to a common catastrophe.

The ecocatastrophe may be an alarmist vision which may never come to pass; to the extent that there is substance to the warning of environmentalists and demographers concerning the perils of untrammeled industrial expansion and population growth, surely, one says, there is a technological solution to the danger. The very world-view which has occasioned the disease will certainly discover the cure. The chapter by Jonathan Turner does not make pleasant reading for the optimist, nor for those committed to the hope of technological solutions to what is basically the most important social problem of all—the very viability of life in an environment assaulted by growth of a particular type of social system.

For those of us in American society who pride ourselves on limiting our families to two children and recycling our aluminum beer cans, the fact remains that we are participants in a lifestyle which uses up 35 percent of the world's minerals and energy resoures, and contributes one-half of the world's industrial pollutants. Bangladesh may, as a national entity, have the fastest growing population and an equally rapid rate of starvation, but it is the fluorocarbons in our deodorant sprays that may cause decomposition of the ozone shield and an increase in the amount of ultraviolet radiation around the world. We may, with Garett Hardin, argue that the pressure of population against food resources must be met by a "life boat" philosophy which consigns the hungry of the world to their fate, but what of the lifeboat itself if the affluent societies flood it with industrial wastes?

The thrust of Turner's argument is that the problem of pollution and of overpopulation are basically bound to the existing social order. The impetus to ravage the environment in order to produce more and more products to meet an exaggerated standard of consumption springs not from technology or rational productive methods themselves, but from the idolatry of technology, the quest for profit, the disregard of nature, and the many vested interests wielding institutionalized resistance to solutions to pollution and overpopulation. These, while effective, challenge existing privilege and profit. Turner's viewpoint is pessimistic; his solutions are disagreeable, since they in effect mean relinquishing "freedoms" heretofore viewed as inalienable, for example, to have as many children as one wishes and to submit to centralized governmental control over broad areas of life. Implicit in Turner's discussion is an even more radical solution, namely, to replace our present mode of control and utilization of our technologically sophisticated and enormously efficient productive apparatus with a more humane set of goals administered for the benefit of all people.

Problems with Mass Education in America

David W. Musick

The United States system of mass public education is seen by many as the chief avenue for personal and occupational success. While securing an education is a major concern for the entire American working population, it has special significance for the lower classes who are told that the path from poverty to full and fruitful participation in American society is academic achievement. This belief was forcefully stated by the United States Supreme Court in its landmark 1954 decision on school desegregation:

[Education] today is a principal instrument in awakening the child to cultural values, in preparing him for later professional training, and in helping him to adjust normally to his environment. In these days, it is doubtful that any child may reasonably be expected to succeed in life if he is denied the opportunity of an education. Such an opportunity, where the state has undertaken to provide it, is a right which must be made available to all on equal terms. (Brown vs. Board of Education of Topeka, 1954:453)

The U.S. Supreme Court was not outlining a new social policy so much as reasserting one of the basic principles upon which the nation had been built: access to public education facilities should be available to all, on equal terms, be they immigrants from Western Europe, Africa, or the rural South. It was the cleverest of social policies, providing a means for directing the actions of masses of people with potentially disparate goals while promising to be the "great equalizer of the conditions of men—the balance wheel of the social machinery" (Mann, 1973:318). The Supreme Court was also reaffirming what was one of the most unimpeachable axioms of the social sciences —the relationship between academic achievement and occupational status and income (Blau and Duncan, 1967:179–80; Ellis, 1917:14–50; Glick, 1954:183–194; Ritzer, 1972:354–55; Thomas, 1956:343–57).

Inequality in America has increasingly been attributed to the inability of certain groups to reach higher levels of educational achievement. Poor, uneducated parents, having limited access to education themselves, are ill-equipped to instill within their children motivation and skills which would enable them to take advantage of those educational facilities available (Council of Economic Advisors, 1964:69–70). Belief in the imperative of acquiring the skills and attitudes necessary for full participation in American society through education culminated in President Johnson's declaring "war" on poverty. This declaration gave birth to one of the largest programs of social action in America's history. The government set out to eliminate poverty not by redistributing income or providing jobs for the poor, but by teaching skills and attitudes which, in turn, would eventuate in the acquisition of better jobs and higher incomes.

Several years later the program was described as "a series of well-intended skirmishes," rather than an all-out attempt to wage war on poverty (Levitan, 1967). Operation Head Start, a massive attempt to provide preschool education for children of the poor, failed to produce measurable gains in educational achievement (Jensen, 1969:3; Miller, 1969:251). Compensatory education, a program aimed at lessening the achievement gap between disadvantaged and more affluent school-age children, had not produced the expected positive results. After evaluating compensatory education programs throughout the nation, the U.S. Commission on Civil Rights concluded:

The commission's analysis does not suggest that compensatory education is incapable of remedying the effects of poverty on the academic achievement of individual children. . . . The fact remains however, that none of the programs appear to have raised significantly the achievement of participating pupils, as a group within the period evaluated by the commission. (U.S. Commission on Civil Rights, 1967:138)

The war on poverty in general, and particularly in its effort to provide avenues of educational attainment for the poor, had failed. But why? Is Banfield correct in asserting that:

The lower-class individual lives in the slum and sees little or no reason to complain. He does not care how dirty and dilapidated his housing is either inside or out, nor does he mind the inadequacy of such public facilities as schools, parks, and libraries; indeed, where such things exist he destroys them by acts of vandalism if he can. Features that make the slums repellent to others actually please him. (1970:62)

Others have proposed the alternative explanation that attempts at educational intervention failed because they were not guided by sound social research and theory. Daniel Moynihan, in his analysis of the failure of the community action part of the war on poverty, discussed this possibility:

This is the essential fact: The government did not know what it was doing. It had a theory. Or, rather, a set of theories, nothing more. The U.S. Government at this time was no more in possession of the confident knowledge as to how to prevent delinquency, cure anomie, or overcome that midmorning sense of powerlessness, than was it the possessor of a dependable formula for motivating the Vietnamese villages to fight communism. (1969:170)

Moynihan was not alone in his condemnation of social action guided by "unquestioned" social theory.

Social scientists have come to realize that programs of social intervention can work only when guided by reliable theory which, in education or any other area, results from continually reassessing what is known about a phenomenon and conducting investigations to close gaps in knowledge. If public education is to remain a viable tool for equalitarian purposes, new approaches are needed, beginning with the critical examination of what is presently known about the conditions which facilitate educational achievement.

It is in this context that we study the major problems confronting public education in the United States. It is known that a child's educational success or failure will, in large part, determine his subsequent life chances. Yet there is little agreement regarding what factors are most influential in shaping educational outcomes. In this essay, we will review what is believed to be known about selected aspects of the structure and functioning of mass education in American society.

FUNCTIONS OF EDUCATION

Social order or integration is promoted by teaching common values, attitudes, motivations, and skills in the classroom which guarantee the smooth fit of successive generations of students into the society's work force. Talcott Parsons elaborated the socializing function of public education in a positive light in his classic essay on "The School Class as a Social System" (1959:298). For Parsons, socialization, "the development in individuals of the commitments and capacities which are the essential prerequisites of their future role performance," is the predominant business of the school class, "from entry into first grade until entry into the labor force or marriage." He argues that socialization through schooling is necessary, for without it children would be ill-equipped to make the transition from consummatory familial relationships to the contractual role expectations of adulthood. That is, public education performs a "sorting service" by passing children out into the occupational world according to gradients of talent and motivation. Parsons concluded that the main criterion for the educational selection process is reducible to "a single main axis of achievement." His views are summarized in the statement that:

Probably the most fundamental condition underlying this process is the sharing of common values by the two adult agencies involved—the family and the school. In this case, the core is the shared valuation of *achievement*. It includes, above all, recog-

nition that it is fair to give differential rewards for different levels of achievement, so long as there has been fair access to opportunity, and fair that these rewards lead on to higher order opportunities for the successful. There is thus a basic sense in which the elementary school class is an embodiment of the fundamental American value of equality of opportunity, in that it places value both on initial equality and on differential achievement. (1959:210)

Parsons' depiction of the functions of American education underlie much of the educational theory now being called into question.

Ralph Turner, in another classic essay, "Sponsored and Contest Mobility and the School System" (1960) further developed the prevailing sociological assumptions that the only impediments to success in the American educational system are low levels of talent and motivation. In England, children with talent and motivation are identified at the earliest possible point in the education process, sponsored through school and on to elite status in society. This is not the case, however, in the United States. Turner concluded, "since the 'prize' of successful upward mobility is not in the hands of an elite to give out, the latter cannot determine who shall attain it and who shall not" (1960:856).

If we are to believe the most noted sociological analysts, schools in America are indeed structures of opportunity. Educators and policymakers alike have assumed that children must only learn their culture and work hard to achieve success —assuming normal intelligence. But modern learning takes place within a large, highly complex structure, called a social institution, and an examination of its features must also be included in any complete explanation of problems with mass education.

THE STRUCTURE OF EDUCATION

The origin of many problems with American education can be traced to the political decision to provide public elementary and secondary schooling for all children. In Table 1 we may see the implications of such an ambitious policy decision for the structure of public education. By the 1969–70 school year public elementary and secondary schools had assumed responsibility for educating more than 45 million children. When over 15 million college and university students, 3 million teachers, and 300,000 administrative personnel are included, education emerges as the major occupation of 3 out of every 10 persons in the United States.

The influence of this national institution is most important within the youth population where almost 9 out of every 10 persons between the ages of 5 and 17 are enrolled in public schools. As a result, it is difficult to isolate the problems of "youth" from problems with mass education in American society. Because education is perhaps the only major structure in modern societies designed to control the behavior of youths, its successes and failures command focused attention from the "adult world." Adults, comprising a more completely integrated component of society, view the workings of teachers with students—schools with masses of youths—with concern. It troubles many that in the 1969–70 school year the United States spent over 40.5 billion dollars on public education—and possibly for a "product" of less utility than in past years. No longer are students at any level easing almost effortlessly into their societal obligations or areas of interest. Neither government, the church, nor industry knows just what to expect from public education today.

If we are to understand why there is a misalignment between education and society, we must begin to look at how the institution of education has reacted to the strains of increasing size and the demand for a functionally trained product to populate our industrial society.

Bureaucratization

A major consequence of the rapid expansion of education has been the inevitable bureaucratization of public school structures which, while probably necessary, dictates a particular pattern of learning.

Table 1. Summary of Enrollments and Expenditures in Public Elementary and Secondary Schools for the Years 1869–70, 1929–30, and 1969–70

Pupil Enrollments and School Expenditures	Year		
	1869–70	1929–30	1969–70
Total Enrollment in Elementary and Secondary Day Schools (Thousands)	6,872	16,790	45,619
Percent of Population 5–17 Years Enrolled	57.0	81.7	86.9
Total Expenditures for all Schools (in thousands of dollars)	$63,397	$2,316,790	$40,683,429

Source: W. Vance Grant and George Lind, *Digest of Educational Statistics, 1973*, U.S. Government Printing Office, 1974.

Charged with coordinating the activities of large numbers of students and teachers, schools implement standardized rules to regularize behavior. These lead to the emergence of a "bureaucratic ethic" stressing more the moving of children up the educational ladder, maintaining control, and imparting limited but measurable skills, than promoting the acquisition of knowledge in a humane, innovative environment (Turner, 1972:188–9). In other words, the sheer size of the organization and its resultant complexity influences the nature of the learning experience.

Paralleling Weber's (1947) classic analysis, sociologist Amitai Etzioni (1964:53) argues that bureaucracies are characterized by:

1. Rules and regulations that force standardized and equal handling of individual cases;
2. Systematic division of labor, rights, and power;
3. A hierarchy of offices;
4. Authority based on knowledge and ability rather than inherited position;
5. Administration separated from ownership;
6. Freedom from outside control of monopoly; and
7. Rules and records embodied in written rather than oral communication.

A closer look at the outstanding features of America's mass educational bureaucracy uncovers many problems which threaten to impede learning.

Mass Production of Students

Standardized rules and regulations and the need to develop equal (mass) handling of individuals have tended to force the setting of narrow educational goals and rigid methods. In today's schools, only certain information and courses of study are deemed worthy of pursuit. Unfortunately, Anglo middle-class values and teaching philosophies have frequently comprised the sole criterion for making these decisions. A pattern of learning requiring teachers to impart only knowledge and skills which lead to success either in the American job market or in seeking further education—principal concerns of the middle class—fostered political and economic elites. Other forms of knowledge and intellectual enterprise are deemed "frills" and are discouraged.

This situation is due, at least in part, to the strong belief current in the United States that the major function of the school system is to train persons for jobs in society. In an era of shrinking educational support, schools faced with limiting curricular programs are on firmer ground by retaining that part of the school structure which is of demonstrable utility in preparing children for competition in the job market or higher education.

Concurrent with the shift toward utilitarian values in education, there have evolved preoccupations with measuring intelligence [1] and the acquisition of job skills. The first is usually measured by utilizing one or more IQ tests, while a host of standardized achievement and "skills" tests have been developed by educators and employers to measure the latter. This feature is perhaps most important for that considerable segment of the school-age population belonging to racial and ethnic minorities. Minority children are asked to turn their backs on much of what they have learned from their families in the preschool years. They

[1] In traditional educational circles, this concept has come to connote a person's capacity to absorb new information and to work with abstract symbols (Jensen, 1969:5–13).

are told there is only one pathway to success in American culture and are required to follow it regardless of prior training or personal bent. In other words, unless children can fit the mold of American corporate-industrial success, they are automatically relegated to a human "junk pile" of educational failures.

Many fear that the training of successive generations of "organization men" by the schools has become dysfunctional. They argue that schools are so preoccupied with fitting children to the mold of success that young Americans no longer possess the creative ability and self-reliance needed to solve major social problems, organizational or otherwise. Social critic Paul Goodman (1960) suggests that a form of social organization requiring standardized rules and regulations and unimaginative equality in the handling of individuals cannot help but conflict with the goals of American education, in particular developing previously untapped talent.

Law and Order in the Classroom

Another disturbing side-effect of the attempt to mass educate practically every American child (using standardized criteria) is the near pathological obsession of parents and teachers alike with maintaining order in the classroom. In response to nearly universal parental demands that "law and order" be upheld (Silberman, 1970:145), schools maintain standardized class sizes, require that teachers work from preprogrammed (and often stale) lesson plans, and that children be kept "in line," regardless of the costs. Thus, teachers are often unable to take advantage of natural events occurring throughout the school day to extemporize perhaps more effective and appropriate learning experiences.

Sociologist Howard Becker (1952b) suggests that such emphasis on "law and order" contributes to two major problems confronting the American school teacher and seriously detracts from her primary function of teaching. First, the teacher-pupil relationship is pursued in an environment of tension because the children must not be allowed to go beyond some subjectively determined, and variable, limit of behavior. Second, teachers as primary advocates of societal norms make commitments to teacher-student relationships in the context of the "moral acceptability" of their students. That is, many children to whom teachers are assigned are reprehensible because they violate basic middle-class moral standards. They dress shabbily, are not scrubbed, exhibit loud and aggressive behavior, lack ambition and proper work habits, and some lack the sexual inhibitions of the middle class. Failing on "disciplinary" and "moral acceptability" grounds, these children frustrate their teachers.

Based on interviews with 60 teachers in the Chicago school system, Howard Becker (1962a) also noted the importance of teacher perceptions of student class characteristics in determining patterns of teacher-pupil interaction. Teachers encounter three types of problems with pupils during the course of their day-to-day activities: teaching—that part of change in a child's skills and knowledge which is attributable to the teacher's direct efforts; discipline—maintaining order and control in the classroom; and moral acceptability—cleansing the child of reprehensible personal traits. Conflict and fear of loss of control in the classroom are common and constantly shape the pattern of teacher-student interaction. In general agreement with Becker's observations, Edgar Friedenberg (1965: 472) concluded:

The teacher feels that the lowest group, "slum" children, is difficult to teach, uncontrollable and violent in the sphere of discipline, and morally unacceptable on all scores, from physical cleanliness to the spheres of sex and "ambition to get ahead."

Consequently, teacher perceptions of lower-class children often result in an emphasis on discipline which detracts from the primary teaching function of schools. Teachers develop specialized techniques for dealing with lower-class discipline problems, ranging from subtle gestures of contempt to nominally illegal corporal punishment. Teachers are often happy to "get just the basics" across to lower-class children, feeling that this satisfies their responsibility as educators.

Social Class Dynamics in the Classroom

Educator Alan Wilson's study (1960) of schools in Berkeley, California, suggests that a crucial factor in shaping children's academic success is the socioeconomic status of their classmates. Lower-class black and white children in middle-class elementary schools perform better than similar children in lower-class school environments. More significant is his finding (Wilson, 1963) that the assigning of grades by teachers is influenced by the social class composition of schools. Middle-class children in lower-class schools receive relatively more A and B grades than middle-class children with comparable achievement scores in middle-class schools. This suggests that teachers adopt grading criteria based, at least partly, on subjective considerations.

There is substantial evidence suggesting that teacher perceptions and expectations result in the creation of "self-fulfilling prophecies" which have serious consequences for children's educational success or failure. Rosenthal and Jacobson (1968a; 1968b) investigated this phenomenon in a South San Francisco elementary school. All children in kindergarten through the fifth grade were given a standard intelligence test on the pretext that investigators from Harvard were trying to refine an instrument designed to identify "academic blooming." The following year 20 percent of the children were randomly selected and classified as potential "academic spurters." This information was casually "leaked" to their teachers. In a retest four months later, using the same instrument, the potential academic spurters "from whom teachers expected greater intellectual gains showed such gains" (1968a:6). The largest gains were found among the youngest children, those from the lowest grades being presumably the most malleable. The children labelled "spurters" were also evaluated more favorably by their teachers than were the others. Rosenthal and Jacobson argue that the academic gains of the sample children can best be explained by the subtler features of teacher-pupil interaction. For example, "Her tone of voice, facial expression, touch and posture may be the means by which—probably quite unwittingly—she communicates her expectations to the pupils" (1968a:7). During the same period, undesignated children who evidenced significant gains on the intelligence tests were denied recognition by teachers for their improvement. The *true* academic spurters were portrayed by teachers as displaying undesirable behavior. They evidently violated the expectations of their teachers, thus contributing to the teacher's feelings of conflict and anxiety.

Ray Rist (1970) made an observational study of a single group of black elementary school children spanning two and a half years, attempting to determine the importance of initial expectations held by teachers for children's future academic success or failure. Rist observed that in initial meetings with kindergarten children the teacher evaluated them regarding the degree to which they fit her idealized conception of the child most likely to succeed academically. These preconceptions were, in large part, based on social class criteria. On the strength of this initial screening procedure, the class was divided (physically and reputationally) into "fast learners" and "slow learners." "Fast learners" received "the majority of the teaching time, reward-directed behavior, and attention from the teacher. Those designated as 'slow learners' were taught infrequently, subjected to more frequent control-oriented behavior, and received little, if any, supportive behavior from the teacher" (1970:414). Throughout the remainder of the school year, these patterns of teacher-pupil interaction persisted, resembling "caste-like characteristics." Thus, teachers' initial expectations, coupled with abrasive patterns of interaction between "favored" and "slow learning" students, resulted in a widening gap between the amount of academic material they covered during the year. This process of differentiation continued in following years with teachers relying progressively more on achievement and intelligence data to justify their actions.

Attempts by individual teachers to overcome the constraints of the bureaucratized classroom and adapt their teaching to the needs of their students are likely to meet with frustration if not professional and personal disaster. For example, Jonathan Kozol, a Rhodes scholar and author who tried his hand at teaching children in the Boston public school system in the 1960s, met with little success in his attempts at resisting the constraints of bureaucratization. He was fired from his "entry level" teaching position for lacking "the personal discipline to abide by rules and regulations, as we all must in our civilized society" and because he was "obviously unsuited for the highly responsible profession of teaching" (Kozol, 1967:226).

His offenses were debatable. He sought to bring learning alive for young Negro students by teaching them the classic poems of Langston Hughes (a black man) and Robert Frost. He read to them from Yeats and captured their interest with pictures by Paul Klee. These offenses, according to noted educator Robert Coles, threatened "his standing, his job, his yearly income, his day-to-day relationship with his peers." His gifted teaching could not be tolerated by a "hopelessly insensitive bureaucracy" (Kozol, 1967:ix).

If there is a lesson to be learned from Kozol's frustrating experiences, it is that mass educating the poor might be impossible within a structure too inflexible to accommodate their special needs and too large to appreciate their unique traits and experiences. It is worthwhile to note that these problems are not confined to schools in Chicago and Boston. Nor, for that matter, are effects of mass education confined to minorities and the poor. In recent years many aspects of the education process described by Becker and Kozol have been observed, and criticized, by other students of education in American society (e.g., Friedenberg, 1965; Silberman, 1970). Jules Henry (1955) believes urban American middle-class children are taught by their teachers a response system called "docility." He demonstrates in American schools "that aspect of docility which has to do with the teacher's getting from the children the answers she wants."

In studying classroom experiences of middle-class children, Henry observed teachers employing uniquely middle-class techniques to maintain law and order and effect moral acceptability. While teachers of the lower classes must rely on authoritarian control, their middle-class counterparts impart docility by taking advantage of students' "fear of loss of love." By offering acceptance to only those children able to guess the routinized answers to standardized questions, teachers reward docility and extinguish creative thought. The goals of the bureaucracy are met; encouraging docility and imparting limited but utilitarian skills and attitudes. But at what price? Henry writes "[t]his kind of docility can be more lethal than the other [lower-class], for it does not breed rebellion and independence, as struggle against authoritarian controls may, but rather a kind of cloying paralysis, a sweet imprisonment without pain" (1968:318).

Teacher Autonomy

Where teachers once commanded several subject areas and interacted with children over a wide range of ages, they now specialize by age group (elementary, junior high, or high school) and subject matter. This, combined with the tendency of bureaucracies to stratify hierarchically, has stripped teachers of much control over what and how they teach.

In many cases, this could be a positive function of bureaucratization. It could afford teachers more time and opportunity to develop their knowledge and teaching skills in areas dictated by their own interests. But there is a greater tendency for the needs of the bureaucracy to dictate teaching assignments. For example, if a school had in its employ three teachers trained in math and enrollments warranted retaining only two, the expendable math teacher might be kept to serve as head coach of two varsity sports or reassigned to English or driver's education. Perhaps matching teacher's skills and knowledge to class subjects be-

Table 2. Structural Profile of American Educational Bureaucracy

Characteristics	Consequences
Large size	Forces use of "mass education" techniques
Standardized rules and regulations and equality of handling	Requires preparing lesson plans far in advance, dictates teaching of subject matter dictated only by job and future educational concerns.
	Teachers must maintain "law and order" by imparting docility to lower- and middle-class children.
Division of labor rights and power	Teachers become age-group and subject matter specialists.
Hierarchically ordering of offices	Authority transfers from teachers to multiplying administrative statuses.

comes a tedious and unwieldy administrative assignment in large schools; so difficult, in fact, that administrators react by changing their attitudes regarding the educational process. They assume that anyone certified (by the organization) to teach can handle practically any subject "at this level." Thus, teachers could often be ill-matched by training and interest with their subjects and students. If these conditions were widespread in education, they would surely result in a weakening of the quality of experiences shared by teachers and the young.

Finally, as administrative statuses in education (principal, counselor, registrar, auditor, and so on) have proliferated, fewer decisions regarding schools are made by teachers. Rather school boards and administrators set policy, leaving teachers the choice of either obeying the rules, seeking alternative careers, or resisting by means once considered "beneath" professionals.[2]

In sum, the most dominant feature of American education is also a major

---

[2] While this point is beyond the scope of the present essay, it is important to note that more teachers are seeking shelter from the educational bureaucracy under the cloak of unions and other collective organizations. Many consider affiliating with such groups to be in conflict with other aspects of the teaching (profession) role. Such role conflict, of course, has consequences for the quality of teaching. For a more complete discussion of role conflict among teachers, see Edward Gross, "Sociological Aspects of Professional Salaries in Education," in Robert R. Bell and Holger R. Stub (Eds.), The Sociology of Education: A Source Book, (Homewood, Illinois: Dorsey Press, 1968); Gerald H. Mueller, "Bureaucracy and Teacher's Sense of Power," School Review, 1964, 72, p. 152; S. Rettig and B. Passamanick, "Status and Job Satisfaction of Public School Teachers," School and Society, 1959, 87, pp. 113–116; G. G. Gordon, "Conditions of Employment and Service in Elementary and Secondary Schools: Teacher Status and Role Expectations," Review of Educational Research, 1963, 33, p. 382.

source of its problems. On the one hand, no one has found a more efficient means of organizing a large-scale complex of human activities than bureaucratization offers. Yet, as Table 2 indicates, organizational considerations may quickly supercede traditional educational values and produce many subtle but constricting impediments to learning.

Many of the current features of education we have discussed result in its being less than the most attractive career choice for persons gifted with the skills of a teacher. This has not always been the case. Writer Kurt Vonnegut, Jr. (1970: vii), speaking of his early educational experiences, reminds us that learning can involve exchanges between the brightest of people—and show positive results.

One thing that was lucky for me: my high school years were from 1936 into 1940, and the Great Depression was still pretty mean, and the smartest people in town had turned to teaching. I don't think the smartest people do that any more. Times change.

We may conclude that many problems with mass education in American society are directly related to the way it has become structured. This suggests that those wishing to improve the quality of learning in schools must begin to pay serious attention to the ways that common *forms* of education make "work" of interaction between teachers and students. But the American educational institution has traditionally resisted change. In the following section we will examine common patterns of educational control and funding and how these have precluded meaningful reform.

THE FUNDING AND CONTROL OF EDUCATION

Since mass education is organized bureaucratically, we would expect to find a centralized pattern of funding and control for schools. This is not yet the case, however, in American society. Sociologist Jonathan Turner (1972:200–204), in his discussion of who should run and fund American schools, presents us with data suggesting that American education is far from the ideal bureaucracy described by Etzioni (1964). He feels that schools are frequently ineffective, not because bureaucracies are necessarily inoperable, but because their structure only in part fits Etzioni's model.

School Funding

American school financing comes from divergent sources, more than in any other industrialized society. Several branches of the federal government channel funds to local school districts. State governments share revenues from income and sales taxes with districts within their political boundaries. But federal and state aid combined pale, when compared to the support given American schools by local property owners. Local school boards and political leaders rightly surmised that if they allowed federal and state agencies to support local school districts, this would lead also to the centering of educational control in the hands of the higher governmental bodies. Thus, they relied heavily on the willingness of local property owners to subsidize local schools in order to maintain what today's Supreme Court terms "local standards."

Local school boards vary in size and complexity from "minibureaucracies" in large metropolitan areas to small aggregates of political-minded and influential citizens in communities of smaller size. School boards are that part of the educational bureaucracy which formulates and enforces most of the standards by which day-to-day public education is

run. The resultant fragmentation of control guarantees that the remarkable cultural and geographical heterogeneity of American society is transmitted into the decision-making process governing our schools. This means that in 1975, children in West Virginia and Boston who attended the same kinds of schools learn markedly different lessons. West Virginia parents have demanded that the writings of Allen Ginsburg, Malcolm X, Dick Gregory, and Eldridge Cleaver be banned from their children's books. These children are also screened from the emergence of urban black America. They are bound by the conservative, rural, blue-collar values of their parents.

At the same time, Boston parents are levying another kind of local control over their schools. While the Boston school board is under instruction from the courts to develop an effective plan for racial desegregation in its public schools, a formidable segment of the community refuses to comply. Consequently, children unfortunate enough to have the wrong skin color are forced to watch contesting groups of parents flail away at one another like boom-town gladiators. These racial conflicts are waged over questions of whether or not black children should be accorded the same educational considerations as Anglos. Judging from these and other available examples, it would appear that local control does not always result in the best possible learning environment for children.

Similarly, the American pattern of decentralized school funding and control results in wide gaps in the quality of school resources and programs. This was recognized in 1971 in the California Supreme Court ruling that the use of local property taxes to finance education "discriminates against the poor . . . [and]

makes the quality of a child's education a function of the wealth of his parents and neighbors" (Turner, 1972:200). But the California decision is currently lost in a torrent of recent federal court decisions. This suggests that American society is not yet ready to give equal economic resources to all children.

Changing Control

Local school boards have feared that if state and federal agencies were to provide the bulk of funds, control of public education could be easily wrested away. But as the cost of education continues to increase, the willingness of local property owners to underwrite the schools has flagged. Consequently, school boards are in financial crises; they are being forced to exchange local autonomy for auxiliary economic support from state and federal sources. With federal and state school funds channeled through state regulatory agencies (usually a state board of education), local school boards are forced to obey new centralized regulatory policies. For example, many state boards have assumed the responsibility for establishing general criteria regarding teacher certification and curricula for all school districts within their political boundaries. But frequently, local boards still retain enough strength to circumvent these policies.

As federal funds comprise increasingly larger portions of local school boards' budgets, however, the balance of control over public education will begin to shift toward the national government. As this trend continues, the Federal Office of Education, a branch of the Department of Health, Education, and Welfare, will probably emerge to control all formal education in the United States. A shift in structure giving rise to a more clear-cut hierarchy of offices and power should improve education's posture in dealing with the society-wide problem of disseminating quality education to all children, regardless of race, creed, color, or national origin.

Centralized federal funding of schools could easily remove the roadblocks of "localism" and "regionalism" which have maintained the present pattern of grossly inadequate economic support for schools serving rural and disadvantaged children. Equal educational opportunity could be provided by implementing a society-wide policy of total racial desegregation of public school facilities. Such policies, when introduced by local school boards, have been alarmingly susceptible to regional manifestations of traditional American racist values. While centralizing school control at the federal level would not automatically make America less racist, a national administrative hierarchy would be physically removed from local influences, and hence more able to use the threat of withdrawing funds to induce compliance to desegregation directives.

But what of a bureaucracy's tendency to go stale with growth? We suggest that educators of today must begin building into the formal structure of American education "regenerative mechanisms" designed to change its conservative bent. For example, if the Department of Health, Education, and Welfare were to create two equal status branches—the Office of Education, regulating today's traditional educational system; and the Office of Experimental Education, to develop innovative and more effective teaching technologies—education could renew itself from within. The Office of Experimental Education (OEE) would fund, and perhaps eventually certify, new kinds of schools and learning situations.

Free schools, "Montessori-type" schools, schools without failure, token economies, and educational co-ops (neighborhood and otherwise) could be evaluated regarding their effectiveness at teaching important technoindustrial skills and attitudes and at instilling within children a deep commitment to learning. As new and more effective teaching methods emerged, they could be adopted by the Office of Education and become part of the general public education system. (This is already done in piecemeal fashion by the federal government's Educational Research Information Center.) Instead of encouraging docility and mediocrity, a federal educational system so structured *could* provide much richer learning experiences for its youth.

But problems with mass education in America do not lie solely in its organization and pattern of funding and control. Schools consist of people, some older and teaching, most young and learning. The children come in different colors with different patterns of appearance, speech, and behavior. Teachers are mostly middle-class and white, and deeply committed to the traditional American belief that "white is better."

RACISM IN EDUCATION

The exploitive and often violent pattern of American interracial behavior is of considerable importance in comprehending educational problems. By 1960 approximately two-thirds of the black and Anglo-American population had left the farm to reside in metropolitan areas, which suggests that industrialized cities offered opportunity to both races. But it does not mean that economically and politically dominant Anglos sought meaningful racial integration. Alexis de Tocqueville (1945) observed in the nineteenth century that belief in the superiority of white-skinned racial groups to blacks and other dark-skinned minorities was strong among Americans. There has been little appreciable change since.

Instead of meeting in social, political, and religious intercourse, urban Anglos and blacks lived in close proximity to their jobs in the city and limited social contacts to the cold contractual economic sector (Banfield, 1973). According to Michael Harrington, (1969) urban minorities (and other societal undesirables) were traditionally cloistered in an "other America" within major cities. Dark-skinned outcasts were pushed as far from sight into the decaying inner city's core as technology would allow. Black laborers were needed to stoke the fires of an industrializing society, but granting marginal status to them in the work force was not meant to imply social parity. Blacks were allowed to rent the city's oldest, most inhospitable slums, to be educated in grossly unequal schools, to be taught largely by culls from the Anglo school system, and to walk the streets closely monitored by police. Their living conditions were dictated more by what the country could spare for an economically necessary but socially undesirable population than an open-door policy toward entry into the Anglo-American "melting pot." Describing Harlem, Harrington (1969:67) summarizes the effect American racism has had on Anglo-black relations:

There is, on the very surface of Harlem life, the imminence of the Man.

The Man is white. He has many guises: as policeman, as judge, as rent collector— as authority made tangible. He is to be feared and hated, for the law is especially swift and hard upon the crimes and vices that grow within these crowded, littered streets. Ultimately he becomes anyone with a white skin. ("Offay," the old Negro slang term for a white, is foe in pig latin.) Because of this, Harlem is a place that is suspicious of all outsiders from the world of white America. It is stunted and sick, and the bread of its poverty has the taste of hatred and fear. . . . Harlem, for all its brashness, for all the ubiquitous rhythms of rock'n'roll, is afraid. And for good reason. The white has been the Man, and in many cases he still is.

As the American economy has become stronger and technological advances allow middle-class Anglos to move to the suburbs, the split between major racial and ethnic groups only widens. Anglo parents, aided by government subsidies and legal guarantees of suburban racial homogeneity, seized the opportunity to put greater physical and social distance between their privately owned homes and the decaying rentals of the urban poor— black and white alike (Banfield, 1973). These trends are illuminated by statistics from the Bureau of the Census indicating that by 1960, 80 percent of urban blacks resided in the central city while more than 50 percent of the nation's urban Anglo population fled to the suburbs (Pettigrew, 1967:11). Direct interracial contact has been reduced by suburbanization; but problems brought on by unequal living conditions have worsened. It is out of this societal context that our system of public education has developed in the midst of exploitation, hatred, and fear between Anglo-Americans and dark-skinned minorities.

Separate school systems emerged; one to create a highly educated white population, the other patterned after its elegant stepsister, but imparting only the most basic cultural values and simple job skills

to "inferior" minorities. This bittersweet relationship between industrializing Anglos and their necessary but culturally "inferior" labor force is not unknown in the history of societies. It resembles, in many ways, the ambivalent patterning of relationships between dominant goups in some modern Scandinavian countries and their imported laborers. On the one hand, these countries have advanced technologically and industrially to the point where the birth rate among native-born persons no longer meets the need for workers. But many Scandinavians find these guest labor forces culturally offensive and are considering legislation which would provide for their mandatory departure in the event of an economic down-swing. This suggests that, in general, societies make only minimal commitment to the welfare of groups, however necessary, which are defined as visually, culturally, and behaviorally inferior. When minorities occupy such devalued statuses in any society it would be surprising to find the political system stressing their welfare— in education or any other sphere of society.

In spite of its structural problems, Anglo-American education has become a vast system of primary, secondary, and higher level schools capable of producing large numbers of highly skilled workers. This is most visible at the university level where a plethora of excellent graduate science, philosophy, literature, and art schools exists. Not only have Anglo schools produced historically unprecedented technological advances, but they have contributed to remarkable improvement in the general Anglo literacy rate. From 1870 to 1969 the proportion of illiteracy among American whites has dropped from 11.5 to 0.7 percent.

But minority (predominantly black) schools have historically been given less help—and hope. From the beginning, blacks, the poor, and other minority children were forced to attend "special schools." Frequently, but not always, these schools were housed in buildings not unlike the crumbling tenements surrounding them. Black parents wanted their children to attend neighborhood schools, but were allowed to do so only when it kept them in their place—the "other America." Moreover, black children are instructed according to Anglo rules and mass education procedures stressing standardized teaching techniques and Anglo middle-class values. Yet, black children in segregated schools learn neither as much nor as fast as Anglos. For example, in the period from 1870 to 1969, black illiteracy was reduced from 79.9 to 3.6 percent. One wonders whether Anglo parents would tolerate a school system incapable of imparting to almost four out of each one hundred children the most basic reading and writing skills.

Even though children in America's devalued schools are predominantly black, Chicano, or Puerto Rican, local school boards, administrators, and teachers for the most part ignore the possibility that black (Chicano, Native American, and so forth) culture influences children's behavior and could be used to promote learning. In fact, schools are not above casting out teachers who dare use unauthorized techniques and materials—black music, poetry, or ideology—in the classroom (Kozol, 1967).

When necessary the legal system has stepped in to protect Anglo America from educational infiltration. Historian Meyer Weinberg (1967) documents this in his important but largely unnoticed review of the American court systems' contribution to racism in education. During education's formative years, black parents regularly went into America's local courts to plead that their children should be allowed to attend "neighborhood schools." They argued it was unfair to require black children to walk farther, across more dangerous terrain, and past Anglo schools, to attend obviously inferior, segregated schools. In the vast majority of cases, courts ruled against minority parents. When questions of gaining black access to Anglo schools were aired, courts apparently saw little need to provide equal justice (Weinberg, 1967:2–27).

Local school boards also contributed significantly to the national segregation effort (Pettigrew, 1967; Weinberg, 1967). In fact, most school boards in the country have gerrymandered districts and attendance lines at one time or another in order to keep their school system racially separate. Anglo America's commitment to the racial homogeneity of public education has nowhere been more forcefully stated than by the nineteenth-century northern mayor who told a committee of black adults:

"I propose to keep the niggers out of school with white children. . . . I don't care where they live, but I will keep them out of the schools with the White children of ———— if I have to use every policeman I have got in the city to do it." (Weinberg, 1967:34)

The federal government, influenced by a racist cultural milieu, would probably not have interceded had it been able. During the emergent stages of public education, a strong states' rights and laissez-faire ideology kept government too weak to intervene. This situation did not change until the mid-1960s when the government finally found and flexed its organizational muscle in defense of minority children. Buttressed by the heretofore unheeded *Brown vs. the Board of Education of Topeka* (1954) Supreme Court ruling, which directed states to provide the opportunity of an education "to all on equal terms," the United States Congress commissioned a group of sociologists to:

conduct a survey and make a report to the President and the Congress, within two years of the enactment of this title, concerning the lack of availability of equal educational opportunities for individuals by reason of race, color, religion, or national origin in public educational institutions at all levels in the United States, its territories and possessions, and the District of Columbia. (Coleman, 1966:iii)

The federal government was about to wage an all-out war on school segregation and wanted evidence of racism in education as armor against inevitable Anglo opposition.

James S. Coleman (1966) of the Johns Hopkins University and Ernest Q. Campbell of Vanderbilt University, were enlisted to design and conduct the survey. From the beginning, their project suffered the problems of much large-scale social research. Congress, ready to act and in a hurry for answers, gave Coleman and Campbell only two years to design and implement the survey of 4000 schools and over 570,000 children. During this time they were to gather data, analyze and interpret it, and report their findings. Lacking a sufficient time for truly critical and complicated social research lessened any chances of obtaining credible answers to their questions. Also, several of the largest school systems in the United

States refused to grant the investigators access to children and information, and these were, consequently, eliminated from the study. All this seriously compromises the ability to draw generalizations from the school survey to educational opportunity in larger school systems. Finally, many have criticized Coleman and Campbell for placing too much reliance on schools, teachers, and administrators for information regarding their own part in providing—or denying—equal educational opportunity. It is possibly naive to assume that the very parties suspected of racism would be willing to give accurate reports of their activities. Also, possibly because of the number of students involved, the investigators failed to gather information on the *quality* of relationships between teachers and students, a critical error if the previously reported work of Becker and Henry is to be considered.

In view of these serious problems with sampling, search design, and interpretation, *Equality of Educational Opportunity* (Coleman et al., 1966) and portions of *Racial Isolation in the Public Schools* (Pettigrew, 1967)—major reports of the survey's findings—were far from definitive. Yet Congress and the American courts were ready to act on racial imbalance and took what suited their purpose from the reports. The following survey findings set the stage for America's first attempt to correct its racist system of education:

Racial concentration into separate schools is indeed even more widespread and severe than anticipated. The vast majority of Black children are concentrated in central city public schools while Anglos attend suburban and private schools. (Pettigrew, 1967)

National figures on population movement suggest these patterns will continue and worsen in the future. (Pettigrew, 1967)

Black students on the average begin school with less verbal ability than Anglos, by the sixth grade they are one and one-half years behind, and by the 12th grade they are three years behind with eighty-five percent falling below the Anglo average. (Coleman, 1966)

Black students in schools with an Anglo majority perform better academically than those in predominantly Black schools. (Coleman, 1966)

The performance of Anglo students is undisturbed by Black attendance. (Coleman, 1967)

Congress felt it had clearly documented American educational inequality and discovered its solution—school desegregation. Shortly thereafter, federal machinery was started to force open the doors of Anglo schools. Congress passed legislation providing vast funds for school buses and new programs in Anglo schools. The American court system reversed its earlier posture and began ordering school boards to eliminate racial considerations from boundary decisions and move toward racial symmetry in school-by-school enrollments.

Predictably, there was no stampede of school boards to plan genuine desegregation efforts (Weinberg, 1970). They chose to retreat and retrench around two new educational practices devised to preserve racial imbalance. First, school systems all over the country quickly announced they were obeying court decisions and congressional directives by adopting open registration policies. Children within school districts would be allowed to select the school which they wished to attend, enrollments permitting, with only one qualification. Their parents must either provide transportation to and from school or pay the school district for transportation. This served the purpose of allowing minority children to attend distant Anglo schools if only their parents could find a way to pay for it. School gates were opened with only residential segregation and black poverty left as impediments.

Federal revenues in hand, school districts also initiated "compensatory" educational programs to intensify efforts at reducing the Anglo-black achievement gap. For the most part, compensatory education took place in the same segregated context which meant failure for earlier generations of black children. Compensatory education turned out to be little more than a new attempt to preserve an old American tradition—segregated and unequal schools.

To no one's surprise, open enrollment policies and compensatory education failed to close the black achievement gap and resulted in little school desegregation. Consequently, court orders soon forced many local school boards to plan and initiate programs of school desegregation in order to achieve racial balance. A few cities, perhaps anticipating court intervention, voluntarily desegregated their school systems.

It should not be assumed that American society, through its schools, was now ready to openly embrace black America on equal terms. To head off anticipated resistance by Anglo parents, in the vast majority of cases, only black students were uprooted, bused across town, and dropped into threatening new circumstances. In socially enlightened cities, such as Berkeley, California, blacks and Anglos equally shared the burden of moving to new schools, but in most cases school boards forced black children to sacrifice far more than their Anglo peers.

SCHOOL DESEGREGATION PERSPECTIVE

Historian Meyer Weinberg (1970:204), an expert on school desegregation, warns that the fight against racism in education is often misunderstood due to popular confusion over meanings of words. *Segregation* is the more or less formal separation of various distinguishable groups by social design. We often think of unequal educational opportunity only in terms of black and white—insurgent Negroes and Anglo schools. But racial segregation is a narrower, perhaps more intense, concomitant of segregation by social class in the United States. As Harrington (1969) noted, the "other America" is only part black. In raw numbers, many American children shuttled through grossly inferior school systems—ghetto schools, rural schools, factory schools—are white. The price they are asked to pay for success is much higher than for more advantaged children. Their failures are tolerated, if not expected, but because their families live in the shadow of poverty, minority children bear a double burden. Not only are they poor, but also distinguishable by skin color or accent. Thus, racial segregation bears the seemingly unlimited ability of economic and political elites to channel the society's efforts and resources into separatist and exploitive domestic policies.

Desegregation is the planned, and politically enforced, removal of major social barriers to significant interracial interaction. In schools, this means the forced removal of formal and covert barriers to the use of Anglo, advantaged schools by blacks and other minorities. But this should not be confused with integration.

Integration is the utopian goal of persons dedicated to democratic and humanistic ideals. It implies that the allocation of scarce resources—power, privilege, education, health, and dignity—be determined solely on the basis of personal achievement and compassion and not ascribed characteristics. In education this would mean that decisions regarding where children go to school would not be influenced by skin color, hygiene, and the fatness of parental pocketbooks, but by considerations of fairness and aptitude.

In view of these important distinctions, it should be obvious that school desegregation is only the first step down a long, difficult path to meaningful social integration. In fact, many argue that trying to achieve social integration through schools—ignoring neighborhood segregation and economic inequality—will meet with about as much success as Native Americans have realized in negotiating treaties with the U.S. government.

As desegregation schemes proliferated, spurred by an adamant Supreme Court and Congress, evidence in support of racial mingling mounted. At first, the pro-desegregation reports came from liberal, and often optimistic, school administrators. They were blatantly subjective and rarely supported by rigorous evaluation efforts. Later, as the first large school systems desegregated, more reliable data appeared to corroborate Coleman's early conclusions (Weinberg, 1970:378–9). In fact, from 1968 through the early 1970s, the utility of school desegregation as an egalitarian measure was so commonly accepted that arguments against it were, for the most part, summarily rejected.

This rare consensus between the government, courts, and educational scholars was shattered in the summer of 1972 by David Armor, a sociologist who himself conducted early prodesegregation research. Armor (1972) reported findings from his own study of desegregation in Boston's suburbs and from his interpretation of reports on desegregation programs in four northern cities: White Plains, Ann Arbor, Riverside, and a combined program in Hartford and New Haven, Connecticut. He concluded: "None of the studies were able to demonstrate conclusively that integration has had an effect on academic achievement as measured by standardized tests" (1972:99). Moreover, Armor argued that early reports of positive gains in such areas as levels of aspiration, self-concept, and achievement motivation, were misleading. If anything, his data suggested that "under the circumstances obtaining in these studies, integration heightens racial identity and consciousness, enhances ideologies that promote racial segregation, and reduces opportunities for actual contact between the races" (1972:102).

Armor's challenge to the assumption that desegregation is an effective procedure for achieving equality in education unleashed a torrent of controversy on two fronts. In academic circles, Armor's ideological heresy was attacked with rare fervor (Pettigrew et al., 1973:89–117). Perhaps more importantly, Armor's words rekindled the flame of racial separatism which had been weakened, but not extinguished, by the short-lived antisegregation approach of the sixties. First in the popular press (Hodgson, 1973:35–46), then in government and the courts, the advisability of school desegregation was called into question. With remarkable haste, a sizeable antibusing bloc formed around a coterie of scholars who argued that the ability of schools to shape skill

levels and attitudes had been exaggerated. The traditional beliefs that schools are incapable of helping minorities, that the black-Anglo achievement differences might ultimately be tied to inherent racial differences, found renewed credibility. Racism had once again gained the upper hand. It was easily overlooked that American black children were struggling to overcome the effects of hundreds of years of racial discrimination in one short childhood, and classrooms became the site for continuing America's racial cold war.

PERSPECTIVE

The importance of public education in determining future lifestyles cannot be overestimated even by those who look at children and schools with the most racist and conservative myopias. Most people must concede that success and failure in school is directly, and causally, related to success and failure, in obtaining access to society's higher forms of cultural and educational structures, seeking secure and rewarding employment, and realizing enough culturally ingrained personal goals to possess a deep sense of self-worth. But schools also exert subtler influences. Lawmaking bodies in most states have enacted statutes which equate many common manifestations of failure in school with juvenile delinquency. Not only children who commit crimes against persons and property, but also those who are habitually truant and the schools' most serious behavior problems are hurled into the gnashing machinery of the juvenile justice system and are frequently defined as societal failures. In most cases, modern schools look on with cold indifference as children are shuttled from the part of society which is supposed to nurture, train, and even succor them, into an abyss of probation departments, courts, and "Orwellian" correctional facilities.

Even the vast majority of persons who achieve in school and are destined to obtain position, influence, and wealth are touched heavily by the problems of mass education. To contemporary race-related issues, they all too often bring plantation attitudes and stereotypes, lessons well-learned in school. Well-educated social leaders continue trying to placate serious and often well-armed minorities with tired slogans—"as long as the grass grows and the river flows," "now, these things take time," and "if you want to make it in America, you're going to have to pull yourselves up by the bootstraps." From our poverty programs, designed to fatten the purses of middle-class Anglo businessmen, to the governments' abandonment of the fight to achieve universal school desegregation, the dominant majority is still maintaining the traditional racist attitudes and values imparted by schools.

Perhaps most significant of all its deficits is education's apparent tendency to promote docility and complacency in all children, black or white, rich or poor. Who could estimate the cost to society of training a population of followers—unquestioning, servile, and barely moved by Watergates, wars, and waste? How might such a society muster enough energy and wisdom to wage the frequent "revolutions" Thomas Jefferson felt were so important to the maintenance of democracy?

Yet, critical as education may be to the future of America, its problems must be analyzed and corrected in concert. The problems of structure, funding and control, and racism combine in subtle and complex ways to produce failure and, at best, only a qualified success. No program or explanation which focuses on one type of problem while ignoring the others will prove of much utility. We must acknowledge that societies, and their parts, are extremely complicated and delicately interrelated. Studies, descriptions, and resulting social programs must take this into account or finite resources and energies will continue to be squandered while the chasm between races continues to grow.

There has been a tendency by students of educational achievement to emphasize the influence of one set of factors—parents' characteristics and attitudes, or teacher-school factors—to the exclusion of the others. Even when lip-service is paid to the multiple and complex causes of academic achievement in the early school years, little effort is expended in determining the relative importance of these factors. Almost no attempt has been made to delineate their interrelationships.

We must learn from our educational failures that piecemeal solutions to general and related social problems will not work. In concert, a centralized agency—most likely the federal government—must take major responsibility for funding and control of education, build in new mechanisms to promote creativity and autonomy for teachers and students alike, and seriously outlaw racial discrimination in both its formal and informal curricular manifestations. Nothing short of this will force change upon today's very complex system of public education.

References

Armor, David J. "The Evidence on Busing." *Public Interest*, 1972, 28, 90–126.

Banfield, Edward C. *The Unheavenly City*. Boston: Little, Brown, 1970.

Banfield, Edward C. *The Unheavenly City Revisited*. Boston: Little, Brown, 1973.

Barry, E. Raymond, Hewitt, Robert R., Gerard, Harold B., Miller, Norman, and Singer, Harry. *Factors Contributing to Adjustment and Achievement in Racially Desegregated Public Schools*. Riverside, Ca.: Riverside Unified School District, 1966.

Becker, Howard S. "Role and Career Problems of the Chicago Public School Teacher." Unpublished Ph.D. dissertation. Chicago: University of Chicago, Department of Sociology, 1951.

Becker, Howard S. "The Career of the Chicago Public School Teacher." *The American Journal of Sociology*, 1952, 52, 470–477. (a)

Becker, Howard S. "Social Class Variations in the Teacher-Pupil Relationship." *The Journal of Educational Sociology*, 1952, 25, 451–465. (b)

Blau, Peter M., and Duncan, Otis Dudley. *The American Occupational Structure*. New York: Wiley, 1967.

Brown versus Board of Education of Topeka, U.S. 347, No. 5, 1954, 493.

Cohen, Wilbur J., and Sullivan, Eugenia. *Poverty in the United States*. Health, Education, and Welfare Indicators, 1964.

Coleman, James S., with Campbell, Ernest Q., Hobson, Carol J., McPartland, James, Mood, Alexander M., Weinfeld, Frederick D., and York, Robert L. *Equality of Educational Opportunity*. Washington, D.C.: U.S. Government Printing Office, 1966.

Coleman, James S. A *Brief Summary of the Coleman Report*. Equal Educational Opportunity edition, *Harvard Educational Review*. Cambridge, Mass.: Harvard University Press, 1969.

Council of Economic Advisers. *Economic Report of the President*. Washington, D.C.: U.S. Government Printing Office, 1964.

Criswell, Joan H. "A Sociometric Study of Race Cleavage in the Classroom." *Psychology Archives*, 235, 1939.

Deese, J. "Skilled Performance and Conditions of Stress," In R. Glaser (Ed.), *Training Research and Education*. Pittsburgh: University of Pittsburgh Press, 1962. Pp. 199–222.

Ellis, A. Caswell. "The Money Value of Education." In Department of the Interior Bureau of Education Bulletin No. 22. Washington, D.C.: U.S. Government Printing Office, 1917. Pp. 14–50.

Etzioni, Amitai. *Modern Organizations*. Englewood Cliffs, N.J.: Prentice-Hall, 1964.

Friedenberg, Edgar Z. *Coming of Age in America*. New York: Knopf, 1965.

Glick, Paul C. "Educational Attainment and Occupational Advancement." In *Transactions of the Second World Congress of Sociology*. London: International Sociological Association II, 1954. Pp. 183–194.

Goodman, Paul. *Growing Up Absurd*. New York: Vintage, 1960.

Grant, W. Vance, and Lind, C. George. *Digest of Educational Statistics*. Washington, D.C.: U.S. Government Printing Office, 1974.

Harrington, Michael. *The Other America*. Baltimore: Penguin, 1969.

Henry, Jules. "Docility, or Giving Teacher What She Wants." *Journal of Social Issues*, 1955, 2, 33–41.

Hodgson, Godfrey. "Do Schools Make a Difference?" *The Atlantic*, 1973, 231, 35–46.

Horowitz, E. "The Development of Attitudes toward the Negro." *Psychology Archives*, 194, 1936.

Jencks, Christopher. *Inequality: A Reassessment of the Effect of Family and Schooling in America*. New York: Basic Books, 1972.

Jensen, Arthur R. "How Much Can We Boost IQ and Scholastic Achievement?" *Harvard Educational Review*, 1969, 39, 1–123.

Katz, Irwin. "Review of Evidence Relating to Effects of Desegregation on the Intellectual Performance of Negroes." *American Psychology*, 1964, 19, 381–399.

Kozol, Jonathan. *Death at an Early Age*. Boston: Houghton Mifflin, 1967.

Levitan, S. A. *The Design of Federal*

Antipoverty Strategy. Ann Arbor: University of Michigan Press, 1967.

Lewis, Oscar. *Five Families.* New York: Basic Books, 1959.

Lewis, Oscar. *The Study of Slum Culture—Backgrounds for La Vida.* New York: Random House, 1968.

Mann, Horace. "Twelfth Annual Report of Horace Mann as Secretary of the Massachusetts State Board of Education." In Henry Commager (Ed.), *Documents in American History,* 9th ed. New York: Appleton, 1973. Original date 1848.

Merton, Robert K. "The Self-Fulfilling Prophecy." *Antioch Review,* 1948, 8, 193–210.

Merton, Robert K. *Social Theory and Social Structure.* New York: Free Press, 1957.

Miller, Walter. "The Elimination of the American Lower Class as National Policy: A Critique of the Ideology of the Poverty Movement of the 1960s." In Daniel P. Moynihan (Ed.), *On Understanding Poverty.* New York: Basic Books, 1969. Pp. 260–315.

Moynihan, Daniel P. *Maximum Feasible Misunderstanding: Community Action in the War on Poverty.* New York: Free Press, 1969.

Parsons, Talcott. "The School Class as a Social System: Some of Its Functions in American Society." *The Harvard Educational Review,* 1959, 29, 297–318.

Pettigrew, Thomas F. *Racial Isolation in the Public Schools.* Washington, D.C.: U.S. Government Printing Office, 1967.

Pettigrew, Thomas F., with Useem, Elizabeth L., Normand, Clarence, and Smith, Marshall. "Busing: A Review of 'The Evidence.'" *Public Interest,* 1973, 30, 88–134.

Radke, Marian, with Sutherland, Jean, and Rosenberg, Pearl. "Racial Attitudes of Children." *Sociometry,* 1950, 13, 154–171.

Rist, Ray C. "Student Social Class and Teacher Expectations: The Self-Fulfilling Prophecy in Ghetto Education." *Harvard Educational Review,* 1970, 40, 411–451.

Ritzer, George. *Man and His Work: Conflict and Change.* New York: Appleton, 1972.

Rosenthal, Robert, and Jacobson, Lenore F. "Teacher Expectations for the Disadvantaged." *Scientific American,* 1968, 218, 3–7. (a)

Rosenthal, Robert, and Jacobson, Lenore F. *Pygmalion in the Classroom.* New York: Holt, Rinehart and Winston, 1968. (b)

St. John, Nancy. "Desegregation and Minority Group Performance." *Review of Educational Research,* 1970, 40, 111–133.

Sarason, S., Davidson, S., Lighthall, F., and Ruebush, K. *Anxiety in Elementary School Children.* New York: Wiley, 1960.

Silberman, Charles E. *Crisis in the Classroom.* New York: Random House, 1970.

Thomas, Lawrence G. *The Occupational Structure and Education.* Englewood Cliffs, N.J.: Prentice-Hall, 1956.

Tocqueville, Alexis de. *Democracy in America.* New York: Vantage, 1945.

Turner, Jonathan H. *American Society: Problems of Structure.* New York: Harper & Row, 1972.

Turner, Ralph H. "Sponsored and Contest Mobility in the School System." *American Sociological Review,* 1960, 25, 855–867.

U.S. Commission on Civil Rights. *Racial Isolation in the Public Schools.* Washington, D.C.: U.S. Government Printing Office, 1967.

Vonnegut, Kurt, Jr. "Preface." In John Birmingham (Ed.), *Our Time Is Now.* New York: Praeger, 1970. P. vii.

Wagenschein, Miriam. "Reality Shock." Unpublished M.A. thesis. University of Chicago, Department of Sociology, 1950.

Weber, Max. *The Theory of Social and Economic Organization,* A. M. Henderson and Talcott Parsons, trans. Glencoe, Ill.: The Free Press, 1947.

Weinberg, Meyer. *Race and Place: A Legal History of the Neighborhood School.* Washington, D.C.: U.S. Government Printing Office, 1967.

Weinberg, Meyer. *Desegregation Research: An Appraisal.* Bloomington, Indiana: Phi Delta Kappa, 1970.

Wilson, Alan B. "The Effect of Residential Segregation upon Educational Achievement and Aspirations." Doctoral dissertation. University of California at Berkeley, 1960.

Wilson, Alan B. "Social Stratification and Academic Achievement." In A. H. Passow (Ed.), *Education in Depressed Areas.* New York: Bureau of Publications, Teachers College, Columbia University, 1963. Pp. 217–235.

Yarrow, Marian R. (Issue Ed.). "Interpersonal Dynamics in a Desegregation Process." *Journal of Social Issues,* 1958, 14, no. 1.

Suggested Reading

General References

BROOKOVER, WILBUR B., AND ERICKSON, EDSEL L. *Sociology of Education.* Homewood, Ill.: Dorsey Press, 1975.

SEXTON, PATRICIA CAYO. *The American School.* Englewood Cliffs, N.J.: Prentice-Hall, 1967.

BELL, ROBERT R., AND STUB, HOLGER R. (Eds.). *The Sociology of Education: A Sourcebook.* Homewood, Ill.: Dorsey Press, 1968.

PAVALKO, RONALD M. (Ed.). *Sociology of Education: A Book of Readings.* Itasca, Ill.: F. E. Peacock Publishers, Inc., 1968.

GRANT, W. VANCE, AND LIND, GEORGE. *Digest of Educational Statistics.* Washington, D.C.: U.S. Government Printing Office, 1974.

Brookover and Erickson is a highly regarded general education text. Sexton is considerably shorter but, nevertheless, comprehensive in its coverage of major educational topics. Bell and Stub and Pavalko are books of readings which, combined, include many of the classic educational essays of the twentieth century. For the reader who is untroubled by information presented in tabular form, *The Digest of Educational Statistics* is a rich source of information on public schools of all types.

Organizational Analyses of Educational Problems

SILBERMAN, CHARLES E. *Crisis in the Classroom: The Remaking of American Education.* New York: Random House, 1970.

HOLT, JOHN. *The Underachieving School.* New York: Dell, 1969.

KATZ, MICHAEL B. *Class, Bureaucracy, and Schools.* New York: Praeger, 1975.

TURNER, JONATHAN H. *American Society: Problems of Structure.* New York: Harper & Row, 1972.

In Silberman's fine book we find what might be the most complete, sensitive, and critical analysis of education, in its many modern forms, of our age. John Holt's *The Underachieving School* examines the tyranny of testing, the rat race for college, the failure of ghetto school programs, compulsory attendance, reading failures, and teachers who talk too much. This, like his many other books, has become a standard among educators, even though he doggedly illuminates their shortcomings. Michael Katz rightly argues that problems with modern education can only be completely understood by studying their origins. *Class, Bureaucracy, and Schools* is an historical analysis of the American educational institution from its beginnings to its present listless monolithic state. Finally, in chapter 8 of his award-winning structural analysis of problems with American society, Jonathan Turner provides us with a short but powerful overview of contemporary educational problems.

The Disaffection of Youth From Schools

The following books, some through empirical social science research, others using the wealth of their authors' perceptions and experiences, explore the reasons why so many children, in one way or another, turn away from school often long before law and custom allow for "honorable" departure. In Friedenberg we learn how a teacher's (mistaking the researcher for a high school student) following him into the restroom and observing his actions over the locked enclosure is related to her ability to serve as a guide through the deepening web of cultural knowledge that awaits students in high school. His is a study of growth and acquiesence in the public school system. Paul Goodman's *Growing Up Absurd* breathes life into the idea that adults, blindly wed to the American system, are the architects of their children's mediocrity, and, he argues, much dulling of the youthful mind occurs in school. Birmingham and Kunen are students. Each has tasted reprisal for seeking awareness and voicing dissent while still in school: Each exemplifies the kind of student good teachers long for, yet each has been tuned out and turned off by his educational experience.

Rosenthal and Jacobsen experimentally demonstrate that teachers base their evaluations of children on rumor and innuendo as much as performance. *Death at an Early Age* depicts rampant teacher racism destroying the life-chances of black Boston schoolchildren. In *Teachers and Students*, The U.S. Commission on Civil Rights documents that Southwestern schoolteachers have much less regard for Mexican-American children than their Anglo counterparts, and that teachers spend considerably less time educating Chicano children than whites.

FRIEDENBERG, EDGAR Q. *Coming of Age in America.* New York: Vintage Books, 1965.

GOODMAN, PAUL. *Growing Up Absurd.* New York: Vintage Books, 1960.

BIRMINGHAM, JOHN (Ed.). *Our Time Is Now: Notes from the High School Underground.* New York: Bantam Books, 1970.

KUNEN, JAMES SIMON. *The Strawberry Statement: Notes of a College Revolutionary.* New York: Avon Books, 1969.

ROSENTHAL, ROBERT, AND JACOBSON, LENORE. *Pygmalion in the Classroom.* New York: Holt, Rinehart and Winston, 1968.

KOZOL, JONATHAN. *Death at an Early Age.* Boston: Houghton Mifflin, 1967.

U.S. COMMISSION ON CIVIL RIGHTS. *Teachers and Students: Differences in Teacher Interaction with Mexican American and Anglo Students.* Washington, D.C.: U.S. Government Printing Office, 1973.

Racism in Education

WEINBERG, MEYER. *Race and Place: A Legal History of the Neighborhood School.* Washington, D.C.: U.S. Government Printing Office, 1967.

U.S. COMMISSION ON CIVIL RIGHTS. *Racial Isolation in the Public Schools.* Washington, D.C.: U.S. Government Printing Office, 1967.

COLEMAN, JAMES S., ET AL. *Equality of Educational Opportunity.* Washington, D.C.: U.S. Government Printing Office, 1966.

WEINBERG, MEYER. *Desegregation Research: An Appraisal.* Bloomington, Ind.: Phi Delta Kappa, 1970.

JENSEN, ARTHUR, AND OTHERS. *Environment, Heredity and Intelligence.* Cambridge, Mass.: Harvard Educational Review, 1969.

In his first book Meyer Weinberg demonstrates how white parents, local courts, and school systems worked together to promote racist values throughout most of American public education's history. *Racial Isolation in the Public Schools* and Coleman's massive survey of almost 600,000 students and 4000 schools stand as landmark studies documenting rampant segregation and unequal educational opportunity in America's schools, although both rely on questionable data. Nevertheless, they served as a basis for the torrent of court desegregation orders flowing forth in the late 1960s. Weinberg's *Desegregation Research* is a craftsmanlike blend of historical and social science information on American education's short-lived embrace with desegregation. *Environment, Heredity, and Intelligence* combines Arthur Jensen's provocative and politically volatile essay on genetic determinants of black intelligence with rebuttals from assorted critics. In this volume dogma reigns over a paucity of data.

Educational Inequality, Jobs, and Money

JENCKS, CHRISTOPHER, ET AL. *Inequality: A Reassessment of the Effect of Family and Schooling in America.* New York: Basic Books, 1972.

SEWELL, WILLIAM H., AND HAUSER, ROBERT M. *Education, Occupation, and Earnings: Achievement in the Early Career.* New York: Academic Press, 1975.

BERG, IVAR. *Education and Jobs: The Great Training Robbery.* Boston: Beacon Press, 1971.

Christopher Jencks has done perhaps the most sensitive and rigorous thinking about the causes of inequality to appear in print in the last few decades. He concludes that inequality, in its many forms, is more properly caused by the fact that some Americans are allowed to make far too much money while millions of others reap only subsistence, or less, for their toil. He likens attacking widespread economic imbalance through schools and families to hunting elephants with fly-swatters. The Sewell and Hauser volume is the latest in their impressive string of research reports on the relationship between socioeconomic background, academic ability and educational achievement, occupational achievement, and earnings. Berg's provocative *"The Great Training Robbery"* questions whether there really is a relationship between academic ability, educational achievement, and job performance in massified, mechanized American society.

Restructuring American Education

RIST, RAY C., (Ed.). *Restructuring American Education*. New Brunswick, N.J.: Transaction Books, 1972.

COMMITTEE FOR ECONOMIC DEVELOPMENT. *Innovation in Education: New Directions for the American School*. New York: Committee for Economic Development, 1968.

The former represents the best current social scientific thinking on alternatives to modern public education practices; the latter reflects the business community's recommendations.

Blacks, Chicanos, and the Health Care System

Daryl D. Enos

Blacks and Mexican-Americans in the United States receive poorer medical care, die younger, and are ill more often than whites in our society.[1] This article describes and analyzes the characteristics of our medical care system and of these two population groups that contribute to this severe social problem. The last section will discuss some proposed solutions.

In the first month of life, a black child has a much greater chance of dying than a white child of the same age. Approximately three times more black children than white die between the ages of one month and one year. All through life illness occurs more frequently among blacks in this society. They are twice as apt to contact pneumonia and influenza than any white group. Perhaps most dramatically, a newborn black child has a life expectancy that is about 10 percent less than for the majority of our population.[2]

Health conditions for Mexican-Americans have not been as well studied as for the blacks, but they too suffer an unusually high incidence of illness and early death. It has been noted that Chicanos have higher than average rates of tuberculosis, infant mortality, and chronic diseases (Burma, 1970:327). As with blacks, adequate medical care is difficult for the Chicano to obtain. The events contained in the testimony of a Los Angeles Mexican-American to a United States Senate Health Subcommittee are both illustrative and common:

I had to take my daughter in [to a doctor] at the age of 8 months. . . . very much underweight . . . temperature, very high, 103, difficulty in breathing . . . I have to call first. . . . I was informed that I could not take the child as it was noon and the doctors had to take a lunch break and they were only able to take care of emergencies. . . . Nevertheless, I was able to force my way, and I do mean force my way, in order to get a doctor to see the child. The baby was found to have a touch of pneumonia, was put under oxygen and was kept in the hospital. (Kennedy, 1973:72)

It is ironic that while they have unusually severe health problems, blacks and Chicanos until very recently have received much less medical care [3] and the care they do get is generally inferior to what other population groups receive. They

---

[1] Because of the size of their population, and because many of the dynamics of their health conditions are similar, our analysis in this article concentrates on blacks and Mexican-Americans ("Chicanos" is a synonym for Mexican-Americans). Some limited, published information is available on the health problems of American Indians, low-income Asians in this nation, and Puerto Ricans.

[2] *Report of the National Advisory Commission on Civil Disorders*, Otto Kerner, chairman (New York: The New York Times Company, 1968), p. 270; *Vital Statistics of the United States*, Vol. II, Section 5, Life Tables, p. 5–5, U.S. Department of Health, Education, and Welfare, Public Health Service and Mental Health Administration, National Center for Health Statistics, (1967).

[3] The facts and possible implications of recent increases in number of visits to physicians by low-income persons will be discussed in the last section.

also frequently must make use of county hospitals, community health clinics, and other forms of "charity care."

It often requires a special effort from those who receive adequate health care to understand the numerous and drastic consequences insufficient and inadequate medical care has on the lives of many of our ethnic minorities. Frequent illness means a special difficulty in obtaining and maintaining employment, and indeed a very high proportion of the heads of black households are too sick to work.[4] The absence of sufficient medical care means that ethnic minorities frequently see physicians only when their health conditions have deteriorated to the point of being an emergency. Perhaps most tragically, the current medical situation means that black and Chicano parents encounter special difficulties in meeting their responsibility of providing adequate health care for their children.

It is important to understand that a number of factors have caused the poor health, underutilization and inferior quality of care for blacks and Chicanos. Two general conditions have combined to produce this situation:

Poverty It is now a well-known fact that a higher proportion of blacks and Chicanos live in poverty than is true for our white majority population. They are more apt to be unemployed or underemployed, and they have much smaller incomes than the rest of society (Bureau of Labor Statistics and Bureau of the Census, 1967; Rowan, 1968:10). Better than one-third of all black and Chicano

families have incomes below the poverty level as defined by the U.S. Social Security Administration, whereas the same figure for whites in our society is slightly more than 11 percent. The stark reality is that poverty causes ill health, since it adversely affects the quantity and quality of medical care received.[5]

Our Health Care Delivery System The system for delivering health care in this country has developed and currently operates in ways most appropriate for middle- to upper-income Anglo families. No similar system exists for low-income blacks and Chicanos.

DEFINITION OF THE PROBLEM: THE MAJOR COMPONENTS AND CHARACTERISTICS OF OUR HEALTH CARE SYSTEM

This section describes the major components of our health care system, shows how they affect one another, and describes what functions they perform in providing health care to our population. We will also analyze some of the major characteristics of the system, such as its financial structure and the orientation of its treatment. We will conclude this section of the article by describing how this society recently came to be interested in and define the problems of health for low-income blacks and Chicanos.

Like our educational and employment systems, our health care delivery system makes certain assumptions about the characteristics of the population it serves.

[4] *Report of the National Advisory Commission on Civil Disorders, op. cit.,* p. 269 ff; "Disability Days, United States, July 1963–June 1964," *Vital Statistics: Data From the National Health Survey,* Series 10, No. 24, U.S. National Center for Health Statistics (Washington, D.C.: U.S. Government Printing Office, November 1965).

[5] Even the phenomenon of sudden or "crib death" is related to low-income status. See *Sudden Death in Infants,* U.S. Department of Health, Education, and Welfare, Public Health Service, National Institute of Health, National Institute of Child Health and Human Development, Public Health Service Publication No. 1412 (1963).

First, it assumes that patients have the capacity to pay for their medical care either directly, or indirectly through their insurance policies, union, or employer health plans. (Medicare and Medicaid present some contradictions to this assumption.) Generally, medical providers are paid fees for their services by the patient or his "representative." Second, it assumes that patients have the ability and inclination to obtain care as needed and are able to perform a good deal of self-care and self-diagnosis.[6] Patients must make frequent decisions about whether they need medical attention and which provider they should see. Third, it is assumed that patients are, on the average, basically healthy and are apt to remain that way. In general, when the individual feels something is wrong he goes to a primary care physician (generalist, internist, and so on). The generalist either prescribes treatment (often instructions for the patient to follow), or refers the patient to the hospital or a physician who specializes in the specific health problem. The patient then must get to the hospital or specialist, make the family and personal arrangements involved, follow a new set of instructions, and be concerned with how these new medical expenses will be paid. Many of the components of our system of medical care function to deny quality care to low-income blacks and Chicanos.

Components of the System

THE DOCTORS Physicians control most of the care we receive. At the beginning of an illness they perform the examination, make the diagnosis, and prescribe

[6] Our continuing concern with healthful diets is a good example, and the encouragement of women to perform self-diagnosis for breast cancer is another.

treatment. They are responsible for deciding what other medical services (for example, medicine, hospitalization) we should or should not receive. There is little doubt that they are the elite of our health care system.

Physicians are an elite in our society in general. They have the highest average income of any occupational group in the United States—over $50,000 per year, as compared to less than half that amount for lawyers (Samuelson, 1973:88–89). They are predominantly male Caucasian. Blacks comprise less than three percent of our physicians and only a slightly larger percentage are women (Wertz, 1973:275). Physicians are not apt to be personally familiar with the difficulties of abject poverty or minority status. Approximately 90 percent receive their medical training in this country. Until recent years, more than 60 percent were members of the American Medical Association, a powerful organization which has significant influence on the laws affecting medical care which are considered by the United States Congress.

THE HOSPITALS Hospitals are probably second only to physicians in affecting the way our care is provided. As anyone with any hospital experience knows, it is expensive, and daily service charges for general care hospitals have increased by more than 12 percent per year since 1967. The average length of stay for a patient entering the hospital is approximately eight days, although it is more than ten days for low-income persons. The charges for a hospital stay usually include a flat rate for occupying the bed and individual charges for the units of medical services that are provided. It is ironic that those who can least afford to pay for hospitalization go more often and stay longer.

The proper functions to be performed by general hospitals in the United States are subject to debate. First, the majority of money spent for medical care in this nation is for hospitalization. As we increasingly focus on the costs and method of financing medical care, hospitals will continue to be a central subject for discussion. Second, hospitals elicit strong emotions among many people. The significance we ascribe to hospitals is realistic and to be expected since it is the place where we are apt to experience many significant events of our lives: childbirth, illness and recuperation, and death. As we continue to discuss changes in our health care system generally, and the issues of increased and improved care for minorities specifically, hospitals, the functions they perform, and their "humanism" or lack of it, will be a center of attention.

There are many different types of hospitals. The majority are nonprofit, usually owned and operated by a community, a university, or by a religious organization. Other hospitals are "proprietary," owned and operated for profit by physicians or other individuals and groups. Some hospitals are government owned and operated, most notably those for military veterans. In addition to general hospitals, there are "special care" hospitals, providing care for special medical problems, such as forms of paraplegia or mental illness. The term "extended care facility" usually refers to a rehabilitation type of hospital where patients are sent to recuperate but are regarded as not needing the intensive care available in short-term general hospitals. Nursing homes are not really hospitals but institutions where patients can receive some limited medical care and stay for a lengthier and less expensive period of custodial care than in general hospitals. Elderly and low-income persons usually comprise the vast majority of nursing home patients.

THE NURSES The nursing profession increasingly is seen as vital to any effort at expanding the medical care provided to low-income groups. This is partly because how they perform their work results from the way physicians practice medicine. Typically, doctors are extremely busy, darting from office to hospital, adhering to a difficult work schedule, and frequently behind in that schedule. Nurses often have more time for the patient and usually perform as an assistant to the doctor, carrying out his orders. One of the big issues in health care today revolves around whether the nurse should engage in some tasks usually reserved for the doctor, and perhaps even do so without his direct supervision. This issue is particularly significant for under-served and low-income areas since nurses could provide less expensive limited care where there is a scarcity of physicians. Not surprisingly, many doctors oppose the expansion of the nurse's role.

Physicians are not the only barriers to major changes in the nursing profession. It is often said that there are too many nurses today. In fact, the ratio of nurses to 1000 persons in our population has increased by 30 percent in the past 20 years (Freeman et al., 1972:210). This has meant a declining interest in increasing the quantity, and, somewhat illogically, the quality of nursing through such things as federally funded training projects. Unlike doctors, nurses have a tendency to be less involved in their profession and professional associations, probably because the majority are women and have different employment patterns than male physicians. About one-third of all registered nurses in the United States are not employed in nursing. The American Nurses Association has a membership of only one-third of the actively engaged registered nurses. However, those nurses organized into professional interest groups are often influential during legislative considerations of public health laws.

OTHER HEALTH PROVIDERS   Health providers other than physicians and nurses are less visible to the public eye, but are very critical in the delivery of care. There are a large number of such providers including dentists, inhalation therapists, podiatrists, optometrists, osteopaths, chiropractors, psychologists and laboratory technicians. There is also a wide variety of nonmedical healers such as faith healers, whose methods have not been accepted by traditional medicine, but who nonetheless have many patients.

The variety of health providers other than nurses and physicians can be bewildering even for a knowledgeable layman. After discussing most of the providers, such as inhalation therapists and laboratory technologists, a recent report on California Health Manpower stated that the "other allied health occupations which provide personal health care services are too varied and the available statistics too few to permit detailed coverage in this report" (California Department of Public Health, 1971:28). The report then listed 17 positions (exclusive of nursing) in allied health occupations for which California community colleges (two-year institutions) are providing instruction. The uses, evaluations, and demand for the services of these allied health personnel vary substantially with

the physician controlling the patient flow, and with the patient's capacity to pay.

THE EDUCATORS   Educators and trainers of health manpower principally include high schools, colleges, universities, and medical schools. There are, in addition, a number of "private schools" that provide students with training, for example, as medical receptionists or dental assistants. There are also some government supported programs with instruction in health occupations. Regardless of the type of institution providing the training, there are a number of critical problems pertaining to our health manpower. We do not estimate the manpower demand (the numbers of health professionals of the various occupations needed by the system) far enough in advance to permit us to regulate the supply of health professionals to fit that demand. Most agree that there is a physician shortage and perhaps a surplus of nurses. But the need for the numerous other health professionals, and the degree of any surplus or deficit, is difficult to estimate and probably changes frequently. If there are deficiencies in the supply of health professionals for one or more of the professions, then the employing medical provider and the patients suffer. If there is a surplus, then the health professionals themselves suffer through low wages or unemployment. This is an especially disastrous occurrence for minorities who frequently suffer employment discrimination.

PAYMENTS   In 1950, direct payments of medical bills by patients, family, or friends, amounted to more than 68 percent of all personal health care expenditures. In 1971, that figure was only 37.2 percent (Schwartz, 1972:116). What occurred during those two decades was a massive shift from direct payment of medical bills to payment by third-party payers (insurance companies, government, unions, and so forth). In 1970, the 72 Blue Shields in the nation served a total of 65,530,827 persons as clients and served as fiscal agents for an additional thirteen and one-half million persons whose medical costs were paid by government through "the blues" to the medical providers (Bureau of Public Health Economics, 1971:1031). In that same year, more than 94 percent of our population under the age of 65 had some form of private health insurance. It should be remembered that the blacks and Chicanos are much less apt than Anglos to have such insurance.

It is frequently argued that the increasing financial role of third-party payers results in increased costs per unit of medical care. When the patients pay the medical bills directly they are more apt to complain if the charges are too high. When government or an insurance company pays the medical bill, patients worry less about the costs. This process often ends up hurting the patient most even though he or she does not know it.

Consider the situation, which appears to exist in a large California county, where there are too many hospitals with more total beds than are needed. Under these conditions, the vacancy rates become too high (occupancy rates too low) for the hospitals to pay their bills or make profits. The result is that the hospitals increase their daily bed rates and service charges. The insurance companies pay the higher charges, increase the policy premiums their clients must pay, and the

reason is cited as "the escalating inflation in medical costs." Those who have no insurance policy must also pay the higher rates.

HEALTH PRODUCTS Manufactured health products sold in 1967 probably amounted to more than five billion dollars. More than four billion of that total was spent for drugs. Physicians receive much of their information on drugs available for patient treatment from the drug salesmen who visit them in their offices. Drug companies maintain large research teams endeavoring to invent new drugs or improve old ones, and these items are occasionally sources of significant medical discoveries. The most important point about this component in our medical care system, however, is the increasing expenditure for expensive medical equipment. X-ray machines that can cost more than $100,000, expensive heart pumps, and kidney machines are only a few examples of a growing variety of medical equipment found in hospitals and clinics. Partly because hospitals and clinics compete for patients, they usually try to purchase their own medical equipment rather than share it with one another. As with any business, the cost of this equipment is passed on to the consumer. Low-income patients are least able to pay for this luxury of competition versus cooperation in the use of medical equipment.

MEDICAL AGENCIES The regulatory, research, and planning agencies affecting the medical care system, like the catalogue of allied health professionals, are too numerous and changing to list in their entirety. There are the National Board of Medical Examiners; the various agencies under the U.S. Department of Health, Education, and Welfare; Regional Medical Programs and the apparently defunct Comprehensive Health Planning; usually a state department of public health (as in California); and many other agencies. For our purposes it is only important to note that there is a wide variety of these agencies engaged in many different and often conflicting operations. Efforts at changing the health care system or expanding care provided to the low-income groups are often frustrated by this fact.

Governmental expenditures in health care have grown rapidly in recent years. Monies for medical research, health projects in underserved areas, and the provision of care to the medically indigent are massive. Whether one favors or opposes the fact, there is little doubt that public expenditures for health, which totaled more than 28 billion dollars in the 1970–71 fiscal year, result in numerous and powerful governmental influences over our medical delivery system. Physicians have been slow to recognize or understand these influences.

Characteristics of the System

The major method of medical care delivery is through the physician's office where he functions as a solo practitioner or as a member of a very small group of physicians. The image projected by our medical care system is that of a plethora of private physicians available to the public. It is a system where a declining percentage of those physicians (the generalists—general practitioners, internists, and pediatricians) are necessary preliminary contacts before other providers are seen. Thus, the patient receives secondary medical care (hospitals, drugs, special-

ists) only after referral by the generalists. The fact that independent physicians serve as the major source of care in our large metropolitan areas has led many to conclude that our medical care system is a "nonsystem."

Physicians dominate the provision of care in the United States. This is of critical importance in considering the inappropriateness of the system for minority group members. The doctor is the symbol and substance of the provision of care in this nation, yet he is almost always white, almost never speaks Spanish, and usually is a male. This is not the individual physician's fault, but we know enough about the emotional content of the medical situation to recognize that patients feel more comfortable and secure if physicians (or at least their assistants or nurses) are of the same ethnic, racial, or lingual background. It should be remembered that the existence of complicated medical machines and the complexity of medical jargon are features of the average medical situation which are not conducive to calmness.

Our medical system is largely curative, that is, patients seek and providers give medical care when there is reason to believe the patient is ill. We do engage in some preventative activities, such as regularly scheduled physical examinations, but these activities are less used by minorities and low-income groups.

There has been much recent discussion of preventative versus curative medicine. On the face of it, it is obviously better to prevent illness than to wait for it to strike and then make efforts at curing it. But other than a few specific activities, such as physical examinations or innoculations, there is little agreement on the nature of preventative medicine. Preventative medicine frequently means little more than "educating" the patient about his or her good health and how to maintain it. Again, however, education for better personal health assumes that the patient receives the information (goes to school, watches television, reads the material in the doctor's office) and has the means for carrying out the instructions (money to have a regular physical examination, methods for providing "better diets").

Almost all medical care in this country is provided on a fee-for-service basis. That is, a unit of care is provided and the patient, or a third-party payer, must pay for that unit of service. As one writer notes, doctors "are independent entrepreneurs who see patients and charge fees for the services performed" (Schwartz, 1972:29). The key point in this method of paying for care is that those who cannot afford to pay, or do not have adequate health insurance, do not get the medical care they need.

Most of us in this country do well enough receiving our medical care principally from the vast array of private practitioners or small group providers. We even like the variety, and having a physician practicing in his private office lets us be assured that "we can have our own doctor." We also survive, perhaps even enjoy, going to the Anglo male physician, and the fact that he speaks no Spanish is of little concern to us. We manage to pay our medical bills, except during catastrophic illness, or at least we make sure our employment has a health insurance benefit connected to it. Despite the fact that we only infrequently get involved in preventing our illness, we manage to live fairly long and healthy lives. But this is true for most of us, not all of us. It became publicly apparent in the 1960s that low-income minorities, and poor citizens

in general, did not receive the same care available to and used by the majority. This society's attention to and definition of that fact occurred in the context of the civil rights movement and the more generalized concern for all the consequences of poverty.

The Beginnings of Change

The pronouncements and decisions of the United States Supreme Court arouse much public attention because they frequently have implications for the entire society. Such was the case with the U.S. Supreme Court's decision in Brown versus Board of Education in 1954, in which the court ruled that segregation in public education was unconstitutional. The mood of black civil rights leaders following the 1954 decision was one of optimism, but this optimism was quickly dampened by the stubborn opposition of many Southern whites. Direct confrontations began to occur frequently. In late 1955 a bus boycott occurred in Montgomery, Alabama, following the arrest of a black woman who refused to give up her seat to a white man. In 1956 there was mob violence at the University of Alabama in opposition to the admission of a black student; and in 1960, four black students in North Carolina who had been denied lunch counter service staged a "sit-in." All of these actions were widely reported and much discussed by our mass media. The "black problem" just wouldn't go away.

In 1959, Oscar Lewis's *Five Families* was published which maintained that many human beings live in a "culture of poverty." In 1962, *The Other America* by Michael Harrington emerged, "and legend has it, introduced liberal America to the larger dimensions of poverty. . . .

both books caught us all unaware" (Sackrey, 1973:7).

The year 1960 saw the first nationally televised campaign for president of the United States. One of the candidates, John F. Kennedy, chose to use the media and his campaign generally to focus public attention on the living conditions of the poor members of our society (Smith and Zietz, 1970:150). Though later as president he achieved only limited legislative success in initiating programs dealing with poverty, Kennedy as a candidate caught the attention and imagination of the younger segments of American society and popularized a concern for ethnic minorities and the poor.[7] Significantly, Kennedy also made it clear that he regarded Mexican-Americans, as well as blacks, as unhappy victims of poverty. Mexican-Americans as well as blacks had become "news."

Kennedy's assassination in November 1963 made his policy proposals almost sacrosanct, and the stage was set for the passage of a large number of federal programs. The entire "war on poverty" was constructed following the Economic Opportunity Act of 1964. Most significantly for our considerations here, President Johnson in 1965 signed into law a bill which not only provided medical assistance for the aged (Medicare) but for some of the indigent of all ages as well (Medicaid). Medicaid made assistance available to persons on public welfare and encouraged states to provide similar assistance for others with little income or personal wealth. Observers from all viewpoints, from those supporting "socialized medicine" to those opposing any governmental interference in the medical system, share one basic assumption: The passage of Medicaid was one of the most important events in the history of our medical care system. The national government had accepted the obligation of promoting massive financial assistance for medical care for some of those who could not afford such care.

A small number of common beliefs about poverty were articulated during the 1960s that have significance for our concern with minorities and medical care.

1. Poverty influences the lives of the poor in their attitudes, their family life, their housing, their education, their occupations, *and* their health. The consequences of poverty usually influence the person's life in any one, or all, of these areas.
2. The greater number of people experiencing poverty are white, but a higher percentage of our black and Chicano population are poorer than whites. For example, blacks are three-and-one-half times as apt to be at the poverty level as Anglos (Kain, 1969:2). Blacks and Chicanos frequently face the dual disadvantages of poverty and ethnic discrimination.
3. Society has an obligation to assist the poor in all these fields. It even has the obligation to assist them in their ability to obtain health care.
4. The health care needs of poor blacks and Chicanos are somewhat different than those for poor whites.

POOR HEALTH AND HEALTH CARE: THE CAUSAL PROCESSES

The poverty living conditions of many minority citizens result in severe illness and special health needs. One of the most dramatic public utterances to illustrate this basic principle is attributed to the health commissioner of New York City. He is reported to have said that

[7] The Area Redevelopment Act (1961) and the Manpower Development and Training Act (1962) are most notable.

"poverty is the third leading cause of death in New York City" (Will and Vatter, 1970:121).

As of 1968, one out of three persons in families with incomes under $2000 suffered chronic conditions that limited their activity. That figure was seven percent for families with incomes over $7000. Members of the lower-income families averaged 50 days of disability per year and had an average of 10.2 days hospital stay, whereas the higher-income group members had 14.3 disability days per year and averaged 7.2 days per hospital stay.

Low income leads to illness in a number of ways. Influenza and pneumonia are twice as high among blacks as whites, partly due to housing and heating conditions. Sanitation conditions are frequently deplorable in low-income neighborhoods, often resulting in rat infestation. It is estimated that there were 14,000 cases of rat bite in this country in 1965. Tuberculosis is twice as frequent in low-income neighborhoods; there is much more venereal disease; whooping cough, amoebic infections, and high blood pressure are much more frequent; and sugar diabetes appears frequently among Mexican-Americans.

Poverty and hunger go together, and constant and severe hunger is unhealthy. It has been recently estimated that 25 million citizens of this nation lack sufficient money to keep themselves adequately fed (Milbauer and Leinwand, 1971:13). The health results are illnesses associated with vitamin or protein deficiency and deaths attributable to severe diarrhea or even starvation. Anemia, blindness, and brain damage are other forms of ill health caused by the lack of proper food.

The values, procedures, and characteristics of the personnel of our medical system often alienate blacks and Chicanos, relatively few of whom work as medical providers. The reasons are partly attitudinal, having to do with minority group beliefs that our health delivery system is by and for Anglos only. Our method of medical delivery assumes that the patient possesses specific items of knowledge, e.g., how to pick the appropriate physician (location, type of specialty, and so on), and that the ability to communicate with the physician is present (telephones, commonality of language). It assumes, for example, that the patient knows that internists now function in ways similar to general practitioners, and that you "should" see a generalist before you see a specialist. It assumes that patients understand and are able and willing to follow referral instructions, even if they are being referred to a hospital or specialist who may be some distance away. In general, it assumes that the patient has the resources to receive his or her medical care from a variety of sources, in a variety of locations, and at different times.

Our system also places emphasis on the efficiency, professionalism, and objectivity of medical providers. Many of these values are incompatible with the resources and even attitudes of low-income blacks and Mexican-Americans who have been frequently heard by this author to complain at state legislative hearings that providers have no concern for the well-being of their patients.

The following is an illustrative account of medical care for Mexican-Americans in the Rio Grande Valley written by an anthropologist only a decade ago:

Professional physicians are viewed with suspicion and hostility by conservative members of the lower class who generally regard the germ theory of disease as a fraudulent scheme to help Anglo doctors and nurses extract exorbitant fees from the gullible. The Mexican-American skeptic in this case reasons that germs which cannot be seen cannot exist. . . .

The typical physician and nurse fail to achieve the close effective relationship with the Mexican-American patients which is so characteristic of the curandero-client (folk healer) relations. The most obvious reason for this failure is the language barrier between the Anglo physician or nurse and the Mexican-American patient who speaks little English. A second reason is the authoritarian relationship which the physician and nurse assume with the Mexican-American patients. The patient feels that the doctor and nurse are unconcerned with his welfare, his feelings, and the obligation of his family. (Burma, 1970:333)

The problem is largely one of manpower; whites provide the medical care. We have already discussed the small number of blacks and women who are physicians. According to the 1970 census, only 1309 of the total 22,356 physicians, dentists, and related professionals operating in Los Angeles county were Spanish-speaking/Spanish surname. That figure represents slightly more than five percent of the total physicians, while the Spanish-speaking/Spanish-surnamed population is 18 percent of the total.

The comments of an observer of the medical system and its populations in a small California community perhaps best summarize the key points here:

Since medical systems are integral parts of the cultures in which they occur, they cannot be understood simply in terms of curing practices, medical practitioners, hospital services and the like. Medical systems are affected by most major categories of culture: economics, religion, social relationships, education, family structure, language. Only a partial understanding of a medical system can be gained unless other parts of the culture can be studied and related to it.

Whenever individuals from one culture, with their particular beliefs about health, illness, and the prevention and cure of disease, come to live as members of minority groups within another culture which has a vastly different medical system, emotional and social conflicts often result when illness brings members of the two groups together. (Clark, 1957: 21–22)

Too often for the good health of the minority groups, these differences between the medical system and minority population cultures result in no contact between the two at all.

Minority groups have achieved less formal success in our educational systems. Education and income are related, and we have already seen how critical good income is to good health. But educational achievement is important to the patient's good health for a number of other reasons. The patient must, of course, be able to comprehend verbal and written medical instructions, a task which is difficult for almost any layman. The higher one's educational achievement, the more reading that person does. Printed material is an important source of information on personal health, including not only printed materials in doctors' offices, but also various magazine, journal, and newspaper articles.

Medical providers often avoid minority group areas and patients. This pattern is two-sided. In a fee-for-service system, the doctors naturally locate where they can receive frequent and higher fees, and that is not in a poverty neighborhood. In Chicago, there are roughly twice as many physicians per 100,000 residents in the nonpoor as in the poor communities. The pattern is almost universally true in our major metropolitan areas, and the relative absence of doctors in rural areas has been well documented (Schwartz, 1972:71; Will and Vatter, 1970:124).

There is also some evidence that discrimination against ethnic minorities and members of low-income groups is widespread among medical providers. In one study, it was found that occupationally "striving" public health nurses regarded their most difficult clients to be members of the lower class in a ratio of almost 3 to 1 (Friedson and Lorber, 1972:276). Discrimination from physicians is not surprising since so few are blacks or Chicanos and so many are from middle- or upper-income families.

Low income minority groups often do not have the resources, time, or willingness to receive care from the private individual/small group provider system. As director of a community service project in Los Angeles, this author recently received a report from one of his staff which dramatically illustrates the problem. The project involved the use of a local Spanish-language-only television station to broadcast brief public service messages on health care and the coordinated operation of a hotline where viewers could call and receive information on public health agencies, health programs, and medical providers. The facts in the case make it clear that the following version is substantially accurate.[8]

The viewer, who had seen one of our announcements on the availability of the hotline, called and gave the following account of his situation. He was a Mexican-American male, in his middle fifties, and the head of a large family. Until recently, he had been employed with the same local firm for ten years. During his employment he had suffered an illness that

his own physician had diagnosed as a heart attack. The company's physician told him he had not suffered a heart attack, and he returned to work where he was soon fired. Since becoming unemployed he had suffered at least three heart attacks and was scheduled the following morning to enter a local hospital for examinations and possible surgery.[9] The income for his family was slightly more than $200 per month, his rent was $130 per month (for one room), and the family was left with approximately $20 per month for food. His problem, as stated to us, was that he had no transportation nor money to get himself and his wife to the hospital the following morning and had no way to get her back home. The distance was more than 20 miles by bus, requiring over four transfers, and neither he nor his wife spoke much English.

Low income people who are exhausted by the struggle to survive from day to day may avoid the medical system because it is an additional "hassle." It is not uncommon for those of us who have adequate income, our own cars, good educations, health insurance, and a background similar to that of our physician, to be skeptical of the argument that large numbers of people in our society cannot respond adequately to the health care delivery system. It is also easy to dismiss the type of tragic health problems, such as those of the Chicano heart attack victim, as exceptional cases. But the evidence of ill health and early death are too apparent to support either skepticism or apathy.

Our fee-for-service method of obtain-

---

[8] The report of this incident is on file in the office of the station manager, KMEX, Channel 34, Los Angeles.

[9] There was no apparent explanation as to how his hospitalization, tests, and surgery were to be paid for, though Medicaid might have been the source.

ing and paying for care and the frequent occurrence of low income and high unemployment among our minority groups has meant that they have received substantially less medical care than the average Anglo and middle-income citizen. On the average, low-income families spend a minimum of 25 percent less for their medical care than do middle-income families.[10] The reasons that poor black families (and low-income families in general) spend substantially less for medical care are easy to enumerate. Their incomes are lower, so they have less money to spend and must make choices about what to purchase, health care frequently being delayed. There is evidence that low-income families pay more for many things they purchase, such as food, thereby receiving less for their money and having less purchasing power.[11]

Historically, low-income families have visited physicians and dentists substantially less often during a year than middle-income families, and as many as 50 percent of the Mexican-American families in many communities have no family doctor (Burma, 1970). While victims of poverty have seen physicians less often, they spend more time in the hospital than most of us. They are ill frequently, even chronically, and as a result, they are often in need of hospitalization for an extended period.

We have indicated that better than 90 percent of our citizens have some form of private health insurance. The evidence indicates that a like percentage of black and Chicano families have *no* private health insurance at all (Kosa, Antonovsky, and Zolo, 1969:187). One of the reasons for this is that citizens often get

health insurance as part of their employment, and blacks and Chicanos are frequently unemployed. This is a serious problem given the growing proportion of medical bills paid through health insurance.

Medicare and Medicaid may have reversed the phenomena of less frequent utilization of physicians by the poor. As of 1969, physician visits for the low-income groups was slightly higher than for either the middle- or upper-income groups (4.6 to 4.0 per capita visits), a marked contrast to 1964 (Andreopoulos, 1974:163). However, low-income children under the age of 15 years still visit physicians less frequently than youths in middle- and upper-income groups; the number of per capita physician visits were 2.8, 3.6, and 4.3 respectively for 1969. Nonwhites over 65 years of age also visited physicians less frequently than whites during that year, regardless of income level.

The increased number of visits to physicians by low-income adults should not be taken as an indication that the problem is solved. Things have improved, but it must be remembered that the low-income groups are more frequently ill than the middle-income group, and probably need to visit physicians *substantially* more often. In addition, quantity does not guarantee quality of medical care, and it may well be that physician services provided under Medicaid and Medicare are often inferior, as has been charged.

RECENT HISTORY AND SOME PROPOSED SOLUTIONS

Our attention to and definitions of poverty, the problems of administering

[10] *Report of the National Advisory Commission on Civil Disorders*, 1968.

[11] *Report of the National Advisory Commission on Civil Disorders*, 1968:272.

Medicaid nationally, and our concern for the health of blacks and Chicanos have resulted in a large number of proposed programs and solutions to many of the problems we have been discussing. There are a number of proposals to expand the federal government's role in guaranteeing medical care for United States residents. In June 1974, there were at least five such major national health insurance proposals before Congress. Two of these proposals, one supported by the Nixon administration and one supported by Senator Edward Kennedy, have drawn national attention and illustrate the major issues faced by all of them.

The Nixon administration's bill would have provided coverage for all residents of the United States: those who are employed, those who are low-income, and those who are aged. Regarding the first group, all employers would be obligated to offer their employees health insurance. The employers would eventually absorb 75 percent of the premium payments for this private health insurance, but employees would also make contributions. The federal government would continue to make grants to the states for payment of medical services for the poor, disabled, and uninsurable (Medicaid), and states would continue payments to providers for these services. Benefits currently provided would be included. Medical assistance for the aged (Medicare) would be continued through the Social Security tax mechanism. The program, which would require six billion dollars in new federal funds, also had provisions for those individuals who do not fall into one of the three major categories identified above.

The benefits for all groups were quite comprehensive. No limits were established on hospitalization and physician's services, and we have already seen how important these components of the delivery system are to good health care. It also provided for home health services, a declining type of service wherein nurses or other similarly trained persons provide care for patients in their homes. This provision would be particularly significant for the aged. It provided dental coverage for children under the age of 13 years, a significant time in a person's dental history. The plan also would have assumed all costs of a medical illness after they reached a certain "catastrophic" level. The definition of "catastrophic" would vary with the income and personal situation of the patient.

One of the most significant organizational aspects of the Nixon plan was that it would be administered through Blue Cross/Blue Shield and private health insurance mechanisms. The insurance carriers would underwrite the employer's group health plans for his employees, and would administer the various government financed benefits. It was this major role of insurance firms which most displeased Senator Kennedy and his forces.

The Kennedy proposal, which is supported by much of organized labor, also establishes compulsory national health insurance providing a comprehensive range of benefits to all U.S. residents. The medical services to be provided are almost the same as for the Nixon plan, except there are some limits on physician's services, and the definition of catastrophic illness is somewhat different. There are three primary differences between the Nixon administration's proposal and the Kennedy plan.

First, Kennedy proposes to abolish Medicaid and provide the same health coverage for all income groups. His position is partly that Medicaid maintains a two-class system of medical care—care for the poor and care for the nonpoor. Instead, his plan would establish a national health security board as part of the United States Department of Health, Education and Welfare. A payroll tax would be levied on employers, employees, and the self-employed, and these monies would go into a trust fund to be administered by the health security board. Employers would pay into the fund at a rate of at least three percent on the first $20,000 of wages, and employees would pay no more than one percent, with payments being less for low-income workers. The health security board, to be appointed by the president, would establish broad policies and priorities, and regional or subregional HEW agencies would administer the program locally. There would be no direct payments by patients to medical providers for the covered services; payments would be made through HEW offices. Again, both the employed and those currently under Medicaid would have their medical coverage under the same health security board mechanisms.

The second difference is that the role of insurance companies is minimal in the Kennedy plan. Direct payments are made to medical providers by the federal government and not by insurance companies. Moreover, the federal government would have a substantial role in evaluating whether or not the services provided were of adequate quality. The third difference is that the Kennedy plan places a greater emphasis than did Nixon's proposal on the development of large medical groups providing care by prepayment of a fixed premium rather than fee-for-service. These organizations are referred to as health maintenance organizations (HMOs). A fully developed HMO is a large group of medical providers who practice together, often in the same location, provide a complete range of medical services, and do so for an amount of money which is paid to them regularly, and in advance, regardless of the illness or health of their patients. These three characteristics of HMOs—group practice, complete range of services, and prepaid financing of health care—will be discussed below.

All of the major national health insurance proposals seem to accept certain common principles. Although they disagree on the methods, they all are based on the belief that the federal government must guarantee adequate medical care to the citizenry. They seem to recognize that low-income citizens still do not receive adequate medical care, despite Medicaid and its benefits. They also assume that only the very wealthy have enough money to pay for any illness that might arise; that severe illness is often too expensive for the middle-income citizen as well; and that all citizens must therefore be protected from the financial disaster associated with these catastrophic illnesses.

Prepaid health care is increasingly viewed as a necessary alternative to the fee-for-service system we now have. Under prepayment, an agreement is made with a medical provider, either an individual provider or a large medical group, in which regular payments in a specified amount are made to the provider, and the provider agrees to make certain services available to some population group. For example, a labor union may sign a prepayment contract with a large medical clinic, paying that clinic a set amount per month for each of its union members, and receiving in return a guarantee that its members can receive certain medical services as needed. Individuals can also enter into these agreements on their own behalf. When prepayment arrangements are with large medical groups who provide a full range of services, these groups are referred to as HMOs.[12] Kaiser-Permanente on the West Coast is the largest prepaid group medical organization in the United States.

Controversy continues concerning the prepayment principle. Its advocates argue that the fee-for-service method often encourages doctors to provide more medical care than a patient may need since he is paid according to how many services are provided. The fee-for-service system also encourages physicians to avoid low-income and rural areas, and it results in inadequate medical care for those who cannot pay the fees. Opponents of the prepayment method, however, also have their arguments. If a medical provider's income is a fixed amount on a regular basis, he will be encouraged to provide less medical care than may be needed because he will want to keep his costs down. In addition, the argument goes, it will destroy the entrepreneurial spirit in medical providers, making them less innovative and unwilling to work as hard as physicians presently do. It is evident that neither the fee-for-service nor prepayment methods are perfect, and that both will probably be used.

The recent growth in interest and support regarding prepayment was largely the result of the government's initiation of Medicaid. For the first few years, Medicaid operated through our traditional fee-for-service medical system. People on Medicaid received identification

[12] Sometimes the prepaid arrangement is made with only one type of provider, for example, a dentist. We currently prepay our health insurance premiums, but under this system, prepayment is made to the medical group.

saying they were entitled to these medical benefits, and they sought out the physician of their choice, who billed Medicaid according to a specified fee for each of the services provided. California and New York were among the first to discover that this approach has major fiscal disadvantages for government. As a result, California now has the bulk of prepaid group health programs for Medicaid recipients in the country, and New York has the largest single program.

The important point is that there is an obvious compatability between prepayment of medical care and government paying for that care (such as Medicaid/Kennedy proposal). Government budgets its programs in advance of the actual expenditure of the money. If government is to budget for medical services under fee-for-service, it must guess as to the amount of illness and costs of services received by the covered population. If it budgets under prepayment, government need only know how many people will be covered in order to know how much money it will need. Fiscal predictability is increased.

Costs for medical care are not only more predictable, they may be more controllable under a prepayment system. If the physician or other medical provider is paid according to the number and type of services provided, then government can control costs only by controlling the services provided, a risky business indeed. If the physician is paid according to the number of people he agrees to serve, then government can control costs simply by agreeing to the desired amount of payment per person. Physicians can, of course, decide not to enter into prepaid contracts under government programs, but to date that has not presented an insurmountable problem.

Many proposals support the increased development of large medical delivery organizations known as large group practices. As noted earlier, the currently predominant method of physician organization is the private independent physician as a solo or small group practitioner. Approximately one in every five physicians practices as a member of a small group of three or more doctors. Only about five percent of our physicians practice in groups that have 25 physicians or more (Schwartz, 1972:32). Critics of this situation argue that solo/small group practice is a wasteful form of doctor organization.

It appears that the formation of large medical groups can have a number of benefits. First, there is some evidence that medical costs can be reduced through large group practices since there is a sharing of overhead, expensive medical equipment, offices, and other medical personnel. In addition, expensive drugs may be purchased more reasonably if a medical group makes a massive purchase, thereby receiving discounts, savings on which are passed on to the patients.

The central characteristic of large medical groups, however, and the key to their benefits for low-income blacks and Chicanos, has to do with the idea of coordinated medical care. It should be remembered that we have portrayed the current medical system as involving a plethora of solo/small group general practitioners who refer patients to an array of secondary medical providers such as specialists and hospitals. In this system, medical care is not coordinated in the sense that the various providers seen by any one patient are usually at different locations, only in occasional and brief communication, and keeping separate medical records. The ideal large medical group, however, approximates a "supermarket of medical care." All, or almost all, medical services are at the same location or at least in close proximity. There is a physician or group of physicians who manage the patient's case, and geographical proximity is one of the factors that contributes to closer communication between the medical providers. Records are centralized, and any provider working on the case benefits from the ideas and information of other involved providers.

The ideal model does not always work in fact. Proximity does not gurantee communication. An additional problem of large medical groups has to do with their very size. Large organizations of any type have a tendency to become impersonal and to operate on a mass of rules and regulations. Sometimes the patient must see the doctor currently on duty, regardless of preference. This tendency is most often expressed by patients of large medical groups by the complaint, "I don't have my own doctor."

Cost savings and coordinated care, however, make large medical groups of value to low-income blacks and Chicanos. If transportation is difficult, it is easier to get to a single medical facility than to many different ones. For low-income individuals, any cost savings that might be passed on to them is a help. Most importantly, if the care is carefully coordinated between the various medical providers, combined support and guidance for the patient can be maximized. Thus, many large medical groups have preventative programs and make use of medical social workers who work with patients on the personal aspects of their health problems.

Various proposals have been made for increasing the output of services currently delivered by physicians. The obvious approach is to increase the actual number of physicians through building new medical schools or increasing the enrollment of current ones. Increasing enrollment usually involves some attention to providing financial aid for medical training to lower-income persons. Another approach is to shift some of the services currently provided by physicians to other medical professionals. Nurses are most commonly mentioned as the group who might receive these added tasks and responsibilities. A common example is the use of nurses to perform physical examinations or provide elementary medical care under the direction of a physician. The expanded use of physician's assistants, who appear to be midway between the doctor and the nurse on the occupational ladder, has also been widely discussed, particularly as a result of the return of numerous Vietnam War veterans who have had medical training.

Whatever methods are used, it seems clear to most observers that an expanded output in the services currently provided by physicians is indicated. There are parts of the country where no doctor exists, or where the ratio of physicians to patients is such that new members of the community can find no doctor of their own. The rule of supply and demand with reference to the cost of medical care is also at work here. It is frequently noted that medical schools produce few more physicians today than they did at the turn of the century. The consequences are quite clear. As long as physicians' services are limited, the costs for those services will remain high, as will the incomes of physicians.

Medical educators, medical providers, and government itself all seem to share the objective of getting more blacks and Chicanos, as well as other ethnic minorities, into medicine as a profession. Educators do it out of conscience, local student or community pressure, or their legal obligations to governmental rules under affirmative action. The federal government has affirmative action legislation which says that their own agencies, and any agencies over which they have jurisdiction, must have minority group members as students, patients, or employees. Many medical providers, observing the changing orientation of educators, the rules and regulations of the federal government, and noting the pressures of minority consumer groups, find themselves also looking for blacks and Chicanos interested in the medical profession.

These good intentions, however, have been hampered by sad realities. If blacks and Chicanos are to become physicians, they must have attended and succeeded at a creditable undergraduate college, and until recently there have been few of these students in any of our colleges. In addition, black and Chicano students show particular interest in the social sciences and are often uninterested in a premedical academic career. Despite these problems, in 1972–73 minority students comprised 10.2 percent of the country's total medical student body as compared to 5 percent in 1969–70. The number of blacks in medical school more than doubled during that period, and the number of Chicano students studying medicine increased more than four times.

There is some tendency for blacks and Chicanos to focus their aspirations on the medical professions that require shorter educational experiences. This is particularly true for those professions, mentioned above, which require only a two-year college program. Two-year community colleges usually have open admissions policies, and inadequate high school transcripts serve as no barrier.

In addition to increasing the numbers of blacks and Chicanos in medicine as a profession, there are a number of programs that serve to bridge the gap between the medical system and these populations. Some of these programs are directed at the system itself. For example, seminars in the medically related attitudes and conditions of Chicanos or blacks, focused primarily on medical providers as the learners, are not uncommon. Other efforts are in the direction of establishing consumer advisory committees to give the provider advice, sometimes unwanted, on medical care for the poor or minority groups. Many cities have health rights organizations which perform a watchdog function in making sure the provider does not violate the rights of his minority group patients.

Programs directed toward the black or Chicano as medical consumer usually attempt to maximize his efficient utilization of medical care. There are some programs, often poorly financed and managed, which provide transportation to medical care and related babysitting services. Other efforts are made to provide the black or Chicano consumer with information about various medical providers so he or she can make an informed choice. Project Search, for example, provides Los Angeles residents using it with information such as whether a physician has a Spanish-speaking receptionist or nurse. There are projects where a citizen can dial a particular phone number and receive recorded information on certain health problems.

These various proposals, projects, and activities elicit strong emotions from many individuals and groups involved in our health care system. The AMA has frequently denounced HMOs, and con-sumer groups can often be heard blaming physicians for all our social ills. In the midst of this controversy, the less emotional observers generally recognize that we are experiencing pains resulting from the fact that our health care system is in a period of major adjustment.

Many of the proposed solutions described above are oriented towards the special health problems of low-income groups or blacks and Chicanos. But national health insurance, for example, will affect the health care provided for all residents of the United States. We now recognize that adequate health care can be too expensive for any of us, and that health insurance policies as currently established do not provide adequate coverage. It is significant that the same report mentioned earlier which shows an increased use of physicians by the low-income groups also shows that middle-income citizens are seeing physicians less often than in 1964. The current and future adjustments of our health care delivery system should have similar benefits for the entire citizenry.

This period of adjustment for our health care delivery system is painful for many of those directly involved. Physicians frequently feel uncertain and threatened about the changes. National health insurance could result in government control over the practice of medicine. HMOs can mean a reduction in incomes and, perhaps most significantly for doctors, involve an increasing role for consumers in judging the appropriateness of their health care.

Many consumers are also experiencing uncertainty over health care and its changing nature. The public is often much skeptical about the efficiency of our national government, and increased federal involvement in our health care could mean more bureaucracy and less care.

Despite the complexity of the problems and the uncertainty and fears of many of those involved in health care, changes in the system will undoubtedly continue and increase in the next few years. Our system is outdated, does not meet enough of our health needs, and is too expensive for our methods of financing it. Any satisfactory solution to the problems we have discussed must involve the principle that low-income citizens can receive the medical care they need despite their incapacity to pay for it. The nation seems to be moving toward the acceptance of that principle. Our decision to guarantee medical care for the poor (Medicaid) has influenced most of the major proposed solutions outlined above. Medicaid provides a form of health insurance for low-income citizens; the national health insurance proposals provide it for all citizens. The fiscal problems of Medicaid, particularly in California and New York, led to an expanded interest in and use of the prepayment mechanisms and health maintenance organizations, and both the Kennedy and Nixon plans have encouraged HMOs. Group practices have blossomed to serve Medicaid patients, encouraging new public interest in that form of provider organization. And medical organizations providing care to Medicaid patients have frequently experimented with the expanded use of nurses in medical care and with various methods for increasing the numbers of blacks and Chicanos they employ as health professionals. It is ironic that our first national effort at guaranteeing medical care for those in poverty, a group long ignored, will undoubtedly have major consequences for the medical care we all receive.

References

Andreopoulos, Spyros (Ed.). *Primary Care: Where Medicine Fails*. New York: Wiley, 1974.

Bureau of Labor Statistics and Bureau of the Census. "Social and Economic Conditions of Negroes in the United States." Washington, D.C.: U.S. Government Printing Office, 1967.

Bureau of Public Health Economics, School of Public Health, The University of Michigan, *Medical Care Review*, November 1971.

Burma, John H. *Mexican-Americans in the United States: A Reader*. Cambridge, Mass.: Schenkman, 1970.

California Department of Public Health, Office of Comprehensive Health Planning. *California State Plan for Health Statistical Supplement, California Health Manpower*. Sacramento, Ca., 1971.

Clark, Margaret. "Sickness and Health in Sal Si Puedes: Mexican Americans in a California Community." Unpublished thesis, University of California at Berkeley, 1957.

Freeman, Howard E., et al. (Eds.). *Handbook of Medical Sociology*. Englewood Cliffs, N.J.: Prentice-Hall, 1972.

Freidson, Eliot, and Lorber, Judith. (Ed.). *Medical Men and Their Work*. Chicago: Aldine, 1972.

Kain, John F. (Ed.). *Race and Poverty: The Economics of Discrimination*. Englewood Cliffs, N.J.: Prentice-Hall, 1969.

Kennedy, Edward M. *In Critical Condition: The Crisis in America's Health Care*. New York: Pocket Books, 1973.

Kosa, John, Antonovsky, Aaron, and Zolo, Irving K. *Poverty and Health: A Sociological Analysis*, Commonwealth Fund Books. Cambridge, Mass.: Harvard University Press, 1969.

Lewis, Oscar. *Five Families*. New York: Basic Books, 1959.

Milbauer, Barbara, and Leinwand, Gerald. *Hunger*. New York: Simon & Schuster, 1971.

Rowan, Helen. "The Mexican American." Paper prepared for the U.S. Commission on Civil Rights, 1968.

Smith, Russell E., and Zietz, Dorothy. *American Social Welfare Institutions*. New York: Wiley, 1970.

Sackrey, Charles. *The Political Economy of Urban Poverty*. New York: Norton, 1973.

Samuelson, Paul A. *Economics*. New York: McGraw-Hill, 1973.

Schwartz, Harry. *The Case for American Medicine: A Realistic Look at Our Health Care System*. New York: McKay, 1972.

Wertz, Richard W. *Readings on Ethical and Social Issues in Biomedicine*. Englewood Cliffs, N.J.: Prentice-Hall, 1973.

Will, Robert E., and Vatter, Harold G. (Ed.). *Poverty in Affluence: The Social, Political, and Economic Dimensions of Poverty in the United States*, 2nd ed. New York: Harcourt, 1970.

Suggested Reading

FREEMAN, HOWARD E., LEVINE, SOL, AND REEDER, LEO G. (Eds.). *Handbook of Medical Sociology*. Englewood Cliffs, N.J.: Prentice-Hall, 1972.
Especially pages 63–101, 206–227, and 315–336. These three articles deal with the relationship between medical care, medical problems, and patient characteristics.

KENNEDY, EDWARD M. *In Critical Condition*. New York: Pocket Books, 1973.
Superficial review of the inadequacies of health care systems based on personal experiences expressed in congressional hearings.

KOSA, JOHN, ANTONOVSKY, AARON, AND ZOLO, IRVING K. *Poverty and Health: A Sociological Analysis*. Cambridge, Mass.: Harvard University Press, 1969.
An insightful discussion of the relationship between poverty and health.

MCKINLEY, JOHN B. (Ed.). *Politics and Law in Health Care Policy*. Prodist, N.Y.: Milbank Memorial Fund, 1973.
This is a sophisticated series of articles dealing with health care systems as a totality, with special emphasis on policy issues and changes within the system.

TAYLOR, CAROL. *In Horizontal Orbit, Hospitals and the Cult of Efficiency*. New York: Holt, Rinehart and Winston, 1970.
Study of the hospital as a social system with special emphasis on the relationships between the patient, physician, and nurse. Also the social and cultural influences on the hospital are discussed.

TUNLEY, ROUL. *The American Health Scandal*. New York: Harper & Row, 1966.
A somewhat dated, but still useful, critique of the inadequacies of the health care system.

The Captive Couple

The Burden of Gender Roles in Marriage

Nona Glazer-Malbin

In Gilbert and Sullivan's musical the soldier gets a cramp trying to play the role of the poet . . . everyone gets a cramp, physical or mental, when playing roles. Cramps of the soul, cramps of the body, arthritis of the emotions.   Anais Nin *

Wives, submit yourselves unto your own husbands, as unto the Lord.   Ephesians 5:22

Thus, full freedom in marriage can become generally operative only when the abolition of capitalist production, and of the property relations created by it, has removed all those secondary economic considerations which now exert so powerful an influence on the choice of a partner.   Frederick Engels, 1884 **

"The battle of the sexes." The refrain runs through folk wisdom, songs, jokes and quips, through Hollywood films and classical theatre, through Western philosophy and religion, a reflection of deeply rooted beliefs women and men have about the relationship between the sexes. The theme is touched with irony for if there is a "battle of the sexes," romantic love has taught the warriors themselves to believe that the most satisfying human relationship in industrial society is between a woman and a man, within marriage. Peasant societies may stress parental bonds, clan bonds, or other ties of the extended family. Socialist societies may stress social class and responsibilities to the proletariat, to the state and to the party. But, in capitalist societies the expectation is that the single most satisfying tie is in a family, in heterosexual, monogamous marriage. Even those who reject the legal commitment of marriage still usually expect to find most of these satisfactions within a paired "marriage-like" arrangement.

While many aspects of conventional marriage may be examined for their contribution to current marital woes, I will be concerned in this article with the problem of gender roles in marriage for both sexes, roles which I see supporting as well as reflecting the ambivalences women and men have learned to feel about each other. The general thesis of my comments can be briefly stated: The burden of gender roles basically lies in a division of labor within the family which leads each person to be interdependent with another of the other sex in highly stylized ways. This division of labor, by sex, promotes specialization which limits the ability of each sex to participate fully in society, to contribute maximally to society, and to develop the self fully. Current gender roles make the functioning of people outside the institution of heterosexual, monogamous marriage difficult.

The accepted family model leads to different views of how gender roles constitute marital problems. The more the family is seen as responsible to the needs

* Anais Nin quoting Otto Rank in *The Diary of Anais Nin*, Vol. 2, 1934–1939 (New York: Harcourt Brace Jovanovich, 1967), p. 7.
** *The Origin of the Family, Private Property and the State.* (New York: International Publishers), p. 67.

of society, the less men and women may deviate from prescribed roles, and the greater appears each member's responsibility for the family's success. The less the family is seen as responsible to society, the greater appears the individual's freedom as far as developing new social roles are concerned, and personal freedom appears more dependent on social organization rather than individual will or decision.

GENERAL PERSPECTIVE

In what sense are gender roles[1] in the contemporary family in the United States a "social problem"? As Donald Ball (1972) notes, what is considered a social problem depends on what is considered *not* to be a problem, what *is* thought to be healthy, normal, desirable. Therefore, to say the contemporary family faces gender role problems means that we have a picture or pictures, however hazy and full of contradictions these may be, of a normal, desirable family life. For example, extramarital sexual relationships are considered to be a problem if we believe that a sexually exclusive relationship (monogamy) is "normal." Divorce is a social problem if we believe

[1] A word about "gender roles," used here instead of the more familiar "sex roles." *Sex* is a biological concept, referring to the division of most species into female and male, based on genes, hormones, and developmental phenomena. Since for humans, role assignments are socially made and the content of roles socially constructed, the ways in which females (girls and women) and males (boys and men) behave cannot be understood by a reference to a biological factor. *Roles* are social, *gender* identity and assignment are social whatever their biological aspects. Hence, gender is a preferable term to sex in this context because the former takes this social nature of roles into account (Money and Ehrhardt, 1972).

that marriage ought to last for the lifetime of the partners.

In many Western countries marriage is seen as problem-ridden. To many, the high divorce rate is a sign of problems. Equally threatening signs are the increasing discussion and practice, even if limited, of alternatives to conventional marriage. Communes, "living together," marriage contracts, group marriage, "swinging," family networks, homosexual and lesbian pairings, the acceptability of single-parent families, and of singlehood —with or without children—as a permanent way of life may be interpreted as evidence that "marriage is in serious trouble." These challenge quite diverse aspects of traditional marriage and provide alternatives to gender roles, private property, lifetime commitments, sexual exclusiveness, sexual preferences, procreation and child-rearing practices, emotional fidelity, and the need to marry at all in order to lead a satisfying and responsible life (Glazer-Malbin, 1975).

MODELS OF THE FAMILY

Models of the family, held by social scientists and the public alike, can be categorized into three general types. Following Ball, I would note that not only do social problems imply notions of the "good," but each model also implies solutions to social problems. We do not always select a solution that matches our model well, but certain kinds of social policies do follow from assumptions about the basic nature of the family, of each sex, and their respective roles in the family. Moreover, each view of the family I discuss below emphasizes a certain perspective but does not exclude, consistent or not, other assumptions about the family. For example, a view may emphasize how the family fulfills functions for the society and still recognize that it can be seen as a system of interacting persons.

Societal Functions and Individual Responsibility

A major view of the family is captured in a definition taken from a widely respected family text written for undergraduates. To Nye and Berardo (1973: 33), the family is typically "at least two adults of the opposite sex living in a socially approved sexual relationship, along with one or more of their own or adopted children." [2] In this conception, the family is the basic and universal social institution and the structure through which important societal needs are met (Parsons, 1951; Zimmerman, 1947). Specifically, society needs new members, and the family performs the function of reproducing. Society needs members who behave more or less in accord with social norms, accept the dominant ideology, attempt to realize certain goals, and so on, and the family socializes the young. Sexuality is seen (with lenses apparently borrowed from Victorian times) as so potentially disruptive of human relationships as to need careful regulation, and the family performs this function by largely limiting sexual expression to the family setting. Society needs to insure that its members survive physically and so family members together produce goods, though in industrialized societies, some family members, usually adult men and unmarried older children of both sexes, leave the household to "work";

[2] Nye and Berardo note that the family may be combined into composite units, into (a) the polygamous family; and (b) the extended family (1973:36–42).

the family as a unit is consuming. This view of work assumes that activities which have *use-value* only, such as childcare, cooking, cleaning, sewing, grocery shopping, and so on (the activities usually done by a woman for her own household) are not "production" because they are done for family members rather than for the market economy. When the same activities are done by a paid worker in the home or in a setting outside the home (e.g., in daycare centers, food processing plants) then the activities have *exchange-value* (Benston, 1969). The assumption that productivity involves only goods and services that can be exchanged with nonfamily persons is a good example of how basic definitions of institutions are related to our views of the family. In this case, the traditional view that wives do not "work" rests partly on the arguable contention that an activity that does not make a direct contribution to the market economy is not work.

The structure of the isolated nuclear family—a unit of husband, wife and their offspring—is explained as adaptative to the needs of an industrial economy. This isolated form makes it easy for families to move vertically on the social class ladder as well as geographically in pursuit of economic security or advancement. Furthermore, the isolation of the nuclear family makes it important that men devote considerable energy (as well as anxiety) to occupational success, since the isolation of the family makes its well-being depend heavily on the man's role in the economy. The intrapersonal and interpersonal difficulties with the isolation of the family and the subordinate position of the woman are relatively ignored, the presumed fit between the structure of the family and the structure of the economy being evaluated as "functional" (Parsons, 1951). In the family needed by society, successful family function is regarded as attainable mainly by individual effort. Family problems (for example, quarreling, sexual dysfunction, economic crisis) are seen as due to the individual's failure to perform family roles well.

An analysis of the black family in the United States shows how conceptions of the family as an institution meeting "society's" needs (rather than class or individual needs) can generate an individualistic social policy. This particular example is of special interest since it focuses on gender roles in the family. The Moynihan report, written in 1965 to inform policy-makers in the federal government about the social conditions of blacks, concludes that the black family is "the fundamental source of the weakness of the Negro community at the present time" (Moynihan, 1965:4). According to the report, black children, especially boys, fail to develop the character and ability needed for successful living because they grow up in a woman-dominated rather than the "normal" man-dominated home. Moynihan noted that unemployment of young black men reflects a lack of job training and job opportunity, that the black family is "battered and harassed by discrimination, injustice, and uprooting . . . ," and that the 1965 federal minimum wage of $1.25 per hour is hardly sufficient to support a couple, let alone one with children. However, the family is viewed as at fault for the plight of blacks, because a woman-dominated household ill-prepares children for a society which, Moynihan writes, "presumes male leadership in private and public affairs. The arrangements of society facilitate such leadership and reward it.

"A subculture, such as that of the Negro

American, in which this is not the pattern, is placed at a distinct disadvantage" (Moynihan, 1965:29). One may legitimately ask: Why must the black family train the sexes to conform to male domination and female subordination but not to white domination? The answer is partly that by 1965, many Americans, including those with the power to shape social policy, overtly rejected racism as a legitimate social form while still taking sexism quite for granted. Not considering whether male supremacy might be a form of discrimination against females, or why black men must conform to some idealized white version of masculinity before being eligible for jobs, Moynihan neglects other questions about social structure. For example why is the federal minimum wage level so low that full-time, year-round workers cannot support themselves adequately, or why does job discrimination continue with the support of corporations and labor unions alike? Nor, does he wonder about the lack of job training. Instead, the burden of the black problem is placed in the lap of the family, and the mother's lap at that, because she gives her sons an inappropriate model of feminine competence. Moynihan does not, interestingly, refer to black daughters, who presumably would also suffer, since they would not be well adapted to the *subordinate* gender role of women accepted in the United States.

Behavioral System, Relational Responsibility

A second perspective is to see the family as a system of interacting personalities, as a system within which members carry out social roles. This view is held by many sociologists and social psychologists and is also the dominant view of the family held by marital counselors. Rather than emphasizing how society needs certain functions performed for its survival, the emphasis is on the functioning of the family. The concern is with feelings, attitudes, roles, personalities, role expectations, and the complementarity of roles, a more individualistic approach than the first view. Variations in this approach examine interaction as it occurs over the family life cycle (Duvall, 1957), in relationship to persons outside the family, such as friends (Nye and Berardo, 1973) and to the individual family's culture.

While these approaches vary in the details of the framework used to investigate the family, they converge in their similar focus on the *relationship between family members* rather than on the relationship of the family to society. Problems such as marital dissatisfaction, sexual dysfunction, physical violence, and so on, are examined as problems of intrapersonal and interpersonal origins; this is true even though there may be the recognition that the family is shaped by extrafamily factors such as gender role expectations (for example, Turner, 1970:249–282).

To this array of problems faced by a family follow two basic solutions: (1) Mental health solutions, in which the roots of family conflicts are treated as located in the personalities of the family members and how they relate to each other. These difficulties are approached with a variety of counseling techniques— individual therapy, cojoint family counseling, encounter groups, sensitivity training, behavior modification. (2) Given the situational aspects of the family's experiences, changes in the immediate family environment may also be sought. Since interpersonal problems may arise out of the context in which the family finds itself, changing the situation is seen as a solution to altering family relationships. For example, a woman, overly dependent for emotional support and intellectual stimulation on her husband and children, may be advised to work outside the home, develop her talents, do volunteer work. Through the establishment of new sources of personal satisfaction and new social relationships the marital problem of over-dependency may be attenuated. Basically, the solutions to the family's problems are located within the power of the family circle itself.

Cultural System, Societal Responsibility

The third model sees the family as a cultural invention reflecting the organization of social institutions outside it, particularly the nature of economic organization. The family is seen as a product of economic development (a traditional Marxian view), and of societal views about social equality, sex differences, sexuality, the nature of the children, and also as an institution which reflects the societal structure of power relationships (sexism). While this model, on the surface, may seem to be the same as the institutional model, it diverges from it in important ways (Engels, 1891; Mitchell, 1971; Vajda and Heller, 1971). The model does not assume that the family must fulfill certain universal tasks for society (reproduction, production, socialization, sexual). What the family *is* becomes a serious question: Do the Israeli kibbutz, the Oneida commune, a contemporary American commune, a stable homosexual pair, a contract marriage, or newly married 65-year-old pair qualify as "families"? Donald Ball provides a definition of the family "based upon the empirical realities of the actual social arrangements of the contemporary everyday-anyday world":

any cohabiting domestic relationship which is (or has been) sexually consequential, i.e., gratification for members, or the production of offspring. These are the relationships most often associated with the emotions of love and the home, whether members are conventionally situated or otherwise. (Ball, 1972:302)

This definition is noteworthy in several ways: (1) It ignores the sex of the relating individuals, and therefore implies that the division of labor (by sex or otherwise) is not an imperative for the existence of a family; (2) it makes no assumption about the permanency of a relationship; (3) it makes no assumption about economic cooperation (though it does about domestic cooperation, assuming a shared residence); (4) formal, public acknowledgement, whether by civil or religious bodies, is absent; and (5) it does make an important statement about commitment and attachment, deriving these from psychological commitment rather than from functionally complementary behaviors. His definition means that childless families, short-term living groups, homosexual couples, group marriage, and communes are "families" rather than "social problems."

Using this definition of "family" allied with the view of social forces as affecting the family, infinite possible living arrangements arise. Now the question is: What forms of social organization do we want, how *can* we live (not how must we live), and what "family" forms will most adequately meet human needs? Mitchell summarizes this:

What is the family? And what are the actual functions that a woman fulfills within it? Like woman herself, the family

appears as a natural object, but is actually a cultural creation. There is nothing inevitable about the form or role of the family, any more than there is about the character or role of woman. It is the function of ideology to present these given social types as aspects of Nature itself. . . . The apparently natural condition can be made to appear more attractive than the arduous advance of human beings towards culture. (Mitchell, 1971)

GENDER ROLES IN THE MARRIAGE RELATIONSHIP

Generally, when "American marriage" is discussed reference is to upper-middle- or middle-class style. However, there is a good deal of variation by social class as well as by race and ethnicity, though it is often difficult to separate their effects. The family which meets the American ideal has a separate household of husband, wife, and their offspring—what Parsons calls the isolated, nuclear family, presumably with the partners being in a first marriage or in remarriages which followed the death of the earlier mate rather than divorce.

Working-Class Marriage

While there is certainly variation within the working class, marriage usually fits Bott's *segregated conjugal role relationship*.[3] Marriage is highly functional—with

[3] Elizabeth Bott has classified husband and wife role relationships as (a) *segregated conjugal role-relationship* where activities of each are different and separate but fitted together, and where activities are carried out separately by each, without reference to each other. Each mate has clear tasks and many separate interests and activities. The mates have different leisure activities and each has friends outside the home; (b) The *joint conjugal role-relationship* in which joint activity is usual. The spouses expect to carry out activities together and there is little difference in the tasks and interests each

the partners concerned primarily with earning a living, having and caring for children, homemaking—and it is less focused on companionship than spouses (especially the wife) may desire (Komarovsky, 1967). First, there is a sharp distinction in gender roles wherein women do "women's work" and men do "men's work." The major aspect of "men's work" is being the breadwinner, while the major work of women is childbearing and childcare, homemaking, and husbandcare (being emotionally supportive, understanding, uncritical, physically attractive, and sexually available). The labor force activity of wives is seen as supplementary and secondary to the main responsibilities of housecare, childcare, husbandcare. This is despite sizeable contributions made by women to family income (Cymrot and Mallan, 1974).

Second, while men are supposed to be the major decision-makers, working-class women exercise considerably more power than is the ideal and more than their middle-class sisters (Steinmann and Fox, 1974). Third, the strongest emotional ties—friendship or the confidant relationship—do not exist between spouses as often as in the middle class. Strong ties with childhood friends and kin are maintained by both partners and leisure is often divided along sex lines (men play cards or pool with their friends, women visit and shop with their friends). In mixed sex activities, the participants may readily divide into same sex groups. Fourth, men tend to be lower in self-disclosure than women, and lower than their wives would like them to be, having learned that it is "masculine" to keep ones troubles to oneself as well as to not

___
pursue. Family activities are planned together, much leisure is spent together, and many tasks are exchanged.

expect that women are interested or capable of talking about "masculine" interests such as sports, politics, autos and the job (Komarovsky, 1967).

Fifth, sexuality is less likely to be a mutually satisfying recreational activity than in the middle class, congruent with the general lesser degree of closeness between working-class compared to middle-class partners. Women also appear to enjoy sex less than their mates and less than women in the middle class (Rainwater, 1968). Women are less satisfied than men with particular aspects of their marriage, though they are as likely as men to report being happily married. Finally, marriage itself is more important to women than men, providing them with work—housecare, childcare, and husbandcare—and with a status—"somebody's wife." It is a paradox and reflection of gender role socialization that marriage is more likely to provide men than women with their sole important interpersonal relationship.

Black Working-Class Families

There has been a good deal of discussion particularly in the past decade about the problems of the black family, and a good deal of commentary about the meaning of the greater frequency of woman-headed households among blacks compared to whites. This structural difference has lead some social scientists to talk about "black matriarchy," suggesting that women dominate in the home more frequently than men do. (However, it may be that a white male social scientist bias that the "normal" family is man-headed and man-dominated leads to the choice of the description "matriarchy" over "egalitarian.")

Actually, since the "woman-headed" household means that a man is not present, as Staples notes, it cannot be that the woman dominates the man. The meaning has more to do with socialization of children, especially feelings of hostility that black mothers supposedly engender in their sons, as well as the suspicion of men which they teach their daughters. This view of relationships between the sexes, as well as the modeling of children's behaviors, needs investigation with detailed descriptions of interaction between spouses and comparative data on the behavior of black children from two-person and mother-headed households (Staples, 1970b). While we may be cautious about the differences in the emotional tone of husband-wife relationships which distinguish black from white couples, in the area of women's employment there are well-substantiated differences. Black wives, living with their mates, are much more likely to work outside the home than comparable white women—54 percent compared to 41 percent in 1973 (Hayghe, 1974).

If there is a striking difference between working-class black and working-class white wives it is that the former appear to reject the double standard as far as sexual activities are concerned; to believe that women have the same rights as men; and to accept a less passive role in general than white women do. Hence, black women may be more assertive in their interactions with men, more willing to be straight forward about what they want. The sexual and interpersonal realm in which black women play a more egalitarian role than white women may engender the accusation that black women dominate their men. After nearly a decade of the reawakened women's movement and the reexamination to which sex roles have been subject, it may be time to change the description of black working-class

relations from "woman-dominated" to "egalitarian."

Middle-Class Marriage

Just as in the case of working-class couples, there is variation within the middle class with patterns ranging from a sharp division between the sexes—the segregated conjugal role-relationship—to complete joint conjugal role-relationship. Nevertheless, middle-class marriage can more often be described as joint conjugal than segregated. Shared activities have particularly to do with the companionship component of the relationship though it involves household activities and childcare, too, although women clearly retain the overwhelming responsibility for the last two activities. To some degree, the companionship role may be a case of the wife more often meeting her husband's needs (as a companion, and emotionally and sexually) rather than companionship being a reciprocal relationship (Bernard, 1971; Glazer-Malbin, 1975a). More emphasis is placed on couple relationships, and though each partner may also have their own friends, their main socializing is as a couple. Women may also play a significant part in their husband's career success, socializing with and entertaining his work colleagues and their mates. Motherhood occupies a prominent place in the lives of women, decreasing their involvement with their mates and diverting their energies from activities outside the home (Bart, 1971; Lopata, 1971).

The general substance of middle-class marriage is that it is a central focus for women, particularly, and for men, even if work takes a more important place. The family is a haven for men from the pressures of the job and the drive to succeed, and for women, the major defining factor in their lives. The greater importance of the couple relationship in middle-class compared to working-class marriage is evident in the relative trauma and problems which follow marital loss (death or divorce). Middle-class women who have centered their lives on their spouses have far greater initial difficulty in adjusting to the single status than working-class women who are embedded in a more dependable supportive network of old friends and family. Middle-class women, however, given their greater resources (education, interpersonal skills, political knowledgeability, and so on) eventually are able to make a better adjustment to the absence of the mate (Lopata, 1973).

THEORETICAL OBSERVATIONS ABOUT GENDER ROLES

The roles which husband and wife fulfill in marriage have been viewed as complementary, each role organizing tasks for the survival of the family and society. It is assumed that the man's role focuses on *instrumental tasks*—such as making a living for the family, representing the family to the community on civic and political matters, assuming the major decision-making responsibility on issues affecting the family, etc.—and that the woman's role focuses on *socioemotional tasks*—socializing the children, providing love and emotional support to family members, managing the emotional relationships between family members, and so forth (Parsons and Bales, 1955). (The ideology of sex differences has been so pervasive that one investigator considered "shopping" to be a wife's socioemotional task!) The theory has been criticized

repeatedly since people do not play such segregated task roles in small groups (Aronoff and Crano, 1975) or in the family (Levinger, 1964). Most recently, women's role as a food provider has been examined across 862 societies of varying types showing that women are not restricted to socioemotional tasks; women contribute *significantly* to the subsistence of the family, providing 41 percent or more of the food in 45 percent of the societies; and between 20 and 40 percent of the food in another 41 percent of the societies (Aronoff and Crano, 1975).

Goode (1960) has suggested that while the organization of roles may be adapted to the demands of the industrial society, husbands and wives may experience considerable stress from these socalled adapted roles. I shall take that one step further in the following discussion, questioning the harmony between the family roles and society.

The protest movements of the 1960s focused concern on human liberation, supporting the reawakening of the women's movement which developed in the latter years of that decade. The challenge to gender roles in marriage reconsiders a woman and a man's lifetime commitment to interdependence emphasizing procreation, sexual exclusiveness, and adherence to complementary roles (even if the roles do not fit the neat division into instrumental and socioemotional) within a residentially isolated nuclear family. The most usual departure from this pattern is serial monogamy, one partner at a time in a cycle of marriage-divorce-remarriage. More recently, alternative life styles have moved away from isolated residences, sexual exclusiveness, procreation, heterosexual exclusiveness, one-couple households. However, any and all of these can occur easily *without* changes in gender roles and, therefore, gender roles have been approached by feminists as a separate issue.

Analysis of gender roles in conventional marriage relationships suggests the following conclusions which depart from the view that roles in marriage are "complementary" and that such roles are not problematic for the society.

Divergence during life-cycle of marriage. Gender roles pattern the involvement of each mate so that there are separating rather than converging or compatible degrees of involvement in (a) their separate responsibilities in the division of labor; and (b) supportive social networks outside the family unit. The separate and conflicting demands are such that the mates must choose between fulfilling role obligations as opposed to interpersonal demands in the husband-wife relationship.

Privilege-penalty effects. Every apparent privilege in a gender role can be examined for accompanying penalties which involve overwhelming responsibilities, restricted competencies, excluded positive experiences—the less than autonomous functioning of the person. (Autonomy is not irresponsibility; it means self-direction, not automatically conforming to social demands.) De Beauvoir (1953) suggested that marriage is always something different for man and for woman, with the sexes being necessary to each other but without reciprocity, and that marriage is for both a burden and a benefit. I will illustrate this in my discussion of the burdens of sex roles.

Dependency effect. Presumably the division of labor in marriage relieves social institutions outside of the family from considerable responsibility—for dependent women and for dependent children, in particular. Moreover, the adaptation of

roles to society presumably means stable families. Neither of these is the case: the divorce rate was estimated at 4.7 (per 1000 population) in 1974 following a high of 4.4 in 1973 compared to rates of 2.1 to 2.6, 1950–1967 (Waldman, 1975). Among persons under 70 years in 1970, 14 percent of white men, 28 percent of black men, 15 percent of white women and 32 percent of black women had been divorced at least once. Mother-headed households changed from 3.0 percent for once-married white women and 7.1 percent for once-married black women in 1940 to 6.2 percent and 20.2 percent respectively, in 1970.[4] Death also brings a change in marital status affecting women more often than men. Among couples married between 30 and 55 years, 9 men in 1000 and 23 women in 1000 become widowed in a 12-month period. Men (divorced or widowed) are more likely than women, given ageism, to remarry (Glick and Norton, 1971). Given the differential rate of remarriage, there are large numbers of children who live in one-parent families: In 1974, 1 of 10 white children and 4 of 10 black children lived with their mothers (father absent) (Waldman, 1975).

Gender roles do not appear to promote stable marriages, and the dissolution rate has serious consequences for the lives of those from dissolved marriages. Gender roles—outside of marriage, as well as in marriage—promote the dependency of women and children on the family unit. Hence, after dissolution, institutions outside the family, particularly social welfare agencies, are faced with trying to cope

---

[4] There has also been an increase in mother-child households headed by never-married women, from 28,000 white and 18,000 black households in 1940 to 63,000 white and 166,000 black households in 1970 (Cutright, 1974).

with exwives who may often find themselves without financial support from their former mates and who cannot earn a living for themselves and their children. These women may find it exceedingly difficult to integrate themselves into social networks which include complete families, to provide models for the children, as well as social and emotional support.

THE BETTER HALF: WHICH HALF?

Theories about the democratization of the American family, which predated the current women's movement, saw the marriage as basically egalitarian, especially in the middle class (Blood and Wolfe, 1960; Burgess, 1953). Recent writers have noted theoretical flaws and questionable interpretations of data and suggested, more cautiously, that egalitarianism in marriage had been greatly exaggerated (Bernard, 1971; Gillespie, 1971; Goode, 1960). Moreover, the analysis of marriage as egalitarian has ignored the different effect upon each sex of marital dissolution, effects which arise partly from the differing responsibilities for housework, production, reproduction and childcare, marital power, and sexuality.

Housework

First, some observations about the relevance of housework to equality in marriage (see Mainardi, 1970). The discussion of housework (and to a lesser degree, childcare tasks) is to some "trivial"; Farrell (1974) says men have more difficulty discussing housework than any other topic including homosexuality. This is a reflection of how women's work is evaluated, as well as a lack of understanding

about how housekeeping (and childcare) shape the economic situation of women. (Women themselves may interpret serving their mates as a sign of love and men frequently support this view: A professional in her early 60s explained to me that she "loved" serving her spouse (also a professional) while a man professor (married to a woman physician) contended that housework chores sapped men's energies, diverting them from important scholarly pursuits.) The housework-is-trivial thesis ignores the effect of a server-served role on the development of and the disrupting effect for an egalitarian relationship—when the man believes the activities of his wife aren't of much importance. (According to Bart (1971) women's restriction to housework and childcare as a career seems connected to particular psychiatric problems.) The effect of the dual, indeed, triple responsibilities of the wife-mother-worker roles (43 percent of married women living with their husband are in the labor force) on the woman's energy and general psychological well-being, not to mention her performance on her job, has also been overlooked. (See Syfers, 1972, for an elaboration of a wife's usefulness from the point of view of a married woman.)

Women's responsibility for housekeeping and childcare weakens her economic condition, forcing her into marginal participation in the labor force—marginal because these responsibilities confine her to intermittent or part-time work. Yet, women are distributed throughout the class system because of their affiliation with husbands. In contrast, the social class placement of men is on the basis of their own work and is maintained quite apart from their affiliation with particular women. (A woman may help or hinder her husband's career advancement, but his class affiliation is not ascribed on the basis of marriage to her.) The connection becomes evident with the high divorce rate which has exposed the weak economic condition of women who drop into a lower social class after divorce. For example, 16 percent of all women and 34 percent of all minor children involved in divorces in 1968 were on welfare in 1968 in two of the state of Oregon's most heavily populated counties (Funkhouser, 1970). While work has become increasingly social—production is cooperative in factories—housework remains private, where the worker (the wife) remains isolated from other workers.

Housework is not a minor activity estimated in dollar values, but an important economic contribution which wives (as well as other family members) make to the family's standard of living (Pyun, 1969; Walker and Gauger, 1973). In fact, men's participation in the work force depends upon the existence of an underclass (wives) who by performing all or nearly all housework release men to give their maximum energy to their job. Finally, though housework has become easier (the vacuum takes the place of the carpet beater), standards of home living have risen while the servants upon which even families with rather modest incomes could once have depended have disappeared.

The burden of women being so totally in charge of these activities created burdens for men in their role in production, discussed below. Exactly what other problems arise for men is not clear. Minimally, men have reported that marital dissolution would create serious problems for them in doing household chores, exceeded as a problem only by loneliness among working-class men; middle-class men saw themselves as even less able to cope, but other problems equalled or exceeded household chores (Glazer-Malbin, 1975).

Marital Power

The difficult problem of assessing marital power begins with the meaning of power. It is asserted that "women run the country" (including presumably their husbands and children) because they are the primary purchasers, spending the family's income for food, clothing, household furnishings, as well as for major appliances, medical care and leisure activities; and because they decide on family meals, are responsible for the children's daily care, for arranging the details of family outings and the couple's leisure. This interpretation of women's power is questionable, overlooking that those who are in social positions which involve implementing goals may or may not have the power to decide a critical issue: exactly *what* goals are to be pursued. This interpretation is akin to believing that workers have considerable political and economic power since they assemble autos, pick crops, or build oil rigs.

Critics of studies of marital power have also noted that all decisions in marriage are given equal weight, for example, a decision about what job the husband should take (affecting all aspects of family life) is considered of the same importance as where to go for a two-week vacation; what house or apartment to take is considered of the same importance as what doctor to consult when someone is sick (Blood and Wolfe, 1960; Safilios-Rothschild, 1969).

Power relationships are still dominated by men (Goode, 1963) because husbands have more resources than wives (Gillespie, 1971). Women are socialized to function less autonomously during the court-ship years than men, and hence may see themselves as less able than men to make good decisions. The legal system, much more importantly, supports the hus-band's superior power, giving him the right to decide on family residence, sur-name, and places on him the responsi-bility for supporting the family. In many states he is given the power to manage and control family income and property, and must give his permission before his wife can start her own business, trade in the commodity market, or obtain credit (Weitzman, 1974). Women, as already noted, have a weak position in the labor force; less education than their husbands; are subject to physical coercion (includ-ing rape, since by law a husband cannot rape his wife); and given the suburbani-zation of metropolitan United States, are more isolated from a support network of friends and kin than twenty years ago (Gillespie, 1971).

The gender role burdens here are both obvious and subtle. For women, there is the obvious problem of being deprived of control over critical aspects of their own lives, deprivation with legal sanction. For men, there is the necessity of appear-ing to know the correct choice, and then, of bearing the lonely responsibility of having been incorrect. Men may also have the need to remain in control of situa-tions, as a way of coping with the inevi-table expectation that they have been given that responsibility and must reas-sure themselves of their ability to exer-cise control, to avoid blame for situations which might slip out of their control. At a more subtle level, the counterpart in a woman's behavior may be elaborate ma-nipulative devices by which she can exert some control over the situation without violating the norm of masculine superior-ity nor—the other side of the coin, the importance of which females learn early in life—without hurting a delicate mascu-line ego (see Farrell, 1974).

Production

The economic vulnerability of women is well-documented in government statis-tics: Women are concentrated in sex-segregated, low-pay, low-status jobs, and they are the last hired, first fired (in spite of affirmative action). Men earn more than women (comparing median wages) in every occupation but kindergarten teachers. This is true even in those occu-pations in which women are the majority of workers as in the five occupations listed in Table 1, occupations which in-clude one-quarter of all women workers. Women are from 65 to 98 percent of the workers in each occupation, while earning from 40 to 82 percent of what men earn. The income gap is not ex-plained by educational differences for among full-time, year-round workers, women earn substantially less than men with comparable education (U.S. De-partment of Labor, 1971). The lower in-come of women is explained by discrimi-nation in the labor force, for example, men are hired for career line positions while women from the same college with equal academic achievements are hired for dead end clerical jobs. Just as impor-tant is the marginal position of women in the labor force, for women leave the labor force in their late twenties to take on parenthood tasks, to reenter consid-erably later (Sommers, 1974). Parent-hood decreases the likelihood that women can earn as much as men regardless of education and occupation since women are pulled out of the labor force during the crucial years, when men are forging ahead.

Table 1. Median Annual Earnings of Women and Men
in the Top Five Occupations of Women Workers

Occupation *	Median Annual Earnings			
				Earnings of Women as Percent of Men's Earnings
			Percent	
	Women	Men	Women	
Public elementary school teachers	$6883	$8366	84	82
Secretaries	$4803	$7536	98	64
Bookkeepers	$4477	$7401	82	60
Retail sales-clerks	$2208	$5482	65	40
Waitresses/waiters	$1662	$3894	89	57

Based on data taken from Tables 1 and 2 in Dixie Sommers, "Occupational Rankings for Men and Women by Earnings," *Monthly Labor Review*, U.S. Dept. of Labor, August, 1974.
* These are the five occupations women are most likely to enter, including 25.4 percent of the female labor force.

Economic dependency means for women little freedom to insure budget expenditures with which their mates disagree: piano lessons for a child, a new living room chair, babysitting while mother is rehearsing for a play, are costs that more than one wife of affluent professionals report meeting by part-time work, believing that their housekeeping and childcare activities are simply in exchange for room and board but not "luxury" items. Equally important, women are restricted in their capacity to leave an undesirable marriage as reflected in the divorce rate which is higher before the advent of children and after the youngest enters school.

Nor does court-ordered child support after divorce provide for offspring as Eckhardt (1968) shows. One year after the court has ordered child support, only 38 percent of the fathers are in full compliance, a figure which drops to 19 percent by the fifth year and 13 percent by the tenth year. Legal action is rarely taken—by order 19, 9 and 1 percent of women,

one, five, and ten years, respectively, after the court order.

Women's dependency has sharp repercussions on men's role in production, a role which for men is one of the main burdens of gender roles in marriage. Men's burdens rests on women's exclusion and/or marginal position in the labor force. For practical purposes, the family relies on the man's work, so the husband finds he has no or little freedom to endanger his job (for example, by criticism, by friction with employer or coworkers, by union organizing, innovation, and so forth) or to leave easily a job that is dissatisfying. Furthermore, being a "man," manliness, masculinity, these are measured by the extent that one "makes it" in the labor force. (The operative verb, interestingly, also applies to sexual relationships with women.) Much of men's work, however, is monotonous and/or psychologically unrewarding, at best; at its worst, it is dangerous to the man as well as to others in the society.

Much of this may be forgotten by women, who, financially dependent on higher-income men, isolated by house-care and childcare, seek work as a route to self-fulfillment (Friedan, 1963).

Boys apparently learn early in life—certainly by adolescence—that they must focus on a career because they will some-day support a family. Girls may, in their early years, aspire to occupations which require considerable training and considerable energy and time in adulthood, but they learn—possibly also by adolescence —that high aspirations are not appropriate for them and they lower their ambitions. The sexes, however, do not appear to differ from each other according to Maccoby and Jacklin (1974) in the pressures experienced from parents to achieve, nor in motivation to achieve. Women have a lesser sense of control than men which may effect their achievements in career situations, which are much less structured and more "out of control" than school. Of course, the organization of post-college living, training programs, the possibility of promotion discourage women from high achievement in the economy (Maccoby and Jacklin, 1974).

The effectiveness of the ideology of masculine responsibility for family income is such that men may accept responsibility, or fear that others may see them as responsible, for unemployment which is a result of the business cycle; they see their inability to find a job as evidence of personal culpability (Bakke, 1940; Sennett and Cobb, 1972). Furthermore, many men do not want their wives to work for pay and especially do not want their wives to earn more than they do.

After the dissolution of marriage, ali-mony is often resented by husbands since women's prior housework and prior and future childcare is not seen as a contribution to family income. Child support is also resisted; from the man's perspective he must provide financial support for children over whom he has minimal control and with whom, in fact, he may have little or no contact. Father and children may meet in highly stylized situations—the weekend outing—in which interaction centers around doing something together rather than the day-by-day concerns of the child. And, of course, his attempts to reestablish a life by remarrying may be sharply curtailed by his financial obligations to his first family.

Childcare

In American society, by custom and by law, it is assumed that the mother will bear the major day-by-day responsibility for a couple's children, *after* divorce as well as during marriage (Weitzman, 1974). This assumption is so embedded in the culture that until recently social scientists studied "maternal deprivation" when the mother was out of the home (either missing or in the labor force) but not the more neutral "father absence" when the man was missing (Wortis, 1971). This assumption persists in spite of considerable evidence disputing the view that children need a mother's fairly constant presence to avoid personality problems, delinquency, or identity problems, and evidence that fathering is important, too. (See Laws, 1971, for a review of the relevant literature; Biller, 1971.)

The high divorce rate has implications for childcare. According to Brown (1975), as the economic value of children declined with industrialization men gave up their legal rights to the sole custody of children, and women began to assume custody; as children are now a cost rather than a value, women are almost forced to take responsibility for them. Though the woman is asked to give up or give second place to the occupation during marriage, with child custody she is frequently left with the financial responsibility for children as well as for herself. She must somehow manage to add the role of breadwinner to her duties while her former husband and the children's father may curtail his roles, lessening both the financial and emotional responsibilities of fatherhood.[5]

Sexuality

The double standard for sexuality has certainly lessened. Yet remnants still remain: in court judgments in which adolescent girls (but not boys) may be adjudged delinquent for engaging in sexual relations (Chesney-Lind, 1973); in the belief that the sexual arousal and satisfaction of women must be tied, unlike for men, to feelings of love, a belief which persists in spite of evidence to the contrary (Schmidt et al., 1973); in the assertion that increased impotency problems of men are a function of the increased demands, sexual as well as nonsexual, of women.

Concepts of woman's sexuality and the

[5] Mulligan has suggested that a situation of structurally extant polygamy has evolved in which an upper-middle-class and professional-class man's current wife performs certain functions (sexual, companionship, household) while the man remains dependent on his exwife for the care and socialization of his children—and is dependent on other women such as secretaries and domestic workers for services once performed by a wife (Mulligan, 1972).

role which men play in female responsiveness have undergone considerable change. The late nineteenth-century concept of sexuality stressed the relative lack of sexual responsiveness of women (good ones) and the lustful nature of women (bad ones), and the uncontrollable sex drive of men, containable by appropriate behavior of women (good ones), as well as the man's finding sexual satisfaction with prostitutes and servant girls (bad ones). Gradually, under the impact of Freudian theory, female sexuality was given legitimacy, but, in Freud's view, it was still curtailed by the generally infantile nature of women. One of the developmental tasks he assigned to the female was that of refocusing her sexual interests from an "immature" interest in the clitoris (an organ whose only known purpose is sexual pleasure) to a "mature" interest in vaginal sensations. With this came a gradual belief that female sexual satisfaction depended on the sensitivity of the man, with men being assigned the responsibility for the orgasmic responses of their partners. That view encouraged male sensitivity to woman's sexual needs, but also placed a burden upon men for the responses of another, while still treating women as objects. Most recently, a new shift has been observed with the advent of the pill which made reproductive control far simpler than it had been (quite aside from alleged dangers). Recreational sex is now something for women. Furthermore, the Masters and Johnson findings of the greater orgasmic potential of woman compared to men has lead to new theories of how female sexuality threatens men (Nissen, 1971).

For women, there are additional burdens—the pursuit of multiple orgasms and the pressures of sexual "freedom."

While she is now seen as entitled to sexual pleasure, no longer judged a "bad girl" if she engages in premarital or extramarital sexual activity, "compulsory sex" may now be a problem. She is now *supposed* to engage in sexual relationships, without heed to her preferences, to demonstrate that she is neither frigid nor lesbian, neither a "tease" nor a puritan (Decter, 1972; Mitchell, 1971).

Ageism and Sexuality

There is yet another burden related to sexuality that women must face: ageism. The ideal "sexy" American woman is young, blond, barely pubescent, hairless and lithe, to whom (as Slater [1970] notes) full sexuality is implicitly denied, since she is unmarried. The young married adult woman is comparatively de-sexed, more often shown as a mother-drudge in media presentations than as erotically attractive. The problem for women is the differential standard of sexual attractiveness. Age in a man is an honor and sexual liasons with considerably younger women are acceptable and in fact may increase his status with other men (De Beauvoir, 1972). Yet, older women are considered unattractive "objects," and an older woman-younger man liason is a subject for jokes. Perhaps nothing contradicts the conclusion that the double sexual standard has disappeared so much as the process of aging in which older women are treated as obsolete objects and older men as respected, honored, and sexually attractive. Such ageism contradicts the research which shows that while men decrease in sexual capabilities with age (a decline with clear psychological and sociological, as well as physiological, roots), there is

little diminution in the sexual capacity of women (Masters and Johnson, 1966).[6]

Men's Sexuality

Men's socialization into sexuality develops a focus on genital sensations, on penis size, on "making it" and "making out" (Farrell, 1974). This relatively (a) excludes diffuse sexual sensations, the ability to enjoy a total sexual experience; and (b) encourages a constant anxiety over genital potency, to the relative exclusion of concern with the interpersonal aspects of human sexuality. Men are taught to see women as sex objects with limited concern for the women's feeling and without the awareness that treating women as objects leads one to objectify the self, in this case, the man sees himself as a "performer," a "make-out artist," a "stud," rather than a human being. Sexuality may take on the quality of work in which the man searches in sexual relationships for evidences of excellence in performance rather than gratification or pleasure from the experience itself (Brissett, 1967).

If sex is something with which women barter (for future dates, for presents, and the ultimate, for marriage) then men are placed in a market position, too, rather than in a potentially warm, mutually supportive interpersonal relationship. While women are well into accepting sex as enjoyable apart from deep feelings of love

6 Differential standards of sexual attractiveness can be seen in the statistics on marital status for persons 65–74 years of age: Among whites, 79.6 percent of men are married, and 47 percent of women, while among blacks, 68.6 percent of men and 35 percent of black women. Among those 75 years old, 61 percent white and 41.9 percent black men compared to 19.8 percent white and 14.1 percent black women are married.

or life-long commitments, men have not received equal social support for dispensing with sexual activity as a test of "masculinity," and instead enhancing their sexual experiences emotionally and diffusely. This problem is related to one which has been labeled variously "low self-disclosure" (Jourard, 1971) or "emotional constipation" (Farrell, 1974), the inhibiting of the emotional repertoire of men, the restriction of their skills at knowing or being open about their emotional needs. (This is counterpoint, of course, to women learning to suppress rational-assertive behaviors.)

The Life Cycle

Gender roles in marriage entail not only conflicting and exclusive responsibilities, but diverse and sometimes incompatible patterns of change and involvement with others, and in both genders, the preoccupation with diverse activities. Each sex is focused, by the division of labor, on quite separate experiences over the life cycle, experiences for the woman geared to marrying and then assuming the roles of housewife and mother; and those for the man geared to occupational preparation and an eventual 45–50 year full-time, year-around participation in the labor force.

The preparation of women and men for their adult roles, however, does not appear to differ markedly.[7] Adult life is

[7] Maccoby and Jacklin (1974) conclude after analyzing several hundred studies, most of which were of white, middle-class American children and adults in educational settings, that the sexes do not differ from each other in their interaction with parents and other adults. Boys and girls do not appear to differ in behaviors related to success in jobs, for example, in self-esteem, in learning rote and simple tasks, in delaying gratification, analytical styles, in achievement motivation. Moreover, boys and girls have the same confidence in their ability to do well *until* the

difficult for married women and men in spite or perhaps because of the similarities in early socialization. Women, trained like men for the world outside the home, but under pressure to marry, experience considerable stress as wives. Housewives are more likely than working women to report symptoms of mental health problems; married women have more symptoms than unmarried women; married women commit more crimes than unmarried women (Bernard, 1972). A closer look at the life cycle of the married woman, comparing it with that of the married man may indicate some of the problems. Lopata (1971) has constructed a life cycle of roles for the American housewife upon which I draw heavily in the following, and I have constructed a comparable cycle of roles for the American man.

(1) *Family-centered* infancy, gradually expanded by *school-centered, work-centered* activities. The experience is similar for both sexes (Maccoby and Jacklin, 1974).

(2) *Young adulthood:* Roles cease to be symmetrical: for women, this means *becoming a housewife*—multidimensional, nonfamily focused life gradually shifts to wife-housewife roles, in which earlier relationships (family, friends, coworkers, housemates, neighbors) are greatly lessened. For men, this means, most importantly, *becoming a worker,* secondarily, becoming a husband: The multidimensional, nonfamily focused life is modified by the relinquishment of earlier relationships, but a good portion of the man's life is only moderately affected. He con-

courtship age (18–22 years) when women conform to the gender-role-designated expectation that they exhibit less initiative and more dependence than men. (This is the age when men, especially middle-class, are selecting lifetime occupations.) Research also shows that neither earlier nor later in life do the sexes differ in self-confidence.

tinues involvements connected to his major defining role as a worker.

(3) *Young adulthood-stage two:* For the woman, there is the *expanding circle and peak stage* (Lopata, 1971) in which her life is constricted by the care of a new child with a shift in her concern from husband to offspring. For the man, there is continued job focus which may be intensified by both his new financial responsibilities and what he may experience as his wife's loss of interest in him. Roles may be complementary for *family* functions, but not for the marital relationship.

(4) *Middle years:* For the woman, there is the *full-house plateau* (Lopata, 1971) in which the woman, with several small children, is heavily involved in childcare responsibilities, and then, gradually, often with some labor force participation (30 percent of married women living with their husbands with children under 6 years old worked in 1972) (Cymrot and Wallan, 1974). For the man, the period is likely to be one of *expanding work and work-connected activities* (especially for the middle-class white-collar or professional worker). After the gradual departure of the children (for jobs, schooling, marriage), the wife may turn to alcohol or tranquillizers, or enter upon a severe depression, a fit candidate for Portnoy's mother (Bart, 1971).

(5) *The later years:* For women, this is the period of the *shrinking circle* (Lopata, 1971), when family life has been diminished by the departure of children. While the wife may be free of major childcare responsibilities from her late thirties and early forties, the husband has remained immersed in the world of work. Her major occupation—mother—has ceased or sharply diminished while his continues.

SOLUTIONS TO THE BURDENS OF GENDER ROLES IN MARRIAGE

Several different approaches exist to the solution of the problem of gender roles in marriage: reform feminism, socialism, and socialist feminism.[8]

Reform Feminism

The reform approach to the improvement of the condition of women in marriage is similar to the liberal approach to the improvement of the condition of men: One deals directly with the concrete everyday problems which people face. Today, reform approaches to the condition of women include a long list of goals, such as upgrading the status and pay of childcare jobs, the development of a network of childcare centers, physical planning to reduce the distance between residence and place of work, and identical educational experiences for girls and boys (Rossi, 1964). Other goals include: low-cost abortion on demand; changing the image of women in the mass media; equal access to higher education and to jobs; the desegregation by sex of job want ads; equal pay for equal work; protection of rape victims; decriminalizing prostitution; giving married women the right to domicile choice, surname, investments, and credit in her own name. This list could continue indefinitely, but these examples illustrate

[8] Radical feminism which takes sexism as the basis for women's condition takes also a separatist position, advocating that women, temporarily at least, do not involve themselves with men. The problem of gender roles in marriage is immediately solved by no marriage. The content of gender roles *in* marriage has no features distinct from socialist feminism and aspects of reform feminism.

In addition, of course, some see the problem with gender roles as being that the sexes are rejecting their psycho-biologically ordained and/or sociologically necessary roles. The nuclear family would in this view be stronger and better if each sex returned to the traditional division of labor with women leaving the labor force, men regaining their authority in the family, and so on (Goldberg, 1973).

the varieties of goals which are attempts to change the condition of women. While not all are directly concerned with the family, nearly all can be indirectly linked to women's status in the family, to wives' socialization for dependency and objectification, to women's adaptability and responsibilities in marriage, and to women's resources outside the marriage relationship (e.g., their ability to support themselves adequately which in turn affects their resources *in* marriage). Each of these affects the burdens of gender roles for husbands as well.

What might be changed by the success of reform feminism? Inevitably, as in any movement which includes so much diversity, there is no simple answer. Successful reform would necessitate: (1) W*oman's equality in the labor force* (equal education, access to jobs, and pay for equal work, and maternity benefits). Changes should most likely include the legitimizing of part-time work, an acceptance of part-time workers as being on the usual career path, with the usual promotions, salary increases, and other job benefits; (2) *legal equality in marriage*, which would include women having the right to establish their own residences, use their own names, and control their own bodies—sexually and in reproduction; and alleviation of their complete legal responsibility for housework and childcare; (3) alleviation of the husband's sole responsibility to provide financial support for his mate and their offspring, and the *sharing* of that responsibility on some negotiated basis; (4) the availability of low-cost, 24-hour-a-day, 365-day-a-year *childcare centers*; and low cost or free *abortion* on demand. Other changes might include *divorce insurance* or perhaps *houseperson insurance* which would protect partners and their off-spring by providing short-term support for the reestablishment of altered lives (e.g., lawyers fees, counseling services for all family members, training for a partner who may have opted to be the "houseperson" rather than labor force participant, and perhaps a guarantee of schooling for offspring).

Since the reform feminists are concerned with allowing women (as well as men) new options, the family of the future could be traditional *with* the sex-segregated conjugal role, or joint conjugal roles, or variations on these. Most likely, women and men would *share* housework, rather than men "helping women," or men could opt to be househusbands; women and men would *share* childcare, rather than men "helping" women, or men could opt to be the parent primarily responsible for day-by-day childcare; women and men would *share* financial responsibility for the family, rather than women's work being supplemental (to keep the family from poverty or to provide luxuries), or one or the other could opt for the provider role; housework and childcare would be considered *work* rather than "nonwork," so that 5, 10, or 20 years of doing these activities would be considered equal to the work of the partner in the labor force and worth an entitlement in future earnings of that partner; there would be a single emotional and sexual standard with concern about mutual support and satisfaction ("open marriage" where one or both partners seek sexual-emotional-intellectual extramarital partners does not seem a frequent possibility).

If these changes occur, it is possible that contrary to the expectation that divorce may increase, I would suggest that divorce is just as likely to decrease, since women would enter marriage as economic and legal equals of men. This would mean that women would initially have more power in negotiating decisions than they now have, that husbands would not have the threat power of expecting women to conform or be divorced; furthermore, the dissolution of marriage would no longer leave women with the responsibility for childcare and for the reestablishment of their lives financially without serious consideration of their contribution as wives and mothers and homemakers to the now dissolved marriage.

Several problems seem possible: (1) The family would remain *privatized* with all the emotional difficulties entailed now, since except for reliance on childcare centers, most of the changes advocated affect women and men as separate individuals. Furthermore, no support systems (formal or informal) seem likely to be generated which would integrate people more fully into society (nor would the society be changed in such a way that people might be more in control of major institutions). An important component of support systems is structural changes which would encourage people to live other than in single family homes, with members of the conjugal family or other relatives. For example, tax laws, subsidies, housing and overall community design could be used to help make large households of unrelated individuals an economically and emotionally attractive life style.

(2) Reform feminism is not concerned with eliminating class connected inequality, for example, the condition of poor welfare mothers is viewed as a woman's issue rather than a social class issue. The changes would affect women *in* their respective classes rather than women as a class in themselves, class inequality would be untouched by these changes. For example, women in upper-status occupations experience less pay discrimination relative to men than women in lower-status occupations. The availability of daycare could be used to force poor women into jobs which pay below or barely equal minimum wage. Thus, daycare would then be subsidizing business rather than mothers and children.

(3) The question of the desirability of using the masculine model for changing the status of women arises. At issue here is whether or not the lives which men currently lead—some aspects of which have been discussed—are ideal models for people. Is the ideal model, for example, a work-oriented, success-minded person concerned with personal goals in a social world predicated upon competition and individualism? Is what is best for society and for the individual a system which isolates people from each other by the emphasis on outdoing others?

(4) Changes in the social condition of women without making other changes is problematic and will require: (a) Changes in the structure of the family, with its traditional responsibility for its members, especially the dependency of members on its own wage earners for schooling, medical care, and general welfare of its members. (b) the economic equality of women, including the right to employment. (c) changing housework (food preparation, laundry, housecleaning, clothing care, home repair, etc.) from a private to the public domain; and the emancipation of children from economic dependence on parents.

Socialist Perspective

Engels (1891) provides an analysis of the condition of women. Based on ethnographic data which has subsequently been discounted, his theory still provides the most adequate interpretation of the status of women, as well as of ethnographic data more recent than that to which he had access (Gough, 1972; Sacks, 1974). Engels concludes that women's inequality stems from the control of the tools of production by men. He argues that when both sexes have equal access to control over the means of production, that is, the means which provide for subsistence, there are no classes, no relationships of economic subordination and superordination. Engels sees *wives* as the first class, subordinate to *husbands* as the latter move from hunting and gathering to herding and farming. Men's ownership of herds and of cultivated land is an extension of the usual individual ownership of tools. Prior to herding and farming, however, when hunting and gathering is pursued, tools cannot confer special economic powers on their owners, for such activities do *not* involve reproduction. Additional products are not generated, for there is only that which exists in nature. But domesticated animals and cultivated land involve exactly that dimension of additional production. Tools are no longer a simple means of subsistence, but a means of acquiring economic power.

Furthermore, women's work does not lend itself to this acquisition of surplus since the sole means of production women have is human reproduction. With the acquisition of surplus by men, women become dependent on them and women's work ceases to have equal economic value with men's. Household work does not have the visible *value added* quality that domesticating animals and plants have: women's household work has no exchange-value but only use-value

(Benston, 1969). Women's reproductive role becomes bound to the protection of private property (property meaning that which has productive capacity, *not* personal consumable property), such a protective function being exactly that of women's premarital virginity and marital sexual exclusiveness, insurance that a man's property goes to his biological offspring.

From Engels theories comes the socialist belief that women's conditions can only be changed by the advent of socialism, and that women should devote their political energies to the establishment of socialism rather than to the alteration of their condition as women. It is believed that the disappearance of capitalism would mean the establishment of sex equality by an automatic elimination of the basis of problems which women experience as wives, daughters, lovers, workers, mothers, political beings, and so forth.

Such has not proven to be the case. The status of women in socialist societies —in the USSR and China, for example— is better, legally, politically, economically, than in capitalist societies, and vastly better than the condition of women in those societies before socialism. That socialism has not meant sex equality is nevertheless visible in the employment, political, sexual and reproductive, household, and parenting aspects of women's lives. In Soviet society, for example, while women are employed in all sectors of the economy, and dominate in some such as medicine, they are comparatively few in other professions, or in administrative posts including medicine. Women are underrepresented in politics (a constant 20 percent membership of the communist party from 1950 to 1968). Access to abortion and birth control, as well as easy divorce, which followed the revolution, was later taken from Soviet women, not to be returned until the 1960s. Women are less likely than men to complete higher education. The Soviets have taken for their own the bourgeois concepts that household work is of low value because it has use-value rather than exchange-value, and household work and childcare are basically women's work. Hence, the Soviet woman continues to be responsible for the very aspect of the economy which is *private* and has no income. Some improvements have been made—daycare is available for example, though not sufficiently so that there is not dependency on the grandmothers to play an important role in childcare. Soviet women bear the responsibility of both their work outside the home and the gamut of housework: shopping, cleaning, meal preparation and clean-up, clothes care, and all related chores. These are still "woman's work," unshared except minimally with the husband, and neglected by the technologists who have paid only scant attention to socializing home-related activities (Kharchev and Golod, 1972; Sommerville, 1972).

Similarly, women in China, while they have experienced enormous changes in their legal status, economic rights, political rights, educational rights, and have had the official support of the communist party, especially since the Cultural Revolution, for "holding up half of heaven," are by no means equal with men. Like their Soviet counterparts, urban women who are not housewives (20 percent of the population is urban) are predominantly in certain sectors of the economy. Rural and urban women are underrepresented in managerial jobs and political offices. In marriage, women have the major responsibility for childcare, birth control, and household activities, and they have limited control over their bodies (abortion except for therapeutic reasons needs the permission of the husband) (Glazer-Malbin, 1975b). Divorce is discouraged. Currently the Chinese are waging a campaign which includes "criticizing Confucius" who taught the Three Obediences: that women should obey the father when young, the husband when married, and the sons when widowed; and that women should adhere to the Four Virtues: compliance with a feudal ethical code; limited speech; adornment to please men; and willingness to do all household work (Peking Review, 1975).

One other system needs some commentary—the Israeli kibbutz. The kibbutzim (which in 1969 numbered 253, including 3 percent of the Israeli population of 2,841,000) are organized along socialist principles. In the early days, women and men were recognized as equals, and women were brought into agriculture, the productive sector of the economy, rather than being segregated in the nonproductive work of housekeeping and childcare. Women were supposedly encouraged to take an equal part in the political and administrative activities of the kibbutz. Machinery, buildings, housing, and funds were and are held collectively, though people do have small amounts of personal property—for example, radios, clothing, and books. Health care and retirement are provided for, while decisions about schooling (and its financial support) as well as work assignments, capital expenditures, and kibbutz goals are made by the office holders and managers of the various sectors, along with members. Children are raised communally, living in children's houses; food is eaten in communal dining rooms in the ideal model. And decisions about children's education and later job assignments are not the parents'.

Sex equality, however, does not now characterize the Israeli kibbutz, and there is some question whether it ever did. The masculine model of sex equality was used —that is, women do men's activities but the compliment is *not* returned by men doing women's activities. In the early years, women did jobs in agriculture, while childcare and household work was communalized—but *women*, not men, performed these communal services. With the advent of immigrants (Blumberg, 1974), there was even less reason for supporting the participation of women in agriculture, and women increasingly worked in the service sector. Finally, disputes developed about communal childcare and communal meals, with some kibbutzim adopting modified privatized versions of these activities; Children were more often allowed to sleep in their parents' apartments and food preparation and eating was done in private apartments. Women today play a vastly curtailed role in production and politics compared to men, compared to the model suggested by ideology of the founding kibbutzim and compared to the early kibbutzim.

Socialist Feminism

Socialism as a basis for the liberation of women neglects the distinction between origins and maintenance of the social condition of sexism. (1) *Origins.* Housework is not dealt with except to continue seeing it as having use-value but not exchange-value. There are at least two alternatives. One is to move women into "productive" labor, labor for exchange-value. The second is to reevaluate housework as well as childcare and to consider these activities worthy of income (as the Israeli kibbutz). Yet, the bourgeois notion that homemaking/childcare/husbandcare are not "productive" labor remains an implicit assumption in socialist societies. Work is so analyzed in Chinese society, for example, where to "release *women* from family drudgery, canteens, nurseries, kindergartens, and creches have been set up" and mills are established on communes to help *women* (Glazer-Malbin, 1975b; Peking Review, 1975).

(2) *Maintenance.* If sexism is not taken seriously as a social fact, then women do not attain equality with men —witness the USSR, China, and the Eastern European countries. For example, the movement for women's rights faltered in the Soviet Union. Immediately after the revolution women were given rights in marriage, in the control of pregnancy, in divorce; but shortly thereafter these rights were rescinded. The Chinese take the problem of women considerably more seriously, concerning themselves with changing ideology and *men's* behaviors, not just women's. Popular materials (such as, *Chinese Literature, China Reconstruct*) contain stories demonstrating that women's equality does *not* automatically follow from the movement toward socialism, but has to be dealt with as a separate issue. Official Chinese policy (for example, the address of the head of the Chinese delegation to the International Women's Year Conference in Mexico City, 1975) nevertheless contends that women's equality has been established while urging that the people "criticize Confucius and Lin Piao," both of whom are shown in official propaganda to have denigrated women.

Essentially, socialist feminism means a concern with sexism—women's condition

—as an issue which can be separately analyzed apart from socialism, but as an issue which is also linked with socialism. The condition of women depends on attitudes of men and women which support the subordination of women as an underclass, as the support system for men; and historical conditions have demonstrated that women are not automatically equal with men when socialism is established.

A comprehensive statement about a revised family under socialism was written by two Hungarians, Mihaly Vajda and Agnes Heller (1971). The complete restructuring of the family into a commune would create (1) "a democratically structured community; (2) guarantee many-sided human relations including those between children and adults; (3) guarantee the development and realization of individuality. The basic precondition of this is the free choosing and rechoosing of human ties even in childhood. (4) eliminate both the conflict originating in monogamy and those in its dissolution." All members of the commune which people choose to enter participate in the labor force; all members participate in the collective tasks within the commune. The commune assumes basic responsibility for the children so that one or the other partners may leave while the children remain in the group. The commune takes no position on sexuality, advocating neither monogamy nor polygamy nor promiscuity. The dissolution of a marriage leaves the children in their home and the former partner as well. Unattached as well as attached individuals are included. Housework (at least at first) is shared by all communal members, rather than being transferred to a service industry. Children are respon-

sible for contributions to the commune (study, instead of work) and participation in housekeeping. Moreover, children participate in deciding on the course of their own activities rather than being subject to the authority of their natural parents, as in present-day nuclear families.

Since, however, these authors do not discuss separately the status of women in the family, whether these conditions would or would not alleviate sexism is not clear, nor is it clear what measures would be taken to prevent a situation similar to that of the Israeli kibbutz, or the gradual reemergence of the importance of the biological family (Talmon, 1972). It does, however, deal directly with restructuring the family as an institution and institutions outside the family, rather than restructuring roles while maintaining the basic components of the present-day family—nuclear, isolated, with children "belonging" to their biological parents. It is a solution which seems to me more sociologically sound than an emphasis only on gender roles in the family or only on making basic economic and political changes. Whether American women and men would accept such changes, adapting them to the particular culture of the United States, is an involved question, a subject for another essay.

References

Aronoff, Joel, and Crano, William D. "A Re-Examination of the Cross-Cultural Principles of Task Segregation and Sex Role Differentiation in the Family." *American Sociological Review*, 1975, 40, 12–20.

Bakke, E. Wight. *The Unemployed Worker.* New Haven, Conn.: Yale University Press, 1940.

Ball, Donald W. "The Family as a Sociological Problem: Conceptualization of the Taken-for-Granted as Prologue to Social Problems Analysis." *Social Problems*, 1972, 19, 295–305.

Bart, Pauline. "Depression in Middle-Aged Women." In Vivian Gornick and Barbara K. Moran (Eds.), *Woman in Sexist Society*. New York: Basic Books, 1971. Pp. 163–186.

Benston, Margaret. "The Political Economy of Women's Liberation." *Monthly Review*, 1969, 21, 13–27.

Bernard, Jessie. 1971. *Women and the Public Interest*. Chicago: Aldine, 1971.

Bernard, Jessie. *The Future of Marriage*. New York: World, 1972.

Biller, Henry B. *Father, Child, and Sex Role*. Lexington, Mass.: Heath, 1971.

Blood, Robert O., Jr., and Wolfe, D. M. *Husbands and Wives*. Glencoe, Ill.: Free Press, 1960.

Blood, Robert O., Jr., and Wolfe, Donald M. "Negro-White Differences in Blue-Collar Marriages in a Northern Metropolis." *Social Forces*, 1969, 48, 59–63.

Blumberg, Rae Lesser. "Structural Factors Affecting Women's Status: A Cross-Societal Paradigm." Paper presented at the International Sociological Association, Toronto, August, 1974.

Bott, Elizabeth. *Family and Social Network*. London: Tavistock, 1957.

Brissett, Dennis, "Sex as Work." *Journal of Orthopsychiatry*, 1967, 15, 8–18.

Brown, Carol. Personal Correspondence, 1975.

Burgess, Ernest W., and Locke, Harvey J. *The Family from Institution to Companionship*. New York: American Book Co., 1953.

Chesney-Lind, Meda. "Judicial Enforcement of the Female Sex Role: The Family Court and Female Delinquent." *Issues in Criminology*, 1973, 8, 51–69.

Cutright, Phillips. "Components of Change in the Number of Female Family Heads Aged 15–44: United States, 1940–1970." *Journal of Marriage and the Family*, 1974, 36, 714–721.

Cymrot, Donald, and Wallan, Lucy B. "Wife's Earnings as a Source of Family Income." *Research and Statistics Note*, No. 10, DHEW Pub. No. (SSA) 74–11701.

de Beauvoir, Simone. *The Second Sex*. New York: Knopf, 1953.

de Beauvoir, Simone. *The Coming of Age*. New York: Putnam's, 1972.

Decter, Midge. *"The New Chastity and Other Arguments against Women's Liberation."* New York: Coward McCann, 1972.

Duvall, Evelyn. *Family Development*. Philadelphia: Lippincott, 1957.

Eckhardt, Kenneth W. "Deviance, Visibility, and Legal Action: The Duty to Support." *Social Problems*, 1962, 15, 470–477.

Engels, Frederick. *The Origins of the Family, Private Property, and the State*. New York: International Publishers, n.d. Originally published in 1891.

Farrell, Warren. *The Liberated Man*. New York: Random House, 1974.

Ferriss, Abbott L. *Indicators of Trends in the Status of American Women*. New York: Russell Sage Foundation, 1971.

Firestone, Shulamith. *The Dialectic of Sex*. New York: Morrow, 1970.

Friedan, Betty. *The Feminine Mystique*. New York: Norton, 1963.

Funkhouser, Erma. "The Asundered." *Bulletin of Oregon Health*, 1970, 48. Oregon State Board of Health, Portland, Oregon.

Gillespie, Dair L. "Who Has the Power? The Marital Struggle." *Journal of Marriage and the Family*, 1971, 33, 445–458.

Glazer-Malbin, Nona. "Man and Woman: Interpersonal Relationships in the Marital Pair." In *Old Family/New Family*. New York: Van Nostrand, 1975. Pp. 27–66.(a)

Glazer-Malbin, Nona. *Notes from China*. Unpublished manuscript, 1975.(b)

Glick, Paul C., and Norton, Arthur J. "Frequency, Duration, and Probability of Marriage and Divorce." *Journal of Marriage and the Family*, 1971, 33, 307–317.

Goldberg, Steven. *The Inevitability of Patriarchy*. New York: Morrow, 1973.

Goode, William. *Family Patterns and World Revolution*. Glencoe, Ill.: Free Press, 1960.

Gornick, Vivian, and Moran, Barbara K. *Woman in Sexist Society*. New York: Basic Books, 1971.

Gough, Kathleen. "An Anthropologist Looks at Engels." In Nona Glazer-Malbin and Helen Y. Waehrer (Eds.), *Woman in a Man-made World*. Chicago: Rand McNally, 1972. Pp. 107–118.

Hayghe, Howard. "Marital and Family Characteristics of the Labor Force in March 1973." *Monthly Labor Review*, 1974, 97, 21–31.

Jourard, Sidney. *The Transparent Self*. New York: Van Nostrand, 1971.

Kharchev, Anatole, and Golod, Serge. "The Two Roles of Russian Working Women in an Urban Area." In A. Michel (Ed.), *Family Issues of Employed Women in Europe and America*. Leiden: E. J. Brill, 1971. Pp. 32–42.

Komarovsky, Mirra. *Blue-Collar Marriage*. New York: Vintage, 1967.

Laws, Judy Long. "A Feminist Review of the Marital Adjustment Literature: The Rape of the Locke." *Journal of Marriage and the Family*, 1971, 33, 483–516.

Levinger, George. "Source of Marital Satisfaction among Applicants for Divorce." *American Journal of Orthopsychiatry*, 1964, 34, 804–866.

Lopata, Helena Z. *Occupation: Housewife*. New York: Oxford, 1971.

Lopata, Helena Z. *Widowhood in an American City*. Cambridge, Mass.: Schenkman, 1973.

Maccoby, Elanor Emmons, and Jacklin, Carol Nagy. *The Psychology of Sex Differences*. Stanford, Ca.: Stanford University Press, 1974.

Mainardi, Pat. "The Politics of Housework." In *Discrimination against Women*. Hearings before the Special Subcommittee on Education and Labor, 91st Congress, Part 1. Washington, D.C.: U. S. Government Printing Office, Committee on Education and Labor, 1970. Pp. 265–268.

Masters, William H., and Johnson, Virginia E. *Human Sexual Response*. Boston: Little, Brown, 1966.

Mills, C. Wright. *The Sociological Imagination*. New York: Oxford, 1959.

Mitchell, Juliet. *Woman's Estate*. New York: Pantheon, 1971.

Money, John, and Ehrhardt, Anke A. *Man & Woman, Boy & Girl*. Baltimore: Johns Hopkins University Press, 1972.

Morgan, Robin. *Sisterhood Is Powerful: An Anthology of Writings from the Women's Liberation Movement*. New York: Vintage, 1970.

Moynihan, Daniel P. *The Negro Family: The Case for National Action*. Washington, D.C.: U.S. Government Printing Office, 1965.

Mulligan, Linda W. "Wives, Women, and Wife Role Behavior: An Alternative Cross-Cultural Perspective." *International Journal of Comparative Sociology*, 1972, 13, 36–47.

Nissen, Ingjald, "The Role of the Sexual Constellation. *Acta Sociologica*, 1971, 52–58.

Nye, F. Ivan, and Berardo, Felix M. *The Family*. New York: Macmillan, 1973.

O'Brien, John E. "Violence in Divorce-Prone Families." *Journal of Marriage and the Family*, 1971, 33, 692–698.

Parsons, Talcott, with Bales, Robert F., Zelditch, Morris, Olds, James, and Slater, Philip. *Family, Socialization, and Interaction*. Glencoe, Ill.: Free Press, 1955.

Peking Review. "Great Changes in Status of China's Women." July 4, 1975 (27), 16–18.

Pyun, Chong Soo. "The Monetary Value of a Housewife: An Economic Analysis for Use in Litigation." *American Journal of Economics and Sociology*, 1969, 28 271–284.

Rainwater, Lee. "Sexual Behavior and Family Planning in the Lower Class." In Clark E. Vincent (Ed.), *Human Sexuality in Medical Education and Practice*. Springfield, Ill.: Charles C. Thomas, 1968. P. 595.

Rossi, Alice. "Equality between the

Sexes: An Immodest Proposal." *Daedalus*, 1964, 93, 607–652.

Sacks, Karen. "Engels Revisited: Women, the Organization of Production, and Private Property." In Michelle Zimbalist Rosaldo and Louise Lamphere (Eds.), *Woman, Culture, and Society*. Stanford, Ca.: Stanford University Press, 1974. P. 352.

Safilios-Rothschild, Constantina. "Family Sociology of Wives' Family Sociology?" *Journal of Marriage and the Family*, 1969, 31, 290–301.

Schmidt, Gunter, Sigusch, Valkmar, and Schofer, Siegrid. "Responses to Reading Erotic Stories: Male-Female Differences." *Archives of Sexual Behavior*, 1973, 2, 181–199.

Sennett, Richard, and Cobb, Jonathan. *The Hidden Injuries of Class*. New York: Random House, 1972.

Slater, Phillip. *The Pursuit of Loneliness*. Boston: Beacon Press, 1970.

Sommers, Dixie. "Occupational Rankings for Men and Women by Earnings." *Monthly Labor Review*, 1974, 97, 34–51.

Sommerville, Rose. "The Urban Working Woman in the USSR: An Historical Review." In Andree Michel (Ed.), *Family Issues of Employed Women in Europe and America*. Leiden: E. J. Brill, 1971. Pp. 91–103.

Staples, Robert. "Educating the Black Male at Various Class Levels for Marital Roles." *The Family Coordinator*, 1970, 19, 164–167.(a)

Staples, Robert. "The Myth of the Black Matriarchy." *The Black Scholar*, 1970, 1, 8–16.(b)

Steinmann, Anne, and Fox, David J. *The Male Dilemma: How to Survive the Sexual Revolution*. New York: J. Aronson, 1974.

Syfers, Judy. "I Want a Wife." *Ms.*, 1972, Spring, p. 56.

Talmon, Yonina. *Family and Commu-*

nity in the Kibbutz. Cambridge, Mass.: Harvard University Press, 1972.

Turner, Ralph H. *Family Interaction*. New York: Wiley, 1970.

Udry, J. Richard. *The Social Context of Marriage*. New York: J. B. Lippincott, 1966.

U.S. Bureau of the Census. *Statistical Abstract of the United States: 1972*, 93rd ed. Washington, D.C., 1972.

U.S. Department of Labor. "Fact Sheet on the Earning Gap." Washington, D.C., February, 1971.

Vajda, Mihaly, and Heller, Agnes. "Family Structure and Communism." *Telos*, 1971, 7, 99–111.

Waldman, Elizabeth. "Children of Working Mothers." *Monthly Labor Review*, 1975, 98, 64–67.

Walker, Kathryn E., and Gauger, William H. *The Dollar Value of Household Work*. Ithaca, New York: Cornell University, 1973.

Weitzman, Lenore J. "Legal Regulation of Marriage: Tradition and Change." *California Law Review*, 1974, 62, 1169–1288.

Wiseman, Jacqueline P. *People as Partners*. San Francisco: Canfield Press, 1971.

Whitehurst, Robert N. "Violence in Husband-Wife Interaction." In Suzanne K. Steinmetz and Murray A. Strauss (Eds.), *Violence in the Family*. New York: Dodd, Mead, 1974. Pp. 75–82.

Wortis, Rochelle Paul. "The Acceptance of the Concept of the Maternal Role by Behavioral Scientists: It's Effect on Women." *American Journal of Orthopsychiatry*, 1971, 41, 733–746.

Young, Michael, and Willmott, Peter. *The Symmetrical Family*. New York: Pantheon, 1973.

Zimmerman, Carle C. *Family and Civilization*. New York: Harper's Social Science Series, 1947.

Suggested Reading

BERNARD, JESSIE. *The Future of Marriage*. New York: World Publishing, 1972.
Changes in American marriage and prospects for the future with a look at some problems in contemporary marriage.

DAVID, DEBORAH S., AND BRANNON, ROBERT (Eds.). *The Forty-Nine Percent Majority: Readings on the Male Sex Role*. Reading, Mass.: Addison-Wesley, 1976.
A variety of writings from fiction and social science, by women and men on the experience of being a man and relating to men.

FIRESTONE, SHULAMITH. *The Dialectic of Sex*. New York: Bantam, 1971.
The subjugation of the second sex in partriarchical marriage; the politics of the relations between women and men is analyzed.

GLAZER-MALBIN, NONA (Ed.). *Old Family/New Family*. New York: Van Nostrand, 1975.
Articles on the varieties of new life styles—communes, lesbian community, swinging, living together—and a look at couples; and the development of sisterhood and brotherhood.

MITCHELL, JULIET. *Woman's Estate*. New York: Pantheon, 1971.
Sophisticated analysis of women's social condition in relationship to the nature of social organization and psychology. Includes well-known essay: "Women: The Longest Revolution."

OAKLEY, ANN. *Sex, Gender and Society*. New York: Harper & Row, 1972.
Exceptionally well-written and documented statement about the sources of gender differences which draws on a variety of social sciences disciplines.

PLECK, JOSEPH, AND SAWYER, JACK. *Men and Masculinity*. New York: Spectrum, 1974.
Collection of essays from a wide array of sources on men's roles in contemporary society, including in marriage, mainly from a social psychological perspective.

SECOMBE, WALLY. "The Housewife and Her Labour under Capitalism." *New Left Review*, 1974, 83, 3–24.
The political economy of being a housewife; a consideration of the relation of the role to the necessities of capitalism. An overlooked topic with considerable implications for family change.

WEITZMAN, LENORE J. "Legal Regulation of Marriage: Tradition and Change." *California Law Review*, 1974, 62, 1169–1288.
An examination of the implications of the marriage laws for sex roles, and of the contradictions between newly developed practices—and some not so new practices—and the legal system.

ZARETSKY, ELI. "Capitalism, the Family, and Personal Life." *Socialist Revolution*, 1973, 3 (1, 2), 69–125; 3 (3), 19–70.
Discussion of the relationship between the movement of economic production for the market from the household, the development of the concept of a "personal life" and the privatized family, and the position of family members.

The Ecosystem

The Interrelationship of Society and Nature

Jonathan H. Turner

For generations humans have sought to master and control their environment. Through most of human history only the most precarious mastery has been possible as people attempted to defend themselves from the vicissitudes of their natural surroundings. Only a few hundred years ago, with the advent of the Industrial Revolution, human societies gained a degree of control over nature that previously would have been considered impossible. About the middle of this century, the abuse of this limited measure of power over nature became apparent (Osborn 1948, 1953; Carson 1962). The warning signals were all too visible as cities lay under blankets of smog, rivers vomited dead fish, giant lakes began to lose their ability to support life, the soil was converted to a storage bin for killer pesticides, and the ocean's life forms became repositories of deadly chemicals.[1]

Solutions will come only by making changes in the structure and culture of the world's societies, especially that of the United States—the world's biggest polluter. The study of ecological problems must therefore begin with an appreciation of how basic ecological processes have been disrupted by the evolution of human societies.

[1] For Sources on the nature and scope of the current ecological crisis see Blau and Rodenbeck (1971); Burch (1971); Burch, Cheek, and Taylor (1972); Campbell and Wade (1972); Commoner (1966); Detwyler (1962); deVilleneuve (1973); Falk (1971); Helfrich (1970); Linton (1970); Murphy (1967); and Train et al. (1970).

THE NATURE OF ECOSYSTEMS

All life is dependent upon other life forms and elements of the physical environment. This fact is the basic contingency of existence for all biological entities, from microorganisms to humans. The term *ecosystem* denotes the complex webs of functional relationships among plant and animal species and between all species and the physical environment.[2] This web of mutual dependencies is so complex as to render the understanding of a small pond difficult, much less an entire nation or the whole world. Despite the complexity of concrete ecosystems, the general processes of their operation are understood. And it is the disruption of these processes that is now a cause of serious alarm (Boulding, 1970; Hardin, 1968).

Ecosystems are composed of complex chains, flows, cycles, and patterns of interdependence among species and minerals. One of the most critical processes in ecosystems is that of energy flow from the sun to all life forms on earth. To simplify what is a fantastically detailed process, emissions of the sun's radiant energy are converted to chemical energy by the photosynthesis process in plants;

[2] Currently there are a wide variety of works on the nature of ecosystems. For source works see Duncan and Schnore (1964); Ehrlich and Ehrlich (1970); Ehrlich, Hodlren, and Holm (1971); Kormondy (1969); Kuntz (1971); Odum (1969); and *Scientific American* (1970, 1971).

this energy then flows through the ecosystem in extended "food chains" as varieties of life forms called herbivores consume plants, and in turn are consumed by other organisms labeled carnivores. In these chains, the consuming organism extracts the chemical energy from the plant or organism consumed and utilizes it to build and maintain its own body— thereby storing it for another organism in the food chain. At each juncture in these feeding chains, some chemical energy is always lost as heat, for the transfer of energy from one life form to another is never complete. In simplified form, the flow of energy through ecosystems follows the general pattern outlined in Figure 1.

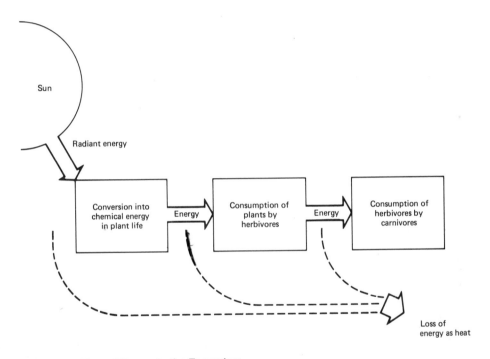

Figure 1. The Flow of Energy in the Ecosystem

Another critical ecosystem process is the cycling of key substances. One such cycle involves the conversion of the carbon dioxide released by respiring organisms into oxygen by plants, thereby enabling animal life to exist. An equally important cycle involves the circulation of such important minerals as nitrogen, phosphorus, sulfur, magnesium, and some fifteen other essential nutrients. These minerals cycle by virtue of the activities of billions of microorganisms, such as bacteria and fungi, known as decomposers (Kormondy, 1969). Unlike most herbivores and carnivores, decomposers do not typically ingest food; rather, they release enzymes produced in their bodies into dead plant and animal material and then simply absorb the material broken down by their enzymes. In addition to supplying the energy needs of their own bodies, however, decomposers "mineralize" organic matter and make it available directly to plants, and indirectly to herbivores and carnivores. For in the process of photosynthesis plants not only require water and the carbon dioxide released by animals, but they also need a variety of inorganic compounds, such as nitrogen, phosphorus, sulfur, and magnesium. Thus, as plants are consumed by herbivores, and then herbivores by carnivores, not only is energy transferred, but life-sustaining minerals also are cycled. But unlike energy in these feeding chains, none of these mineral nutrients are lost, because the activities of decomposers reinsert these vital minerals into the energy chain. Figure 2 shows the cycling of oxygen and other inorganic compounds.

At the heart of ecosystem dynamics,

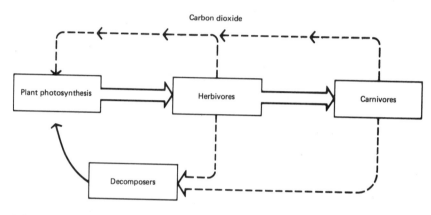

Figure 2. Mineral Cycles in the Ecosystem

then, are the complex patterns of interdependence among millions of plants and animal forms which allow for the one-way flow of energy and the cycling of life-sustaining inorganic compounds. To the extent that the flow of energy or the cycling of crucial compounds is disrupted, the capacity for life on earth is diminished (Woodwell, 1967). Furthermore, any species that attempts to alter drastically the conditions of its dependency runs the risk of setting off a chain of events that threatens those life forms upon which it is dependent for its own existence (Hill, 1970).

Diversity represents a source of stability in ecosystems, or more accurately, orderly change. Because the web interconnecting life forms is so incredibly diverse and complex, changes introduced at one point in the ecosystems will encounter considerable resistance. Typically, change will be gradual, thereby giving plants and organisms time to adjust and adapt to changing environmental conditions. For if change were rapid, the life elements of an ecosystem would not have sufficient time to adapt, thus setting off widespread destruction as the sudden death of some species assures the successive termination of other dependent species.

To understand the processes of change in the structure of ecosystems it must be recognized that:

1. Undifferentiated ecosystems will change more rapidly than highly differentiated ones composed of diverse relations among a wide variety of species. Forces

operating to simplify ecosystems will therefore make them unstable.

2. A seemingly small change introduced at one point in the ecosystem can become, under certain conditions and over time, amplified into large-scale disruption and change in the structure of a large eco-space.

3. Because of lag effects, it is sometimes difficult to comprehend the ultimate result of changes introduced into ecosystems. This can result in a situation where the point of no return in the destruction of an ecosystem is passed long before it is recognized that little can be done to reverse a destructive chain of events.

These principles of change in ecosystems make an assessment of the world ecological system difficult. It is clear, however, that the evolution of human society has:

1. stripped the world's ecosystem of much of its natural diversity

2. introduced massive changes in the flow of energy and cycling of minerals, the amplified impact of which cannot be known

3. already caused unknown amounts of irreversible destruction.

These facts make imperative the analysis of the relationship between society and the ecosystem (Iltis, 1970).

SOCIETY AND THE ECOSYSTEM

The energy and mineral consumption of the 3.5 billion humans on earth far exceeds what is necessary for their biological subsistence. Unlike other social organisms, such as bees and ants, human societies reveal complex cultures composed of elaborate systems of symbols: language, music, knowledge, ideologies, and values. The organization of these systems ultimately dictates what level of consumption is appropriate, for the consumption of energy and materials is as much a function of values as the anatomy of humans. Patterns of social organization among humans are partly a reflection of values—of how humans *should* be organized. But they also reflect the impact of many other cultural components, such as technology (knowledge); geographical conditions; size and composition of the population; and the availability of natural resources.

The impact of the human species on the world's ecosystems can only be comprehended through the analysis of these cultural components and the organization of the societies of which they are a part. Modern societies like the United States currently have the most disruptive effects on the world's ecosystem, discharging such large quantities of wastes and pollutants that the survival of the world's ecosystem now is threatened (Freeman, 1970; Goldman, 1970; Mix, 1966). At the most general level, the relationship between industrial societies, including the United States, and the world's ecosystem is shown in outline in Figure 3 (Turner, 1972a:239).

In column 2 of Figure 3, the cultural values and structure of an industrial society are viewed as encouraging high levels of consumption. Extravagant consumption generates a demand for industrial and agricultural goods, which stimulates high levels of production requiring large quantities of energy. These influences are reciprocal, for once an extensive productive system exists, this system encourages consumer demand and sustains the cultural values and structural arrangements in the society that give rise to an industrial form of economic organization.

This type of social system is capable of

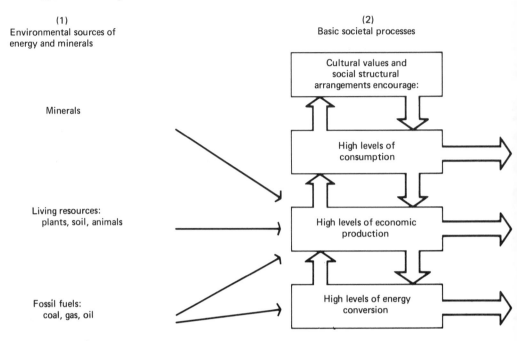

Figure 3. Society and Ecological Disruption

extracting wide varieties and vast quantities of energy and minerals from the ecosystem, as shown in column 1. High levels of extraction are possible because industrial systems (a) possess the technology to extract resources; (b) have the machines to implement this knowledge; (c) maintain cultural values encouraging manipulation and control of the environment; and (d) have an institutional structure capable of organizing the technology, machines, and men necessary to realize these cultural values. Industrial societies extract enormous quantities of fossil fuels (stored plant energy) and inorganic minerals, cultivate vast tracts of land or soil for intensive plant agriculture, and breed and slaughter large herds of diverse animals.

The conversion of resources to energy, the production of goods, and their consumption by individuals in industrial societies generates huge quantities of waste residues, as is indicated in column 3, "societal wastes." On a level unparalleled in human history, industrial societies now discharge garbage, junk, slag, pesticides, organic wastes, chemicals, scrap, radioactivity, carbon monoxide, sulfur, heat, and other residues into the renewable resources of the ecosystem: air, soil, and water (column 4). Under ordinary circumstances, each of these resources is capable of rejuvenating itself through the flows and cycles of energy and minerals through the ecosystem. While substitutes for diminishing stock resources, such as coal, oil, and gas, can be found to supply human societies with energy, there is no substitute for the depletion of renewable resources. Life simply cannot be sustained without air, water, and soil.

It is becoming increasingly evident that these renewable resources are not inexhaustible, as once naively believed. The death of lakes, the fact that no soil

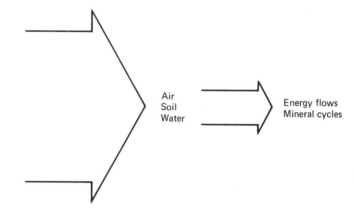

(3)
Societal wastes

(4)
Renewable resources as
a refuse for wastes

(5)
Disruption of basic
ecological processes

Garbage, trash,
sewage, junk, carbon
dioxide, heat,
chemicals, organic wastes

Pesticides, industrial
slag, organic wastes,
chemicals, trash, scrap,
radioactivity, heat

Heat, nitrogen oxides,
carbon monoxide, ash, sulfur,
radioactivity

Air
Soil
Water

Energy flows
Mineral cycles

in the United States is devoid of DDT, the inability of some rivers and streams to support life, and the smog-laden air of American cities all show that the re-juvenating capacities of the air, water, and soil are being seriously taxed. Critical food chains and mineral cycles are being interrupted and altered in ways that could foretell large-scale ecological dis-ruption (column 3) and potentially, an ecocatastrophe of proportions great enough to cause the death of all human life on earth.

Recall the three principles of ecological change enumerated earlier to visualize the ecological specter now facing hu-mans. Large-scale agriculture which uti-lizes chemical fertilizers and pesticides has simplified the world's ecosystem to an alarming degree, making it vulnerable to rapid and destructive alterations. For ex-ample, pesticides not only kill their tar-get species, but many others, thereby re-ducing the number and diversity of insect organisms in the ecosystem. And further, these same pesticides and chemical fer-tilizers run off into rivers, streams, lakes and the ocean, joining the other wastes of the urban-industrial complex to create a deadly mixture that suffocates wide varieties of life and perhaps the basic source of air on earth, the oceans' phyto-plankton. Industrial and other emissions into the air kill many plant forms, thus further reducing the diversity of species in the world's ecosystem. The accumula-tion of compounds in the upper reaches of the atmosphere can, in the long run, create a "green-house effect" killing un-told plant forms and thereby decreasing even further the diversity of life on earth.

The very process of simplification means ecological disruption, but it does not reveal the amplification of this dis-ruption over time and space. With the "lag effects" of change, current levels of "tolerable" ecological disruption and simplification may have set into motion irreversible processes of destruction. Some biologists have asserted that the point of no return on the road to ecocatastrophe may be reached within the next decade. Unless human societies undergo profound reorganization, particularly of their industrial systems, the renewable resources sustaining life will lose their rejuvenative capacity.

Industrial societies have created and now perpetuate the discharge of wastes causing ecological disruption. Why do industrial societies continue to pollute? Why is affecting change in economic production and consumption so difficult? Why are currently available means for pollution abatement not used? What changes in the nature of society will be necessary to assure survival on the "spaceship Earth"? These and similar questions require an analysis of social systems such as that of the United States, for unless the cultural values and patterns of social organization perpetuating pollution are understood, it will be difficult to find solutions to ecological problems (Odum, 1969).

AMERICAN SOCIETY AND THE ECOSYSTEM

With only one-fifteenth of the world's population, the United States extracts thirty-five percent of the world's minerals and energy and accounts for one-half of the industrial pollutants emitted into the world ecosystem. Even more disturbing is the fact that most societies in the world are attempting to emulate America's capacity to extract resources, produce goods, and unwarily consume. Thus, although the pollutants of the United States, Russia, Western Europe and Japan already pose a deadly threat, the expansion of industrial production in the "Third World" nations could seriously aggravate existing problems in the world ecosystem.

By analyzing American society it is possible to derive some clues as to what causes high levels of ecological disruption in industrial societies. Hopefully, the lessons learned from this analysis can provide some guidelines for solutions not only to America's problems, but also to those of other societies in the world.

America's Culture of Pollution

One of the ironies of human existence is that those values channeling human effort toward increased prosperity, health, and well-being can become dangerously inappropriate. To have the values of a "frontier society" dominate in a system with the disruptive capacity of the United States appears to have created serious ecological problems. And yet, these values are built into the fabric of American society. They legitimate those institutional arrangements in the economy, polity, legal system, and community structure causing pollution, while in turn these structures sustain and support the dominant values. It is this reciprocity between social structure and cultural values which makes change in American society—indeed in all societies—more difficult.

What are these dominant values?[3] At the most general level, four complexes of values encouraging ecological disruption in the United States can be isolated:

1. The growth ethic
2. The consumption ethic

[3] For other discussions of how values affect pollution see Campbell and Wade (1972); Moncrief (1970); Turner (1972a).

3. Technological idolatry
4. Nature as a free good

THE GROWTH ETHIC   A concern with expansion and progress has pervaded the United States since its early beginnings. Values emphasizing economic growth were necessary for the industrialization of American society. Only through the ever increasing investment of capital in the economy could the productive apparatus expand to provide the levels of material well-being associated with the modern American way of life. Unfortunately, the economy has now become organized around the ethic: "The more the better." For an underpopulated, agrarian society where the land, the air, and the water seemed inexhaustible, this value was probably appropriate. By using these renewable resources as a refuse dump, a considerable amount of time, money, and effort was saved—thus allowing industrialization to occur that much more rapidly. But as is now evident, these renewable resources are not inexhaustible because of the ever-increasing burden being placed upon them. Yet, even in the face of the disruptive capacity of the American economy, the growth ethic still dominates as economic "health" is measured by the annual growth in the gross national product (GNP), as presidents extol the virtues of a trillion dollar GNP, and economists lament a slow growth quarter.

To reduce the possibility of a severe ecological crisis the growth ethic would have to be supplanted by values more congruent with the realities of the late twentieth century. New cultural premises must begin to guide the conduct of human affairs; values emphasizing stability, no growth, the recycling of wastes, and the sanctity of the rejuvenative abili-

ties of water, air, and soil (Boulding, 1966; Daly, 1973; Ehrlich and Ehrlich, 1970; Goldman, 1972; and Luce, 1970). Such a shift in values, however, appears difficult to implement since existing institutional patterns revolve around premises of growth.

THE CONSUMPTION ETHIC   Americans value the purchase and consumption of increasing quantities and varieties of economic commodities. Such consumption is considered a reflection of both individual and societal progress and prosperity. These needs for consumption create economic demand and hence increase economic productivity; once a large productive apparatus exists, it has a vested interest in manipulating the value of materialism by stimulating needs for consumption; in turn such stimulation generates greater economic demand leading to increased production, and so on in an endless consumption-production cycle. Fanned by the consumption ethic, economic production results in the wholesale dumping of harmful residues into the ecosystem. When high levels of consumption are encouraged, a disposal crisis is created, as, for example, when the amounts of phosphates dumped into America's sewers no longer can be absorbed or when the American landscape becomes scarred with vast quantities of solid wastes.

IDOLATRY OF TECHNOLOGY   Americans have an abiding faith in and reverence for the application of technology. American society has in the past resolved a wide variety of problems with a simple solution: the application of more science. Such a solution usually has resulted in widespread ecological damage because the users of technology have been concerned with immediate payoffs rather than the long range consequences of their activities. The faith is so strong that many citizens and politicians are now awaiting the technological breakthrough that will resolve the world's ecological problems. Actually remedies to most ecological problems already exist but remain unused because their application incurs too many "costs" for consumers, producers, and politicians. To continue to wait is to delay action on acute problems, while perhaps allowing them to amplify to a point where no scientific or technological solution could be effective.

When efforts are undertaken to cope with ecologically related problems, technology is often employed indiscriminately. For example, the problem of feeding the world's growing population has been turned over to United States agricultural "experts" who have created a Green Revolution through the excessive use of chemical fertilizers and pesticides —thereby feeding the world's population in the short run, while potentially disrupting the ecosystem's capacity to support this population in the long run. Frequently, no action is taken at all to cope with the problems. The problem of providing birth control for the alarmingly high birth rates in some countries has been assumed by United States medical "experts" who await the better contraceptive, while time is lost in altering the familial, economic, and governmental structures that will ultimately reduce birth rates. Thus the idolatry of technology is now an inappropriate value. Ecological problems are not so much technological as they are social, structural, and cultural in nature.

NATURE AS A FREE GOOD When renewable resources were considered inexhaustible, nature was defined as a free good. The pioneer conception of unbounded resources meant that the air and water could be used as free refuse dumps, in the pursuit of profit and the better life (Murphy, 1967; Revelle, 1968). This value on free access to nature is clearly inappropriate in the face of the potential exhaustion of renewable resources. It will be difficult, however, to change American values to emphasize nature as a "common good," which is increasingly in short supply and for which one must pay. As industries pay for pollution, prices will rise; as government monitors and regulates industry, taxes will increase; and as local communities modernize their garbage and sewage treatment facilities, property taxes will soar. When unsupported by existing fiscal arrangements in society, the introduction of new values will encounter stiff resistance.

These four value complexes—the growth ethic, the consumption ethic, idolatry of technology, and nature as a free good—shape social action in America. At the same time, they are supported and sustained by the structure of American society. This mutual support makes the introduction of new values most difficult, since such an introduction must encounter the resistance of established modes of conducting human affairs.

AMERICA'S STRUCTURE OF POLLUTION
As ecosystems reveal structure, so do social systems. Social structure can be viewed as those relatively stable ways in which human activity becomes patterned and organized. Much like ecosystems, social systems are constantly in flux. Yet, it is possible to identify for any society a particular pattern of organization or social structure.

It is convenient to visualize two

generic structures organizing the human species: (1) *communities* and (2) *institutions*. *Communities* are those structures which organize human populations into residential patterns where individuals secure and consume the commodities for their survival. *Social institutions* are those patterns of organization that resolve enduring problems of survival facing human populations: securing sustenance from the environment (economy), maintaining order and resolving conflicts (law), making decisions (polity), and protecting and raising the young (family).

Communities and institutions are not mutually exclusive; they overlap, interpenetrate, and affect each other. As energy flows and mineral cycles in the ecosystem operate simultaneously, so do the processes making up the basic structures of society such as the operation of the family, economy, and polity in any community (Turner 1972b). But when the analysis of society is undertaken, it is wise to focus on the separate impact of structures on the ecosystem, for in this way a more complete understanding of the diverse sources of pollution is possible.

AMERICAN COMMUNITIES AND THE ECO-SYSTEM Most Americans reside in urban communities. In fact, a population of 210 million resides in less than two percent of the total land area of the United States. Such a population density assures that large quantities of waste residues will be dumped into a small ecological space in concentrated and toxic quantities. These pollutants not only diminish the rejuvenative capacity of the renewable resources surrounding urban regions, but in accordance with the principle of "amplification," they extend their disrup-

tive impact across vast geographical territories. And due to the "lag effects" of pollutants, it is not possible to comprehend fully just how much disruption already has occurred. More important than the effects of residential concentration, however, are the consequences of the particular *pattern of urban organization* in America. In 1800 only a few cities exceeded 100,000 in population; by 1880, twenty cities had surpassed the 100,000 mark with New York and Philadelphia becoming two of the largest urban areas in the world. The spectacular rate of urban growth can be accounted for by the rapid industrialization of the United States and the resulting flood of eager workers into the emerging urban-industrial areas. Urban-industrial cities required cheap sources of power, ready means for transporting raw materials and finished products, and most important, free waste disposal. This was essential for the *rapid* growth of the American industrial complex; thus, early industrial centers settled along major waterways—America's lakes, rivers, and bays. The water could be used to generate power, to transport materials and products, and to discharge wastes.

These events created a *pattern* of urban-industrial organization that inevitably caused ecological problems with subsequent expansion. This pattern was legitimated by dominant American values: growth of the urban-industrial complex was considered desirable; the indiscriminate application of technology to enhance growth was viewed as appropriate; the consumption of increasing quantities of goods was seen as an important goal of every individual American; and the use of the renewable resources of nature was considered essential for profit, progress, and productivity. This established pattern of urbanization, reinforced by these values, now poses a problem: Industry continues to use the urban environment as a refuse dump. Technological solutions are available (Revelle, 1968) but they involve costs—lower profit margins for manufacturers and higher prices for consumers.

The *rate* of the rural to urban population shift and the influx of immigrants created additional destructive patterns of urban organization. As New York, Philadelphia, Boston, Chicago, and St. Louis grew from small towns to major urban centers, their sewage treatment facilities were overwhelmed by the organic wastes of the foreign and domestic immigrants seeking a better life. The result was the discharge of untreated wastes into adjacent waterways, a practice that then did not seem abhorrent because of the dominance of the "nature as a free good" value. However, the sewage systems in America's older cities now pose a severe ecological problem, even with the application of sewage treatment technology (Blake, 1956; Daly, 1959; McClane, 1968). Many cities remain a major source of water pollution because their sewage systems represent an elaborate combination of pipe laid one hundred years ago and modern treatment facilities. For example, New York, Cleveland, Chicago, and many old smaller cities treat organic wastes by the use of interceptor sewers which have been constructed to catch and then conduct the wastes from the original sewers to modern treatment plants (Revelle, 1968). During rainy seasons and peak periods of use, this makeshift system often breaks down as interceptor sewers are overwhelmed, with the result that untreated sewage passes directly to the adjacent waterways. This legacy assures continued water pollution

in the decades to come, especially since remedies are incredibly expensive and thus unlikely to be implemented.

Industry concentrated in urban areas used the air as a refuse for pollutants; however, it has been estimated that one-half of the sulfur oxides, hydrocarbons, and nitrogen oxides, as well as three-quarters of the carbon monoxide, that create smog are emitted by automobiles (Steif, 1970). Early urbanization was accomplished without the automobile, but the subsequent growth of the metropolitan region—the decaying core city surrounded by affluent suburbs—was achieved by the mass utilization of cars and trucks. In contrast to the fixed trolley system of early cities, the car gave people flexibility and choice in the selection of their place of residence. The flexibility of truck transport for industry was similarly exploited. The result has been increasing dependence upon cars for the movement of individuals and upon trucks for the dissemination of goods and services in urban areas. And in some urban centers —most notably Los Angeles—the entire metropolitan area is built around motor transportation, thereby creating a deadly smog problem while making alternative transport systems politically and economically unfeasible. If the current energy crisis, including gasoline shortages, should stimulate a search for alternatives, it is still unlikely that the use of cars as a principal means of transport will be supplanted in the near future.

Thus an increasing reliance upon a polluting transport system was built into the initial growth of the metropolitan area in the United States. The short run consequences are, at the very least, discomfort and a decline in the quality of life; at most, they may cause death to those with respiratory problems and shortened life for the young raised in smog. It is the long range prospects of smog that are especially disquieting. If the smog discharges of urban America accumulating in the outer reaches of the atmosphere continue, what will be the consequences for the world ecosystem? Opinion varies on whether such accumulations would cool the earth down by insulating it from the sun, or increase the earth's temperature by trapping heat within the atmosphere and preventing its escape into space. In either case, the ecological disruption to energy flows and mineral cycles would be extensive.[4]

To attack the pollution problems generated by current patterns of urban organization would require an efficient and effective community political system. Since pollutants do not stop at the boundaries of metropolitan areas, the urban political system will need to be drastically altered. However, the historical development and subsequent evolution of metropolitan regions has created a pattern of political decision-making that will inhibit concerted and comprehensive political action by America's communities.

Because American cities grew so rapidly in a period of weak federal government, they were unplanned and unregulated. In an era where the intervention of the federal government in local affairs was considered inappropriate and where there was no federal income tax to give national government financial leverage, the cities evolved as politically autonomous entities. Autonomy is reinforced by values such as "laissez-faire" and "states

rights," and there are few clear and stable lines of communication and decision-making between the cities and the federal government.[5]

As it became possible to live outside the large core cities, suburban residents began to desire local control of their taxes and government; at the same time, short-sighted big city governments perceived the suburbs as a liability since they had to provide too many services, such as fire protection, police, and education, and capital improvements like streets, lights and sewers, for all too small a tax return. Coupled with the desire of rural legislators to keep the large cities from expanding and consolidating statewide power, the cities stopped (or were stopped from) annexing their suburbs, thus creating the political partitioning of the large decaying city from a series of autonomous and affluent suburban communities (Greer, 1966). The end result has been wasteful and expensive duplication of services in each community and the political fragmentation of America's metropolitan regions into often competing and jealous governmental bodies. As long as political power remains so fragmented, it will prove difficult to have *regional* planning, waste standards, land-use controls, effluent and sewage treatment plants, and effective alternatives to smog-producing automobile transportation.

Because of this lack of regional planning, it is likely that federal programs and revenue-sharing funds would be wasted as communities fought over their fair share, duplicated their efforts, and

[4] For some interesting source works on the problem of air pollution see Battan (1966); Carr (1965); Esposito (1970); Goldsmith (1969); Graham (1968); Griffin (1965); Peterson (1970); Stern (1968); and Wolozin (1966).

[5] The fact that the executive Department of Housing and Urban Development is only a decade old underscores the lack of long-standing lines of communication and decision-making between cities and the federal government.

worked at cross purposes with each other. It is obvious that pollution problems do not recognize community boundaries; this suggests the need for governmental bodies for ecological territories rather than arbitrary political borders. Yet the very fact that the creation of effective regional government appears so difficult to envision underscores the extent to which ecological disruption is built into the American community structure.

As a discussion of community structure reveals, basic institutions such as the economy and polity are involved in the pollution problem. It is important to analyze these institutions as entities in their own right that cut across not only communities but the entire society. When this kind of analysis is undertaken, attention is drawn to the dominant social institutions in America that contribute to ecological disruption: (1) the economy, (2) the legal system, and (3) the political system.

THE ECONOMY AND THE ECOSYSTEM
The economy of a society extracts stock resources, such as oil, coal, gas, and various minerals. These resources then are used to create energy which, in turn, powers the continually expanding and productive apparatus of industrial societies. The conversion of energy, the production of goods, and their consumption is accompanied by the discharge of enormous quantities of waste residues (see Figure 3).

Ecological disruption occurs in both the industrial and agricultural sectors of the economy. In the agricultural sector, the use of pesticides, inorganic fertilizers, and other chemical substances has had a number of consequences. First, the use of pesticides to maintain single crop agricultural production has simplified the

ecosystem. One result has been to increase the vulnerability of the ecosystem to diseases and pests, thus further increasing reliance upon the use of chemicals. Simplification fosters an escalating dependence upon those very substances that caused it since the natural sources of resistance to insects or diseases, such as other pest-eating insects, have also been killed. Chain reactions have been set in motion the amplified impact of which over time has yet to be determined. It is unclear just how long the ecosystem can absorb these disruptive chains of events, especially as the world moves to feed its rapidly expanding population.

Second, an equally dangerous consequence of the use of chemical pesticides in agriculture, especially the group of chemicals known as chlorinated hydrocarbons (of which DDT is the most conspicuous example), is that they accumulate and thus increase their toxic impact on the ecosystem.[6] Unlike many chemical substances, chlorinated hydrocarbons do not break down but are passed along in food chains without dissipating. As some organisms are eaten by other larger organisms in food chains embracing thousands of species, these chemicals are passed up the chain at nearly full strength. Because some of the energy in this food is lost as heat (see Figure 1), the concentrations of harmful chemicals as a proportion of organic matter increase as they move unaltered up the food chain. For this reason animals at the end of the food chains, such as humans, are likely to contain high levels of toxic chemicals in their tissues.

[6] For some interesting analyses of the toxic impact of agricultural residues see Carr (1966); Carson (1954); Coffman (1969); Mellanby (1967); Rudd (1964); Wesley (1967); and Wurster (1971).

In the industrial sector similar processes of disruption occur; wastes have immediately disruptive effects, and often accumulate as toxic substances in vital food chains (Abelson, 1970; Marquis, 1966). Then, for both industrial and agricultural production, the chemical and organic wastes utilize the soil, the water, and the air as a conduit to amplify their destructive impact across the world ecosystem. When renewable resources are used in this way their rejuvenative capacity decreases as waste residues accumulate. For example, recent studies have revealed that the ocean's phytoplankton, which provides the earth with 80 percent of its air, is accumulating chemical substances that may eventually prove toxic to these vital life forms. Also, it is rare to find any soil in the United States completely free of residues of DDT. What level, then, of DDT in the soil will kill the bacteria and fungi critical for the circulation of life sustaining nutrients? (See Figure 2.) The fact that the ban on DDT in the United States has been lifted for some industries, such as the lumber establishment, reveals not only that the ecosystem has been stripped of its natural resistance to lumber-killing life forms, but also that ecological considerations will usually be seen as less important than perceived (or promoted) economic crises.

This situation is likely to persist because the American economy is structured around continued expansion (Boulding, 1970; Hill, 1970; Miles, 1970; Murphy, 1967). Monetary stability, employment of the work force, and even political stability are dependent upon a small but steady rate of growth in the GNP—from four to ten percent per year. Economic growth is now artificially maintained by a variety of tactics, revealing that growth is required not so much for supporting population as for the maintenance of profits for corporations. For example, advertising is used to stimulate needs for increasing quantities of commodities. Further, it has created for consumers a state of psychological obsolescence for their current goods, thus allowing industry to bring out "improved" models of what is essentially a version of the same old thing. Consumers now are exposed to an endless variety of slightly modified products, packaged in "new," "more convenient," and nondegradable ways—to stimulate increased demand and the expectation that "new" products are always better. Manufacturers currently build products that are less durable and that deteriorate at a rate commensurate with economic growth. Consumers believe that it is critical to have a specialized gadget, from an electric can-opener to an electric toothbrush, to perform each specialized task. And, a gigantic credit industry has emerged to facilitate the realization of the consumers' demand beyond their immediate capacity to pay. With unclean air, heavily chlorinated water, and the disruption of life by an energy crisis, the actual result of needless consumer demand, unnecessary productivity, and wasteful consumption has been to decrease in absolute terms the quality of life in America.

The obvious solution to this problem is a slowdown or outright stoppage in the rate of economic growth (Boulding, 1966; Daly, 1973). Yet, such a radical solution would require vast readjustments in the structure of the economy. For instance, full employment would be impossible, especially with an expanding population. In turn, this situation would require more widespread and routine reliance on mechanisms for getting income to individuals, such as welfare, income guarantees, or "make work" projects provided by the government. These solutions are contrary to basic American values—the "work ethic," in particular. To provide income to a large and relatively permanent nonworking labor force, the corporate tax structure would have to be changed so that the federal government could increase its revenues and thus give income to consumers whose purchases will maintain the corporate system. Americans would have to recognize the degree to which they have been manipulated into a state of believing that perfectly useful goods are "outdated" and obsolete, and thereby in need of replacement. Along with this recognition, consumption habits would also have to change as individuals began to use recyclable and degradable goods, for Americans would have to become accustomed to the shortages created by the energy crisis as the full magnitude of the ecological crisis became evident. But to effect change in consumption habits would necessitate even more direct governmental regulation of the market in order to control supply and demand, thus assuring cries of "socialism" and other epithets.

Such an exercise of government power, however, would have to circumvent the influence of economic interests, for the biggest polluters are also the most powerful forces in American society. Polluting corporations exert disproportionate influence on national decision-making while pressing for their primary interest—making money. The proecology advertising campaigns mounted by the biggest corporations in America should not conceal the fact that these same corporations lobby most effectively against any legislation that decreases their profits. This inability of the political

processes to become liberated from the power of America's corporate structure represents another obstacle to implementing ecologically beneficial changes in the economy.

THE LAW AND THE ECOSYSTEM   Because the initial growth of the nation took place in an era dominated by the cultural values of growth, technology, consumption, and nature as a free good, little legal regulation of communities and industries occurred. About the turn of the century, the Bureau of Reclamation was established and the National Park Service was expanded, stimulating the passage of limited conservation laws. But it was not until the Dust Bowl of the 1930s that legislators revealed any sensitivity to the danger of unregulated use of renewable resources, and enacted the Soil Conservation Act (Boulding, 1970). After this belated but promising beginning, the thousands of conservation laws enacted over the last forty years still have done little to prevent ecological disruption. Most conservation laws are part of an "administrative handbook" telling corporations how to apply for resource extraction rather than controlling it.

It is not surprising that the many explicit antipollution codes enacted since the 1930s are ineffective. There are several reasons for this (Turner 1972a:243–244).

1. Conservation and antipollution laws typically are written in ambiguous language. Coupled with the court system's favoritism of economic interests, agencies charged with enforcing these vague laws are reluctant to press charges in court for fear of having the law, and thereby their function, invalidated (Murphy, 1967).

2. Existing antipollution laws usually carry very weak civil penalties and seldom

are backed by criminal sanctions. Should an agency finally take action against an offending industry or community, it usually secures a "cease-and-desist" order which requires the violator to stop its illegal activities. Only after such an order is ignored are minimal civil penalities sought. If all industries have to fear is a series of warnings, backed by weak civil penalties and no criminal sanctions, then there is little reason to obey the law. Companies faced with relatively minor fines view noncompliance as just another "cost" to be absorbed and passed on to the consumer. Until companies are confronted with criminal penalties, heavy civil damages, and perhaps dissolution of the corporation, antipollution laws will not be effective. The most comprehensive and unambiguous federal antipollution law ever enacted—the Clean Air Act of 1970—carries no criminal penalties.

3. The vast majority of laws do not attack the source of pollution. More typically they require treatment of pollutants after they have been created. The Clean Air Act did not specify that the internal combustion engine must be replaced but only that the ultimate emissions of this engine must be reduced; should it prove impossible to meet the standards imposed by the Clean Air Act, valuable time will have been lost in developing an alternative to the internal combustion engine. Because time is a critical consideration, antipollution laws should go directly to the source by prohibiting the· use or production of commodities generating pollutants.

4. Finally, many state antipollution laws have "grandfather clauses" which allow industries that polluted before the enactment of the law to continue their harmful activities. One result is that outmoded and highly polluting industries are encouraged to continue, while new industries which must utilize expensive antipollution equipment are discouraged from becoming established in a given area. Thus in the end, these laws often perpetuate the very industrial processes that they were designed to discourage.

Inducements to pollution are found in other types of statutes. Present tax codes encourage unnecessary pollution; for example, depletion allowances, which allow corporations extracting resources to deduct from their taxes the "depletions" of resources, encourage rapid and sloppy extraction methods. Property tax laws permit lower tax assessments for land as resources are extracted, once again providing inducement to careless and rapid extraction (Murphy, 1967). Under some state statutes, legally imposed fines for pollution can be deducted as a business expense. When corporations are found liable for their pollutants (and rarely is this the case), they are allowed to deduct as a business expense the costs of cleaning up their effluents.

Until state and federal tax laws reward careful resource extraction, while heavily penalizing polluters, American industry is unlikely to initiate a serious antipollution effort (except perhaps in their advertising). To solve these problems, a comprehensive national body of laws carrying severe criminal and civil penalties will be necessary. This new federal body of law will have to involve a coordinated writing and rewriting of pollution, conservation, and tax laws.

What is needed is a set of clear *national* quality standards for the air, soil, and water, with no region in America excepted. Aside from the reticence of federal legislators to enact such bold legislation, there are a number of fundamental problems. Determining what the standards should be, how much pollution is tolerable, when pollution does begin to harm the ecosystem, and the short-run *and* the long-run consequences of pollutants is extremely difficult. This makes it hard for legislators to set renewable resource quality standards, assuming the will to do so.

In this current state of ignorance, legislators tend to write ambiguities into pollution laws, especially when pressured by well-organized lobbying interests (Graham, 1966). For example, the Water Quality Act of 1965 established vague water quality standards which could be suspended upon a "due consideration to the practicability and to the physical and economic feasibility of complying with such standards . . . as the public interest and equities of the case may require." Coupled with the court's typically sympathetic attitude toward communities and industries, the Water Quality Act has proven almost unenforceable, since it is all too easy to see the way pollution serves the public interest (lower taxes, for example) or the "equities" of the case (jobs for workers in industry).

In the Clean Air Act of 1970, tolerable emissions are stated clearly and deadlines for compliance with these standards are explicit. But auto makers have now been granted the allowable one-year extension to meet the required standards (excluding California); and currently, with the energy crisis and the specter of economic recession resulting from enforcement of the standards, there is considerable pressure to suspend or weaken the law. If unambiguous standards for clean air cannot be maintained, it is unlikely that similar standards can be set for emissions into the soil and water which, in both the short and long run, represent a much more dangerous threat to ecological balances than does air pollution. This is especially likely to be the case, since pollution of the soil and water is not as directly observable and hence not as alarming to the public. Also the interaction of pollutants with the water and soil is more complex than with the air and legislators can always cry ignorance about what standards to establish.

Should quality standards for air, water, and soil ever be enacted, the next step would be to make communities and industries pay for *all* their remaining pollutants discharged into the environment. Such laws would contain the following basic formula: the more pollutants, the more the offender must pay, and if the offender is a private corporation, the less costs should be passed on to consumers. Such laws could serve as incentives for industries to clean up the last of their harmful emissions. Enacting such a body of law, however, poses the major problem of determining how to devise the formulas for assigning costs. There is much ignorance concerning which interacting pollutants in different environments over varying lengths of time cause the most harm to the ecosystem. Of all emissions, those into the air can most easily be calculated because they can be measured and their interaction with other chemicals and ecosystem processes is more easily assessed than those discharged into the water and soil (Ehrlich, 1971; Murphy, 1967). Yet unless some steps are taken to construct cost formulas for polluters of soil and water as well as air, there will be little incentive for industries and communities to cease their harmful activities.

Further, a rewriting of tax laws will be necessary. No longer should industries be given depletion allowances and lowered tax assessments for harmful resource extraction, nor tax write-offs for cleaning up their mistakes. Accompanying this, laws should be written encouraging research on pollution control and installation of emission control devices. One approach would be to allow high tax write-offs for antipollution activities, although such a law would have to be monitored carefully by the Internal Revenue Service to insure that industries do not simply rename their previous activities as "antipollution research, development, and implementation." Another strategy would be to enact laws requiring industries to reinvest a certain percentage of their net profits into pollution control, while forbidding these corporations to pass their costs onto consumers.

To legitimate these new types of laws, and to force their enactment where legislative bodies hesitate, it has been proposed that a constitutional amendment containing an Environmental Bill of Rights be passed (Ehrlich 1971; Nader, 1970). In the present legal morass, the doctrine of "balance of equities" has evolved and now guides all too many pollution suits. This doctrine requires the courts to weigh the "good" (a clean environment) against the "bad" (high taxes, unemployment, and so forth) consequences of a ruling in favor of environmentalists. The result has often been for the courts to rule that the economic benefits of pollution outweigh the costs of personal health and ecological disruption. A constitutional amendment containing a forceful Environmental Bill of Rights would put an end to such decisions. Such an amendment would uphold these human rights (1) to drink clean water, (2) to breathe clean air, and (3) to enjoy natural beauty (Ehrlich, 1971; Landau and Rheingold, 1971:37–39). Without such a constitutional amend-

ment, there are no established legal traditions with which to press environmental lawsuits. Probably the most applicable of existing legal traditions are the doctrines of "nuisance" and "trespass" (Ehrlich and Ehrlich, 1970:267–274; Landau and Rheingold, 1971). It is not stretching the issue to visualize pollutants as a nuisance to public health and as a trespass on individuals' air, land, and water. Yet these doctrines are not likely to prove effective. In the case of the doctrines of nuisance, for example, several limitations exist:

1. Only those whose property is affected can initiate the suit.
2. A clear causal relation between the damaged property and the nuisance must be established (a difficult task in the light of the complex interactions among pollutants and the ecosystem).
3. The doctrine can be invoked only when the nuisance is considered to cause more harm than good.

Furthermore, the utilization of all existing legal doctrines was dealt a blow by the United States Supreme Court in December 1973. In a landmark water pollution case, the Court ruled that citizens of each state bringing suit in a federal court must demonstrate damage to their property or health. This ruling severely limits the capacity of environmental groups to bring class action suits. Each plaintiff must now document $10,000 in damages—a difficult task when hundreds of plaintiffs in several states are involved in a class action suit. The extent to which the American legal system has institutionalized patterns of ecological disruption is thus clearly evident. The federal government's past record on first enacting and then implementing major social reforms has not been impressive over the last twenty-five years. Until the laws are changed, little progress will be made in averting world ecological dissipation. If there should be significant legal change, will there be implementation? For in the end, the law is only what the government chooses to enforce (Wheeler, 1970).

POLITICS AND THE ECOSYSTEM The cost of saving the environment will be high, perhaps as much as $50 billion per year for at least a decade, to restore the environment, and close to that amount thereafter just to maintain the ecological balances. The reason for the high costs are varied: tax incentives for polluters to clear their refuse would tax the federal treasury; revenue sharing with cities attempting to revamp their antiquated sewage systems would also be costly; and the giant federal bureaucracy needed to implement, monitor, and enforce antipollution codes would be expensive.

Currently demands are escalating for money in domestic spheres (Sprout and Sprout, 1971a), such as welfare costs, national health care, education, law enforcement, maintenance of agricultural and industrial subsidies, and allocations for foreign aid. Moreover, the combined expenses of the executive departments such as Interior, Labor, Commerce, Housing and Urban Development, will undoubtedly increase in the coming decades. Some of the monies for pollution control and other domestic programs can come from closing tax loopholes, raising corporate and individual taxes, and the increasing tax revenues of an expanding economy (a self-defeating source of pollution control revenue).

However, if Americans are to continue to enjoy their current life style *and* fight pollution, a reordering of national priorities will involve taking money from the single most expensive item on the federal budget, the military. The military presently spends from forty to fifty percent of all federal revenues. Unless Americans wish to have higher taxes, poorer schools, expensive health care, decaying cities, less police protection, vast poverty, *and* widespread pollution, then the logical place to secure resources is from the military. This reordering of priorities would not be easy because the political power of the military is considerable—another example of how pollution is built into American political structure (Sprout, 1970).

The military is now a giant state-corporation which, through the awarding of defense contracts, directly and indirectly controls as much as thirty percent of the GNP. Unlike other "corporations," the military markets an illusive product: deterrence and defense. This illusiveness is one of its major sources of power. Since 1960, the period of biggest military expansion, American citizens have continuously been informed by the military of a missile, bomber, antiballistic missile, fighter plane, megatonnage, submarine, survival, and security "gap." Through fear-mongering tactics the Pentagon has been able to codify an ideology justifying its continued grasp on tax resources. Some of the tenets of this ideology include:

1. Additional weaponry increases America's deterrence capacity.
2. The United States would be overrun without continued military buildup.
3. The United States must be prepared to deal with all military contingencies.
4. Defense spending is necessary for continued economic prosperity. (See Melman, 1970: 103–183; and Turner, 1972a: 178–181.)

Many of the new weapons promoted by the Pentagon are probably superfluous. It is doubtful that the United States could be overrun, and a doubling of the current overkill capacity will make it no safer from invasion. The lesson of Vietnam makes it clear that the United States cannot police the world or deal with every contingency. Defense spending produces few goods that can be used by the American public and is thus inflationary.

Strategies invoking the Pentagon ideology only represent the most visible bases of power. For ultimately the Pentagon maintains its power through its current web of dependencies of economic and political interests. Because some of America's largest corporations are under Pentagon control, they help lobby for military spending. These corporations—such as General Dynamics, Lockheed, and Boeing—cannot survive without defense contracts. In turn, smaller companies depend upon these larger corporations for subcontracts and join in lobbying activities. Labor unions have now joined the lobbyists, since defense cuts mean the loss of jobs. Some states—such as Texas, Washington, Alabama, California, and South Carolina—have a large proportion of their economy structured around military activities, thereby making their senators and congressmen allies for the maintenance of the Pentagon. In addition to the lobbying activities of those sectors of the society dependent on the military budget, the Pentagon itself has mobilized a propaganda machine costing hundreds of millions of dollars per year. The formal budget for military lobbying is set at $30 million dollars (by an act of Congress in 1971), but it is estimated that the Pentagon actually spends over $200 million in such activities (Turner, 1972a:197).

The combined impact of this lobbying by the Pentagon and its allies cannot be matched by any other group or coalition of groups in America. The fears of Americans over deterrence capacity and the pervasive influence of the Pentagon ideology makes it seem unlikely that sufficient monies to fight pollution can be taken away from the military.

There are additional problems inherent in the structure of the American political system. The financial power of America's large corporations, most of which pollute, is extensive and continues to skew decisions in both the House and Senate in favor of polluters. These interest groups —oil companies, auto makers, associations of manufacturers, and labor unions —maintain extensive staffs of professional lobbyists who possess considerably more money and influence than representatives of environmental organizations such as the Consumers Union, The National Wildlife Federation, or the Sierra Club. Passing effective legislation is also difficult because of the collective power of diverse *local* interests. In order for any piece of legislation to get to the floor of either the Senate or House, it must first pass through the appropriate committee, which has the power to pigeonhole, rewrite, stall, or kill any bill. Since committee chairmen are selected on the basis of seniority, they tend to come from rural districts or states where interests are stable and conservative. In such areas, senators and congressmen can be consistently reelected *if* they accede to the interests of their constituency; and thus, they come to dominate the chairs of important committees. This situation reveals that local, rural, and conservative interests have a disproportionate power over legislation on national issues. Antipollution legislation threatens in different ways a number of these interests, thereby making its passage through congressional committees difficult. This kind of resistance is encountered by all national legislation, from welfare to tax laws, but because antipollution legislation inevitably must require higher taxes, lower profits, and economic reorganization, it will always encounter even stiffer resistance.

Should national and comprehensive legislation on air, water, and soil quality standards be passed by Congress, its implementation will prove difficult because of the current *pattern* of governmental administration in America (Revelle, 1968). The United States is organized as a federalist political system and considerable power resides in local governments. One of the administrative problems for all types of national legislation, from health care to welfare, is the coordination of city, county, and state governments with the federal agencies. It is perhaps inevitable that state and local governments will often have conflicting interests, making it difficult to implement legislation. To prevail, antipollution agencies would have to wield enormous power. Even the public in the post-Watergate era is likely to resist the allocation of such power. Yet without it, it will be difficult to avoid the rivalries and antagonisms among diverse governmental bodies and effectively implement on a national scale antipollution legislation.

Another problem with the current administrative pattern is that regulating agencies often do not exercise their mandated powers. For example, the U.S. Department of Agriculture has often failed to curtail the use of pesticides, especially the dangerous chlorinated hydrocarbons. A suit by the Environmental Defense Fund forced the Department to ban the use of DDT, but this ban now is being relaxed under pressure from the lumber industry. Indeed, federal agencies often are co-opted by those very industries they are established to regulate. The Department is supposed to regulate the pesticide industry but has consistently encouraged the use of pesticides while under-emphasizing research on and use of alternative forms of pest control (Ehrlich, 1971). Further, agencies frequently fail to argue for tougher standards where those existing are weak or ambiguous (Nader, 1970). This failure now is justified by a governmental ideology that is invoked to legitimate the lackluster enforcement of the law:

1. *No one* can meet the minimum standards. Or, if this is not satisfactory:
2. Conditions would be *worse* without us. Or, if this is still unsatisfactory:
3. There are _____ (fill in the blank) extenuating circumstances that prevent enforcement. (See Murphy 1967, p. 107)

A final impediment to affective administration of regulatory law in America lies in the consistent failure of agencies to use even the limited sanctions at their disposal.

This administrative pattern now seems endemic in America and its failings are likely to be repeated even should antipollution laws be enacted. A supra-agency with power over all other agencies might well be necessary for effective enforcement. One difficulty in establishing such an agency centers around lines of authority to other executive departments in the federal government, as well as to state and local governments (Goldman, 1970). At minimum, an antipollution agency would probably require authority over the Departments of Health, Education and Welfare, Commerce, Interior, Agriculture, Transportation, and Housing and Urban Development. These executive departments would oppose the creation of this supra-agency and, should it be established, would likely work to undermine its effectiveness. In July 1970 President Nixon formed the current Environmental Protection Agency to consolidate pollution control policy and activity. This agency has yet to prove its effectiveness, even for the enforcement of the Clean Air Act, and has had difficulty asserting any authority over other executive departments. If this situation proves typical, then the administration of environmental law will become as ineffective as in the past.

The prognosis is not bright. The administrative problems involved in creating a system of accountability represents a roadblock to monitoring industry and communities. Furthermore, the governmental agency charged with enforcing what would inevitably be a somewhat arbitrary set of cost formulas would be resisted by industry and communities. It is possible to visualize a poorly funded agency so embroiled in legal battles that it cannot enforce even minimal national quality standards for air, water, and soil (Sprout & Sprout 1971b).

Americans can probably expect in the coming decades to live in a "threshold environment" where the air, water, and soil are maintained at minimal levels for the support of what will very soon be a declining style of life. This situation will be complicated by another force in America: population growth. Should the population continue to expand, the already harmful impact of the community and institutional structure in America will be exacerbated.

The Small but Deadly Population Bomb in America

The human species has been multiplying at an accelerating rate. For example, from 1850 to 1930, a mere eighty years, the earth's population doubled from one to two billion (Appleman, 1965). Currently the world's population is set at 3.5 billion, soon to double again (Ehrlich, 1970; Hardin, 1969; Miles, 1970; and Wald, 1970). The rate of population growth in industrial societies is much slower than that of underdeveloped nations; and once these latter societies become industrialized, their rates of population hopefully will decline. The large populations of the undeveloped world do not represent so much of an ecological problem in the present; the real danger is their rapid growth, coupled with industrial expansion, *in the future.* Currently, it is the comparatively "small" populations and "low" rates of growth of industrialized nations that pose the present threat to the ecosystem. For, as the demands of these "small" populations are met with the destructive techniques of mass agriculture and industrial production, large quantities of waste residues are cast into the ecosystem (Miles, 1970; Stockwell, 1968).

The patterns of population growth in the United States and elsewhere in the industrial world hopefully will become more prevalent, but the changes needed to bring this drop in the birth rate, industrialization, urbanization, and mass production, will probably be more harmful to the ecological system than continued growth of the Third World populations with low economic demands. The possibility of the American system becoming the world pattern is disquieting:

The consumption of goods produced by polluting industrial and agricultural processes and the disposal of wastes by each American is fifty times that of an individual in a nonindustrial nation (Wald, 1970). It is not pleasant to contemplate the prospect of the ecological damage to be wrought by a reduction in that ratio from 50/1 to 25/1, or 10/1, or 1/1. It must be recognized that the United States causes more pollution with its current population of 210 million than the 2.5 billion inhabitants of the underdeveloped world combined. It consumes one-third of all resources and causes one-half of the world's industrial pollution (Davis, 1970; Price, 1967). With an additional 100 million citizens by the year 2010—ignoring what is occurring in the rest of the world—the United States alone may have disrupted the ecosystem beyond the point of rejuvenative return.

Much publicity has been given recently to the drop in the United States birth rate to a point of "no growth." Hopefully, this recent trend will endure; but even if it does, it will not immediately become translated into a stable population, since the current child-bearing population will live for another fifty to sixty years. Hence, their children and their grandchildren and even great grandchildren could be added to the population. Thus, even should the birth *rate* stay at the zero level it is inevitable that the United States will grow to perhaps as much as 300 million before it finally stabilizes.

One problem with extrapolating from current birth rates is that they fluctuate enormously. During the 1930s there was widespread concern with the fact that the birth rate was so low. With World War II came the baby boom; and now, there

has been a marked drop in the birth rate. It would appear that the long-range trend in the United States has been a progressive decline in birth rate, periodically reversed. These periodic reversals pose the real threat to the ecosystem, because they increase the absolute population base and hence the demand for industrial and mass agricultural goods.

Perhaps the world's ecosystem can support an American population of 300 million, but if the United States rate is allowed to jump, even if only briefly, world ecological disruption will escalate rapidly. To understand how the United States can remain at a zero population growth requires an examination of those institutional conditions that could potentially cause a small but disruptive increase in the population.

FAMILY AND POPULATION GROWTH   The American family is undergoing change and reorganization. Male-female relations are becoming more egalitarian; women now work in close to one-half of all families and childless marriages have increased. These factors help account for the decline in the birth rate. But the structure of the family in America, and the values legitimating this structure, maintain the potential for a rise in the birth rate.

A list of dominant cultural values encouraging childbirth is revealing: One of the most important goals of marriage is to bear and raise children; self-worth, psychological fulfillment, and even sexual adequacy still are defined by child-bearing; zygotes in the womb still are revered as true life by a large segment of the population; babies still are supposed to hold a special status in the family; child-rearing is considered a right rather than a privilege; and regulation of family patterns by the state is considered abhorrent. Whether these values are good or bad is not at issue, but they make possible a sudden increase in birth rate, while hindering the federal government's capacity to intervene in family life to prevent excess childbirth.

These values are sustained by and legitimate the behaviors of family members. Despite the publicity given to alternative forms of family life, most women are thrust into the housekeeping, child-bearing, and child-rearing role (Day, 1968; Turner, 1972a:258). As long as the major source of reward for women in the family stems from the performance of this role, the potential for increased birth rates remains. To implement change, involves such measures as the expansion of occupational opportunities for women, and their resocialization, alteration of men's attitudes, and revision of the interpersonal relations between men and women in the family. These changes are necessary, and while it is possible to observe some small movement in this direction, the change must come rapidly and be permanent to avoid ecological disaster.

Combating the values and dominant structural arrangements of the American family are the weak family planning programs of various private groups, and, to a limited extent, the federal government (Berelson, 1969; Davis, 1967). Such programs emphasize the voluntary use of contraceptives with the result that there is no established way to prevent people from voluntarily deciding to have more babies. As long as the federal government leaves programs of population control to private organizations, it increases its incapacity to act in a crisis. Should the

federal government need to intervene hastily, it would possibly violate individuals' civil rights (Day, 1968). The dominance of the voluntary family planning concept thus deflects political attention from the establishment of a clear federal policy emphasizing compulsory contraceptive measures for families whose size has reached a designated limit (McKinley, 1967; Westoff and Westoff, 1971).

THE ECONOMY AND POPULATION GROWTH
The current structure of the American economy depends upon economic growth which requires a growing population. Economic interests are thus likely to oppose any policies that would stem growth. While it is hard to see any pressure at the present time, should a drop in the rate of population growth (fifty to sixty years down the road) begin to cause a decrease in consumer demand, the potential is always there. Lest it be thought that this possibility is remote, it can be noted that in Japan there has been a relaxation of pollution standards because they cut too sharply into the rate of economic growth. As soon as such a connection is made between profits and population, pressures for population growth could suddenly spring from economic interests. It must be remembered that each baby in its 70-year lifetime will consume directly and indirectly: "26 million gallons of water, 21 thousand gallons of gasoline, 10 thousand pounds of meat, 28 thousand pounds of milk and cream, $4,000 to $8,000 in school building materials, $6,300 worth of clothing and $7,000 worth of furniture" (Ehrlich, 1971:139). In view of the money spent on these goods, it would seem unlikely that industry and commerce would stand back and let govern-

mental policies cut into these profits (Turner, 1972a:203).

THE LAW AND POPULATION GROWTH

Early America was a frontier society attempting to fill its vast lands and supply a labor pool for its emerging factories. Even as the government began to find it necessary to regulate communities, industries, and education, it dared not intervene in the family life that had literally stocked the territories and industries of modern America. The end result has been a legal barrier to the enactment of laws for regulating and controlling population (Ehrlich and Ehrlich, 1970). More than legal inattention is involved because American law actually encourages population growth.

In a landmark decision the United States Supreme Court recently indicated that states could enact laws which would enable women openly to seek abortions. Tax laws should be rewritten so that they no longer penalize childless couples; in fact, for families with more than two children, severe tax penalties should be levied. Although a careless writing of such laws might discriminate against the poor, it would be possible to have progressive penalties as family income increases—thereby removing the potential inequity. Another indirect incentive to population control would be the enforcement of existing civil rights laws or the ratification of the Equal Rights Amendment. This legal activity could open up new lines of employment for women, thereby providing a meaningful alternative to the wife-mother role in the family. Social Security laws could be rewritten increasing the retirement benefits of childless couples, thus removing the fear of many adults that without

children they will be left financially vulnerable in their old age (Ehrlich and Ehrlich, 1970:253).

The use of direct and indirect incentives now appears to be the only legal way to implement population policy, for in the landmark *Criswold* v. *Connecticut* decision in 1964 the Supreme Court ruled that the family is immune to the coercive powers of the state. Although there are dangers in granting these powers to the state, there are equal dangers in its incapacity to halt a sudden increase in the rate of population growth.

GOVERNMENT PROGRAMS AND POPULATION GROWTH

In contrast to the administrative problems of enforcing national resource quality standards (see the earlier discussion of the polity), the implementation of population standards would be comparatively simple (Turner, 1972a:265). However it would be difficult to secure enactment by Congress.

In Table 1, the major population control programs are listed in order of their probable effectiveness. As can be seen, the most effective programs are the most politically infeasible. Current family planning programs and community sex education programs (as opposed to a national program), have probably helped reduce the rate of growth to zero over the last year.

But an involuntary population control program (1 in Table 1) would be the most effective in stopping a sudden rise in the birth rate, since it would prevent families from having more than two children. Naturally, the specter of forced abortions or compulsory sterilization is not a pleasant prospect, and hence such a program is politically infeasible. The next most effective program would be a

Table 1. Programs of Government Control of Population Growth

Population control program	Feasibility and effectiveness		
	Probable effectiveness	Administrative feasibility	Political feasibility
(1) Involuntary population control	High	High	Low
(2) Institution change	High	Moderate	Low
(3) New tax incentives and penalties	High	High	Low
(4) Sex and population clinics	Moderate	High	Moderate
(5) Voluntary family planning	High	High	Moderate

concerted effort by the government to reorganize the institutions of the economy and family (2 in Table 1) as discussed earlier. Given the economic disruption that would occur under such programs, such action is politically infeasible. The third possibility would be the enactment of new tax laws as discussed in the previous section. Such changes are difficult, especially when they involve family matters, and hence are politically infeasible. A system of national population control clinics is the next most effective program. These clinics would make available and encourage abortions and sterilizations. Such clinics are administratively viable, since they could utilize the existing administrative machinery of the veterans hospitals. Currently, some states and many communities have sex education courses, but rarely do these explore the implications of childbirth on the ecosystem. Under a national program, this connection between population size and ecological disruption could be mandated and easily implemented through the existing administrative liaisons between the federal government and state boards of education. In light of the resistance sex education has encountered in many communities, population control training is

not likely to be well received—thus giving such a program only a moderate chance of enactment. A national program of family planning could be enacted, since Congress has already enacted in 1970 a Family Planning and Population Act which provides free contraceptives to the poor through nonprofit agencies. It is unclear whether an expanded program, reaching into the lives of the affluent, would be so easily tolerated as it is for the poor; but it would seem that a voluntary program would have high political feasibility and could be easily administered through existing state public health agencies.

Since the politically feasible programs cannot prevent an increase in the growth rate, it appears that the incapacity to control population size is now built into the American political system. To wait for ecocatastrophe is to assure that legislation will be hastily conceived and abusive. It is far better to begin serious consideration of "mutual coercion" of population limits "mutually agreed upon" by the citizens of a democracy (Hardin, 1968). The political system in the United States must set up the administrative structure to coerce families to limit their size since the "spaceship Earth" may not be able to tolerate a larger population in America—the most deadly population of all the world's societies.

THE WORLD ECOSYSTEM: PROSPECTS FOR THE FUTURE

Analyzing the relationship between society and nature has required an appreciation of the structures of both ecosystems and social systems. Only by understanding the basic elements and processes in both is it possible to comprehend the ways in which society has interacted with the ecosystem to create a problem of survival. Ecosystems consist of incredibly complex flows of energy and cycles of minerals through the millions of life forms on earth. Social systems are composed of humans organized into complex webs of interrelationships which are mediated by cultural symbols. It is this organization of the human species into sociocultural entities that now threatens the flow of energy and cycling of minerals in the ecosystem—thereby creating not only a crisis of survival for humans, but for the other life forms of the planet as well.

What intensifies the crisis is the fact that the structure of ecosystems is now highly vulnerable to change from the pollutants of human societies, whereas the structure of social systems appears highly resistant to the changes which could restore more harmonious relations between society and nature. While the details of ecological disruption must be left to biologists, a cursory appreciation of the structure of ecosystems reveals that human society has (a) stripped the world's ecosystem of its natural diversity and hence stability; (b) altered the flow of energy and cycling of minerals to an un-

paralleled degree, thereby setting off a chain of events the fully amplified impact of which cannot be known; and (c) generated unknown amounts of irreversible destruction to plant and animal species.

American society is largely responsible for this disruption which is alarming in itself; but equally disturbing are the worldwide processes of restructuring human societies along the American pattern. While there are differences with respect to ideology and specific forms of economic and political organization, industrial and industrializing societies look much alike. All are dominated by cultural values emphasizing economic growth, higher levels of consumption, the worship of technology or knowledge, and the utilization of nature as a refuse dump. All reveal community structures and institutional arrangements that not only generate enormous quantities of waste residues, but also seem resistant to abating the discharge of these wastes.

Finally, it can properly be asked whether there is hope for corrective action, and, what such action will require of Americans. It does appear that there is growing consciousness of ecological problems in America and elsewhere in the world; and perhaps this awareness can be translated into action. Corrective action, however, will require major adjustments for most Americans: Pollution control will cost money in higher taxes and prices; it will cost jobs in private industry; it will make "luxuries" of many goods and services heretofore taken for granted, and it will require a willingness to save, conserve, and recycle. These kinds of changes in the "American way of life" will be required. The next two decades will probably reveal whether or not Americans are willing to make the necessary sacrifice.

References

Abelson, P. H. "Methyl Mercury." *Science*, 1970, 169, 237–238.

Appleman, P. *The Silent Explosion.* Boston: Beacon, 1965.

Battan, L. J. *The Unclean Sky: A Meteorologist Looks at Air Pollution.* New York: Doubleday, 1966.

Berelson, B. "Beyond Family Planning." *Science*, 1969, 163, 533–542.

Blake, N. M. *Water for the Cities.* Syracuse, N.Y.: Syracuse University Press, 1956.

Blau, S. D., and Rodenbeck, J. (Eds.). *The House We Live In: An Environmental Reader.* New York: Macmillan, 1971.

Boulding, K. E. "The Economics of the Coming Spaceship Earth." In H. Jarret (Ed.), *Environmental Quality in a Growing Economy.* Johns Hopkins Press, 1966.

Boulding, K. E. "No Second Chance for Man." In *The Crisis of Survival.* Glenview, Ill.: Scott, Foresman, 1970.

Burch, W. R. *Day Dreams and Nightmares—A Sociological Essay on the American Environment.* New York: Harper & Row, 1971.

Burch, W. R., Cheek, N. H., Jr., and Taylor, L. *Social Behavior, Natural Resources, and the Environment.* New York: Harper & Row, 1972.

Campbell, R. R., and Wade, J. L. (Eds.). *Society and Environment: The Coming Collision.* Boston: Allyn & Bacon, 1972.

Carr, D. N. *The Breath of Life.* New York: Norton, 1965.

Carr, D. N. *Death of the Sweet Waters.* New York: Norton, 1966.

Carson, R. L. *The Sea Around Us.* New York: Signet Library, 1954.

Carson, R. L. *The Silent Spring.* Boston: Houghton Mifflin, 1962.

Coffman, R. "Are Fertilizers Polluting Our Water Supply?" *Farm Journal*, 1969, 46, 46–50.

Commoner, Barry. *Science and Survival.* New York: Viking, 1966.

Daly, H. E. (Ed.). *Toward a Steady-State Economy.* San Francisco: Freeman, 1973.

Daly, R. *The World Beneath the City.* New York: Lippincott, 1959.

Davis, K. "Population Policy: Will Current Programs Succeed?" *Science*, 1967, 158, 730–739.

Davis, W. H. "Overpopulated America." *The New Republic*, 1970, 162, 48–52.

Day, A. T. "Population Control and Personal Freedom: Are They Compatible?" *The Humanist*, 1968, 28, 7–10.

Detwyler, R. (Ed.). *Man's Impact on Environment.* New York: Knopf, 1962.

deVilleneuve, R. (Ed.). *The Enemy Is Us: A Rational Look at the Environmental Problem.* Minneapolis: Winston Press, 1973.

Duncan, O. D., and Schnore, A. "The Eco-system." In C. A. Faris (Ed.), *Handbook of Sociology.* Chicago: Rand McNally, 1964.

Ehrlich, P. R. *The Population Bomb*, rev. ed. New York: Ballantine, 1971.

Ehrlich, P. R., and Ehrlich, A. H. *Population, Resources, Environment: Issues in Human Ecology.* San Francisco: Freeman, 1970.

Ehrlich, P. R., Hodlren, J. P., and Holm, R. W. *Man and the Ecosphere.* San Francisco: Freeman, 1971.

Esposito, J. C. *Vanishing Air: The Ralph Nader Study Group Report on Air Pollution.* New York: Grossman, 1970.

Falk, R. A. *This Endangered Planet: Prospects and Proposals for Human Survival.* New York: Random House, 1971.

Freeman, A. M. "Cleaning Up Foul Waters. I—Pollution Tax." *The New Republic*, 1970, 162, 18–21.

Goldman, M. I. (Ed.). *Controlling Pollution.* Englewood Cliffs, N.J.: Prentice-Hall, 1967.

Goldman, M. I. "From Lake Erie to Lake Baikal—From Los Angeles to Tbilisi: The Convergence of Environmental Disruption." *Science*, 1970, 170, 37–41.

Goldman, M. I. *Ecology and Economics:*

Controlling Pollution in the 70's. Englewood Cliffs, N.J.: Prentice Hall, 1972.

Goldsmith, J. R. "Los Angeles Smog." *Science Journal*, 1969, 45, 84–92.

Graham, F., Jr. "The Infernal Smog Machine." *Audubon*, 1968, 70, 720–726.

Graham, F., Jr. *Disaster by Default: Politics and Water Pollution.* New York: Evans, 1966.

Greer, S. *Urban Renewal and American Cities: The Dilemma of Democratic Intervention.* Indianapolis: Bobbs-Merrill, 1966.

Griffin, C. W., Jr. "America's Airborne Garbage." *Saturday Review*, 1965, 48, 8–12.

Hardin, G. "The Tragedy of the Commons." *Science*, 1970, 168, 42–49.

Hardin, G. *Population, Evolution and Birth Control.* San Francisco: Freeman, 1969.

Hardin, G. "Parenthood: Right or Privilege?" *Science*, 1970, 169, 427–28.

Helfrich, H. W. (Ed.). *The Environmental Crisis—Man's Struggle to Live with Himself,* New Haven, Conn.: Yale University Press, 1970.

Hill, G. "A Not So Silent Spring." In *The Crisis of Survival*, Glenview, Ill.: Scott, Foresman, 1970.

Iltis, H. H. "The Optimum Human Environment." In *The Crisis of Survival.* Glenview, Ill.: Scott, Foresman, 1970.

Kormondy, E. J. *Concepts of Ecology.* Englewood Cliffs, N.J.: Prentice-Hall, 1969.

Kuntz, R. F. "An Environmental Glossary." *Saturday Review*, 1971, 54, 81–88.

Landau, N. J., and Rheingold, P. D. *The Environmental Law Handbook.* New York: Friends of the Earth/Ballantine, 1971.

Linton, R. M. *Terracide: America's Destruction of Her Living Environment.* Boston: Little, Brown, 1970.

Luce, C. F. "Energy: Economics of the Environment." In W. Helfrich, Jr. (Ed.). *Agenda for Survival.* New Haven, Conn.: Yale University Press, 1970.

Marquis, R. W. *Environmental Improvement: Air, Water and Soil.* Washington, D.C.: Graduate School Press, 1966.

McClane, A. J. "The Ultimate Open Sewer." *Field and Stream*, 73, May 1968.

McKinley, P. "Compulsory Eugenic Sterilization: For Whom Does the Bell Toll?" *Duquesne University Law Review*, February, 1967.

Mellanby, K. *Pesticides and Pollution.* New York: Collins, 1967.

Melman, S. *Pentagon Capitalism: The Political Economy of War.* New York: McGraw-Hill, 1970.

Miles, R. E. "Whose Baby Is the Population Bomb?" *Population Bulletin*, 25, February, 1970.

Mix, S. A. "Solid Wastes: Every Day, Another 800 Million Pounds." *Today's Health*, 44, March, 1966.

Moncrief, L. W. "The Cultural Basis for Our Environmental Crisis." *Science*, 170, October 30, 1970.

Murphy, E. F. *Governing Nature.* New York: Quadrangle Books, 1967.

Nader, R. "Corporations and Pollution." In *The Crisis of Survival.* Glenview, Ill.: Scott, Foresman, 1970.

Odum, E. *Fundamentals of Ecology,* 2d ed. Philadelphia: Saunders, 1959.

Odum, E. "The Strategy of Ecosystem Development." *Science*, 1969, 169, 262–69.

Osborn, F. *Our Plundered Planet.* Boston: Little, Brown, 1948.

Osborn, F. *The Limits of the Earth.* Boston: Little, Brown, 1953.

Peterson, E. "The Atmosphere: A Clouded Horizon." *Environment*, 1970, 12.

Price, D. O. (Ed.). *The 99th Hour—The Population Crisis in the United States.* Chapel Hill: University of North Carolina Press, 1967.

Revelle, R. "Pollution and Cities." In J. Q. Wilson (Ed.), *The Metropolitan Enigma.* Cambridge, Mass.: Harvard University Press, 1968.

Rienow, R., and Leona, L. *Moment in the Sun: A Report on the Deteriorating Quality of the American Environment.* New York: Ballantine, 1969.

Rudd, R. L. *Pesticides and the Living*

Landscape. Madison: University of Wisconsin Press, 1964.

Scientific American. The Biosphere. San Francisco: Freeman, 1970.

Scientific American. Energy and Power. San Francisco: Freeman, 1971.

Sprout, H. "The Environmental Crisis in the Context of American Politics." In *The Crisis of Survival.* Glenview, Ill.: Scott, Foresman, 1970.

Sprout, H., and Sprout, M. "Ecology and Politics in America: Some Issues and Alternatives." Morristown, N.J.: General Learning Press, 1971. (a)

Sprout, H., and Sprout, M. *Toward a Politics of the Planet Earth.* Philadelphia: Van Nostrand Reinhold, 1971. (b)

Steif, W. "Why Birds Cough." In *The Crisis of Survival.* Glenview, Ill.: Scott, Foresman, 1970.

Stern, A. C. (Ed.). *Air Pollution.* New York: Academic, 1968.

Stockwell, E. G. *Population and People.* Chicago: Quadrangle Books, 1968.

Train, R. E., et al. *Environmental Quality: The First Annual Report of the Council on Environmental Quality.* Washington, D.C.: Government Printing Office, 1970.

Turner, J. H. *American Society: Problems of Structure.* New York: Harper & Row, 1972. (a)

Turner, J. H. *Patterns of Social Organization: A Survey of Social Institutions.* New York: McGraw-Hill, 1972. (b)

Wald, G. "A Better World for Fewer Children." In *The Crisis for Survival.* Glenview, Ill.: Scott, Foresman, 1970.

Wesley, M. *The Tainted Sea.* New York: Coward, McCann & Geoghegan, 1967.

Westoff, L. A., and Westoff, C. F. *From Now to Zero: Fertility, Contraception and Abortion in America.* Boston: Little, Brown, 1971.

Wheeler, H. "The Politics of Ecology." *Saturday Review,* 1970, 53, 21–24.

White, L., Jr. "The Historical Roots of Our Ecological Crisis." *Science,* 1967, 155, 1203–1206.

Wolozin, H. (Ed.). *The Economics of Air Pollution: A Symposium.* New York: Norton, 1966.

Woodwell, G. M. "Toxic Substances and Ecological Cycles." *Scientific American,* 1967, 216, 216–221.

Wurster, C. F. "DDT and the Environment." In W. Helfrich, Jr,. (Ed.), *Agenda for Survival.* New Haven, Conn.: Yale University Press, 1971.

Suggested Reading

CAMPBELL, R. R., AND WADE, J. L. (Eds.). *Society and Environment: The Coming Collision.* Boston: Allyn and Bacon, 1972.
  A good series of readings on the problems that current patterns of social organization create for the ecosystem.

CARSON, R. L. *The Silent Spring.* Boston: Houghton Mifflin, 1962.
  The classic and original statement of the impending problems to the environment.

DUNCAN, O. D., AND SCHNORE, A. "The Eco-system." In R. A. Faris (Ed.), *Handbook of Sociology.* Skokie, Ill.: Rand McNally, 1964.
  A good analytical discussion of society and the ecosystem.

EHRLICH, P. R., AND EHRLICH, A. H. *Population, Resources, Environment: Issues in Human Ecology.* San Francisco: Freeman, 1970.

Two biologists discuss the problems facing the ecosystem through population pressures.

LANDAU, N. J., AND RHEINGOLD, P. D. *The Environmental Law Handbook.* Boston: Little, Brown, 1970.
A summary of existing environmental laws and how they might be used to prevent ecological disaster.

MURPHY, E. F. *Governing Nature.* New York: Quadrangle Books, 1967.
A scholarly discussion of the practical and political problems regulating environmental quality in America.

Part V

Criminal Justice and Social Problems

Fascination with the police and their activities undoubtedly stems from the fact that they are the most visible strand of the web of social control we call the criminal justice system. Police are armed and sometimes use their weapons, bringing to consciousness the role and threat of force in social life. Police enforce laws and carry out the mandates of persons in authority, which sometimes prove unpopular with one segment of society or another. For some, they are the last bastion of order and decency, for others, they are the henchmen of the ruling class.

Like the media image of the confrontation between prosecutor and defense attorney in a hushed and tense courtroom, such caricatures of the police, the courts, and other components of the criminal justice system divert attention from important problems in the administration of criminal justice. To be sure, the legitimacy of the laws enforced by the criminal justice system is a fundamental concern. Earlier chapters have suggested the need for reform or more fundamental change in the present structure of society which would have major implications for the system, for example, greater access by the poor to legal services.

There is, however, the proximate concern to how the present system works and the nature of the problems it poses. Sanders addresses himself to this latter issue. He describes the component agencies of the criminal justice system—the police, the district attorney, the public defender, the courts, and the correctional system, pointing out that each is a distinct but interrelated organization with its own internal structure and bureaucratic criteria of success.

For example, Sanders notes that a prime indicator of efficiency for the police is the "clearance rate," that is, the "clearing" of a crime by the arrest of a suspect. The district attorney's office is concerned with gaining convictions, and cases forwarded by the police to the district attorney for prosecution are evaluated in part with respect to the likelihood of conviction. Some cases thought to be settled by the police through an arrest are dismissed by the district attorney due to insufficient evidence or procedural irregularity. The district attorney's concern for his or her record of conviction and the expeditious handling of cases leads, with the cooperation of the public defender or private attorney, to an informal "bargaining" process in which the original charge is reduced in return for a guilty plea.

The prosecutor's concern for a conviction is not necessarily contradictory to the police concern with clearing crimes by arrests, except for the fact that the main external control exercised over the police is through the exclusion of illegally obtained evidence—what the police tend to view as legal "technicalities." Prosecutors, already concerned to maximize conviction may dismiss charges against a defendant in the anticipation of the case being thrown out of court. From the point of view of the police, this means that someone who is patently guilty is allowed to go free. This situation encourages what Sanders delicately refers to as "inventiveness" on the part of the police in obtaining evidence, despite the restrictions posed by the civil rights of defendants, even to the point of falsified testimony. Different criteria of "efficiency" and the strains generated by bureaucratic pressures and distinctive occupational "world-view" lead to various distortions in the administration of justice which Sanders describes in fine detail.

Like Himelson in the article following, Sanders is concerned with the correctional system. Conceding the difficulties in interpreting the statistics on recidivism, or repeated crimes by persons processed through the correctional system, Sanders suggests that prisons are either remarkably successful in reforming their charges or dismal failures, depending on point of view. He argues that it is difficult to conceive of a system better designed to create career criminals than the prison system, so the estimated one-third recidivism rate he cites may be seen as an encouragingly low figure, indicating that prisons succeed in some degree of rehabilitation despite the obstacles Sanders notes.

The irony of Sanders' remarks is brought home in the essay by Himelson. He discusses four areas in which criminal rehabilitation is attempted: the juvenile court, prisons which have indeterminate sentences, parole, and probation. In each, three different approaches to rehabilitation may be employed at different times or in different jurisdictions: psychotherapy, education, and cultural reorientation. With the exception of a handful of projects, research has indicated that attempts to rehabilitate criminals have been far from successful. A number of reasons for the failure of rehabilitation has been advanced—

the inmate social system prevents it, the goal of rehabilitation conflicts with the goal of protecting society from the criminal, bureaucratic rigidity subverts it, and the stigma of involvement in the criminal justice system undermines it, factors similar to those cited by Sanders.

The apparent failure of rehabilitation has served as ammunition for certain critics of the criminal justice system who claim that strict enforcement of the law, closing legal loopholes, and lengthy incarceration under rigorous prison conditions are the "cure" for what they take to be a crisis of "law and order," as Sanders points out. In addition to simple incarceration without rehabilitation, Himelson discusses a set of further alternatives to the rehabilitative goal; reduction in the number of criminal laws (thus reducing the number of offenses for which someone may be sent to prison), various diversion programs (where arrested persons are referred to social agencies or simply released), and the formation of self-help groups.

Himelson is not sanguine concerning the overall effectiveness of these solutions, holding out only the hope that they will provide a greater sense of confidence in the integrity of the criminal justice system. As Sanders points out in his conclusion, more radical critics would wish for more.

Criminal Justice and Social Control

William B. Sanders

A predominant institution of social control in America is the criminal justice system. Composed of the police, prosecution and defense, the courts and corrections, the criminal justice system is intended to control law violators and at the same time to protect the rights of all citizens, including suspected criminals. By examining a society's criminal justice system, we learn not only about social control, but also about dominant values, social structures, and social problems in that society.

Before proceeding with an examination of the criminal justice system, several concepts need clarification: the notion of "social control" and its relationship to the criminal justice system, the underlying theory of law in an avowedly democratic society and the issues posed by the use of force and the notion of democracy; and finally, the idea of "criminal justice" itself.

Social Control

Social control refers to those systems that keep people in compliance with norms. William Goode (1972:507–508) outlines four social control systems: force, prestige, wealth, and love. Of these four systems of control, we will be concerned only with the first, force, for it is the use of force (including force-threat) that is the primary tool of the criminal justice system.

Typically, we understand force in terms of *overt* force, such as a criminal being subdued at gunpoint by the police (Goode, 1972:510). However, overt force only operates when other more subtle kinds of social control break down. Similarly, force-threat, such as the high visibility of police in the streets, signals that more common and less obtrusive agencies of control are not operating.

As a social control mechanism, the criminal justice system is primarily responsible for enforcing the formal norms or laws of society; and in this context, we refer to "legitimate coercive force" (cf. Bittner 1970:36–47). Now it may be that those who must obey the law do not see the law as a good one, or it even may be that the population sees those in power as illegitimate (Goldhamer and Shils, 1964:134). However, we use the term "legitimate force" as employed by criminal justice agencies to refer to the force used to order legal compliance as opposed to the force a mugger would use to relieve a passerby of his or her pocketbook. The ultimate legitimacy of force rests with the people's willingness to be governed.

Democratic Legal Ideals

In a democratic society, the laws are supposed to reflect the popular will of citizens. Ideally, compliance with the laws is synonymous with compliance with the popular will. All citizens are held accountable for compliance and all are treated equally by social control agencies. No one is supposed to be treated differently because of race, sex, political affiliation, or social status.

The democratic process of choosing lawmakers is designed to ensure that everyone has a voice in the initiation and enactment of laws. The rights of due process are intended to act as safeguards for the equal treatment guaranteed under the law. If representatives are elected by popular vote to make the laws that the populace must follow, the democratic ideal is realized. Similarly, in a democratic society, a defendant's guilt or innocence is determined by a jury of his peers. By being provided with a defense counsel, the defendant in court, whether rich or poor, has the same chance of being exonerated as anyone else. Thus, the *intended* processes are in accordance with democratic ideals.

Given that American society holds democratic values to be a basis of government and that the procedures regulating the social control agencies are responsible for a large part of the governing duties, can force be justified? My answer is a qualified "yes," for the exercise of the force is intended to preserve democratic ideals. However, the qualification is that the force is just only if actual social control practices live up to those ideals. Later we will examine the empirical evidence concerning the actual working of the criminal justice system, but first a closer look at the meaning of the term "criminal justice system" is needed.

The Criminal Justice System

The term "criminal justice system" is used to refer to the various agencies that make up the system. This usage is more a convenience than a reflection of a truly integrated system. Actually, the police, the prosecution-defense, the courts, and correction agencies are semiautonomous organizations with distinct goals. There are, of course, system-like features to the relationship among the agencies, since

there is input and some feedback among them, but there is no overarching "criminal justice system" as such. Therefore, in this evaluation each agency must be considered more or less separately as a unique organization, and it is necessary to understand that each develops its own independent processes of measuring success. By looking at the bureaucratic criteria that these agencies set up to measure success, the extent to which democratic values and procedures are carried out can be determined and an overview of the criminal justice system provided. At the same time, the extent to which the components of the criminal justice system are interrelated can be gauged.

MEASURES OF SUCCESS OF SOCIAL CONTROL AGENCIES

In our consideration of the various criminal justice agencies and the criteria by which they are judged, we find the police evaluated by their "clearance rate" (Skolnick, 1967). The clearance rate refers to the percent of crimes known to the police and considered to be "solved" (Skolnick, 1967:168). This does not necessarily include conviction, and if they believe that a defendant "got off" because of a "wily" defense attorney or on a "technicality," this does not prevent them from seeing the case as being solved, or cleared (Sanders, 1974). Therefore, because the clearance rate is determined by the police—they decide when a crime is solved —their goal and evaluation is not dependent on prosecution or the courts.

The prosecutor, while dependent on the police for input, is not wholly dependent on them for meeting his goal; he is evaluated in terms of his "conviction rate" or the percentage of convictions he is able to produce for the cases he prosecutes (Mayer, 1971:138–153). The conviction rate can be kept high by prosecuting only those cases where he has a "sure thing." Such cases usually entail a guilty plea and thereby avoid a trial. If the prosecutor is uncertain as to whether he can get a conviction, even though he believes the defendant guilty, the charges can be dismissed for lack of sufficient evidence. Doing this does not affect his conviction rate since there was a decision not to prosecute.

More immediately, the prosecutor's goal is to "produce" (Blumberg, 1967; Sudnow, 1965). The prosecutor must "produce" by clearing up those cases he has been given "to work" (Blumberg, 1967:59), for example, by setting up a trial with judge or jury. Since trials are time-consuming, obtaining guilty pleas or dismissals are the most expedient courses of action.

If, however, the prosecutor dismisses every case where there is no guilty plea, the police, newspapers, and others can apply pressure in the form of editorials, news stories, and features that make evident the high number of dismissals. Such pressure is detrimental to the image of the prosecutor's office, and to avoid a high dismissal rate, the prosecutor makes a deal with the defense attorney to reduce the charges against the defendant in return for a guilty plea. Inherent in this "deal" is an assumption held by both prosecution and defense that the defendant is guilty of some crime (Sudnow, 1965). A trial is avoided, thereby saving the attorneys time: the prosecutor gets a conviction, and the defense attorney gets his client off with less punishment than the law prescribes for the crime with which the defendant was originally charged.

The goals of the courts, officially to ensure due process, justice, and the rule of law, have been displaced by bureaucratic administrative goals based on maximum production and career enhancement. Concern over backlogs on the court calendar, crowding in the jails produced by those awaiting trial, and pressure to have "justice" done has led to an assembly line production in the criminal courts (Packer, 1968). There is a direct conflict between the police goals of apprehending criminals and the court's goals of clearing the calendar, for it is the volume of arrests that leads to the court backlog.

Finally, the correction system must process those referred to them by the courts. Correctional administrators' main concerns are controlling those who have been sentenced and maintaining them until their time is served. This too is handled with bureaucratic dispatch, with an eye to minimizing costs and conflicts. Rehabilitation programs are minimal since correction agencies are largely concerned with maintaining control over their charges. Thus, the organizational problems of correction agencies supercede the larger ideal goals of the system.

THE AGENCIES AND PROCEDURES IN THE CRIMINAL JUSTICE SYSTEM

Now that we have a general overview of the criminal justice system and an understanding of some of its problems, we can look at each of the agencies in the system as a separate organization and explore its *actual* as opposed to its ideal procedures.

When the system is examined in this way, many of its problems can be seen to be specific to the individual organizations. Later, the specific problems within the individual agencies will be related to the context of society as a whole.

The Police

The police mandate is a dual one: to enforce the law and maintain order (Bittner, 1969:170). Law enforcement involves crime prevention, crime detection, and apprehension of criminals; maintenance of order refers to the settlement of disputes among citizens who accuse one another of being at fault (Manning, 1971: 151) and control over personal disorder—such as is created by drunks and the like, public disorder or riots—and structural disorder such as in traffic jams (Stinchcombe, 1963). The means for enforcing the law and maintaining order are those that exist within the framework of "due process" and protection of individual rights (Manning, 1971:159).

COERCIVE FORCE Underlying all police authority is nonnegotiable coercive force (Bittner, 1970:36–47). Manifested in guns, clubs, handcuffs, and chemical sprays, police force is the most immediate and visible. However, the police rarely use these weapons, and when they do, as is the case with handcuffs, it is not so much to subdue a resisting suspect as it is to satisfy departmental policy requirements. Police force exists mainly as a potential threat backing up the institution's power to carry out its mandated duties.

The extent to which coercive force is used documents the unwillingness of a people to be governed (Goode, 1972:

507–508). As the use of weapons increases, the willingness of the people to submit to police authority, more or less voluntarily, decreases. During the 1960s and early 1970s when the urban ghettos exploded in riots and students engaged in violent demonstrations to end the war in Vietnam, police arsenals grew. For example, after the Detroit riot in 1967, the Detroit police department ordered an improved arsenal that included 100 Stoner machine guns (Joyce, 1971). A person struck by a bullet from a Stoner will literally be ripped apart by the small calibre projectile, which tumbles while in flight and upon impact.

Such a purchase of weapons is more indicative of the fear of danger than of what routine law enforcement and order maintenance actually entails. The danger is both real and imagined, for, on the one hand, policemen do confront suspects who use and carry weapons, as was dramatically illustrated in the shoot-out between the Los Angeles police and members of the Symbionese Liberation Army. Most policemen, however, retire without ever having to shoot their guns at suspects.

Occupationally, the death rate for police personnel is 33 per 100,000 (Robin, 1963), significantly higher than the homicide rate for the population as a whole which stands at 5.1 per 100,000 (President's Commission, 1967a:21). However, the death rate for police includes accidents, and not all policemen who are killed in the line of duty are murdered. Furthermore, the number of suspects killed by police is six times greater than the number of police killed, making the criminal's occupation a good deal riskier.

Compared to other occupations, police work is relatively safe. Miners are killed at a rate of 94 per 100,000; agriculture workers at a rate of 55; construction workers at a rate of 76; and transportation workers at a rate of 44 (Manning, 1971:158). However, when police are killed by felons, or by others who resist police force, their deaths are not "accidents." The danger that occasionally occurs in police work is generalized and magnified to include more than is ordinarily considered reason for alarm (cf. Goffman, 1971).

In their training, police recruits are told to be ever alert, for even though their daily routine may not necessarily involve danger, they must be ready for it at all times (Harris, 1973). Continual alertness prepares the police for situations in which they will have to employ their weapons and skills in self-defense; however, it may lead them to use force where no actual danger exists. A toy gun may be seen by a policeman as the real thing, with the possible result that the officer kills innocent citizens. By the same token, a routine traffic stop may produce a dead police officer who did not take precautions in approaching the car.

The potential for danger is thus seen to be everywhere in police work, and mistakes in the assessment of a situation are often fateful (Goffman, 1967). If it were merely a matter of knowing when a situation would be dangerous or safe, there would be little problem in the use of coercive force; but this is not the case, and it is inevitable that on many occasions too little or too much force will be employed by the police.

The extent to which the police use excessive or undue force has been examined in numerous studies. William Westley (1953) found that police employed violence on those who were perceived as a threat to police authority, and in turn, this threat was a challenge to their masculinity (Harris 1973:92). Westley pointed out that when the police encountered what they considered to be disrespect, they would harass the person until he or she said or did something that could be construed as resisting arrest. Then they would proceed to "subdue" the suspect. In this context, police violence stems from "character contests" (Goffman, 1967) rather than from law enforcement, and instead of being legally warranted is culturally prescribed for handling character challenges (cf. Miller 1958).

The evidence supporting the contention that police use force unnecessarily when their authority is challenged is mixed. Albert Reiss (1970) found that in 3826 observed encounters with citizens, there were 37 incidents where police used excessive force. Reiss used explicit criteria for excessive force. Included were physical assault without arrest; the use of force against mere verbal resistance or where an assault was unnecessary; situations in which a large number of other police were available for nonviolent subduing tactics; the use of force persisting after the suspect had been subdued and handcuffed. In 39 percent of the cases where such force was used, there was an "open defiance" to police authority, and in 9 percent the suspects resisted arrest (Reiss 1970:79).

While this tends to confirm the hypothesis that police use excessive force when their authority is challenged, it does not show that whenever there is open defiance or antagonism towards police excessive force is employed. In another observational study by Reiss (1971: 142), in 13,939 encounters between police and citizens, the citizens acted antagonistically in 1149 cases. However, in only 3 in 1000 cases did the police use excessive force (Reiss, 1971:142). Thus, while there was a threat to police authority in 10 percent of the encounters between police and citizens, in only 0.3 percent of the cases did the police employ violence. If Westley and Harris are correct in their assessment of why police employ undue force, it is surprising that so little use of force was observed in encounters between police and citizens who failed to respect police authority. In Reiss' study, force may not have been used because observers accompanied the police, and although it would seem unlikely that the police would use unnecessary brutality *at all* in front of observers, in almost forty incidents they did; therefore, we cannot say that the little brutality that was observed was any more or less than normal.

Racism has been cited as a cause of police brutality. This may be the case with individual police officers, but in looking at patterns, Reiss (1970:73) found that in 4604 encounters with whites, police used excessive force in 27 situations, and in 5960 encounters with blacks, 17 cases resulted in excessive force. That is, whites were twice as likely to be subjected to excessive force. Moreover, it was more likely that a black citizen would be subjected to excessive force by a black policeman. In 71 percent of the cases where black policemen used excessive force, the victim was black, and in 67 percent of the cases where white policemen used excessive force, the victim was white (Reiss, 1970:75). It is true that in Reiss' study black policemen were more likely to police black areas and therefore were more likely to encounter blacks; however, since

the majority of the police were white, they had ample opportunity to encounter blacks, especially given the ecological distribution of crime and criminal suspects.

The use of coercive force by the police can be considered legitimate only so long as it is used where legally sanctioned. The extent to which police engage in brutality reflects the degree to which they are out of control, either in terms of institutional goals and values or departmental regulations. If the police control the civil population, we need to know who controls the police.

WHO CONTROLS THE POLICE?   As long as the police use their coercive force in the manner intended by the government, the problems that occur cannot be blamed on the police; rather, they must be blamed on the legislature and the courts, who provide the guidelines for employing coercive force. However, if the police employ their power in a way not intended by the government, then the responsibility belongs to the police. The problem is, "Who controls the police?"

If a person is arrested for murder, and the police take that person into the back room of the police station and beat a confession out of him, there is a good chance that the person will go free. On the other hand, if the police advise the same suspect of his rights to remain silent and to have an attorney present, and the suspect elects to do so, the police may have a good deal of work to do in order to gather the evidence needed for a conviction. Assuming that the suspect is guilty, the first route saves time and effort, but if the suspect goes free, the police have failed in their mission. Therefore, the advising the suspect of his rights is preferable since only in this way can a conviction hold. In the first instance the suspect would go free because the police did not follow the Supreme Court's decision in the case *Miranda vs. Arizona*, which provided that a suspect must be advised of the rights guaranteed him by the Constitution. By nullifying police work that does not conform with the Miranda decision and with other case rulings handed down by the judiciary, the courts are able indirectly to control police behavior (Packer, 1970:465). Such an approach to control of the police only applies to cases that are brought to the attention of the courts. If the police decide to harass various groups without the intention or hope of conviction, court decisions have no impact and no control; additionally, there are no sanctions brought directly against the police for their misconduct.

A citizen review board representative of the community provides another means of control. However, even though such review boards would constitute a more direct form of control through scrutiny of all complaints against the police, they lack the consistency provided by case law. A "law and order" board may allow the police free reign, while another may restrict the police to the point that they are rendered ineffective. Decisions would be made on an ad hoc basis and, unlike the specificity provided in the various legal codes, the regulation patterns of citizen review boards change with their composition. Reliance on such boards would be like reliance on legislatures that change without providing laws that continue over from one group of legislators to the next.

Most police departments prefer to control the police by means of self-policing units. These units, "Internal Affairs Divisions," are designed to seek out and eliminate crooked cops. However, while it is admittedly important for police departments to have such units, they are not the most effective devices for dealing with the broader spectrum of illegal police conduct. A policeman who neglects his duty or who accepts bribes is bound to reduce departmental efficiency in terms of the number of arrests produced by the department. But a policeman who is somewhat inventive in circumventing citizens' rights and making arrests may enhance the department's image, especially in cases involving "dangerous felons." Policemen well understand what it is to lose a case because of legal "technicalities" which typically involve rights that are due every citizen. Generally, the loss of such a case is taken by internal affairs as indicative not of police illegality, but rather of legal technicality and, therefore, out of their jurisdiction. Since the men who make up the internal affairs divisions themselves "understand" these problems of "due process" that confront the police, they are sympathetic with the arresting officer and not with the person who "got off on a technicality." Complaints of illegal police behavior, other than outright corruption, are unlikely to be heard sympathetically. If citizen's boards are unstable, internal affairs divisions are less than open-minded in their attempts to control police behavior.

THE POLICEMAN AS SOLDIER-BUREAU-CRAT Organizationally, police departments have a tradition of being difficult to control (Rubinstein, 1973:12–25). As managers of social control agencies in a democratic society, police administrators need to control their officers so that they do not trample citizens rights, but at the same time, they want to make sure that these officers are doing the work—enforcing the law.

Egon Bittner (1970) characterizes the role of the policeman in terms of the exigencies of police work, calling him a "soldier-bureaucrat." On the one hand, the police have a quasimilitary function in their use of force, while on the other hand, they must operate within a bureaucratic framework. The trappings of the soldier are evident in the uniform and weapons, but far more pervasive if less visible is the massive amount of paperwork required in modern policework. Indeed, when questioned as to their biggest problem, police complained not of citizen disrespect, low pay, or Supreme Court decisions making their work more difficult, but of the amount of paperwork that had to be completed by the average police officer (Sanders, 1974).

The role of the soldier-bureaucrat began with attempts to transform police departments from slovenly collections of corrupt and lazy policemen to highly efficient organizations of professional law enforcement officers. By introducing quasimilitary organization and discipline, it was hoped that the police officers would be efficient as well as controlled (Bittner, 1970:53). This "professionalization" had the immediate effect of changing the image of the cop on the beat from that of a slow-witted lout whose ambitions were linked to political favors to that of a spiffy figure who appeared the model of efficiency. The old "watchman" style of organization, based on political patronage and an order-maintenance mentality was replaced by "legalistic" organizations that were geared to specialization, with rewards based on merit (measured in arrest rates) and with a law enforcement

orientation (Wilson, 1968). However, the rewards were geared to good performance *inside* the department, not *outside* where the routine work was situated (Bittner, 1970:54–55). Officers were evaluated by the number of arrests and traffic tickets and not in terms of keeping the peace and stopping crime. Ironically, if an officer were successful in reducing crime, he would joepardize his ability to make arrests and thereby satisfy departmental criteria.

The paperwork load on the police grew in response to two organizational pressures. First, by laboriously writing down everything they did, the police officer's rendered their activities accessible to monitoring by superiors. In this way police activities could be controlled. However, if no arrest is made, no report need be written; hence, other devices for "handling the situation" are often seen to be preferable to making an arrest that would entail massive report writing. But since the efficiency of officers is measured in terms of the arrests they make, they have to do the paperwork if they hope to get ahead.

Secondly, paperwork serves an investigative purpose. Detectives rely on the initial report from patrol in order to investigate a crime (Sanders and Daudistel, 1974:172). Initially, there is no way to predict whether a report might be informative (Sanders, 1974). A patrol report could prove helpful in an investigation, but in most situations it is of little use except to note that further investigation was futile. As a result, reports have to be written even though they generally end up filed away and forgotten.

Not only is the police officer required to write a report on almost everything he does, from transporting a prisoner to finding a homicide victim, he is required to write a report that shows his actions to be in accord with the law. The "law" is generally interpreted to be what the prosecutor would accept as a legally executed action. Where illegal actions occur it is possible to omit them from the report or to take the more drastic step of lying in the report. For example, most felony arrests are made on the basis of "probable cause" (LaFave, 1965), which means that the police officer must show that he has good reason for suspecting a defendant to have committed a felony. If an officer is walking by an open door and he sees a bag of heroin in the house, he has "probable cause" to make an arrest. But if a policeman breaks into a house without a search warrant and then finds the heroin, any arrest is illegal and would be thrown out of court. In a recent article (*Time*, February, 4, 1974), it was reported that a number of arrests had been made on the basis of bags of heroin being "in plain view" through open doorways. Of course, it is highly improbable that heroin dealers or users would leave their doors open with heroin "in plain view." Rather, it appears that the police falsified reports and testimony. Even though false testimony about actual innocence or guilt is rare, a result is that police credibility among judges and juries has been seriously hurt.

POLICE DISCRETION If a police officer witnesses a misdemeanor, he can choose to make an arrest or not. If he has probable cause to believe that a felony has been committed and knows who committed it, or if he witnesses a felony, he again has the decision whether or not to make an arrest. This power to decide whether or not to enforce the law in situations that are viewed as being un-

equivocally illegal is the power of police discretion. There are only vague guidelines covering police actions in regard to whether or not the law should be invoked (LaFave, 1965), and other than various civil actions that can be taken against them for not enforcing the law, there is little that can be done to assert control over the police.

It is important to understand the processes involved in situations of police discretion, for the decision to make an arrest sets in motion the mechanisms of the criminal justice system. The decision to arrest occurs typically in situations where the law has been broken, for the police are rarely accused of making arrests where no crime has been committed. Rather, since violation of the law is supposed to be the sole basis for an arrest, the concern is that other considerations enter into situations where the police must make such a decision.

Numerous studies have been made of police discretion, but two of the most important concern police who had contact with juveniles. Although police have some discretion in their treatment of adults, they have far greater leeway in their handling of juveniles. The greater number of alternatives available to police in dealing with juveniles make such encounters a rich source of data.

A study by Irving Piliavin and Scott Briar (1964) found that beyond the seriousness of the crime, whether or not the police would arrest a juvenile depended largely on the youth's demeanor. Juveniles who were uncooperative with the police in discretion situations were seven times more likely to be arrested than were juveniles who were cooperative. Juveniles who showed remorse, appeared "clean cut," and generally presented themselves as respectful to the police were likely to be merely warned or given an informal reprimand, while those who acted "tough," had greasy hair, and displayed their contempt for the police received the more serious dispositions, such as detention. Thus, instead of basing their decisions on the offense, the police made decisions on the basis of the youth's personal characteristics.

In contrast with the Piliavin and Briar study, a more recent study by Black and Reiss (1970) found that even though there were variations in demeanor of juvenile suspects, there was a weak relationship between a youth's actions after the crime and the severity of the sanctions he received. They found that arrests were highest for antagonistic suspects and ones who were very deferential and lowest for those who were civil (1970: 75). These were all nonfelony situations.

Often, the police encounter with a juvenile is occasioned by a complaint from an adult about the youth's behavior. When the researchers examined the complainant's preference for an arrest, they found a more dramatic relationship. In those situations where the complainant and suspect were both present, the police would generally go along with the complainant's wishes. In no cases where the complainant preferred an informal disposition (for example, warning by police) did the police make an arrest. Moreover, the researchers found that blacks were more likely than whites to demand that an arrest be made—21 percent versus 15 percent (Black and Reiss, 1970:71). While the demeanor of a suspect may thus play some small part in juvenile arrests, the desire of the complainant is far more influential in the police officer's decision making.

Another variable studied in police discretion was the organizational style of the police department. James Wilson (1968) found that the form of the organization and departmental policy determined the extent to which police used the arrest as a means of handling a situation. In the "watch-man" style organizations, most situations are handled as order maintenance instead of law enforcement problems. If the officer can handle the situation without making an arrest, he will do so since it involves less effort, and there is little incentive to work hard. Therefore, fewer arrests are made where "watchman" style policies are in effect. At the other extreme are "legalistic" styles of organization which place the emphasis on technical efficiency as measured in numbers of arrests. Commonplace situations are treated as law enforcement problems; therefore, arrests are more likely to be used to handle problematic situations. Finally, some organizations have a "service" style. These organizations are most commonly found in communities with a high consensus of values, and where the police administrators are very concerned with their public image. The police in service-style organizations respond to all types of calls for order maintenance and law enforcement but are more likely to handle a situation without making an arrest. The police in such departments are expected to exercise their discretion not in terms of the law, but in terms of the community views.

OCCUPATIONAL CULTURE OF THE POLICE
In order to understand police actions, it is necessary to understand their world view, to catch a glimpse of the world as they see it, the problems of their work, and the kinds of situations that policemen routinely encounter. Police work generates distinctive experiences to those

involved, and collectively, police develop a set of beliefs that articulate these experiences.

The first thing that must be understood is that virtually every police organization is designed to handle unpleasant situations. Police officers are forced by the structure of their work into encountering misery. When a child drowns in the family swimming pool, a police officer will be forced to witness parents anguished over their child's death. When someone has been the victim of a crime, a police officer must encounter the victim. Any and all types of trouble are relayed to the police, and members of the police department come to see and experience these problems much more frequently than the average person.

Additionally, there is the possibility of intentionally inflicted physical danger in their job. They cannot, like the rest of us, organize their lives to minimize contact with the ugly and saddening aspect of life, for their experience is structured in accordance with their duty to seek out and neutralize the bad. There is no reason to "call the cops" when everything is working out as people wish; only when things go wrong are the police summoned.

As a result of, and in response to, the experiences police encounter in their occupations, they come to have certain assumptions about the nature of the social world. Peter Manning (1971:156) outlines the following postulates that are prompted by the occupational culture of the police:

1. People cannot be trusted: they are dangerous.
2. Experience is better than abstract rules.
3. You must make people respect you.
4. Everyone hates a cop.
5. The legal system is untrustworthy; policemen make the best decisions about guilt or innocence.
6. People who are not controlled will break laws.
7. Policemen must appear respectable and be efficient.
8. Policemen can most accurately identify crime and criminals.
9. The major jobs of the policeman are to prevent crimes and to enforce the laws.
10. Stronger punishment will deter criminals from repeating their errors.

These assumptions about the social world are not independent of the police officer's experience. They articulate what happens in the everyday world of police activity, and in so doing provide the police with a way to understand the events and people they encounter. Experiences thus interpreted by these prior assumptions are then used to document the validity of the police perspective on events. We can see an intimate and circular relationship between the police officer's way of looking at things and his actual experience.

We can characterize this viewpoint as "police cynicism" (Niederhoffer, 1967: 98–108) and think of it as an occupational attitude. The extent to which cynicism influences police actions is difficult to measure when we isolate it from the occasions on which it serves to color a police officer's view of people and situations. Ideally, the criminal justice system in a democratic society holds that all persons are innocent until proven guilty, and that the police officer's role is not to make judgments as to innocence or guilt, but rather to act as a "fact gatherer." Because police are guided by a set of assumptions that contradict these ideals, that is, by occupational cynicism, the administration of justice *in fact* is something other than what it is meant to be. This is not to say that the police corrupt the ideals, but rather that the social situation is structured to defeat that ideal.

To illustrate this further, consider the earlier point about the character of encounters between the police and the public. Police must face all of the ill will humans visit upon one another. The victim of an assault is found unconscious, bleeding, and with his front teeth knocked out. The police are called and they pick up a suspect whom they believe is responsible. When the victim regains consciousness, he identifies the suspect as his assailant. Before the identification, the suspect had proclaimed his innocence and protested that the police are harassing him; however, when he is identified by the victim, the suspect changes his story and says that the victim started the fight. Such incidents are used as a basis on which to interpret future protestations of innocence or any other accounts offered by suspects to show themselves in a favorable light. Instead of suspending assumptions about innocence or guilt until the time of trial, the police learn to operate on the assumption of guilt. Their cynicism articulates their experiences, and their experiences fortify such cynicism.

Once the police have made an arrest, the suspect (now called the "defendant") is turned over to the judicial process. The police distrust lawyers and the court system in general, and except for attempting to stay on good terms with the prosecutor's office and supplying him the necessary evidence to obtain a conviction, the police have little influence on what happens after they have made an arrest.

Prosecution and Defense

The prosecution and defense ideally represent the "adversaries" in the criminal justice system which is intended to further the democratic ideal of equal treatment. Representing the "people" is the prosecutor. He is usually a deputy district attorney (DA), and he decides whether a suspect who has been arrested should be prosecuted. On the other side, representing the person who has been arrested, is the defense attorney. Defense counsels are of three types: (1) the private attorney retained by the defendant; (2) the court appointed attorney whom the court pays to represent the defendant; and (3) the public defender who is a full-time employee of the court. The provision of a defense attorney for the accused is intended to safeguard the defendant from being convicted because of his unfamiliarity with the law and legal procedures.

Under the adversary concept, the prosecution and defense are joined in combat over the question of the defendant's guilt. Such conflict is the subject matter of numerous television series, movies, and books. While occasionally a courtroom drama will take place that resembles these fictional accounts, it is the exception rather than the rule. What little conflict there is between prosecution and defense attorneys is for the benefit of the audience in court. The prosecutor puts on a show to demonstrate that the district attorney is "cracking down" on crime, and the defense attorney demonstrates that the money his client invested is being earned (cf. Goffman, 1959).

The extent to which the adversary system lacks substance documents the erosion of democratic values, and points to both the problems of perfunctory judicial process and unequal treatment. Not even operational justice is realized as the two sides go through ritualized motions. Furthermore, if neither the defense nor the prosecution are willing to go through the adversary procedure, except in unusual cases, only those who can afford to stir up public notice will be likely to receive the full benefit of the available adversary roles. By examining the structure of the relationship between the prosecution and the defense in the context of the courthouse bureaucracy, we can explore the root of the problem.

THE BEST OF ADVERSARIES A popular characterization of what typically takes place between prosecution and defense is "bargain justice" (President's Commission, 1967a:9–12). This model pictures the defense attorney making a deal with the prosecutor. He agrees to have his client plead guilty if the prosecutor will reduce the charges. They barter over the terms of the agreement with each side trying to get the better of the bargain. The defense is pitted *against* prosecution in the role of an opponent; thus, to speak of "bargain justice" still preserves the sense of an adversary system.

A more accurate characterization of the relationship is that of two bureaucrats who must meet certain production demands while at the same time maintaining some quality control. The production demands are generated by the police, who bring in any number of people who must be processed through the system. Quality control alludes to the problem of having to see that defendants "get what they have coming to them" or "get what they deserve" (Sudnow, 1965). If a defendant gets "too much" for his crime or "too little," there is a failure in quality control; therefore, the prosecutor and the defense attorney operate within a framework of tacit agreements as to what a crime, under various conditions, is

"worth." For example, a first degree burglary may be "worth" a charge of "petty theft" for a first-time offender, but for a repeated offender, first-degree burglary may be "worth" second-degree burglary, which carries stiffer penalties.

Moreover, the "worth" of a case is settled between the prosecution and defense attorneys, and not between the prosecutor and the defendant. If the defendant wants to bypass the defense attorney simply by entering a plea of guilty, he will not receive the same treatment received by a defendant who is represented by an attorney. An unrepresented defendant is more likely to receive the penalty prescribed by law for the offense to which he enters a plea of guilty, while a represented defendant, charged with the same crime under the same circumstances, will probably receive less than the crime's "worth"[1] as established between prosecution and defense.

We can better understand the operation of defense and prosecution in the criminal justice system by viewing their work in terms of a bureaucratic model (Blumberg, 1967). Instead of being adversaries, they are cooperating bureaucrats who must get their job done in what they take to be an efficient and effective fashion. Jury trials are slow and costly and they slow down production. By establishing a case's "worth," the cooperating attorneys save additional time that might have been spent quibbling over what penalty a defendant should receive. However, the criminal justice process was not designed to be bureaucratically efficient, and makeshift efficiency has been achieved at the expense of due process.

---

[1] This term was used by an assistant district attorney in the seminar of Donald R. Cressey, Spring 1973.

PROFIT AND JUSTICE As in any other business transaction, private defense attorneys are expected to render services for fees paid. In the best tradition of the free enterprise system, there is the belief that "you get what you pay for." While it is generally assumed that those who pay for private attorneys "get more" than those who are represented by public defenders, value received may not be a function of the private attorney's skills but rather of the characteristics of the clients. A number of studies have shown that clients who are able to make bail and better able to afford private attorneys are more successful in "getting off" (Skolnick, 1970:421) than those who cannot afford bail. Moreover, the very wealthy (for example, those involved in organized and white-collar crime) can better protect themselves with a battalion of lawyers than can the poor, who are typically represented by public defenders. The "deal" of unsupervised probation given former Vice President Agnew not only points to the value of highly skilled private attorneys, but also it shows that clients who have high status and the characteristics which accompany those in high positions receive more lenient justice. However, because persons of wealth rarely are charged with crimes, we will consider the financial transaction between the more typical and less affluent criminal defendant and the private attorney.

Abraham Blumberg (1967:110–115) describes the financial relationship between private attorneys and their clients as a "confidence game" in which the attorney is the con man and the client is the mark. In other words, the lawyer somehow cheats his client as a routine practice. In exchange for a sum of $500 to $1500, the defendant "gets" to enter a plea of guilty to a lesser charge than the one of which he is accused (Blumberg, 1967:112). Compared with what a defendant who uses the services of a public defender "gets" for pleading guilty (Skolnick, 1970:414–423), the client of the private attorney is indeed fleeced. As was pointed out earlier, there is a going "rate" or "worth" that is established between the defense and prosecution attorneys, and whether the defense attorney is public or private, the "worth" is the same. Therefore, if a client pays a private attorney for the same "justice" he could have had for nothing, he has been "conned." If, on the other hand, there are courts where a better bargain can be had by a private attorney, then, "justice" can be bought. Either way, the arrangements between the prosecutor and defense attorney suggest that no justice is being done.

THE PRESSURE TO PLEAD GUILTY A guilty defendant who pleads guilty to receive a lesser sentence than he deserves gets a better deal than an innocent defendant. An innocent person faces pressure to make a deal and plead guilty in the interest of saving time and avoiding possible incarceration. If the sentence is probation or a small fine, the innocent defendant will be told that even though he is innocent, it may be better to plead guilty and "get it over with" than to chance a trial that may result in a conviction. Even if his attorney believes him to be innocent, legal fees may amount to more than the fine; thus, financially, the defendant is often better off to plead guilty and keep his legal expenses at a minimum. Because of the fee structure of private attorneys and the typical course of action that is taken jointly by the prosecution and the defense, in the system that was designed above all to protect the rights and welfare of the innocent, it is precisely the innocent who are least protected and most vulnerable.

The commonsense understanding of "defense" portrays an attorney shielding his client against a torrent of accusations; however, a closer examination of the role of the defense attorney shows that he serves to oil the gears of the criminal justice system. He prepares the defendant to move through the system with the least inconvenience to the court organization, including his adversary, the prosecutor. To expedite the procedures of the system, it has been shown that a plea of guilty is the most "practical" course of action for everyone except the innocent. This necessitates that the defense attorney assume his client to be guilty in most cases and operate on that assumption.

The percentage of cases that are handled by a plea of guilty has steadily increased as plea bargaining has become more popular. The 1967 President's Task Force on the courts show that the majority of cases resulting in a conviction are based on a guilty plea (President's Commission, 1967b:9). The main source of pressure to plead guilty is not the prosecutor's office, as would be expected under an adversary system, but from the defense attorney. For example, Blumberg (1967:92) found that in over half of the cases, the defense counsel was most influential and most likely to make the initial suggestion of a guilty plea (see Table 1).

Table 2 shows that the "privately retained" attorney, whom the defendant must pay, waits until the later stages of contact before suggesting a guilty plea. Blumberg points out that by waiting, the private attorney keeps his client in a stage of agitation and is better able to collect his fees. In effect, the attorney "cons" his client into believing that a great deal of legal work is being accomplished and that the counsel is making important contacts in the courthouse on behalf of his client (Blumberg, 1967:110–115).

Table 1. Source of First Suggestion to Plead Guilty

Person or Official	First Suggested Guilty Plea		Most influence in decision to plead guilty	
Judge	4	(0.6%)	26	(3.6%)
District Attorney	67	(9.3%)	116	(16.0%)
Defense Counsel	407	(56.2%)	411	(56.7%)
Probation Officer	14	(1.9%)	3	(0.4%)
Psychiatrist	8	(1.1%)	1	(0.1%)
Relative (Wife)	34	(4.7%)	120	(16.6%)
Friends and Other Relatives	21	(2.9%)	14	(1.9%)
Police	14	(1.9%)	4	(0.6%)
Fellow Inmates	119	(16.4%)	14	(1.9%)
Others	28	(3.9%)	5	(0.7%)
"No Response"	8	(1.1%)	10	(1.4%)
TOTAL	724	100.0%	724	99.9% *

* Rounded to nearest tenth

Source: From *Criminal Justice,* Copyright 1967 by Abraham S. Blumberg, by permission of the Publishers, Franklin Watts, Inc.

Table 2. Type of Counsel, Stage of Contact, and Suggestion to Plead Guilty

Stage of Contact	Privately retained		Counsel Type Legal aid		Assigned	
First	66	(34.7%)	237	(48.6%)	28	(59.6%)
Second	83	(43.7%)	142	(29.1%)	8	(17.0%)
Third	29	(15.3%)	63	(12.9%)	4	(8.5%)
Fourth or more	12	(6.3%)	31	(6.4%)	5	(10.6%)
"No Response"	0	(0.0%)	14	(2.9%)	2	(4.3%)
TOTAL	190	100.0%	487	99.9% *	47	100.0%

* Rounded to the nearest tenth.

Source: From *Criminal Justice*, p. 93, Copyright 1967 by Abraham S. Blumberg, by permission of the Publishers, Franklin Watts, Inc.

The private attorney who immediately suggests a guilty plea has less time to "perform" for his client and to collect his fees.

The Courts

When we think of courtroom activities, we are likely to envision the dignified proceedings popularized in television dramas. In some courtrooms, this is certainly the case; however, in the lower courts, which handle all misdemeanors, "petty offenses," and the initial phases of felony cases, dignity and due process are the exception rather than the rule. As the President's Commission pointed out:

The Commission has been shocked by what it has seen in some lower courts. It has seen cramped and noisy courtrooms, undignified and perfunctory procedures, and badly trained personnel. It has seen dedicated people who are frustrated by huge caseloads, by the lack of opportunity to examine cases carefully, and by the impossibility of devising constructive solutions to the problems of offenders. It has seen assembly line justice. (1967a:128)

Under these conditions, "justice" becomes a random event. If a person receives justice in the sense of due process, it is not because the situation fosters justice, but because that person was lucky. Some situations that are typical of our lower courts and that constitute a parade of delayed justice or a high-speed assembly line will be discussed in the next section of this unit.

PRETRIAL DETENTION AND COURT BACKLOG Before an accused citizen is tried for the crimes he has been charged with, there is a period of delay. The delay between arrest and release, or conviction and sentencing, is less than 25 hours for over half of the defendants brought before a police or magistrate's court (President's Commission, 1967a:131). However, for the others, final disposition takes days, weeks, and even months.

If an individual cannot pay the bail or bond, he must remain in jail. Thus, many who have not been convicted of a crime serve time in jail. If these people are found innocent of the crimes with which they have been charged, their "jail sentences" have been served unjustly. In some cases, it is possible to serve more time in jail awaiting trial than would be required were the defendant convicted of the crime. Those who must wait in jail are most likely to be the poor who cannot afford bond or bail. The bail system works in the following way. A defendant comes before the judge who sets the bail at a given rate. For a fee of roughly 10 percent (but sometimes as high as 20 percent) of the bail, a defendant can pay a bondsman to post bail (President's Commission, 1967a:37). If the defendant can afford the entire bail, he will be refunded that amount when he shows up for trial. On the other hand, if the defendant uses a bondsman, he will be charged the percentage of the bail taken by the bondsman. Thus, if bail is set at $1500 and the bond is 10 percent, the defendant pays $150 he will never see again. It does not matter if he is innocent or guilty.

Bail amounts vary from place to place. In New York, for example, it was found that 25 percent of the defendants were unable to pay a bail of $500, 45 percent failed at $1500, and 63 percent could not pay a bail of $2500 (President's Commission, 1967a:37). When we examine the percentage of those who could afford bail, we can see that the ability to pay bail is determined by where one is arrested (See Table 3).

In locations where a high percentage of people are unable to make bail, it is probable that bails are excessive. Since the disadvantaged are the most likely to be charged with crimes in any location, cities and counties with a low percentage of defendants unable to make bail approach justice, while those with the highest percentage are the least just. This point was made by President Lyndon Johnson when he signed the Bail Reform Act of 1966.

The defendant with means can afford to pay bail. He can afford to buy his freedom. But the poorer defendant cannot pay the price. He languishes in jail for weeks, months and perhaps even years before trial.

Table 3. Percentage of Felony Defendants Able to Post Bail by Jurisdiction

	Felony defendant unable to make bail
Large Counties:	
Cook (Chicago)	75%
Hennepin (Minneapolis)	71%
Jefferson (Louisville)	30%
Philadelphia	14%
Small Counties	
Brown, Kansas	93%
Rutland, Vermont	83%
Putnam, Missouri	36%
Anchorage, Alaska	28%
Catoosa, Georgia	6%

Source: President's Commission, *Task Force Report: The Courts* (U.S. Government Printing Office, 1967b), p. 37.

He does not stay in jail because he is guilty. He does not stay in jail because any sentence has been passed.

He does not stay in jail because he is any more likely to flee before trial. He stays in jail for one reason—because he is poor.

There are hundreds, perhaps thousands, of illustrations of how the bail system has inflicted arbitrary cruelty: A man was jailed on a serious charge brought last Christmas Eve. He could not afford bail and spent 101 days in jail until a hearing. Then the complainant admitted the charge was false.

A man could not raise $300 bail. He spent 54 days in jail waiting trial for a traffic offense, for which he could have been sentenced to no more than five days.

A man spent two months in jail before being acquitted. In that period he lost his job, and his car, and his family was split up. He did not find another job for four months. (Johnson, 1966)

The logic of bail is simple if not simple-minded. If a defendant pays a certain sum of money to the court, he is more likely to return to court so that he will not lose his money. If the bail were proportionate to the income of the accused, there would be some validity to the logic of bail, but since it is set in relation to the crime charged and not to the defendant's ability to pay, it favors rich over the poor, and the system lacks reason from the standpoint of equal justice. Where "O.R." (own recognizance) release exists, this inequality is banished, for no bail money is necessary for release before trial. O.R. will be discussed later as a possible solution to the problem of judicial inequities.

ASSEMBLY LINE JUSTICE In order to clear up the court backlog the judicial process must be quick. The longer courts take to try cases, the longer the accused must wait in jail. One way to proceed is to take shortcuts by means of such strategies as plea and sentence bargaining. This reduces the number of jury and judge trials, and even if the defendant is convicted, he can begin serving his sentence without doing "dead time" (time that does not count toward serving a sentence) in a county jail. The other route to quick disposition is to have more courts and judges available to handle the increase in cases. So far, the former method has been adopted, and the results, some of which have been discussed, have led to "justice" on an assembly line.

Herbert Packer (1964:1–68) contrasts two models of the criminal justice system. One is the "due process" model, which Packer characterizes as an obstacle course. The other is the "crime control" model, which resembles an assembly line. The "obstacles" that Packer refers to are the constitutional guarantees to a trial by jury and other safeguards, as well as anything else that gives a defendant every possible chance of exoneration. Packer is not critical of the "obstacles," but he points out that due process was not designed for speedy adjudication. In their attempts to be more efficient in controlling crime, the courts have come to "produce" justice more rapidly at the cost of due process. They have developed an administrative and managerial focus with defendants being smoothly and rapidly processed. The doctrine of *legal* guilt, that is, guilt by legally obtained and presented evidence, has been supplanted by the doctrine of *actual* guilt, or guilt in the eyes of the police. As a result, there is the assumption of guilt until proven innocent. Assuming guilt, the courts can operate quickly by processing guilty pleas; otherwise they must go through the slower process that is involved in adversary decision-making.

DRUNK COURT AS AN ASSEMBLY LINE Under the doctrine of equal justice, all people should receive the same time and consideration in court. However, as is true of so many other "ideals" of the criminal justice system, we find a different reality. The prime example is drunk court, which processes men and women charged with drunkenness and/or disorderly conduct. Since 42.5 percent of all arrests are for drunkenness and disorderly conduct (President's Commission, 1967a:20), the drunk court cannot be taken as an exception; more people are processed through drunk courts than any other.

In Jacqueline Wiseman's (1970:86–105) study of one urban drunk court, it was found that, on the average, the defendant was given 30 seconds for his "day in court." The assembly line metaphor is thus transformed into reality. The courtroom was located on the same floor as the jail, and the defendants were marched from their cells to a holding room adjoining the court. Two lines of men and women were brought into the courtroom and made to stand behind a pipe railing. (Defendants who had paid bail were seated.) As each person's name was called, he or she would move down the line against the railing to the point nearest the judge and enter a plea. The defendants were lined up in such a way that they came up in the order the judge would call, and the line moved like a queue at the movies. As soon as the first of the two lines ended, the second line would move up to the railing, and a new line would be brought in to take the place of those who had moved up. In this way not a moment was lost as the court meted out "justice."

The judges in the court were rotated weekly, and the man who appeared to make the juridical decisions was known to the defendants as the "Knocker" (Wiseman, 1970:95). Since the Knocker was not rotated, he knew more about the defendants than the judges did, and sometimes, when a defendant gave a false name, it was the Knocker who spotted him. He would tell the judge if the defendant previously had been warned by another judge and would generally supply the judge with information about sentencing. As one observer noted,

The Knocker spoke to the judge in just about every case. However, I do not know what he said. He may just be reading to the judge the official records, or he may be giving his personal judgment about the possibility of the defendant being picked up again in the near future. One thing seems clear: the judge receives his information from the Knocker just before he hands out the sentence. (Wiseman, 1970:95)

Thus, in many respects, the judge's presence is ritualistic while the fate of the defendants is determined by the Knocker.

Typically, the first appearance for the drunk court defendant is his last. At that time, formal charges are announced en masse, a plea is entered, and the defendant is sentenced. With rare exceptions, the defendants enter a plea of guilty and hope for the best. If a defendant pleads not guilty, a court date will have to be set and a trial held; however, as one defendant found when he entered a not guilty plea:

The judge told me if I didn't think I was guilty to plead not guilty, which I did. He moved my case ahead 30 days and I spent 30 days in jail, was found guilty and sentenced to 30 days. (Spradley, 1970:181)

Another strategy used by judges to encourage guilty pleas was to dismiss the charges against anyone pleading not guilty, revoke the suspension of a previous sentence, and send the defendant to jail. This worked in most cases since the majority of defendants had recently been arrested on the same charges and had been given suspended sentences. A man with a 30-day suspended sentence risked having his suspension of sentence revoked and serving 30 days in jail for pleading not guilty. Thus, whether a defendant believed himself to be guilty or not, he would plead guilty and hope to receive a suspended sentence.

The drunk court was not only an assembly line, it was also a "guilty court." By a "guilty court" I mean that it was a court where there was not only an assumption of guilt, guilt was taken as a condition of being a defendant in the first place, and there was no chance to introduce proof of innocence. The "fact of guilt" in an adversary model of justice is determined *after* the defense and prosecution have presented their testimony, but in drunk court, the "fact of guilt" was established as soon as an arrest was made. The court served as no more than a sentencing agency. It was, however, a paragon of efficiency, for it could process up to 120 defendants in an hour. The danger of such courts, which already administer "justice" to 42 percent of all defendants, is that as cries for efficiency increase, their assembly line methods may come to be used for all criminal cases.

Corrections

The final organ of the criminal justice system is the correctional system. The correctional system involves three different types of agencies that are geared to correct and punish. First there are those that incarcerate prisoners, generally known as jails or prisons. Jails are used for short-term incarceration, usually less than a year and are situated in local communities under city or county jurisdiction. Prisons, on the other hand, are for longer sentences, and are under either state or federal jurisdiction. New York's Sing Sing prison and California's Folsom and San Quentin prisons are well-known state prisons, and the old federal prison at Alcatraz, which is no longer in use, is the best known federal facility.

The second type of agency is a system of monitoring convicted offenders by local, state, or federal probation officers. The offender is free from incarceration, but he is required to report periodically to his probation officer and meet any requirements that have been set up as conditions of his probation. The third type, the parole board, differs from the probation agency in that it administers and supervises the activities of a person who has been released from prison. All aspects of corrections are designed to provide some form of supervision and control over those convicted of breaking the law, and although the methods differ, the ends are the same.

PRISON RECIDIVISM "Recidivism" refers to the proportion of people who are released from prison that later return. It is a measure of the ability of the prisons to rehabilitate convicts, although other forces that are independent of the prison play a role in recidivism. In a recent evaluation of the success of prison and parole, the California Department of Corrections found that from 1962 through 1969 the rate of recidivism was cut almost in half. Table 4 shows the decrease in recidivism.

The "technical violators" column reflects violations of parole conditions (for example, failure to report to parole officer), and a return for such violations does not necessarily mean that the exconvict had committed any crime. Importantly, slightly less than half returned to prison for committing a new felony. By 1969, about 75 percent were successful after two years of release, and of those returning to prison, only two-fifths were reincarcerated for new felonies.

Another way in which parolees were evaluated by the California Board of Corrections was to keep track of those whose record showed a favorable outcome and those who showed an unfavorable one. The "favorable outcomes" were divided into "clean" records for those who were not found to have engaged in any type of criminal conduct and "other" for those who had gotten into relatively minor trouble. The "unfavorable" records included those who had been returned to

Table 4. Recidivism Rates in California, 1962–1969

Year of Release	Return to Any Prison	With New Felonies	Technical Violators
1962	46.9%	20.1%	26.8%
1963	44.8	15.2	29.6
1964	41.4	15.4	26.0
1965	38.3	14.9	23.4
1966	36.0	14.0	22.0
1967	35.9	11.8	23.1
1968	30.4	11.4	19.0
1969	24.7	10.0	14.7

Source: California Department of Corrections, "Returns to Prison —One Measure," Human Relations Agency, 1972.

prison, had served local jail terms for more than 90 days, and one parolee who had run away for at least six months. Here the picture is not so bright, but it does show some improvement over the years. (See Table 5.)

In the President's Commission *Task Force Report* (1967b:259), the national rate of recidivism was vaguely put at between "one third and two thirds." The "two-thirds" rate of recidivism has been cited frequently as actual, but as Daniel Glaser (1964) has pointed out, the reported high rate reflects poor methodology more than the actual rate of recidivism. Glaser found that only about 31 percent of exconvicts were reimprisoned, and although this figure is lower than what was found in California for the same period, we can assume that the national rate of recidivism stands at about one-third.

Depending on how we view the one-third rate of recidivism, prisons can be seen as greatly successful or as massive flops. If we attribute the success or failure to the prisons alone, incarceration would have to be taken as a failure since it does not function properly a third of the time. However, if we look at the prisons in the context of society, the two-thirds success rate is outstanding. Those who enter prison experience a devastating life, and when they are released, many of the prob-

Table 5. Outcome after Release from Prison

Year of Release	Favorable Outcome Clean	Other	Unfavorable	Pending
1962	22.9%	20.2%	56.9%	—
1963	28.3	17.7	54.0	—
1964	30.3	17.2	52.5	—
1965	27.7	21.6	49.7	1.0
1966	29.2	21.0	48.7	1.1
1967	28.3	21.5	48.3	1.9
1968	29.2	22.9	46.1	1.8
1969	31.4	23.9	42.8	1.9

Source: California Department of Corrections, "Returns to Prison—One Measure," Human Relations Agency, 1972.

lems persist. We shall examine some of the problems encountered by those who have been convicted.

STIGMA, ASSIMILATION, AND OPPORTU- NITY If a conscious attempt were made to devise ways to transform a person into a criminal, no better method could be found than the one used in this country to "rehabilitate" prisoners. First, the person is stigmatized with the criminal label (Becker, 1963; cf. Goffman, 1963) so that he comes to see himself as a criminal. The police would be routinely notified of the person's presence in town so that if any trouble occurred, they could pick the person up and question him. Whenever the person went to look for a job, he would tell his prospective employer that he had been in trouble with the law, and to prevent his lying about this matter, potential employers would be provided with his criminal records. In short, we would have everyone know that the person was a criminal so that they could treat him accordingly. This would insure a continuing criminal identity.

A second major strategy would be to assimilate the person into a criminal subculture (Cohen, 1955) so that he could learn criminal behavior patterns if he did not already know them (Sutherland and Cressey, 1970). Studies of prisons have found that inmates are assimilated into a prison "culture" (Clemmer, 1940). In addition to learning that no cooperation should be given the officials or staff in the prison, the inmates learn that their loyalty should be given to fellow inmates. Thus, the "convict code" (Wieder, 1969) that is fostered in prison communities serves to pull the inmate further out of the law abiding and into the criminal way of life.

Once out of prison, it might be assumed that the exconvict could escape his ties to prison culture. In some instances this may be true, but with the attitudes and skills learned in prison, he is less likely to break with his past than one who was never exposed to the prison world. Moreover, the failure of halfway house projects, where the inmates are gently reintroduced into society was accounted for by both laymen and sociologists as being due to the convict code that operated beyond the prison walls (Wieder, 1974). Thus, even systematic attempts to reassimilate convicts into society can fail because of the strength of prison-fostered assimilation into criminal worldviews.

Third and last, we would want to provide every opportunity for a life of crime and cut off every opportunity for a noncriminal career (Cloward and Ohlin, 1960). If we took care to meet the first two criteria, we would ensure ample opportunity to satisfy the third.

When the recidivism rate of one-third is reexamined, it can be asked: Why did so few of those who were processed through the criminal justice system enter into stable criminal careers? Why didn't more become hardened criminals? Society has provided a system of incarceration and supervision that virtually guarantees criminal behavior, but only a third of those who we attempt to make criminals are successful. What went wrong?

It may be the case that the criminal justice system, taken as a whole, is hiding a good deal of recidivism. Returning to the California Department of Corrections statistics, only 31.4 percent in 1969 had a "clean" record, and even though exconvicts are not reimprisoned, this does not mean that they are leading noncriminal lives. Robison and Takagi (1970:234) point out that the policy of parole departments may influence the violation rate figures more than the actual rate of "technical" violations. That is, if the policy is a "get tough" one, then regardless of parolee behavior, more men on parole will be returned to prison. For instance, between 1960 and 1965 there was an increasing number of unfavorable outcomes for parolees, but during the same period, there was almost a constant rate of parolees who returned to prison for committing new felonies (Robison and Takagi 1970:234). They suggest that since the rate of recidivism for new felonies was the same, it is unlikely that the increase in technical violations could be attributed to characteristics of the inmates on parole. Conversely, if the parole department's policy was oriented to "showing" the success of parole program, we would expect fewer technical violations. If the rates of parolee failure as the result of technical violations and failure as the result of new felonies are compared (see Table 4), it is evident that there was roughly a 33 percent drop in returns because the highest rate of technical violations of new felonies was from 1963 to 1969. There was almost a 50 percent decline in technical violations during that same period. By merely changing departmental policy from "get tough" to "show success," parole can be seen either as more or less effective.

With this discussion of recidivism, the full cycle of the criminal justice system has been completed. At the outset, the police provide as input a criminal suspect to be run through the defense-prosecutor complex, through court, into a holding pattern in corrections, and out as a parolee. We might say that the only thing that the criminal justice system produces as a "system" is a parolee. The goals of the distinct agencies are set more in accord with immediate bureaucratic demands than with such long-range and broad ends as justice or due process. The displacement of goals is the problem, for the ideals of due process are consistent with democratic government, and when the ideals are not met problems occur. In part, this distance between ideal and actual may be a result of the administration of the ideals by means of bureaucratic mechanisms or it may be a distance that is inevitable in mass society.

POSTSCRIPT ON SOLUTIONS

As we have seen, one problem often leads to another, even more difficult problem in the criminal justice system. The public demands law and order creating pressure on the police to enforce the law. Police organization and methods of training are "professionalized" and the number of arrests soar. This brings an overload of defendants to be prosecuted and defended. District attorneys and defense counsels begin expediting the judicial process through bargain justice. Those who will not cooperate by pleading guilty to a crime must wait in jail for their trial, and the jails overflow. This brings pressure on the courts to speed up their trials, which leads to assembly line justice. At the end of the line are the understaffed probation and parole offices and overcrowded, poorly financed prisons. They are expected to "correct" those who have been convicted, but they are only marginally successful, and the cycle starts all over again.

The solutions to these problems are not simple. Moreover, there is considerable disagreement over the approach to take in addressing deficiencies in the criminal justice system. Three perspectives on criminal justice will be considered briefly.

Punitive Perspective

The first approach can be called the "punitive" viewpoint, or, alternatively, the "law and order" perspective. It rests on rather implicit assumptions since its advocates place a heavy emphasis on a fixed but vaguely specified "human nature" which limits the available options in dealing with crime and criminals. A favored stance of politicians and editorial writers, it is probably the most widespread popular notion of how the dilemmas in the criminal justice system (and crime in general) can be handled. The following represents a good example of this perspective:

Remedy: Demand Respect for Law

The remedy is . . . plain. It is simply to insist that our governments, State and federal, reassume and discharge their first duty of protecting the people against lawless invasions of their persons and property and from assaults upon their liberties by demanding and commanding respect for law and legal processes through the impartial, even handed, vigorous, swift and certain enforcement of our criminal laws and the real and substantial punishment there under of all conduct that violates those laws.

These are not platitudes, but are fundamentals and vital, as every thinking man should see, to the survival of our nation.

In no other way can we orderly resolve the issues that confront and divide us, or live together in peace and harmony as a civilized nation of brothers under the fatherhood of God. (From an address by Charles E. Whitaker, associate justice of the Supreme Court [retired], before a meeting of the Tennessee Bar Association, Nashville, Tennessee, on June 7, 1965).

This "get tough" position assumes the basic strength of our criminal justice system but suggests that "*they* aren't doing their job." There is little interest in rehabilitation, but instead, punishment is viewed as sufficient correction. If recidivism occurs, the criminal should simply be punished again. All the courts have to do is to see to it that criminals receive the punishment prescribed by the law.

When we get to the specific problems in the criminal justice system, such as overcrowding in the courts and prisons, this approach simply advocates building more prisons and courtrooms. Similarly, the problems encountered by the police can be lessened by hiring more officers to increase the certainty of arrest. In this way there will be more respect for the law, for those who violate it will receive full legal sanctions.

Some politicians take this position and blame the rising crime rate on Supreme Court decisions which make police work more difficult. Decisions such as *Mapp vs. Ohio* which specifies legal requirements for search and seizure and the famous *Miranda vs. Arizona* decision which requires police to advise a suspect of his rights to counsel are cited as examples of cases which "hand-cuff" the police. However, the law and order perspective does not necessarily blame criminal activity on legal constraints over the police. It would be more accurate to say that this position sees the solution in terms of better training and the use of sophisticated technological developments rather than changing the law. This perspective sees the criminal justice system and the legal process in general as sound. If judges were stricter, and the police were permitted to do their job unfettered by constraints flowing from an excessive concern for the rights of the accused, the "problems" of the criminal justice system would be considerably lessened.

Ameliorative Perspective

A second general approach to the problems in the criminal justice system can be characterized as the "reform," "liberal," or "ameliorative approach." From this perspective, there are a number of things wrong with the criminal justice system, and by examining the specific causes of these problems, the various agencies and processes can be repaired. This approach sees the problems stemming from social changes outpacing policy changes, and by updating the policies of the various agencies, including modernization and expansion, the problems can be solved.

Unlike the punitive perspective, where the distinct agencies in the criminal justice system and the system as a whole are viewed as basically sound, the ameliorative approach forces us to see the structural and procedural problems. By employing the methods of social science, it attempts to find the causes of the problems in the system and then to solve them by using social science theories.

The tenets of the democratic process are at the heart of this approach, including egalitarian treatment of those encountering the criminal justice system, and due process strictly interpreted. Additionally, this perspective holds that the criminal justice system should serve as a rehabilitating institution and not merely a punitive one.

Perhaps the best example of the ameliorative approach is seen in the report by President Johnson's Commission on Law Enforcement and Administration of Justice, entitled *The Challenge of Crime in a Free Society*. The report was compiled by a number of recognized authorities in the field of criminal justice and social science. Every aspect of the criminal justice system was examined, and the commission compiled a massive number of research reports before making its recommendations, which included hiring minority group police officers, requiring baccalaureate degrees for policemen, developing and enunciating policies regulating police discretion, and raising police salaries. Among recommendations for court reform were that pretrial release without financial conditions be initiated, conditions of plea bargaining should be openly announced, and that mandatory minimum prison sentences should be removed so that judges can exercise greater discretion. Decriminalization of drunkenness and drug treatment and research programs were also suggested as means to reduce pressure on the criminal justice system.

In effect, these solutions add up to "modernizing," "repairing," or "fixing up" the criminal justice agencies. It is not unlike a plant being modernized so that it can produce better products more efficiently and effectively. Envisioned in the overall recommendations are the best of both worlds. The criminal justice system would be more effective in controlling crime and at the same time be more just in its procedures. Moreover, all of this could be done by making minimum alterations and without disturbing the larger social structure.

Critical Perspective

The final approach to social problems in the criminal justice system holds that the problems in criminal justice are merely indicative of the overall social structure and institutions. By confronting the major institutions on a broad front, the problems will be solved, and all that the reform accomplishes is to prop up a basically unsound social structure.

One of the most articulate proponents of the critical approach to criminal justice is Richard Quinney. Quinney (1974) points out that reforms in the criminal justice system are designed to subdue crime stemming from poverty, racial inequality, and campus unrest. Instead of attacking the real problems which are seen to be exploitation of the poor, racism, and political repression, the criminal justice reforms serve to more effectively manage or control the consequences that flow from these conditions, while preserving the existing social and economic arrangements which cause them.

Quinney (1974:391) claims that such reforms are only stop gap measures and are doomed to failure. Since they do not attack the real problems, they will not reduce crime. Failure of reform will induce the power structure to institute repressive measures to preserve the social and economic system upon which the power is based. The inexorable result is a repressive state unless fundamental changes occur in the existing social order.

The solutions proffered by the "critical theorists" involve the complete restructuring of a society in which power over critical areas of public and private life is presently in the hands of a ruling elite. Since this power arrangement is based on capitalism, capitalism must be replaced. As Quinney (1974:393) notes,

A vision of a decent, humane, socialist society must be developed. It is in the struggle to transcend capitalist society that the details of an alternative existence will emerge. The values that characterize a truly decent society will be based on equality and cooperation. Socialism, as a process, means the democratic, decentralized, and participatory control of the activities that affect one's life. Alienating, destructive forms of production, consumption, and social relations will be eliminated. Our task, in the political struggle, is to develop forms that will promote equality, nonalienating activity, and the other requirements of a decent society.

This sweeping solution is directed not only at the criminal justice system, but at the existing social institutions which give rise to the problems seen in the criminal justice system.

CONCLUSION

This discussion has merely scratched the surface of the problems in the criminal justice system, and the solutions are far more detailed and complex than what we have presented. However, this essay should serve as a window through which a glimpse of the problems of criminal justice can be seen and a keyhole for solutions. Further readings in this area will provide richer grounds for understanding these problems and solutions, and even though the problems are far from simple and remedies do not abound, it is an area of intense interest, one where new and fresh minds and ideas are sorely needed.

References

Bittner, Egon. "The Police on Skid-Row: A Study of Peace Keeping." In Richard Quinney (Ed.), *Crime and Justice in Society*. Little, Brown, 1969. Pp. 169–193.

Bittner, Egon. *The Functions of the Police in Modern Society*. Washington, D.C.: U.S. Government Printing Office, 1970.

Black, Donald J., and Reiss, Albert J. Jr.

"Police Control of Juveniles." *American Sociological Review*, 1970, 35, 63–77.

Blumberg, Abraham. *Criminal Justice*. New York: Franklin Watts, 1967.

California Department of Corrections. "Returns to Prison—One Measure." Human Relations Agency, July, 1972.

Clemmer, Donald. *The Prison Community*. North Quincy, Mass.: Christopher Publishing, 1940.

Cloward, Richard A., and Ohlin, Lloyd E. *Delinquency and Opportunity*. New York: Free Press, 1960.

Cohen, A. K. *Delinquent Boys*. New York: Free Press, 1955.

Daudistel, Howard C., and Sanders, William B. "Application of the Law: An Examination of Rule Use by Police Officers." Paper presented at the Pacific Sociological Association Convention (March), 1974.

Douglas, Jack (Ed.). *Understanding Everyday Life*. Chicago: Aldine, 1970.

Garfinkel, Harold. *Studies in Ethnomethodology*. Englewood Cliffs, N.J.: Prentice-Hall.

Glaser, Daniel, *The Effectiveness of a Prison and Parole System*. Indianapolis: Bobbs-Merrill, 1964.

Goffman, Erving. *The Presentation of Self in Everyday Life*. New York: Doubleday, 1959.

Goffman, Erving. *Stigma*. Englewood Cliffs, N.J.: Prentice-Hall, 1963.

Goffman, Erving. *Interaction Ritual*. New York: Doubleday, 1967.

Goffman, Erving. *Strategic Interaction*. Philadelphia: University of Pennsylvania Press, 1969.

Goffman, Erving. *Relations in Public*. New York: Basic Books, 1971.

Goldhamer, Herbert, and Shils, Edward A. "Power and Status." In Lewis A. Coser and Bernard Rosenberg (Eds.), *Sociological Theory*. New York: Macmillan, 1964. Pp. 134–143.

Goldstein, Herman. "Police Discretion: The Ideal versus the Real." *Public Administration Review*, 1963, 23, 140–148.

Harris, Richard. *The Police Academy: An Insider's View*. New York: Wiley, 1973.

Hersey, John. *The Algiers Motel Incident*. New York: Knopf, 1968.

Johnson, Lyndon B. *Weekly Compilation of Presidential Documents*, 819, June 27, 1966.

Joyce, Frank. "Death of Liberalism." In Irving Louis Horowitz (Ed.), *The Troubled Conscience*. Palo Alto, Ca.: James Freel Associates, 1971.

LaFave, Wayne. *Arrest: The Decision to Take a Suspect into Custody*. Boston: Little, Brown, 1965.

Leiter, Kenneth. *"Telling It Like It Is: A Study of Teachers' Accounts."* Ph.D. dissertation, University of California, Santa Barbara, 1971.

Manning, Peter. "The Police: Mandate, Strategies and Appearances." In Jack Douglas (Ed.), *Crime and Justice in American Society*. Indianapolis: Bobbs-Merrill, 1971.

Mayer, Martin. "Hogan's Office: A Kind of Ministry of Justice. In Donald R. Cressey (Ed.), *Crime and Criminal Justice*. Chicago: Quadrangle Books, 1971.

Miller, Walter B. "Lower Class Culture as a Generating Milieu of Gang Delinquency." *Journal of Social Issues*, 1958, 14, 5–19.

Niederhoffer, Arthur. *Behind the Shield: The Police in Urban Society*. New York: Doubleday, 1967.

Packer, Herbert. "Two Models of the Criminal Process." *University of Pennsylvania Law Review*, 1964, 113, 1–68.

Packer, Herbert. *The Limits of Criminal Sanctions*. Stanford, Ca.: Stanford University Press, 1968.

Packer, Herbert. "Who Can Police the Police?" In Richard Schwartz and Jerome Skolnick (Eds.), *Society and the Legal Order*. New York: Basic Books, 1970.

Pilliavin, Irving, and Briar, Scott. "Police Encounters with Juveniles." *American Journal of Sociology*, 1964, 70, 206–214.

Polsby, Nelson W. *Community Power and Political Theory*. New Haven, Conn.: Yale University Press, 1963.

President's Commission on Law Enforcement and Administration of Justice. *The Challenge of Crime in a Free Society.* Washington, D.C.: U.S. Government Printing Office, 1967. (a)

President's Commission on Law Enforcement and Administration of Justice. *Task Force Report: The Courts.* Washington, D.C.: U.S. Government Printing Office, 1967. (b)

President's Commission on Law Enforcement and Administration of Justice. *Task Force Report: Corrections.* Washington, D.C.: U.S. Government Printing Office, 1967. (c)

Quinney, Richard (Ed.). *Crime and Justice in Society.* Boston: Little, Brown, 1969.

Quinney, Richard. *Criminal Justice in America: A Critical Understanding.* Boston: Little, Brown, 1974.

Reiss, Albert J., Jr. "Police Brutality: Answers to Key Questions." In Michael Lipsky (Ed.), *Police Encounters.* Chicago: Aldine, 1970. Pp. 57–83.

Reiss, Albert J., Jr. *The Police and the Public.* New Haven, Conn.: Yale University Press, 1971.

Robin, Gerald D. "Justifiable Homicide by Police Officers." *Journal of Criminal Law, Criminology and Police Science,* 1963, 54, 225–231.

Robison, James, and Takagi, Paul T. "The Parole Violator as an Organization Reject." In Robert M. Carter and Leslie T. Wilkins (Eds.), *Probation and Parole: Selected Readings.* New York: Wiley, 1970. Pp. 233–254.

Rubinstein, Jonathan. *City Police.* New York: Ballantine, 1973.

Sanders, William B. "Detective Story: A Study of Criminal Investigations." Ph.D. dissertation, University of California, Santa Barbara, 1974.

Sanders, William B., and Daudistel, Howard C. "Detective Work: Patterns of Criminal Investigations." In *The Sociologist as Detective: An Introduction to Research Methods.* New York: Praeger, 1976. Pp. 166–183.

Skolnick, Jerome. *Justice without Trial.* New York: Wiley, 1967.

Skolnick, Jerome. "In Defense of Public Defenders." In Richard D. Schwartz and Jerome Skolnick (Eds.), *Society and the Legal Order.* New York: Basic Books, 1970. Pp. 414–423.

Spradley, James P. *You Owe Yourself a Drunk: An Ethnography of Urban Nomads.* Boston: Little, Brown, 1970.

Stinchcombe, Arthur L. "Police Practice, Types of Crimes and Social Location." *American Journal of Sociology,* 1963, 69, 150–160.

Sudnow, David. "Normal Crimes: Sociological Features of the Penal Code in a Public Defender Office." *Social Problems,* 1965, 12, 155–276.

Sutherland, Edwin. *White Collar Crime.* New York: Holt, Rinehart and Winston, 1949.

Sutherland, Edwin, and Cressey, Donald R. *Principles of Criminology,* 8th ed., Philadelphia: Lippincott, 1970.

Time Magazine, February 4, 1974, 104, 96.

Werthman, Carl, and Pilliavin, Irving. "Gang Members and the Police." In David J. Bordua (Ed.), *The Police: Six Sociological Essays.* New York: Wiley, 1967.

Westley, William. "Violence and the Police." *The American Journal of Sociology,* 1953, 49, 34–41.

Wieder, D. Lawrence. "The Convict Code: A Study of Moral Rhetoric." Ph.D. Dissertation, University of California, Los Angeles, 1969.

Wieder, D. Lawrence. "On Meaning by Rule." In Jack Douglas (Ed.), *Understanding Everyday Life.* Chicago: Aldine, 1970.

Wieder, D. Lawrence. *Language and Social Reality.* The Hague: Mouton, 1974.

Wilson, James Q. *Varieties of Police Behavior.* Cambridge, Mass.: Harvard University Press, 1968.

Wiseman, Jacqueline R. *Stations of the Lost: The Treatment of Skid Row Alcoholics.* Englewood Cliffs, N.J.: Prentice-Hall, 1970.

Suggested Reading

BLUMBERG, ABRAHAM. *Criminal Justice*. Chicago: Quadrangle Books, 1967.
Blumberg's work deals with all aspects of criminal justice, but it is especially good for his discussion of the structure of lawyer-client relationships and the role of the judge in the criminal justice process.

HARTJEN, CLAYTON A. *Crime and Criminalization*. New York: Praeger, 1974.
This work examines the relationship between people becoming criminals and the process whereby suspected criminals are brought into the criminal justice system. Hartjen argues that much crime is due to the very process designed to control it.

PACKER, HERBERT. *The Limits of Criminal Sanction*. Stanford, Ca,: Stanford University Press, 1968.
In addition to dealing with the effects of criminal sanctions in relation to its detrimental effects on certain types of crime, Packer provides two models for analyzing the criminal justice process. He shows the conflicting goals of crime control and due process to be a central dilemma in the study of criminal justice.

PLATT, ANTHONY. *The Child-Savers: The Invention of Delinquency*. Chicago: University of Chicago Press, 1969.
Platt traces the development of juvenile justice from its origins in the United States up to the present. The misplaced benevolence of the "child-savers" has resulted in a harsher system of justice than the adult process.

REISS, ALBERT J., JR. *The Police and the Public*. New Haven, Conn.: Yale University Press, 1971.
A good overview of the various organizational and situational issues in police work. The data in this work is based on over 5000 observations of police mobilizations by researchers who rode with police patrols in Boston, Chicago, and Washington, D.C.

RUBINSTEIN, JONATHAN. *City Police*. New York: Farrar, Straus, 1973.
This work is based on a study in Philadelphia by Rubinstein who rode with the police as an observer for several months. The book provides insight into the formal structure of police organization and process and the informal arrangements developed by the police to circumvent the formal policy.

SANDERS, WILLIAM B., AND DAUDISTEL, HOWARD C. (Eds.). *The Criminal Justice Process*. New York: Praeger, 1976.
This collection of readings emphasizes the situational contexts of the criminal justice process. The critical decisions made in the criminal justice system are bound to key situations where a defendant is either released from or brought deeper into the system, and the readings examine how these situations are resolved one way or the other.

Criminal Rehabilitation

Alfred Himelson

Criminal rehabilitation refers to those deliberate attempts to change or modify persons convicted of criminal acts, in such a way that 1) they are less likely to commit crimes in the future and 2) they can be restored to some "normal" state. During the past three-quarters of a century, this concept of "criminal rehabilitation" has been considered an important element in our system of justice. But it has hardly lacked controversy regarding its nature and use. Its proponents see its successful employment as a necessity if we are to reduce crime. They point to the number of serious crimes committed by those released from jails and prisons where proper "treatment" is lacking (Clark, 1970). They also believe the rehabilitation ethic furthers the humane treatment of prisoners. Their position is frequently supported by editorials in many of our most prestigious newspapers which declare that one of the ways we can have safer streets is a greater application of progressive programs of criminal rehabilitation. On the other side, the opponents of rehabilitation do not see it as stopping or significantly reducing crime—but actually aggravating the problem by reducing periods of incarceration and by advocating permissive standards of behavior.

This general criminal rehabilitation movement differs from earlier attempts in several ways (see Mennel, 1973). Efforts by individuals and institutions in the nineteenth century to change criminals were carried out by people who could best be described as "amateurs." They were amateurs in the sense that they had not received formal academic education to prepare them for their job or mission. There was no licensing board or graduate school to certify that they were competent to pursue their work. Many were possessed by a religious zeal that drove them to perform good works. It is therefore not surprising that many of them were clergymen or exclergymen (for some historical background to this period see Mennel, 1973).

But what occurred in the twentieth century represents a real break from the preceding period. Increasingly the work of criminal rehabilitation has been performed by those we occupationally title as professionals or in some cases "quasi-professionals." These were people who had the benefit of some specialized form of higher education. They saw themselves and were perceived by others, as "experts" in this field; they applied "scientific" methods in their attempts to change criminals. The attempt to use a so-called scientific language further distinguished their efforts from those of the preceding era. The twentieth century rehabilitators had been strongly influenced by the positivistic school of criminology (Jeffrey, 1962). They were convinced that the scientific model which had proved so fruitful in studying physical processes could be transferred directly to their work. This meant that they viewed their task in a highly mechanistic manner. Their criminal subjects were to be dealt with as one would deal with a faulty machine. The medical terminology adopted in many criminal rehabilitation programs was consistent with this mechanistic worldview of their subjects, some of them saw offenders as "sick"—in a way similar to that in which a physician would view a patient. Criminal behavior was considered symptomatic of some underlying disorder—emotional or otherwise.

Most of these highly deterministic conceptions of human behavior held by the rehabilitationists stressed the irrational side of man. They did not center on his capacity for exercising free will but rather on the uncontrollable forces driving him to criminality. This was in direct philosophical conflict with one of the main underpinnings of American criminal law. In the legal system the concept of the *reasonable person* is central to its operation. The reasonable person is one who knows the difference between right and wrong and can assess the consequences of his or her act. This does not mean that people are necessarily law-abiding, but if they do commit a criminal act they do so with a knowledge of what will happen to them if they are apprehended. A small percentage of adults are judged by the court not to possess the characteristics of the reasonable person—the insane or senile, for example. But the overwhelming bulk of defendants in criminal cases are tried as "reasonable persons." They are not excused from committing criminal acts because of their social, physical, and emotional backgrounds. Only the evidence relevant to the crime itself is to be considered. This system of law is seen as one of the major pillars of a democratic society; for it is intended to make us responsible for our conduct and because the concept of the "reasonable person" is then expanded into other areas

such as the electoral process (Allen, 1964).

But once the defendant is found guilty and has been committed to the custody of some governmental organization, then a different process is set into motion. Whereas the notion of the reasonable person was central to the conduct of the trial, during the period when efforts at rehabilitation are being attempted this concept is often denied. The fact that the person committed a crime is itself defined as an indication of his or her "unreasonableness."

It is this movement from a system of *equal justice* (consideration of the act, not the person) to one of *individualized justice* that is the concern of the next section.

INDIVIDUALIZED JUSTICE

The last two decades of the nineteenth century saw a general demand for the reformation of several aspects of American life. Working conditions, housing, public health, and civic government were some of the areas where improvement was demanded. One of the changes advocated in the criminal justice system was for individualized justice to be given greater weight in the decision of what to do with the convicted party. "Individualized justice" means that factors other than merely the nature of the crime are taken into account in determining what shall be done (Pound, 1930). Thus the individual's general circumstances, past history, and future potential serve as a valid guide for the decision by the judge or other officials (Pound also used the term "socialized justice" in discussing this process, 1942).

There were two sometimes contradictory points of view involved in pressing for an extension of individualized justice. On one side were those whose primary concern was the present or future welfare of the convicted person. Many of those who advocated this concern came from (or were influenced by) the newly emergent occupation of social work. This group felt that many of those who were convicted in the courts were the victims of their social circumstances; rather than be punished, they should be helped. A second group also supported individualized justice as a means of achieving greater protection than was afforded by the criminal law. Many in this group were strongly influenced by the positivistic school of criminology which expounded the belief that society is best protected by attempting to change, in any way necessary, its convicted criminals (see Jeffrey, 1962; Matza, 1964).

Four separate but somewhat ideologically related developments came out of the increasing application of the notion of individualized judgment: the juvenile court, the indeterminate sentence, parole, and probation. These became the important elements in the establishment of the basic governmental framework within which most efforts at criminal rehabilitation take place.

The Juvenile Court

One of the consequences of the struggle to insure that children would not be abused and would be given opportunities for healthy development was the creation of juvenile court. The court was set up to act in the role of the wise and powerful parent. The atmosphere in the court was to be such that a more personal pattern of communication between the youth and court members would be possible. Criminal court procedures which stressed adversary relationships were viewed as harmful to the interests of the youth. The rules of evidence, because they severely narrowed the range of permissable communication, were perceived as constituting a hindrance to creating the proper atmosphere for juvenile court proceedings. For similar reasons lawyers were excluded from the court. Until quite recently there was no necessity for a determination of the youth's guilt or innocence of the charge. What mattered was dealing with their individual circumstances. The juvenile court probably represented the most complete form of individualized justice adopted in the United States (see Caldwell, 1961, and Lemert, 1970, for a history of the Juvenile Court).

The Indeterminate Sentence

Many years elapsed from its first appearance in the United States until a significant number of states adopted some version of the "indeterminate sentence." It was to be one of the major victories of the proponents of individualized justice and was the instrument par excellence of those who had been influenced by the doctrines of positivistic criminology. For the positivist, the criminal act was no longer the center of attention. The characteristics of the person were to be the focus of inquiry—followed by various "scientific" attempts to modify the criminal. But the proponents saw that the time necessary for this modification varied between individuals. Some "offenders" were more resistant to change than others. The adoption of the indeterminate sentence supposedly provided the rehabilitators a means of assuring sufficient time for the modification of prisoners or wards (Johnson, 1974; Rubin, 1949).

The indeterminate sentence operates in a number of states in a typical way. A defendant is found guilty of a felony and is sentenced by the judge to state prison. By state statute, for that crime there is a minimum and maximum sentence that can be served within the prison system. In many states which have this system the judge does not set the actual length of sentence that is served. This is done by some administrative body, often a parole board, and oftentimes the setting of the length of sentence is delayed until the offender has served some time in confinement—perhaps undergoing "treatment" in some program. If the staff believes the inmate has progressed sufficiently, they will recommend his or her release. If they see little progress and there is a formidable record of institutional infractions by the inmate, the recommendation will be for the prisoner to be confined for a longer time.

Parole

Further restraints were placed on most of those released from prisons. This new legal status in which they found themselves was a further indication of the expansion of "individualized justice" in the United States. They were on *parole*, that is, they were still legally serving their sentence, but outside prison walls. Parole officers were assigned to help and counsel them or to make recommendations to higher authority when the parolees were detected engaging in "deviant" or criminal behavior. The parole officers in many states also had the power of arrest and detention. In each state some version of the parole board possessed the legal authority to determine when men and women on parole should be returned to prison to complete their terms. The legal grounds for this return were that the parolee had violated certain conditions they had agreed to before leaving prison.

Parole was an acceptable institution to both those factions making up the proponents of individualized justice. Those concerned with the welfare of the offender saw parole as a means of shortening the time spent in what they saw as repressive institutions. On the other hand, those influenced by the positivistic orientation viewed parole as another means of "treating" and controlling criminals. Instead of being in prison the treated criminal was out in the community. Many of the experiments in "criminal rehabilitation" were conducted by parole organizations. (See President's Commission, 1967, for background and history of parole.)

Probation

A fourth development was that of *probation*. The term refers to a legal status in which the convicted person is placed in lieu of serving time in jail or prison. In most jurisdictions the legal power to place an individual on probation is granted to the criminal court judge. Some form of supervision in the community is required for those on probation. Revocation of probation can lead to the jail or prison sentence being imposed. The creation and growth of probation probably represents the triumph of that faction of advocates of individualized justice who were concerned with the welfare of the individual, although the positivists in general could see some value in this method of treatment. It still represented control over the individual by the state.

APPROACHES USED IN REHABILITATION [1]

A belief in the necessity of changing convicted criminals was common to all those advocating rehabilitation, but their views on how to achieve this differed. The different approaches have been classified under three main approaches. They are the *psychological*, concerned with the link between crime and the inner man; *education-socialization*, emphasizing the necessity of developing knowledge and skills; and *cultural reorientation*, which attempts to change the norms and values of prisoners. It is obvious that many programs are a mixture of more than one approach, whereas others utilize only one of them. In examining various programs we should be careful to look beyond its language; for the words are often used for purposes of rhetoric, while the program has some other emphasis.

There is one other basic dimension which must be scrutinized; this is the degree of voluntarism permitted inmates and residents in their participation in these programs. Generally, criminal rehabilitation efforts have carried an aura of total or semicoercion with the subjects having little option about whether to participate or not. This emphasis on coercion was compatible with the mechanistic conception of the problem by the rehabilitators. Voluntary participation, on the other hand, is most identified with the emergence of self-help groups run by the subjects themselves.

The first approach to be examined is

[1] This discussion is drawn from material which first appeared in Himelson, 1968.

the psychological—which is concerned with the link between crime and the so-called "inner man." The psychological approach can be split into two groups of programs. The first emphasizes personality factors either through modification or management. The second uses psychological learning theory to bring about the modification of behavior (although some of its proponents claim that it also leads to more drastic personality changes).

Personality Modification or Management

Under this heading may be found those efforts at criminal rehabilitation which involve the central belief that further crime and delinquency of criminals can be avoided or lessened by working with such areas as their feelings, emotions, anxieties, and psychological concepts of self. In more ambitious instances drastic personality modification may be attempted.

Despite the broad variety of programs that fit under this heading, they share a common perspective: recidivism is mainly caused by internal psychic problems. This has been called the "sick" model which assumes that when certain people (1) are tense, anxious, or (2) are troubled by unresolved antecedent traumas and driven by neurotic forces, or (3) are uncertain of their identity, suffering from low self-esteem, possessing inadequate patterns of interpersonal communication, or (4) suffer from a character weakness that is manifested in hedonistic, immature behavior, they are more likely to return to various forms of crime and delinquency. (For an early formulation of this idea see Healy, 1910.)

Many of the individuals influential in

the growth of the criminal rehabilitation movement were caught up in Freudian and similar psychologies. For many years much of what the general public imagined rehabilitation to be was displayed in the work of the prison psychiatrist of the analytic orientation, the psychiatric social worker, and the casework oriented probation officer-counselor. The terms used in working with convicted offenders or those coming from the juvenile court process began to be the same as those used in the general field of mental health. The techniques and definition of goals were also quite similar or identical. The process was called "treatment" or "therapy."

The ideal situation for the practitioner was to have few patients, be able to spend large blocks of time with them, and to be reasonably unfettered by institutional rules and regulations. This supposedly made possible the emergence of the necessary patient-therapist relationship. Often the unconscious (a concept of great importance to the analytic psychology of the time) was the primary target of the therapist. Once freed of the effects of the repressed childhood or adolescent traumas (and able to work through their fixations) that were instrumental in forming their criminality or delinquency, the inmate or delinquent could now go forth and lead a law-abiding life. Robert Lindner's *Rebel without a Cause* (1944) was a dramatic example of this "genre" (see also Alexander and Healy, 1935).

The basic question of the validity of this approach for rehabilitation will be dealt with later, but there was one serious obstacle to actualizing this version of the psychological treatment approach. It was an expensive process. There was little money in the various budgets to hire the necessary therapists; and where there were funds it was often difficult to attract professionals to work within criminal justice institutions. These budgetary and manpower problems coupled with the fact that it was possible to "treat" relatively few patients (inmates, probationers, and so forth) in the one-to-one therapy situation, meant that a small number ever received this treatment for any duration.

The techniques of group counseling and group psychotherapy, used widely during World War II, replaced the individual session as the modal setting for "treatment" in the ensuing years. Group psychotherapy, in large measure initiated as an expedient way of dealing with the massive number of military patients during the war, was later seen as having many superior characteristics compared to the individual session format. According to the proponents the group atmosphere was more "real" than the strictly therapist-patient setting and the peer pressures generated in the group were believed to be potent forces for inducing individual change (see S. R. Slavson 1954, for a description of the use of group techniques with delinquents).

Group counseling, a less intensive form of group interaction, began to be widely used in the late 1940s in some prison systems. California extended its use to a majority of inmates during the 1950s (Eaton, 1962). The way it was implemented allowed the general body of prison employees to be used in its supervision. During this decade it was common to see female secretarial help, prison guards, and members of the civilian work force leading inmate groups (Eaton, 1962:152–156). The theory of group counseling posits that one of the major reasons that men and women turned to crime is that they possess inadequate patterns of communicating with others and are therefore unable to share their problems, feelings, and emotions with other people. One of the major tasks of the group leader is to facilitate the beginnings of this communication among inmates. Once this process begins to happen positive group interaction occurs spontaneously (Fenton, 1961).

A consciously stated attempt to achieve an ever greater sense of "reality" in the therapeutic situation was embodied in the concept of the therapeutic community first attempted in England by Maxwell Jones. The Therapeutic Community amalgamates the "sick model" of the client with the notion that psychic change takes place best in a setting that represents a miniature of the outside world. Typically a unit of some institution is taken over for this type of treatment and all the subjects live together. A series of definitions and goals are imparted to the participants and the staff. Some of these more important definitions are (a) that all that takes place in the unit is part of the treatment process (not just what occurs in special group settings), (b) that all patients should be treated equally, (c) that in order to facilitate open communication, status differences between patients and staff should be minimized during the group sessions, and (d) that patients within the unit are encouraged to participate in decision-making.

Two types of patient-staff meetings were typically part of this program. The *large meeting*, which everyone in the program attended, was devoted to dealing with the daily problems that arose from living together. While this daily group session was more oriented to problem solving, it still was considered an essential part of the treatment process for each person present. The use of *small group meetings* was similar to the use of such groups in traditional group psychotherapy; that is, for treatment of a more intensive nature (Jones, 1953, 1962; Rapoport, 1960).

Often times therapeutic community type programs were centered in what have been titled *halfway houses*. These are generally residential centers for either (1) people who have been released from custodial institutions or (2) those for whom the halfway house is being used in lieu of being placed in custodial institutions. The implicit assumption underlying the use of the halfway house for those coming from custodial institutions is that individuals leaving lock-up or regimented places after lengthy incarceration need some intermediate situation before they can adjust to the normal, everyday world. During their period of incarceration they have become dependent on their warders to take care of them. Now they must slowly rid themselves of this dependency, regain their confidence and self-esteem, and reestablish their ties with people on the outside. What places the halfway house idea under the psychological approach is the belief by proponents of the idea that without the presence of such an institution as the halfway house, intense stress and anxiety will arise within ex-prisoners, and that these emotional disturbances, which cannot be resolved, will lead them back to committing crimes and serious delinquencies (Geis, 1966; Miller, Himelson, and Geis, 1967; Wieder, 1969, 1974).

In addition to offering various kinds of psychological treatment many halfway houses provide job placement services and also serve the function of a temporary, low cost hotel for the destitute exprisoner. But all these services are provided with the central purpose of the halfway house in mind: to promote the psychological well-being of their subjects and supposedly lessen their probability of criminal behavior either during their stay or after they leave.

Reward and Punishment

Of the current attempts at criminal rehabilitation perhaps the most in fashion are those loosely lumped under the title of behavior modification. They have been derived out of certain psychological learning theories and are attempts to produce persistent law-abiding behavior in those who have been criminals through a system of controlled reward and/or punishment (Franks, 1969; Skinner, 1969; Tharp and Wetzel, 1969).

Those using punishment depend upon linking the appearance of some form of pain or trauma (psychological or otherwise) to follow the committing of deviant acts. This form of aversion therapy has been utilized in the treatment of alcoholism and various other addictions and afflictions (for example, eneurisis). Drastic forms of punishment have been one of the oldest forms of intervention by the state in dealing with its convicted criminals. While they did not bear the rhetoric of modern day "treatment" to the survivors, their intent was probably viewed in a similar way as so-called aversion or modification techniques today (Andrews, 1960).

A decade or so ago some psychologists and social psychologists became disenchanted with punishment technique and turneJ to learning principles using rewards. Their disillusionment was probably a mixture of concern over the ethical problems posed by the scientific application of punishment, the lack of tangible results of punishment, and the increasing popularity of the use of rewards in a broad range of areas (for example, programmed instruction).

In criminal rehabilitation, especially in juvenile rehabilitation, this led to the development of programs of token economics. If an inmate or resident performed some approved task he was given a token which could be saved or used, for example, for increased canteen privileges. The scheme calls for an initial phase in which the reward is administered soon after the occurrence of the approved behavior. Continuing approved behavior may lead to increased privileges (through the accumulation of tokens or points) and could result in larger rewards such as furloughs or release from the institution. The long-range purpose is to establish a permanent or long-lasting link between positive, law-abiding behavior and the receiving of rewards (Kazdin and Bootzen, 1972).

There are obstacles, however, to this coming about. The first, of course, is that the inmate or resident who goes back into the community may not be able or willing to equate rewards within an institution (which may make life more comfortable or lead to an earlier release) with those rewards on the outside which come from law-abiding behavior. Secondly, even within the institution there may be some forces that limit the intended operation of the reward system.

In a sense, the token economy system is like an industrial piecework system. The more you produce (perform approved acts), the greater the reward. But industrial sociologists and psychologists long ago demonstrated that that system does not operate unhampered. There are group pressures that operate to limit the rate of production; and the rate buster—

in industry the ones who exceed these un-official quotas—is negatively sanctioned in various ways by their fellow workers (Homans, 1950).

There is no reason to believe the same would not be true in a prison or institutional environment and that the inmate social system would exert pressure on various inmates not to exceed their quota of rewards. It is possible, given the focus on the individual rather than the social system, that much of this institutional rate-setting would go unnoticed by the staff.

The Education-Socialization Approach

Programs that see the rehabilitation of "offenders" being furthered by such means as academic education, vocational training, enhancement of instrumental interpersonal skills and the like, we have classified under education-socialization. Some of the basic beliefs underlying the education-socialization approach are (1) that the clients come from an impoverished environment, or (2) that they lack both the knowledge of and the skills to take advantage of alternative life styles, or (3) that opportunities are lacking which would enable them to meet the types of aspirations set by the society, or (4) that their antisocial acts are related to the deprivations imposed by exterior environments in which they find themselves a part. Underlying the education-socialization approach is the assumption that given a brighter set of alternatives most criminal offenders, in some way, will choose one of them in preference to the limited vistas and opportunities they supposedly had prior to this new exposure.

The education-socialization approach is hardly a new theme in criminal rehabili-tation and reform. A great deal of attention was focused on it during the nineteenth-century (Mennel, 1973). In the mid-twentieth century, additional theoretical support for this approach came from a group of sociological writers who were influenced by the theories of Emile Durkheim (1933, 1951). For example, Robert Merton (1957) in his oft-quoted essay "Social Structure and Anomie," discussed the consequences for individuals of their having to deal with strong and pervasive American norms of being "successful" without the availability of the legitimate institutional means of reaching the goals.

Cloward and Ohlin (1960), in a work geared primarily toward explaining the etiology of lower-class group delinquency, added an additional dimension to the original Merton formulation. They elaborate the Mertonian theme that delinquency is an adaptation to blocked goal attainment. They argue that the delinquent alternative occurs not only when "legitimate" avenues for success are blocked, but also when illegitimate paths are also not open. It is when illegitimate careers are not open that individuals pursue deviant careers that are not structured within organized crime— or within associations of highly skilled and organized criminals. These efforts bring in less rewards and have a higher probability of failure. Prisons and jails are filled with those who have made this type of adaptation.

In their writings, Cloward and Ohlin were not necessarily espousing the education-socialization approach as a treatment technique for those already considered persistent offenders against societal laws. They are careful to point out that the etiology, persistence, and cessation of delinquency are probably each subject to a different set of dynamics, and should not be considered as a unity. Others, however, have designed rehabilitation and prevention programs based on Cloward and Ohlin's reasoning, for example, the major "war on poverty" program in Harlem (HARYOU, 1964).

Institutional programs are designed to increase legitimate opportunities for ex-offenders who are seen as lacking the basic skills to get along without turning to crime. Vocational training, a basic academic education, and the learning of how to approach and get what you want in legitimate endeavors are usually the areas stressed within this perspective (Dickover et al., 1971; McCollum, 1975; Pownall, 1975).

CULTURAL REORIENTATION

The rationale generally advocated for programs classified under this heading is that inmates and parolees hold a set of norms and values which are either in conflict with those of the general society or are in conflict with the special set held by the captors. Key to this notion is the conception of the criminal or delinquent subculture the norms of which provide a kind of legitimacy for the criminal behavior of the subject. Some of these norms are that it is alright to commit illegal acts because (1) everyone is crooked, (2) the victim had it coming to him, and (3) the criminal is the victim of social circumstance (Sykes and Matza, 1957).

The correctional worker who adopts the cultural reorientation approach tries to subvert the inmates' or exoffenders' belief in crime as a legitimate activity. Programs emphasizing cultural reorienta-tion are less concerned with whether the subjects are "sick" or "healthy" in the clinical sense. They are basically concerned with weaning people away from criminal activity by changing their perspectives. These activities often take place within special living groups—where the inmates in the program are isolated from the main body of prisoners (Himelson and Thoma, 1968).

SELF-HELP COMMUNITIES

Perhaps the most significant development in cultural reorientation has been in the creation of self-help communities. These organizations are often composed of people who define their difficulties as stemming from a common problem such as drug addiction. Many of these self-help organizations have rejected using professionals to help solve their individual problems. They believe that, in general, these professionals have not been successful, and that their presence would prevent the growth of the kind of group solidarity which they believe to be necessary for a successful operation. One of the earlier and best known of these organizations is Synanon. It was founded in Southern California in the late 1950s as a self-help community for persons with a history of heroin addiction (see Casriel 1963; Volkman and Cressey 1963; Yablonsky 1965).

At first glance self-help organizations such as Synanon appear to be using a predominately psychological approach. Their language and the use of group processes appears to indicate this. But closer inspection shows that their primary concern is that the specific behavior of their members conforms to the norms and values of the group or community. One unique way that some of these self-help groups differ from official or quasi-official programs of cultural reorientation is that they do not so much attempt to change the norms and values of their residents as provide them with alternate ways of life that are lived within the residential center and which do not bring them into conflict with the law.

Various techniques have been developed within these centers to reach their goals. Perhaps the most significant has been the creation of systems of reward through the use of an occupational stratification system. Newcomers entering into the self-help community, no matter what their background, start at the bottom of the occupational ladder. They do menial jobs and have little say in the operation of the organization. If they show diligence in their occupational role and also indicate their acceptance and involvement in the group's culture they are promoted. Each advancement indicates their greater involvement in the life of the organization.

The various self-help groups have differed from each other on what the eventual goal for each individual should be. Some, such as Synanon, believe that the members should stay within the organization for the rest of their lives—only in this way can they permanently overcome their problem and have a fulfilled life. Other groups, such as Seattle's Family House, have questioned this view for fostering an almost total dependency on the organization, thus denying any hope for returning to a normal life on the "outside." This latter group of self-help organizations advocates long periods within their environment with eventual graduation to the outside. The former members

continue contact with the group but live and work away from the organization (*Corrections Magazine*, 1974).

EVALUATION

Until the post-World War II period there was little solid data available on the success or failure of rehabilitation programs. What articles were published in journals by the creators and operators of various programs tended to follow a pattern. After detailing the theoretical framework, describing the subjects, and relating the happenings that occurred during the program's operation, the authors often concluded by presenting some statistic that indicated that the program had been a success and extolled the virtues of it being generally used. But had they really succeeded? Because of the deficiencies in the techniques of evaluation there is no way of knowing.[2] What were these deficiences?

First were the problems of selection. This involves asking such questions as what kind of subjects had been in the program? Were they typical of the general body they had been selected from? Favorable results might be accounted for by the fact that only the subjects most likely to succeed in any case were placed in this special program. This would represent a "stacked deck," whether it resulted from deliberate intent or by accidental circumstance.

The second problem was that of comparison. The question must always be

---

[2] Articles of this sort still occasionally appear in some journals, but a great deal of useful information is available from programs that have been well researched and evaluated.

asked, what would happen to these or comparable individuals if they had not gone through this special program or had been involved in some other experience. One way of finding out is to conduct the program as part of an experiment with the inmates, residents, or subjects being designated the experimental group and a comparable group of individuals who are not part of the program being defined as the control group. As discussed later, this does not totally eliminate the evaluation problems.

Many studies have been carried out since the 1950s which have taken the above factors into account. But with the increasing methodological sophistication other problems in evaluation were noted. For example, it is not always possible or desirable to use the experimental framework. There may not be sufficient subjects available for placement into two or more study groups, or perhaps the program designer wants to retain a more "natural environment" for the program and therefore wishes to avoid the inquiries, anxieties, and conflicts that often develop among both staff and subjects when they are assigned into different groups.

One alternate to depending upon experimental situations is by using risk prediction scores (Mannheim and Wilkins, 1955). These scores are derived from specially devised scales and give a group prediction as to how many under ordinary circumstances will "fail" and how many will succeed. It is then a fairly simple matter to derive these scores for some special program group and then calculate how many should succeed or fail. One then asks if this number differs significantly from the actual outcome of the program.

CRITERIA FOR MEASURING THE SUCCESS OR FAILURE OF PROGRAMS

Choosing the proper criteria for evaluation is often times a difficult process, and one that requires more than merely knowledge of what is satisfactory for purposes of statistical manipulation. Analyzing and interpreting data without having intimate knowledge of the circumstances of its collection is perilous in the best of circumstances. This is certainly true in dealing with crime rates. The "problematic" nature of police statistics is well known; such factors as the percentage of crimes reported, police manpower allocation, and current policy, can drastically affect the reporting of crime. What is less publicized and perhaps at a lower level of awareness is that these same or similar problems are present within most organizations involved in criminal rehabilitation.

Say that a group of men in a prison are participating in a special therapy program typical of those in the California Department of Corrections in the 1960s. The program operates under the belief that their criminality is linked to the anxiety and stress that results from their unresolved psychological problems. Three times each week they are engaged in group therapy sessions. The length of the treatment for each man is one year. He is then released from the prison on parole. How is the degree of success of this program to be measured? The first step in evaluation would be to see if any type of change had taken place during the program. There are several ways this might be done. In the first method a "movement scale" is used (Segal, 1972). The movement scale measures change along a series of observable behavioral dimensions (for example, frequency of verbal participation). This charts progress or retrogression during the inmate's participation in the program. A second method would be to test the inmates with various psychological scales, at the time when they first enter the program and at the time of their departure. A third area is that of attitudes. Such items as satisfaction with program, satisfaction with self, and confidence regarding post-prison life can be measured with paper and pencil tests (see Glaser and Stratton, 1961, for a general discussion of measuring inmate change).

Many programs have been able to demonstrate their ability to change the behavior of inmates in the program, of producing positive shifts as measured by psychological testing, and graduating people from the program with positive attitudes. But are these measurements of the program sufficient for a final evaluation? The answer is no. In almost all circumstances the crucial test of the success or failure of a program will depend on what happens to the subjects *after* they leave prison or some kind of institution. No matter how dramatic are changes within prison they must be shown to persist on the outside in some measurable way if they are to be a demonstration of "rehabilitation." What criteria can demonstrate this "success"? Generally, conviction for crime and return to prison for parole violation are the two criteria most often used, as will be discussed later. Both generate their own problems in interpretation.

Parole is legally considered to be still serving one's prison sentence, and therefore under the legal jurisdiction of the prison system. Decisions regarding lengthening or shortening of sentences, discharge or return to prison are in most states the legal prerogative of the parole board. Prior to the inmate's departure from prison he is informed of behavior which is regarded as not permissible on the outside, and which can result in his return to prison, if the parole board so decides. In fact, in many states the inmate signs an agreement to this effect (Irwin, 1970:208–211). The wording of the rules which define the proscribed behavior is generally ambiguous. For example, "the parolee must maintain regular employment." How is one to interpret the word "regular" and to take account of conditions in the job market which might make having employment very difficult. Another typical condition is that he must conduct himself as a good citizen; but this also allows for a wide latitude in interpretation. Where is the line drawn between inconsequential and serious deviance (see Irwin, 1970, for a general discussion of this area)? It is clear that the rate of return to prison for violation of the parole rules, given the ambiguous nature of these rules, can vary dramatically from year to year and from one parole board or panel to another. These decisions on parole revocation are particularly sensitive to general or special interest political pressures. In most states parole board members are political appointees. Periods when there are demands for increased "law and order" lead to a lower tolerance for many forms of deviance; and it is in these periods that returns to prison for technical violations are likely to increase.

If this is the case, then it is possible that the behavior of groups of men on parole may not appreciably vary from year to year, but their failure rates will vary because of changing patterns of official behavior; that is, changing patterns of decision-making by official boards (see Robison and Takagi, 1970 for an interesting examination of this area).

There is another area that makes certain kinds of rehabilitation data in many ways as problematic as police statistics. It is known that the discretion used by individual police officers can drastically affect rates of arrest and so on (Black, 1970; Reiss, 1971). The same is true of parole and probation officers (Robison and Takagi, 1968). Frequently there is a negotiation process that takes place between the officer and the parolee or probationer. Typically some form of deviant behavior has come to the attention of the parole or probation officer. The rules of the organization may require some official action to be taken, such as incarceration. But if the parolee or probationer has previously shown conforming behavior, or has a steady job, or a reasonably good family situation, then the officer may be reluctant to invoke the official policy and thereby seriously damage the individual's present situation. An informal warning is given to the person with an admonition that there be no repetition. The result is there is no record of the deviance and there is also a somewhat reduced probability of revocation of the parole or probation status by some board or judge because of the lessened visibility of the parolee or probationer.

SERIOUS CRIME

In spite of the problematic nature of general crime statistics, certain of them have distinct advantages for evaluating programs of criminal rehabilitation over such measures as parole technical violation (or revocation of parole) or therapists' judgments. Their most important advantage is that they are usually derived and recorded in a system that is relatively independent of the system in which rehabilitation takes place. Especially in large cities the police, district attorneys, and courts are independent of and maintain very limited contact with such organizations as prison and parole systems. In fact, anyone who has had extended contacts with both types of organizations is aware of how little each generally knows about the other's work and structure. The result is that police arrests and the court trials of men and women on parole or in other program situations are not ordinarily influenced by whether they are part of some special rehabilitation program or not. This independence is not found within such an organization as a prison system. The parole board is usually aware of which inmates or parolees are or have been in which program and they may take this information into consideration in making their decision.

The second reason for using criminal convictions as a primary criteria lies in this instance, not in the methodological advantages, but in the fact that crime represents the area of behavior most crucial to validating the usefulness of various forms of criminal rehabilitation. If ex-offenders are better adjusted, happier, and more confident but the number of criminal convictions stays the same or increases, then it is likely that there will be a judgment that the program is not successful and should be abolished.

GOOD TIME

There is one other measure, while not having the importance of criminal convictions, is useful in measuring the effectiveness of a program. This has been titled "good time"—and refers to the number of days each present or former program subject spends in the community—and not in jail, prison, or whereabouts officially unknown. Since the financial cost of maintaining someone in prison or jail is so much greater than the cost of their parole supervision in the community, any program which increases this time in the community or good time and at the same time does not show an increase in criminal convictions among its subjects has also achieved some measure of success. It has saved money for the state and its citizenry in addition to furthering social goals (see Burkhart and Sathmary, 1962; Himelson and Thoma, 1968, for an example of the use of good time).

EVALUATION AND THE PROBLEM OF UNCERTAINTY

Is it really possible to measure the consequences of programs of criminal rehabilitation? Most knowledgeable researchers in the field will answer yes, if the rigorous conditions of that most desirable form of research—the experiment—are carried out. That is, if proper experimental and control groups are defined and designated and an acceptably unbiased sampling and assignment procedure is carried forth. That it is not quite that simple has been known for some time. More than three decades ago, during the course of evaluating the results of the famous Western Electric studies, the investigators realized that their very presence in the study, by creating special experimental conditions, and the subsequent measurement of these conditions

had introduced an additional unintended variable into the system which effected the outcome of the research. This discovery was given the title of the "Hawthorne effect" and researchers now routinely look for its presence in experimental situations; although its effect is often difficult to measure (Roethlesberger and Dickson, 1939).[3]

But there is a second problem of measurement in addition to the "Hawthorne effect" that produces uncertainty in interpreting the findings in certain areas of social research, and especially in studying the modification of deviant behavior. The difficulty of interpreting the results of California's first Narcotic Treatment Control Program (NTCP) provides a clear example of how this second problem of uncertainty applies in the study of such situations.

This program was created by the California State Legislature in 1959 as a means for the treatment and control of opiate addiction (Burkhart and Sathmary, 1962; Himelson and Thoma, 1968). The program was intended to run for five years and was to be operated on an experimental-control basis that would allow a careful evaluation of the results. The subjects of the experiment were men paroled from California prisons who had a history of opiate use, that is, were heroin addicts. They were assigned into experimental and control groups by a random selection process. The selection was performed by the prison system's parole research staff. The original experimental design of NTCP was built around two independent variables which were the

[3] In the physical sciences the delineation of the Heisenberg effect first called to attention the problem of separating the observer from the observed (Brooks, 1965; Heelan, 1965; Price, 1965).

| CASELOAD | NALLINE TEST | |
SIZE	Test Used	Not Tested
30 Man	NTCP EXPERIMENTAL GROUP	THIS CELL NOT UTILIZED
70 Man	CONTROL GROUP I	CONTROL GROUP II

size of parole agent caseloads and the use of the nalline test.

The size of parole agent caseloads refers to the number of men on parole supervised by a parole agent at any given time. The assumption was that having a smaller caseload would allow the specially trained agents to carry out the prescribed "treatment" approach. The reduced size was set at approximately 30 cases and constituted the experimental factor. The regular caseload size in the parole division at this time was slightly in excess of 70 parolees per agent. This constituted the control factor.

The second variable that was included was the use or absence of the nalline test, a physiological test for determining the presence of opiates in the individual. The use of the test was the experimental variable and nonuse the control.

The table below shows the experimental design.

One of the major indicators that the treatment program was successful would be significantly less opiate use among the experimentals compared to the controls. Table 1 is reproduced from the report and shows the comparison of detected opiate use for the three groups for each of three follow-up periods.

For those being tested regularly (experimental group and control group 1) detection of opiate use could have taken place in a number of ways: (1) through the nalline test, which was the most frequent mode of detection, (2) by the subject admitting use to the parole agent, or (3) through police investigation. For those not being tested, detection took place through the latter two modes.

Table 1 clearly shows that in all three follow-up periods the control group without either experimental condition had the lowest percentage of detected opiate use.

At least two interpretations can be made from these results: The first is that

Table 1. Number of Los Angeles Area Subjects with Various Parole Periods during Program Phase II, and Percent Detected Using Narcotics

Parole Period	NTCP Experimental Parolees		Control Parolees without Nalline Testing		Control Parolees with Nalline Testing	
	No. of Subjects	Percent Detected	No. of Subjects	Percent Detected	No. of Subjects	Percent Detected
6 months	460	36.5	105	21.9 *	93	35.5
12 months	302	48.7	60	31.7 *	50	56.0
18 months	78	65.4	19	47.4	20	60.0

* Chi-square P = less than .01
Source: Burkhart and Sathmary, 1962.

the control group without either experimental variable had less detection or use because subjects in this category were not exposed to other addicts at the center where the nalline test was given. Some have claimed that these forced associations have led to reinforcement of addict identification. Secondly, subjects not receiving nalline were not subjected to constant hypodermic needle injections—which some have conjectured lead to a persistence of what they title the "needle culture." But another equally plausible interpretation can be made from the data, that is, that nalline is an effective detector of use—and the higher percentage in the experimental group as compared to the no-nalline group is because of test efficiency. This kind of interpretation was not provided for in the original description of the experimental design—which talked about the reduction of drug use through treatment—but was given by the research and operational staff as an explanation of why the experimental group had done "worse." Which interpretation or alternate interpretations should be adopted? There is no way of resolving this dilemma (Himelson, 1968; Martinson, Kassebaum, and Ward, 1964).

Given these methodological problems the results of these types of programs in criminal rehabilitation must remain uncertain—no matter how sophisticated the experimental techniques adopted. In fact, greater effort may only confound the problem further. For example, one might suggest self-reporting techniques such as have been used in trying to assess the extent of youth delinquency (Short and Nye, 1958). But since the behavior is illegal and negatively sanctioned if detected, the subjects in "rehabilitation" programs will not readily admit to it, nor would there be any way of estimating

how many should have truly reported opiate use. It merely adds one more set of statistics to confound the interpretation.

In this particular example the use of such "modern" detection devices as the nalline or the urinalysis test does not solve this methodological problem either. Subjects being tested develop all sorts of avoidance techniques to "beat" the test. Nalline testing during the period reported on was on a once a week basis. Introduction of daily, in place of weekly, testing for example, even if practical, would have further compounded the experimental situation, for the rate of addicts absconding (running from parole) would have risen dramatically as would the rate of detection. But what this increased failure rate was due to would still remain uncertain. In other words, increasing the intensity of the measurement would have a high probability of further confounding the assessment.

It is obvious in this particular experiment that confusion is introduced by using the nalline test as both an independent variable and as one means of measuring the dependent variable. But this problem is present in all such deviance intervention research no matter how well carried out. For (1) greater intervention almost always implies greater visibility of the experimental subjects and (2) more intensive measurements of the dependent variable may very well lead to the measurement itself becoming an unintended independent variable of uncertain effect. Thus the more one looks the greater the probability of finding the occurrence of "criminal" behavior, but if one looks too hard, the original experimental situation will no longer be present. This evaluation problem applies to all types of criminal rehabilitation programs, although it is certainly most severe for programs like our example.

Thus far we have looked at the historical and philosophical framework of criminal rehabilitation; this was followed by an examination of the various "treatment" approaches; we then considered some of the methodological problems in evaluating rehabilitation programs. In the next section the concern is with their effectiveness.

EVIDENCE: HAS REHABILITATION WORKED?

Any systematic review of adequate studies of criminal rehabilitation must lead the reader to the conclusion that with the exception of a handful of projects, these programs have not been able to achieve what they set out to do. The fact that this failure was universally experienced, in different parts of the North American continent, by different governmental entities, and by professionals and other practitioners *using all the various approaches* (i.e., psychological, education-socialization, cultural reorientation), leaves little doubt that the criminal rehabilitation movement has not "delivered"—even on its own terms (Robison and Smith, 1971; Martinson, 1974).

In one or two instances where at first glance there seemed to be the possibility of a real breakthrough, a reanalysis of the program results showed something else. What apparently had changed was not the behavior of subjects but that of the administrative and program staff who were not catching and/or punishing their experimental subjects while the control group was being dealt with more harshly (Lerman, 1968; Robison and Smith, 1971; Martinson, 1974).

These dismal conclusions apply to government-run rehabilitation efforts and to most private programs operated by staffs of professionals. An evaluation of privately operated self-help groups and movements is a more difficult task. Since the members are self-selected volunteers (in a sense that they had a choice between entering the self-help group and some more negative experience), it is almost impossible to make a comparison of what happened to them with some other group's experience. It is even more difficult to compare them with some coercive government programs.

Secondly, they can be judged using a different kind of criteria as to what constitutes success and failure. Because the self-help groups offer either very long-term or lifetime residence and membership they can provide an alternative, lawful way of life that is all encompassing. If we assume that while in these programs the residents are law-abiding, then the criteria of success for such a program will be the continual increase in the numbers of people in residence. Every member in residence means one fewer possible law-violator on the streets. Some programs, for example, Synanon, appear to be successful when judged in these terms. However, there are objections by critics of these programs who believe that no program should be considered successful unless the residents have been prepared for a "normal" independent life outside the organization (*Corrections Magazine*, 1974:19).

Two other favored notions of criminal rehabilitators also have not led to successful outcomes. Despite the ever-persisting optimism that some typology will be discovered that will exert almost magical properties for treatment, none has yet appeared.

The second notion highly regarded in the field is that of caseload size, that is, the number of inmates, residents, and so on, that each professional or agent is responsible for treating and supervising. Despite almost 20 years of evidence that small caseload size has not been a factor associated with program success, practitioners still mention this as a crucial factor in program design (Bailey, 1966; Martinson, 1974).

REASONS FOR FAILURE

Inmate Social Systems

Beginning with Donald Clemmer's book *The Prison Community* (1958), first published in 1940 and further discussed and elaborated on in a series of articles and books during the 1950s and 1960s, a picture of what has been called the inmate social system and structure has emerged (Schrag, 1961; Sykes, 1958). According to this perspective, this social system is oriented around a series of opposition norms that stress noncooperation with the staff, a lack of trust in the motives and loyalties of staff members, and cooperation and solidarity with other inmates. The opposition not only extends to resisting various aspects of the prison routine and control, but also extends to programs of "criminal rehabilitation." These programs are often seen by the inmates or residents as another means of control by the staff. Therapy or rehabilitation are viewed by many inmates as illegitimate attempts to foist a definition on the inmate concerning what he was and what his problems were. All the various kinds of treatment models, except perhaps those classified under education-socialization, encounter this opposition. Learning a trade or going to school are not seen by inmates as necessarily "selling out."

Inmates or residents seldom accept as accurate the image of themselves as sick. They also oppose attempts by the staff to culturally reorient them to a way of life that would indicate disloyalty to fellow captives (Allen Sillitoe's [1959] *The Loneliness of the Long Distance Runner* is a poignant description of this loyalty).

Examples of this type of opposition are apparent in many of the group therapy, counseling, and therapeutic community programs operating within adult and juvenile institutions. These kinds of activities require personal candidness, disclosure about the behavior of others, and a temporary dropping of various role definitions. But "snitching" (informing), even when the purpose is ostensibly self-improvement, runs counter to the central inmate norm of not providing any important personal information to the staff about yourself or other inmates (Malcolm Braly's [1967] novel *On the Yard* provides a view of this treatment setting).

Inmates and residents often participate in these programs voluntarily, but while there are some who genuinely seek the benefits, others (probably the great majority) feel that having this kind of "treatment" activity on their records would be favorably viewed by parole boards, institutional staffs, or other governmental functionaries, and would lead to an earlier release. They go through the treatment ritual but without possessing the motivation necessary to produce change (Braly, 1967).

Role and System Conflict

Another reason often advanced for the failure of programs to produce positive changes is that there is an inherent conflict between the goals of rehabilitation and the protection of the general society (see Miller, 1973, for a discussion of the various points of view). Those who are convinced of this conflict believe that the progressive changing of criminals requires that they not be taken permanently out of circulation for every crime and deviance. It may take some period of time for the treatment program to take full effect, and the offender has to have an opportunity to learn from his failures. This reasoning is based on the analogy of a child learning to walk. The child constantly falls down, but each time is encouraged to get up and keep trying. The rehabilitators recognize that some social harm will come from giving their subjects continued freedom, but their priority is to make the individual law-abiding in the long run. They feel they must take short-run chances. However, various administrative, political, and public groups do not see this position as at all acceptable. They say that if people in rehabilitation programs are committing criminal acts, they should be dealt with like any other person accused of the same act. In fact, not to do so merely encourages these and other offenders to continue to violate the law. Since this group of officials and public often has the final say as to what will be allowed, the limits of what is permissible in rehabilitation programs is considerably narrowed, to the dismay of the rehabilitators who see success just around the corner if they could have their say.

Bureaucratic Rigidity

When the results of a rehabilitation program are not what its designers had predicted, there is a search for what went wrong. The character of this search and its consequences have been described in detail in Himelson (1968) and will be summarized here. There is a morality play script that is often invoked to explain the outcome. The title of the play is "The Good Professionals versus the Bad Bureaucrats." It describes a group of highly educated, skilled, idealistic professionals (drawn from psychology, social work, and so forth) formulating exciting programs that will finally save the lives of many whose fate up until this time was to be, forever, criminals. But, the script goes on to show that the professionals can't really carry out these ideas, for at every step of the way they are frustrated by bureaucrats who have other interests to protect and by a bureaucracy whose built-in inertia and insensitivity to necessary change enervates anyone who tries to proceed at an urgent pace.

The theme seems plausible. After all, many American social scientists have berated bureaucracy as an organizational type. On the other hand, while sometimes being described in comedy terms by the media, these professionals seldom have their idealistic credentials challenged. The question is not so much one of idealism as of effectiveness and flexibility. By flexibility I mean the ability to change perspectives in the face of solid evidence that what one is doing does not work. Are the professionals more flexible than the bureaucrats, or even as flexible?

Thomas Kuhn (1963) has pointed out that most or all so-called scientific endeavors are carried out within the framework of what he calls a "paradigm." The basic structure within which one works is spelled out by the paradigm. It assumes that fundamental theoretical problems have been resolved and that if one works properly within this framework the results will usually be successful or at least provide a clue for future success. Physicists working within the Einsteinian paradigm of relativity assume that certain relationships are valid on the basis of the paradigm and try to elaborate on relations within its boundaries.

But sometimes a crisis in acceptance occurs when there is continual failure to achieve results predicted by the paradigm. Scientists will not lightly discard a paradigm which has successfully provided their basic orientation for so many years. They may blame their talents, tools, or techniques for lack of confirmation. But eventually if this failure repeatedly takes place in the work of a number of scientists, a basic reconsideration of the paradigm will take place. This is what happened with Newtonian physics, which had served as the basic paradigm for a considerable time (Kuhn, 1963). The training of physical scientists makes possible this reconsideration. While they are taught to master the paradigm, they are also taught to see themselves as possible discoverers of uncharted areas. Michael Polanyi has called this desire for exploration "the heuristic passion" (Polanyi, 1958).

Why has this paradigmatic reconsideration so seldom taken place in the field of criminal rehabilitation? Given the numerous results reported from well-designed and evaluated programs, this lack of paradigmatic soul-searching is, on the surface, rather odd. Its absence is especially puzzling among those professionals who have used some version of the psychological approach for their program rationale. For this type of program has been numerous, well-researched, and well-staffed.

The "heuristic passion" of the physical scientist appears to be frequently lacking in the "helping professional." The helping professional seems to approximate more closely the "true believer" than the scientist. There is seldom an effort to blame the intrinsic faults of the paradigm for the lack of success and to consider some other approach (Himelson, 1968).

This lack of searching for alternatives is in large measure associated with the type of graduate education these professionals were required to complete in schools of social work, psychology, counseling, and so on. Mastery of the paradigm was valued during their education, but seriously challenging its basic tenets, even as an exercise to develop problem-solving abilities, was often discouraged. Being intellectually critical could lead to one's expulsion from these schools or to voluntarily dropping out (Butler, 1959).

But it is not only the lessening of critical faculties that results from a one-sided reliance on this kind of training. There also results an equating of the professional role with the particular paradigm being emphasized. For many of them, giving up the paradigm would mean giving up the professional role. To understand their reluctance it is necessary to look at the social context in which many of these programs operated. When the innovators first came into the prison setting they were scoffed at by the traditional correctional workers and called, "do-gooders," "social workers," "convict-lovers," and so forth. They (the innovators) saw themselves as the bearers of a new, scientifically derived knowledge that was humanistically oriented. Their mission was to change the typical climate —lessen what in their opinion were its "punitive aspects" and replace them with an emphasis on humanistically oriented treatment. In their eyes the contest was often between those that were punishment-oriented and those who advocated what we have titled the personality approach of treatment. The innovators saw victory in terms of having this latter paradigm prevail.

They further resisted reconsidering their basic approach because they were unprepared to deal with failure. They believed that the basic problem had been solved by the paradigm, and therefore if a particular program did not work it was because they were not doing enough. Often doing more meant trying to increase the intensity of the treatment (Himelson, 1968). Another often heard remedy was the development of classification or typology systems. The program people reasoned that all inmates, residents, or patients are not alike; therefore, one of the major reasons for the lack of positive results was the lack of differentiation among the subjects. The belief is that there is an optimal treatment for every offender (see Wilkins 1969:89–103, for a discussion of the classification and typology of offenders).

The bureaucrats at the top of the organizations carrying out programs of criminal rehabilitation owe no particular loyalties to the treatment paradigms. They do not see their roles tied to any specific type of program. They are simply interested in results. While they may have been won over by the treatment fashion of the day or have not seen any other alternative available at the time, they are not committed in the way that the helping professionals are. If an approach has persistently failed to lead to successful results, the so-called bureaucrat has eventually turned to a new approach. With the availability of fairly sophisticated research evidence, they have been able to make these judgments with some confidence. They have seldom made public announcements about the ineffectiveness of an old program—to do so would not be politically expedient. Rather, an ineffective program has been quietly phased out or relegated to obscurity. Thus, the top bureaucrats can be and often are more flexible than many of the professionals, and in my estimation the morality play is indeed a work of fiction.

Stigma and Labeling

The entire question of stigma and labeling has achieved recent prominence in the fields of criminology and deviance (Foster et al, 1972; Goffman, 1963; Harris, 1975; Lemert, 1967; Rosenhan, 1973; Scheff, 1974; Schur, 1971; Thorsell and Klemke, 1972). But long before this academic interest, the difficulties which the excon had in getting a decent job and being socially accepted were well known to the general public. The label of criminal or excon not only carried the connotation of having committed a criminal act in the past, but also indicated to many that the individual continued to be untrustworthy and morally suspect. This resulted in men and women being denied satisfactory jobs even though there appeared to be no apparent relationship between their past criminal activity and their potential as employees. The operation of this exclusion resulting from stigma was not always apparent. Often a kind of scientific rationality was invoked to explain not hiring. Thus, when an exconvict approached a potential employer and demonstrated the necessary skills for the job, he was often not hired. The actual reason he was not given the job was in most instances that the employer was influenced by stigmatic considerations or he felt his other employees would be disturbed by his hiring the ex-offender. But if he does not give the person the job the employer is publicly rejecting the strongly held American value that a man or woman should be given a second chance. To avoid making this rejection of the value apparent, other reasons are invoked. Some of the most often used are problems of security, insurance, or fidelity bonding. Despite the fact that these are occasionally legitimate barriers to employment, in the majority of instances the real barriers are the employers themselves (Himelson, 1966).

This rejection from the pursuit of normal moral careers has been advanced by some in the field of criminal rehabilitation (especially those advocating the education-socialization approach) as a major reason for lack of results. They claim that no matter how good the program, any benefits are washed out by societal rejection and the ensuing alienation of the exprisoner.

ALTERNATIVES TO REHABILITATION

Given the fact that the criminal rehabilitation movement has completely failed to achieve its objectives, what alternative means might be adopted in dealing with the problem of the criminal offender? In trying to assess the desirability of various alternatives three factors should be kept in mind regarding each. (1) Is the approach compatible with the present aims of our political-legal system? (2) How much economic cost is involved? (3) From the technical point of view will the approach work?

REDUCTION IN THE NUMBER OF CRIMINAL LAWS   This first alternative is not aimed at doing more, but rather at doing less. Its purpose, by eliminating a number of criminal laws, is drastically to reduce the number of persons being dealt with by the criminal justice system. Those supporting this approach decry the present tendency to deal with many social problems through use of the criminal law. There is special concern about the effects of enforcement of laws regarding so-called victimless crimes (Morris and Hawkins, 1970; Schur and Bedau, 1974). Proponents of this approach believe that by eliminating many of these laws, a number of positive benefits will be realized: (a) With fewer cases on the calendar the criminal courts will be more likely to function without having to resort to the routine form of plea bargaining which presently demeans the criminal law process in so many jurisdictions; (b) The police will have greater resources to concentrate on the more serious crimes (with reduced opportunities for police corruption); (c) Those no longer defined as criminals by the law no longer have to be "rehabilitated." This is consistent with the libertarian approach to individual conduct which advocates the maximum possible latitude for voluntaristic, individual behavior which does not directly harm others, with the minimal amount of governmental coercion (supposedly, the point of view of the founding fathers); (d) The drastic depopulating of our jails and prisons that probably would result from reducing the number of criminal laws, may not further rehabilitation, but would make for more humane conditions for the remaining prisoners.

DIVERSION   An alternative that not only has been considered but also applied is that of diversion. By diversion is meant preventing persons arrested or detained by police authorities from entering various parts of the criminal justice system (that is, courts, jails, prison, parole, and so on). These kinds of programs have been most frequently used in dealing with youth detained by the police for relatively minor offenses. Rather than locking them up for any appreciable time, the police have referred youths to such organizations as social welfare agencies or simply released them without further action. These programs are based upon the premise that much of youth deviance is transitory and will not recur, or at least infrequently, if youths are not "hardened" through negative labeling or contact with more sophisticated deviants in penal institutions. Often times these diversion programs have rehabilitation aspects attached to them (for example, referral to treatment in a social welfare setting)—programs which are probably as ineffective as their institutional counterparts (Empey, 1973; Martinson, 1974).

INCARCERATION Another alternative to the policy emphasizing rehabilitation is that of placing in institutions the more serious offenders and *not being concerned with their reformation*. The primary purpose is to take them out of circulation and thus protect others. They would not be denied access to programs for self-improvement during confinement, but they would participate on a voluntary basis, without necessarily receiving any reward (for example, early release) for their actions.

Among the proponents of this approach are two general groups who have supported its implementation. The first group is made up of people whom Packer (1968) has called proponents of the "crime-control" model. Their major concern is getting criminals off the streets and into jails and prisons. The longer the period of incarceration the better. They feel that the emphasis on rehabilitation has led to shorter periods of confinement without any compensatory benefits. The second group consists of those who are primarily emphasizing the constitutional rights of individuals. Packer calls this the "due process" approach. This latter group has been very critical of what they see as the highly coercive nature of participation in criminal rehabilitation programs (that is, inmates must be active in these programs if they want to be released). They have also been concerned with what they believe to be the brainwashing aspects of many rehabilitation programs, which they view as a violation of the rights of prisoners.[4] Furthermore, they believe the removal of coercive rehabilitation will eliminate much of the hypocrisy they consider to be practiced by prison systems, who often use the rhetoric of rehabilitation to carry out policies of punishment.

SELF-HELP GROUPS While self-help groups which provide a total community arrangement appear to be a promising alternative to governmentally operated programs of criminal rehabilitation, their overall effect cannot be decisive because of the relatively small number who are long-range members of these organizations. Since membership in these self-help communities is voluntary, this will probably always be the case. Their for-

[4] The crime control and due process proponents—while they may agree on the deemphasizing of criminal rehabilitation—diverge widely on other issues. The former generally advocate incarceration for a wider range of crimes and for longer periods of time than do individuals of the latter persuasion.

mation can be encouraged through a relaxation of zoning regulations that allows for their existence in desirable locations, a lack of harassment by law enforcement, and perhaps a very modest degree of governmental economic support. But too great an effort or financial expenditure on the part of federal, state, or local government will lead to greater governmental control over these programs with the usual result of a pernicious draining of their vitality and autonomy.

CONCLUSIONS

It is abundantly clear that from the technical point of view the criminal rehabilitation movement has completely failed, but serious objections to the continuance and further creation of criminal rehabilitation programs are not held only on the grounds of their inefficiency. We discussed earlier that the criminal justice process is usually split into separate and contradictory phases. The trial portion operates on the assumption that the defendant is a "reasonable person"; later, however, the same person as prisoner in a rehabilitative setting is often treated as unreasonable and irrational.

There are critics who claim that because the rehabilitative phase frequently emphasizes this deterministic view of human behavior it undermines notions of personal responsibility and therefore negates some of the basic notions of the law and of a democratic society (Allen, 1964). For these critics, effective rehabilitation programs would be as great or perhaps a greater disaster than the present record of ineffectiveness, for it would indicate that men and women can be coerced through various techniques into becoming something and someone they do

not choose to be of their own volition. The critics posit the greater danger that these same techniques might be generalized for political and other purposes. But the general futility of programs of criminal rehabilitation, at least up to this point, should somewhat allay their fears.

The lack of results in criminal rehabilitation has other implications besides those for ethics and politics. Seriously brought into question is a whole model of what can best be described as behavioral utopianism—the belief in the possibility of bringing about drastic, rapid, and long-lasting changes in complex human behavior through the deliberate intervention of special agents of change (see Kristol, 1974, for a general discussion of this utopianism). In many programs these agents were specially trained professionals, operating from various behavioral paradigms, using different metalanguages, and devising various classifications and typologies. Each created a slightly different behavioral image of the prisoner or resident, but most of the images portrayed the object of rehabilitators' efforts—the criminal—as a faulty machine, similar to other faulty machines, repairable through mass production techniques which if not presently known, were soon to be discovered. The total lack of results of these programs calls into question the validity of the whole superstructure, not only for the treatment of criminals but for other attempts in such areas as mental health and poverty. In these other fields similar evidence is accumulating.

If we accept the utter futility of pursuing further efforts in coercive criminal rehabilitation, what shall we advocate in its place? If we have learned anything from recent experience it is not to put all our eggs in one utopian basket. A moderate implementation of the four alternatives previously presented would appear to represent the best strategy. (1) Through the legislative process there should be a significant reduction in the range of behavior covered by the criminal law; (2) those caught up in it for trivial reasons should be diverted from the criminal justice system; (3) jails and prisons should be used for the purpose of protecting others in the society or for symbolizing the extreme gravity of a crime; and (4) we should encourage use of private, voluntary, self-help communities for those who feel they need these kinds of environments.

None of these alternative actions will solve the majority of the problems of crime and delinquency. Their solution lies elsewhere and with different remedies. But they will help restore a greater confidence in the integrity of our criminal justice system. Their implementation may also help reduce the cost of government and represent one step toward reversing the dangerous trend toward an ever-increasing criminal justice establishment.

References

Alexander, Franz, and Healy, William. *Roots of Crime*. New York: Knopf, 1935.

Allen, Francis. *The Borderland of Criminal Justice*. Chicago: University of Chicago Press, 1964.

Andrews, William. *Bygone Punishments*. New York: Frederick Publications, 1960.

Bailey, Walter. "Correctional Treatment: An Analysis of One Hundred Correctional Outcome Studies." *Journal of Criminal Law, Criminology and Police Science*, 1966, 57, 153–160.

Black, Donald J. "Production of Crime Rates." *American Sociological Review*, 1970, 35, 733–748.

Braly, Malcolm. *On the Yard*. Boston: Little, Brown, 1967.

Brooks, Harvey. "Scientific Concepts and Cultural Change." In Gerald Holton (Ed.), *Science and Culture*. Boston: Houghton Mifflin, 1965. Pp. 71–87.

Burkhart, Walter, and Sathmary, Arthur. *The Narcotic Treatment Control Program*. Research Report No. 19. Sacramento: California Department of Corrections, 1962.

Butler, Ruth. *An Orientation to Knowledge of Human Growth and Behavior in Social Work Education*. New York: Council on Social Work Education, 1959.

Caldwell, Robert. "The Juvenile Court: Its Development and Major Problems." *Journal of Criminal Law, Criminology and Police Science*, 1961, 51, 493–511.

Casriel, Daniel. *So Fair a House*. Englewood Cliffs, N.J.: Prentice-Hall, 1963.

Clark, Ramsey. *Crime in America*. New York: Simon & Schuster, 1970.

Clemmer, Donald. *The Prison Community*. New York: Rinehart and Company, 1958. (First issued 1940.)

Cloward, Richard, and Ohlin, Lloyd. *Delinquency and Opportunity*. New York: Free Press, 1960.

Corrections Magazine. "From 'Bums' to Businessmen: The Delancey Street Foundation." 1974, 1, 13–28.

Dickover, Robert, Maynard, Verner, and Painter, James. *A Study of Vocational Training in the California Department of Corrections*. Research Report No. 40. Sacramento, Ca.: Research Division, Department of Corrections, 1971.

Durkheim, Emile. *The Division of Labor in Society*. New York: Macmillan, 1933.

Durkheim, Emile. *Suicide*, edited by George Simpson. Glencoe, Ill.: Free Press, 1951.

Eaton, Joseph. *Stone Walls Not a Prison Make*. Springfield, Ill.: Charles C. Thomas, 1962.

Empey, LaMar. "Juvenile Justice Reform: Due Process and Deinstitutionalization." In Lloyd Ohlin (Ed.), *Prisoners in America*. Englewood Cliffs, N.J.: Prentice-Hall, 1973. Pp. 13–48.

Fenton, Norman. *Group Counseling*. Sacramento, Ca.: Institute for the Study of Crime and Delinquency, 1961.

Foster, Jack, Dinitz, Simon, and Reckless, Walter. "Perceptions of Stigma Following Public Intervention for Delinquent Behavior." *Social Problems*, 1972, 20, 202–209.

Franks, C. M. *Behavior Therapy: Appraisal and Status*. Chicago: Aldine, 1969.

Geis, Gilbert. *The East Los Angeles Halfway House for Addicts*. Sacramento, Ca.: The Institute for the Study of Crime and Delinquency, 1966.

Geis, Gilbert. "Ethical and Legal Issues in Experimentation with Offender Populations." *Research in Correctional Rehabilitation*. Washington: Joint Commission on Correctional Manpower and Training, 1967. Pp. 34–41.

Glaser, Daniel, and Stratton, John. "Measuring Inmate Change in Prison." In *The Prison: Studies in Institutional Organization and Change*. New York: Holt, Rinehart and Winston, 1961.

Goffman, Erving. *Stigma: Notes on the Management of Spoiled Identity*. Englewood Cliffs, N.J.: Prentice-Hall, 1963.

Harris, Anthony R. "Imprisonment and Expected Value of Criminal Choice: A Specification and Test of Aspects of the Labeling Perspective." *American Sociological Review*, 1975, 40, 71–87.

HARYOU (Harlem Youth Opportunities Unlimited). *Youth in the Ghetto*. New York, 1964.

Healy, William. "The Individual Study of the Young Criminal." *Journal of the American Institute of Criminal Law and Criminology*, 1910, 1, 50.

Heelan, Patrick. *Quantum Mechanics and Objectivity. A Study of the Physical Philosophy of Werner Heisenberg*. The Hague: Martinus Nijhoff, 1965.

Himelson, Alfred. *Risk and Rehabilitation*. Sacramento, Ca.: Institute for the Study of Crime and Delinquency, 1966.

Himelson, Alfred. *When Treatment Failed*. Unpublished Ph.D. dissertation, University of California at Los Angeles, 1968.

Himelson, Alfred, and Thoma, Blanche. *The Narcotic Treatment Control Program: Phase III*. Sacramento: California Department of Corrections, 1968.

Homans, George. *The Human Group*. New York: Harcourt, 1950.

Irwin, John. *The Felon*. Englewood Cliffs, N.J.: Prentice-Hall, 1970.

Jeffrey, C. Ray. "Criminal Justice and Social Change." In F. James Davis, H. H. Foster, C. Ray Jeffrey, and Eugene Davis (Eds.), *Society and the Law*. New York: Free Press, 1962. Pp. 264–310.

Johnson, Elmer H. *Crime, Correction, and Society*. Homewood, Ill.: Dorsey Press, 1974.

Jones, Maxwell. *The Therapeutic Community*. New York: Basic Books, 1953.

Jones, Maxwell. *Social Psychiatry in the Community, in Hospitals, and in Prisons*. Springfield, Ill.: Charles C Thomas, 1962.

Kazdin, A. E., and Bootzin, R. R. "The Token Economy: An Evaluative Review." *Journal of Applied Behavioral Analysis*, 1972, 5, 343–372.

Kristol, Irving. "Utopianism, Ancient and Modern." *The Alternative*, 1974, 7, 5–9.

Kuhn, Thomas. "The Function of Dogma in Scientific Research." In A. C. Crombie (Ed.), *Scientific Change*. New York: Basic Books, 1963. Pp. 347–395.

Lemert, Edwin. *Human Deviance, Social Problems and Social Control*. Englewood Cliffs, N.J.: Prentice-Hall, 1967.

Lemert, Edwin. *Social Action and Legal Change*. Chicago: Aldine, 1970.

Lerman, Paul. "Evaluating the Outcome of Institutions for Delinquents." *Social Work*, 1968, 13, 55–64.

Lindner, Robert. *Rebel without a Cause*. New York: Gwen and Stratton, 1944.

Mannheim, Herman, and Wilkins, Leslie. *Prediction Methods in Relation to Borstal Training*. London: Her Majesty's Stationary Office, 1955.

Martinson, Robert. "What Works?—Questions and Answers about Prison Reform." *The Public Interest*, 1974, 9, 23–54.

Martinson, Robert, Kassebaum, Gene, and Ward, David. "A Critique of Research in Parole." *Federal Probation*, 1964, 28, 34–38.

Matza, David. *Delinquency and Drift*. New York: Wiley, 1964.

McCollum, Sylvia. "New Design for Correctional Education and Training Programs." In Paul F. Cromwell, Jr. (Ed.), *Jails and Justice*. Springfield, Ill.: Charles C. Thomas, 1975. Pp. 197–210.

Mennel, Robert. *Thorns and Thistles*. Hannover, N.H.: University Press of New England, 1973.

Merton, Robert. *Social Theory and Social Structure*. Glencoe, Ill.: Free Press, 1957.

Miller, Donald, Himelson, Alfred, and Geis, Gilbert. "Community's Response to Substance Misuse." *International Journal of the Addictions*, 1967, 2, 305–310.

Miller, Walter B. "Ideology and Criminal Justice Policy: Some Current Issues." *Journal of Criminal Law and Criminology*, 1973, 64, 141–162.

Morris, Norval, and Hawkins, Gordon. *The Honest Politician's Guide to Crime*. Chicago: University of Chicago Press, 1970.

Packer, Herbert L. *The Limits of the Criminal Sanction*. Stanford, Ca.: The Stanford University Press, 1968.

Polanyi, Michael. *Personal Knowledge*. Chicago: University of Chicago Press, 1958.

Pound, Roscoe. "The Individualization of Justice." In *The 1930 Yearbook*, National Probation Association, 1930.

Pound, Roscoe. "The Rise of Socialized Criminal Justice." In *Social Defenses against Crime 1942 Yearbook*, National Probation Association, 1942.

Pownall, George A. "Employment Problems of Released Prisoners." In G. R. Perlstein and T. R. Phelps (Eds.), *Alternatives to Prison*. Pacific Palisades, Ca.: Goodyear Publishing Company, 1975. Pp. 238–246.

President's Commission on Law Enforcement and Administration of Justice. *Task Force Report: Corrections*. Washington, D.C., 1967.

Price, Don. "The Established Dissenters." In Gerald Holton (Ed.), *Science and Culture*. Boston: Houghton Mifflin, 1965. Pp. 128–143.

Rapoport, Robert. *Community as Doctor*. London: Tavistock, 1960.

Reiss, Albert J., Jr. *The Police and the Public*. New Haven, Conn.: Yale University Press, 1971.

Robison, James, and Takagi, Paul. *Case Decisions in a State Parole System*. Research Report No. 31. Sacramento, Ca.: Research Division, California Department of Corrections, 1968.

Robison, James, and Takagi, Paul. "The Parole Violator as an Organizational Reject." In Robert Carter and Leslie Wilkins (Eds.), *Probation and Parole*. New York: Wiley, 1970. Pp. 233–254.

Robison, James, and Smith, Gerald. "The Effectiveness of Correctional Programs." *Crime and Delinquency*, 1971, 17, 67–80.

Roethlesberger, F. J., and Dickson, W. J. *Management and the Worker*. Cambridge, Mass.: Harvard University Press, 1939.

Rosenhan, D. L. "On Being Sane in Insane Places." *Science*, 1973, 179, 250–258.

Rubin, Sol. "The Indeterminate Sentence: Success or Failure." *Focus*, 1949, 28, 47.

Scheff, Thomas. "The Labeling Theory of Mental Illness." *American Sociological Review*, 1974, 39, 444–452.

Schrag, Clarence. "A Preliminary Criminal Typology." *Pacific Sociological Review*, 1961, 4, 11–16.

Schur, Edwin M. *Labeling Deviant Behavior*. New York: Harper & Row, 1971.

Schur, Edwin, and Bedau, Hugo. *Victimless Crimes*. Englewood Cliffs, N.J.: Prentice-Hall Inc., 1974.

Segal, Steven. "Research on the Outcome of Social Work Therapeutic Interventions: A Review of the Literature." *Journal of Health and Social Behavior*, 1972, 13, 3–17.

Short, James F., and Nye, F. Ivan. "Extent of Unrecorded Juvenile Delinquency." *Journal of Criminal Law, Criminology and Police Science*, 1958, 49, 296–302.

Sillitoe, Allen. *The Loneliness of the Long Distance Runner.* New York: Knopf, 1959.

Skinner, B. F. *Contingencies of Reinforcement: A Theoretical Analysis.* New York: Appleton, 1969.

Slavson, S. R. *Re-Educating the Delinquent.* New York: Harper & Row, 1954.

Sykes, Gresham. *The Society of Captives.* Princeton, N.J.: Princeton University Press, 1958.

Sykes, Gresham, and Matza, David. "Techniques of Neutralization: A Theory of Delinquency." *The American Journal of Sociology*, 1957, 22, 664–670.

Tharp, Roland, and Wetzel, Ralph. *Behavior Modification in the Natural Environment.* New York: Academic Press, 1969.

Thorsell, Bernard, and Klemke, Lloyd. "The Labeling Process: Reinforcement and Deterrent." *Law and Society Review*, 1972, 6, 393–403.

Volkman, Rita, and Cressey, Donald. "Differential Association and the Rehabilitation of Drug Addicts." *American Journal of Sociology*, 1963, 69, 129–142.

Wieder, Donald L. *The Convict Code: A Study of a Moral Order as a Persuasive Activity.* Ph.D. dissertation. University of California, Los Angeles, 1969.

Wieder, Donald L. *Language and Social Reality: The Case of Telling the Convict Code.* The Hague: Mouton, 1974.

Wilkins, Leslie T. *Evaluation of Penal Measures.* New York: Random House, 1969.

Yablonsky, Lewis. *The Tunnel Back: Synanon.* New York: Macmillan, 1965.

Suggested Reading

ALLEN, FRANCIS. *The Borderland of Criminal Justice.* Chicago: University of Chicago Press, 1964.
A competent presentation of the position of those opposing the criminal rehabilitation movement on legal and philosophical grounds.

BRALY, MALCOLM. *On the Yard.* Boston: Little, Brown, 1967.
A novel written by an exinmate which vividly portrays inmate life.

IRWIN, JOHN. *The Felon.* Englewood Cliffs, N.J.: Prentice-Hall, 1970.
A sociological analysis of the life of the convict and the problems faced after release.

MARTINSON, ROBERT. "What Works?—Questions and Answers about Prison Reform." *The Public Interest*, 1974, 9, 23–54.
A summary of the results of various kinds of rehabilitation programs to date.

MATZA, DAVID. *Delinquency and Drift.* New York: Wiley, 1964.
The first section of the book contains a though-provoking analysis of the influence of positivism in the development of Western criminology and corrections.

MENNEL, ROBERT. *Thorns and Thistles.* Hannover, N.H.: University Press of New England, 1973.
One of the few works that makes an attempt to describe the early development of juvenile justice systems and programs in the U.S.

MILLER, DONALD, HIMELSON, ALFRED, AND GEIS, GILBERT. "Community's Response to Substance Misuse." *International Journal of the Addictions,* 1967, 2, 305–310.
A brief, concise analysis of what went wrong with a parole department-operated halfway-house program for addicts.

MORRIS, NORVAL, AND HAWKINS, GORDON. *The Honest Politician's Guide to Crime.* Chicago: University of Chicago Press, 1970.
This book attempts to deal with some of the major issues in criminal justice and penology and presents some alternatives to replace what is being done presently.

ROBISON, JAMES, AND SMITH, GERALD. "The Effectiveness of Correctional Programs." *Crime and Delinquency,* 1971, 17, 67–80.
An evaluation of some of the important shibboleths used as the basis for devising prison, parole, and probation programs.

Part VI
Postscript

The growth of government at all levels in the past forty years is in part a response to the attempt to meet the social needs generated by the rapid expansion of the American economy and to undercut or divert the discontent and protest resulting from the contrast between great wealth and dismal poverty. As a result, the affairs of millions have come to be administered in one respect or another by bureaucratic agencies of the state or affected by some state or federally funded program. With the availability of large amounts of tax-derived funds as well as a burgeoning faith in and impetus to rely upon a bureaucratic response to societal troubles, the liberal or reform approach to social problems tends to generate a plethora of programs and policies aimed at effecting change in the behavior of individuals or organizations the conduct of which has been officially defined as "problematic." The increase of private, community-based self-help organizations in recent years has tended to reproduce the programatic approach of governmental agencies on a smaller scale.

John Berecochea poses a pertinent question for partisans of one or another program: How do you know it works? On the surface, this challenge has a conventional ring since governmental funding agencies and legislative bodies increasingly require some systematic evaluation of the programs they support. Berecochea provides a concise summary of the issues involved in evaluating the effectiveness of a program aimed at ameliorating some problem, including the pitfalls of faulty research design, the problems emerging from the difficulty in determining if the program was actually implemented, and the perplexities of deciding among alternative explanations of the results once in hand. His chapter, in effect, furnishes an introduction to the elements of evaluation research and should equip the student with at least rudimentary critical tools for assessing claims to program effectiveness.

Berecochea's concerns are not narrowly technical, however. He is careful to make explicit what he sees as basic assumptions in the methodological practices of evaluation and in the design and administration of social programs—assumptions that might be questioned apart from finding specific procedural weaknesses in particular evaluation studies or deciding that a program is or is not "effective." He urges a skeptical stance in assessing solutions to social problems, not merely at the level of rigorous evaluation but in terms of more fundamental questions such as: Even if the program *works* is the solution it offers good in terms of one's values? Is the behavior or condition remedied by the program really in need of change? Will a program be adopted just because it is effective? Will it be abandoned just because it is *in*effective? What alternative solutions are excluded from consideration?

Berecochea's skepticism is parallel to the critical attitude adopted by Hadden and Lester in the introductory article. The attempt to ameliorate social problems through the administration of programs aimed primarily at modifying the behavior of disadvantaged and stigmatized populations prove difficult to evaluate or are found to be ineffective but are nonetheless robust in the face of alternative approaches which do not vest power in the hands of established bureaucracies or take aim at current power arrangements in society. The solution to social problems, like their definition, reveal a great deal about their architect and the larger interests served.

How Do You Know It Works?

John E. Berecochea

The intent of this article is to provide the reader with an understanding of the commonly used strategies and techniques for determining if a program or policy designed to alleviate a social problem actually does so. Even at the elementary level of this exposition, it will be found that the task is much more complex than it would appear from the simplicity of the question "How do you know it works?"

The opening paragraph reflects two difficult and unhappy choices. First, this treatise will focus on traditional ways of determining whether a program or policy works and, second, it will be rather pervasively skeptical.

The Heavy Arm of Tradition

The decision to limit this presentation to traditional methods of evaluation was based on the fact that most readers of this text will be examining the claims of others about effectiveness rather than doing the research themselves, and, by definition, most such studies are done in traditional ways. When closely examined there are several assumptions underlying the traditional strategies and techniques for testing effectiveness. These assumptions are embedded in both the methodological practices and the programs and policies tested. It would be possible to separate out the assumptions underlying the methods and programs or policies in the abstract, but in practice they are inextricably intermixed.

With no order implied, the first assumption is that reliable and valid so-cially useful knowledge can be gained by viewing the social world as if it were understandable by the use of causal relationships. The second assumption is that social phenomenon can be understood by methods of analysis which treat the social world as if it were separable along various dimensions which can be analytically manipulated in such a way as to accurately account for observed or observable social change.[1] For example, it is assumed that a workable theory of juvenile gang formation could be devised on the basis that the formation of gangs is the result of certain knowable combinations of characteristics of the social environment and the people in it. The third assumption is that the alleviation or elimination of the social problem is desirable. Witchcraft and homosexuality are, for example, social problems about which there has been or is some disagreement as to the desirability of elimination or alleviation. Belief in social harm by witches no longer prevails in the United States and the belief that homosexuality is morally, legally, individually, or socially harmful is under sustained and growing attack.[2]

The fourth assumption seems to be embedded in the practice of evaluational research rather than in the methodologi-

[1] A different set of assumptions, simply stated, is made by Mao Tse-Tung (1967).

[2] An analysis of witchcraft and witches as deviance is given by Kai T. Erickson (1966). The decriminalization of homosexuality is supported by Edwin M. Schur (1965:67–119). William Simon and John H. Gagnon (1967) argue for the position that homosexuality and heterosexuality are not distinct categories.

cal techniques themselves, but it is nonetheless an assumption, and a critical one. This assumption is that managers of the program being evaluated will produce a more effective program if they allocate some portion of the available funds to the evaluation of the program either by their own staff or by researchers connected with such external organizations as universities, private research outfits, or the staff of the agency which provides (all or part of) the funding for the operation of the program. To date, this assumption seems to have received scant attention. However, the writings of those people and groups now often referred to as "activists"—public interest groups such as those originated or spawned by Ralph Nader, community organizers such as Saul Alinsky, Marxist politicians/theorists, and "anticolonialists"—are developing a body of practices and theories which should be consulted by anyone who might wish to assess effectiveness in ways other than those presented herein (Alinsky, 1972; Barrera and Vialpondo, 1974; Carmichael and Hamilton, 1967; Fanon, 1968; Memmi, 1967; Nader and Ross, 1972; Mao Tse-Tung, 1966).

The critical differences between these alternatives and those presented herein are two. One is the relative emphasis on practice versus theory. These alternatives emphasize everyday active involvement in the production of social change as the basis for the development of theory. Theoretical propositions grow out of practice, and those propositions developed out of practice which do not lead to change are modified. As applied, this has resulted in an interest in change which is easily recognizable by those involved in the practice as well as those involved as targets of the change. The other critical difference is in the locus of the

"program." The traditional techniques of evaluating programs were developed to examine those carried out by such conventional social institutions as the government (for example, social welfare, public health, and law enforcement agencies), public charities (such as, church-related welfare agencies, national youth organizations, and blood banks), and professional service associations (for example, physicians, psychologists, and lawyers). The alternative strategies and techniques of the "activists" were developed by the people who are the objects of the traditional social-problem programs just indicated. Some of these alternative groups include those typically identified as activists, militants, liberation fronts, socialists, and community organizations representing such groups as prisoners, blacks, homosexuals, mental hospital patients, students, ghetto residents, native Americans, Africans in European colonies, and the poor and racially oppressed worldwide.

A most happy development in the area of social problems in particular and for all people in general would be a synthesis of the traditional and alternative methods of developing and testing solutions to social problems. Such a development seems possible.

The Importance of Skepticism

The behaviors and conditions which come to be identified as a social problem are most often undesirable for the people directly affected (for example, alcoholism, poverty, and suicide) or the larger society (example, crimes of violence, overpopulation, and environmental pollution); it is thus important to the aggrieved parties that they be solved or alleviated. A hardy dose of skepticism is helpful in examining the programs and policies designed to alleviate the social problem(s) in that there is a tendency to believe that the programs or policies which come to be established are doing the job and those charged with carrying them out are both ideologically and materially committed to seeing them as effective. When the program or policy is or becomes governmental, the tendency toward self-perpetuation probably becomes even greater.

To take but one example, the threat of military attack upon the United States of America is a problem which has spawned the national defense system comprised of both the military and the industries which supply goods and services to the government. At least one "private" company which supplies military hardware was given governmental security for a loan amounting to millions of dollars because the failure of the company would have resulted in massive unemployment and a serious threat to the well-being of the economic elite.[3] The failure of the military policy of deterrence to produce a market situation in which the need for hardware could be met by ordinary procurement procedures was thus extraordinarily rectified and the ordinary policies and programs were continued because other interests became paramount. Similarly, it has been claimed that juvenile reformatories (or correctional institutions) continue to exist not because of any claims of rehabilitative effectiveness made by those who operate or fund them, but, rather, because they serve to keep the poor in their place (Liazos, 1974).

[3] For a thorough treatment of the virtually autonomous, post-"military-industrial complex" see Seymour Melman (1970). For a treatment of war as a social problem, see Irving Louis Horowitz (1966).

TOWARD A DEFINITION OF TERMS

The relatively succinct definitions which follow are intended to provide a basis for beginning. They are *not* meant to be memorized as the word of God or any of his or her temporal standins. The meanings of the terms will shift as the presentation moves on, and any ultimate meanings will be left to the cataloguers and those who believe that such god-like qualities as omniscience and knowledge of ultimate realities are open to the human intelligence.

The three key words for the task at hand are "know it works." For the sake of convenience and in order to tie these words from the title to the traditional works in the area, substitutes will be used; methodology (for know), program (for it) and effectiveness (for works) will be used.

Program

The term program will incorporate programs as such, as well as policies; programs and policies are distinguishable in the abstract, but they often merge together in practice. A program is any set of activities designed to accomplish some goal or set of goals. Typically, these activities are carried out by a single organization. These organizations include the government and its various divisions, private welfare organizations, and self-help organizations, among others. Aid to families with dependent children, police athletic leagues (for children), and Alcoholics Anonymous are programs, for example.

A policy may be defined as a set of principles to be used as guides in deciding what is to be done now and in the future given a choice of actions in the light of existing conditions. Policies are designed to achieve some valued end(s) or goal(s). Policies are themselves chosen from among alternatives and the principles may be put in priority orders. For example, politicians and bureaucrats in the United States have, in effect, decided to deter (rather than ignore or promote) the recreational use of opiate drugs by a policy of criminal punishment, stressing severity over certainty, and excluding medical treatment.[4]

Some other examples of programs and policies are cash assistance to the aged, the criminal justice system in general, and probation; in particular, public information campaigns to limit family size, racial/ethnic integration, air pollution controls, medical control of deviants not defined as criminal, capitalist expansion, and so forth.

Effectiveness

Effectiveness refers to the degree to which a program (or policy) achieves its goals. In some cases, goal achievement hardly requires investigation. For instance, the goal of outlawing the production and sale of alcoholic beverages was accomplished by the Eighteenth Amendment to the United States Constitution, although the goal of eliminating the consumption of alcoholic beverages was not; prohibition probably helped to create the bases for contemporary organized crime, and pro-

[4] The development of the criminalization of opiate use in America and an analysis of the severe penalties imposed is provided by Alfred R. Lindesmith (1947:179–203). The medical profession's exclusion from the treatment of opiate addicts and their active involvement in abandoning the medical treatment of addicts is treated by David E. Smith and George R. Gay (1972).

hibition was subsequently repealed by the Twenty-first Amendment.

The story of prohibition provides a good example of one of the major problems of assessing effectiveness. The problem is how to measure effectiveness. One reason that this is a problem is that a program typically has more than one goal and they are often at odds with each other. Related to the problem of mixed, incongruent goals is the fact that different groups interested in the program have different interests in the accomplishment of the goals, so that success in one of the goals may be irrelevant to another group with different goals, or even a failure for those with opposite goals. Some goals are so obscure as to defy measurement and some are such that making them explicit would cause embarrassment. Measurement of a program's effectiveness may be irrelevant to changes in it.

If the program of political education carried out by the Women's Christian Temperance Union and related or sympathetic organizations was intended to eliminate the drinking of alcoholic beverages, then it was probably a failure. However, this could not be reliably or accurately determined in that measures of alcohol consumption during the period of prohibition were extremely difficult, if not impossible. However, if the goal was to assert as governmental law that the values of the advocates of temperance were the values of the country, than the program was a smashing symbolic success, except that there is some question about whether the temperance group activities were responsible for the enactment of prohibition. The repeal of prohibition was not due to research showing its failure to eliminate or reduce the use of alcohol (that is, its "effectiveness"); rather, repeal was due to the ascendance into political power of those groups for whom temperance was not symbolic of their values.[5]

Methodology

Finally, there is the issue of methodology. Most generally, methodology refers to the strategies and techniques used to learn about the phenomenon of interest; that is, what we do when we want to generate new knowledge about some topic. Strategy is the determination of what information is needed and can be obtained, how the information is to be organized so as to make sense, and how it is to be collected and analyzed. Technique refers to specific steps taken in collecting, organizing, and analyzing the information.

EVALUATION

As indicated earlier, the methods for examining effectiveness to be discussed are based upon the concept of cause. Other concepts of the sources of change are available; indeed, these other sources of change are critical in the evaluation of effectiveness (cause), for it is the elimination of these and other sources of change as possible causes of the program/policy's apparent effects which leaves the program/policy as the only viable alternative explanation for the change (or deviation from the expected).

[5] Probably one of the best program evaluation studies, although not intended as such, is Joseph R. Gusfield's *Symbolic Crusade: Status Politics and the American Temperance Movement* (1966). An outline of two approaches to organizational analysis—one centering on specific goal attainment and one centering on organizational survival—is provided by Amitai Etzioni (1960).

The Concept of Cause

The concept of cause is simple in principle but elusive in practice. In principle, it is the idea that some event or condition produces some other event or condition. For instance, putting a match to an open container of gasoline causes a fire, at least under certain conditions. Similarly, wealthy, upper-status, well-educated parents produce children who are also wealthy, upper-status, and well-educated, at least under certain conditions.[6] However, if the oxygen is removed from the room in which the gasoline and match are brought together or if the child is raised in an orphanage for children of the poor, low-status, and uneducated, the postulated causal relationships will most likely not hold. Thus, certain conditions must be present for causal relationships to hold.

The typical method used to infer a causal relationship is to introduce the causal agent into a situation which is identical to another situation in all regards except for the presence of the (presumed) causal agent and then observe the result or lack thereof. There are at least two requirements of this method. The presumed causal agent must be present under one condition and absent under the other, and no other causal agent may be present or its effects must be separable and known.

Although it may seem abstract or actually unrelated, the goals of a program are

[6] Peter Blau and Otis Dudley Duncan (1967) have studied these variables extensively using high-level sociological mathematical theory. Christopher Jencks et. al. (1972) have used equally high-power methods and theory to reach different conclusions. For a critique of the latter, see "Review Symposium on Inequality: A Reassessment of the Effect of Family and Schooling in America by Christopher Jencks and others," (1969).

a part of the program (that is, the causal agent whose effect is to be determined). As was indicated earlier, the goals of social programs are rarely, if ever, singular and explicit; indeed, they are multitudinous and vague. If the analyst is to conduct an evaluation, some limited number of explicit goals must be determined. Some examples of prison programs may help to clarify this and related points.

The larger, "more advanced" prisons of the United States, and other countries, have engaged in a wide variety of treatment or rehabilitative programs for a century and more. Most analysts have taken for granted the claim that the purpose of these programs was and is to correct the prisoner so that he or she will no longer commit crimes, or, at least, fewer. What seems more likely is that these programs were introduced and have been continued to achieve better control of the prisoners, that is, to keep the prisons from "blowing up." [7] Seen from this point of view, the failure of prison programs to reduce recidivism is irrelevant. More importantly, for the purpose at hand, the question is not whether prison schools, for instance, reduce recidivism— a question which might be answered by comparing the recidivism rate of some set of people receiving the school program with some set receiving no schooling—but, rather, whether prison schools keep prisons from blowing up. The conceptualization of the goal and causal agent would have to be changed.

Rather than a model positing that people sent to prison commit crimes because they are ignorant, which would call for a

prison school program to achieve the goal of reducing recidivism, the model required might posit that prisons blow up because the prisoners have nothing to do which they find interesting and valuable, and having nothing to do results in their causing trouble for the prison operators. This reconceptualization changes the causal agent from the impartation of knowledge to the provision of activities to occupy the prisoners' time in legitimate and interesting ways. Comparing those in school with those in athletic programs, for instance, would *not* make the two groups equivalent in all regards but for the presence or absence of the causal agent in that athletic programs are also a way of occupying prisoners' time in interesting, legitimate activities.

The presence or absence of the causal agent can present analytical problems in another way; it too is not immediately apparent. It is, "Was the program actually implemented?" It may be necessary to make the program itself the object of inquiry. If this is not done, one might conclude that such and such a solution is not effective when the plain "facts" are that it was never actually implemented. For example, it might be concluded that group therapy in prison is ineffective without noting that the therapists and patients were engaged in activities only dimly related to therapy (Manocchio and Dunn, 1970; Wright, 1973: 152–60). Or, one might find that job training in prison was ineffective, but fail to notice that the jobs for which the prisoners were being trained either did not exist or today employ a different technology than that being taught in the prison. It might be said that these programs (causal agents) exist in name only —a critical situation which would not be-

[7] See Sheldon Messinger. For some notes and references on the development of a macroscopic analysis of the development and functioning of prisons in America, see Paul Takagi (1974).

come known unless it was remembered to ask, "Was the program actually implemented."

Finally a program might be a failure due to the presence of some counteracting agent or condition. For example, vocational services to parolees might fail to reduce recidivism because there are *no* jobs to go to due to a rise in unemployment, or direct financial stipends to parolees may produce no reduction in returns to prison because the system for dispensing the money might make the parole agents more aware of the behavior of the parolees (Berecochea, 1974).

Common Sources of Error in Imputing Cause

The discussion of the conditions for imputing causality has so far been rather general. The purpose of this section is to present some categories of more specific extraneous sources of change.[8] This section may, then, be considered as a specification of the above.

MATURATION People change for many reasons; one set of reasons is captured by the concept of maturation or aging. As a result of physiological changes and patterned social conditions associated with these changes, people change from birth to death in their use of language, physical strength, fund of knowledge, sexual activities, and in many other ways. These maturational or age-related changes occur among virtually all members of a given society almost without regard to the pres-

[8] The classical work on designs for controlling error in research keyed to application in the field setting is Donald T. Campbell and Julian C. Stanley (1963). It is quite compact and easy to read; because it is so, no attempt will be made to repeat its contents herein.

ence or absence of a program, and these changes are sometimes associated with the changes the program is designed to induce. For instance, it would appear that criminal involvement is extremely low among children, increases very sharply with the advent of puberty, and then declines, more gradually, with advancing age. Thus any changes in criminal involvement associated with a program designed to produce such a change would have to rule out maturation or aging as the cause of the change. If, for example, the propensity of convicted criminals to commit further crimes was apparently reduced after ten years of some sort of treatment, one would need to take into account the fact that those who began the treatment at the age of twenty-five, for instance, would be thirty-five at the completion of the treatment.

SELECTION Another contender for the explanation of change induced by a program is captured by the concept of selection. Neither the reasons nor degrees are well known, but it is clear that people differ in their likelihood of engaging in any given kind of behavior.

If these differences are thought of as reflecting differences in tendencies to act in certain ways, then people exposed to the program would be expected to differ from those not so exposed because they were selected for exposure to the program on the basis of the difference in their dispositions. Programs for narcotic addicts are an example of this process; with some probably uncommon exceptions, people are exposed to programs designed to eliminate their addiction to opiates because they are addicted (among other reasons). People exposed to such programs would be expected to use narcotics more than those who were not exposed because they were selected for such exposure due to their addiction. Two variates of the selection process are less obvious and consequently more important.

It is not uncommon for large-scale programs, especially governmental, to develop programs within programs. Typically these special programs are seen by their developers and supporters as the solution to problems not otherwise soluble. It is also not unusual for those who would otherwise be more likely to exhibit the desired change to be selected for the special program. Thus a comparison of those selected with those not selected would probably show more change among those exposed to the special program due to the effects of selection (rather than the treatment).[9] For example, it might be determined by some community-service group that sending juveniles to reformatories is not effective in reducing their likelihood of further troubles with the law. The reformers might then decide to put pressure on the judges to place more juveniles on probation by getting people in the community to improve the programs for juveniles on probation. Those for whom the improved community programs were most applicable would be expected to do better (as

measured by further criminal involvement) than those for whom no program was applicable and who were therefore sent to the reformatory. The difference in subsequent criminal involvement between those placed on the improved probation program and those sent to the reformatory could then be attributed to the selection process itself rather than the program.

This last example must not be carried beyond its specific point, however. It might well be that the apparent effectiveness of the treatment or help provided to the juveniles placed on probation (rather than sent to the reformatory) was entirely due to selection, but the program might well be termed a success nonetheless because it did reduce commitments to the reformatory. However, this distinction too must be kept clearly in mind, for failure to do so would obscure the most interesting aspect of the study: it might well be that commitments to reformatories could be reduced without any special treatment or help at all for those diverted.[10] The social reformer might then seek to develop other ways of making it easier for judges to reduce their commitments to reformatories rather than trying to develop "more effective" treatment or helping programs for the juveniles.

Self-selection may also produce spurious

[9] Gene G. Kassebaum, David Ward, and Daniel M. Wilner (1971) used a classical experimental design to study the effects of a group counselling program in a prison setting; their study showed no effect upon recidivism, while a prior study which used statistical matching to control for selection effects showed a positive impact upon recidivism. The strong inference is that the positive effects shown by the first study were really the effects of selection which had not been fully controlled by the less adequate research design. The first study was Robert M. Harrison and Paul F. C. Mueller (1964).

[10] California apparently reduced commitments to adult and youth state correctional institutions by giving thousands of dollars to the counties for each person given probation instead of a commitment to a state institution, using the counties' commitment rate per 100,000 population during a base period as the standard for determining reductions in commitment rates. The counties were required to use the money to improve their probation programs. It seems likely that it was the "bribe" as much as anything else which caused the reduction. The program has been described and given a limited analysis in Robert L. Smith (1971).

relationships. For instance, the claims by such groups as Synanon—a self-help, voluntary program using group confrontation and support techniques for illicit drug users who wish to become completely abstinent—that they have high success in the production of abstinence may be valid, but the requirement that those who wish to enter Synanon must be committed to complete abstinence from all drug use makes it seem likely that such groups as Synanon would have higher success rates than that for programs having no such requirement. Any "positive" difference in success rates could be attributed to nothing more than membership in a group such as Synanon being an identifier of those who are committed to abstinence.[11]

CONTAMINATION Yet another source of error in attributing causality to a program may be captured in the concept of contamination. This occurs when the presence or absence of the presumed causal agent (program) is associated with the presence or absence of some other agent which is the cause of the change. There are several types of contamination.

Perhaps the best known type of contamination is known in sociology by the name "Hawthorne effect." In this situation it is not the treatment itself which produces the effect, but rather the fact that any kind of special treatment was given. Generally, the Hawthorne effect is used to refer to the production of change in a desired direction, but there would

seem to be no reason why the term should be limited to situations in which the change is in the desired direction.[12] Prisoners provided with a course in sociology might increase their conformity with prison rules because they see the mere fact that they were given the course as an expression of the prison operators' good will, or they might reduce their conformity because they see their being given the course as a one-sided attempt to induce conformity in the guise of giving the prisoners what they want.

Another type of contamination is commonly referred to as the "Rosenthal effect." This term refers to the tendency for experiments to confirm the researcher's expectation (hypothesis) as a result of the expectation itself. For example, children given a special reading program might well improve in their reading comprehension not because the program itself was effective but because the children improved their comprehension out of their desire to please the teacher whose desire for improved performance was made evident by the introduction of the program. Researchers in this area have designed rigorously controlled experimental studies under both laboratory and field conditions which indicate that when all conditions other than the experimenters' expectations of the outcome are equivalent, the outcome will conform to the experimenters' expectations.[13]

Lest the reader be led to the dismal conclusion that this phenomenon means

[11] Synanon and Alcoholics Anonymous seem to work, for those who want them to; see Rita Volkman and Donald R. Cressey (1963); Harrison M. Trice and Paul Michael Roman (1970). However, the conclusion that they work (that is, that the people who participate in them are better able to remain abstinent because of the programs) is based on theory or faith rather than upon experimental proof.

[12] For a further statement of the "Hawthorne effect" thesis and a critique of the logic which was used to derive the thesis, see Alex Carey (1970).

[13] See Robert Rosenthal and Lenore Jacobsen (1968). For a strong methodological critique, see Richard E. Snow (1969). But there is other evidence (Friedman, 1967).

that no valid test of effectiveness of a program is possible, let it be quickly noted that the number of studies has never been counted or empirically estimated, but it would seem reasonable to intuitively estimate that many thousands of studies have been done in which the experimenters' hypotheses have not been confirmed, even though they were dearly held. The solution to the problem posed by the Rosenthal effect is not to give up in despair, but to attempt to discover the conditions under which it occurs and then develop methods for gaining control over these conditions. One of the likely candidates for these conditions is the presence in a study of a researcher who is committed to a certain outcome coupled with a research design devised and/or implemented by the researcher; such studies must be subjected to strenuous skepticism, regardless of the seeming elegance of the design, expertness of execution, or honesty of the researcher.

Another type of contamination (or confounding) is produced by differential response to the phenomenon upon which the criterion measure is developed. In psychology, this type of error is captured by the term "halo effect." This term derives from psychometric studies in which it has been found that when raters judge the behavior, characteristics, talents, or whatever of people (and other entities) they tend to make their ratings of the person or entity on various dimensions more similar to each other than they are. In particular, a person who is seen by the rater as outstanding on one trait is likely to be rated as outstanding on other traits; thus the term "halo effect" (Guilford, 1954:279). The obverse might be called the "satanic effect." In studies of the effectiveness of programs,

this type of contamination is likely to be produced under two conditions.

One condition is that in which the people exposed to a program are so exposed because of some wrong they have done or some "evil" condition. The tendency for "badness" to be seen as a product and producer of "badness" might result in a tendency to rate the people poorly on the criterion used to measure effectiveness. For instance, children from poor families without both parents in the home who are committed to a reformatory for being absent from school and staying out after curfew might be more likely than other children to be identified as having committed a crime because "we all know" that such children "have delinquent tendencies." Thus a measure of program effectiveness for the reformatory based on the subsequent criminal involvement of those committed to and released from it might be low due to the tendency of the police to define behavior of the releasees as criminal because they come from poor families without both parents.[14]

ERRORS IN THE USE OF COLLECTIVITIES
The sources of error in imputing a causal program impact have so far centered on studies in which identifiable, individual actors are the object of the program and study, but not all social programs and studies are of this type. For instance, the criminal law is at least partially intended to deter people in general from committing acts defined as crimes. Popula-

[14] Indeed, this is a central theme of a major body of work in social psychology known as "labelling theory". Among other themes, it holds that peoples' behavior is defined as deviant because the people are themselves defined as deviant. For a fuller view, with a critique, see Edwin M. Schur (1971).

tion-size control programs and policies are intended to limit the number of children produced by people in their fertile years. Ecology programs are designed to protect the environment from corporate and individual actors who would do irremediable life-threatening damage to the environment. Such programs and policies generally require different modes of study and the problems of inferring causal effects from the programs/policies are also different, in some ways. However, at certain levels of abstraction, the concepts used in the earlier discussion to capture sources of error in causal inference may also be used here.

The concept of maturation or aging may be extended to include changes over time. One of the more common sources of possible error in inferring that a change is due to a program or policy is to attribute changes which would have occurred over time to the program/policy under study. This type of error seems to be especially likely in examining new programs or policies. A brief digression will be necessary to make this point.

In the state of Connecticut a severe crackdown on speeders was introduced as a result of a sharp increase in motor vehicle fatalities. The fatality rate had shown a slight increase over the period from 1951 through 1954, though the fluctuation was considerable with some years showing an increase and some showing a decline over the prior year; the 1955 rate was substantially higher. The motor-vehicle fatality rate went down after the crackdown. The problem was to determine whether the decline in the fatality rate was due to the crackdown (and to determine, as well, if there was indeed a crackdown). After all, the rate did fluctuate greatly and the decline might well

have been normal, that is, the result of other factors. After considerable analysis of existing data using advanced statistical techniques, the answer provided by the analysts to both questions was a qualified yes; there probably was a crackdown on speeders and it probably did result in a decrease in the motor-vehicle fatality rate.

This is an example of the general methodological problem of separating the effects of "natural" time-related changes from the effects of a program interjected at some point in time chosen because of a high rate of occurrence of the problem. Rates of occurrence of some event over time are sometimes used to define a new social problem or to justify doing something more or new to solve or alleviate an old problem which has "grown worse." It would not be unexpected for the rate to change (decrease) with the introduction of the new program, or somewhat thereafter, as a result of the tendency for high rates to be rare. Indeed, a competent statistician working with adequate data and some luck could greatly increase the odds that a program would be termed successful by instituting the program at a high point in the rate which is so unlikely that a lower rate would be expected in the near future. The "best" time to introduce a program woud be during a period of steady decline in the rate used to measure the problem. Put this baldly, such a procedure would be obviously dishonest. But sometimes it is not known that the problem was decreasing (as measured) until after the program has been introduced or changed. Programs are sometimes introduced or changed exactly because the problem has reached a high point; a high point which might happen to be a rare event which would be expected to change anyway. Fortunately, there are statistical methods which can be used to estimate the probability that a change in rates constitutes a significant deviation from the historical trend.[15] However the statistical techniques themselves do not tell you what caused the change.

When dealing with programs intended to have an effect on the entire area in which it is applied or to segments of the population as a group, a major problem is to devise a satisfactory test condition. For instance, the problem might be a high birth rate and the program might be a public education campaign designed to encourage the use of such birth control techniques as vasectomies and intrauterine devices. A desirable procedure from a methodological point of view would be to randomly divide a set of appropriate communities into one group which would receive the program and one set which would not. Failure to randomize might produce communities which are not comparable on relevant characteristics thereby confusing the effects of these differences with those of the program, if any. By way of an example, a campaign for birth control devices applied to predominantly Catholic communities would probably produce some effect on birth rates, but comparing their subsequent birth rates to predominantly protestant communities without such a program would be likely to show that the communities which had the program had higher birth rates because of differences in religious principles. Comparing the *differences* in the birth

[15] For the analysis of the Connecticut program and programs (reforms) brought in as a package to solve some "crisis" in a social problem for which there are historical statistics and no opportunity for a comparison group, see Donald T. Campbell (1971).

rates from before to after the introduction of the program in the communities receiving it with the *differences* over the same time period in the communities not receiving the program would be desirable, but it could be that both would show an equal change due to the forces which brought about a program in the Catholic communities being sufficient in themselves to produce a decline in the protestant communities. If the reduction associated with the program were no different from that associated with no program, it would be assumed (perhaps incorrectly) that the program had no unique effect (especially if it were not known that the communities happened to differ on the "degree of Catholicism").

Similar problems occur in studies which are more clearly in the policy rather than the program area. A common procedure used in the empirical analysis of a proposed policy is to divide a larger sociopolitical area into a number of smaller areas which differ on one or more variables associated with the policy. For instance, one of the prevalent themes in the discussion of the criminal justice system is the relative importance of the severity versus the certainty of punishment in the prevention of crime. In conventional policy terms, the issue might be put, "Given fixed resources, which would be better—a higher degree of certainty of punishment or a higher degree of severity of punishment?" This question has been investigated by comparing the crime rates of states which have varying degrees of punishment certainty and severity. The problem is that other variables having unknown relationships with the crime rate may systematically vary with variations in the degree of certainty or severity. This means that the associated variations in the crime rate might be due to the other variables rather than the differences in punishment severity or certainty (Tittle, 1969; Tullock, 1974). For instance, a finding that a higher probability (certainty) of punishment was related to a lower level of crime could be the result of a high average income which might also produce high levels of certainty.[16]

The problem missed by this example arises when the "true" causal variable which produces the change is not known but is associated with the presumed causal variable so that the inference is incorrect but now known to be so.

A Note on Theory

Those who have read widely in the social sciences will have come across statements of the need to develop theory. Often this call for theory stems from the desire to become scientific, but there is a much more practical and pressing basis for the call. Most of the prior discussion has been devoted to an elaboration of one idea— "It might have been something else." The problem is that there are an infinity of "something elses" and no amount of time and resources would be sufficient to investigate them all. One of the things which a theory does is to identify those variables and processes from an infinite number which might explain the phenomenon of interest. By identifying the causal variables and processes, alternative explanations of any observed changes or differences may be more thoroughly and efficiently tested.

[16] After much research, capital punishment presents an even more difficult problem. It is not clear whether capital punishment bears any relationship to homicide rates, and, if it does, what the nature or direction of the relationship is. See William C. Bailey (1973) and Hugo Adam Bedau (1967).

Designs for Controlling Error

Several techniques have been developed for eliminating or controlling the sources of error in attributing causal effects to programs. They are not foolproof, but they can generate more confidence in the conclusion that a program does or does not have an effect (Campbell and Stanley, 1963). They have been touched upon already; they will now be discussed more explicitly.

THE CLASSICAL EXPERIMENT Elaborating on one of the prior examples, imagine two identical rooms both containing an open bowl of gasoline and a person holding a match. Imagine further that in one room the match is lit and held within a fraction of an inch from the surface of the gasoline while in the other room the match is not lit. The gasoline will burn in one of the rooms but not in the other. From this experiment it would be reasonable to conclude that the stipulated difference caused the gasoline to burn.

Now imagine two identical communities in which ten percent of the population are experiencing some sort of social problem. A program designed to cause the elimination of the problem is introduced into one of the communities but not the other on the basis of a toss of a coin. Subsequently none of the people in the community with the program experience the problem while ten percent do so in the other community. This would be a classical experiment, and it would be concluded that the program caused the elimination of the problem. There is a parallel here between the causal conception underlying the program and problem and the causal conception underlying the experiment. But these conceptualizations must be expanded if they are to be useful, as the social world is more complex than these concepts as they stand. However, these concepts are basic to the experimental method. More to the point, the social world can seldom be made as simple as that just outlined.

Most complications of the basic model arise from two sources; one derives from the evident fact that the social world is inextricably interlinked in ways which are only barely known (that is, theoretically explainable) and the other is due to the effects (artifacts) of experimentation. Put somewhat differently, the classical experiment is a rather weak instrument with which to study the social world in that only a necessarily few influences on the phenomenon under study can be incorporated in the study design and the low level of theoretical knowledge means that more important influences not included within the design might well unknowingly produce the results attributed to the influences incorporated in the study. The unknown influences may be external or the result of the study itself.

With regard to the influences other than those due to the conduct of the study itself, there are two basic ways of handling extraneous influences on the phenomenon under study. One is to manipulate directly the extraneous variables and the other is to randomize them so that they will not have a systematic effect.

When variables other than the program are directly manipulated it is essential that the program and other variables not be confounded with each other. For instance, a study of the effect of an English for Spanish-speaking students program designed to reduce the school drop-out rate might be introduced in several schools and not in several others. Such programs cost money; this money could be obtained by reallocating resources from other programs in the same schools. If this were done, any change (or lack thereof) in the drop-out rate could be attributed to either the program or the reallocation of resources or some combination of the two. For instance, the schools might cut back their utilization of part-time instructors who might well be Spanish-speaking teachers in other areas who taught courses in subjects of special interest to the Spanish-speaking students thereby reducing the attractiveness of the school and consequently lowering the attendance rate. A more obvious example would be to couple the English for Spanish-speaking students with a Spanish for English-speaking faculty in all the departments of the schools with the special program for the students. There would seem to be nothing wrong with such a combination, but if all the experimental schools got both of the programs and none of the controls got them, it would be impossible from the experiment alone to determine if the results were due to the student or faculty program or both. There are methods for examining the independent effects of the two programs and their combined effects (Kerlinger, 1973).

Continuing the above example, there are many influences upon drop-out rates, so many that they cannot all be simultaneously controlled by direct manipulation. In experimental designs, these other variables are controlled by randomization. The schools (having some minimum number of Spanish-speaking students) which might be candidates for the program would no doubt differ on a number of variables related to dropping out of school. Randomly dividing them into two groups would produce two sets of schools which would be expected to have equal, or nearly equal, distributions on the variables other than the program which might effect the drop-out rates. However, this method of achieving control over "extraneous" influences on the dependent variable (school drop-out rate) requires a "large" number of units (schools); it would not work in the case of just two schools, but it would for, say, thirty. Unfortunately, there is no magic number, although a statistician can work out the minimum number needed given such information as the variability in the drop-out rates, the size of the reduction in the rate which is desired or expected (for whatever reason), and how much confidence in the conclusion is desired.

People too vary with regard to their propensities to engage in different kinds of activities and in their social positions. The techniques used to control for the influence of these differences parallel those outlined above in the school example. For instance, if the social problem were heroin addiction and the program were methadone maintenance provided by a clinic open to all addicts, an experimental test of the effectiveness of methadone maintenance in reducing heroin addiction among those on the program would require the following conditions.

First it would be necessary to isolate one set of addicts who were maintained on methadone and another set who were not. Second, the two sets of people would have to be equally likely as a set to possess or not possess any biographically or socially connected characteristics which might effect their use of heroin. Some idea of the range of such "extraneous" variables which might produce or

inhibit the results (or lack thereof) to be attributed to the program may be obtained from the following, incomplete list.

1. Age—heroin use seems to increase with age up to a point and then decrease.
2. Marital status—addicts who are married seem more likely to cease use than others.
3. Motivation—this is an almost hopelessly vague concept, but there is little doubt that some people want to quit while others do not and the motivation to quit comes and goes.
4. Occupation—it would appear that people who are regularly employed are less apt to continue heroin use.
5. Place of residence—for whatever reasons, the areas typically called ghettoes seem to engender heroin use.
6. Availability—some heroin addicts quit because they lose their connection with their supplier.

This listing could be greatly extended (Schasre, 1966; Waldorf, 1970) and parallels could be found for other social-problem programs "applied to" individuals. But the point is not to list every possible influence on heroin use, rather it is to demonstrate that there are many influences on behavior which is the object of social programs and they must be controlled if any changes in the behavior are to be attributed to the program. That is, if selection into the program were to happen in such a way as to result in more of the people in the experimental group being married than in the control group, a finding of higher abstinence in the experimental group could be attributed to this difference rather than the program. The study design itself would not rule out, or make unlikely, the alternative explanation that the difference was due to the difference between the people rather than the presence or absence of the program.

The ideal way to "rule out" such alternative explanations is to randomly place the people (heroin addicts in this case) in the program or in the control group. In most situations, random assignment to treatment and control groups is at least technically possible, although political obstacles may impede the idealist in his or her pursuit of "perfection." The case of methadone maintenance offers another kind of obstacle to the pursuit of the ideal design.

One of the more important possible sources of error in attributing a causal effect to a program is known in medical research as the "placebo effect." This concept refers to the process by which the patient's belief that the treatment (for example, medication) works results in the elimination or alleviation of the malady. Giving inert medications such as sugar pills and injections of saline solutions, for instance, has been found to alleviate warts, ulcers, depression, and disruptive behavior by inmates of mental hospitals and training schools for juvenile delinquents (Frank, 1973). Such an effect might also be present in the case of methadone maintenance for opiate addicts. The technique used to control for the placebo effect is to create two treatment programs: one in which the medication is given and one in which an inert medication is given but the patient is led to believe that he or she is receiving the "real" medication. This approach is very valuable; but it is difficult, if not impossible, to apply in some cases. Methadone maintenance may be one of these cases.

Patients on methadone develop a tolerance to opiates which means that relatively high doses of opiates will have no deleterious effects. The methadone

patient who also used heroin would suffer no harm. However, if the patient were really receiving a placebo, tolerance would not have developed and a "shot" of heroin could result in the patient's death. The "ideal" experiment may not always be possible.[17]

THE QUASI-EXPERIMENT   It is often very difficult if not effectively impossible to test a social program by the use of a classical experiment. It might even be argued that the classical experiment is undesirable due to its unrealistic character.[18] The distinguishing characteristic of the quasiexperiment is that the experimental and control groups are not created by a random technique; rather, they are created by some systematic process. Because the treatment and control groups are systematically created, it is not possible to rule out differences other than the treatment as likely explanations of any difference in the criterion, or lack thereof.

One technique used in the design of quasiexperiments treats those on a waiting list for the program as the control group. This has been done, for example, in the assessment of psychotherapy, a halfway house for narcotic addicts, and a summer placement program designed to promote democratic ideals among young, possible future leaders (Berecochea and

[17] For a quasiexperimental evaluation using a waiting list and matching, see Welton A. Jones and John E. Berecochea (1973). For a discussion of methadone maintenance programs, see Paul Danaceau (1974). That massive doses of "street" heroin far beyond the possibility of obtaining and injecting would be required to produce death is argued in *Heroin Maintenance: The Issues* (1974). It may thus be that a placebo study could be done, but not all physicians would agree.

[18] See Egon Brunswik (1957). The alternative of quasiexperiments is ably presented by Campbell and Stanley (1963).

Sing, 1972; Eyesenck, 1966; Hyman, Wright, and Hopkins, 1962). Although differing in the ways in which they were studied, these evaluations each identified people who were placed on waiting lists to determine if those who received the program changed any more or less or differed on the criterion from those who were scheduled to receive the program but did not or had not yet. The idea behind this technique is that people on a waiting list are similar to those who actually receive the service in their social, psychological, and biographical characteristics. These are reasonable assumptions given certain conditions. The first set of conditions is that the placement on the waiting list as opposed to provision of the treatment is *not* related to the person's problems, motivations, or any other variable which would be related to (a) the effectiveness of the treatment, (b) the person's likelihood of showing a change, or (c) differences on the measures used to assess the impact of the program.

This set of conditions is probably seldom met. In any ongoing program there are good reasons to believe that people selected for treatment will be ˋselected on the basis of something about them. The most obvious reason for this is the desire of those running the program or providing a service to choose those who are most likely to show improvement so that the program or service will show some positive results. A somewhat less obvious reason is the tendency for people who are less in need of the program to be more able to gain the assistance provided by the program, in one way or another. For example, city residents on a waiting list for a junior college computer training program might well enroll in a commercial computer training program, especially if they were somewhat better off financially. Or the financially better off people on the waiting list might obtain training in a more lucrative field. A comparison five years later on annual income of those who received the computer training at the junior college with those who were on the waiting list might favor the people on the waiting list due to their differences in financial well being or the subsequent training their received. Any study using a waiting list or other control group *not* based on random allocations should show a comparison of the experimentals and controls on various measures; these measures should include such widely available and relatively powerful variables as sex, marital status, and occupation.

The second condition which must be met for the waiting-list quasiexperiment is that they do not significantly differ in what happens to them after they are assigned or not assigned to the treatment and before the outcome measures are taken (except, of course, for the provision of the treatment to the experimentals). If, for example, the waiting list for the computer training program were at the commercial school and the junior college subsequently opened a computer training program, there would be a good possibility that those on the waiting list would actually receive the training at the junior college thereby cancelling the critical difference. Or, people waiting for an opening in a halfway house might be provided with lodgings elsewhere. That the control group receive no "treatment" is, of course, a condition for the classical experiment as well, but it seems more likely to be violated in the quasiexperiment in that the researcher has less control over the situation in which a quasiexperiment is conducted. All other conditions for a classical experiment should also be met, if possible. Several relatively uncomplicated expositions are available.[19]

Another approach is possible when there is continuous intake of relatively large numbers of people in relatively short periods of time, such as applications for drivers' licenses in a large city. The procedure is to randomly or systematically alternate the "service" over short periods of time by either providing it in one set of periods and not in the other or by varying the types of service (Harrington, 1973).

Another way of assessing the effectiveness of a program or policy is to make before and after comparisons of the "treated group" only; the lack of a control group makes this design nonexperimental in the classical sense. The study discussed earlier of the crackdown on motor vehicle speeders in Connecticut was such a study; motor vehicle fatalities were lower after the crackdown then they were before, probably as a result of the program. A crackdown on parking violations was examined by determining the number of such violations before and after the increased enforcement activities. The conclusion was that increased certainty and severity of punishment did reduce parking violations on a college campus among some people. More generally, the conclusion was that the tendency to draw absolute conclusions about the effectiveness or ineffectiveness of punishment as a deterrent must be replaced by theory and research which seeks to determine those circumstances

under which particular forms of punishment have some or no effect.[20]

The major problem with before and after comparisons of this sort is the possibility that the change might have occurred anyway. That is, for unknown reasons, the motor vehicle fatalities and parking violations might have changed anyway. They are included here as quasi-experiments because they do not have a control group which does not receive the treatment as a test condition for determining what change would have occurred without the treatment program/policy.

There is a class of studies which attempts to overcome the lack of a "true" control group that is so common as to merit separate treatment.

STATISTICAL MATCHING This technique has been used in studying the effects of time served in prison on recidivism, vocational training for parolees, and the effect of different kinds of welfare on worker morale, among other things (Chapin, 1947; Jaman, Dickover, and Bennett, 1972; Witt, 1968). This type of study is also typically *ex post facto* in that the groups studied are formed after the people or other units have already been "treated" (Greenwood, 1945).

Statistical matching studies start with those who have been exposed to the program, and information on their characteristics is collected. Those not exposed to the treatment are then matched with those exposed on the characteristics related to the outcome measures. This same technique is also used to compare those who receive more of the treatment with those who receive less. For instance,

[19] Besides Campbell and Stanley (1963), see Glenn H. Bracht and Gene V. Glass (1968). Although it is relatively old, Lindquist (1953: 1–12) gives a good treatment of internal and external threats to the validity of experimental studies.

[20] For the "crackdown" study, see Campbell (1971); for the parking violation study, see William J. Chambliss (1969); for the theory, see Chambliss (1967).

a study of the effects of time served in prison matched a group of releasees from prison who had served a shorter term with those who had received a longer term. They were matched on the crime which resulted in their commitment to prison and on their past criminal record because these variables are related to both time served in prison and recidivism (the outcome measure used for the study) (Jaman, Dickover, and Bennett, 1972). Some variables used in matching are age, sex, educational level, race, occupation and, when available and appropriate, scores on attitude, intelligence, and personality tests.

When matching is done with any but a very large sample, it becomes very difficult, if not impossible, to find matches for all of the treated units. The unmatched treated people or units must then be dropped or the matching made less precise. The exclusion of cases necessarily produces a set of treated cases which are not representative of all those receiving the treatment. This, in turn, means that the conclusions from the study cannot be generalized to all people receiving the treatment. Thus, the decision to continue or drop the program, to the extent that the decision rested on the results of the study, would be based on the statistical artifact of how many matches could be found. In other words, it would mean that the decision about the effectiveness of the program would be at least partially based on a nonrepresentative sample, perhaps as small as 50 percent or less, of those treated.

As indicated earlier, the number of cases which have to be dropped can be reduced by making the matching less precise; for instance, instead of matching on the person's age to within five years, the range might be extended to ten. How-

ever, the reduction in the precision increases the probability that the groups will differ sufficiently to make the comparisons on the outcome measures of no relevance to the test of the program's effectiveness.

Another approach to matching is referred to as "frequency matching." In this approach, the individuals are not matched, but the two groups are made to be the same in their overall distributions on the matching variables. For example, they might be made to have the same distributions on sex, age in five-year intervals, and major occupational categories. Frequency matching is also done by dropping cases from the study.[21]

As must be clear by now, the major problem with all matching studies is that the groups might well differ substantially on some variables which actually produce the difference in the outcome measures attributed to the program. Classical experimental tests have yielded findings of no difference for programs/policies that previous matching studies had "shown" to make a difference. Returning to previous examples, it has been found in an experimental study that shorter and longer prison sentences may have no impact on subsequent levels of recidivism. Prior matching studies of various sorts had seemed to indicate that longer sentences induced higher levels of recidivism, at least for some kinds of prisoners. The experimental study showed no such differential effects. It would appear that the studies which matched those with shorter and longer sentences were not sufficiently

[21] The classical treatment is by F. Stuart Chapin (1955); for an up-to-date treatment that promises to reduce some of the loss problem, see Robert P. Althauser and Donald Rubin (1970). For an extensive, clear, and concise discussion of precision versus frequency matching, see Bernard S. Phillips (1971:108–12).

controlled to remove all of the differences other than time served, even though the matching was relatively extensive in some of the studies. The differences in recidivism associated with shorter and longer prison terms which were found in some of the other studies were apparently due to something other than time served.[22]

CORRELATIONAL APPROACH   Correlational studies attempt to achieve an answer to the question of effectiveness in a different manner from those so far discussed. Some would argue that correlational techniques are an attempt to achieve by statistical techniques what the experimental method tried to achieve by direct manipulation, while others would argue that correlational techniques are worthwhile and valid in their own right. This issue is of no great importance for this presentation.

The thinking behind the correlational approach is similar to that behind matching. It starts with the concept that the unit of analysis may be described by measurable variables such as age, occupational level, personality dimensions, and so forth, which vary across people, collectivities of people, or other units. From prior research, theory, or hunch, it is asserted that some of these variables are associated with the variables which the program is designed to change and that these variables are, or may be, related to both program involvement and its effects, if any. The variables are then used to estimate what would happen to the people or other units of analysis independently of the program. This estimate becomes the standard of comparison.

For instance, the effects of a year of graduate education on income was estimated by using parental income and social status, cognitive skills, and racial/ethnic group to determine how much income a sample of people would have, and this estimate was then used as the standard against which to compare the income of those in the sample with a year of graduate education. It was found that a year of graduate education probably resulted in an increase (over the standard) of less than five percent. A simple comparison of those with and without a year of graduate education, with no statistical controls for variables related to both graduate education and income, showed an income gain of about seven percent. Similar results were found for elementary, secondary, and college education. The authors' concluded that increasing education does little to increase incomes. Although not related to the immediate point, they also concluded that education probably works to engender more inequity in income rather than less, although this conclusion was more speculative. They also used the same approach to examine the probable relative effects of such policy relevant variables as the quality of schools, type of curriculum, and racial segregation.[23]

This technique differs from the matching technique in many ways. The most practically important way is that no cases are excluded by the analytical technique; this means that the results of the analysis are generalizable to the entire population from which the sample was drawn. Because no cases are thrown out, the analysis requires fewer cases. Also, in compari-

[22] Differential effects were postulated by Donald L. Garrity (1961); Daniel Glaser (1964: 301–3). For the experimental study, see Berecochea, Jaman, and Jones (1973).

[23] Jencks et al., 1972. A conceptually similar approach which can be used when it is only possible to classify people on several sets of categories is provided by Morris Rosenberg (1970).

son to the matching technique, there is no loss in precision; that is, for instance, exact age may be used rather than matching on age within some interval such as five years.

The principal problem with this type of approach is that the present state of theoretical knowledge is such that few if any of the variables which social problems programs are designed to effect can be predicted with great accuracy. This means, for the correlational model, that variables not included in the statistical analysis have an effect on the outcome variable. If these other variables are also related to exposure to the program so that those exposed to the program differ on them in some systematic manner, then the attribution of a causal effect to the program would be at least partially erroneous. For example, it might be that people who attend college earn more money, not because they are more privileged to begin with and not because of the formal skills which they acquire in school, but rather because jobs which are limited to people with a college education are seen as being worth higher salaries while jobs which do not require a college education are seen as less worthy, even though the required skills and the contributions of the jobs are equivalent. Prison guard and prison counsellor jobs might be a case in point.

Adequacy of Information, or Convincing Others

The primary purpose of collecting and analyzing information about the workings of a program is to tell a story which others will believe to be an adequate representation of what happened. All science is, in fact, an effort to do things in such a way that others will or could believe the story. There are two principal ways in which the information collected for the story may undermine confidence in the story; these threats will be referred to as problems of reliability and validity.

RELIABILITY Information is said to be reliable when it can be replicated. Various techniques are used to produce reliable information and to test for it. Some examples may help to get across the key points.

Imagine two people observing the same situation and counting the number of times some act such as lighting a cigarette occurs. The measure of frequency of cigarette lighting is held to be reliable if the two observers come up with the same count independently of each other. When the two counts diverge, the measure is said to be unreliable. Few if any measures are reliable in the sense of perfect agreement, but some measures deviate from perfect agreement by only slight amounts while others diverge greatly.

The same idea may be applied to self-reporting questionnaires; in this situation, the observers are replaced by the questionnaire which is administered twice to the same people and the similarity of the responses is used as the reliability measure. In order to reduce or eliminate memory or practice effects, alternative forms of the questionnaire may be used or the questionnaire may be administered at different times. If reliability is found to be too low, the instrument may be corrected to improve it (Peak, 1953).

Unreliability can also be introduced in the process of transferring the observational or self-reported data to computer cards or other instruments used to perform the statistical analysis. This can result from "human error," inadequate instructions to the coders (transcribers), "cheating" resulting from boredom or the inherent ambiguity of the social world.[24]

VALIDITY   The problem of measurement validity is much easier to state than solve. A measurement device, be it a psychological test administered by a trained professional to measure self-esteem or a count of the number of cigarette papers sold in different communities to measure marijuana use, is designed to assess some aspect of a phenomenon under study. If it assesses that aspect of the phenomenon which it was designed to, then it is valid; if it does not, it is not. That is, if the self-esteem test measures self-esteem or if the volume of cigarette paper sales measures marijuana use, then they are valid; if they do not, they are not. Of course, there are degrees of validity. The problem is that there are no foolproof methods of measuring validity. A little bit of thought will reveal possible sources of error (invalidity) in any social measurement; this is not the place to catalog them or to present the various techniques used to generate and determine degrees of validity (Peak, 1953). Rather, two rules-of-thumb will be provided.

If the effects of a program on one aspect of a social problem are assessed by a single measure, give considerable thought to the adequacy of the measure as an indicant of the social problem. If there is some question as to its validity (adequacy), then consider its inadequacy in terms of the conclusion that the program does or does not work. If the inadequa-

cies are biased with respect to the program, then the conclusion as to the effectiveness of the program must be discounted (to some degree). If not, a conclusion based on a measure of low validity need not be thrown out as useless. For instance, arrest rates have poor validity; indeed, they are notoriously so.[25] Given two large sets of cities randomly assigned to experimentally controlled levels of presentation of violence in the public media, a finding of a direct correlation of changes in crime rates (using arrests as the measure) with the amount of violence in the public media would support the conclusion that there is a causal connection, even though the arrest rate is a poor measure of criminality. However, if the study was instead based on a comparison of cities in which there "happened" to be more violence presented in the media with those in which there "happened" to be less, the conclusion that there is a causal connection would be vitiated by, among other things, the low validity of arrest rates as a measure of crime. Because arrest rates reflect variables other than the amount of crime committed in a city, it could be that the correlation was really due to (1) higher crime rates producing more media coverage, (2) media attention to violence producing pressure on the police to make more arrests, (3) higher unemployment rates producing more crime resulting in greater media attention to violence to

[24] On coding errors, see Kathleen S. Crittenden and Richard J. Hill (1971); on "cheating" in the coding of information, see Julius Roth (1970); on the inherent ambiguity of the social world and the problems of coding, see Harold Garfinkel (1967:186–207).

[25] For a conventional treatment of the problems of using criminal statistics, see Edwin H. Sutherland and Donald R. Cressey (1970:25–47); for a conventional treatment of the history and problems of juvenile and adult criminal statistics, see Thorsten Sellin and Marvin E. Wolfgang (1964:7–70); for a radical history and fundamental criticism of criminal statistics as measures of criminal behavior, see Jack D. Douglas (1971:47–78, 79–132).

divert attention from the level of unemployment, or (4) those who control the media also controlling the police.

The experimental study would, of course, have some of the same measurement-validity problems as the "accidental" study. The manipulation of the amount of violence in the media would be controlled, but all the factors influencing the criterion measure—crime rates—would not be. Increased exposure to media violence could produce more reporting of crime by the victims or greater police attention to reports of crime, for instance. But such sources of measurement invalidity as the thing being measured—criminal acts—producing both the experimental variable—degree of media exposure—and the criterion—crime rates—would be avoided or reduced as would such exogenous processes as the degree of unemployment producing both higher media coverage of violence and higher crime rates.

When there are no sufficiently valid measures available, multiple measures should be used. In the above example, several alternatives might be used:

1. Claims to insurance companies for losses and personal injury due to theft, robbery, and so forth
2. Deaths due to other than natural causes or suicide
3. Hospital admissions for injuries due to assault, and so forth
4. Questionnaire surveys ("victim" surveys)
5. Inventory shrinkages
6. Prices paid by pawn shops
7. The "street price" of heroin

Each of these measures is less than perfectly valid, as a measure of crime, but together they would provide a much more valid indication of the level of crime than would arrests alone or any one measure alone. Each has its own set of biases, but the biases are not all the same; they reflect different influences operating in different ways. A finding that cities in which more attention is paid to violence in the media also have higher crime rates as measured by these indices would lend credence to the causal inference that media attention influences the amount of crime in the cities. The conclusion would be further strengthened by using several different measures of media attention to violence.

SPECIFIC THREATS TO VALIDITY There are at least a dozen threats to the validity of measurement devices. Most are threats to the validity of the social scientist's favorite method of collecting data —the interview/questionnaire.[26] A questionnaire is a set of questions typically written on one or more pieces of paper which the respondent is asked to answer by writing them out or by checking (or otherwise indicating) his or her choices of responses from among those provided by the researcher. In an interview, the questions are asked orally and the responses are recorded by the interviewer. It is probably best to prepare the questions for the interview in advance and keep them fairly similar across the respondents. The questionnaire/interview is unsurpassed in the breadth of information which can be collected in a short period of time and without a great deal of loss waiting for the behaviors of interest to occur (or not occur). Because the questionnaire/interview is probably the most commonly

[26] These are taken from a classic and entertaining work replete with references on the problems of obtaining valid measures of behavior, Eugene J. Webb et al. (1966:10–34).

used technique for gathering information and because more is known about the sources of invalidity for them, most of the following discussion will be centered on threats to the validity of information so obtained.

1. Receiving a questionnaire/interview is not an everyday affair; being questioned puts the person on notice that he or she is the object of study. As has been indicated earlier, this special attention itself may produce an effect which would be confused with the effects of the program. Being questioned about a public education program, for instance, might be the only exposure which the person has and this single exposure might produce a favorable (or unfavorable) rating of the program. In an experimental design, this would be handled by doing the questioning after the introduction for the experimentals and at the same time for the controls. If before and after measures are necessary or desired, it is best to use two control groups: one which would be questioned "before" and "after" and one "after" only. The after-only control group would provide a baseline for assessing the effects of being questioned. These techniques, and others, may also be used to control for some of the other sources of error listed below (Campbell and Stanley, 1963). Less obvious data collection devices such as cameras, sound recorders, photoelectric counters, and human observers can also put the person on notice if the instrument or observer is clearly visible.

2. A variant of the above is the patterning of responses to those which the person believes to be expected from the wording of the questions, what is known about the study, or what is otherwise thought to be appropriate or desirable by the respondent. For instance, a uniformed policeman asking people if they feel safer from crime after some program might produce a positive response due to acquiescence to authority.

3. Questionnaires/interviews can also produce change in themselves by causing the person questioned to ponder issues not considered before or to revise beliefs and opinions as a result of the questions themselves. Few people, for instance, have given intensive thought to a program which would allow thieves to anonymously sell their loot to an organization which would turn the goods over to the owner. A series of well-designed questions might induce acceptance (or rejection) of such a proposal where no opinion existed before.

4. People have proclivities which can reduce the validity of various measures. Some people have a tendency to answer "yes" or to "agree" with statements while others do not, or do so to a lesser degree. Thus, a questionnaire designed to test for anti-Catholicism which worded all or most of the questions in such a way that an answer of "yes" (or "agree") would be taken to be an expression of anti-Catholicism would be confounded with the tendency to say "yes" (or "agree"). Similar tendencies exist for endorsing strongly stated rather than weakly stated items and for checking boxes on the right (or left).

5. Who asks the question can also be important; different answers to some questions are elicited by questioners of different ages, sexes, and racial-ethnic groups, and these effects vary depending upon their combinations in the questioners. Further, respondents of different ages and so forth answer questions differently depending upon the age and so

forth of the questioner. For example, whites may be less likely to give obviously racist responses to a black interviewer.

6. When the information needs require more than one administration of the questionnaire/interview or when the information is collected over an extended period of time, changes or differences in the questions can have a confounding effect. Perhaps less obviously, words change their meaning over time. Some years ago, a question which asked people how often they "got high" would have produced an answer reflective of alcohol use, today it would be more likely to reflect marijuana use. During the period of rapid change in the use of this phrase, which was also a period of increasing use of marijuana, a measure of the effectiveness of an antimarijuana campaign among middle-aged, middle-income people using before-and-after answers to the question about "getting high" might produce a "positive finding" in that the meaning of the phrase would have changed so that it reflected relatively frequent use of alcohol before the campaign and relatively less frequent use of marijuana afterwards (with the actual rate of marijuana use not changing, or increasing somewhat).

7. The purpose of questionnaires/interviews is to provide information not just about those questioned but about some larger population of which they are a part (except for those relatively rare cases in which everyone of interest is questioned). It is therefore necessary to be sure that the people questioned are representative of those to whom the obtained information is to be generalized. The preferred method is to pick those to be questioned using a random technique. But even random selection is no guarantee of the representativeness of the re-

sponses, as responses might not be obtained from all those selected. Personal questioning and other means of obtaining responses to questionnaires or interview schedules is hindered by differences in life styles. Housewives and children are more likely to be home during certain times of the day than are others; very poor people—especially if they are not married—are less likely to have a fixed abode, some interviewers avoid some "parts of town," and so forth. When these people are missed or more than their share are questioned, the generalizability of the obtained responses is threatened. Even the well-financed and planned U.S. Census which is designed to include everyone in the country misses millions of people, and they are characteristically different from those not missed.

8. Behavior varies over time periods, thus observations at different times will produce different results. For instance, television watching is much more common during the evening hours, the behavior of people on downtown streets varies by hour of day and day of week due to shifts in the populations drawn there, and behavior in gambling casinos is likely to vary by season of the year due to status differentials in vacation periods. Interviews and questionnaires also are subject to time-associated differences such as those due to seasonal fluctuations in unemployment rates and holiday periods which might influence both who responds and the responses themselves.

9. Behaviors and the people engaging in them also vary over locations. For instance, expressions of homosexual behavior are much more common in some cities than in others and in some social settings than others. The principal issue for program evaluations is that the mea-

sure used to assess the outcome of the program hold time and place constant or randomize them. For example, if the program were designed to reduce the fear of being robbed while on vacation, it would be best *not* to take the before and after measures during different seasons of the year.

Much information can be gained from records maintained for purposes other than program evaluation. Some examples are vital statistics records, business sales records, newspaper files, arrest reports, floor wear in public buildings, congressional testimony, and insurance claims. The value of these sources is that they are not directly influenced by their use for data collection to assess the impact of a program (unless such use is made known). There are, however, some other problems. The major problem is selection as to what to record and what to keep for how long once recorded. The next two items discuss the use of records for measurement purposes.

10. Births and deaths are probably almost all recorded, but "illegitimate" births and deaths are probably recorded less fully or promptly. The major problem with governmental crime figures is the much less than complete recording of crimes and the biases which exist in every stage of the processing of those suspected, prosecuted, and convicted. Newspapers are very selective in what they report, but an assessment of their content would be essential in most any study related to community-leadership opinion. Indeed, it is the very selectivity of their reporting which makes them useful. Business records are excellent sources of information, but their private ownership and limited useage by social scientists makes it impossible to offer any general guidelines.

11. Records accumulate rapidly and are expensive to store; they typically lose their usefulness to those who produce them as time elapses. Any factor which is associated with selective retention is a threat to their validity as measures of anything other than the factors affecting their retention. Thus, sales records are probably more likely to be retained if the bill is not paid. Using year-old sales records to obtain a before-program measure of average expenditures on various goods and services would probably yield a biased measure.

These are but the major threats to the validity of measures. More exist and much more detail could be provided about each, but the purpose of this presentation is to alert the reader to the more common problems of making inferences about variables and populations rather than to catalog them all or present the various methods which have been developed to overcome and assess them. Reference to any of the standard works on measurement and sampling should be made for further detail (Cochran, Mosteller, and Tukey, 1970).

If there is any general guideline which can be drawn from what has been learned about influences upon the validity of measurement, it is that no one measure can be totally valid. Whenever possible, multiple measures of the variable of interest should be used. For instance, there is some indication that a much more accurate count of the number of narcotic addicts in a town would be obtained by using records of the police *and* noncriminal treatment centers (Weissman, Giacinti, and Lanasa, 1973).

CONCLUSIONS

Most studies of social programs and policies end with one or more conclusions.

Like the commencement exercise which marks graduation from school, the conclusion section of a report is the traditional place for putting a fine finish on the rough production which preceded it and a place for the expression of exhortations only loosely connected with what went before. A skeptical eye is especially helpful when reading the conclusion sections of reports, including this one. And the true skeptic is suspicious of everything, including that which works and that which does not.

Suppose It Works

No study can ever produce certainty in its conclusions; such is the nature, it would seem, of human existence. The belief that something works does not mean that either part of the question need be accepted as defined for the purposes of the study. That which works is not necessarily good, unless goodness is equated with effectiveness; and just because a program/policy reduces a social problem, one need not conclude that the social problem is bad.

In some societies freedom of speech is considered to be a social problem and the government effectively limits such freedom by suppressing it through the use of spies and the legal harassment of those who speak freely; this need not mean that the tactics are good or that free speech is bad. For another example, it might be found that executing everyone who was suspected of using heroin for recreational purposes would virtually eliminate heroin addiction, but this would not mean that it is a good thing to do so or that heroin addiction should be eliminated. Or, just because some form of social program might keep everyone in school until the age of eighteen, it does not necessarily follow that keeping everyone in school until the age of eighteen is desirable.

The "fact" that a program/policy works does not mean that it will be adopted. For instance, there is good reason to believe that a policy of more evenly distributing the profits of American corporations so that everyone would have sufficient funds to adequately feed, house, clothe, entertain, and transport themselves would greatly decrease crime and improve mental health, but there is also good reason to believe that this will not happen to any substantial degree. This is because those who control the distribution of corporate profits think that they benefit from a disproportionate distribution more than they would do from an equitable one. Similarly, a program which is effective may cost more than it is worth, so to speak. Thus, individual psychoanalytic therapy *might* be quite effective in reducing crime among the poor, but it is not likely to be widely adopted because it is very expensive.

But there are other factors besides expense which might limit the adoption of a program or policy which appears to be selective; one is organizational survival. The Roman Catholic church has taken the position that birth control techniques such as intrauterine and contraceptive pills are sinful in that they artificially obstruct the purpose of sexual intercourse which is to procreate children. Thus the church cannot endorse the use of such techniques to limit family size, even though such techniques are quite effective and overpopulation is a serious social problem (Davis, 1973; Schnore, 1966).

Another kind of issue is posed, or made more clear, by success. The criminal justice system in the major cities of the United States have developed effective techniques for arresting, holding, prosecuting, adjudicating, and punishing people involved in so-called mass riots. The people who are arrested are effectively processed and the due-process requirements are minimally met. By virtually all system standards, the policies and procedures have been a success in the more recent situations. But this success loses much of its sweet smell if the purported problem is viewed differently. If the so-called riots are seen as protests against harassment by law-enforcement agencies and exploitation by the economic system, then the successful criminalization of the rioters takes on a different meaning. It becomes a successful collaboration between the government and the economic system to define the failure of the government and economic systems to meet the human needs of people as criminality on the part of those who express their objections in ways which threaten the interests of the government and economic systems. Success, and claims of success, are best not taken lightly (Balbus, 1973; Marx, 1971).

Suppose It Doesn't Work

A single test of a program or policy is never sufficient to reach the conclusion that it does not work. Likewise, multiple tests of one type of program or policy are not sufficient to reject the theory upon which they are based. But multiple tests of multiple programs which show that they do not work are sufficient basis to question the underlying theory. In other words, a motive *may* be provided for questioning the underlying theory, but not always.

The failure of a program can lead to even greater faith in the program, with the evidence of failure either rejected outright or attributed to contingencies which

leave the faith in the program unchallenged (Himelson, 1968). But if cognitive dissonance reduction or some other mechanism does not save the day for the believer, the theory may be challenged. For instance, a large number of programs and policies designed to rehabilitate people committed to prison and/or placed on parole have been tested many times. Only rarely have they been successful (Lipton, Martinson, and Wilks, 1975; Robison and Smith, 1971). All of these programs and policies are based on the notion that the criminal is somehow sick, or at least different from normal, (noncriminal) folk. The theory leads to the conclusion that they must somehow be reformed or rehabilitated. Upon examination, it turns out that there is little or no support for the underlying theory. About all that can be said with any certainty about people committed to prison and/or placed on parole is that they have been convicted of a crime and that they are virtually all from the lower socioeconomic classes. The finding that commitments to prison go up with increases in unemployment levels and that most crimes involve economic gain would indicate that the problem of crime is largely a function of economic problems and that the solution would be institutional rather than personal, but such solutions are seldom even suggested (Gordon, 1971; Quinney, 1973).

A program which continues to exist even though it is widely held to be a failure merits investigation to determine if the proper criterion has been used. To take but one example, if public welfare (also known as public assistance and poor relief) is seen as a vehicle for making people self-sufficient ("getting them off the rolls") and the provision of an adequate income for those without any other source of income, then there can be little doubt that welfare has been a failure. However, if the purpose of welfare is seen as keeping the surplus population in capitalist countries from revolution or serious disruption of the status quo, then it has been rather successful (Piven and Cloward, 1971). The point of this example, whether it be accurate or not, is that the success of a program may depend upon what the purpose of the program is thought to be, which in turn determines what measures of success will be used; and the purpose and outcomes are not necessarily those defined by those who run and authorize the programs.

References

Alinsky, Saul D. *Rules for Radicals: A Practical Primer for Realistic Radicals.* New York: Vintage Books, 1972.

Althauser, Robert P., and Rubin, Donald. "The Computerized Construction of a Matched Sample." *American Journal of Sociology,* 1970, 76, 325–46.

Bailey, William C. "Murder and Capital Punishment: Some Further Evidence." Cleveland, Ohio: Cleveland State University, 1973.

Balbus, Isaac. *The Dialectics of Legal Repression: Black Rebels before the American Court.* New York: Russell Sage Foundation, 1973.

Barrera, Mario, and Vialpondo, Geralda. *Action Research in Defense of the Barrio.* Los Angeles: Aztlan, 1974.

Bedau, Hugo Adam (Ed.). *The Death Penalty in America: An Anthology,* rev. ed. New York: Anchor Books, 1967.

Berecochea, John E. "Correctional Research." *Federal Probation,* 1974, 38, 59–61.

Berecochea, John E., Jaman, Dorothy R., and Jones, Welton A. *Time Served in Prison and Parole Outcome: An Experimental Study, Report Number 1.* Sacramento: California Department of Corrections' Research Report No. 49, October 1973.

Berecochea, John E., and Sing, George E., Jr. "The Effectiveness of a Halfway House for Civilly Committed Narcotic Addicts." *International Journal of the Addictions,* 1972, 7, 123–32.

Blau, Peter, and Duncan, Otis Dudley. *The American Occupational Structure.* New York: Wiley, 1967.

Bracht, Glenn H., and Glass, Gene V. "The External Validity of Experiments." *American Educational Research Journal,* 1968, 5, 437–74.

Brunswik, Egon. *Perception and the Representative Design of Psychological Experiments.* Berkeley: University of California Press, 1957.

Campbell, Donald T. "Reforms as Experiments." In Francis G. Caro (Ed.), *Readings in Evaluation Research.* New York: Russell Sage Foundation, 1971. Pp. 233–61.

Campbell, Donald T., and Stanley, Julian C. *Experimental and Quasi-Experimental Designs for Research.* Chicago: Rand McNally, 1963.

Carey, Alex. "The Hawthorne Studies: A Radical Criticism." In Dennis P. Forcese and Stephen Richer (Eds.), *Stages in Social Research: Contemporary Perspectives.* Englewood Cliffs, N.J.: Prentice-Hall, 1970. Pp. 352–69.

Carmichael, Stokely, and Hamilton, Charles V. *Black Power: The Politics of Liberation in America.* New York: Vintage Books, 1967.

Chambliss, William J. "Types of Deviance and the Effectiveness of Legal Sanctions." *Wisconsin Law Review,* 1967, 67, 702–19.

Chambliss, William J. "The Impact of Punishment on Compliance with Parking Regulations." In William J. Chambliss (Ed.), *Crime and the Legal Process.* New York: McGraw-Hill, 1969. Pp. 388–93.

Chapin, F. Stuart, *Experimental Design*

in Sociological Research. New York: Harper & Row, 1955.

Cochran, William G., Mosteller, Frederick, and Tukey, John W. "Principles of Sampling." In Dennis P. Forcese and Stephen Richer (Eds.), *Stages of Social Research: Contemporary Perspectives.* Englewood Cliffs, N.J.: Prentice-Hall, 1970. Pp. 168–86.

Crittenden, Kathleen S., and Hill, Richard J. "Coding Reliability and Validity of Interview Data." *American Sociological Review,* 1971, 36, 1073–80.

Danaceau, Paul. *Methadone Maintenance: The Experience of Four Programs.* Washington, D.C.: Drug Abuse Council, 1974.

Davis, Kingsley. "The Population Explosion." In Martin S. Weinberg and Earl Rubington (Eds.), *The Solution of Social Problems: Five Perspectives.* New York: Oxford, 1973. Pp. 85–98.

Douglas, Jack D. *American Social Order: Social Rules in a Pluralistic Society.* New York: Free Press, 1971.

Erickson, Kai T. Wayward Puritans: A Study in the Sociology of Deviance. New York: Wiley, 1966.

Eyesenck, H. J. *The Effects of Psychotherapy.* New York: International Scientific Press, 1966.

Etzioni, Amitai. "Two Approaches to Organizational Analysis: A Critique and a Suggestion." *Administrative Science Quarterly,* 1960, 5, 257–78.

Fanon, Frantz. *The Wretched of the Earth.* New York: Grove Press, 1968.

Frank, Jerome. *Persuasion and Healing: A Comparative Study of Psychotherapy,* rev. ed. Baltimore: Johns Hopkins University Press, 1973.

Friedman, Neil. *The Social Nature of Psychological Research: The Psychological Experiment as Social Interaction.* New York: Basic Books, 1967.

Garfinkel, Harold. *Studies in Ethnomethodology.* Englewood Cliffs, N.J.: Prentice-Hall, 1967.

Garrity, Donald L. "The Prison as a Rehabilitative Agency." In Donald R. Cressey (Ed.), *The Prison: Studies in Institutional Organization and Change.* New York: Holt, Rinehart and Winston, 1961. Pp. 358–80.

Glaser, Daniel. *The Effectiveness of a Prison and Parole System.* Indianapolis: Bobbs-Merrill, 1964.

Gordon, David M. "Class and the Economics of Crime." *Review of Radical Political Economics,* 1971, 3, 51–75.

Greenwood. E. *Experimental Sociology: A Study in Method.* New York: King's Crown, 1945.

Guilford, J. P. *Psychometric Methods,* 2nd ed. New York: McGraw-Hill, 1954.

Gusfield, Joseph R. *Symbolic Crusade: Status Politics and the American Temperance Movement.* Urbana: University of Illinois Press, 1966.

Harrington, David. *An Evaluation of the Driver Test as an Examination for Drivers Previously Licensed in Another State.* Sacramento: California Department of Motor Vehicles' Research Report No. 44, December 1973.

Harrison, Robert M., and Mueller, Paul F. C. *Clue Hunting about Group Counselling and Parole Outcome.* Sacramento: California Department of Corrections Research Report No. 11, May, 1964.

Heroin Maintenance: The Issues. Washington, D.C.: Drug Abuse Council, 1974.

Himelson, Alfred N. "When Treatment Failed: A Study of the Attempt of a Public Service Organization to Change the Behavior of an Intransigent Population." Ph.D. dissertation, University of California at Los Angeles, 1968.

Horowitz, Irving Louis. "The Conflict Society: War as a Social Problem." In Howard S. Becker (Ed.), *Social Problems: A Modern Approach.* New York: Wiley, 1966. Pp. 695–749.

Hyman, Herbert H., Wright, Charles R., and Hopkins, Terence K. *Applications of Methods of Evaluation: Four Studies of the Encampment for Citizenship.* Berkeley: University of California Press, 1962.

Jaman, Dorothy R., Dickover, Robert

M., and Bennett, Lawrence A. "Parole Outcome as a Function of Time Served." *British Journal of Criminology*, 1972, 12, 5–34.

Jencks, Christopher, et al. *Inequality: A Reassessment of the Effect of Family Schooling in America.* New York: Basic Books, 1972.

Jones, Welton A., and Berecochea, John E. *California Department of Corrections' Methadone Maintenance Programs: An Evaluation.* California Department of Corrections' Research Report No. 49, October, 1973.

Kassebaum, Gene G., Ward, David, and Wilner, Daniel M. *Prison Treatment and Parole Survival: An Experimental Assessment.* New York: Wiley, 1971.

Kerlinger, Fred N. *Foundations of Behavioral Research*, 2nd ed. New York: Holt, Rinehart and Winston, 1973.

Liazos, Alexander. "Class Oppression: The Function of Juvenile Justice." *Insurgent Sociologist*, 1974, 5, 2–24.

Lindesmith, Alfred R. *Opiate Addiction.* Evanston: Principia Press of Illinois, 1947.

Lindquist, E. F. *Design and Analysis of Experiments in Psychology and Education.* New York: Houghton Mifflin, 1953.

Lipton, D. R., Martinson, R., and Wilks, J. W. *The Effectiveness of Correctional Treatment: A Survey of Treatment Evaluation Studies.* New York: Praeger, 1975.

Manocchio, Anthony J., and Dunn, Jimmy. *The Time Game: Two Views of a Prison.* Beverly Hills, Ca.: Sage Publications, 1970.

Mao Tse-Tung, *On Practice: On the Relation between Knowledge and Practice, between Knowing and Doing.* Peking: Foreign Language Press, 1966.

Mao Tse-Tung, *On Contradictions.* Peking: Foreign Language Press, 1967.

Marx, Gary T. "Civil Disorder and the Agents of Control." In Marx (Ed.), *Racial Conflict.* Boston: Little, Brown, 1971. Pp. 286–306.

Melman, Seymour. *Pentagon Capitalism: The Political Economy of War.* New York: McGraw-Hill, 1970.

Memmi, Albert. *The Colonizer and the Colonized.* Boston: Beacon Press, 1967.

Messinger, Sheldon. "Strategies of Control." Ph.D. dissertation, University of California at Los Angeles, 1969.

Nader, Ralph, and Ross, Donald. *Action for a Change: A Student's Manual for Public Interest Organizations*, rev. ed. New York: Grossman Publishers, 1972.

Peak, Helen. "Problems in Objective Observations." In Leon Festinger and Daniel Katz (Eds.), *Research Methods in the Behavioral Sciences.* New York: Dryden Press, 1953. Pp. 292–9.

Phillips, Bernard S. *Social Research: Strategy and Tactics.* New York: Macmillan, 1971.

Piven, Frances Fox, and Cloward, Richard A. *Regulating the Poor: The Functions of Public Welfare.* New York: Vintage Books, 1971.

Quinney, Richard. "Crime Control in Capitalist Society: A Critical Philosophy of Legal Order." *Issues in Criminology*, 1973, 8, 75–99.

"Review Symposium on Inequality: A Reassessment of the Effects of Family and Schooling in America by Christopher Jencks and Others." *American Journal of Sociology*, 1973, 78, 1523–44.

Robison, James O., and Smith, Gerald. "The Effectiveness of Correctional Programs." *Crime and Delinquency*, 1971, 17, 67–80.

Rosenberg, Morris. "Test Factor Standardization as a Method of Interpretation." In Dennis P. Forcese and Stephen Richer (Eds.), *Stages in Social Research: Contemporary Perspectives.* Englewood Cliffs, N.J.: Prentice-Hall, 1970. Pp. 261–73.

Rosenthal, Robert, and Jacobsen, Lenore. *Pygmalion in the Classroom: Teacher Expectation and Pupils' Intellectual Development.* New York: Holt, Rinehart and Winston, 1968.

Roth, Julius. "Hired Hand Research." In Norman K. Denzin (Ed.), *Sociological Methods: A Sourcebook.* Chicago: Aldine, 1970. Pp. 540–57.

Schasre, Robert. "Cessation Patterns among Neophyte Heroin Users." *International Journal of the Addictions*, 1966, 1, 23–32.

Schnore, Leo F. "Population Problems in Perspective." In Howard S. Becker (Ed.), *Social Problems: A Modern Approach*. New York: Wiley, 1966. Pp. 625–54.

Schur, Edwin M. *Crimes without Victims: Deviant Behavior and Social Policy*. Englewood Cliffs, N.J.: Prentice-Hall, 1965.

Schur, Edwin M. *Labelling Deviant Behavior: Its Sociological Implications*. New York: Harper & Row, 1971.

Sellin, Thorsten, and Wolfgang, Marvin E. *The Measurement of Delinquency*. New York: Wiley, 1964.

Simon, William, and Gagnon, John H. "Homosexuality: The Formulation of a Sociological Perspective." *Journal of Health and Social Behavior*, 1967, 8, 177–85.

Smith, David E., and Gay, George R. "A Brief History of Heroin Addiction in America." In Smith and Gay (Eds.), *It's So Good, Don't Even Try It Once*. Englewood Cliffs, N.J.: Prentice-Hall, 1972.

Smith, Robert L. *A Quiet Revolution: Probation Subsidy*, U.S. Department of Health, Education and Welfare Publication Number (SRS) 72-26011. Washington, D.C.: U.S. Government Printing Office, 1971.

Snow, Richard E. "Unfinished Pygmalion." *Contemporary Psychology*, 1969, 14, 197–9.

Sutherland, Edwin H., and Cressey, Donald R. *Criminology*, 8th ed. Philadelphia: Lippincott, 1970.

Takagi, Paul. "The Correctional System." *Crime and Social Justice*, 1974, 2, 82–9.

Tittle, Charles R. "Crime Rates and Legal Sanctions." *Social Problems*, 1969, 16, 409–23.

Trice, Harrison M., and Roman, Paul Michael. "Delabeling, Relabeling and Alcoholic's Anonymous." *Social Problems*, 1970, 17, 538–46.

Tullock, Gordon. "Does Punishment Deter Crime?" *Public Interest*, 1974, 36, 103–11.

Volkman, Rita, and Cressey, Donald R. "Differential Association and the Rehabilitation of Drug Addicts." *American Journal of Sociology*, 1963, 69, 129–42.

Waldorf, Dan. "Life without Heroin: Social Adjustment during Long Term Periods of Voluntary Abstention." *Social Problems*, 1970, 18, 228–43.

Webb, Eugene J., et al. *Unobtrusive Measures: Nonreactive Research in the Social Sciences*. Chicago: Rand McNally, 1966.

Weissman, James C., Giacinti, Thomas G., and Lanasa, Francis W. "Undetected Opiate Use." *Journal of Criminal Justice*, 1973, 1, 135–44.

Witt, Leonard R. *Final Report on Project DEVELOP*. Albany: New York State Division of Parole, 1968.

Wright, Erik Olin. *The Politics of Punishment: A Critical Analysis of Prisons in America*. New York: Harper & Row, 1973.

Suggested Reading

BLALOCK, HUBERT M., JR. *Causal Inference in Nonexperimental Research*. Chapel Hill: University of North Carolina Press, 1964.

A primer for using regression analysis to attribute causal relationships to changes and differences in rates computed over social areas and units of time. Requires some statistical knowledge for development and implementation, but understandable as prose.

CAMPBELL, DONALD T. "Reforms as Experiments." In Francis G. Caro (Ed.), *Readings in Evaluation Research*. New York: Russell Sage Foundation, 1971. Pp. 233–261.
Brings together methodological concepts and statistical techniques for estimating whether a policy or program change introduced in an entire area produced a significant change in relevant rates from what they would have been expected to have been.

CAMPBELL, DONALD T., AND STANLEY, JULIAN C. *Experimental and Quasi-Experimental Designs*. Chicago: Rand McNally, 1963.
The classic, clear and concisely written treatise on the use of experimental and quasiexperimental designs in field or applied settings.

KERLINGER, FRED N. *Foundations of Behavioral Research*, 2nd ed. New York: Holt, Rinehart and Winston, 1973.
A thorough statement of the basic principles of research design, measurement, and statistical analysis primarily oriented toward basic research.

MILLER, DELBERT C. *Handbook of Research Design and Social Measurement*, 2nd. ed. New York: David McKay, 1970.
Good compendium of multitude of social measurement instruments including citations to basic works and applications.

MUELLER, JOHN H., SCHUESSLER, KARL F., and COSTNER, HERBERT. *Statistical Reasoning in Sociology*, 2nd. ed. Boston: Houghton Mifflin, 1970.
Very readable exposition of basic principles of descriptive statistics, correlation and association, sampling, and statistical inference techniques.

OPPENHEIM, A. N. *Questionnaire Design and Attitude Measurement*. New York: Basic Books, 1966.
Simple presentation of basic processes in the design of questionnaires and measurement of attitudes—a basic guide.

ROSENBERG, MORRIS. *The Logic of Survey Analysis*. New York: Basic Books, 1968.
A well-written guide to the use of cross classifications for the analysis of data classifiable into categories rather than measurable on dimensional variables. Presentation is keyed to the attribution of causal relationships to changes and differences in categorical measures of individual actors.

SUCHMAN, EDWARD A. *Evaluation Research: Principles and Practices in Public Service and Social Action Programs*. New York: Russell Sage Foundation, 1967.
Basic methodological text emphasizing multiple, interrelated goals, barriers to their achievement, the place of evaluation in administration of programs, and the place of administration in evaluation research. Probably the best evaluation treatise on public health programs.

WEBB, EUGENE J., ET AL. *Unobtrusive Measures: Nonreactive Research in the Social Sciences.* Chicago: Rand McNally, 1966.
Contains thorough analysis of threats to the validity of all methods of collecting information about the social world. A well-written and enjoyable presentation of a multitude of ordinary and ingenious ways of collecting information. Centers around the concepts of ruling out alternative explanations and the use of more than one measure of variables to reduce biases.

Index